SYSTEMATIC THEOLOGY

SYSTEMATIC THEOLOGY

— Volume 2 —

Wolfhart Pannenberg

Translated by

Geoffrey W. Bromiley

William B. Eerdmans Publishing Company
Grand Rapids, Michigan

T&T Clark Ltd
Edinburgh

Originally published as *Systematische Theologie*, band 2
© 1991 Vandenhoeck & Ruprecht, Göttingen, Germany

English translation copyright © 1994 Wm. B. Eerdmans Publishing Co.
255 Jefferson Ave. S.E., Grand Rapids, Michigan 49503

Published jointly 1994 in the U.S.A. by
Wm. B. Eerdmans Publishing Co.
and in the U.K. by
T&T Clark Ltd
59 George Street
Edinburgh EH2 2LQ Scotland

Printed in the United States of America

02 01 00 99 98   6 5 4 3 2

Library of Congress Cataloging-in-Publication Data

Pannenberg, Wolfhart, 1928- .
    Systematic Theology. Translation of: Systematische Theologie.
    Includes bibliographical references and indexes.
    1. Theology, Doctrinal. I. Title.
    BT75.2.P2613   1991   230′.044   91-26339
    ISBN 0-8028-3707-7

British Library Cataloguing in Publication Data

A catalogue record for this book is available from the British Library.

ISBN 0 567 09598 3

CONTENTS

v

ABBREVIATIONS

AB	Anchor Bible
AC	Apostolic Constitution
ANET	*Ancient Near Eastern Texts Relating to the Old Testament*, ed. J. B. Pritchard, 3rd ed. (Princeton, 1969)
ARG	*Archiv für Reformationsgeschichte*
BKAT	Biblischer Kommentar: Altes Testament
BSLK	*Die Bekenntnisschriften der evangelisch-lutherischen Kirche*, ed. E. Wolf (Göttingen, 1967)
CA	Confession of Augsburg
CChrSL	Corpus Christianorum, Series Latina
CD	Karl Barth, *Church Dogmatics*, 4 vols., ed. G. W. Bromiley and T. F. Torrance (Edinburgh, 1936-1969)
CR	*Corpus Reformatorum*, ed. W. Baum et al. (Braunschweig, 1863)
CSEL	Corpus Scriptorum ecclesiasticorum latinorum
DS	*Enchiridion Symbolorum*, ed. H. Denzinger
EDNT	*Exegetical Dictionary of the New Testament*, 3 vols., ed. H. Balz and G. Schneider (Grand Rapids, 1990-1993)
EK	*Evangelische Kommentare*
EKK	Evangelisch-katholischer Kommentar
EvT	*Evangelische Theologie*
HDG	*Handbuch der Dogmengeschichte* (Freiburg, 1956ff.)
HTR	*Harvard Theological Review*
HWP	*Historisches Wörterbuch der Philosophie*
IKZ	*Internationale kirchliche Zeitschrift*

Int	*Interpretation*
KuD	*Kerygma und Dogma*
KZ	*Kirchliche Zeitschrift*
LCC	Library of Christian Classics
LThK	*Lexikon für Theologie und Kirche*, 10 vols., 2nd ed. (Freiburg, 1957-1965)
LW	Luther's Works
ND	*The Christian Faith in the Doctrinal Documents of the Catholic Church*, ed. J. Neuner and J. Dupuis (Dublin, 1976; revised ed., New York, 1982).
NTD	Das Neue Testament Deutsch
NZST	*Neue Zeitschrift für systematische Theologie*
OTL	Old Testament Library
PG	*Patrologia Graeca*, ed. J. Migne
PhB	Philosophische Bibliothek
PL	*Patrologia Latina*, ed. J. Migne
PRE	*Paulys Real-Encyclopädie der classischen Altertumswissenschaft*
RAC	*Reallexikon für Antike und Christentum*, ed. T. Klauser (Stuttgart, 1941-)
RE	*Realencyklopädie für protestantische Theologie und Kirche*
RGG	*Religion in Geschichte und Gegenwart*
SBAW	Sitzungsberichte der bayerischen Akademie der Wissenschaften
SBT	Studies in Biblical Theology
ScEc	*Sciences ecclésiastiques*
SJT	*Scottish Journal of Theology*
SP	*Studia Patristica*
TDNT	*Theological Dictionary of the New Testament*, 10 vols., ed. G. Kittel and G. Friedrich (Grand Rapids, 1964-1976)
TDOT	*Theological Dictionary of the Old Testament*, ed. G. J. Botterweck and H. Ringgren (Grand Rapids, 1974-)
TEH	Theologische Existenz heute
TLZ	*Theologische Literaturzeitung*
TP	*Theologie und Philosophie*
TQ	*Theologische Quartalschrift*
TRE	*Theologische Realenzyklopädie*
TSK	*Theologischen Studien und Kritiken*
VF	*Verkündigung und Forschung*

VT	*Vetus Testamentum*
WA	Luthers Werke, Weimarer Ausgabe
ZAW	*Zeitschrift für die alttestamentliche Wissenschaft*
ZEE	*Zeitschrift für evangelische Ethik*
ZKG	*Zeitschrift für Kirchengeschichte*
ZKT	*Zeitschrift für katholische Theologie*
ZST	*Zeitschrift für systematische Theologie*
ZTK	*Zeitschrift für Theologie und Kirche*

FOREWORD

The first volume of this systematic presentation of Christian doctrine pursued the question of the truth of talk about God into the
field of the religions which with their different and in many ways
contradictory truth claims compete with one another in both historical
controversies and present-day religious pluralism. Christianity, despite
and even with its summoning to a unique divine revelation, is one of these
religions that contend with one another for ultimate truth about the
world, humanity, and God.

The fact of these conflicts among religions is obvious enough in
the life of people of very different cultures. Only a so-called theology of
religions in the industrial societies of the West closes its eyes to this truth,
depicting the many religions as in principle unconflicting ways to the same
God. In the event this type of theology plays into the hands of the prejudice that the advanced secularism of the modern public has against all
religious truth claims, treating the differences in religious confession
merely as private matters of no public interest. This view evades the reality.
Even today it is still being confirmed again and again that the deepest
cultural differences have religious roots. Modern secularism, which would
like to suppress this fact, is itself a by-product of the cultural tradition so
strongly shaped by Christianity. Secularism, then, provides no basis on
which to convince the religious traditions of other cultures that their truth
claims are irrelevant. Christianity, too, has to cling to the truth claim of
the revelation on which it rests. To make this claim with any credibility,
we must first consider the many other claims and the related contestability
of truth. In so doing we do not relativize the claim to the truth, even the

definitive and absolute truth, of the revelation of God in Jesus Christ. Only in so doing, indeed, do we make this claim with material seriousness and with tolerance.

The claim to a truth that is given to all people with the revelation of the one God of all people, the Creator of the world, in the person and history of Jesus of Nazareth, is the starting point of the Christian mission to the world and the source of its power. Christian theology has developed in the service of this truth claim, seeking to clarify it, to strengthen it by a systematic presentation of Christian teaching, but also again and again to test how far it may be made. Theologians can do justice to this task only if they examine the Christian truth claim as impartially as possible. They cannot begin, then, with a firm presupposition of the truth of Christian revelation. If they did, they would make this truth a matter of mere subjective conviction, which would be little more than an objective untruth and perhaps even an in many ways attractive fable.

The systematic presentation of Christian doctrine that I have undertaken in this work deals with the question of the correctness of its truth claims as an open one. The claims are open to possible confirmation in the history of human experience and reflection, but also open to provisional confirmation in a logical account of their contents. That in itself is no little thing. It is by no means self-evident today that the truth claims of Christian doctrine may even be regarded as open. Many champions of the public culture of secularism have long since answered the question in the negative. We have to be able to offer good reasons both to ourselves and to others if it is to be clear that the truth claims of religious statements, in principle if not in every detail, must be treated as serious and worth discussing. The second and third chapters of Volume 1 were meant as an introduction to this issue. The fourth chapter showed how, in the field of competing religions, we might present the truth claims of the biblical, or more specifically the Christian, belief in God. These claims found initial, comprehensive, theoretical formulation in the NT itself, in the assertion of the eschatological revelation of the Creator God in the person and work of Jesus of Nazareth.

The chapters that follow develop this claim by means of a systematic presentation of the doctrine of God, the world, and humanity, also of reconciliation and redemption. In the process we keep in view the plurality and debatability of all religious truth claims. In the competition of religions the issue is whether in the light of one specific understanding of ultimate and in the main divinely conceived reality, the world and humanity as they are can be comprehended in a more appropriate and nuanced way than in terms of rival approaches.

The systematic presentation of Christian doctrine does not attempt a comparative evaluation of the Christian and other religious interpretations of the world and human life from the standpoint of the given understanding of the reality of God. This might be the task of a philosophy of religion. Christian theology has simply to show how the event of revelation which the Christian faith claims makes it possible to develop an integrated interpretation of God and humanity and the world which we may with good reason regard as true in relation to the knowledge that comes from experience of the world and human life, and also to the knowledge of philosophical reflection, so that we can assert it to be true vis-à-vis alternative religious and nonreligious interpretations. A comparative discussion and appraisal of the opposing truth claims of different interpretations has to presuppose expositions of the views that are to be compared. The presentations might not always be available in a complete or satisfying form for all the religious traditions that merit consideration. We have here one of the difficulties and limitations of the task of religious philosophy. Caution is thus necessary as regards the possibility of a definitive judgment in this field. Christian theology may be content to give as impressive an account as possible of the Christian interpretation of God, the world, and humanity relative to the good reasons for the truth claims which it makes. Part of this will be accepting into its own sense of truth the situation of Christianity itself in a world of disputed truth claims and thus showing tolerance to other opinions. The ability to assess realistically the particular and provisional nature of Christian teachings and the related ability to show toleration are themselves important arguments in favor of the justice of the Christian truth claim.

In offering an integrated interpretation of God, the world, and humanity from the standpoint of the event of revelation on which the Christian faith rests, the details condition one another. If, in the light of the Christian doctrine of God, the world and human life are seen to be grounded in God, then conversely we have to consider a reformulation of the Christian understanding of God from the standpoint of experience of the world and humanity and the related reflection. The deliberations on the doctrines of God and the Trinity in Volume 1 have shown to what degree the redefining of the relations of these doctrines to their historical origins, of the motifs in their development, and of the involved philosophical conceptions, is normative for the redefining of their content. In the process, of course, modern ideas of history and hermeneutics, and therefore of the relation of humanity, history, and religion, are at work, as are the connections with cosmic reality that are contained not merely in philosophical conceptions. The present volume, however, will deal with knowledge derived from experience of the world and humanity from the standpoint of the Christian understanding of God.

This mutual conditioning of our understanding of God and the world does not rule out our giving precedence to the concept of God in understanding humanity and the world, nor vice versa. Any serious talk about God implies the requirement that we think of the reality of humanity and the world as determined by God and established through him. Conversely, the possibility of an integrated interpretation of the world, including humanity and its history, in terms of the concept of God will already be a test of the possible truth of this concept even though the interpretation of the world may be debatable at many points. The more such a presentation is in harmony with the data of knowledge derived from experience, the more illuminating it will be for the truth claim which the relative understanding of God is making. At all events it will carry with it a proof of the way in which the function of constituting a concept of the world that is in some way implicitly bound up with the concept of God is capable of a more or less detailed presentation.

In this sense the doctrine of creation with which the volume starts will be an explication and confirmation of the Christian understanding of God. Modern theology has not always estimated the full weight of this fact. The task of offering a doctrine of creation that is in keeping with its importance has often been neglected. It will thus receive special attention in this volume. Nevertheless, for the Christian doctrine of God demonstration of the view of God by developing a corresponding view of the world is not enough, for in particular human reality in its facticity would not then, or not yet, be congruent with the Christian view of God. Reality as it is does not everywhere bear clear witness to a loving and almighty Creator as its origin, and human beings do not consistently relate to the divine reality by thanking God for their existence or honoring him in his deity. As the Author and Consummator of the actual world, including humanity, the God of the biblical revelation can be understood as its Creator only from the standpoint of a reconciliation of the world to himself. But the reconciliation of the world with God which Christian faith finds grounded and anticipated in the death of Jesus remains, thus far at least, incomplete as regards the reality of the human race and its history. It finds definite realization already only in the faith consciousness of Christians and the fellowship of the church, and even there we see tensions and breaks between the reality of faith and the reality of life. Volume 3 will deal with the at least partial achievement of reconciliation in the life of the Christian community and individual Christians relative to the world as a whole that has yet to be reconciled and redeemed.

Creation and reconciliation are thus closely linked as regards demonstration of the Christian understanding of God in its relation to cosmic reality. In a certain sense creation will be complete only with the eschatological consummation of the world. Hence the final chapter on eschatology in Volume 3 will not only form the horizon for the preceding discussion of the church and the faith life of individual Christians. It will also conclude the presentation, which we begin here, of the understanding of the world that corresponds to the trinitarian understanding of God according to the Christian faith. The Christian sense of the provisional and significatory nature of all forms of the manifestation of God's lordship, and therefore of the actual truth of God, will be especially dealt with in Volume 3. Related to Christian awareness that the consummation of the world and of individual salvation has still to come is the sense that only God's own future can definitively answer the question of the truth of the Christian revelation and Christian faith, though this truth is everywhere at work where the Spirit of God and of Christ may blow. Thus deciding the truth of God's revelation and bringing about its public acknowledgment are God's own affair. They will have to be left open, then, even at the end of this presentation of Christian doctrine. On this side of the consummation of the truth of God in the history of the world, the sense of the provisional and broken nature of its present actualization among us remains one of the conditions of the credibility of Christian proclamation and theology.

In this volume, too, I have to express my thanks for a great deal of help. My secretary Gaby Berger assisted me in preparing the manuscript for press. My assistants Dr. Christine Axt-Piscalar, Walter Dietz, and Friedericke Nüssel, as well as Markwart Herzog and Olaf Reinmuth, helped to correct the proofs and to check quotations. The first three also prepared the indexes. Thanks also are due to all those who encouraged me to go ahead with a work at the beginning of which, in the light of Luke 14:28ff., I wondered if I would ever be able to bring it to completion.

Munich, November 1990					Wolfhart Pannenberg

CHAPTER 7

The Creation of the World

I. CREATION AS THE ACT OF GOD

§ 1. God's Outward Action

The doctrine of creation traces the existence of the world to God as its origin by moving from the reality of God to the existence of a world. It does so by means of the concept of divine action.[1] Only thus do we arrive at the definition of the divine origin of the world as creation. The world is the product of an act of God. To say this is to make a momentous statement about the relation of the world to God and of God to the world. If the world has its origin in a free act of God, it does not emanate by necessity from the divine essence or belong by necessity to the deity of God. It might not have existed. Its existence is thus contingent. It is the result and expression of a free act of divine willing and doing. Unlike the Son, it is not in eternity the correlate of God's being as the Father.

But does there not have to be a world of creatures, or a relation to it, if God is to be thought of as active? Christian doctrine denies this by describing the trinitarian relations between Father, Son, and Spirit as themselves actions. To these the divine actions in the creation of the world are added as actions of a different kind, as outward actions.

The Greek fathers used the term "activity" (*energeia*) only for the common outward action of the three persons with reference to the world of creatures.

---

1. See vol. I, 367ff., 384ff.

1

Athanasius formulated the concept of the unity of the work of the Trinity in correspondence to the indivisibility of the divine nature. He thus opposed Origen's doctrine of three different circles of operation on the part of the divine persons.[2] The Cappadocians untiringly made unity of operation a proof of the essential unity of Father, Son, and Spirit.[3] Augustine, too, spoke of the indivisibility of the divine operation along these lines (*De trin.* 1.4[7]: *inseparabiliter operentur* [CChrSL, 50 (1968), 24f.]; cf. *De trin.* 4.21[30].203.31f. etc.), and Ambrose had done so before Augustine (*De fide* 4.8.90 [CSEL, 78, 187f.]). Yet Augustine did not call the intratrinitarian relations of begetting and breathing "operations" or "actions," but "works" *(opera).* The Latin Scholastics were the pioneers in this regard.

Richard of St. Victor's doctrine of the Trinity seems to have been the starting point. He made "procession," which was until then used more specifically for the Holy Spirit, a general term for all the trinitarian processes.[4] The term could even be used for God's outward action.[5] Similarly "action" in the sense of the inner action of intellect and will came into use for the trinitarian relations. Augustine's psychological analogies provided material for this development. The idea of inner action in acts of intellect and will was expounded as a basis for the thesis of divine relations (Aquinas *ST* 1.28.4c). Thomas could also use "operation" instead of "action" (1.27.3c). The whole discussion of intellect and will in God could then come under the concept of operations in the sense of inner action (1.14. Introduction). As Thomas saw it, the fact that God is the living God rests especially on these operations (1.18.2c; cf. 1c).[6]

2. Cf. Athanasius *Ad Serap.* 1 (PG, 26, 596A). On the opposition to Origen see D. Wendebourg, *Geist oder Energie. Zur Frage der innergöttlichen Verankerung des christlichen Lebens in der byzantinischen Theologie* (Munich, 1980), p. 173. Cf. also vol. I, 261.

3. Basil *De Spir. S.* (PG, 29, 101C-D, 133B-C), Gregory of Nazianzus *Or.* (PG, 36, 116C, etc.), Gregory of Nyssa *Ex comm. not.* (PG, 45, 180). Cf. Wendebourg, *Geist oder Energie,* pp. 222f., and pp. 201f., 214f., and (on Didymus the Blind) 187ff.

4. F. Courth, "Trinität in der Scholastik," *HDG,* II/1b, 67, does not deal with this generalizing of the term. Cf. esp. Richard of St. Victor *De trin.* 5.6ff. (PL, 196, 952ff.). Peter Lombard (*Sent.* 1.13.1, 2) refers to procession in regard to the origin of both the Son and the Spirit from the Father. With Augustine the distinction is that the procession of the Spirit is not by begetting but by giving or as gift (*De trin.* 5.14.15 [PL, 41, 920f.]). For Eastern criticism of this more general use of the term, which is presupposed in the Scholastic view of processions as operations or actions, cf. P. Evdokimov, *L'esprit saint dans la tradition orthodoxe* (Paris, 1969), 69, in which we read that viewing generation and procession as two processions is an arbitrary abstraction, for in no sense can we number them together as two. The generalizing of the term does not seem to derive from Augustine's work. We find examples in pre-Nicene theology in the West. Thus Tertullian calls the Son the Word that proceeded from the one God (*Adv. Prax.* 2, 7: *processerit;* I owe this reference to A. Ganoczy). I am unable to say whether the Scholastic use went back to this or developed independently.

5. Thomas Aquinas *ST* 1.27.lc.

6. Cf. already Augustine *De trin.* 6.10, 11; 15.5.7.

The earlier Protestant dogmatics took over this usage to a large extent, though with reservations respecting Scholastic psychology. In this theology the concept of divine action came at the beginning of the doctrine of creation as a transition from the doctrine of the Trinity to presentation of the economy of the divine action in creation. In Amandus Polanus (1690) the concept served expressly as a basis for the Reformed doctrine of the eternal decrees of God.[7] On the Lutheran side we find similar discussions especially in the Jena school of J. Musäus and J. W. Baier[8] and also in D. Hollaz.[9] But Wittenberg theology held aloof, tending to use the term "divine action" only for God's outward works,[10] though not wholly excluding a use for intratrinitarian relations.[11]

The acts of the trinitarian persons in their mutual relations must be sharply differentiated from their common outward actions. This differentiation finds support in the rule that posits an antithesis between the inseparable unity of the trinitarian persons in their outward action relative to the world and the distinctiveness of their inner activities relative to one another, which is the basis of the personal distinctions of Father, Son, and Spirit.[12]

The common thesis that the inner works of the Trinity are separable and the outward works inseparable is not, then, a mere "Augustinian rule of thumb."[13] It is rather the result of the development of views of the divine action in Latin theology, which is described above. Only the second part of the statement actually comes from Augustine, who in this regard was simply following the teaching of the Cappadocian fathers, as we showed above. In regard to the indivisibility of

7. A. Polanus, *Syntagma theologiae Christianae* (1609; Hanover, 1625), pp. 236aff.

8. J. W. Baier, *Compendium theologiae positivae* (1686, 3rd ed. Jena, 1694), ch. 1, § 37 (p. 151); ch. 2 § 1 (p. 156); J. Musäus, *De Deo triuno theses* (Jena, 1647), pp. 12ff. (theses 52ff.).

9. D. Hollaz, *Examen theologicum acroamaticum* (Stargard, 1707), I, 508ff. Hollaz speaks of actions, not works (as Polanus does), in these introductory remarks to his doctrine of creation.

10. Cf. A. Calov, *Systema locorum theologicorum*, III (Wittenberg, 1659), pp. 882ff.; also J. Gerhard, *Loci theologici* (1610ff.; ed. F. Franz; Leipzig, 1885), II, 1a.

11. Cf. J. A. Quenstedt, *Theologia didactico-polemica sive systema theologicum*, I (1685, repr. Leipzig, 1715), p. 589 (beginning of ch. 10 on the actions of God in general and particularly in creation); cf. H. Schmid, *Doctrinal Theology of the Evangelical Lutheran Church* (Philadelphia, 1961), p. 161.

12. Thus Quenstedt points out that we cannot equate inner and outer works of the Trinity because the latter, even though inner acts of the subject, relate to an outer object (*Theologia*, pp. 589f.).

13. Cf. C. H. Ratschow, *Lutherische Dogmatik zwischen Reformation und Aufklärung* (Gütersloh, 1966), II, 156, cf. p. 158.

the outward work of the trinitarian persons, Quenstedt in 1685 referred to an "Augustinian rule" (p. 328), which gave rise to the impression that Augustine himself had formulated the rule. The first part of the rule, which speaks of intratrinitarian relations, could well have been formulated first when the terms "operation" and "action" came to be applied to these relations. In the older Protestant theology the formula in its extended form came into use around the middle of the 17th century. We see this from the 1659 observation of Calov regarding the personal actions within the Trinity, which is to the effect that the rule should be kept that the inner works are separate (*Systema*, p. 882). Musäus referred to a rule of theologians (*De Deo triuno*, thesis 94).

The application of the idea of divine action to the intratrinitarian relations of Father, Son, and Spirit in Western theology might seem to be a deviation from the teaching of the Greek fathers, who laid such stress on the unity of the divine action by limiting it to God's outward relations. Nevertheless, Western theology clung expressly to the indivisibility of God's outward action. Again, the extension of "action" to intratrinitarian relations cannot mean that the trinitarian persons are independent of one another in their mutual acts in the same way that the Creator God is independent of the world that he creates. At this point the Western extension of the concept ran into a difficulty that remained concealed only because the hypostatic autonomy of the divine persons was traced back to inner acts of the one divine subject in knowledge and volition. The difficulty is this: Are the acts of the divine persons in their mutual relations less free than their common outward action in bringing forth the world? Or does the act of creation for its part, notwithstanding its freedom, have a share in the reference of the divine persons to one another that leaves them indivisible?

In spite of this problem the Western extension of the idea of divine action was in many ways a great gain in theological insight. In the first place it was a gain for the actual understanding of God that God should be thought of as active. The advantage of this view is clear in comparison with the Palamist doctrine of divine "energies" that are uncreated but still distinct from the divine essence.[14] Western theology avoids the inner contradiction of this idea of uncreated divine works by linking the concept of God's eternal activity in himself to the trinitarian relations. Of itself this means that God does not need the world in order to be active. He is

14. Cf. on this Wendebourg, *Geist oder Energie*, pp. 39-43.

in himself the living God in the mutual relations of Father, Son, and Spirit. He is, of course, active in a new way in the creation of the world. It is part of the concept of action that one who acts leaves the self by an act of freedom, producing something different from the self or acting on it or reacting to it. This is true within the unity of the divine life as regards the relations of the trinitarian persons. But with the creation of a world all the persons, acting together, move out of what they have together, namely, the divine essence. Thus the creation of the world, with the related economy of the divine action, differs from the activity of the living God in the mutual relations of Father, Son, and Spirit.

Extension of the idea of divine action to the intratrinitarian relations also brings a gain in theological insight from another direction. The doctrine of the indivisible unity of the three persons in their common action quickly came under attack. Alleged against it were biblical statements that speak uninhibitedly of action by one or another of the persons individually. Ambrose and Augustine both saw the objection.[15] One might counter it by saying that in such sayings the common work of the three is appropriated to one of them. But how these appropriations are grounded in God's trinitarian life is just as unclear as is how one gains knowledge of the distinction of the persons in view of the indivisible unity of their divine action. But linking intratrinitarian relations to the idea of God's action as Creator, Sustainer, Reconciler, and Consummator of a world of creatures makes possible a clarification of these difficulties by enabling us to think in trinitarian fashion of the relation of the one God to the world, i.e., as Creator, Reconciler, and Consummator, so that the reciprocal action of the persons always lies beyond the relation of the one God to creatures and the relation of creatures to the one God. The action of the one God in relation to the world is not wholly different from the action in his trinitarian life. In his action in relation to the world the trinitarian life turns outward, moves out of itself, and becomes the determinative basis of relations between the Creator and the creatures.

This matter has been expressed in the theological tradition by adding to the principle of the common working of the persons the thesis that it is according to

---

15. Ambrose *De fide* 4.6.68 (CSEL, 78, 180, 32-35); Augustine *De trin.* 1.4.7 (CChrSL, 50, 36, 22-24), where Augustine argues that as the three are inseparable, they work inseparably.

the order of the divine persons (Hollaz, *Examen*, § 510; cf. Quenstedt, *Theologia*, p. 589). Along traditional lines the order is that of the relations of origin between Father, Son, and Spirit. In their outward working the persons work according to these relations, with the Father as unbegotten origin, the Son as begotten by the Father, the Spirit as proceeding from the Father and received by the Son. On the distinction grounded in this order the appropriations rest: creation to the Father, reconciliation to the Son, and eschatological consummation to the Spirit. This insight might be extended along the lines of the exposition in vol. I (pp. 308ff.), and the thesis might be advanced that the common outward action of the trinitarian persons expresses the reciprocity of their relations.

With the trinitarian mediation of God's outward action a further question arises concerning the unity and inner cohesion of the different phases of the saving economy of the divine action. The unity of action, which finally rests on the unity of the acting subject, links a variety of elements into a unity of process in the course of events. This is true of any action that takes place in time, no matter whether the one who acts has a place in time and with the goals of the action aims at a future distinct from the present, or whether only the object of the action has its existence in time and takes shape under the conditions of temporal processes. Only in the latter sense may we say of God's action that it is structured by the distinction and coordination of means and ends, and we may say even this only with reservations. Human action brings results that are owed to the linking of means and ends. This is so because humans usually do not try to achieve their goals directly by single acts but only by an interconnected nexus of acts. For in their acts they must use as means to the achievement of the goals conditions and materials that are posited for them. In this sense we cannot apply the structure of ends and means directly to the idea of divine action. To do so would be to make God a needy and dependent being.[16]

But the structure of ends and means also has the function of binding into a unity a variety in the temporal sequence of its elements and of doing so in such a way that the unity of the series has its basis in the end. In the light of this function of integrating a series of events into a unity based on its end, we *can* speak of the ends and means of the divine action. This does not mean that God can accomplish his goals only by the use of suitable means. The creative action of Almighty God can of itself

16. On this point see vol. I, 375f., 386f.

reach all its ends directly in the form of "basic actions,"[17] by simple acts of will. Nevertheless, when the divine action produces finite creatures that are subject to temporal and temporally limited relations, it produces finite events and beings in the nexus of a temporal sequence in which their existence is referred to a future fulfillment.

Talk about the means and ends of the divine action, then, simply expresses the relations between finite events and beings as God himself wills them, though naturally from the standpoint of their reference to a future that transcends their finitude. We will have to support and expound this more fully later. Here we may simply state that the temporal order in which creaturely things and events stand as such enables us to describe their relation to the divine action in terms of a plan (Isa. 5:19, etc.) — a plan that God himself follows in the process of history. If the destiny of all creaturely occurrence and existence is oriented to fellowship with God himself, then this idea takes the conceptual form of a plan of salvation. At this point the relation of the outward divine action to a goal acquires the form of trinitarian mediation inasmuch as the fellowship of creatures with their Creator is to be thought of as participation in the fellowship of the Son with the Father through the Spirit. The saving decree or plan (Eph. 2:9ff.) that lies behind the course that the history of creation follows and into which all events are integrated can thus be proclaimed as already manifest in Jesus Christ, in his obedience to being sent by the Father. In this context we may also say that though God is independent in himself, yet with the act of creation and in the course of the history of his creatures he makes himself dependent on creaturely conditions for the manifestation of his Son in the relation of Jesus to the Father. It is not as though God were referred to different means for the accomplishing of his ends. The point is that this is the actual way in which a multiplicity of creatures will be brought into the eternal blessedness of the fellowship of the Son with the Father. For God's action no creature is merely a means. By the ordering of its existence to the *kairos* of the manifestation of the Son, each creature has a part in the saving purpose of the Father.

The developed structure of God's outward action embraces not only the creation of the world but also the themes of reconciliation, redemption, and consummation, which are usually differentiated from

17. Cf. T. Penelhum, *Survival and Disembodied Existence* (London, 1970), p. 107; cf. p. 40, with a reference to A. Danto, "Basic Actions," *American Philosophical Quarterly* 2 (1965) 141-48.

creation. In a broader sense the fulfillment of the creature might be included in the concept of creation. But if we follow the traditional path and speak of creation more narrowly in distinction from reconciliation and consummation, even then the thought of God's outward action embraces more than the act of creating. Creating is simply the first step in an economy of divine action that includes and expresses God's relation to the world in all its aspects.

Do we have to speak of a plurality of divine acts? Or does the eternal self-identity of the one God exclude the idea of a sequence of different acts, so that strictly God's action from all eternity is single? Under pressure from the postulate of the simplicity of God the theological tradition has in fact maintained that in itself God's action is single and identical with his essentiality.[18] At the same time the scriptures speak quite freely and expressly of a variety of divine acts, e.g., the many acts (Ps. 78:11: 'aliloth) that God causes his people to see (cf. 77:12), the great acts of God (106:2: geburoth), or quite simply his acts (111:6: ma'aśaw). These can be summed up in a collective plural. Thus Josh. 24:31 says that the elders of Israel knew all Yahweh's action (kol-ma'aśeh yhwh; cf. Exod. 34:10; Jub. 2:7, 10), i.e., in the exodus and the wilderness wanderings. The Hebrew Bible uses this collective plural for history as a whole (cf. Isa. 5:19; 28:1; Ps. 92:5f.), there again conceiving of the multiplicity of God's acts as a unity, but as a structured and differentiated unity.

The real multiplicity within the unity of the divine action is no mere appearance. Nor is it proper only to the creaturely side. It is proper to God's own action as well. This fact comes to expression at least where it shows itself to be connected with the trinitarian distinctions in the life of God. God's reconciling action, which begins with the incarnation of the Son, is really something new as compared with the establishment of creaturely existence, though it has to do with the consummation of creatures and therefore also with the work of creation. Therefore, we might say very generally that what is new is that the sequence of the divine action, and therefore its multiplicity, is grounded in the trinitarian plurality of

18. Cf. Aquinas ST 1.30.2 ad 3, which refers to only one operation, which is God's essence. This is true even of the trinitarian processions (1.27.4 ad 1), since they are grounded in acts (1.27.1, 5). As regards the Trinity the older Protestant theology agreed with Aquinas in seeing a real distinction of the inner divine processions and persons. As regards the divine action Calov could use the identity of the essential internal actions (like will and intellect) with the divine essence as a reason to focus the idea of action on God's external actions (Systema, pp. 883f.).

the divine life. Therefore, the unity of this divine action in the economy of God's history with his creation is not lost by reason of the plurality of events. We will speak of this again at the end of this chapter.

First, however, we have to deal with creation as a special work of God. At issue primarily is the divine act of creation as the free origin of a reality distinct from God. The action of the trinitarian persons in their mutual relations is also free, but not in the sense that the Father might cease to beget the Son, that the Son might reject the Father's will, or that the Spirit might glorify something other than the Father in the Son and the Son in the Father. The origin of the world as creation by God's free action tells us that even if the world had not come into existence, nothing would have been lacking in the deity of God. This is, of course, more a statement about the world, about the contingency of its existence, than it is about God. For in his freedom God has from all eternity decided to be the Creator and Consummator of a world of creatures. Hence the thought that God might not have made the world rests on an abstraction from God's actual self-determination, which must be grounded in the eternity of his essence and cannot be conceived of as external to God's concrete reality. All the same, from the standpoint of God the origin of the world must still be viewed as contingent, for it derives from the freedom of God in his trinitarian life.

§ 2. The Nature of Creation

The concept of creation developed in Israel as an extension of saving faith in the covenant God, who elects and acts in history as also the beginning of all occurrence. As von Rad put it, the beginning of this covenant history was dated back to creation.[19] This view has been attacked with the argument that Israel already shared in Near Eastern ideas of the world and creation and understood its own specific experiences of history and God against this background.[20] Certainly the cosmological and cosmogonic ideas of ancient Near Eastern religions were never wholly alien to the

---

19. G. von Rad, *OT Theology*, 2 vols. (New York, 1962-65), I, 139.
20. Cf. H. H. Schmid, "Schöpfung, Gerechtigkeit und Heil. 'Schöpfungstheologie' als Gesamthorizont biblischer Theologie," *ZTK* 70 (1973) 1-19, esp. 11f. For a similar view cf. R. P. Knierim, "Cosmos and History in Israel's Theology," *Horizons in Biblical Theology* 3 (1981) 59-123.

ancestors of Israel. Therefore, concepts of a divine origin of the world order were not just extrapolations from experiences of God's action, especially in the exodus, the Red Sea deliverance, and the gift of the promised land.

Since early days the divine origin of the earthly world seems to have been ascribed to the Canaanite God of heaven El, who is called "the Creator of the earth" in the Karatepe inscription in Cilicia and who links Israel's early days to Ugarit.[21] Abraham is said to have identified the God whom he worshiped with El.[22] We see this especially in the story of his meeting with Melchizedek, the priest of El Elyon of Jerusalem, whom Abraham blessed in the name of El Elyon who made heaven and earth (Gen. 14:19). Since Abraham's God was later equated with Yahweh, the God of Sinai and the exodus (Exod. 3:6), Yahweh also came to be understood as one with the creator-god El. Here we need not discuss further the undoubtedly complex religious processes that lie behind the identification of Yahweh, El, and the God of the patriarchs.[23] The important point is that there was no mere adjustment of the deity of Yahweh to that of El or that of a patriarchal deity, should that have been a separate object of

21. Cf. W. H. Schmidt, *Königtum Gottes in Ugarit und Israel* (2nd ed. 1966), pp. 23ff. on the creative function of El. For the inscription see *ANET*, pp. 653f. Cf. also F. Stolz, "Strukturen und Figuren im Kult von Jerusalem," BZAW 118 (1970) 102-48; F. M. Cross, *Canaanite Myth and Hebrew Epic* (Cambridge, MA, 1973), pp. 1-75; idem, "אל," *TDOT*, I, 242-61.

22. Materially cf. also H. H. Schmid, "Jahweglaube und altorientalisches Weltordnungsdenken," in *Altorientalische Welt in der alttestamentlichen Theologie* (Zurich, 1974), pp. 31-63, esp. 38ff. Schmid rightly points out that we do not have here a careful or considered identification but an approximation of the context of experience of Yahweh worship to that of El or Baal religion to the extent that necessarily parallel or even identical expressions arose. El traditions seemed clearly relevant to Yahweh (pp. 46f., n. 58).

23. In "The Religion of the Patriarchs in Genesis," *Biblica* 61 (1980) 220-23, J. van Seters throws doubt on the theory of a specific patriarchal deity different from Yahweh and on a worship of El unrelated to the figure of Yahweh. But Exod. 6:3 states expressly that the patriarchs did not yet know the identity of the God Yahweh whom they worshiped, and the story in Exod. 3 agrees with this. The use of *'ēl* in Isa. 43:5, 10; 45:22; 46:9, which van Seters adduces in favor of a late dating of the references in Genesis, is undoubtedly the expression of an "increasing effort to identify Yahweh with the one universal deity reflected in the use of the term *el*" (p. 230), but this does not rule out the adoption of archaic reminiscences (cf. p. 221) that the tradition had preserved, which might have taken on new relevance in the situation of exile and which could give the argument the validation of traditional language. In view of the evidence in Exod. 3 and 6:3 and the uncontested significance of El in Canaanite testimonies from the second and early first millennia B.C., it seems most plausible to assume with Cross that the patriarchs worshiped El or a particular form of El, though it is an open question whether, along the lines of the theses of A. Alt, there perhaps stood in the background an originally independent nomadic deity that came to be fused with El.

cultic veneration. What happened was that Yahweh took over the tradition of the patriarchs, including the figure of El, and also of the El of Jerusalem. The process probably lasted until well into the period of the monarchy. But with the appropriation there was also a transformation of the cosmogonic functions related to El and more strongly to Baal.

In this regard von Rad's thesis that the biblical belief in creation had its origin in Israel's experience of Yahweh's acts in history contains an abiding kernel of truth. The ideas of the world's order and origin may not be new, but their character changes under the influence of Israel's experiences of the divine action in its history. This is a matter of supreme theological relevance, for connected with it is the distinctive nature of biblical ideas of God's creative action as compared with other conceptions of the world's origin, even though other cultures might also trace the world to a divine origin.

The motive behind the appropriation and alteration of the cosmological functions of El and Baal by Yahweh is Yahweh's holy zeal, his exclusive claim to worship, which comes to expression in the first commandment (Exod. 20:3 and esp. Deut. 6:14f.).[24] This claim made it impossible to think that the God of Sinai and the historical election and leading could be different from the author of the world and its order. The cosmic order and origin were traced back to the God of salvation history, and thereby unlimited power came to be seen in God's historical action. Not merely El was equated with Yahweh but also Baal, who unlike El sustains and renews the world as well as establishing it.[25] With the motif of the chaos dragon this creative activity of Baal was also transferred to Yahweh.[26] In both nature and history the universe is then the field of Yahweh's acts.[27] In the exilic psalms of complaint the chaos motif took on new relevance (Pss. 74:12ff.; 77:12ff.; 89:6ff.), since Yahweh had again to snatch the cosmos from chaos by his primal power. In Ps. 104:5ff., however, the earth has been established once and for all and is protected against the waters of chaos.[28]

24. Cf. W. H. Schmidt, "Die Frage nach der Einheit des Alten Testaments — im Spannungsfeld von Religionsgeschichte und Theologie," *Jahrbuch für biblische Theologie* 2 (1987) 33-57, esp 42ff.

25. Cf. Schmidt, *Königtum Gottes*, pp. 61f.

26. Ibid., pp. 46ff. Cf. J. Jeremias, *Das Königtum Gottes in den Psalmen. Israels Begegnung mit dem kanaanäischen Mythos in den Jahwe-Königs-Psalmen* (Göttingen, 1987), esp. pp. 29-45 on Ps. 29:3ff.

27. Ibid., p. 44.

28. Ibid., pp. 29, 49.

In Deutero-Isaiah, belief in creation becomes an argument for the expectation of a new saving action on the part of Yahweh that will demonstrate afresh his power over the course of history.[29] How closely the action in creation is here linked to the bringing forth of something historically new emerges in the use of creation terminology for the divine action in history. Thus the new thing that is coming is "created" (Isa. 48:7; cf. 43:19). As Yahweh "fashioned" light and "created" darkness, so he works salvation and catastrophe in history (45:7).[30] The question thus arises for theology whether the term "creation" may be reserved for the beginning of the world or whether we must expound it as the epitome of God's creative action in world history. Tension between these two aspects marks the biblical testimonies to God as Creator.

In connection with the exilic renaissance of belief in creation and a theology of creation, the first chapter of Genesis calls for evaluation. Here, in distinction from Deutero-Isaiah, God's creative action occurs at the beginning or founding of the world. It does not serve as an example or proof of anything historically new in the present. The founding of the world at the first has contemporary relevance, rather, in that the concern is with an order that stands unshakable right up to the present. In this regard the account corresponds to cosmogonic myths, especially the Babylonian Enuma Elish epic, which stands behind it. Nevertheless, the description of the divine creative action in Gen. 1 differs profoundly from the mythical presentation. The unrestricted nature of Yahweh's action corresponds to what we read in Deutero-Isaiah and the Psalms concerning the action of the one and only God in creation and history.

The Genesis story gave classical expression for ages to come to this unrestricted nature of God's power in creation. It did so by focusing on the divine Word of command as the only basis of the existence of creatures. Whether this version crowded out an earlier version,[31] or whether command and record went together from the very first,[32] it is clear in any case that creation on this view did not need to include a battle with chaos as

29. Cf. R. Rendtorff, "Die theologische Stellung des Schöpfungsglaubens bei Deutero-jesaja," *ZTK* 51 (1954) 3-13, esp. pp. 6f. on Isa. 40:12-17, 21-24, 27-31; 44:24ff., and p. 8 on 54:4-6.

30. Ibid., p. 11.

31. Cf. W. H. Schmidt, *Die Schöpfungsgeschichte der Priesterschrift* (2nd ed., Neukirchen-Vluyn, 1967), esp. pp. 169ff., cf. 115ff.

32. So O. H. Steck, *Der Schöpfungsbericht der Priesterschrift* (Göttingen, 1975), pp. 14-26, 246ff.

it did in the Babylonian epic or a struggle with the sea like that of the Ugaritic-Canaanite Baal, of which we still find echoes in the Psalms. The effortless nature of the simple command illustrates the unrestricted nature of the power at the disposal of the Creator.[33]

This idea, too, may be of mythical origin.[34] It was perhaps suggested in Israel by the prophetic view of the working of God's Word in history.[35] The idea that all things come into being through a magically operative word or through the royal command of God may be found as early as the third millennium in the Egyptian Memphis theology. It was related there to the royal God Ptah,[36] and then later in the Apophis myth it was ascribed to the sun-god Re.[37] No literary connection has been found between these texts and Gen. 1,[38] but at all events the concept of creation by the divine Word is not as such the unique feature in the biblical view of creation.

What is distinctive is that which creation by the Word demonstrates, which is the unlimited freedom of the act of creation, like that of the historical action of the God of Israel. The uniqueness of this concept stands in close relation to the uniqueness of the biblical God, which is the basis of the decisive difference from analogous cosmogonic ideas in ancient Near Eastern cultures. This unlimited freedom of the creative action later found expression in the formula "creation out of nothing" (first found in 2 Macc. 7:28; cf. Rom. 4:17; Heb. 11:3).[39]

In 2 Maccabees the phrase does not rule out any forming from existing matter. It simply means that the world was not previously there.[40] In Hellenistic Jewish writings we find the idea of creation out of shapeless primal matter (cf. Wis.

---

33. In Pss. 29, 93, and 104 God's kingship, like El's but unlike Baal's, is without beginning or end, not attained by a fight with chaos. Cf. J. Jeremias, *Königtum,* p. 27 on Ps. 93:1f., pp. 38f. on Ps. 29:3, 10, and pp. 42f.

34. We are not to say too quickly that creation by God's sovereign Word of power is antimythical, as does L. Scheffczyk (*Einführung in die Schöpfungslehre* [1975, 2nd ed. 1982], p. 11), clear though the difference may be from ideas of a battle with chaos. A middle position in this regard is the focus on the voice of Yahweh in Ps. 29:3ff., an idea that played a role in the Baal myth (Jeremias, *Königtum,* pp. 41f.).

35. The conjecture of Schmidt, *Schöpfungsgeschichte,* pp. 175f.

36. *ANET,* p. 5 (ll. 53ff.).

37. Ibid., pp. 6f.

38. So Schmidt, *Schöpfungsgeschichte,* p. 177.

39. Cf. also 2 Bar. 21:4; 48:8. For further examples cf. U. Wilckens, *Der Brief an die Römer,* 3 vols., EKK (Zurich/Neukirchen, 1978-82), I, 274, n. 887.

40. So G. May, *Schöpfung aus dem Nichts* (Berlin, 1978), p. 7. In an analogous expression Xenophon (*Mem.* 2.2.3) speaks of parents bringing forth their children out of nothing *(ek men ouk ontōn).*

11:17),[41] which recurs in Justin (*Apol.* 1.10.2) and Athenagoras (*Suppl.* 22.2).[42] Among the 2nd-century Christian Apologists Tatian was the first to insist that God must have brought forth the primal matter (*Or.* 5.3) because, as Justin had already taught (*Dial.* 5.4-6), there can be no second uncreated principle alongside God. This theme became pertinent in controversy with Marcion's dualism.[43]

Theophilus of Antioch and Irenaeus of Lyons played a decisive role in establishing the doctrine of creation out of nothing.[44] Theophilus in particular expressly opposed the Platonic idea of matter that was as uncreated as God (*Ad Autol.* 2.4). He argued that the greatness of God and his creative act may be seen only if he does not bring forth out of existing matter like human artists, but brings forth out of nothing whatever he wills. Irenaeus, too, emphasized that of his own free will God brought forth all things (*Adv. haer.* 2.1.1), including matter (2.10.4). At much the same time the renowned physician Galen, criticizing the Jewish doctrine of creation, called a view of this kind unreasonable, as the Platonic philosopher Celsus would also do in the 3rd century.

If the original point of the formula "creation out of nothing" was simply that the world did not exist before, and if the phrase came into dogmatic use in early patristic writings in order to exclude the dualistic idea of an eternal antithesis to God's creative activity, it is best not to follow Karl Barth in giving this "nothing" a reality again under the name of "nothingness" (*CD*, III/3, 289-368), even if it be only as "opposition and resistance" (p. 327), "in face of which God asserts Himself and exerts His positive will" (p. 351). Appeal to Gen. 1 (p. 352) cannot justify such a view, since the primal flood *(tehom)* that is briefly mentioned there is a demythologizing of the Babylonian Tiamat, whereas Barth equates this chaos with his nothingness and evil (pp. 352f.). Gen. 1 makes no reference to any resistance to God's creative activity. The unrestricted power of the divine Word of command rules out any such idea.

The different interpretation of "nothing" by J. Moltmann, which rests on Jewish speculations and which identifies it as the space that God gives creatures as he himself withdraws (*God in Creation* [San Francisco, 1985], pp. 86-88), must also be re-

---

41. May, *Schöpfung*, pp. 6ff., and on Philo, pp. 9ff.
42. Ibid., pp. 122-42.
43. Ibid., pp. 153ff. Prior to Tatian the Gnostic Basilides had taught creation out of nothing (pp. 71f., 74ff.). Cf. H. Chadwick's observations in "Freedom and Necessity in Early Christian Thought about God," *Cosmology and Theology*, ed. D. Tracy and N. Lash (Concilium 166; New York, 1983), pp. 8-13.
44. On Theophilus *Ad Autol.* 1.4, 8; 2.4.10, 13; cf. May, *Schöpfung*, pp. 159f.; on Irenaeus see ibid., pp. 167ff.

jected as a materially unfounded mystification of the subject. In a Christian doctrine of creation the trinitarian explication of the doctrine of creation must replace this thesis of Moltmann's, which in Jewish mysticism had the function of explaining the independence of creaturely existence alongside God. On the logical problem of the phrase "creation out of nothing," cf. E. Wölfel, *Welt als Schöpfung. Zu den Fundamentalsätzen der christlichen Schöpfungslehre heute* (Munich, 1981), pp. 26ff.

The unique character of the biblical concept of God's creative action rules out, then, any dualistic view of the origin of the world. The world is not the result of any working of God with another principle, as, e.g., in the description of the world's origin in Plato's *Timaeus* as the shaping of formless matter by a demiurge.[45] In a very different way a similar dualistic conception has been developed in modern philosophical thinking by the process philosophy of Alfred North Whitehead.[46] Along these lines many theologians, too, resist the classical doctrine of creation out of nothing. In Whitehead especially the difference from Platonic teaching lies in the thought of the creative self-fashioning of each finite being and event. God originates the form, but only in such a way as to give each event its initial aim.

Whitehead's God works by "persuasion," not by mighty creative action. In this regard he is more distant from the Creator God of the

45. On this cf. A. Dihle, *Die Vorstellung vom Willen in der Antike* (1982, repr. Göttingen, 1985), pp. 9, 12ff., 16f. On the reasons for the criticism cf. pp. 21ff. Dihle maintains that the idea of a will independent of intellectual pondering developed in antiquity only later and under the influence of biblical ideas (pp. 29f.).

46. A. N. Whitehead, *Process and Reality* (corr. ed. New York, 1978), pp. 348f.: "Opposed elements stand to each other in mutual requirement. . . . God and the World stand to each other in this opposed requirement. . . . Either of them, God and the World, is the instrument of novelty for the other." Therefore, "It is as true to say that God creates the World, as that the World creates God" and even "He does not create the world, he saves it." Cf. J. Cobb, *A Christian Natural Theology Based on the Thought of Alfred North Whitehead* (Philadelphia, 1965), pp. 203-5, and the comprehensive survey of different theological adaptions of Whitehead's concept of God in R. C. Neville, *Creativity and God: A Challenge to Process Theology* (New York, 1980), pp. 3-20. Neville focuses on purely immanent criticism of Whitehead's doctrine of God and the different attempts of his followers to overcome its inconsistencies. W. Temple had already offered an express theological criticism from the more theistic standpoint of a personal and purposeful God in *Nature, Man, and God* (London, 1934; 4th ed. 1949), pp. 257ff. L. Gilkey, *Maker of Heaven and Earth* (New York, 1959), pp. 48ff., finds in Whitehead's view of God's relation to the world a modern version of Platonic spirit-matter dualism in the context of differentiation of the Christian doctrine of creation from this thinking by the formula "creation out of nothing." Cf. also Moltmann, *God in Creation*, pp. 78f. Later Gilkey, like Temple before him, deals critically with the distinction between God and creativity in *Reaping the Whirlwind: A Christian Interpretation of History* (New York, 1976, 1981), pp. 248f., 414, n. 34.

Bible than Plato's demiurge. But the idea of a God who works by persuasion and not by sheer power has given the concept much of its
attraction.[47] There are features in common at this point with the traits
of patience and kindness that characterize the biblical God in his dealings
with his creatures as in love he seeks them even to the point of suffering
with those who have gone astray. Behind the biblical statements, however,
there is always the fact that the creatures owe all that they are to God's
almighty creative action. Once having called them into existence, the
biblical God then respects their independence in a way that is analogous
to Whitehead's description. There is truth in the contention that to attain
his ends in creation, and especially the end of the creature's own fulfillment, God works by persuasion and not by force. But the patience and
humble love with which God seeks his creatures are divine in the sense
that they do not proceed from weakness. They are an expression of the
love of the Creator, who willed that his creatures should be free and
independent.

Process theologians have rightly argued against the doctrine of
creation out of nothing that the existence of wickedness and evil in the
world causes it difficulty. It would seem that in his omnipotence a Creator
who acts with unrestricted freedom should have been able to create a
world without wickedness and evil. Their presence in creation has always
given rise to doubt whether God as an almighty Creator could be the God
of love whom Christians proclaim. By restricting the power of God, the
theological adherents of Whitehead's process philosophy seem at a first
glance to be able to offer a more illuminating answer to the experience of
wickedness and evil than the Christian doctrine of creation.

In truth, however, this teaching leads to the result that the creature
does not depend on God alone but on other powers, so that it cannot
rationally put full trust in God alone for the overcoming of evil in the
world. The devout in ancient Israel would rather trace back evil and
misfortune to their God (Jer. 45:4f.; Isa. 45:7; Amos 3:6) than recognize
a power of evil that is independent of God. Thus even Satan is a servant
of God in Job 1:6. In this way God alone will reverse the destiny of those

47. Cf. L. S. Ford, *The Lure of God: A Biblical Background for Process Theology*
(Philadelphia, 1978), esp. pp. 20ff.; J. Cobb, *God and the World* (Philadelphia, 1969), ch. 2,
"The One Who Calls" (pp. 42-66, esp. 63); J. Cobb and D. R. Griffin, especially on creation
out of nothing; cf. Ford, "An Alternative to *creatio ex nihilo*," *Religious Studies* 19 (1983)
205-13.

who suffer, even though it is beyond human understanding why he permits suffering and the dominion of evil in the world, and their persistence.

An attempt has sometimes been made to justify biblically Whitehead's version of the relation between God and the world by pointing out that the formula "creation out of nothing" is postbiblical and that the idea of continuous creation does better justice to the biblical witness.[48] As regards the formula, of course, continuous creation comes from an even later period (the Western Middle Ages; see below, pp. 40ff.) than does creation out of nothing. It also presupposes the strict concept of creation out of nothing by seeing in God's preservation its continuation. For this reason we cannot set the two formulas in antithesis to one another.

OT statements about creation in, e.g., Pss. 104:14-30; 139:13; 147:8f. refuse to limit the creative power of God by linking it with preexistent matter. Like the thought of creation by the Word in Gen. 1, they imply the unrestricted freedom of God's creative action that the phrase "creation out of nothing" would later express (cf. P. Hefner in *Christian Dogmatics*, ed. C. E. Braaten et al. [Philadelphia, 1984], I, 309ff., esp. p. 310). In this respect the statements in the Psalms are not in tension with the account in Gen. 1. The only difference is that they do not limit God's creative action to the beginning of the world. They are not dealing, however, with the same issue as the formula "creation out of nothing." In the fathers this phrase was simply meant to reject any correlation of God's creative action with a principle distinct from God. The biblical statements offer no basis for the view that the formula rejected.

The reason that the biblical belief in creation that found classical expression in Gen. 1 could not make any concession to a dualistic cosmogony also differentiates it from the opposite view of the relation of God to the world in the act of its creation. If a dualistic view of the world's origin limits the Creator's freedom in his almighty working, the divine freedom in the systems of a philosophical monism falls victim to an iron necessity governing the cosmic process subsequent to its origin. On this view God himself seems to be tied to the logic of his own nature, the logic that everything has to happen as in fact it does.

Ancient views of *heimarmenē* prepared the way for this type of monism. It came to full development when *heimarmenē* was no longer seen as the fate that rules

48. Cf. the influential work of I. G. Barbour, *Issues in Science and Religion* (Englewood Cliffs, NJ, 1966, 1968), pp. 383ff.; see also R. J. Russell, "Contingency in Physics and Cosmology: A Critique of the Theology of Wolfhart Pannenberg," *Zygon* 23 (1988) 23-43, esp. 25.

over the gods but as the divine power over the cosmos, as in the older Stoicism of Chrysippus, who could equate the *pneuma* that permeates the world with Zeus and his providence.[49] Stoic monism, of course, did not as yet regard the world as a necessary development from its divine origin, for it found in the visible cosmos the body of the *logos* that is ruled and ordered by the latter's *diakosmēsis*.[50] The difference from the biblical doctrine of creation was unmistakable, but this view did not stand in antithesis to a system of emanation.

To many, Neoplatonism offers an example of such a system. But the philosophy of Plotinus made only sparse and restricted use of the idea of the procession or outflowing of *nous* and the world soul from the One,[51] and it traced the existence of a visible world to a fall of the soul, i.e., the world soul, which by wanting more produced time and the transitory world (Plotinus *Enn.* 3.7.11). The emergence of the visible world does not follow necessarily from the nature of the One or *nous*. Rightly, then, the common view that Plotinus taught an emanation of the visible world from the One has come under criticism.[52] The situation is different in Proclus in the sense that he abandoned the element of freedom in the Platonic thesis of the origin of time from a fall of the world soul, in favor of a continuous procession of the stages of being from the One.[53]

By way of Pseudo-Dionysius the Areopagite and the *theologica Platonica* the thoughts of Proclus made their way into the discussions of Latin Scholasticism.[54] Approaches to monistic thinking might be found already in Arabic Averroism. The Scholastic doctrine of God warded off both dangers by developing a psychology of the cooperation of will and intellect in God, with an increasing emphasis on the will.

Spinoza's criticism of the anthropomorphism of the ideas of will and intellect in God[55] was thus a precondition of the revival of philosophical monism. Through Spinoza, monism became a challenge in the modern period to the

49. M. Pohlenz, *Die Stoa. Geschichte einer geistigen Bewegung,* 2 vols. (Göttingen, 1959), I, 102ff. (cf. II, 58ff.).

50. Ibid., I, 78f. and the examples in II, 45f.

51. Cf. K. Kremer, "Emanation," *HWP,* II (1972), 445-48, esp. 446.

52. W. Beierwaltes, *Plotin über Ewigkeit und Zeit* (1967, 3rd ed. 1981), pp. 17ff., sees in the interpretation of the teaching of Plotinus as an emanation system a misunderstanding of the depiction of the origin of *nous* and the soul from the One, since in the process this remains as it is (cf. pp. 166f.).

53. On the differences between the systems of Proclus and Plotinus cf. W. Beierwaltes, *Denken des Einen. Studien zur neuplatonischen Philosophie und ihrer Wirkungsgeschichte* (1985), pp. 155-92, esp. 170f. on Proclus's criticism of the derivation of time from a fall of the soul in Plotinus.

54. The Areopagite, however, avoided the danger of emanationism, according to J. Meyendorff, *Christ in Eastern Christian Thought* (Washington, D.C., 1969), pp. 73f. See also W. Beierwaltes, "Andersheit. Grundriss einer neuplatonischen Begriffsgeschichte," *Archiv für Begriffsgeschichte* 16 (1972) 166-97.

55. On this see vol. I, 375f.

Christian understanding of God in his relation to the world. Hegel gave it its most nuanced shape, in which it absorbed the Christian doctrine of the Trinity and took the form of an interpretation of this doctrine. Here it found its focus in the thesis that the element of otherness in the divine unity could achieve its full right, i.e., the right of difference, only by emanation of the world of the finite from the Absolute.[56] Because of its affinity to Christian theology this Hegelian monism has to rank as a special challenge to it and was felt as such from the very first. In materialistic forms of modern monism[57] the opposition to Christian faith is much more obvious because it usually involves a contesting of God's existence altogether.

It is essential for the Christian understanding of God's freedom in his activity as Creator that he did not have to create the world out of some inner necessity of his own nature. If he did, he would be dependent in his very essence on the existence of the world. This would be true even if we merely thought of the world as a tiny aspect of his divine self-actualization. Such a view, which grants the world only a very insignificant being, would be incompatible with Christian teaching on the other side as well. We see this from the saving economy of the divine action, which aims at the consummation of creation.[58] The freedom of the divine origin of the world on the one hand and God's holding fast to his creation on the other belong together. The nature of the link may be deduced from the concept of divine love as the world's origin. God's love and freedom are inseparably related, but we must not misconstrue the freedom of love as caprice. At the same time, we are also not to view it as an emotional force that overpowers all personal freedom. The trinitarian explication of the concept of divine love avoids both these misconceptions. Hence the biblical concept of creation needs a trinitarian basis if it is to be proof against misunderstandings and shortsighted criticism.

56. G. W. F. Hegel, *Lectures on the Philosophy of Religion*, III (London, 1896), pp. 1ff. Cf. the text of the Lasson ed. (PhB, 63, 85), and *Logik*, II (PhB, 57, 485), to the effect that in the sphere of the divine idea the difference is not yet otherness but remains perfectly clear to itself. Hegel speaks expressly of necessity in the development of the Absolute in the first part of his *Lectures on the Philosophy of Religion* (PhB, 59, 185f.). On the criticism of Hegel by J. Müller, *Die christliche Lehre von der Sünde* (1838, 3rd ed. Breslau, 1849), I, 552, cf. my discussion in *The Idea of God in Human Freedom* (Philadelphia, 1973).

57. Cf. "Monismus," HWP, VI (1984), 132-36.

58. For a similar judgment cf. Gilkey, *Maker of Heaven and Earth*, pp. 58ff.

§ 3. The Trinitarian Origin of the Act of Creation

The contingency of the world as a whole and of all individual events, things, and beings has its basis in the omnipotent freedom of the divine creating. Precisely by this freedom of its origin, that things are or are not becomes an expression of divine love. God had only one reason to create a world, the reason that is proclaimed in the fact of creation itself, namely, that God graciously confers existence on creatures, an existence alongside his own divine being and in distinction from him. Part of this creating is the continuity of creaturely existence. Only as it continues to be does creaturely existence acquire the independence of its own being distinct from God's. We see here the intention of the Creator, which is inseparably connected with the act of creation and which has the existence of creatures as its goal.

Strangely, Hans Blumenberg completely overlooked this aspect in his criticism of the Christian concept of God's omnipotent freedom as the origin of the world. Blumenberg saw in the contingency of the creature only the correlate of blind caprice (*Die Legitimität der Neuzeit* [Frankfurt am Main, 1966], pp. 102-200). Purely arbitrary action, however, is not compatible with the eternity of the Creator God. Even as a free act the creation of the world has to stand in relation to God's eternity as an act of the eternal God. Essential to the idea of caprice is the element of the momentary or ephemeral. Relation to what precedes and follows excludes pure caprice. But we have to posit such a relation in all God's actions, even where something totally new takes place. At least in retrospect we can still see a connection with what precedes. This is true of the relation of the divine action in creation to God's intratrinitarian life.

The act of creation, then, is not an expression of pure caprice. Furthermore, a God who made the world out of pure caprice would not be the author of a world that is upheld. The idea of divine caprice as the origin of the world is incompatible with God's creative will constantly to preserve the world. We shall see that the God of the Bible even holds fast to his creatures beyond the end that is posited with their finitude, i.e., with a view to the eschatological consummation of his creation. The free origin of a lasting creation has to be viewed as the expression of an intention to create this reality that is different from his own, which has its basis in the eternity of the Creator.

But how are we to reconcile such an eternal intention with the freedom of the act of creation? Moltmann seeks a solution to this problem in the older Reformed doctrine of the eternal decree of the divine will that precedes the act of creation (*God in Creation*, pp. 79ff.). The union of nature and will in the concept of the eternal decree rules out any concept of a capricious God. But is not the freedom of the act of creation lost in this teaching inasmuch as the act seems to be only the necessary expression of God's eternal nature? Karl Barth rightly saw this and tried to correct it by substituting for the doctrine of the eternal decree his own christologically based doctrine of election (*CD*, II/2, 145ff.). Whatever criticisms might be brought against this thesis from the standpoint of election (cf. Pannenberg, "Erwählung III. Dogmatisch," *RGG*, II [3rd ed. 1958], 614-21), Barth did in this way give a trinitarian basis to the whole sphere of God's relations to the world.

We might have expected this from Moltmann too, since he argues so forcefully for the trinitarian meaning of the Christian belief in God. Like similar constructions in other confessional traditions, however, the older Reformed doctrine of the eternal divine decree was the expression of a nontrinitarian monotheism that Moltmann rightly criticized. Did not this mean, however, that it could not really protect the freedom of the divine act of creation? The attacks of Lutherans of the day on the Reformed doctrine of the decree as fatalistic determinism certainly did not do justice to the good intentions of the Reformed theologians, but did they not correctly show how unattainable is the notion of a union of nature and will in the concept of the eternal decree? Such a concept is far too close to the idea of emanation. Theology has to develop the thought that the creation of the world is an expression of the love of God (Moltmann, pp. 75f.) along trinitarian lines, and to seek here an answer to the question regarding the freedom of the divine act of creation.

The very existence of the world is an expression of the goodness of God. This statement of the Christian belief in creation relates first to the person of the Father. God is Father as the origin of creatures in their contingency by granting them existence, caring for them, and making possible their continued life and independence.

The goodness of the Father as Creator, by which he gives and upholds the existence of his creatures, is not different, however, from the love with which the Father from all eternity loves the Son. The Son is the primary object of the Father's love. In all the creatures to which he addresses his love he loves the Son. This does not mean that he does not love the creatures as such, each in its own distinctiveness. The love of the Father is directed not merely to the Son but also to each of his creatures. But the turning of the Father to each of his creatures in its distinctiveness is always mediated through the Son. The Father's love for his creatures is not in competition with the love with which from all eternity he loves the Son. The creatures are objects of the Father's love as they are drawn into his eternal turning to the Son. In other words, they become the object of the Father's love because the eternal Son is manifested in them.

In the Son is the origin of all that differs from the Father, and therefore of the creatures' independence vis-à-vis the Father. In this statement I am trying to repeat materially what the NT says about the mediation of the Son (Heb. 1:2) or the divine Logos (John 1:3) in creation. We have to recall that all the statements about the eternal Son of the Father are based on statements about the man Jesus in his relation to his heavenly Father. The concrete relation of Jesus to the Father always combines divine and creaturely aspects of the relation, for over and above the historicity of the relation, Christian doctrine affirms that God is essentially as he is shown to be by Jesus. The relation to Jesus as Son is intrinsic to the eternal deity of the Father.

Decisive in this regard is the self-distinction of Jesus from the Father, by which he lets God be God as Father over against himself, differentiating himself as a mere creature from the Father, subjecting himself to the one true God, letting his life be totally determined by him, as his message demands, for the future of the human relation to the divine rule, and thus letting the Father be the one God in testimony to his sole deity. This event of the self-distinction of Jesus from the Father constitutes the revelation of the eternal Son in the earthly existence of Jesus. By the humility of his distinction from the Father as the one God to whom alone all honor is due, Jesus proves himself to be the Son. Hence we have first a *noetic* basis for his eternal sonship in this distinction from the Father. But are we not also to seek in the self-distinction of the eternal Son from the Father an *ontic* basis for the existence of the creature in its distinction from the Creator? The self-distinction of the Son, which corresponds to the fatherly address to him and which gives the Father alone the honor of being the one God, forms a starting point for the otherness and independence of creaturely existence. For if the eternal Son in the humility of his self-distinction from the Father moves out of the unity of the deity by letting the Father alone be God, then the creature emerges over against the Father, the creature for whom the relation to the Father and Creator is fundamental, i.e., the human creature.[59] With this creature, however,

59. This situation is as K. Rahner described it in principle in his "Theology of the Incarnation," in *Theological Investigations* (23 vols.; London, 1961-92), IV, 105ff. (also with some differences in his *Foundations of Christian Faith* [New York, 1978], p. 225): When God wills to be not God, human beings come into existence. Rahner can thus regard the assumption of human nature by the Logos in the incarnation as the creation of humanity by the Logos, adducing the saying of Augustine regarding creation by assumption (PL, 42, 688, quoted by Rahner in *LThK*, V, 956). To this idea Rahner then links the thought of the

the existence of the world is posited, for it is the condition of the possibility of this creature.[60]

We have here the same theme as that of the confession of the deity of Jesus, but now in the mode of an inversion. As Jesus shows himself to be the eternal Son of the Father in his obedience as the Son, the distinction of his humanity from the eternal God is not sidetracked, for as an acknowledged distinction from the one God it is the condition of the sonship of Jesus. The ongoing difference of the human Jesus from the eternal God, and therefore also from the eternal Son, means materially that the eternal Son not only precedes the human existence of Jesus but is also the basis of his creaturely existence. The existence of Jesus, like that of all creatures, has its basis in God, the Creator of the world. With his difference and self-distinction from God, however, it is grounded in the self-distinction of the eternal Son from the Father. Hence the eternal Son is the ontic basis of the human existence of Jesus in his relation to God as Father. But if from all eternity, and thus also in the creation of the world, the Father is not without the Son, the eternal Son is not merely the ontic basis of the existence of Jesus in his self-distinction from the Father as the one God; he is also the basis of the distinction and independent existence of all creaturely reality.

Conversely, it is only on the condition thus formulated that in the creaturely existence of Jesus there can be manifested the eternal Son of the Father who is the Creator of the world. The creaturely existence of

---

self-emptying of the Logos in the incarnation by assuming, and of assuming by self-emptying (*Theological Investigations*, IV, 117; cf. *Foundations*, p. 226). If we follow up this line of thinking, we cannot see in the self-emptying any loss of essence on the part of the Logos. It is the self-actualization of the Logos in the other, in the act of the creation of humanity. In the first instance, at any rate, we have here an act of the Logos, the second person of the Trinity. Certainly it corresponds to an action of the Father, i.e., his sending by the Father. But the Son is the primary subject, though he does not act alone, but in fellowship with the Father through the Spirit.

60. Materially these statements correspond to Barth's theses that creation is the external basis of the covenant (*CD*, III/1, 94ff.) and that the covenant is the internal basis of creation (pp. 228ff.). But Barth moves on from the election of the Son to the concept of the covenant, not from the self-distinction of the Son to the existence of the creature (the human creature and the world of creatures). Hence the total picture is different. In contrast to my presentation it centers on the subjectivity of the Father as the electing God. Rahner, however, argues from the self-distinction of the Son from the Father (see n. 59 above). Barth's orientation to the idea of the electing God leads him to the concept of the covenant; less significance then attaches to creation at the beginning (see below, pp. 38f.). I myself take the same path as Rahner does in his incarnational theology, moving on from the thought of the eternal Son to the concept of humanity. Reflection on the world as the external basis of human existence refers only to the relation between humanity and world *within* creation.

Jesus actualizes in the course of his life the cosmic structure and destiny of all creaturely reality as in distinction from creation Jesus *assumes* his distinction from God the Father and totally affirms and accepts himself as God's creature, and God as his Father. This presupposes that Jesus is not just creature but human creature. As such he is not just factually different from God. He is also aware of this difference, of the finitude of his existence in distinction from the eternal God. Having religion is a mark of the uniqueness of the human creature among all others. Awareness of God in distinction from everything finite is the supreme expression of the human ability to distinguish and to be oneself when with the other.[61] The determination of everything finite, i.e., distinction from the Infinite and from everything else that is finite, is thus a theme for the human creature.

But it does not follow that human beings accept their own finitude. They usually live in revolt against it and seek unlimited expansion of their existence. They want to be like God. Jesus, however, accepted his finitude, and with it the finitude of the human creature and of all creaturely existence in relation to God, by honoring God as his own Father and Creator, and as the Father and Creator of all creatures. To honor God as the one God of all creatures, however, is not possible without drawing all other human beings, and in the first place the people that is elected to bear witness to God's deity, into recognition of the deity of God and his unrestricted lordship over their lives. Jesus, then, put his own existence in the service of the glorifying of God. In this obedience of the Son the structure and destiny of creaturely existence found their fulfillment in Jesus of Nazareth. In this way the eternal Son is the ontic basis of the creaturely existence of Jesus and all creaturely existence. As such he was manifested in the historical relation of Jesus to the Father.

As regards his function as the mediator of creation, the NT develops the idea of the Son of God in connection with the Jewish concept of preexistent divine wisdom (Prov. 8:22-31) and expresses it in terms of the concept of the Logos (Col. 1:15-20; Heb. 1:2f.; John 1:1ff.).[62] In *Jesus — God and Man*, § 10.3, I linked these NT sayings to another group of NT christological statements, those pertaining to the election or predestination of Jesus Christ to be the Head of a new humanity (Heb. 1:2: "whom he appointed the heir of all things, through whom also he

---

61. In proof cf. my *Anthropology in Theological Perspective* (Philadelphia, 1985), pp. 62ff., 66ff.
62. Cf. H. Hegermann, *Die Vorstellung vom Schöpfungsmittler im hellenistischen Judentum und Urchristentum* (1961).

created the world"; cf. Col. 1:16, 20; Eph. 1:10). What is said here about the Son as Mediator of creation has primarily a "final" sense. It is to the effect that creation will be consummated only in Jesus Christ.

Yet true though this is in the light of the NT statements, it is not the only aspect of the Son's mediation of creation. The final ordering of creatures to the manifestation of Jesus Christ presupposes that creatures already have the origin of their existence and nature in the Son. Otherwise the final summing up of all things in the Son (Eph. 1:10) would be external to the things themselves, so that it would not be the definitive fulfillment of their own distinctive being. If, however, the creatures have their origin in the eternal Son or Logos, then as creatures aware of themselves they will be alienated from themselves so long as they do not perceive and receive the law of their own nature in this Logos. Thus we read in the prologue to John: "The world was made by him, yet the world knew him not" (1:10b). This situation is presupposed in the event of the incarnation and is the basis of the statement that follows in v. 11 that in the incarnation the Logos came to his own "possession."

The theological tradition has explained the participation of the eternal Son in the act of creation with the help of the idea that the Logos corresponds to the divine intellect, which from all eternity contains within itself the images of things, the ideas. This notion goes back to the link that Middle Platonism made between Plato's doctrine of the ideas and the divine *nous,* or, in Philo, the divine *logos.*[63] Origen incorporated it fully into his systematic presentation of Christian doctrine. According to him the origins, ideas, and forms of all creatures are present in the hypostatic wisdom of God, the Son.[64] He thus calls the wisdom of scripture (Prov. 8:22) the beginning of the ways of God *(initium viarum Dei).*[65] Later patristic authors developed the thought in different ways. Thus Maximus the Confessor suggested that the many *logoi* of individual creatures are all summed up and contained in the one Logos.[66]

63. According to H. J. Krämer, *Der Ursprung der Geistmetaphysik* (Amsterdam, 1967), the corresponding statements in Albinus *Didascalicus* 9f. (cf. pp. 101ff., 111f.) go back to Xenocrates (pp. 121f.) and even to Plato himself (pp. 218f.). On the Logos as the epitome of the ideas in Philo cf. pp. 264-81, esp. p. 276. On Clement of Alexandria cf. pp. 282f., also H. Meinhardt, "Idee," *HWP,* IV (1976), 61f.

64. Origen, *De princ.* 1.2.2: *vel initiae, vel rationes, vel species.*

65. Ibid. 1.2.3. Materially we also find the Philonic idea of the ideas in the Logos in Tatian *Or.* 5.1, though the reference there is to the *logikē dynamis* and there is no mention of the ideas. See M. Elze, *Tatian und seine Theologie* (Göttingen, 1960), pp. 74f.

66. PG, 91, 1081B-C; cf. L. Thunberg, *Microcosm and Mediator: The Theological Anthropology of Maximus the Confessor* (Lund, 1965), pp. 80f.

Augustine thought of the Son as God's creative Word, by which all things are present to God even before they are created.[67] In medieval Scholasticism, however, the doctrine of divine knowledge led to a linking of the thought of ideas in God to the unity of the divine essence. This was especially true of Aquinas, who traced God's ideas of creatures back to knowledge of his own essence as the prototype for different creatures.[68] Aquinas did, of course, relate the creative action of God to the person of the Son, for God creates all things by his Word. On his view, however, this means that the Son, like the Spirit, shares in the act of creation only inasmuch as the processions of these persons are linked to the essential qualities of the divine knowing and willing.[69] The basic idea is that creation as an outward act is to be ascribed to the trinitarian God as subject, so that we need not differentiate the specific contributions of the individual divine persons. This was still the thinking of the older Protestant dogmatics. The three persons do not work, then, as three different causes with common outward working as the result. In its inseparable unity the act of creation corresponds to the inseparable unity of the divine essence.[70] Hence the ancient confession of the mediatorship of Christ in creation, while not denied, is stripped of all function. The Son did indeed participate in creation. But that he did so is simply an implication of the doctrine of the Trinity. It carries with it no specific idea of the nature of the participation.

The concept of a preformation of creaturely things in the divine mind through a variety of ideas brought with it from the very outset many conceptual problems. Thus there was an apparent contradiction with the unity of the divine essence. In addition the linking of God's creative will to a model that was already there from eternity in his intellect, so that the act of creation simply gave existence to the model, constituted a special difficulty. If the solution of Aquinas offered a way out of the first problem, Occam's criticism of the anchoring of the divine ideas in the essentiality of God kept the second to the fore and tried to confront it in the interests of the contingency of creaturely reality and its immediacy to the will of God.[71] Occam's interpretation of the Augustinian doctrine of ideas thus

---

67. Augustine *De Gen. ad litt.* 2.6.12: "the only-begotten Son in whom all things were created before they were created" (PL, 34, 268). In expounding John 1:2 Augustine speaks expressly of the idea in the mind of the artist that precedes the real object (*In Joann.* 1.17 [PL, 35, 1387]). Cf. *De div. quaest. oct.* 46.2 (PL, 40, 30f.).

68. *ST* 1.15.2. For a perspicacious discussion of the ideas in High Scholasticism see K. Bannach, *Die Lehre von der doppelten Macht Gottes bei Wilhelm von Ockham* (Wiesbaden, 1975), pp. 111-248, esp. 135ff. on Henry of Ghent and 154ff. on Duns Scotus; cf. also C. Knudsen et al., "Idee," *HWP*, IV (1976), 86-101.

69. *ST* 1.45.6; cf. art. 6 ad 2.

70. We may simply adduce Hollaz, *Examen*, 513 (see n. 9 above): "As the divine essence is one and indivisible, so the act of creation is one and indivisible."

71. Cf. K. Bannach, *Lehre*, pp. 225-48. Occam rejected any identification of the ideas with the divine wisdom (*Ord.* 1 d 35 q 5 a 3 [*Opera theologica*, IV (1979), pp. 488, 3-7]; cf. Bannach, *Lehre*, pp. 226ff.) and instead related them to the creatures and their creation (pp. 227ff.; cf. *Opera*, IV, 488, 15-18).

tends to dissolve it. Descartes, who at this point as at others followed Occam to a large extent in his views of God and creation, makes the logical inference that God did not need any preceding ideas in creating the world.[72]

Leibniz, however, found in the Cartesian "eternal varieties" ideas in the divine intellect that precede the resolves of the divine will and therefore precede creaturely things.[73] This was the basis of his linking of the divine will to what God's wisdom recognized to be the best of all possible worlds. Leibniz thus came close to the view that Kant later discussed and according to which the cosmic plan is a necessary object of the divine wisdom but is not to be seen as a consequence of this incomprehensible being. On this Kant observed that "the dependence of other things is simply limited to their existence, so that a large part of the basis of so much perfection of the highest nature is withheld from them and allotted to I know not what eternal nonthings."[74]

Realistically appraising the difficulties that have come to light in the history of the notion of divine ideas as various preexistent models of things and their order in the divine mind, modern theology refrains from following this route in its interpretation of the mediatorship of the Son in creation. The notion not only implies a much too anthropomorphic distinguishing and relating of understanding and will in God but fails to do justice to two characteristic elements in the biblical belief in creation — namely, the contingency and historicity of the reality that results from God's creative action.

How, then, are we to understand the mediatorship of the eternal Son in creation and his function as the Logos of all creation? Hegel's philosophy of religion offers a conceptual starting point that takes up in a new way the material concern of the older doctrine of divine ideas united in the Logos, i.e., the concern to understand the creation of the many from the divine unity. Hegel replaced the static concept of an intelligible cosmos of ideas with the concept of a principle that generates the plurality and distinction of creaturely things. He also revived the christological character of the concept in contrast to the medieval and postmedieval

72. R. Descartes, *Meditationes* (Amsterdam, 1685), with objections and answers, pp. 580f. (Answer to Six Objections, n. 6). Cf. E. Gilson on the beginning of part V of the *Discours de la méthode* in *Descartes, Discours de la méthode, Texte et Commentaire* (1925, 5th ed. 1976), pp. 342f.

73. G. W. Leibniz, *Monadology*, §§ 43, 46; *Theodicy*, §§ 180-92.

74. I. Kant, *Der einzig mögliche Beweisgrund zu einer Demonstration des Daseyns Gottes* (1763), pp. 181f., ET *The One Possible Basis for a Demonstration of the Existence of God* (New York, 1979); cf. H.-G. Redmann, *Gott und Welt. Die Schöpfungstheologie in der vorkritischen Periode Kants* (Göttingen, 1962), pp. 99ff., 105ff.

doctrine of ideas in the divine mind. Hegel's thesis is that in the Trinity the Son is the principle of otherness, the starting point for the emergence of the finite as that which is absolutely other than deity.[75] This thesis not only describes the transition from the divine life to the existence of the finite but also offers a reason for the multiplicity of the finite inasmuch as everything finite has the characteristic of being other vis-à-vis the other. Otherness, then, may be seen as the generative principle of the multiplicity of creaturely reality. In place of the static cosmos of ideas that the traditional view of the divine ideas in the mind of God postulated as models of creation, we find here a productive principle behind the emergence of ever new distinctions and therefore of ever new and different forms of finite existence.

Hegel's idea of the emergence of finitude from the Son as the principle of otherness was said to be in need of criticism (cf. n. 56 above) because he linked to it the thought of a logically necessary self-development of the Absolute in producing a world of the finite. This thesis is not compatible with the belief in creation. It occurs in Hegel because he presented the Trinity as the development of an absolute subject after the pattern of the self-consciousness. If we already think of the other in the form of the Son as the product of the moving of the absolute subject out of unity with itself, then it seems plausible enough that this self-alienation necessarily goes on to produce the finite, since only thus do we seriously have the principle of otherness.

But if we think of the life of the Trinity in terms of the mutuality

75. Cf. the references in n. 56 above. Meister Eckhart had already moved in this direction, revising Lombard's separation of the doctrines of creation and the Trinity; cf. L. Scheffczyk, *Schöpfung und Vorsehung* (1963), pp. 80f., also 92ff. on Aquinas. In his *Opus tripartitum* Eckhart related Gen. 1:1 to John 1:1 and concluded that the Word or Son is the "beginning" in which all things were created *(Expositio libri Genesis)*. Appealing to Job 33:14 in the same work, he declared that the generation of the Son and the creation of the world took place in one act. In 1329 John XXII included this statement among the twenty-six condemned theses (DS § 953 = ND § 406/3) because it seemed to deny the origin of the world in time. The condemnation misses the point, however, that the temporal origin has to be thought of as proceeding from the eternity of God (Scheffczyk, *Schöpfung und Vorsehung*, p. 103). Nor does it do justice to the regaining of a trinitarian starting point for the doctrine of creation in Eckhart. Eckhart did not expressly see in the mediatorship of the Son the origin of the otherness of creation in relation to God, though in expounding John 1:1b he did speak of that which proceeds from God being different from God. Even Nicholas of Cusa excluded the thought of *alteritas* from the concept of God and also from that of being *(De visione dei* 14). He defined truth itself as an absence of all otherness *(carentia alteritatis, Compl. theol.* II) and thought there would be no otherness in God's kingdom *(De doctae ignor.* I, 536).

of the relations of the trinitarian persons, no such necessity arises. For each of the persons, self-distinction from the others is a condition of their fellowship in the unity of the divine life, irrespective of the different forms of the self-distinction in each case. Thus the divine life is a self-enclosed circle, which needs no other outside itself. The self-distinction may take on its sharpest form in the Son, but precisely by this act of self-distinction, he too remains in the unity of the divine life because it is the condition of his unity with the Father. Nevertheless, in the event of the incarnation, in the relation of Jesus of Nazareth to his heavenly Father, the Son moved out of the unity of the Godhead. In his awareness of being a mere human, a creature, in his self-distinction from the Father, Jesus recognized the Father as the one God over against himself. In so doing he gave validity to the independent existence of other creatures alongside himself. This was part of the humility of the recognition and acceptance of creatureliness.

Related to it again is the fact that subjection to the Father as the one God of all creatures finds fulfillment in a sending to others in testimony to the deity of God. In this self-distinction from the Father Jesus showed himself to be the Son who is the eternal correlate of the fatherhood of God. Included here is the truth that the relation of the eternal Son to the Father must include at least the *possibility* of his moving out of the unity of the divine life into existence in the form of a creature. We may not speak in this regard of any divine necessity because precisely in his self-distinction the Son remains bound to the Father in the unity of the divine life. Yet insofar as the Son lets the Father alone be God and is aware that as the one God the Father is distinct from himself, it is possible that his sonship may come to realization in that other form, in the distinction of creaturely life that accepts itself in its creaturely finitude and in so doing honors the Father as its Creator.

In this sense we may view the Son's mediation in creation not only as a structural model (and in this way the Logos) of the determination of all creaturely being for fellowship with God by acceptance of its distinction from him, but also as the origin of the existence of creaturely reality. With this we must presuppose that in his moving out of the unity of the divine life, as in all else, the Son is obedient to the Father. The Son is not alone the Creator of the world. He moves out of the deity in execution of the mission that he is given by the Father. Hence the Christian church confesses the Father as the Creator of the world, not the Son, for the only content of the work of the Son is to serve the Father and to bring in his kingdom. The Father thus acts as Creator through the Son. Nevertheless, the Son's moving out of the deity to become the Logos of a world of creatures must be regarded no less as an expression of his own free decision. This is obvious if we are to expound the concept of the divine Logos in terms of the relationship of Jesus as Son to his heavenly Father.

Barth did not do full justice to this aspect in his presentation of the trinitarian origin of creation. He certainly rejected the idea that "exclusively God the Father is the Creator" (CD, III/1, 49). The work of creation is *appropriated* to the person of the Father. According to Barth, however, the Son's part is simply that it was with a view to the Son that the Father created us humans and our world (pp. 50f.). Barth says nothing about the Son's own subjectivity, in spite of assuring us of the mutuality of the love of Father and Son in the Holy Spirit (p. 56). In keeping with this is Barth's teaching about the relation between creation and the covenant. Only in the logic of a plan and its execution (cf. CD, III/3, 4ff.) can creation be presented as the external basis of the covenant and the covenant as the internal basis of creation, i.e., its intended goal. In Barth, however, the subject to whom this action is ordered is the Father, even though from the outset he acts with a view to the Son.

In the free self-distinction of the Son from the Father the independent existence of a creation distinct from God has its basis, and in this sense we may view creation as a free act not only of the Father but of the trinitarian God. It does not proceed necessarily from the fatherly love of God that is oriented from all eternity to the Son. The basis of its possibility is the free self-distinction of the Son from the Father; even as the Son moves out of the unity of deity, he is still united with the Father by the Spirit, who is the Spirit of freedom (2 Cor. 3:17). The Father sends the Son but thereby lays on him no compulsion to follow a command of fatherly love as though by outer constraint. In a free act of fulfilling his sonship, the Son himself moves out of the divine unity by letting the Father alone be the one God. That even in this act of freedom he is one with the will of the Father can be understood only in the light of a third thing, namely, that we have here an expression of the fellowship of the Spirit that unites the two. Thus creation is a free act of God as an expression of the freedom of the Son in his self-distinction from the Father, and of the freedom of the fatherly goodness that in the Son accepts the possibility and the existence of a creation distinct from himself, and of the freedom of the Spirit who links the two in free agreement.

This Christian understanding of the free origin of the world from God differs from both the Neoplatonic and the Hegelian views. The philosophy of Plotinus traced physical existence and the visible world back to a fall of the world soul (*Enn.* 3.7.11). In this respect he followed Plato, who in the great myth of his *Phaedrus* (248c-d) described bodily existence as the result of a fall of souls. Plotinus expanded Plato's conception into the idea of a fall of the world soul due to a restless longing for "more" beyond mere fellowship with the One by the *nous*. This thought of a fall of souls as the origin of physical existence and the visible world found its way into Christian theology in Origen (*De princ.* 1.3.8, also 4.1; cf. Jerome in PL, 23, 368ff.). We also find it in Gnostics like Valentinus (cf. P. Kübel, *Schuld und Schicksal bei Origenes, Gnostikern und Platonikern* [1973], pp. 95f.). The 6th-century church rejected this view along with what it presupposes, i.e., the preexistence of souls (DS § 403 = ND § 401/1: Justinian's 543 edict; DS § 433: condemnation of Origenist teachings by the Fifth Ecumenical Council in 553). This is in opposition to Christian truth, according to which God did not create the visible world as a place of punishment for fallen creatures but as good by its original nature and destiny.

The philosophical monism of Hegel is closer to Christianity, for it arose on the soil of Christian truth and as an interpretation of it. The difference, as noted above, is that Hegel saw creation as necessary, supposedly because the distinction must have its validity in itself (*Philosophy of Religion,* III, 27f.). This necessity is that of the development of the absolute Subject. Though Hegel says that the distinction has its validity (i.e., that of distinction) in the Son, in the determination of the distinction (p. 37), he views the Son only as the logical element of distinction and not personally as a free principle of self-distinction.

On the Christian view creation can be thought of as God's free act because it does not derive from a necessity that flows one-sidedly from the Father, nor from a mistake of the Pneuma, but from the free agreement of the Son with the Father through the Spirit in the act of the Son's self-distinction from the Father, insofar as we have here the transition from the self-distinction of the Son from the Father within the unity of deity to self-distinction from the Father as the one God, and thus to the otherness of a creaturely existence, which is the form of the existence of the Son only in the man Jesus. Thus the Son is the origin of creaturely existence not only as the principle of distinction and self-distinction but also as the link with that which is thus distinct. As in the intratrinitarian life of God the self-distinction of the Son from the Father is the condition of his unity with the Father through the Spirit, so creatures are related to their Creator by their distinction from God and to one another by their distinctions from one another. The distinctions do not have to take the form of separation or conflict, which is what happens when they fall out of the fellowship with God in which they were created by the Son and the Spirit of God. In his linkage with the Spirit the Son acts in creation as the principle not merely of the distinction of the creatures but also of their interrelation in the order of creation. In this sense, too, he is the Logos of creation. He gathers the creatures into the order that is posited by their distinctions and relations and brings them together through himself (Eph. 1:10) for participation in his fellowship with the Father. But this takes place only through the Spirit, for the creative work of the Son is linked at every point to that of the Spirit.

According to the biblical witnesses the Spirit was at work in creation (Gen. 1:2), especially as the origin of life in the creatures (Gen. 2:7; Ps. 104:29f.). On the one side the Spirit is the principle of the creative presence of the transcendent God with his creatures; on the other side he is the medium of the participation of the creatures in the divine life, and therefore in life as such. His working, then, is closely related to that of the Son, though also characteristically different. For the independence and distinction of the creatures relative to God goes back to the self-distinction of the Son, but the Spirit is the element of the fellowship of the creatures with God and their participation in his life, notwithstanding their distinction from him. To be sure, in the Son, too, self-distinction from God and union with him belong closely together, for self-distinction from the Father is the condition of fellowship with him. Nevertheless, we see here the indissoluble interrelation of the Son and the Spirit. The Son is not the Son without the Spirit.

The self-distinction of the Son from the Father is the condition of the distinctiveness that recognizes the other even in this distinctiveness. This applies also to the creaturely other. On this basis there arises the order of the creaturely world in the mutual relations of creatures of different form. With the continued existence of these different forms the independence of creaturely existence in its distinction from God reaches its goal. Creaturely reality would otherwise be no more than the emergence and extinction of a tiny light in God's eternity. The preservation of the creatures is thus related especially to the work of the Son, to the divine wisdom. Naturally the Son is obedient to the Father in the creation and preservation of creatures. In proceeding from the Father and creating the world, he honors the Father as also the Father of a world of creatures, namely, as the Creator of this world. He himself is the Word of the Father, who summons creatures into existence by his Word.

The bringing forth of the creature reaches fulfillment in the creature's continued independent existence, which is the goal of God's creative act. But continued creaturely existence is possible only by participation in God. For God alone has unrestricted duration. All limited duration derives from him. The creatures need participation in God not merely because their existence differs from that of God but also in their life's movement insofar as life finds fulfillment in transcendence of its own finitude. This life of creatures as participation in God that transcends their own finitude is the special work of the Spirit in creation — a work that is very closely related to that of the Son. This is true not merely of individual creatures but also of the dynamic of all creation in the creatures' interaction, i.e., of "the history of nature," to use a phrase of C. F. von Weizsäcker.

The immanent dynamic of the life of creation may be more precisely described as a process of the increasing internalizing of the self-transcendence of creatures. Organic life is the fully developed basic form of this internalized self-transcendence. The stages of the evolution of life may be seen as the stages of its increasing complexity and intensity and therefore of a growing participation of the creatures in God — an ecstatic participation, of course, that is possible only in the medium of life's going out of itself if there is to be no violation of the distinction between God and creature. We shall have to say more about this in the second part of this chapter. In elucidation of the activity of the divine Spirit in creation, however, we may say here that while the results of the elementary events of natural occurrence seem to remain external to them, and while the environment of the lasting forms of inorganic nature and the changes that overtake them also seem to remain external to them, it is a mark of the organic that it has an inner relation to the future of its own changes and also to its spatial environment. We see this in the developmental thrust of plants and the instinctive life of animals. Only in this context may we speak in at least an analogous way of self-preservation, though without self-awareness there can be no expression of a self-relation that must be presupposed for the fully developed structure of self-preservation.[76]

This internalizing of the relation to a future that changes one's own nature implies existence on the far side of one's own finitude. The movement of such self-transcendence, especially its internalizing, may be de-

---

76. Cf. D. Henrich, "Die Grundstruktur der modernen Philosophie," in *Subjektivität und Selbsterhaltung*, ed. G. Ebeling (1976), pp. 97-121, esp. 103ff.

scribed as the participation of creatures in the God who gives them life.[77] Insofar as we may follow Henri Bergson and Teilhard de Chardin in characterizing the evolution of life as a process of producing increasingly complex and therefore increasingly internalized forms, the sequence of forms may be seen as an expression of the increasing intensity of the participation of the creatures in the divine Spirit of life. At no stage does this growing participation in the Spirit eliminate distinction from God, for the creatures share in the life of the Spirit only by moving out of their own finitude. Hence they participate in the divine life only to the extent that self-distinction from God (and therefore the Son) takes shape in them. The work of the Spirit in creation thus converges on the incarnation of the Son, which in the scriptural testimony is in a special way the work of the Spirit, in which creation finds fulfillment by the full manifestation of the divine likeness in humanity.

A trinitarian exposition of the concept of creation makes it possible, then, to relate what is said about creation to the totality of the world from the standpoint of its duration in time. It does not concern merely the world's beginning. To limit it to the beginning, as the OT stories seem to do in accordance with Near Eastern myths of a primal era, is one-sided.[78] Yet what the two Genesis accounts are really seeking to describe is the normative and abiding basis of creaturely reality in the form of depiction of the initial event. Thus preservation goes with creation. Nor are we to view preservation simply as an unchanging conservation of the forms of creaturely existence laid down at the first. It is a living occurrence, continued creation, a constantly new creative fashioning that goes beyond what was given existence originally. Creation, preservation, and overruling thus form a unity whose structural relation has yet to be defined more closely. By the doctrine of the Trinity all three are set in relation to the saving economy of the divine action in the world. God's action, then, is seen to be a single act that embraces the whole cosmic process, that

---

77. This is one of the most important insights in P. Tillich's description of life in his *Systematic Theology* (3 vols.; repr., Chicago, 1961), III, pt. 4. Yet Tillich did not view the ecstatic aspect radically enough, and he thus distinguished from the divine Spirit a spirit that we may ascribe ontologically to creaturely life. Cf. my "Der Geist des Lebens," in *Glaube und Wirklichkeit* (1975), pp. 31-56, esp. 41ff., 51f.

78. On this view of myth cf. my "Christentum und Mythos," in *Grundfragen systematischer Theologie* (2 vols.; Göttingen, 1967, 1980), II, 13-65, esp. 14ff., 29ff.; on its relation to the biblical material see also my essay "Die weltgrundende Funktion des Mythos," in *Mythos und Rationalität*, ed. H. H. Schmid (Gütersloh, 1988), pp. 108-22, esp. 111f.

includes at the same time many individual acts and phases, and that thus leaves room for a plurality of creatures. Conversely, the creatures in their plurality, which is an expression of their finitude, can participate, each in its own place, in the movement of the divine action that permeates all creation, in the taking shape of the Word and the moving of the Spirit.

§ 4. God's Creation, Preservation, and Rule of the World

a. Preservation and Creation

To preserve something in existence presupposes that it exists. Only that which already is can be preserved. Preservation also implies that what is to be preserved does not owe its existence to itself. It would need no preservation if it had the cause of its existence in itself. Insofar as God's creative act establishes the existence of creatures, they are referred primarily to God for their preservation in existence.

The biblical writings bear broad testimony to the fact that God wills to preserve the world that he has made. In the first instance this means that he keeps creation within the orders that he has created. This is the special theme of the Noachic covenant (Gen. 9:8-17). But preservation also involves keeping the circle of the earth intact (Ps. 96:10; cf. Isa. 45:18) and keeping inviolate the orders of nature in the alternation of day and night and the sequence of the seasons (Pss. 74:16f.; 136:8f.). It means, too, that God cares for each individual creature, providing it with food and water at the right time (Deut. 11:12-15; Jer. 5:24; Pss. 104:13ff., 27; 145:15f.). This divine provision for creatures finds especially intensive expression in what Jesus says about the birds of heaven and the lilies of the field (Matt. 6:25f., 27ff.; Luke 12:24ff., cf. v. 6), as God sees to the special needs of each.

In view of the close connection between preservation and provision, theology has often related preservation to providence. But the NT itself does not yet connect the Hellenistic concept of providence with the relation of God to his creation.[79] There are a few express references to preservation, however, most occurring in connection with the creation of the world by the Son (Col. 1:17; Heb. 1:3c). 1 Clement speaks more explicitly of divine providence (24:5). Among the Apol-

---

79. Cf. R. Bultmann, *Theology of the NT,* 2 vols. (New York, 1951, 1955), I, 71.

ogists Theophilus of Antioch also deals with providence, affirming that the works of providence manifest God's deity to us (*Ad Autol.* 1.5f.). In Clement of Alexandria and Origen providence has systematic importance for the interpretation of salvation history as divine education of the race.[80] In this regard Origen viewed the world's preservation from the standpoint of the governance of the world by providence (*De princ.* 2.1, etc.). Later, John of Damascus took a similar course (*Fid. orth.* 2.29). Clement, however, dealt separately with the immutable preservation of the created order, seeing in it an expression of God's rest on the seventh day (*Strom.* 6.16.142.1).[81] Augustine took up this thought and extended it by relating it to Christ's saying in John 5:17: "My father works thus far, and I also work." The seventh-day rest does not have to mean that God is no longer working but simply that he does not bring forth any new creatures. But his work needs continuation, creatures being referred to the fact that God preserves and rules them (*continet* and *administrat*). Without this divine preserving and ruling they would sink back into the nothing from which they were created.[82]

Directly and indirectly by way of Gregory the Great the Augustinian thought that for the preservation of their existence creatures are referred to the Creator passed into the theological thinking of Latin Scholasticism. We thus find it in Aquinas, who says that as light fails when the sun no longer shines, so creatures perish when God no longer upholds them in being.[83] Even for so critical a spirit as William of Occam this thought had such evidential power that he believed that it demonstrated the existence of God.[84]

Like Augustine, Aquinas in *Summa theologiae* related preservation to the divine rule of the world (1.103-5). In the *Summa contra gentiles* he saw both as partial aspects of God's providence (3.64-67, esp. 65). The older Protestant dogmatics followed him at this point.[85] From the time of A. Calov it subdivided providence

80. H. Koch especially has studied early Alexandrian theology from this angle in *Pronoia und Paideusis* (Berlin, 1932).

81. It is not wholly correct to interpret this concept as an expression of continuous creation (cf. Scheffczyk, *Schöpfung und Vorsehung*, p. 49), since Clement regarded the bringing forth of creatures as having come to an end with the seventh day. From the standpoint of the Christian present, creation had long since ended.

82. Augustine, *De Gen. ad litt.* 4.12.22f. (PL, 34, 304). Augustine could also relate the seventh day typologically to Christ and especially to Christ's sabbath in the tomb (11.21).

83. *ST* 1.104.1; cf. *SCG* 3.65.

84. See vol. I, 88.

85. Cf. Hollaz, *Examen*, 645: Conservation is an act of providence by which God sustains all that he has created. Calov equated providence and governance, which embraces preservation (*Systema*, p. 1127; cf. Schmid, *Doctrinal Theology*, pp. 170f., 172).

into preservation, concursus, and overruling. The divine concursus was distinguished from preservation in existence because existence is a basic presupposition of activity. One does not to have to be active to exist, but one must exist, and continue to do so, to be active. Preservation is thus a presupposition of activity. Creatures also need God's cooperation in order to act. This follows from the fact that they need his constant preservation in order to continue to exist.[86] Concursus in creaturely activities, however, does not set aside the independence of the creature as the principle of its activities. The special intentions of creatures in their activities may deviate from the intentions of the divine government of the world that weave the details into a whole.[87] Hence the divine cooperation does not have to be responsible for deviations from the intentions of God's providence. At the same time, the sin and evil in creaturely acts do serve the aims of divine providence.[88]

All that is said about God's preserving and ruling presupposes creation. The reflections of Clement and Augustine on God's rest on the seventh day, which they nevertheless tried to relate to a continuous divine working, presuppose that the creation of the world was complete on the sixth day, as we read in Gen. 1:1–2:3. The divine work that follows is of a different kind, i.e., the work of preserving and governing what was created. In early Christian theology, however, this strict distinction between creation and preservation came into irresolvable tension with another thesis, namely, that as an act of the eternal God, creation itself must also be eternal. As an eternal act of the eternal God, creation cannot be restricted to the beginning of the world. It is contemporary with all created time. It does not take place in time. Time itself came into existence with the creatures.

Early Christian theology could find this idea formulated already in Philo (*Leg. all.* 1.2). Following Philo, Clement of Alexandria expressly denied that the act of creation took place in time, for time itself was created only with being (*Strom.* 6.16.142.4). All that is created was brought forth by the divine Logos. Creation follows in an act. Clement derived this thought from Gen. 1, which first speaks of the creation of heaven and earth "in the beginning" (v. 1) and only then lists

---

86. Aquinas, *SCG* 3.67; cf. 1.105.5.
87. Aquinas traced the difference between the working of creaturely secondary causes and the divine power that is at work in them, not to a difference in intention, but to a defect on the part of the creature, which the divine activity uses an an instrument (ibid., 3.71).
88. Ibid., 3.140.

the specific works of creation (*Strom.* 6.16.142.2). In his exposition of the six-day work of creation Basil of Caesarea defined this thought more precisely by positing for the created world a beginning in creation but describing the divine act of creation itself as the nontemporal beginning of all time (*Hex.* 1.6 [PG, 29, 16C-D]; cf. 3.29 [PG, 29, 9A-B]).

Augustine transmitted the concept to the Latin Middle Ages: As God's Word is spoken in eternity, so all things are brought into existence by it, for the speaking of the eternal Word by God has no end. No other things could have been said. Everything is spoken at once and eternally by God (*Conf.* 11.7.9).[89] Time came into being only with creatures, as the condition of their movement, their coming into being, and their perishing (*Civ. Dei* 11.6).

The existence of creatures has its beginning in the act of their creation. Thus far creation relates to their beginning. It does not follow, however, that the act of creation relates only to the beginning of the world and is thus restricted to this time of the beginning. If it were, it would be an act in time, not an eternal act of God. Time would not then be posited with the existence of creatures. The transition from eternity to time would take place already with God's moving out of the immanence of his essence to the act of creation. If the act of creation were itself already an act in time, we would unavoidably have to inquire into the time preceding it. We would also have to face the notion of a change in God with the transition to creation. For this reason Augustine rejected the idea that the act of creation is an act in time; in eternity there is no change (*nulla mutatio; Civ. Dei* 11.6). Instead Augustine advanced the thesis that the world was created not in time but with time (*non est mundus factus in tempore, sed cum tempore*).

In opposition Karl Barth spoke of a creation in time, and indeed at its beginning (*CD*, III/1, 67-70). Barth agreed with Augustine that time is part of the creaturely world and that in distinction from eternity it came into existence only with the act of creation. Yet he found it "dubious" that Augustine denied "not only a time prior to creation but the temporality of creation itself" (p. 70). In Barth's view Augustine, contrary to his own thesis, ascribes "to the temporal creation as such . . . temporal priority over the emergence of the creature and the beginning of time."

But the thesis was not, as Barth thought, that "God first created, and then

89. Cf. what Augustine says in *De Gen. ad litt.* 5.23 (PL, 34, 337f.) about the way in which God created all things at once and yet in temporal sequence (cf. ibid. 1.10.18 [PL, 34, 253] and 4.35 [PL, 34, 320]).

the creature emerged and time began." Augustine's real point was that the divine eternity and the creative act of the eternal God both precede the creature and are contemporary with it. Barth did not want to rule out the contemporaneity of the act of creation with the existence of the creature, though he emphasized that creation is "the first of God's works" (p. 42), the "beginning of all things" (p. 12), and therefore "not a timeless truth" (p. 60). He rightly argued that eternity for its part is not the negation of time but "the source of time," the unity of past, present, and future (p. 70). This is the element of truth in Barth's criticism of Augustine's concept of eternity.[90]

But in insisting against Augustine that the act of creation took place in time, that "it takes place as history in time" (pp. 69f.), he brought on himself his own criticism of being in contradiction. As Augustine perceived, such statements inevitably imply a time prior to creation (*Civ. Dei* 11.6). Barth claimed, of course, that he did not want to posit a time before creation (p. 70; cf. pp. 79f.). If so, however, he could not really speak of an act of creation in time.[91] In Barth what lies behind this kind of phrase is the idea that God "condescends to his creature . . . by the utterance of His Word and the accomplishment of His work in time" (p. 69). In creation, however, as distinct from the incarnation, the point was to bring forth the "level" of creaturely reality into whose form of existence the Son would enter at the incarnation. This is especially so if with Barth we develop the concept of creation only from the standpoint of the beginning.

The lasting relevance of Augustine's thesis that the world was created with and not in time is not that in this way we defend the immutability of God, as Augustine wished to do. Augustine was simply setting time in antithesis to timeless eternity. This is the weakness of his teaching that time had its origin in God's act of creation.

But its lasting merit is twofold. First, this view avoids the appearance that the world's origin rests on an arbitrary resolve of God. A constitutive factor in understanding the act of creation is that it is an act of divine freedom. But it is not the result of chance, of a capricious whim with no basis in the inner life of God. Second, and above all, Augustine's thesis opposes any restriction of the divine action in creation to the beginning of the world. The eternity of the act of creation offers a pre-

---

90. Cf. vol. I, 404ff.
91. R. Rothe incisively addressed this problem in his *Theologische Ethik* (2nd ed. Wittenberg, 1867-70), I, 193ff. (n. on § 52). The criticism applies also to Luther's response to Augustine, namely, that God created in time and not in a moment (WA, 12, 245, 38). But Luther was concerned not to restrict creation to the beginning but to see God ceaselessly doing new things (WA, 1, 563, 7ff.). Cf. D. Löfgren, *Die Theologie der Schöpfung bei Luther* (1960), pp. 37ff. He was contending for continuous creation, which we shall discuss in what follows.

supposition for the understanding of God's preserving activity as continued or continuous creation.

Already Aquinas could describe and stress preservation as continued creation, not in the sense of a new act of God, but in the sense of the continuation of the act by which he conferred existence on creatures (*ST* 1.104.1 ad 4). This thought took on a deeper and more radical sense in William of Occam by reason of his concept of the contingency of each individual event consequent on its direct dependence on God.[92] Descartes followed Occam, arguing that the existence of the creature depends at every moment on God's creative action, since we cannot infer from its existence at an earlier point its existence at the next. If, however, the creature owes its existence at each moment to God's creative activity, the concept of preservation differs from that of creation only in virtue of its connection with the fact that God has already granted existence to the creature concerned (*Med.* III, 36). The older Protestant dogmaticians spoke similarly, though without the special point that was given by Descartes's atomistic view of time as a contingent sequence of moments. Thus J. A. Quenstedt could define the preservation of the creature as its continued bringing forth, differing only in name from creation.[93] For Hollaz, too, preservation was a continued act of creation differing only in the sense that its product already existed.[94]

Critics of the understanding of preservation as continued creation have objected that it calls into question the independence of creatures and their actions,[95] or at least their identity and continuity.[96] But these fears are groundless if God is faithful to himself in his creative action. The faithfulness of God guarantees as well as makes possible the emergence and persistence of continuously existing forms of creaturely reality and their ongoing identity and independence. Another objection might be that the work of creation is finished (Gen. 2:1).[97] This is in fact the view of the first Genesis account.

92. K. Bannach thus judges rightly that no theologian before Occam had so radical a view of the creatureliness of the creature (*Lehre,* p. 300). In themselves, however, Occam's statements about the unity of creation and preservation hardly go beyond what Aquinas said (cf. p. 213, on *Sent.* II q 11H and q 3 and 4L).

93. *Theologia,* p. 760; cf. Schmid, *Doctrinal Theology,* p. 179.

94. *Examen,* pp. 645f.; cf. Schmid, *Doctrinal Theology,* p. 179.

95. J. F. Buddeus, *Compendium Institutionum theologiae dogmaticae* (Leipzig, 1724), 1.2, ch. 2, § 47.1 (quoted by Ratschow, *Lutherische Dogmatik,* II, 244). Cf. also Müller, *Lehre von der Sünde,* I, 302; Rothe, *Theologische Ethik,* I, 217 (§ 54); F. A. B. Nitzsch and H. Stephan, *Lehrbuch der evangelischen Dogmatik* (3rd ed. Tübingen, 1912), p. 413.

96. Barth, *CD,* III/3, 69.

97. Buddeus makes this his first argument against continuous creation; cf. *CD,* III/3, 68: "We cannot say that He continues to create it. That is unnecessary, for it has already been created, and created well."

But we also must take into consideration other sayings like that of Christ in John 5:17: "My Father is working still, and I am working." The fathers already took note of this saying (cf. n. 82). Are we to relate it only to the preservation of what is already created, or to the bringing forth of something new? The latter is certainly the case in the Pauline saying that the promise of a son to Abraham is parallel to the raising of the dead and the work of creation on the part of the God who "calls into existence the things that do not exist" (Rom. 4:17). Abraham's trust in the promise of a son so late in life is oriented to the creative power of God, which did not merely found the world at the first and without which the event spoken of could not take place. Deutero-Isaiah speaks similarly, using the concept of divine creating *(bara')* for the bringing forth of what is historically new, whether the event be good or bad (Isa. 45:7f.; with a different verb in 43:12, 19; also 48:6f.; Num. 16:30). When we read that God created Jacob (Isa. 43:1) or Israel (43:15), we are to think of God's act of historical election, which gave the people its existence. The new things that take place in nature may also be regarded as creative acts of God (Isa. 41:20; cf. Ps. 104:30).[98] Finally, in eschatological expectation we read of the creation of a new heaven and a new earth (Isa. 65:17f.). All these works — God's action in preserving and ruling his creatures, and also the bringing forth of new things and God's reconciling and consummating of the world that he has created — participate in the quality of his action at the creation of the world.

As an eternal act God's creative action embraces the whole cosmic process and permeates all phases of the divine action in its history.

Friedrich Schleiermacher had a fine phrase for this matter with reference to the incarnation of Christ and the founding of a new common life by him. He spoke of the creation of human nature as only now completed (*The Christian Faith* [New York, 1963], § 89). Nevertheless, he viewed the unity of God's action in the world primarily in terms of preservation and only secondarily in terms of creation (§§ 36ff.). As he saw it, we are constantly existent and in movement (§ 36.1). In its positive content, then, we are to depict the basic feeling of dependence on God as preservation (§ 39). What we say about creation simply supplements the concept of preservation, expressing the dependence that unconditionally embraces all things (§ 36.1). Nothing is excluded from having come into existence through God (§ 40).

98. For further examples cf. W. Kern in *Mysterium salutis,* II (1967), p. 533.

But this account fails to do justice to the theological concern for the freedom of the divine act of creation. Similarly, in Schleiermacher's detailed statements about preservation the element of the divine freedom and the related contingency of creaturely reality are secondary to the integration of everything individual into the nexus of nature (§ 46). Hence the thought of the overarching unity of the divine action in creation, preservation, and overruling is better preserved from the standpoint of continued creation.

Schleiermacher, too, considered the possibility of thinking of all God's actions vis-à-vis the world as creation. Thus he spoke of the creation of the world as one divine act, and with it the whole nexus of nature (§ 38.2). For if with each beginning of a series of acts or effects deriving from this subject, something new is posited that was not previously posited with the same specific nature, a new thing has arisen that can be seen as a creation (§ 38.1). Yet Schleiermacher preferred to use "preservation" for that one creative act, because he began with the feeling of dependence. Even stronger, however, was his interest in thinking of all God's action as a unity.

Müller aimed his criticism precisely at this thesis (*Die christliche Lehre von der Sünde*, I, 300ff.). He was prepared to speak of continuous creation (p. 304) but insisted on differentiating from continuous creation God's preserving action (p. 304), which sustains created forces in each moment of their activity without itself giving any specific determination to the working of creaturely forces (p. 317). Müller found the basis of the distinction between God's sustaining and creative action in the independence of the creature and especially of its activities. This was the presupposition for the concept of sin. On this ground he also had to reject the linking of preservation and world rule, for which Rothe contended (*Theologische Ethik*, I, 215ff.).

The unity of God's eternal essence and therefore of his activity does not prevent us from speaking of a plurality and multiplicity of divine actions that are all summed up in the unity (see n. 18). If the relations of the divine action to God's creatures in their history are not external to the essence of the Creator, since his eternity embraces time, then we may also speak of the acts of God in time and history.

But the creation of the world is not one of God's historical acts among others, for it is not an act in time and history, if only at their beginning. It is the act that constitutes time itself along with all creaturely reality. It establishes not merely the temporal beginning of creaturely existence but even this existence itself in all its range. The fact that God is the origin of this existence finds expression in the tracing back of its beginning to God, which presupposes already the perspective of a time in which creatures have their existence. From this angle the ideas of creation and preservation differ as seen from the standpoint of the creature. Nevertheless, the concept of creation contains more than a mere statement about the world's beginning. Each individual creature — indeed, each event, each moment — has its beginning in God's creation.

The concept of preservation, unlike that of creation, implies of itself a temporal distinction, namely, the distinction between beginning and continuance.[99] In contrast to creation, God's preserving action is always an action of God in time. Yet it is not a single or distinct action, like the call of Abraham or the incarnation. It is a general divine action relative to creatures. In that sense the rule holds good that what God has created he will also preserve.[100] Herein God's faithfulness comes to expression in his creative action. The preservation of creatures is not, of course, the only form of God's faithfulness, his holding fast to his creation. We see it also in the purifying, delivering, reconciling, and consummating of his creatures. All these actions, however, include preservation as a partial element. But they also presuppose the existence, and therefore the creation, of the creatures, as does the act of preservation. Hence the concept of creation relates especially to the creatures' beginning. We see it also in their preserving and overruling, but their beginning relates solely to God's creation and not to the activity that preserves and overrules their existence.

As it is with creation, so also with new and contingent things in world occurrence. There, too, the divine action has a fundamentally creative character. It posits new beginnings. H. L. Martensen gave expression to this relation when he said that preservation succeeds creation insofar as the will to create gives itself the form of law, insofar as it works under the form of the natural and spiritual world order at every stage of development, insofar as it works in, with, and under cosmic laws and cosmic forces. But the activity of creation bursts forth again out of that of preservation. Martensen added that we see this bursting forth of creativity in world occurrence wherever we cannot view something as a mere repetition of what has gone before, but that which is new and

99. Rothe, *Theologische Ethik,* I, 216, cf. 203 (§ 52): "The concept of the act of creation as the creative function of God does not even remotely imply that this function has a beginning." But then preservation has to differ from creation. The two do not coincide as Rothe would have it (p. 216).

100. Cf. J. J. Schütz's hymn "Sei Lob und Ehr" (1675), translated by Frances E. Cox (1858) and appearing in, e.g., *Rejoice in the Lord,* ed. Erik Routley (Grand Rapids, 1985), no. 146.

original manifests itself in its existence.[101] He rightly related to this the concept of miracle.

As the idea of creation traces back the beginning of the world and all finite existence to the freedom of God, the phenomenon of miracles expresses God's creative freedom within the already existent world order.[102] Miracle is what is unusual and seems to be contrary to the nature of things. As Augustine stressed, however, the unusual events we call miracles are not really contrary to the nature of things but merely contrary to our limited knowledge of the course of nature.[103] Aquinas held the same view (*SCG* 3.100; *ST* 1.105.6); unlike Augustine, he also taught that God might act objectively outside the order of nature *(praeter naturam)* as well as within it. Miracle is that which deviates not only from the normal course of a specific kind of event but also from the order of nature as a whole.[104]

This thought started a development that finally brought theology into conflict with the scientific concept of law. First the distinction between what takes place *outside* the natural order and what is *against* it *(contra naturam)* lost its sharpness because the concept of nature was no longer related to the will of God as the author of the natural order but to the experienced course of natural events. Thus Occam described it as a divine intervention in the ordinary course of nature when God alone does what normally is the result of creaturely secondary causes.[105] When this thesis was applied to the concept of law in modern science as it developed from the 17th century on, conflict arose because the idea of a

101. H. L. Martensen, *Christian Dogmatics* (Edinburgh, 1898), p. 126. Cf. Rothe, *Theologische Ethik*, I, 217 (cf. p. 216), where we read that all God's activity vis-à-vis the world is essentially creative on the special side in which, in dealing with the existent world, it is not preservation or ruling because it involves, not mere continuation, but self-development.

102. On this thesis cf. H. Fries, in *Handbuch theologischer Grundbegriffe*, II (Munich, 1963), pp. 886-96; G. Ewald, B. Klappert, et al., *Das Ungewöhnliche* (1969); T. Löbsack, *Wunder, Wahn, und Wirklichkeit* (1976). For a short history of the concept of miracle and a classification of positions adopted toward it in 20th-century theology see B. Bron, *Das Wunder* (1975, 2nd ed. 1979).

103. *De Gen. ad litt.* 6.13.24 (PL, 34, 349). Cf. *Civ. Dei* 21.5.3; 8.5 (on Rom. 11:17, 24).

104. *ST* 1.110.4; cf. 1.105.7 ad 1, in which creation and justification are not regarded as miracles in this sense. In *De pot. Dei* 6.1 ad 1 the possibility of divine miracles against nature in this sense is admitted. Cf. also 6.2 ad 2.

105. *Opera theol.*, VI, 173-78 (3, sent. 6 a 2 O). With regard to its systematic relevance H. Blumenberg described this concept as the paradigmatic reduction of the binding character of nature (*Die Legitimität der Neuzeit* [Frankfurt am Main, 1966], p. 155). It involves not only a favoring of the possible against the actual, as Blumenberg thought, but also an interest in the immediacy of God's creative action in the actual world. Cf. K. Bannach, *Lehre*, pp. 305ff.

temporary suspension shattered the concept.[106] In a way that became a model for the age that followed, Spinoza criticized the possibility of miracles on the ground that the immutability of the natural order is a necessary expression of the immutability of God himself.[107] In his view it would show imperfection in the Creator if the Creator had to intervene in its course to adjust its direction to his will. Leibniz argued similarly in his controversy with Newton and Samuel Clarke regarding God's relation to his creation.

In opposition, Clarke rejected a view of God that the 18th century found especially suggestive, namely, God as a perfect clockmaker whose work functions without further intervention. Against this comparison Clarke observed that such a view delivers up the world to a materialistic fate by banishing from it the activity of divine preservation and overruling. God's cosmic plan is indeed unchangeable, but it is not achieved in an order of things that is present from the outset, nor by a mechanistic functioning. In the process of time it develops through phases of decay, disorder, and renewal. The laws that we formulate at specific periods ("the present Laws of Motion") are not identical with the divine world order but only approximate the real order of nature, which God controls.[108] According to Clarke, then, actual deviations from the formulas that we posit stand in no contradiction whatever to the perfection of God.

By rejecting the concept of an order of nature which lay behind Spinoza's criticism, Clarke in fact went beyond the Christian Aristotelianism of High Scholasticism back to the view of Augustine, who saw no invasion of the divine world order in miracles but related them simply to our limited knowledge of this order. Unusual events do not breach natural laws but manifest the working of hitherto concealed parameters.[109] Nor are we to see only deviations from the usual course of events as miracles. According to Augustine, the existence of the world and humanity is a much greater miracle than all the spectacular events that astonish us because they are unusual. The only problem is that our minds are too

106. Thus J. F. Buddeus referred to the suspension of the order of nature in miracles (*Compendium,* p. 149). This view inevitably invited the sharp rejection that we find in D. Hume: "A miracle is a violation of the laws of nature and as a firm and unalterable experience has established these laws, the proof against a miracle, from the very nature of the fact, is as entire as any argument from experience can possibly be imagined" (*An Inquiry concerning Human Understanding* [1748], 10.1).

107. B. de Spinoza, *Theologisch-politischer Traktat* (1670), ch. 6. Cf. L. Strauss, *Die Religionskritik Spinozas als Grundlage seiner Bibelwissenschaft* (1930, repr. Darmstadt, 1981), pp. 106ff.

108. Cf. G. W. Leibniz, *Die philosophischen Schriften,* VII, ed. G. J. Gerhardt (1890), pp. 354, 357f., 361 (n. 8).

109. Roman Catholic theologians today also reject the idea that miracles break natural laws. Cf. B. H. Fries, *Fundamentaltheologie* (1985), pp. 291ff.; *Handbuch theologischer Grundbegriffe,* II, 889, 895. For a different view cf. L. Monden, *Theologie des Wunders* (1960), p. 51; cf. 54f., 334ff.

dulled to perceive the miracle of creation in what takes place every day.[110] The contingency of creation as a whole expresses itself in each detailed event. Since every moment and every event is contingent, it is ultimately nonderivable. Its occurrence is thus a miracle.

Schleiermacher rightly said that "miracle is simply the religious name for event. Every event, even the most natural and usual, becomes a miracle" once it is related to the Infinite, the Universum.[111] He was close to Augustine in his insight that we are unaware of the true nature of things in our everyday dealings with them because of the dulling effect of what is routine and because of our utilitarian approach to reality. We see things only in their immediate context and not as a manifestation of the Universum. Religious perception, however, sees the deeper nature of everyday events, experiencing them as miraculous, as an expression of the providence of God. The real basis, however, is not, as Schleiermacher thought, that religious perception regards individual events in general as an expression of the Universum. When the Universum is pictured as a fate that rules the world, individual events do not take the form of miracles. For this we must presuppose the contingency of all world occurrence and not just individual events. This presupposition is what we find in the biblical belief in God as the Creator of the world. This belief finds in the incalculability and contingency of each individual event an expression of the freedom of the Creator. Hence with Schleiermacher, and with Augustine before him, we will find the fact of the order of nature, its regularities and enduring constructs, genuinely astounding. The contingency of individual events does not lead us to expect to find the contours of order in the sequence of events. In virtue of the contingency of the elementary fact that things take place and do not take place, individual events are conversely a condition and basis for the construction of every type of form and order. With the contingency of occurrence, then, a direct relation of all individual events to the divine origin of all things is posited, notwithstanding the part played by creaturely secondary causes in what takes place. Since it is not self-evident that anything should take place, not merely the emergence but above all the continuation of creaturely forms and states is at every moment miraculous.

b. *Divine Cooperation in the Activities of Creatures*

If the preservation of creatures by their Creator demands his constant presence with them, his activity cannot be restricted to simply conserving their original constitution. It must also extend to their changes and

110. *In Joann.* 24.1 (PL, 35, 1592f.); cf. *Civ. Dei* 10.12.
111. *On Religion* (New York, 1958), p. 88.

activities. It was particularly in relation to the activities of creatures that the concept of concursus, which we briefly mentioned above, was developed.

The distinction between *concursus* and *conservatio* rests primarily on the fact that for the ontology of Aristotelian Scholasticism the being of creatures (as *actus primus*) must also underlie their activity (as *actus secundus*), whereas creatures still exist even when their activities cease.[112] Modern theology has thrown doubt on the distinction. Thus Johann Christoph Döderlein argued that the preservation of creaturely powers, to which S. J. Baumgarten related the concursus, is included in God's work of preservation.[113] Yet the older Protestant dogmatics did not restrict the divine cooperation in creaturely activities to the sustaining of their powers for action but claimed that God actively influences the acts of creaturely activity. This was the case, even though Lutherans and Reformed differed in detail on whether we are to see simultaneity in the cooperation, as the Lutherans taught,[114] or a creative movement on God's part that precedes the creaturely act *(concursus praevius)*.[115]

112. Cf. S. J. Baumgarten, *Evangelische Glaubenslehre*, ed. J. S. Semler (Halle, 1759; 2nd ed. 1764), I, 807ff. Cf. the formulation of Aquinas in n. 86. On *actus primus* and *actus secundus* cf. *ST* 1.48.5c, 75.2c, and the application to the divine concursus in 105.5c.

113. J. C. Döderlein, *Institutio theologi christiani* (Nuremberg, 1780), I, 586ff. Cf. Baumgarten, *Evangelische Glaubenslehre*, I, 808. I. Dorner, *System of Christian Doctrine* (Edinburgh, 1881), II, 53f., related the doctrine of divine cooperation to the power of self-preservation and thus integrated it into the general concept of preservation.

114. Cf. Calov, *Systema* 6.2.2 (pp. 1204f.); Quenstedt, *Theologia*, ch. 13; Hollaz, *Examen*, 648; Schmid, *Doctrinal Theology*, p. 184. Cf. J. Kösten, *PRE* 4, 263f.

115. K. Barth expressly depicted and discussed this distinction in his extensive account of the divine concursus in *CD*, III/3, 90ff., esp. 94ff., 115ff., 133f., 145f. In spite of his criticism of the determinist tendency in the Reformed position (pp. 115ff.), Barth sought his own solution in the Reformed thesis of *concursus praevius* (pp. 119ff.), though also adopting the doctrine of the simultaneity of the divine and creaturely working (pp. 132ff.). Criticism of the formalism of causal thinking (pp. 101ff.) and the assurance that he does not want "to begin with empty concepts but with concepts which are already filled out with Christian meaning" (p. 117) do not protect Barth himself, however, from a certain formalism. The older Reformed dogmatics, at least, did not restrict God's cooperation in the activities of creatures to preservation of their powers of action. Older dogmaticians had already advanced Barth's solution that God's unconditional and irresistible lordship establishes the freedom of creaturely activity in its "particularity and variety" (p. 146; cf. H. Heppe and E. Bizer, *Reformed Dogmatics* [London, 1950], pp. 254, 266ff.). The Lutheran concern to think of this cooperation in such a way that the sin of the creature is not attributed to God's creative action also fails to receive due justice in Barth, for all his assurances that it is not his intention to ascribe sin to God.

Schleiermacher criticized all such distinctions on the ground that they rest on an abstraction, not merely as regards God's simple action, but also as regards creaturely reality. As he says, a being that is to be posited for itself exists only where there is power, and there is power only in activity. Hence a preservation that does not imply the placing of all the activities of any finite being under absolute dependence on God would be as empty as a creation without preservation.[116]

Those who can no longer follow the Aristotelian ontological tradition can hardly avoid feeling the weight of Schleiermacher's argument. But we must still ask whether there is not some point to distinguishing such abstract aspects. Not infrequently what is undivided in reality can be distinguished abstractly for purposes of knowledge. The best-known example is that of the question of universals, which so deeply agitated the Middle Ages: The universal and the particular are one in concrete reality, but it makes sense to distinguish the two aspects for purposes of knowledge. Might this not also be true of the abstract distinction between God's preservation and his cooperation relative to his creatures?

On the one side the doctrine of divine cooperation with the activities of creatures shows us that creatures are not left to themselves in their activities. On the other side we are not to see in God's working an omnicausality that excludes the autonomy of creatures and their possible deviation from God's purposes.[117] Such deviation might be out of keeping with God's own creative ends, but this risk goes hand in hand with the independence that is given the creature and without which God's creative action could not come to fulfillment in his work.

The most important function of the older doctrine of the divine concursus was to describe God's cooperation in the activities of creatures in such a way as to leave their independence intact so that sin could be ascribed to them as the acting subjects, not to God. Up to the middle of the 17th century this was the main concern of the older Lutheran dogmatics in exposition of the theme. By the end of that century, however,

116. *Christian Faith*, § 46, Appendix.
117. Aquinas raised against such a view the objection that it would negate God's act in creation (*ST* 1.105.5c). The objection applies against Luther's statements in his *Bondage of the Will* (WA, 18, 753, 28-31) to the effect that God does all things in all people, even the wicked. He does so as Creator by giving the creature autonomy and not depriving it of this autonomy. Barth agreed with Aquinas at this point (*CD*, III/3, 145), but without noting that the logic of this thought carries with it a self-restriction on the part of the Creator, which gives his influence on the creature's freedom the form of persuasion and accommodation. Barth showed little appreciation for Quenstedt's stress on this logic (ibid.).

the accent had shifted.[118] The issue now was not so much to leave room for creaturely autonomy as to prevent the autonomy of the creaturely world from becoming total. The trend in that direction was related to the mechanistic physics and the philosophy of nature that developed with Galileo and Descartes.

Descartes developed the thesis that God no longer intervenes in the course of events after the act of creation. Instead, all changes in the world are due to the reciprocal workings of the states of movement assigned to things at their creation.[119] Although Descartes agreed that all created things need ongoing preservation by God, which he equated with continued creation at each moment (*Med.* III, 36), in virtue of the immutability of God he did not think we can ascribe changes in the world (once created) to God. Nor can these changes derive from an inner dynamic of creatures, since each creature is held immutably in the state of movement or rest in which it was created (*Princ.* II, 37f., Descartes's formulation of the principle of inertia). Hence changes can arise only out of the external, mechanical workings of the different creatures and their movements upon one another (II, 40).[120]

J. F. Buddeus saw in this view a denial of God,[121] and no less a figure than Isaac Newton agreed. Newton, too, feared that the basis Descartes laid down for physics had atheistic implications.[122] Newton thought that he himself avoided these implications in his own principles of natural philosophy by viewing absolute space and forces like that of gravity, which does not work through physical contact,

118. On this point see Ratschow, *Lutherische Dogmatik*, II, 228ff. Cf. also the complaint of K. G. Bretschneider, *Handbuch der Dogmatik der evangelisch-lutherischen Kirche* (1814, 1822, 3rd ed. Leipzig, 1828), I, 697f., that the new dogmaticians wrongly neglected the real problem of the doctrine, namely, whether preservation is an ongoing direct act of the divine will or whether God gives creative things the power to persist, so that he no longer works directly but the world is preserved by its own forces.
119. So already around 1630 in the hitherto unpublished work *Le Monde* (vol. XI in the Adam and Tannery edition [1967], pp. 34f.). He presented the same thesis more succinctly in 1644 in *Princ.* II, 36.
120. Descartes states this more plainly in *Le Monde*, ch. 2. From the preservation of matter in the state of movement of the different parts in which it was created, it follows necessarily "qu'il doit y avoir plusieurs changemens en ses parties, lesquels ne pouvant, ce me semble, être proprement attribuez à l'action de Dieu, parce qu'elle ne change point, je les attribue à la Nature; et les regles suivant lesquelles se font ces changemens, je les nomme les Loix de la Nature" (Adam/Tannery XI, 37, 8-14).
121. Buddeus, *Compendium*, p. 286.
122. Cf. A. Koyré, *Newtonian Studies* (London, 1965), pp. 93f.; E. McMullin, *Newton on Matter and Activity* (Notre Dame, IN, 1978), pp. 55f. McMullin has shown that theological interest in the dependence of creatures on God's omnipotent working was one of the roots of Newton's concept of force as a principle that we must distinguish from inert matter (pp. 32ff.).

as an expression of the continued presence and activity of God in his creation.[123] Newton also argued against Descartes that in the course of time all impulses of movement decline (*Opticks* [1704], III, 259, ll. 23ff.), so that for the preservation and renewal of cosmic movements active principles are needed, which as Newton saw it are not material and can work at distances in space (Koyré, *Newtonian Studies*, p. 109). It is not without irony that with his *Principia mathematica philosophiae naturalis* Newton ranks historically as the father of a purely mechanistic explanation of the world (on the reasons for this cf. McMullin, *Newton on Matter and Activity*, pp. 111ff.).

When the principle of inertia, which Newton viewed as *vis insita*, was linked to the relating of moving forces to bodies, which prevailed contrary to Newton's intentions, it took on normative significance for the emancipation of the mechanistic view of sciences in the 18th century from all connections with the theological doctrine of the creation and preservation of the world by divine action. Today, perhaps, the theory has only historical importance, for the field theories and quantum physics of the 20th century have outdated the 18th-century concept of force, and in this connection especially Ernst Mach and Albert Einstein have interpreted the inertia of bodies as an expression of cosmic fields of gravitation.[124] At any rate, however, modern dialogue between scientists and theologians needs to study the process that led decisively to alienation between the scientific worldview and theology if this alienation is to be permanently overcome.[125]

The modern emancipation of the creaturely world from dependence on the continuing cooperation of God reached its first high point with Spinoza's understanding of the physical principle of inertia in terms

123. Cf. G. B. Deason, "Reformation Theology and the Mechanistic Conception of God," in *God and Nature: Historical Essays on the Encounter between Christianity and Science*, ed. D. C. Lindberg and R. L. Numbers (Berkeley, CA, 1986), pp. 167-91, esp. 181-85.
124. Cf. the helpful discussion of R. J. Russell, "Contingency," pp. 31ff.
125. For this reason I have repeatedly stressed how important it is to understand the significance of the principle of inertia in the dialogue between science and theology, especially in "Theological Questions to Scientists," in *The Sciences and Theology in the Twentieth Century*, ed. A. R. Peacocke (Notre Dame, IN, 1981), pp. 3-16, esp. 5f. E. Mcmullin at the end of "How Should Cosmology Relate to Theology?" (pp. 17-57 in the same volume) asks whether these deliberations are meant as criticism of the principle or whether they concern its interpretation (pp. 50f.). Theology should be regarded not as an "autonomous source of logical implication capable of affecting scientific theory-appraisal but as one element in the constructing of a broader world view" (p. 51). I can agree with this to the extent that dialogue between theology and the sciences moves on the plane of philosophical reflection on the construction of scientific theory and not on that of actually constructing such theory. The history of science shows, of course, as we see from the different formulations of the principle of inertia, that this reflection has always affected the process of "scientific theory-appraisal."

of the thought of self-preservation.[126] According to H. Blumenberg, others as well as Spinoza found here an alternative to the theological view that each creature depends on another outside itself for preservation, namely, on God.[127] Blumenberg rightly perceived, then, a link between a concept still presupposed in Descartes's doctrine of continuous creation, that of a contingency of individual events and the referring of all finite beings to preservation by another. He missed the point, however, that the thought of self-preservation does not remove the problem but presupposes it, so that it cannot be an alternative to the theological doctrine of the dependence of all finite beings on their Creator for their preservation in existence. Self-preservation is necessary only relative to the contingency of one's own existence. Since continued existence is so uncertain, special efforts have to be made to safeguard it. The task is imposed especially by the fact of change. The aim is *identity in change.* If there were no change in the states and conditions of existence, self-preservation would no more be necessary than preservation by another. Hence self-preservation is not the same as physical inertia, for inertia in the sense of Descartes and Newton is apart from all change. Persisting implies more than inertia, for it involves an active principle relative to changing conditions of existence — a *connatus* in Spinoza's sense. Self-preservation also involves the further element of a self-relation,[128] whether in the fully developed form of self-awareness or in the rudimentary and unexpressed form of self-familiarity that is proper to every living thing (the *oikeiōsis* of Stoic philosophy). When it comes to full expression this self-relation carries with it an awareness of the contingency and threatened nature of one's own existence and thus poses the task of self-preservation. As Henrich says, that which has to preserve itself has to realize that it never has its absolute basis in itself.[129]

Therefore, self-preservation alone cannot guarantee the continuation of one's own existence and nature. It is always referred to preservation by another. The conditions of self-preservation are dependent on this alien preservation as regards both cosmic factors and one's own activity. In the process the self that is to be preserved is not even there at the outset. As personal identity, it is formed in the process of one's individual life and is

126. B. de Spinoza, *Ethica more geometrico demonstrata,* III, prop. 7.
127. H. Blumenberg, "Selbsterhaltung und Beharrung. Zur Konstitution der neuzeitlichen Rationalität," in *Subjectivität und Selbsterhaltung. Beiträge zur Diagnose der Moderne,* ed. G. Ebeling (1976), pp. 144-207, esp. 144ff., 185ff.
128. Cf. Henrich, "Grundstruktur," pp. 103ff.
129. Ibid., p. 111.

present only by way of anticipation at each moment of self-awareness.[130] Furthermore, even mere persistence in being has an element that aims beyond the momentary state. That which proves able to persist does so not merely in and by virtue of the identity of its momentary state. Its identity is formed in the process of persisting. The principle of inertia in physics may seem to offer a parallel to all persistence in being. But this is only a superficial appearance. If we fall victim to it, we forget the abstract nature of the principle, which does not take account of persistence in changing conditions. The persistence of that which exists concretely must always face the contingency of its own existence and its changing conditions.

Far from being in opposition to the persistence and self-preservation of finite things, the preserving work of God makes possible the independence of creatures that finds expression in the possibility and fact of their self-preservation. God for his part reaches the goal of his creative action only with the producing of creatures that persist and that exist independently insofar as by its very nature this goal had as its object the producing of that which is distinct from the Creator and can exist independently. God's work of preservation is in the service of the independent existence of creatures, and his cooperation with their development is in the service of their independence in action.[131] The question arises, then, whether we can say the same about God's world government.

c. World Government and the Kingdom of God: The Goal of Creation

The divine world government is an expression of the faithfulness of God in the changes of created reality. Faithfulness connects the preservation and overruling of the creaturely world and includes the contingent freedom of God's creative action.[132] The preservation of creatures does not rest simply on a rigid immutability of God, as Descartes assumed, but on the faithfulness of the Creator, in which God's identity makes itself known

130. For a fuller discussion cf. my *Anthropology*, pp. 522ff.

131. This is the point of the Lutheran description of God's cooperation in Hollaz when he speaks of it as simultaneous and by persuasion (*Examen*, 654; cf. Schmid, *Doctrinal Theology*, p. 187). Calov raised against both Calvinists and Thomists the objection that they fell into the Stoic doctrine of fate (*Systema*, pp. 1210ff.; cf. 1205f. on the Thomistic doctrine of *praemotio physica* in *ST* 1.105.1, 2/1.109.1).

132. Barth rightly stressed the basic significance of the faithfulness of God for the theological concept of the divine overruling, especially over against all the unfaithfulness and opposition of creatures (*CD*, III/3, 41, 179, 186).

in the contingent sequence of his actions. God's faithfulness, which proceeds from the mutual faithfulness of the Son to the Father and the Father to the Son, is the basis of the identity and continuation of his creatures. Posited already in the concept of preservation is the element of contingency, of the creatively new at each new moment. But the aspect of changes in the development and history of creatures and their relations to one another is intrinsic to the concept of divine world government.[133]

To say this, however, is not yet to name the object of God's governance, which applies especially to the relations of creatures and the opposition and conflict that arises between them in their struggles to assert and expand themselves. The world as a whole is the concern of this governance. Necessarily, then, it must deal with the relations of the parts to one another.[134] It cannot be equated simply with the providence that sees to the well-being of individuals in isolation. Jesus' sayings about God's care for all his creatures (Matt. 6:26ff.; 10:29f.) rule out any creature having less significance for God as just a means to the higher ends of his world government.[135] Every creature is itself an end in God's work of creation and therefore an end for his world government as well. But the way in

133. Thus F. V. Reinhard defined it as the action whereby God suitably adjusts the mutations of all things to his own counsel (*Vorlesungen über die Dogmatik* [1801], § 62, p. 221).

134. In Bretschneider, *Handbuch,* we read in § 93 that because God's government is over the whole world and therefore over the relations of its parts, it is none other than the governing of the parts whose epitome is the world (p. 614). Among the distinctions between God's preservation and governance of the world that were then discussed, Schleiermacher thought the best was that which relates preservation to the individual positing of creatures but governance to their common life and all that results from it (*Christian Faith,* § 46, Appendix). Yet he saw in this distinction, as in that between creation and preservation, only an abstraction of no significance for our pious self-consciousness. In the older Protestant dogmatics the Reformed rather than the Lutherans stressed the relation of divine government to the totality of the created world, as Aquinas did in *ST* 1.103.3, 5. With some qualifications, Barth did the same (*CD,* III/3, 165ff., 170ff.).

135. Barth rightly rejects any such idea. For him, each creature has "its own significance and validity, its own value and dignity" (*CD,* III/3, 173). But Barth might have turned this insight into a more radical criticism of the structuring of the older doctrine of providence in terms of ends, which is found especially in Aquinas. As means serve ends, so for Aquinas the divine world government subordinates the particular good to the universal good (*ST* 1.103.2, 3). Therefore, God is himself the final end of his action (*SCG* 3.64; cf. *De pot. Dei* 9.9). Aquinas softens the problem by calling the divine goodness (*bonitas*) the end of the order of the universe and saying that this leads all things to their own ends (*SCG* 3.64; cf. *ST* 1.44.4c). Nevertheless, the idea that God, not creatures, is the final end of his world government has a harsh sound and leaves the impression that his rule is one of oppression.

which he has the good of individual creatures in view, namely, with regard for his care for all other creatures, can be very different from what the creatures themselves seek as their good.

At this point we find complaints and protests that the actual direction of the world and its history often enough offers little evidence that a God of love and mercy or even justice controls it.[136] The extent and absurdity of what seems to be meaningless suffering and the triumph and good fortune of the ungodly and the wicked are among the trials of believers. Not everyone can join in Paul Gerhardt's hymn when he says that even though God allows him to be ill, or gives him gall to drink, or plagues him in other ways, he will accept it if it pleases God, since God alone knows what is good or harmful for him. And it is hardest of all to agree with him when in the face of our helplessness at the sufferings of others we are invited to sing that God has never troubled anyone too severely. Yet this is what the Christian doctrine of providence affirms. It involves more than trust in God's daily care, in his direction and aid through life. It stands fast vis-à-vis the absurdity of suffering and guilt. Face to face with the obvious reign of death in the world, faith can make this affirmation only in expectation of the future of God and his rule in a renewed creation, which even death can no longer limit.[137]

Barth rightly perceived that the world government of God is the same as the royal dominion of the God of Israel to which the OT bears witness (CD, III/3, 176ff.). It is also the same as the divine rule whose imminence Jesus proclaimed and that already came in him. If we notice these connections, it ought to be plain that God's world government is not a fixed thing, even though it is beyond the understanding of the creature and manifest in the world only in signs such as the existence of the Bible, the church, and the people of Israel, as Barth thought. We cannot overlook the fact that already the OT statements on the theme are full of

---

136. For an especially emphatic statement of these facts, which from antiquity have cast doubts on the divine world government, cf. C. H. Ratschow, "Das Heilshandeln und das Welthandeln Gottes: Gedanken zur Lehrgestaltung des Providentia-Glaubens in der evangelischen Dogmatik," NZST 1 (1959) 25-80, esp. 76ff., and his criticism of Barth (pp. 57ff.). Nevertheless, Ratschow's demand for reservations regarding not only providence but also preservation (p. 80) is overhasty. Without preservation and world government we cannot think of God as Creator. Ratschow does not go into the relation between the doctrine of God's world government and the biblical concept of his lordship.

137. Hence the last verse of Gerhardt's hymn deals with the eschatological consummation beyond death. W. Lütgert (Schöpfung und Offenbarung. Eine Theologie des ersten Artikels [1934]) saw this point more clearly than did Barth (CD, III/3, 368f.).

tension between God's royal rule from eternity and his royal rule that is being actualized in history and is awaited as the future of the consummation of history. Nor can we overlook the fact that Jesus' message has its starting point in the statement that this future is near at hand. It is this future alone, however, that will determine and manifest openly that the God of the Bible is not just the Creator but also the King of the world, who has by no means lost control of his creation but always has exercised it in the course of its history.

With the tension between the present concealment and the future consummation of God's royal rule over the world, the question arises whether and in what sense the divine world government has a direction, a final structure of action.[138] If God's rule and kingdom will be consummated only in the future, in the eschatological future of God and his coming, even though it is already dawning wherever this divine future is at work in the world, then all God's preceding rule in the world seems to be oriented to this future. But in what sense? Certainly the eschatological consummation is the goal of all creaturely reality (Rom. 8:19ff.). But is it the goal of the divine action?

In the doctrines of creation and providence advanced by medieval Aristotelian Scholasticism, God himself is the final goal of his action.[139] Aquinas appealed in this regard to Prov. 16:4, and the older Protestant dogmatics followed him.[140] This is the only biblical text that, at least in the Latin Vulgate, expressly states that the act of creation had this goal. The other texts adduced either link other events to the goal (cf. John 11:4) or state that God's rule is manifest in works that proclaim his glory (heaven in Ps. 8:1) or that ought, like humans, to give him thanks and honor him in his deity (Rom. 1:21; cf. Luke 17:18). The Vulgate renders the verse in Proverbs as follows: *Universa propter semetipsum operatus est Dominus,* but this translation is not literal. The original speaks of the specific end of each individual creature.[141]

---

138. Cf. vol. I, 386ff.; J. Ringleben, "Gottes Sein, Handeln und Werden," in *Vernunft des Glaubens. Festschrift für W. Pannenberg,* ed. J. Rohls and G. Wenz (1988), pp. 457-87.

139. Cf. n. 134; Aquinas, *SCG* 3.17f. and *De pot. Dei* 9.9. The psychology of the Trinity was the basis of this view; namely, as God knows all things in knowing himself, so he wills what he wills in willing himself. For Aquinas, however, God is not the goal of his action in the sense of gaining something for himself that he did not have before (*SCG* 3.18).

140. Cf. Calov, *Systema,* pp. 900f., who puts this text at the head of his biblical evidences for the thesis. Cf. also Quenstedt, *Theologia,* p. 595 (ch. 10, th. 16).

141. Cf., e.g., O. Plöger in the BKAT series (1984), who translates: "Yahweh created everything for its own purpose," and comments: "For its specific purpose" (p. 186).

In the older Protestant dogmatics the idea of a direct self-reference of the divine action whereby God is its final goal was adopted in the form of the statement that the glory of God and its recognition and praising by creatures is the goal of creation.[142] In the discussions it is not always clear whether this is the goal of the act of creation or of the resultant creaturely reality. Undoubtedly the biblical testimonies tell us that it is the destiny of creatures to praise and honor God and to extol his glory.[143] Herein the existence of creatures, and especially of human creatures, reaches its fulfillment (Rev. 19:1ff.), for thus they participate in the Son's glorifying of the Father (John 17:4). Thus it is our human destiny and the goal of our existence to glorify God by our lives. Our sin is our withholding from God the honor that is due him as Creator (Rom. 1:21). Nevertheless, it is rather a different thing to maintain that the basis of God's resolve to create the world was that thereby he might glorify himself.[144] Certainly the work that God created redounds to his glory. We may say this at any rate in the light of the eschatological consummation of the world and in believing anticipation of this future of God, which will resolve all doubts concerning theodicy. Every creature should confess, then, that the world was made for God's glory.[145]

Nevertheless, the creature was not created in order that God should receive glory from it. God does not need this, for he is already God in himself from all eternity. He does not need to become God through his action or much less become sure of his deity in the mirror of creaturely

---

142. Cf. Hollaz, *Examen,* 3 q 14; Calov, *Systema,* pp. 900, 1141. We might also cite J. Gerhard, *Loci theologici,* II, 15, n. 85, and on the Reformed side A. Polanus, *Syntagma,* p. 265b. The scriptures quoted (Ps. 8:1; Rom. 11:36; Rev. 4:10; 5:13) suggest that we are to think of the glory that God's works bring to him. For other Reformed examples cf. Heppe and Bizer, *Reformed Dogmatics,* pp. 135f.

143. Hollaz, *Examen,* appeals especially to Ps. 19:1.

144. This is the element of truth in the criticism by A. Günther and G. Hermes of the Scholastic doctrine that God is himself the goal of his creative action. Cf. M. J. Scheeben, *Handbuch der katholischen Dogmatik,* III (3rd ed. 1961), p. 40 (n. 92).

145. Vatican I anathematized any contesting of this thesis (DS § 3025). According to Scheeben, *Handbuch,* III, 35, the thesis relates to the *finis operis* (of creation), not to the *finis operantis.* But on the basis of Prov. 16:4 Scheeben, too, saw in God himself the goal of the divine act of creation (II, 222, § 96, nn. 513f.). M. Schmaus, *Dogma* 2 (New York, 1969), pp. 87ff., also teaches that divine self-love was the motivation for the divine act of creation. In opposition Kern, in *Mysterium Salutis,* II, 449, argued that we must not misunderstand the inner goal of created things to honor God as the outer goal of the Creator, as though God sought his own glory in creating the world. God's glory is the intrinsic goal of creation, built into it, part of its nature — indeed, constituting its nature — but is not the extrinsic goal of the Creator in creating it.

praise. A God who first and last sought his own glory in his action would be a model for the attitude that in us constitutes the perversion of sin in the form of self-seeking *(amor sui)*.[146] As the activation and expression of his free love, God's creative action is oriented wholly to creatures. They are both the object and the goal of creation. Herein is his glory as Creator, the glory of the Father, who is glorified by the Son and by the Spirit in creatures.

We cannot say, then, of the divine act of creation that in the first instance God sought his own glory by giving existence to creatures. The same applies to the act of world government. It, too, is an expression of God's love, and it has as its content and object the consummation of creation and creatures. Certainly creatures can achieve the consummation of their creaturely existence only by praising and honoring God as their Creator and thus participating in the glorifying of the Father by the Son in the Holy Spirit. Nevertheless, it holds good here, too, that God sets up his kingdom in the world, not in order to assert himself against it, but in order to redeem and fulfill his creation.

It is inappropriate to use teleological language of God's love, language that subjects God's action to a goal that is not yet present for this omnipotent will but must be reached by employing means. The idea of distance between the goal and the subject of action is not in keeping with God's eternal self-identity as though his identity were the result of his participation in the life of his creatures. The object of the divine will has to be thought of as already realized, even though God ties the realization to the conditions of creaturely life and conduct. It is only on the condition of the trinitarian God's participation in the life of his creatures, and therefore in the distinction of beginning and end that characterizes creaturely life, that we can speak of a differentiation of subject, goal, and object in the divine action.

All this sheds further light on the distinction between God's creation, preservation, and world government. Creation cannot be an act in time. We have to view it as the constitution of the finite existence of creatures and therefore of time as the form of this existence. Preservation presupposes the existence of creatures and consequently the preceding act of creation. It is thus structured in time. The same is true of world government or providence in its orientation to a goal. Preservation and world government differ from creation, then, in that they are expressions

146. Cf. my *Anthropology*, pp. 87ff.

of the participation of God in the life of creatures and therefore in their time-structures. But they differ from one another inasmuch as preservation relates to the origin of creatures in God's act of creation, and providence or world government has a forward reference to their future consummation. What ultimately underlies the participation of God in the life of creatures that works itself out as their preservation and governing is the self-differentiation of the Son from the Father. The Son's moving out of the unity of the divine life makes independent creaturely existence possible. Thus the Son "sustains" the universe (Heb. 1:3) in its creaturely autonomy distinct from God and forms the goal of the divine world government inasmuch as this directs the course of the times to their fulfillment in such a way as "to unite all things in him, things in heaven and things on earth" (Eph. 1:10), i.e., in such a way that all created things participate in the filial relation of Jesus Christ to the Father, in the fellowship with the Father that is mediated by self-distinction from him.

The older Protestant dogmatics did no more than medieval Scholasticism to work out expressly the structural differences between the divine act of creation and the acts of preservation and world government. But it did take account of it by relating the distinctions between preservation, cooperation, and world government to the misuse of creaturely independence.[147] Whereas preservation forms the general condition of creaturely independence, the accompanying cooperation of God in the activity of his creatures has to do with his participation in the independence of their lives, even though the intentions of creaturely conduct may deviate from the norm of the relation of the Son to the Father. World government relates to integrating into God's purposes for the world the actual results of the independent conduct of creature, namely, their failures and the evil that these failures cause.[148] The central theme of the divine world government is God's supremacy over the misuse of creaturely independence. It is here that the idea of world government most clearly goes beyond what we find in the concepts of creation and preservation. World government contradicts the claim made by wickedness and evil that they can oppose God's will as Creator. This aspect of the concept of world government finds expression in the fact that even the consequences of creaturely revolt from the Creator finally have to serve God's purpose

---

147. Cf. ibid.

148. Cf. Quenstedt, *Theologia,* pp. 763f., who sees four specific acts: permitting, impeding, directing, and determining. Cf. Schmid, *Doctrinal Theology,* pp. 189f.

for his creation. God's skill in government shows itself in his constant ability to bring good even out of evil.[149] Its final vindication, of course, will come only with the eschatological transformation and consummation of the world as the kingdom of God.

II. THE WORLD OF CREATURES

After discussing the act of creation in the light of the doctrine of God and in relation to the divine activities of the preservation and overruling of the world, we must now turn to creation itself and interpret it as the work of the trinitarian God. We have here a theme of the utmost importance for the question of the truth of the Christian faith. Only if we can understand the world as the creation of the biblical God and God himself as its Creator can we raise a truth claim for belief in the sole deity of God. Furthermore, only on this same assumption can we set forth the history of Jesus Christ as the reconciliation of the world by the one true God, only then do the proclamation and mission of the Christian church take place in obedience to this one true God, and only then can the Christian hope of the future have a sure basis in him. For this reason Luther in his Large Catechism could say that we believe that the God of the Bible, the Father of Jesus Christ, is the true God because none other could be said to have created heaven and earth (WA, 30/1, 483, on the first article of the creed).

Let us consider what this means. Alternative explanations of the origin of the world are all inadequate. Abstract approximations to the reality of the creaturely world are certainly possible, even without seeing any constitutive relation to God. Theology has to reckon with the fact that right up to our own day there is no general agreement about the Christian truth claim as concerns the understanding of the world as God's creation. Theological statements themselves are all debatable in this area of concern. Nevertheless, theology cannot refrain from describing the world of nature and human history as the creation of God, or from claiming that only thus do we bring into view the true nature of the world.

Theology must make this claim in dialogue with the sciences. It

---

149. Clement of Alexandria described this as the greatest act of divine providence (*Strom.* 1.17.86). Augustine saw it as the reason for the permission of sin and evil by God that he brings good out of it (*Enchir. ad Laur.* 11 [PL, 40, 236]).

may prove to be vulnerable in this regard, and often enough it may fail
to do justice to its task. But this is far better than neglecting that task.[150]
A failure to claim that the world that the sciences describe is God's world
is a conceptual failure to confess the deity of the God of the Bible. To
focus the belief in creation on subjectivity, as an expression of the feeling
of dependence, is no substitute.[151] If we follow such a course, the self-
understanding of faith comes into conflict with our awareness of the world
and easily becomes insincere, and confession of God as Creator becomes
an empty formula. In view of the emancipation of 18th-century science
from belief in God as the world's Creator and Sustainer, all this has become
part of the fate of the Christian faith in the modern world. But theology
cannot make a virtue of the resultant necessity by simply asserting itself
against the scientific view of the world. It cannot ignore what the sciences
have to say about the world. Naturally the tasks that are posed can hardly
be properly discharged in summary fashion.

150. In his survey of the relations between science and theology in the 20th century,
Barbour (*Issues in Science and Religion,* pp. 115ff.) lists three varieties of opposition between
the two: the neo-orthodoxy deriving from Barth, existentialist theology, and linguistic
analysis, which reduces religious statements to subjectivity. E. Schlink in *Ökumenische Dogmatik* (Göttingen, 1983), p. 36, rightly says that the failure to set the world as we now know
it under God as Creator is Docetism in the doctrine of creation (cf. also pp. 75f.). See also
A. R. Peacocke, *Creation and the World of Science* (Oxford, 1979), pp. 46f.; W. H. Austin,
The Relevance of Natural Science to Theology (New York, 1976), pp. 1ff.; and my essay "The
Doctrine of Creation and Modern Science," *Zygon* 23 (1988) 3ff.

151. In his *Der Mensch zwischen Gott und Welt* (Stuttgart, 1952, 1956), pp. 317-50,
Gogarten follows this line of interpretation, which goes back to Schleiermacher. Though he
rightly stresses the causal relation to God as first cause, Gogarten sees no way leading from
the world to God as its Creator (p. 324). Yet this is not to deny that there is a need for
reflection on the belief in creation, and especially on the world as God's creation. If Gogarten
thinks we can avoid this task by noting that belief in creation is a philosophical interpretation
of the world (p. 325), he comes into conflict with the older theological tradition, including
that of the Reformation, and empties the belief of all content.

G. Ebeling (*Dogmatik des christlichen Glaubens* [Tübingen, 1979], I, 264ff., 302ff.)
takes a more nuanced view, though he comes close to Gogarten when he finds a positive
relation between belief in creation and science primarily in the fact that the thesis of the
world's creatureliness opens the door to research. But Ebeling takes too lightly the scientific
challenge to belief in creation (pp. 302f.), in view of more than two centuries' discussion
of the theme. Ebeling is no doubt correct in saying that science does not give belief in
creation its certainty (p. 304), but in no way does this alter the fact that the sense of the
truth of this certainty is tied to the possibility of integrating the scientific understanding of
the world into the Christian view of it as God's creation. P. Hefner rightly calls this a
condition of the coherence of the Christian faith in God: "The doctrine of creation is an
elaboration of how we understand the world when we permit our understanding of God
to permeate and dominate our thinking" (in C. E. Braaten et al., *Christian Dogmatics*
[Philadelphia, 1984], I, 298).

The deliberations that follow may at least point the way, even if several things remain open to question, as in other parts of dogmatics. In distinction from other discussions of the objects of the act of creation, i.e., of the creaturely world, we shall not turn at once to the variety of creaturely forms. We shall first look again at the work of the Son and the Spirit in creation, this time from the standpoint of their immanent working, the principles of cosmic order and dynamics. On the one hand this will make more concrete our trinitarian handling of the doctrine of creation, while on the other hand it will clarify the relation to basic aspects of the scientific description of the world.

§ 1. Plurality and Unity in Creation

The creation of a reality that is distinct from God, but one that God also affirms and thus allows to share in fellowship with himself, is conceivable only as the bringing forth of a *world* of creatures. A single creature would be too tiny face to face with God's infinity. As a finite creature it would have no lasting entity. A finite being is limited by other beings, not merely by what is infinite, but also by other finite things. It has its distinctiveness only vis-à-vis other finite things. Only in this distinction does it exist. Hence the finite exists as a plurality of what is finite.

Creaturely reality, then, is a plurality of creatures making up the world. Plurality results logically as part of the concept of the finite. This does not have to mean that in time creation always existed as a plurality of creatures. Relativist cosmology that sets the beginning of creation before finite time[152] traces the plurality of finite phenomena to a big bang, associating the plurality of material forms and figures with the expansion of the universe. It would be in this way that the Logos would work as the generative principle of the diversity (and therefore plurality) of creatures. At any rate, the cosmogonic idea of the expansion of the universe shows

---

152. For the difficulties of such a view within a physical cosmology cf. McMullin, "How Should Cosmology Relate to Theology?," pp. 17-57, esp. 34ff., who rightly stresses that "the Big Bang cannot automatically be assumed . . . to be either the beginning of time or of the universe . . ." (p. 35). "What one *could* readily say, however, is that if the universe began in time through the act of a Creator, from our vantage point it would look something like the Big Bang that cosmologists are now talking about" (p. 39). Cf. also P. Davies, *God and the New Physics* (New York, 1983), pp. 9ff., 25ff.

that for plurality we need space in which one creature can be at a distance from another. The temporal expansion of cosmic space is a basic condition for the development of lasting forms.[153]

Increasingly diverse phenomena have their inner unity or identity not directly in their own particularity but in their relations to the unity of the world, in the order that links them to the unity of the one world. Theologically considered, the order of the world is an expression of God's wisdom, which is identical with the Logos. If the Logos is the generative principle of all the finite reality that involves the difference of one thing from another — a principle grounded in the self-distinction of the eternal Son from the Father — then with the advent of ever new forms differing from what has gone before there comes a system of relations between finite phenomena and also between these phenomena and their origin in the infinity of God. As the productive principle of diversity the Logos is the origin of each individual creature in its distinctiveness and of the order of relations between the creatures. Thus the different creatures in the created world differ from the one Logos, from whom they all derive. Nevertheless, the Logos is not merely transcendent in relation to the creatures. He is also at work in them as he constitutes for each its own specific existence in its own identity. Order and unity are not just external to the creatures. The greater the independence of the creature, the more plainly it has its specific structure by which it forms a totality in distinction from everything else. Patristic theology expressed the relation between the transcendence and immanence of the Logos by speaking of the many *logoi* of the creatures that are all summed up in the one Logos (see n. 64 above). The *logoi* are also transcendent to the creatures in the sense of the Platonic doctrine of the ideas. Today we prefer to speak of the rise and development of creaturely forms with their own distinctiveness in open connection with the cosmic process.

The uniform order of the world, insofar as it stands over against the plurality of events as the general forms of their conditions of origin, is that of the natural law that governs phenomena. This order is indeed the epitome of the rules for the emergence of phenomena in the process of time, but as such it is abstract, detached from the plurality of creatures in their concreteness. In terms of the order of natural law, creatures seem to be interchange-

---

153. Expansion carries with it the idea of openness to the future. For the correlation between the expansion of the universe and the knowable variety of phenomena, cf. C. F. von Weizsäcker, *Die Einheit der Natur* (1971), p. 365: "The growth of space is in this sense the openness of the future."

able and thus to be no more than indifferent examples of the validity of the law. Necessarily no account is taken of the individuality of the specific event. We still need to show on what this individuality rests. But first we have to consider how abstract the law is in relation to what is individual, and therefore how abstract is any theory of the natural order of occurrence.[154]

At this point the scientific description of reality in terms of natural law must be distinguished from the way in which the divine Logos is the unity of creation in its plurality. The Logos is not the abstract order of the world but its *concrete* order. It is so because in the concept of the divine Logos we cannot separate the eternal dynamic of self-distinction (the *logos asarkos*) from its actualization in Jesus Christ (the *logos ensarkos*). The universal Logos is active in the world only as he brings forth the particular *logoi* of specific creatures. Only in the person of Jesus of Nazareth, of course, is the Logos fully one with the particular *logos* of each creature, namely, with the "flesh" of each individual person. We showed why this is so in our development of the doctrine of the Trinity in vol. I, 263ff., 310f., and we shall have to develop and clarify the reason in our christology. In this chapter we have already reversed the procedure that led from Jesus' relation to God to a statement about the eternal Son (see above, pp. 22ff., 27ff.). The creation of creatures distinct from God rests on the self-distinction of the eternal Son. Because this path was first taken in the man Jesus of Nazareth, we must now speak of an indissoluble relation between the eternal Son as the creative Logos of a world of creatures and the man Jesus in his relation to the Father and these fellow creatures. Because the Logos who permeates the world of creation came to full manifestation in this man, all things in heaven and on earth are summed up in him (Eph. 1:10). As the creative principle of the cosmic order, then, the Logos is not a timeless universal structure like natural law or a theoretical system of order in terms of natural law. It is the principle of the concrete, historically unfolded order of the world, the principle of the unity of its history. The working in creation of the Logos thus includes its entry into the particularity of creaturely reality, its immanence — better, its intervention — which took place supremely in the incarnation as the Logos so united itself to one individual and distinct creature that it became definitively one with it.

---

154. This abstraction is different from that which Ebeling stresses, i.e., the abstraction of science from life (*Dogmatik des christlichen Glaubens*, I, 299, 302). If Ebeling has in view what others call objectivity, the abstraction that we have to explain more precisely is from the reality of nature and not from the subjectivity of human experience.

This unification of the universal Logos with one individual creature is possible only because the creature concerned is universal — just as the Logos, being universal, is also concrete. Not every creature could meet this condition. Elemental events and elemental parts of matter are highly universal in virtue of the simplicity of their structures, which are repeated in innumerable examples, and also in virtue of the fact that their atoms can be the building blocks for more complicated creatures. They are not universal, however, as individual examples. Universal relevance in the sense of a distinctive universality of historical scope and significance mediated by particularity is possible only at the stage of higher complexity, for only here — and especially at the stage of human life — do we find a full development of individuality. At the human stage what is universal in the relation of the creature to the Creator finds thematic expression in the creature, and the working out of this theme is the specific particularity of Jesus. Thus the Logos is concretely united with the plurality of creatures by humanity, or more strictly by the one man who for his part integrates humanity into a unity as himself the "new man."

The incarnation is, then, not alien to the concept of the Logos. It is part of the function of the Logos as the principle of the world's unity, which is not an abstractly descriptive principle but the creative principle. The incarnation is the integrating center of the world's historical order, which is grounded in the Logos and will find its perfect form only in the eschatological future of the world's consummation and transformation into the kingdom of God in his creation. Therefore, the incarnation cannot be an external appendix to creation nor a mere reaction of the Creator to Adam's sin. From the very first it is the crown of God's world order, the supreme concretion of the active presence of the Logos in creation.[155]

As the creation and expression of the divine Logos, each individual creature with its distinctiveness over against all other creatures is related to the Father so as to glorify him as Creator by its creaturely existence. The destiny of creatures corresponds to the relation of the eternal Son to the Father, to the glorifying of the Father by the Son. As the Son glorifies the Father by distinguishing himself from the Father, yet owing himself wholly to the Father even in his distinctiveness, so it is the destiny of each creature to honor the Father as its Creator in its own creaturely distinctiveness. In this way each creature shares in the filial relation of the Logos to the Father.

155. Maximus Confessor, in PG, 91, 1217A; cf. L. Thunberg, *Microcosm and Mediator*, pp. 90ff. On Duns Scotus, *Ord.* 3 d 7, q. 3, cf. W. Dettloff, *TRE*, IX (1982), pp. 223-27.

This is not an abstractly general principle with the creatures as specimens. As the generative principle of otherness, the Son is the creative origin of the particularity of each creature and at the same time the concrete epitome of its varied manifestations. The function of the eternal Son as the Logos of creation includes both these aspects. Furthermore, the relation of creatures to the divine Logos differs from that of concrete examples to an abstract universal in the sense that the destiny of creatures for fellowship with God by recognizing and glorifying him as Creator and Father does not find direct fulfillment in their concrete existence. We shall see that for this purpose there is need of a history that overcomes the trend toward independence from God and the resultant conflicts with fellow creatures.

If we can conceptually explain and elucidate along such lines the function of the eternal Son as the Logos of a world of creatures, then we can see more clearly the relation between the Christian concept of the creation and preservation of the world by the divine Logos and the description of the order of the world in terms of natural law. Such a description, as already emphasized, is marked by abstractness, even though its statements refer to movement and change, to the rise and fall of phenomena in time. Scientific hypotheses of law generally describe processes that can be reproduced and rely on repeatable experiments.[156] They describe the concrete order of events from the standpoint of that which recurs uniformly. Now there can be no doubt as to the great importance of uniformities of this type, not only for technological mastery of natural processes, but also for nature itself. The inviolability of nature's laws is a basic condition for the rise of more complex structures. Yet there is more to what takes place in nature than the uniformity of its processes. This is true at any rate if the course of time, its movement from the earlier to the later, to the future, is irreversible. The irreversibility of time justifies the thesis that in the processes of nature each specific event is unique as such, notwithstanding obvious uniformities with other events. Uniform processes that give us formulas like "If A, then B" are then associated with something different, namely, the contingent sequence of events.[157] Erwin

156. Cf. the contrast between scientific and theological statements in A. R. Peacocke, *Science and the Christian Experiment* (London, 1971), pp. 21f.; A. M. K. Müller, *Die präparierte Zeit* (1972), pp. 264f.; my article "Kontingenz und Naturgesetz," in *Erwägungen zu einer Theologie der Natur,* ed. A. M. K. Müller and W. Pannenberg (1970), pp. 34-80, esp. 66; and the remarks of W. Döring, *Universitas. Zeitschrift für Wissenschaft, Kunst und Literatur* 14 (1959), p. 974.

157. For details cf. my "Kontingenz und Naturgesetz," pp. 65ff.

Schrödinger said already in 1922 that at least for the great majority of processes whose regularity and constancy have led to the development of the postulate of universal causality, the common root of the strict regularity that is observed is chance.[158] The contingency of events is presupposed in scientific hypotheses of law at least in the sense that there is to a large degree abstraction from contingency. It is not a theme as such. The uniformities that can be expressed as laws are the theme, whether the laws be regarded as deterministic or as statistical. But the uniformities do not stand alone. They stand only in relation to that which goes beyond uniformity,[159] i.e., contingent sequences of events.

Reflection on this truth shows that application of scientific formulas to natural events demands the postulating of initial and marginal conditions that we cannot deduce from the formulas and that are thus contingent to them. But even in what is uniform there are constants that as such are contingent.[160] The drift of all this is that the scientific hypotheses of law presuppose that the material of natural events is contingent.[161] The hypotheses formulate the uniformities in events that

158. E. Schrödinger, *Was ist ein Naturgesetz?* (1962), p. 10. His statement rests on the basic significance of statistical uniformities in microprocesses for all macrophysical regularity, and it presupposes the irreversibility of the direction of time (p. 13).

159. C. F. von Weizsäcker also said that we cannot reduce reality to our detailed knowledge of structures in "Kontinuität und Möglichkeit," in *Zum Weltbild der Physik* (sixth ed.; 1954), pp. 211-39, here p. 227 (cf. ET *The World View of Physics* [Chicago, 1952]).

160. In his nuanced analysis of different aspects of contingency Russell has shown that the contingency of constants in nature vanishes on a global view of the cosmos, often by application of an "anthropic principle" that gives final meaning to the constants in nature ("Contingency," p. 35). This is no doubt true, but in my argument the issue in the nomological contingency of nature's constants is simply their relation to the formulas in which they are expressed and not the more comprehensive question of their relation to what Russell calls the "global contingency" of the universe in general. On the anthropic principle cf. nn. 177ff. below.

161. At issue here is Russell's "nomological" contingency, but it is linked with the contingency in the sequence of events that he calls "local" as distinct from global contingency (cf. Russell, "Contingency," pp. 24, 27ff., 30ff.). In general, "contingency" refers to that which is not necessary and which something else might thus replace (cf. the first of the three meanings cited by W. Hoering, "Kontingenz," *HWP*, IV [1976], 1035, though Hoering views it linguistically rather than ontologically; in its ontological form the definition goes back to Duns Scotus, *Ord.* 1 d 2, p. 1, q. 1-2 [Vatican ed. (1950), II, 178, n. 86]). Nomological contingency is always relative to the formulas defining the contingency of a thing (e.g., the condition of its beginning). It does not rule out the possibility that the thing might be necessary by other laws.

The contingency of event, however, is relative to time, not to formulas. It denotes that which is not necessary in terms of the past and presupposes openness to the future. Negatively it takes the form of the indeterminacy of quantum physics or thermodynamics (cf. Barbour, *Issues in Science and Religion*, pp. 298, 303ff., though he does not use the term

may be seen in spite of the contingency of each individual event. In view of the interrelation of statements about laws, a scientific description can approximately reconstruct sequences of events, since the starting and marginal conditions for the application of a given law are themselves the result of other regularities. In such wide-ranging processes as the development and history of the universe as we know it, or of living creatures, we can thus describe the sequence of events as the interaction of laws. But such reconstructions are only approximations to the actual course of events. This is so because the direction of time is irreversible and hence both the world process as a whole and each event in it are ultimately unique.

A description of the nexus of events in concrete processes may also take a different form from that of an exemplification of general rules and their interrelation. Historical narratives do not suppress the contingency of events within a general sequence. The contingent sequence constitutes the whole.[162]

There is, of course, some abstraction, since the narrative is selective. In describing a process we cannot portray all the events concerned but only those that give the process its character and are important for its outcome. Yet there is no abstraction from contingency. The whole sequence, as well as the individual events in it, is irreversible and unrepeatable. The individual events do not have their specific historical importance because they illustrate general laws, though they may in fact do so. They are important because of their place and function in the sequence of the unique process, because of their relation to a historical process whose distinctive shape is discernible only in terms of its outcome.

Along such lines ancient Israel viewed the reality of humanity and its world as a history, namely, as an irreversible sequence of ever new

---

"contingency"). To bring all events and not just indeterminate events under the concept we find that the definition of contingency as what which is not necessary will not suffice. A distinction of that kind limits contingency to that which is not regulated by a formula. If all events as such are contingent, and if what is necessary in the sense of law describes only one aspect of them, we need an extended definition of contingency. The contingent will have to be that which is not necessarily *not*, i.e., what is possible insofar as it takes place (cf. my "Kontingenz und Naturgesetz," p. 75, n. 11). In this sense we can think of all events as contingent, even though the way in which they come to pass conforms to laws. We best describe this as "general contingency," in distinction from Russell's local and global contingency, since it is a feature of every event, though not of the world as a whole. A fundamental and perfectly adequate basis for this view that all events are contingent may be found in openness to the future in a temporal sequence that is irreversible, for this means that every event is unique and unrepeatable and thus transcends the laws to which it conforms.

162. Cf. my *Theology and the Philosophy of Science* (London, 1976), pp. 61ff.

events. In distinction from the anthropological understanding of history in our own time, which has freed itself from its origins in a theology of history,[163] the OT finds in God's action in the contingency of events that which gives the sequence its integrity and meaning. Certainly human acts and purposes have their place in this history, but God ultimately directs its course.[164] Ancient Israel did not set nature and history in antithesis as modern Western thought does. In both realms the actuality of the divine action was considered constitutive.[165] It viewed the orders of the natural world as divinely posited. It traced back their inviolability to a historical event (Gen. 8:22). This idea seems to have been a familiar one in the days of Solomon.[166] Other texts integrate the creation of the world and its orders into God's salvation and covenant history with Israel.

Even in Israel, however, tension developed increasingly between the cosmic action of God, which we see in the regularity of events, and his historical action. This tension found its plainest expression in the Wisdom literature.[167] It was present before the exile but undoubtedly was sharpened by the shattering of confidence in God's saving acts in history when the monarchy came to an end and the Jewish people lost their political independence in the 6th century. In spite of many attempts at mediation in Jewish thinking,[168] the tension between God's action in the order of creation on the one hand and his action in the history of Israel's election on the other found a definitive resolution only with the Christian doctrine of the incarnation of the Logos, who is identical with the wisdom

163. For the classical account of this development cf. K. Löwith, *Weltgeschichte und Heilsgeschehen* (1953). Cf. also G. A. Benrath, *TRE*, XII (1984), pp. 633ff., on "Die Verselbständigung und Säkularisierung der Weltgeschichte."

164. Cf. the basic materials in von Rad, *OT Theology*, II, 99ff.; K. Koch, *TRE*, XII (1984), pp. 572f.

165. G. von Rad, "Aspekte alttestamentlichen Weltverständnisses," *EvT* 24 (1964) 57-98, esp. 65. As von Rad sees it, the OT view of nature is just as opposed to the modern one, and at the same point, as is its view of history (p. 64).

166. Presupposing that Gen. 8:22 was already extant at this time.

167. Von Rad, "Aspekte," pp. 65ff.; cf. idem, *Wisdom in Israel* (London, 1972), pp. 174f., 282ff., in which von Rad stresses more strongly that Israel, with its unique recognition of historical contingency, increasingly had to face the question of the constants in history (p. 290). H. H. Schmid, however, in his "Altorientalisch-alttestamentliche Weisheit und ihr Verhältnis zur Geschichte," in *Altorientalische Welt in der alttestamentlichen Theologie* (Zurich, 1974), pp. 64-90, argues that from the first, Wisdom thinking in Israel had abandoned the frame in which historical experiences were understood.

168. Cf. Sir. 24:8, 11, which states that the wisdom of God found a place of historical residence in Israel and took up its dwelling there. Along these lines Philo interpreted the revelation of God to Moses at Sinai as a revelation of the *logos* that permeates all things.

of God, in Jesus of Nazareth. Here the theme of wisdom is integrated into that of salvation history, and the latter is expanded into a cosmic drama. Christian theology thus had the task of finding a place for Wisdom's concern about the divinely posited natural order in its doctrine of the mediatorship of the Logos in creation.

In the theological tradition this was one of the functions of the thought that ideas in the mind of God are the prototypes of creaturely things and their relations (see above, pp. 25ff.). If instead modern theology seeks a basis for the existence and order of created phenomena in the self-distinction of the Son from the Father and his creative activity, then it must find an appropriate place and rank for the natural order in its understanding of natural events. It will not do for Christian theology simply to set in antithesis to the description in terms of natural law a totally different view of reality as a field of personal experience in the open process of history.[169] This can never be more than a subjective, and therefore impotent, protest against the view of a necessary regulatory nexus in all events. Even the reference to the abstractness of the law formulas cannot by itself change anything as long as we do not consider what they are abstracted from or from what the related description of events remains independent, namely, the contingency of events as the basic character of all occurrence.

If "contingency" is only a philosophical term for what theology must regard as the creative action of God,[170] then we must maintain that it applies to all events and therefore to the world as a whole.[171] Only thus is God seen as the Creator of all things, the Creator of the world. But a necessary condition is that

169. Cf. P. Althaus, *Die christliche Wahrheit* (3rd ed. 1952), pp. 319-23. By contrasting regularity and history, Althaus admirably defines the problem of relating scientific and theological views. By merely opposing them, however, he does not differ basically from Barth, who along the same lines totally ignores the scientific description of the world in his doctrine of creation (cf. *CD*, III/1 [1958], ixf.).

170. E. Brunner, *Dogmatics*, II (London, 1952), p. 12 describes the concept of contingency as no more than a philosophical formulation of the Christian idea of creation.

171. Local contingency as a general characteristic of all events is basic to Russell's "global contingency" ("Contingency," pp. 27ff.), which, according to him, does not require a beginning in time. Medieval theology earlier distinguished between the creatureliness of the world, which shows itself to be rational, and the question of its beginning in time. In my view Russell is wrong when he claims that the idea of the contingency of the universe (pp. 28f.) stands in need of the anthropic principle and that this principle offers a cogent basis for contingency. Certainly the idea that the universe is oriented to humanity might suggest that its contingency is the work of a purposeful will. But this is by no means conclusive. Aristotelian metaphysics earlier offered an instance of teleology without contingency. On contingency cf. T. F. Torrance, "Divine and Contingent Order," in *The Sciences and Theology in the Twentieth Century*, ed. A. R. Peacocke (Notre Dame, IN, 1981), pp. 81-97.

we view even the emergence of regularities, of uniform processes[172] that can be expressed as laws concerning what takes place in nature, as contingent.[173] Only thus can we view God as the Creator of the world of nature as we know it, even in its regulated order, without making a theological assertion that is external to natural occurrence itself.

Even in a scientific description of this occurrence, in spite of all the confusion caused when statements about law are referred to contingent entities, we can still find a basis for the theological interpretation of the reality of nature as the expression and result of contingent divine action. In this regard, of course, we must not miss the point that scientific and theological statements are made on different methodological levels. Physics must inquire into laws, not speak of God's action. The phrase "history of nature," used in cosmological physics, is not itself from physics but from philosophical reflection on theoretical cosmological constructs. The concept of contingency is marginal in the logic of scientific statements. It is a correlate of regularity and not a general characterization. It occurs only as indeterminacy. Yet in connection with the irreversibility of time it provides a basis for philosophical reflection on the scientific description of the world that necessarily leads to the thesis of the contingency of events, and even the contingency of regulated processes, in the context of the open process of a history of nature.

Theology then uses this philosophical reflection to identify the contingency of events both in detail and in the world as a whole as the expression of the creative activity of the biblical God who acts in history. Even the rise of

172. Cf. H. Wehrt, "Über Irreversibilität, Naturprozesse und Zeitstruktur," in *Offene Systeme,* 2 vols., ed. E. von Weizsäcker (1974-81), I, 114-99, esp. 140. The systems observed in nature are always open, for as real systems they are basically temporal, i.e., systems in which temporal processes of change take place. H.-P. Dürr argues that the phenomenon of open (as opposed to closed) systems in thermodynamics is ultimately due to the openness to the future that is posited in principle in quantum physics ("Über die Notwendigkeit in offenen Systemen zu denken," in *Die Welt als offenes System,* ed. G. Altner [1986], pp. 9-31; this volume is devoted to dialogue with I. Prigogine). On different views of open systems cf. n. 277 below.

173. We have here Russell's "absolute nomological contingency" ("Contingency," pp. 35f.), which is closely linked to the thesis that on the presupposition of the irreversibility of time all the natural uniformities that can be expressed in law formulas must be seen as having developed, and as therefore having a "first instantiation" (cf. pp. 36ff.) and being locked in (cf. my "Kontingenz und Naturgesetz," pp. 57ff., 65f., and *Theology and the Philosophy of Science,* 64ff.). In confirmation, modern cosmology teaches that the areas in which most natural laws apply (e.g., in classical mechanics) arose in advanced phases of the expansion of the universe. But when there is no area of application, it makes no sense to speak of a law of nature. On the issue of "first instantiation" from the standpoint of information theory, cf. E. von Weizsäcker, "Erstmaligkeit und Bestätigung als Komponenten der pragmatischen Information," in *Offene Systeme,* 2 vols., ed. E. von Weizsäcker (1974-81), I, 200-221.

uniform processes that can be described in law formulas may then be seen by theology as a contingent positing of the Creator. In this respect theology can appeal to the fact that in a cosmic process characterized by the irreversibility of the flow of time, regular processes and scientific observation must have taken place for the first time in order to be then locked in (first instantiation). This is not to give a scientific proof for the existence of the Creator, since the argument is on a philosophical and theological level. But the truth claim of creation is strengthened by the fact that in principle theology can integrate scientific statements into its coherent description of the world as the creation of God.

Without such a conceptual "synthesis" that allows us to bring even nature's uniformities into a view of the world as God's creation that is marked by contingency and historicity,[174] the regularity of nature would be an argument against the truth of the belief in creation, which is, in fact, how it has usually been regarded in the modern period. The contingency of events in quantum physics and thermodynamics may be seen, of course, as an exception to the normal regulation of events in nature, as gaps in the scientific description of nature, which according to all our historical experience will be closed as research continues. To base what we say about God's work in natural events on these exceptions would be to fall victim to the fatal mistake of seeing God at work precisely in these gaps, so that every scientific advance would be a further blow to theology. The situation is quite different, however, if all events, all the processes that can be described in terms of laws, are seen to be contingent, as the irreversibility of the direction of time suggests. In this case we are not simply dealing with gaps. We have a total understanding of reality that embraces the basic theses of science. In this understanding the fact that events take place according to law has a specific and in many ways a very important place.

The regularity of events in elementary processes is the basic presupposition for the development of permanent forms. Without duration

174. Althaus, *Christliche Wahrheit,* pp. 320f., has two arguments against a synthesis of this kind of historical and scientific approaches. First, faith should not seek for itself a scientific place in physics, namely, in the indeterminacy of individual events in quantum physics. Second, if theology does lay special claim to gaps, i.e., to exceptions to an explanation in terms of law, then regulated events cannot be seen as direct and living acts of God in the way that miracles are. These two weighty obections are related. We find similar reservations in J. Polkinghorne, *One World: The Interaction of Science and Theology* (Princeton, 1986), pp. 71f., commenting on W. Pollard, *Chance and Providence* (New York, 1958).

The only safeguard against the argument that theology is here again claiming a gap in what is normal as the basis of its description of God's action in natural occurrences is to show first that contingency is constitutive for the very concept of laws in nature, and then to claim that contingency thus applies not merely to events that are not regulated by law but to all events in general. We can do this if we show that the contingency of each event is the result of the irreversibility of time. If this argument holds good, only a contesting of the irreversibility of time can weaken the thesis that all events are contingent.

there is no independent existence. The uniformity of events according to law is thus a condition of creaturely independence. If the Creator wanted to bring forth independent creatures, he had primary need of a uniformity of elementary processes. Hence the regulated order of nature does not conflict with the contingent working of God in the producing of creaturely forms but is, in fact, an important means to this end. The uniformity of natural occurrence is on the one hand an expression of God's faithfulness and constancy in his activity as Creator and Sustainer, while on the other hand it is the indispensable basis for the development of ever new and more complex forms in the world of creatures. Only on the premise of the uniformity of elementary processes can thermodynamic variations from stationary conditions be the source of anything new, especially in the rise and development of life and its forms.

Earlier in the modern period it was thought that the independence of more complex creaturely forms is prejudiced if we view them as the result of the operation of laws of nature. This was understandable at a time when nature was construed mechanistically. But the processes of nature do not run in closed and isolated systems (see n. 172 above). Hence with each new form a new totality comes into existence, and it has a retrospective regulatory effect on the conditions of its own existence[175] and asserts itself as a new factor in relation to the environment. The constancy of environmental conditions regulates the persistence and, of course, the perishing of forms. In order for forms to persist in relation to their environment, the environment's stability is a condition of survival. For us humans, however, this stability has become a basis for ever increasing mastery over nature.

God has bound his creative action to the laws of nature, which are grounded in his creative action, but this no more excludes the creation of

---

175. Cf. Barbour, *Issues in Science and Religion,* on the implications of the principle of Wolfgang Pauli (pp. 295f.). On this principle cf. also J. D. Barrow and F. J. Tipler, *The Anthropic Cosmological Principle* (New York, 1986), pp. 302ff. In a review of Barbour's work D. R. Griffin argued that his "relational emergentism" cannot, like Whitehead's process philosophy, distinguish between "compound individuals" and "nonindividuated wholes" (*Zygon* 23 [1988] 57-81, esp. 62). To me this does not do justice to Barbour's interpretation of the Pauli principle. Perhaps the perspective of process philosophy is responsible, since this gives no ontological rank to the emerging totality (cf. my criticism of the implications of Whitehead's event-atomism in my *Metaphysics and the Idea of God* [Grand Rapids, 1988], pp. 113ff.). Process philosophy cannot give an ontologically satisfactory description of complex forms because it must view their unity as something that is ultimately secondary ("compound," in Griffin's language). For good reasons Barbour rejected it.

what is new than does the immediacy of each created form to God. Mediacy and immediacy are not incompatible at this point.[176] The idea that God can bring forth what is new and unusual only by breaking the laws of nature has been overruled by the insight that for all their regularity the laws of nature do not have the character of closed (or, better, isolated) systems. At the same time the mediation of all emerging and perishing by the validity of the laws of nature is a condition if creaturely forms are to achieve the independence vis-à-vis God that lies in the concept of a creature distinct from its Creator. Only on this presupposition can creatures act independently even in relation to God, and this is a condition of their being brought into the relation of the Son to the Father and of thus attaining to fellowship with God. The laws of nature, then, have an indispensable ministering function in the trinitarian history of creation.

From the standpoint of Christian theology the participation of creatures in the trinitarian fellowship of the Son with the Father is the goal of creation. We see this plainly in the incarnation of the divine Logos in Jesus of Nazareth. For the goal of this event was that all might be reconciled in him (Col. 1:20; cf. Eph. 1:10). This goal is achieved only at the human stage, and even there not directly, but only as the result of a history in which human apostasy from God and all its consequences must be overcome. But according to the apostle's statement the destiny of all creation is at stake (Rom. 8:19ff.). All creation waits for the manifestation of divine sonship in the human race, for thereby the corruptibility from which all creatures suffer will be vanquished. Whatever we may say about the immediacy of nonhuman creatures to God, it has at any rate a reverse side in their suffering from corruptibility. If, however, this suffering is overcome by the adoption of humans into the filial relation of Jesus to the Father, the relation of nonhuman creatures to their Creator thereby also comes to fulfillment.

176. From the days of L. Hutter (1618) the older Protestant dogmatics distinguished between immediate and mediate creation (*Loci communes theologici*, III, q. 2) on the ground that in Gen. 1 there was no prior work on the first day of creation but that the works of the next five days presuppose what has already been created (cf. Quenstedt, *Theologia*, p. 594, th. 13; Schmid, *Doctrinal Theology*, p. 169). Reformed theology adopted a similar distinction, though rejecting the idea of Quenstedt and other Lutherans that immediate creation brought forth only unformed matter, a formless chaos, out of which all else was made (cf. the examples in Heppe and Bizer, *Reformed Dogmatics*, p. 187). The distinction was relativized by the express declaration of F. Buddeus that even creatures made with creaturely mediation were still created *ex nihilo* by God (*Compendium*, pp. 212f.: "All things were made *ex nihilo*, some mediately, others immediately"). To this extent each creature is immediate to God, and Buddeus fiercely contested the view that God might have surrendered his creative power to creaturely mediation (§ 8.216).

But are we humans really the goal of creation? The Christian doctrine of the incarnation obviously implies such a view, which we find also in the OT creation stories. In the light of the incarnation, of course, we humans can be called the goal of creation only because in us, or more precisely in Jesus of Nazareth, the fellowship of the creature with the Creator comes to fulfillment as the Son of God comes among us as a man. From this standpoint, however, it is still true that the whole history of the universe is a prehistory to the coming of humanity. For many years such a view seemed incompatible with modern science. As Copernicus showed, the earth is not the center of the universe. We humans thus seemed to be marginal phenomena in the cosmos. Might there not be in other galaxies and solar systems planets on which life might arise and on which there might be intelligent beings? Even on earth, is the evolution of life to end with us? Only the scientific cosmology of the 20th century and its calculations of the age and development of the universe have shown us what cosmological data are indispensable for the emergence of life, and therefore of human life, in the world.

Among these are data regarding light, gravity, electricity,[177] the relation of photons and protons, and the relative strength of nuclear and electromagnetic forces, which are so constituted that there may be only slight change if the emergence of life on earth is not to be impossible.[178] The age of the universe is also seen to be necessary for the formation of the galaxies and the chemical elements and relations that permit organic life.

On this basis many scientists now think that the anthropic principle is plausible, though others contest it. In the weak version of Robert H. Dicke (1961) the principle is that the universe must have features that make possible the emergence of life and intelligent beings. The strong version of the British physicist Brandon Carter (1973) argues that the universe must have been made in such a way that it not only permits the emergence of intelligent beings (and physics) but in the long run will *necessarily* produce them.[179] In both versions the attraction

177. R. Breuer, *Das anthropische Prinzip* (1981), p. 25.

178. Barrow and Tipler, *Anthropic Cosmological Principle*, pp. 5, 125, 175.

179. Breuer, *Das anthropische Prinzip*, p. 24; cf. Barrow and Tipler, *Anthropic Cosmological Principle*, pp. 16ff., 21f. Confusing at first is the linking of the principle to an assertion of the dependence of what is observed both on the nature of the instruments and on the observer (pp. 15ff., 23, also 557). From the days of discussions of quantum physics the associating of instruments and observer has been a common one, but in principle it is dubious, for observers are not tied to a single viewpoint but can enlarge it by their instruments. We humans can also accept data that assign to our existence a marginal role, as the Copernican worldview did, and also at first the theory of evolution.

of the principle is that it gives meaning to the otherwise inexplicable facticity of the constants of nature to which we have referred. The valid argument might be raised against it that it offers no scientific explanation.[180] Nevertheless, it still "reveals an intimate connection between the large and small-scale structure of the Universe."[181] This is especially true of the weak version. The strong form goes much further by claiming that the universe must necessarily produce life and intelligent beings. It thus runs into criticism, and even Barrow and Tipler call it speculative (*Anthropic Cosmological Principle*, p. 23). This is even more true of their own "final anthropic principle," according to which intelligence, having once emerged in the universe, can no longer perish but will achieve mastery over all material processes and itself become immortal.[182]

Recently, then, serious discussion has been devoted to the idea that the goal of the universe and the normative details of its construction are the producing of human life. But the idea is often rejected because of the prospect that further exploration of the cosmos will bring to light nonterrestrial life. The discovery of intelligent life outside the earth has also caused some to have doubts about the Christian doctrine of redemption.[183] But does the redemption which is bound up with the incarnation relate only to earthly humanity? Would intelligent beings in other galaxies need no redemption, or would there be other plans of salvation specifically designed for other worlds? In reply we may say first that though some authors support the possibility of nonterrestrial forms of life and intelligence, other researchers have good reasons for rejecting

180. McMullin, "How Should Cosmology Relate to Theology?," p. 43: "The anthropic principle would tell us to expect these physical features, once we know that this is the universe that has man in it. But to expect them, given the presence of man, is not the same as to explain why they occur in the first place." McMullin refers especially to the relevance (discussed from the time of Collins and Hawthorne in 1973) of the isotropy of the universe, though Barrow and Tipler have reservations here (*Anthropic Cosmological Principle*, pp. 428f.). McMullin's point refers, of course, to all the constants in nature that the anthropic principle claims to "explain."

181. Barrow and Tipler, *Anthropic Cosmological Principle*, p. 4.

182. Ibid., p. 23, cf. 659ff. For a summary and criticism of the steps in the argument, which in many respects leads to an eschatological vision similar to that of Teilhard de Chardin, cf. F. W. Hallberg's review "Barrow and Tipler's Anthropic Cosmological Principle," *Zygon* 23 (1988) 139-57, esp. 148ff., 151ff. Meanwhile F. J. Tipler has further developed the cosmology that he began under the banner of the anthropic principle. Cf. his omega point theory, which assumes that the state of eschatological fulfillment rather than the emergence of humanity is normative for the course of the whole cosmic process ("The Omega Point as *Eschaton*: Answers to Pannenberg's Questions for Scientists," *Zygon* 24 [1989] 217-53).

183. Cf. R. Pucetti, *Persons: A Study of Possible Moral Agents in the Universe* (1969), 125f.; E. McMullin, "Persons in the Universe," *Zygon* 15 (1980) 69-89, esp. 86ff.

it.[184] Second, traditional Christian teaching does make mention of other intelligent beings apart from humans, namely, angels, of whom some need no redemption, while others, having turned against God, are incapable of it.

Hence Christian teaching traditionally developed the incarnation-related thesis of our central position in the universe in spite of the acceptance of other intelligent beings superior to us. It is hard to see, then, why the discovery of nonterrestrial intelligent beings should be shattering to Christian teaching. If there were such discoveries, they would, of course, pose the task of defining theologically the relation of such beings to the Logos incarnate in Jesus of Nazareth, and therefore to us. But the as yet problematic and vague possibility of their existence in no way affects the credibility of the Christian teaching that in Jesus of Nazareth the Logos who works throughout the universe became a man and thus gave to humanity and its history a key function in giving to all creation its unity and destiny.

§ 2. The Spirit of God and the Dynamic of Natural Occurrence

a. The Biblical Starting Point

If we are to regard creatures in their plurality as the work of the Son both as deriving from God and among one another, and if the Son, as the Logos of creation, is the principle of its order, by which all phenomena in their variety are related to one another, then, according to the biblical testimony, the Spirit of God is the life-giving principle, to which all creatures owe life, movement, and activity. This is particularly true of animals, plants, and humans, of which Ps. 104:30 says: "Thou sendest forth thy Spirit; they are created, and thou renewest the face of the ground." In keeping with this is the second creation account, which says that God "formed man of dust from the ground, and breathed into his nostrils the breath of life,

---

184. Barrow and Tipler, *Anthropic Cosmological Principle*, pp. 576-612; cf. 132f. on the evolutionary improbability of the rise of intelligent beings and p. 558 on the related requirements regarding the duration of a planet. On the latter point cf. esp. the discussion of W. Stegmüller in his excellent summary of the problems and results of modern cosmological physics (*Hauptströmungen der Gegenwartsphilosophie*, II [6th ed. Stuttgart, 1979], pp. 693-702).

and man became a living being" (Gen. 2:7; cf. Job 33:4).[185] Conversely, all life perishes when God withdraws his Spirit (Ps. 104:29; Job 34:14f.). The souls of all living things and the breath of all people are in the hands of the Spirit (Job 12:10).

At a first glance this biblical view of life is hard to reconcile with modern opinions. For modern biology, life is a function of the living cell or of the living creature as a self-sustaining (above all self-nourishing) and reproducing system,[186] not the effect of a transcendent force that gives life.[187] It might be suggested that the relevant biblical notions must be regarded merely as the expression of an archaic and outdated understanding of the world, like many other biblical views on natural phenomena. We will have to take up this point later. The direct symbolism of God breathing breath into creatures seems to us today to be more poetic than explanatory. The only question is whether the metaphor carries a deeper meaning that might be illuminating even for the modern understanding of natural processes.[188] If so, it would be worth exploring. Theology can hardly refuse to carry out this exploration, since Paul's statements about the new life of the resurrection as a work of the divine Spirit (Rom. 8:11; cf. 1:4; 1 Cor. 15:44f.) presuppose the OT and Jewish concepts of the relation between the divine Spirit and life (cf. also Ezek. 37:5ff.).

The theme gains in complexity because the first creation story extends the creative work of the Spirit beyond the giving of life to plants and animals and refers it to the whole work of creation (Gen. 1:2). The statement about original chaos leads on to the saying that "the Spirit of God was moving over the face of the waters." The exact meaning of *ruaḥ 'elohim,* translated "Spirit of God,"[189] has been the subject of much debate among exegetes, but only in regard to this one instance.[190] Elsewhere, as the wording suggests, it is always rendered "Spirit of God." Why not here?

185. We must explain more clearly in the next chapter the relation between the divine Spirit and the human spirit.

186. Cf., e.g., L. von Bertalanffy, *Theoretische Biologie,* II (2nd ed., Bern, 1951), pp. 49ff. (on the sustaining function of the cell); M. Hartmann, *Allgemeine Biologie* (Jena, 1953), p. 17; but also J. Monod, *Chance and Necessity* (New York, 1971).

187. Vitalist theories of a special life force ascribe this to the organism itself; cf. the dominant idea in the 18th and 19th centuries that organic forces were functions of physical bodies. See E.-M. Engels, "Lebenskraft," *HWP,* V (1980), 122-28.

188. Cf. my "Der Geist des Lebens," pp. 51-56.

189. Cf. K. Koch, "Wort und Einheit des Schöpfergottes in Memphis und Jerusalem," *ZTK* 62 (1965) 251-93, esp. 275f.

190. See, e.g., Exod. 31:3; 35:31; Num. 24:2; 1 Sam. 10:10; 11:6; 2 Chron. 15:1; 24:20; also Job 33:4 *(ruaḥ 'el),* and often with *yhwh.*

Since we have here a carefully considered text that in other places uses 'elohim as a divine name, we may rightly describe the idea that the reference is to an extremely powerful storm, a hurricane,[191] as grotesque.[192] It seems more likely that an existing theological view of the divine Spirit is at work in Gen. 1:2, one that we can hardly reconcile with the mere physical mobility of wind.[193] We see this when the text speaks of a shaking or vibrating.

But why do we have to regard "Spirit" and "wind" as alternatives? The link to 'elohim suggests that God's Spirit is depicted here in terms of wind, as in Ezek. 37:9f. (cf. v. 5). This view is close to the common idea of the life-giving breath of God, for with both wind and breath we have a movement of air that is otherwise still. We might compare the original meaning of Greek pneuma (as distinct from aēr).[194] As regards Gen. 1:2, then, we should not distinguish wind and breath. Plainly we must associate the reference to the Spirit of God with the creative speaking of God that immediately follows. What we have here is the breath of God that stands in affinity to his speaking.[195] A supporting point is that the speaking and not the Spirit is now the subject of all God's creative work. Are we to conclude, then, that here, in distinction from other OT passages, the divine breath is not itself life-giving or active?[196] The Spirit-wind does at least

191. Cf. G. von Rad, *Genesis: A Commentary* (Philadelphia, 1961), p. 49; C. Westermann, *Genesis 1–11* (Minneapolis, 1984), p. 107.

192. Steck, *Schöpfungsbericht*, p. 235; cf. also Koch, "Wort und Einheit," p. 281, n. 92; B. S. Childs, *Myth and Reality in the OT,* SBT, 27 (1968), pp. 35f.

193. Westermann concludes that to take *ruah* as "wind" is difficult in view of the link to 'elohim (*Genesis 1–11*, pp. 107f.). Childs too, in spite of the verb, sees here the creative Spirit of God in antithesis to chaos. The final question is thus: What view of God is presupposed or possible? For Westermann the only cogent reason for a different translation here is the verb.

194. On the early Greek distinction in Anaximenes and Empedocles versus the later Stoic view, cf. J. Kerschenstein, *Kosmos. Quellenkritische Untersuchungen zu den Vorsokratikern* (1962), pp. 79f.

195. Steck, *Schöpfungsbericht,* p. 236. Steck alludes to the close link between word and breath in Ps. 33:6: "By the word of the Lord the heavens were made, and all their host by the breath of his mouth."

196. Ibid., p. 235. Steck argues that the situation in Gen. 1:2 is before the beginning of the real work of creation. But can we make so clear a distinction? Do we not rather have here the transition to creation? In a long note Steck himself (p. 236, n. 971) asks whether we are not to take Gen. 1:2 more positively as an expression of God's readiness for the work of creation. This view would eliminate the antithesis to other OT ideas of the creative dynamic of God's life-giving work by the Spirit and yet also preserve the uniqueness of the account, i.e., its close linking of the dynamic of the Spirit to the divine speaking (the word in Ps. 33:6).

have the function of moving over the waters of chaos. We do not have here merely a process in God himself. God's breathing is a raging storm, and from its dynamic issues the creative speaking.

The Spirit of God is the creative principle of movement as well as life. The OT developed no general conception of cosmic movement to denote the various movements and activities of creatures. But there is an approach to this in the idea of the creative dynamic of the Spirit of God. The question remains, however, whether this makes it possible to reconcile the statements about the Spirit of God as the origin of life with the modern understanding.

b. Force, Field, and Spirit

The description of forms of movement and moving forces is the central theme of physics today. To describe movement and change physics has developed the concept of force or energy working on bodies and thus producing movement.[197] Classical dynamics tried to trace the concept of force back to that of the body and the impulses that move it, and in this way to base all physics on the body and the relations between bodies. Thus Descartes sought to describe the mechanical effects of bodies upon one another as the transfer of movement from the one to the other.[198]

Newton found inertia in bodies *(vis insita)* but did not limit the forces working upon them *(vis impressa)* to the transfer of movement. He thus worked out the idea of force that is independent of bodies.[199] With his thesis that the alteration of movement is proportionate to force, he limited himself to devising a method of measuring force, regarding the nature of forces as for the most part obscure.[200] Unlike Descartes, Newton took into account nonmaterial forces that act through the soul in analogy to bodily movement. One such force was gravity, which Newton viewed as an expression of the moving of the universe by God with space as his instrument.[201]

197. C. F. von Weizsäcker, "Die Einheit der bisherigen Physik" (1962), in *Die Einheit der Natur*, pp. 133-71.

198. R. Descartes, *Le Monde* (1664, written 1633) ch. 7.2.

199. I. Newton, *Philosophiae naturalis principia mathematica*, I (3rd ed. 1726, new impression Cambridge, 1972), def. 3 and 4; McMullin, *Newton on Matter and Activity*, pp. 43ff., 52f., 80ff.

200. M. Jammer, "Kraft," *HWP*, IV (1976), 1178f., esp. 1179 on *Opticks*, III, q 31.

201. Koyré, *Newtonian Studies*, p. 109, cf. 91. See also McMullin, *Newton on Matter and Activity*, pp. 55ff., and on gravity, pp. 57ff.

The theological implications of this idea that nonmaterial forces cause material changes perhaps contributed to the criticism that 18th-century French physicists up to Ernst Mach and Heinrich Hertz brought against this aspect of Newton's concept of force. Unlike Newton, these physicists sought to reduce forces to bodies or masses (Hertz). If all force comes from bodies or masses, then and only then the understanding of natural events is definitively cut loose from any connection with the concept of God, since God cannot be understood as body.[202] Theological talk about God's working in worldly events then becomes totally nonsensical.[203]

The antireligious ramifications of the reduction of the concept of force to the body and its inert mass enable us to see at once the theological relevance of the changed relation between force and body resulting from the growing significance of field theories in modern physics from the time of Michael Faraday. Faraday regarded bodies themselves as forms of forces that for their part are no longer qualities of bodies but independent realities that are "givens" for bodily phenomena. He now viewed these forces as fields that occupy space in order to avoid the problems involved in the idea of force working at a distance, and he hoped that ultimately all these fields would be reducible to a single all-embracing field of force.[204]

Leibniz had already moved in this direction by seeing in the monads forces that manifest themselves at specific points and deriving the impermeability of matter (its mass) from the concept of force, namely, from the repulsion that it causes;[205] the opposing forces of attraction would then be made responsible for the continuity of natural phenomena.[206] Here, however, force or its manifestation is

202. We may simply recall at this point the arguments of Origen which we summarized in vol. I, 372. Cf. also Aquinas *ST* 1.3.1.

203. We can thus understand the battle of early 18th-century theology for the doctrine of the divine concursus as an indispensable condition of the creaturely faculty of self-movement. Under the circumstances depicted, however, it was bound to fail. Cf. Buddeus, *Compendium,* p. 48. On the concept of force and its history cf. M. Jammer, *Concepts of Force* (Cambridge, MA, 1957); M. B. Hesse, *Forces and Fields. The Concept of Action at a Distance in the History of Physics* (New York, 1961); and W. Berkson, *Fields of Force* (New York, 1974).

204. Berkson, *Fields of Force,* pp. 31 and 58-60, shows that Faraday let a metaphysical position of this kind guide him in his experiments.

205. Ibid., p. 24.

206. On these two forces cf. later Kant's *Critique of Pure Reason* § B 321 and the second part of *Metaphysische Anfangsgründe der Naturwissenschaft* (1786), ET *Metaphysical Foundations of Natural Science* (Indianapolis, 1970). Schelling then came to his idea, increasingly oriented to electrical phenomena, that duality in tension is the basic condition (*Einleitung zu seinem Entwurf eines Systems der Naturphilosophie* [1799], in *Sämtliche Werke,*

linked not to bodies but to spatial points. Faraday linked it to the totality of the field that embraces one or more bodies. In Faraday's view, mass (as the "rate of response to forces," i.e., inertia) depends on the concentration of force at a given point. It thus manifests itself point by point. The material particle is the point of convergence of lines of force, or a cluster of such lines over a given period.[207] This concept of force as field links it to the metric field of space or space-time. Thus A. Einstein in his general theory of relativity (1916) could even try to reduce the concept of force to the metric field of a non-Euclidean space-time.[208] Conceivably the metric field of space-time might itself be reduced to the concept of force.[209] At any rate, field theories see a close link between force and space-time.

The claim that the switch in modern physics to increasingly comprehensive field theories of natural occurrence is of theological relevance finds support in the metaphysical origin of the field concept. The idea of the field of force goes back by way of Stoicism to pre-Socratic philosophy, namely, to the teaching of Anaximenes that air is in the *archē* and that all things originated as compressions of air. Max Jammer thinks that the Stoic doctrine of the divine *pneuma* was actually the direct precursor of the modern field concept. For the Stoics the *pneuma* was a very fine stuff that permeates all things, that holds all things in the cosmos together by its tension *(tonos),* and that gives rise to the different qualities and movements of things.[210] This Stoic doctrine influenced not only the thought of Philo but also what early Christian theology had to say about the working of the divine Spirit in creation.[211] There were fewer contacts with Stoic philosophy in the later fathers, of course, especially after Origen's criticism of the Stoic doctrine of the material nature of the *pneuma* (cf. vol. I, 372, 382). Such problems do not arise with the modern theories, especially now that they have dropped the idea of ether as a substratum.

III, 299). On this cf. F. Moiso, "Schellings Elektrizitätslehre, 1797-1799," in *Natur und Subjektivität,* ed. R. Heckmann, H. Krings, and R. W. Meyer (1985), pp. 59-97, esp. 92ff. Schelling was moving toward an idea of field as a basic model for natural occurrence (p. 94).
    207. Berkson, *Fields of Force,* pp. 52ff.
    208. M. Jammer, "Feld/Feldtheorie," *HWP,* II (1972), 925. Cf Berkson, *Fields of Force,* p. 318.
    209. Berkson, *Fields of Force,* pp. 324f., gives to Faraday's idea of a cosmic field as a field of force the advantage of theoretical consistency, since Einstein's field theory cannot trace back all forces (e.g., gravity) to curved forms of space (i.e., geometrically) but has to allow for energy changes in the field (p. 320).
    210. M. Jammer, "Feld," *HWP,* II (1972), 923. Cf. also Pohlenz, *Die Stoa,* I, 74f., 83, with examples in II, 42f.
    211. R. Rüsch, *Die Entstehung der Lehre vom Heiligen Geist bei Ignatius von Antiochia, Theophilus von Antiochia und Irenäus von Lyon* (1982), pp. 80ff.

But insofar as the field concept corresponds to the older doctrines it is not a mistake, but does justice to the history and concept of spirit, if we relate the field theories of modern physics to the Christian doctrine of the dynamic work of the divine Spirit in creation.

For theology there is in fact a closer relation between its doctrine of the divine Pneuma and the field theories of modern physics than there was in the Middle Ages between this doctrine and the Aristotelian theory of motion. Like the mechanistic description of nature, the theory of motion held by Christian Aristotelians in the Middle Ages regarded the body as the starting point of movement, whether self-movement or movement by others. The question of the relation of natural events to God had to focus, then, on the possibility and necessity of having recourse to a first cause of all movement, to a nonbodily cause of bodily movement, and to the necessity of the activity of this cause in all the activities and operations of secondary causes. If natural bodies might be seen as having the power to move without need of any further causes, the idea of God's working in natural events would be no less unintelligible than superfluous.

Over against this, the renewing of the thought of the primacy of force in Leibniz (with Newton as a precursor) and the development of field theories in physics have made it possible again to relate the function of the divine Spirit in the creation of the world to the way in which physics describes nature.[212] We may refer especially to the concept of all material, bodily phenomena as manifestations of force fields and finally of the one cosmic force field that Faraday had in view.[213] Einstein's metaphysical interests were more in the immutability of law and the geometric order of the field.[214] We recall his skeptical remark about the indeterminism of quantum physics, namely, that God does not throw dice.[215] Behind

212. We must credit T. F. Torrance with being the first to recognize these links and plead for theology's adoption of the field concept: "The field that we are concerned with is surely the interaction of God with history understood from the axis of Creation-Incarnation. . . . Our understanding of this field will be determined by the force or energy that constitutes it, the Holy and Creator Spirit of God" (*Space, Time, and Incarnation* [New York, 1979], p. 71).

213. G. Süssmann, "Geist und Materie," in *Gott — Geist — Materie*, ed. H. Dietzfelbinger and L. Mohaupt (1980), 14-31, esp. 18ff., thinks field theories make possible a nonmaterial understanding of reality.

214. Berkson, *Fields of Force*, pp. 317f.

215. Cf. Einstein's letter to Max Born on 12 April 1926 (*Albert Einstein, Hedwig und Max Born, Briefwechsel, 1916-1955*, kommentiert von Max Born [Munich, 1969], pp. 129f.). Cf. also the letter on 9 July 1944 and Born's comments in his essay on Einstein's "Statistical Theories" in *Albert Einstein: Philosopher-Scientist*, ed. P. A. Shilpp (1951), pp. 163-77. In the same volume V. G. Hinshaw deals with Einstein's recognition of Spinoza in the *New York Times* on 25 April 1929 ("Einstein's Social Philosophy," pp. 659f.). Cf. also I. Paul, *Science, Theology, and Einstein* (New York, 1982), pp. 56f., 122ff.

Einstein and his liking for Spinoza on the one side and the field concept of Faraday on the other, along with the indeterminism of modern quantum physics, there probably lie different theological and metaphysical conceptions of reality.

The principial differences between the ways of describing reality in physics and in theology prohibit us from offering a direct theological interpretation of the field theories of physics. In accordance with the nature of scientific perception (see above, pp. 63ff.), these theories can be seen only as approximations to the reality that is also the subject of theological statements about creation. We see that the reality is the same because theological statements about the working of the Spirit of God in creation historically go back to the same philosophical root that by mathematical formalizing is also the source of the field theories of physics, and the different theories give evidence of the same emphases that we find in the underlying metaphysical intuitions. We also see that the reality is the same because the theological (as distinct from the scientific) development of the concept is in a position to find a place in its reflection for the different form of description in physics, for which there can be empirical demonstration, and in this way to confirm the coherence of its own statements about the reality of the world.

The relation, of course, is not merely an external one. If it were, we would simply have bad apologetics. Theology has to have its own material reasons for applying a basic scientific concept like field theory to its own philosophical rather than scientific presentation. Only then is it justified in developing such concepts in a way appropriate to its own themes and independently of scientific usage. Reasons for introducing the field concept into theology have been given already in the context of the doctrine of God, namely, in interpreting the traditional description of God as Spirit. Criticism of this traditional way of speaking about God as though the reference were to subjectivity *(nous)* led us to the insight (vol. I, 372ff.) that it is more in keeping with what the Bible says about God as Spirit, or about the Spirit of God, to view what is meant as a dynamic field that is structured in trinitarian fashion, so that the person of the Holy Spirit is one of the personal concretions of the essence of God as Spirit in distinction from the Father and the Son.

The person of the Holy Spirit is not himself to be understood as the field but as a unique manifestation (singularity) of the field of the divine essentiality. But because the personal being of the Holy Spirit is manifest only in distinction from the Son (and therefore also from the Father), his working in creation has more of the character of dynamic field operations. Even in the mediatorship of the Son in creation the personal relation to the Father takes full shape only in the incarnation, in the distinction of the man Jesus from the Father, though all creaturely distinction from God and from other creatures is to be understood as deriving from the Son's self-distinction from the Father and its manifestation.

The same applies to the Spirit's work in creation. In distinction from the Son's mediatorship in creation and its significance for the distinction and otherness of every creature, it relates to the link and movement that connects the creatures to one another and to God. To this extent the Spirit's work in creation is by nature more than a field of divine essentiality. It relates plainly to the specificity of the person of the Holy Spirit in distinction from the Son, so that we may rightly refer to the third person of the Trinity. Certainly the difference of creatures among themselves and from God cannot be thought of without the reference to the one who is thus distinct. But the same applies to the Son's own relation to the Father. The Son's fellowship with the Father is always mediated by the Spirit. The Son is the first recipient of the Spirit (vol. I, 315ff.). We thus ascribe to the third person of the Trinity both the positive relation, in the sense of the fellowship of what is distinct, and also the associated dynamic, whether in the trinitarian life of God or in creation. In the conditions of time in creaturely relations the dynamic of the Spirit's working will of course express itself differently than in the eternal fellowship of the Trinity. It has to overcome the rifts that come as creaturely existence makes itself independent. This is possible, however, only in transition through the antitheses and collisions that characterize dynamic relations in creation.

The trinitarian grounding and structuring of a theological account of the participation of the Holy Spirit in the work of creation through field concepts leads us to expect that using this terminology in theology will give evidence both of similarities and of characteristic differences as compared with its scientific use. We may illustrate both by the relations between the field concept and the concepts of time and space.

c. Space and Time as Aspects of the Spirit's Working

When the first creation story speaks of the "moving" of the Spirit of God over the face of the waters (Gen. 1:2), the idea of a surging force is hardly possible without time and space. The storm wind can develop its dynamic only in space, and to sweep forward it needs time. The same holds good — though in softer tones — when we read of the sending forth of the divine breath that renews life on the earth (Ps. 104:30). We must take statements of this kind figuratively, but still must not detach their content from their figurative form by spiritualizing.

Spatial ideas occur elsewhere in biblical statements about God's relation to creation. We read of God's dwelling in heaven. From there his power, or he himself, is manifested on earth (vol. I, 410ff.). The idea of God's transcendence also demands space if it is not to be reduced to the logical distinction of the Infinite from everything finite. The concept of the incarnation, of God's entry into the different sphere of creaturely being, implies a spatial difference that can be overcome only in a temporal process.[216] It is inappropriate, of course, to localize God himself in space, to restrict him to one place as distinct from others, but we do not avoid this by limiting the idea of space to God's relations with his creatures.[217] Precisely the distinction between that which is in relation and the relation itself we owe to the idea of space, and it cannot escape this. We cannot set God's relations to the world in antithesis to his essence, as though this were unaffected by the relations. We have seen already that essence itself is a relational concept (vol. I, 359ff.). But the relations of God to his creatures must be thought of as an expression of the freedom of his essence and therefore must be depicted as grounded in it.

Jewish thought in the 1st century A.D. often used the term "space" *(makom)* as a divine name on the basis of Exod. 33:21 ("Behold, there is a place by me"), Exod. 24:10 LXX, and statements in the Psalms like Ps. 139:5ff. or 90:1.[218] This view influenced both early Christian theology (see n. 224) and Renaissance philosophy. Thomas Campanella linked it to the geometric concept of Bernhardino Telesio and Francesco Patrizzi with an appeal to the infinity of mathematical space.[219] For other 17th-century thinkers like Pierre Gassendi and Henry More, preference

216. According to Torrance, incarnation "asserts the reality of space and time for God in the actuality of His relations with us" (*Space, Time, and Incarnation*, p. 67).

217. Ibid., pp. 23f. H. Heim in *Der christliche Gottesglaube und die Naturwissenschaft*, I (1949), pp. 183f., would distinguish his postulated superpolar space in which God is present for us from the reality of God himself. This space is simply one aspect, a side turned to us, from which space alone God can be accessible to us.

218. Cf. M. Jammer, *Das Problem des Raumes* (1953), pp. 28ff.

219. Ibid., pp. 91ff., 96ff. Jammer thinks this line of thought might also have had an impact on Spinoza (p. 50).

for the Aristotelian concept of space over that of matter that fills space was important in preparing the ground for Newton's physics, especially as regards the theory of absolute space. More, who argued against Descartes in favor of a view of space independent of matter, was not afraid to take the step of identifying God and space.[220]

In combination with the geometric concept, this is the view that Leibniz contested in his letters to Samuel Clarke, suspecting an idea of space as the *sensorium Dei* behind the observations of Newton.[221] Unlike space, God cannot have parts or be made up of parts. Clarke replied that infinite space is undivided as such and is the presupposition of divided space, since spaces and division of space are conceivable only on the premise of unlimited space.[222] Clarke equated this unlimited space with God's immensity. God, then, is not identical with the limited space of geometry. This view overcame in principle the Renaissance idea of infinite space as an empty receptacle of things.[223]

In creating, God gives creatures space alongside himself and over against himself. But his presence still comprehends them. As the early fathers said, God comprehends all things and is comprehended by nothing and no one.[224] In God's own immeasurability itself distinctions are posited and permitted that go with the existence of creaturely finitude.

---

220. For examples cf. ibid., pp. 48f.

221. On this cf. my essay "Gott und die Natur," *TP* 58 (1983) 481-500, esp. 493ff. Especially important is Clarke's observation in the second reply to Leibniz that *sensorium* denotes the place, not the organ, of perception (Leibniz, *Die philosophischen Schriften*, VII, 360).

222. Clarke (cf. Leibniz, *Die philosophischen Schriften*, VII, 368): "Infinite Space is One, absolutely and essentially indivisible: And to suppose it parted is a contradiction in Terms, because there must be Space in the Partition itself." Kant argued similarly in his discussion of space in the *Critique of Pure Reason* (§ A 23). Space must underlie the idea of different places; we can think of many spaces only in space.

223. Cf. Jammer, *Problem des Raumes*, pp. 91f. on Telesio and pp. 83f. on Hasdai Crescas. We find the same idea in Newton's statements about absolute space (cf. ibid., pp. 121f.), though Newton puts it more cautiously and obviously prefers to characterize space as the working of the presence of God. The first move toward overcoming the idea of space as a receptacle may be seen in Clarke's observation regarding the essential indivisibility of infinite space (see n. 221).

224. Cf. Hermas *Man.* 1.26.1, also Aristides *Apol.* 1.4, Theophilus *Ad Autol.* 1.5 and 2.10, Irenaeus *Adv. haer.* 2.1.2 and 2.30.9. Did this view retreat into the background as the fathers turned to a more Platonic or spiritual view? Torrance (*Space, Time, and Incarnation*, pp. 10ff.) finds in this type of statement an alternative to the idea of space as a container. This is illuminating to the degree that spatial comprehending in the patristic statements is meant dynamically as in Stoicism (p. 11), but it does not involve the view of space as a system of relations, which Torrance thinks he sees in Athanasius and the idea of perichoresis (pp. 14ff.).

As regards the concept of space, this means that a plurality of places, and therefore of limited spaces, comes into being with the making of creatures. Presupposed is plurality in God himself, namely, that of his trinitarian life. The eternal contemporaneity of the three persons in their mutual relations might suggest the idea of spatial distinctions and relations in God himself. The trinitarian distinctions, however, are not fixed divisions. In the act of self-distinction each of the persons is one with the other from whom it is distinguishing itself.

We cannot, then, regard the bringing forth of creatures as though creatures were an object of divine self-distinction. Only indirectly do they proceed from the self-distinction of the Son from the Father. In the same way they are willed and affirmed by the Father in his self-distinction from the Son, by which he also accepts the Son in his distinction. The Father wills and accepts them as an expression of the overflowing of the divine love with which the Father loves the Son. Differences in the creaturely world take the form of division, of divided existence, though not to the exclusion of relations between things divided. The space of creatures is constituted by the fact that they are related precisely by their finitude and in their limitation. From this standpoint space is the epitome of relations between divided spaces, between points of space.

Leibniz especially developed this view and set it in antithesis to the idea of absolute space.[225] The Arab philosophy of the Middle Ages prepared the way.[226] But the guiding theological interest that space, like time, could come into being only with the making of creatures derives from Christian theology, and as early as Augustine. Augustine rejected both the idea of infinite space outside our world and that of time before the creation of the world, for we cannot agree with the Epicureans in postulating countless other worlds in addition to that created by the biblical God (*Civ. Dei* 11.5). This would be to bring into question the divine immutability (see above, pp. 37f.). Augustine's argument is that where there are no creatures with mutable movements, there is no time (12.15.2), nor is there any space outside this world of creatures (11.5).

Leibniz's idea of space as the epitome of relations goes further only in categorical precision as Leibniz states that we can think of space neither as infinite substance (alongside God or identical with him) nor as attribute (for things change their places, and therefore the place they take cannot be one of their qualities). The only option is to see space as the epitome of the relations of things

---

225. Leibniz, *Die philosophischen Schriften*, VII, 389-420 (Letter 5 to Clarke).
226. Jammer, *Problem des Raumes*, pp. 52ff.

whether in the concept of God or of creatures. In opposition to Newton's view of an absolute space as the receptacle of things, Albert Einstein backed up Leibniz with his general theory of relativity. B. Riemann had suspected that the metric structure of space might be dependent on the distribution of matter in space. The relativity theory carried this thought further with a geometric interpretation of gravity and in so doing robbed absolute space of its function as a condition of the definition of inertia (namely, the postulate of a "straight-line" movement independent of a system of relations).[227] The relativity theory has led Torrance to go back in theology, too, to a relational definition of space instead of the idea of space as receptacle or container.[228]

In modern discussion characterized by the relativity theory any idea of a relation of partial spaces or places still presupposes a unity of space, in keeping with the argument of Clarke and Kant that a condition of all division and all relation of spaces is the unity of space as an infinite given quantity (cf. Kant's *Critique of Pure Reason*, § B 39). This space, however, is not that of some geometry, which would always mean division by points, lines, surfaces, and bodies. Along the line taken by Clarke, it is the divine immensity, which is indivisible as such but which underlies all ideas of space and their orders and divisions in an intuition of the Infinite as the supreme condition of all human knowledge and all human concepts.

227. Ibid., pp. 178f., 183ff., 192f. Cf. also Einstein's preface to Jammer's work (ibid., pp. xivf.) in which he states that the relativity theory proves that Leibniz and Huygens were right in opposing the postulate of absolute space.

228. Torrance, *Space, Time, and Incarnation*, pp. 11ff., 22ff. (cf. already 4f.), 60ff. It is not clear in Torrance's thought, however, how space and time as a "continuum of relations" in the creaturely sphere (p. 61) relate to what he says about the relation between God and the creaturely world. On the one hand he states that space and time are the medium for understanding the relation (p. 61, cf. 68), but on the other hand he argues that we cannot define the relation in terms of space and time (p. 23 etc.). How, then, are we to understand "the reality of space and time for God in His relation with us" (p. 24)? To say along the lines of K. Heim that an extension of space-time is the "vertical dimension" of the relation to God through the Spirit (*Der christliche Gottesglaube*, p. 72) will hardly suffice as an answer to this question. The relation of space and time to the dynamic of the Spirit needs closer definition. Yet Torrance has seen and formulated what theology has to do at this point. We might note in passing that to link Lutheran teaching on christology and the eucharist to a notion of space as receptacle (pp. 30f.) is not convincing, since with his doctrine of the participation of the exalted Christ in the ubiquity of God Luther was specifically combating a circumscribed view of the session at God's right hand such as Zwingli upheld. Cf. on this H. Grass, *Die Abendmahlslehre bei Luther und Calvin* (1940; Gütersloh, 1954), pp. 53ff.; and J. Rohls, in *Mahl des Herrn*, ed. Garijo-Guembe, Rohls, and Wenz (1988), pp. 164f., on Christ's ascension and omnipresence. The statement of Torrance (*Space, Time, and Incarnation*, p. 32) that Lutheran theology "could only read the language about the body of Christ in heaven to mean that it was confined there as in a container" ascribes to the older Lutheran teaching the very opposite of what it was saying.

The two historically influential concepts of space — i.e., as the epitome of the relations of bodies or spaces and as that which is prior to all division or to every relation of what is divided — do not have to be mutually exclusive. They may go together if we take the first as describing the space of the creaturely world and the second, the immensity of God that constitutes this space.[229] But we must not do as Renaissance philosophy did and equate the infinity of geometric space with the immensity of God. If we do, we arrive either at the pantheism of Spinoza or at the idea of empty space as a container for things yet to be created. Geometric space may well be unlimited and therefore potentially infinite in the sense that it can be expanded without limit, but it is not really infinite.[230] Its potential infinity is only a broken reflection of the infinity of God in the human spirit. By his infinity God is present to all things, constituting the omnipresence of the space of creation. His infinity is also a presupposition of every human view of spatial relations in which things are both distinct and related. The perception of space, which according to Kant is, with that of time, at the basis of all human experience, is a way of intuiting the Infinite. According to Descartes, this intuition is a presupposition of the defining and distinguishing of all knowledge and all ideas.[231] Time and space as forms of perception are thereby also without limit, and they thus precede all the finite contents of experience. But every concept of space suggested by geometry differs from the concept of the space of perception

229. Moltmann, *God in Creation,* pp. 156f., also tries to bring the two concepts together by means of the concept of creation, which distinguishes the space of God from that of the created world. This thought is in keeping with what we said above. But we cannot follow Moltmann's thesis that the space of creation precedes creation, and the spaces created in it, as a third thing between the divine omnipotence and the world of creatures along the lines of the Jewish doctrine of Zimzum (cf. Jammer, *Problem des Raumes,* pp. 37, 50). Opposed to this thesis is the truth that God is omnipresent in the space of creatures. The thesis also opens itself to all of Torrance's objections to the idea of empty space as a receptacle. The idea of empty space between the absolute space of God's presence and the concrete space linked to the existence of creatures involves a hypostatizing of abstract ideas of space that the theory of relativity has outdated. The space of creation is not really distinct from the world of creatures. As the epitome of relations, it is constituted by the presence of the infinite God with his creatures. This is the guarantee of its unity. Only thus can we explain Moltmann's correct statement that by the concept of creation the space of the created world is related to that of the presence of God. The point is that the idea of creation means that the creature is not properly understood in isolation from the presence of the Creator, which is constitutive for its existence.

230. Jammer, *Problem des Raumes,* p. 168, refers to the distinction in geometry between the unlimited and the infinite, which was made by G. F. B. Riemann, *Über die Hypothesen, welche der Geometrie zu Grunde liegen* (1854; Berlin, 1919).

231. Cf. my *Metaphysics and the Idea of God,* pp. 22ff.

as an infinite totality, for it reconstructs the perception of space either for conception or purely conceptually.[232]

The differentiation of space from time is also a work of reflection that distinguishes the togetherness of things in space from their following one another in time. The concept of time proves to be basic in this regard, for it is constitutive for that of space. The simultaneity of what is different constitutes space. Somewhat epigrammatically Georg Picht could thus say that truly "space is time."[233] The implied reduction of space to time is a presupposition for a theological interpretation of the presence of God in space as the dynamic operation of the divine Spirit. This is why we had to discuss space first in this section. The situation changes when we go on to describe the temporal structure as a field of the working of the divine Spirit in his creative activity. The starting point then must be an interpretation of simultaneity.

The constitutive significance of simultaneity for the concept of space

232. The thesis that the immensity of God is constitutive for the space of creatures, and the related theological interpretation of Kant's statements about the infinite totality of the space of perception as a condition of all spatial distinctions and relations, takes up in another form Heim's "suprapolar space," by which God is present with his creation (Heim, *Der christliche Gottesglaube*, pp. 179ff., 183ff.). The problem with Heim's form of the thesis is that in keeping with contemporary discussions of multidimensional spaces, he tried to arrive at suprapolar space by introducing a new dimension, as in the transition from line to depth. In criticism W. H. Austin referred to the quasi-metaphysical character of Heim's statements (*Relevance of Natural Science to Theology*, p. 71). But the rational core of the argument also falls under the criticism that Heim uses paradoxes relative to a specific space as a reason for bringing in a new dimension: "Heim's examples do not establish (or render highly probable) that paradoxicality is either a necessary or a sufficient condition for the presence of a new space" (p. 69). Heim's description of suprapolar space is also "sermonic in style and quite obscure in content" (p. 71), so that it is hard to see whether it really is a space at all (p. 72). In distinction from Heim's argument, our own does not rely on geometric construction by introducing added dimensions. It reflects with Kant on the conditions of spatial concepts that apply also to spatial relations independent of our human perceptions; unlike Kant, however, we go back to the metaphysical background of his argument and do not restrict ourselves to the subjectivity of spatial perception. We do this on the ground that the concept of a knowing subject, like that of any other finite entity, is formed only by circumscription of the intuition of the Infinite (Descartes *Med.* III, 28).

233. G. Picht, "Die Zeit und die Modalitäten," in *Quanten und Felder. Festschrift W. Heisenberg*, ed. H. P. Dürr (1971), pp. 67-76, cited below in its reprinting in Picht's collected works, *Hier und Jetzt* (1980), pp. 362-74. Pointing in the same direction is the fact that filled space is related to the idea of the body; cf. A. Einstein, "Die Grundlage der allgemeinen Relativitätstheorie," in *Das Relativitätsprinzip*, ed. O. Blumenthal (1913, 6th ed. 1958), p. 81. A body is something only if it has duration (G. Schwarz, *Raum und Zeit als naturphilosophisches Problem* [1972], p. 152). This is also true of geometric bodies, for an ideal simultaneity underlies geometric ideas of space. This makes possible the unlimited duration of bodies in geometric conception.

gives philosophical plausibility to the linking of space and time in an idea of space-time as a multidimensional continuum. Nevertheless, the concept of absolute simultaneity has run into difficulties from the standpoint of relativity theory. For many observers there can be no strict simultaneity in many reference systems because determining time depends on light. Yet this does not wholly eliminate simultaneity. It is simply relative to the standpoint of the observer. With it spatial measurements are also relativized. Relative simultaneity is simply that of what is not simultaneous in itself. In the case of our sense of time it is made possible by the phenomenon of the present that bridges time as Augustine first described it.

In his famous treatment of time in book 11 of the *Confessions,* Augustine showed from examples like understanding speech or hearing a melody that human experience of the present is possible only because, beyond the imperceptible point of the Now, memory can preserve what is past and expectation can make present what has yet to come (11.28.38). All this takes place in virtue of "attention." There is thus an "extension of the soul" beyond the momentary Now.[234] We need to distinguish, of course, between the span of time that we can experience as an actual present and past or future events that we can associate with the present by memory or expectation, even though we know them to be distant in time. The strict present, which for its part integrates a series of events, is limited to a few seconds.[235] Yet events that we recall or expect also come within our sense of the present when we experience their contents as a form of reality that stretches across time to the present. The experience of stretching into the present is a more complex and comprehensive form of a present that overarches time.[236]

We have to think of the present of creaturely events for God as also bridging time. On the level of its own creaturely reality, that which is present to God belongs to different times. But before God it is present. In this regard God's eternity needs no recollection or expectation, for it is itself simultaneous with all events in the strict sense. God does not need light to know things. Being omnipresent, he is with every creature as its own place.[237]

234. Cf. my *Metaphysics and the Idea of God;* also K. H. Manzke, "Zeitlichkeit und Ewigkeit" (diss. Munich, 1989), pp. 259-360.

235. E. Pöppel suggests two to four seconds ("Erlebte Zeit und Zeit überhaupt," *Die Zeit. Schriften der Carl-Friedrich-von-Siemens-Stiftung* 6 [1983] 372).

236. Ibid., pp. 373f. To experience duration we need an identification and integration of events and forms of perception in relation to memory (p. 374).

237. The time-bridging character of the divine knowledge as simultaneity with what is not simultaneous explains Kierkegaard's use of simultaneity for faith in Jesus Christ.

Eternity is the undivided present of life in its totality (vol. I, 403ff.). We are not to think of this as a present separated from the past on the one hand or as the future on the other. Unlike our human experience of time, it is a present that comprehends all time, that has no future outside itself. The present that has a future outside itself is limited. A present can be eternal only if it is not separate from the future and if nothing sinks for it into the past.[238]

We are not to think of eternity as the epitome of time. Rather, we are to think of time with its sequence of events — future, present, past — as proceeding from eternity and constantly comprehended by it.[239] Eter-

---

In distinction from mere historical recollection, simultaneity with Christ is mediated by the gift of the Spirit, i.e., by the presence of eternity. With and by the eternal God, the past of the salvation event is also present to believers. Cf. Kierkegaard's observations at the beginning of *Training in Christianity* (Princeton, 1941), p. 9.

238. In "Zeit und Modalitäten," G. Picht rejects the "Greek" concept of the eternal present in favor of the primacy of the future in the understanding of time. This option presupposes a view of the constant present that isolates one of the three modes of time, i.e., the present, from the other two. To understand the eternal present as a present that comprehends time is not to exclude past and future but to include them. It is possible only from the standpoint of a future (or its anticipation) that cannot be infringed upon. We must not confuse the phenomenon of a present that comprehends time with the schema (or matrix) of interlaced modes of time (A. M. K. Müller) or times (Moltmann, in *God in Creation,* 124-39, esp. 128). Müller developed this matrix on the basis of Picht's discussion and his relating of the three modes of time to the modalities of possibility, reality, and necessity ("Naturgesetz, Wirklichkeit, Zeitlichkeit," in *Offene Systeme,* 2 vols., ed. E. von Weizsäcker [1974-81], I, 339f.). Any knowledge that includes all three modalities relates to the unity of time.

In comparison with the normal use of modes of time, however, we have here a higher stage of reflection, whereas the phenomenon of the present that comprehends time belongs to the sense of time itself. Augustine spoke about this in *Conf.* 11.20.26. He was not thinking of a combination — past present, past past, past future, etc. — such as we find in Müller with a view to critical elucidation of the linear nature of the physical understanding of time (cf. "Zeit und Evolution," in *Die Welt als offenes System,* ed. G. Altner [1986], pp. 124-60). A combination might serve this purpose, especially when it causes us to reflect on the historicity of the experience of time. It is doubtful, however, whether it brings us any closer to insight into the nature of time. Basic to talk about interlaced modes of time or times is the underlying relativity of the sense of time but also the phenomenon of the time-comprehending present, which such talk does not really explain. But cf. Müller's *Die präparierte Zeit,* pp. 206ff., on the importance of duration in the experience of time.

239. In modern discussion of the concept of time David Bohm is close to this idea of Plotinus (*Enn.* 3.7) with his doctrine of "implicate order" as the origin of the evolving phenomena of "explicate order" in natural processes; cf. his "Time, the Implicate Order, and Pre-Space," in *Physics and the Ultimate Significance of Time: Bohm, Prigogine, and Process Philosophy,* ed. D. R. Griffin (Albany, NY, 1986), pp. 177-208, esp. 192f.: "The order of unfoldment at a given level emerges from a 'timeless' ground in which there is no separation" (p. 196). In tension, however, is Bohm's idea that we must view time as an abstraction from

nity is constitutive for the experience and concept of time. Only if time is basically a unity, i.e., as eternity, can we understand the nexus of that which is separated in its course.

Plotinus accordingly viewed the soul as the origin of time. For although the soul is implicated in the many, it still shares in the one, and thus the succession of moments of time forms a nexus, a *synecheia hen* (*Enn.* 3.7.11). Plotinus set this grounding of the concept of time in the thought of eternity in antithesis to the Stoic and Epicurean theories of time and also to the Aristotelian thesis that defined time as the enumerating of movement (*Phys.* 219b.1f.), the unit whereby movement being measured being itself a movement. Plotinus argues that here time is always presupposed, so that this description does not explain its nature or constitution.[240]

The same criticism applies to the definition of time in modern physics, which follows the Aristotelian tradition inasmuch as it starts with the measurement of time, so that a unit of movement that serves as a standard — light in relativity theory — is basic.[241] Related to this orientation to measurement is the thesis of the uniformity of segments of time and the neglect of past, present, and future in understanding its nature.[242] All this may be pragmatically fitting for

---

movement (pp. 177, 189). In criticism of attempts to derive the concept of time from specific physical data instead of treating it as the presupposition of specific descriptions of natural processes, cf. Griffin's own discussion of I. Prigogine et al., in ibid., pp. 1-48. Some paradoxes in Bohn's thinking (cf. R. J. Russell, in ibid., p. 216) can be resolved only if we note the prephysical nature of time and its basis in eternity.

240. *Enn.* 3.7.9 and cf. Beierwaltes, *Plotin,* pp. 233ff.

241. Cf Schwarz, *Raum und Zeit,* pp. 183ff., esp. 186ff. On the Aristotelian origin of this view cf. pp. 168ff. Schwarz points to the absoluteness of space-time as defined especially by Einstein. In his relativity theory this replaces the absoluteness of the eternity that constitutes time.

242. This is Müller's so-called manipulated or prepared time (*Präparierte Zeit,* pp. 189ff., 228ff., 264f., 275f.). Picht, on whom Müller primarily relies, refers specifically to the lack of attention that classical physics pays to past, present, and future ("Zeit und Modalitäten," pp. 366ff.). Certainly these are relative to the awareness that orients itself in time and to its position. But the distinction is present no matter what the standpoint, relating to the present of the subject. P. Bieri makes this point in his incisive debate with the analytically based concept of J. E. McTaggart, H. Reichenbach, A. Grünbaum, G. J. Withrow, et al. (*Zeit und Zeiterfahrung. Exposition eines Problembereiches* [1972]), seeing a place only for the distinctions of earlier vs. later (on the assumption of irreversibility) and not the actual past, present, and future of real time, which is physically objective and thus constitutive for subjective experience of it (pp. 142ff., 165ff., 203ff.). The thesis, however, that the presuppositions are not therefore an objectifying of the distinction of modes, especially the future over against what is already factual (155ff., 165ff.), applies only to Reichenbach's arguing on the basis of the difference between the fixed nature of the factual and the indeterminacy of the future, not to the more precise form that it takes in G. Picht and C. F. von Weizsäcker, who link the future to the concept of possibility.

science and its concern for measurement, but it falls short of everyday experience of time, and it also fails to deal with the philosophical question of the nature of time that led Plotinus to his insight that time has its basis in eternity.

We find a remarkable parallel to the teaching of Plotinus in Kant's view of time. This view is remarkable because it stands in tension with Kant's very different anthropologically oriented intention. As regards time as well as space, Kant presupposed a constant unity of time in the concept of different times.[243] The original idea of time is uncircumscribed (30); it is an infinite unity. Materially, then, it does not differ from the concept of eternity. Perhaps Kant did not see this because he was not familiar with the relation between eternity and time in Plotinus (or Boethius) but thought of eternity as timeless. At any rate he tried to base the unity of time as well as space upon human subjectivity.[244] But the subject as a finite entity cannot be the basis of something infinite, of something that for Kant, too, is an infinite totality.[245] At all events, however, it can be the principle of duration without end and therefore of potential infinity. We can understand this only in terms of the constitution of subjectivity itself by intuition of the Infinite as the condition of all the finite contents of the consciousness, including the thought of the ego itself. Fichte came back to this insight of Descartes at the end of his discussion of the constitution of the self-consciousness in terms of a positing of the ego.[246] We cannot conclude, then, that Kant solved the problem definitively by substituting subjectivity for eternity as the constitutive basis of time. Nor did the early Heidegger fare any better when he developed this idea.

Although eternity is constitutive for the nexus of time and of that which is separated by the sequence of moments in time, we cannot derive time from the concept of eternity. Any attempt to conceive of time's origin presupposes time. Rightly, then, Plotinus regarded the transition from eternity to time as a leap. Following Plato in his *Phaed.* 248c.8, he described

243. *Critique of Pure Reason,* § A 31f. For Kant different times are simply parts of the same time, so that a specific time is possible only by circumscribing a single basic time.

244. The argument is that time is based on an inner sense in a "self-affection" of the subject (cf. p. 33). On this cf. Manzke, "Zeitlichkeit und Ewigkeit," pp. 111f., 118f., 152f. Nevertheless, according to Picht the constant present of eternity also served in Kant as a basis for the unity of time, since time for him was immutable in contrast to the changes that take place in it. We have to think of all the flux of phenomena as within time, but time remains and does not change; cf. Picht, "Zeit und Modalitäten," p. 366. To the degree that Kant saw in the constancy of time within the flux of phenomena the basis of the category of substance, the concept really rested on the awareness of time. Nevertheless, the thesis of the immutability of time lies behind the timeless identity of the subject (§ B 132; cf. § A 123).

245. Cf. my *Metaphysics and the Idea of God,* pp. 82ff.

246. Cf. D. Henrich, *Fichtes ursprüngliche Einsicht* (1967).

this leap mythologically as a fall.[247] This idea played a role in Christian Gnosticism. But Christian theology could not adopt it if it was to retain the doctrine of creation. If God positively willed the world and all its creatures, the same applies to the temporal form of their existence. Augustine rightly taught that God created time with all the creatures.[248]

Is time always related also to the finitude of creatures? If by this we mean the separation of earlier and later by the sequence of times, so that the present constantly sinks into the past, a theological objection to the idea of the unrestricted flow of time as thus constituted is that eschatological expectation of Christ is oriented to an end of this time *(aiōn)* (Matt. 13:39f.; cf. 24:3; 28:20) and includes hope of the resurrection of the dead. We shall deal with the related problems more fully in the section on eschatology. For the moment we may simply say that the end of this aeon is more than an epochal turning point in the flux of time.

With the completion of God's plan for history in his kingdom, time itself will end (Rev. 10:6f.) in the sense that God will overcome the separation of the past from the present and the future and therefore the separation of the present from the past and the future that is a feature of cosmic time in distinction from eternity. In the eschatological consummation we do not expect a disappearance of the distinctions that occur in cosmic time, but the separation will cease when creation participates in the eternity of God. Hence the distinction of life's moments in the sequence of time cannot be one of the conditions of finitude as such. For the finitude of creatures, their distinction from God and one another, will continue in the eschatological consummation. Nevertheless, the distinction of life's moments in time has something to do with the finitude of creaturely existence, if only as a transitional feature on the way to the consummation.

Succession in the sequence of time is obviously a condition of the attainment of independence by creatures as essential entities, their independence in relation both to one another and to God. Only in the process of time can a finite being act and thus manifest itself as the center of its own activity. After it has won independence, such a being can be preserved or renewed as its participates in the eternity of God, a point we cannot

247. *Enn.* 3.7.11. Cf. Beierwaltes, *Plotin*, pp. 244-46. Cf. also *Enn.* 2.9.4, where Plotinus argues against the Gnostic idea of the derivation of the visible world from a fall of the soul, holding instead that the world soul brings forth the visible world in recollection of the upper world and thus has to be in constant relation to it.

248. *Civ. Dei* 11.6; cf. 12.15.2. Cf. above, pp. 37ff.

develop further here. To win it and thus to achieve its individuality, a
being needs the conditions of becoming and perishing in time. In saying
this, we see in what sense cosmic time is to be regarded as the subject of
God's creative action. Because the Creator's action aims at the independent
existence of his creatures as finite beings, he willed time as the form of
their existence.

The independent existence of creatures has the form of duration
as an overarching present, by which they are simultaneous to one another
and relate to one another in the distinction of space. Since they do not
have their existence of themselves, their present is distinct from their
derivation as their past. They have, however, another relation to eternity,
which constitutes their origin. For their existence as duration they are
referred to eternity as the future of the good that gives duration and
identity to creatures. But since as creatures they are distinguished by their
independence from their origin in eternity, in the same way they also have
their future outside themselves, although in the duration of their existence
they already exist as an anticipation of the future of their total being.[249]

The future toward which creative forms move in the duration of
their existence has for them an ambivalent face. On the one hand, for the
preservation, development, and consummation of their nature, they are
referred to a future over which they have little or no control, while on the
other hand, since they are finite, the future threatens to end and dissolve
their independent form. It is precisely because of their creaturely independence, and the related distinction from their origin in creation, that
creatures are exposed to the fate of the dissolution of their form.

Origen took the obscure Pauline saying about the futility to which creation is
involuntarily subjected (Rom. 8:20)[250] and related it to the linking of souls to
bodies, which makes them vulnerable to corruptibility (*De princ.* 1.7.5). He did
not regard souls as such as vulnerable. If, unlike Origen, we believe that phenomena of the soul are all rooted in material forms and developments, we see how
totally radical is the Pauline saying. Subjection to the power of corruptibility is

---

249. On anticipation, cf. my *Metaphysics and the Idea of God.*
250. Wilckens, *Römer,* II, 154, argues that we must see God himself as the one who
subjected creation to the power of corruptibility (8:21). In this regard we may think of
God's decisions at the end of the paradise story (Gen. 3:15ff.), but this is an open question
and seems doubtful, since Paul has in mind something that goes back not simply to God
but to the will of God (not merely on account of Adam), and he sees it from the angle of
the overcoming of corruptibility by the liberty of the children of God (Rom. 8:21, cf. v. 19).

according to God's will as Creator. We may find an expression of this fact today in the thermodynamic principle of increasing entropy that affects all natural processes. All forms of energy are continually and irreversibly transformed into heat, and a feature of all cosmic processes is thus the breaking down of differences between them. This principle is so significant for the processes that some have even made it responsible for the irreversibility of time.[251]

Perhaps, however, we should see it instead as a manifestation of this irreversibility.[252] More important than the relating of the directed course of time to the increase of entropy is its relation to the theological problem of evil in the world along the lines of Rom. 8:20. In the hands of the Creator and his world government, of course, physical evil is a means to bring forth new forms.[253] Hence the sway of the entropy principle in natural processes is ambivalent as regards the effects. If we link it to evil, we cannot regard it as a result of human sin. It is part of the cost of the development of independent creaturely forms within the natural order that regulates the general process of the universe.

Even more important is the positive aspect of the future. The future is the field of the possible.[254] It is thus the basis of the openness of creation

251. Davies, *God and the New Physics*, p. 125: "All physicists recognize that there is a past-future asymmetry in the universe, produced by the second law of thermodynamics."

252. C. F. von Weizsäcker, "Der zweite Hauptsatz und der Unterschied von Vergangenheit und Zukunft" (1939), in *Die Einheit der Natur*, pp. 172-82, traces back the irreversibility of time in its future orientation to differences between past and future in the structure of time, e.g., the facticity of the past and the indeterminacy of the future (pp. 180ff.). In his 1948 work *Geschichte der Natur* (1948, 2nd ed. 1954) he then stressed that the irreversibility of time is a "presupposition" of the second law of thermodynamics, not its basis (p. 41). For a full discussion cf. H. Werth, "Über Irreversibilität, Naturprozesse und Zeitstruktur," in *Offene Systeme*, 2 vols., ed. E. von Weizsäcker (1974-81), I, 114-99, esp. 127f., 186ff. Cf. also K. Pohl, "Geschichte der Natur und geschichtliche Erfahrung," in *Die Welt als offenes System*, ed. G. Altner (1986), pp. 104-23, esp. 106f.; also D. R. Griffin (n. 239 above), 18ff. An illuminating distinction is made by P. Bieri, *Zeit und Zeiterfahrung* (1972), pp. 136ff., between the introduction of the "earlier-later" differentiation into physics, which goes back to a prephysics sense of time, and its "objectifying" by the second law of thermodynamics as a direction that applies to natural processes quite apart from all human observation (p. 155, cf. 148).

253. Cf. R. J. Russell, "Entropy and Evil," *Zygon* 19 (1984) 465: "If evil is real in nature, entropy is what one would expect to find at the level of physical processes." But with a reference to the bifurcation theory of Ilya Prigogine (of which we shall have to speak later), Russell stresses that the rule of the entropy principle in natural processes can also be the condition for an irenic perspective, the bringing of "order out of chaos" (p. 466).

254. Müller, *Präparierte Zeit*, pp. 287f. Picht, *Hier und Jetzt*, p. 383, calls possibility "the indirect presence of the future." Cf. also C. F. von Weizsäcker, *World View of Physics*, pp. 186ff. Cf. also E. Jüngel's plea that we should give preference to possibility (and hence to futurity) in an understanding of reality (*Unterwegs zur Sache* [Munich, 1972], pp. 206ff.; cf. vol. I, 420).

to a higher consummation and the source of what is new, i.e., of contingency in each new event. This fact is basic even in relation to the scope of the law of entropy. Without events and the resultant forms, there could be no entropy. Entropy is parasitic in relation to these events and forms.[255] But in the creaturely power of the future as the field of the possible, the dynamic of the divine Spirit in creation expresses itself.

This last statement might seem to be both theologically and scientifically audacious, let alone unfounded. But on closer scrutiny its face changes. As regards theological presuppositions, the NT finds in the Spirit's presence with Jesus Christ and believers the decisive indication of the coming of the eschatological consummation. This is true already in the tradition relating to Jesus. The powerful presence of the divine Spirit in the person of Jesus shows that he is the eschatological revealer of God through whom God's coming kingdom is already dawning. The same applies to Paul's theology in the thesis that the Spirit who is imparted to believers guarantees them a share in the future consummation (Rom. 8:23; 2 Cor. 1:22; 5:5; cf. Eph. 1:13f.).

The basis of this thesis is that the Spirit is the creative origin of the new life of resurrection (Rom. 8:11). In this way the Jewish view of the Spirit as the origin of all life is seen from the new perspective of the eschatological future. The Spirit's function as the origin of all life is now viewed as preparation for the completion of his work by bringing forth the new eschatological life (1 Cor. 15:45ff.). Does not theology have to take this fact into account by trying to find in the life-giving working of the Spirit at creation a working that is preparatory to the creation of eschatological reality? If this is so, however, we have to regard the dynamic of the Spirit in creation from the very outset in terms of the coming consummation, i.e., as an expression of the power of his future.[256] This is true even where the connection with the final eschatological future is not apparent. In the life of creatures this connection is concealed from both general observation and scientific description.

But can we adopt such a view in a philosophy of nature? Can we relate it meaningfully to a description of natural events that can claim universal validity according to modern insights? Can it serve

255. Russell, "Entropy and Evil," p. 458, sees here an analogy to Augustine's view of evil as privation of good (cf. pp. 455f.).
256. For a first sketch cf. my 1967 essay in *Theologie und Reich Gottes* (1971), pp. 18ff.; see also my debate with E. Bloch in *Basic Questions in Theology* (2 vols.; Philadelphia, 1970-71), II, 234ff.

modern science as an integrating interpretation of a correspondingly basic situation?

Among ongoing efforts to find an appropriate philosophical interpretation of the findings underlying quantum physics,[257] we may refer to some observations of Hans-Peter Dürr on quantum field theory that form a starting point for further deliberations.

Dürr first related quantum indeterminacy to the concept of possibility, and this again (cf. Picht and Müller) to the future aspects of events, so that the future as the realm of the possible stands in contrast to the past as the realm of the factual and the present as the point when possibility becomes factual.[258] This description gives the impression of a movement that comes from the future to the present, runs its course in the present, and is then fixed in the past.

Dürr's later formulations do not tally with this, however, since he argues that the present event lays down a field of possibility for the future that covers all space with a layer of probability for the possible emergence of a "part" (p. 20). Does the dynamic then come from the future, to which Dürr allots greater power than he does to the factual (p. 17), or is the future established by the factual as it takes place in the present? Perhaps it would be better to speak of the power of the realm of the future being given concrete form by the event that takes place in the present. This would seem to accord better with Dürr's express intention of replacing the classical line of inquiry into the determination of the future by the past with an approach that gives priority to the future in terms of its greater power than that of the factual.

If we give priority to the field of possibility of future events along such lines (p. 28), do we not have a starting point for a philosophical interpretation of events?[259] A meaningful connection might then be seen between the statement that extrapolation into the future is not possible (p. 17) and the statement that this world in some sense takes place afresh every moment (p. 21). The interest of physicists may still be in the predictability of the future on the basis of past events, even though this may be merely along the lines of possibilities or statistical probabilities.

257. Cf. the survey in M. Jammer, *The Philosophy of Quantum Mechanics: The Interpretation of Quantum Mechanics in Historical Perspective* (New York, 1974); also R. J. Russell, "Quantum Physics in Philosophical and Theological Perspective," in *Physics, Philosophy, and Theology: A Common Quest for Understanding*, ed. R. J. Russell et al. (Notre Dame, IN, 1988), pp. 343-74.

258. Dürr, "Über die Notwendigkeit," p. 17. Cf. also Barbour, *Issues in Science and Religion*, pp. 273f., 278f., 297f., 304f.

259. Account would have to be taken especially of the distinctively holistic character of the data in quantum physics (cf. Russell, "Quantum Physics," pp. 350ff.), which D. Bohm certainly distinguishes from classical field theories as "implicate order" but which has field qualities in the broader sense (cf. Bohm, "Time," pp. 186ff., on "vacuum state").

Philosophical reflection, however, must still take up the question whether this interest does not imply the reversal of the material connection to which Dürr referred. A material basis would then be required for possibility and for a successful application of the reversal. It is still true, however, that scientific description rests on an inverting of the real nexus of events when it describes the causal nexus that defines the future in terms of the factual. Only in the exceptional case of closed determination (p. 28) do we have a full inversion of the nexus in terms of the future. Even then, the contingency of events at every moment is basic (p. 21). Even the regular order of events in the macrocosmic sphere, which makes the world a reliable one for creatures, still rests on the fact that the possibility field of the future constitutes events in the irreversible flow of time.[260]

If we view the occurrence of microevents at each present moment as a manifestation of the future (deriving from the possibility field of future events), this has considerable implications for the philosophy of nature and for theology. It suggests an interpretation of microevents that does not have to choose between an objectivist and an epistemic or statistical interpretation of the findings of quantum physics. An ontological understanding of natural events from the standpoint of the priority of the future[261] is undoubtedly no longer objectivist in the sense of classical physics. Ontologically the possibility field of future events may be seen as a field of force with a specific temporal structure. It has to be understood as such if events that occur contingently derive from it. These events give it contours relative to each present but with no prejudice to the contingency of the events that follow. A constitution of elementary events along such lines also forms the basis for macroevents that take place according to natural law in the classical sense, and in some cases, as Dürr suspects,[262] thermodynamic fluctuations, for example, may affect macroevents as well. This being so, the force field of future possibility is thus responsible for

260. We evade, however, the ontological problems involved in the holism of phenomena in quantum physics (Russell, "Quantum Physics," p. 359) if we ontologize directly the multiplicity of possibilities in terms of actual multiplicity, as in the quantum "many worlds" of H. Everett or the summation of possibilities of R. Feynman, which S. W. Hawking has also adopted (*A Brief History of Time* [Toronto, 1988], pp. 134ff.).

261. I postulated and sketched an eschatological ontology based on the power of the future in the work referred to in n. 256. Some elements in philosophical justification may be found in *Metaphysics and the Idea of God,* esp. in the sections dealing with the relation between being and time (pp. 69ff.) and anticipation (pp. 91ff.). The approach is worked out theologically in the doctrine of creation, in particular in deliberations on the field character of the working of the Spirit.

262. Dürr, "Über die Notwendigkeit," pp. 29ff.

the fact that the process of nature, which as a whole tends toward the dissolution of creatures through increase of entropy, also offers space for the rise of new structures of increasing differentiation and complexity, as actually took place with the evolution of life.

In this respect the field concept undoubtedly takes a new turn vis-à-vis the field theories of physics. This is true at any rate as regards its prior use in physics. Even though field concepts in physics may speak of a force field as the origin of what is possible in the future, we have here an extension of such usage. We are thinking not only of the priority of the future over the present and the past but also of the basic creative dynamic of the field in relation to the phenomena that take place in it.

Jeffrey S. Wicken objected against this that in physics a force field is constituted by the material elements and movements that occur in it, though conversely it also regulates the elements relating to it. The two together form the totality to which the scientific description refers ("Theology and Science in the Evolving Cosmos," *Zygon* 23 [1988] 45-55, esp. 52). This may well be, although Faraday's intuition went further with its postulate of the priority of the field over bodies (see above, pp. 80f.), thus reversing the relation between forces and bodies and seeing bodies as manifestations of force fields. Insofar as there is a mutual relation between bodies and field along the lines of Wicken, as in a gravitational field, we may understand this as deriving from a creative function of the field.

Once material elements in the field appear, they work on the field, as in Dürr's restructuring of the field of possibility from the perspective of each microevent in it. Whether or not we can describe the priority of the field over every kind of material manifestation is a matter that we may leave to advances in physics. By nature the creative working of the divine Spirit cannot be regarded as conditioned by the resultant creaturely phenomena. But for the sake of the creatures this working can adjust itself to the conditions of their existence and activity and thus give them room to affect the field structure of the Spirit's working.

These considerations help to show that the theologically based idea of a dynamic of the divine Spirit working creatively in all events as the power of the future is by no means alien to a philosophy of nature. It stands in a demonstrable relation to the basic data of science. Indeed, it can set scientific descriptions in a new light by putting them on a different plane of argumentation. Confusion with scientifically possible statements is excluded, but there may well be convergence in philosophical reflection on them.

The power of the future that manifests itself in the dynamic of the divine Spirit is not merely to be understood as the origin of the contingency of individual events. It must be seen also as the origin of lasting forms and of the unvarying regularity and reliability in the process of natural occurrence, without which there can be no lasting forms. The future at issue in the dynamic of the divine Spirit is the entry into time of the eternity of God. The unity of life that we see only partially in the sequence of moments in time, and that can find actualization as a whole only in eternal simultaneity, can be attained in the process of time only from the future, which brings it to totality.[263] More precisely, it can be attained only as the integration of moments and events that are always contingent, and therefore apart and separate, in time. The emergence of contingent individual events from the possibility field of the future constitutes, then, only the elementary aspect in the creative dynamic of the Spirit, the beginning of its development. It culminates in the integration of events and moments into a unity of form. Within worldly time it appears as a time-bridging present in the duration of forms. In this duration of creaturely forms, which also brings them together in space, we have a kind of inkling of eternity. The goal of the Spirit's dynamic is to give creaturely forms duration by a share in eternity and to protect them against the tendency to disintegrate that follows from their independence.

We are thus to think of the dynamic of the divine Spirit as a working field linked to time and space — to time by the power of the future that gives creatures their own present and duration, and to space by the simultaneity of creatures in their duration. From the standpoint of the creature, origin from the future of the Spirit has the appearance of the past. But the working of the Spirit constantly encounters the creature as its future, which embraces its origin and its possible fulfillment.

d. Creative Working of the Spirit and Doctrine of Angels

Describing the divine Spirit as a field that in its creative working manifests itself in time and space sheds a new light on the older doctrine of angels. In analogy to the ideas of antiquity, the early fathers found in biblical angels spiritual entities and powers that work in both nature and history either at the command of God or in demonic autonomy against God. Primarily we have here cosmic forces — former deities like the seven

---

263. Cf. vol. I, 403ff., on the link between eternity and time in Plotinus and the modification needed in Christian thought (esp. pp. 408f.).

planetary gods — that in the biblical tradition became creatures of the one God, which we still find in Revelation as seven spirits, lights, torches, stars, or angels (Rev. 1:4, 12ff.; 4:5). We might also mention the angels of the four winds in Rev. 7:1 (cf. Ps. 104:4, quoted in Heb. 1:7). The number four with its reference to the four quarters of heaven is an indication of their cosmic nature. The four or seven archangels of Judaism[264] could well have a similar background, partially in astral ideas going back to Babylonian astrology and linked to the notions of guardian angels for individuals and nations, partly in concepts of natural forces or elements, in connection with which we find angels of fire, water, and air.[265]

Karl Barth's doctrine of angels in CD, III/3 § 51 is the most important discussion of the theme in modern theology, but in the very full exposition of the biblical statements about the function of angels it does not go into this aspect. Unlike the tradition, especially Aquinas in ST 1.50-64 and 106-14 (cf. CD, III/3, 393ff.), Barth refused to examine the nature of angels. He regarded any study leading to a philosophy of angels as an aberration (pp. 410ff.) and not sufficiently oriented to what scripture says about them. Scripture itself, he said, tells us nothing about the nature of angels (p. 410), focusing instead on their function and ministry (pp. 459ff.), which Barth thought he could define comprehensively as the ministry of witnesses to God and his kingdom (pp. 461, 497ff.). Barth did not fail to speak about the activity ascribed to angels in the Bible (pp. 499ff.), but he subordinated this to the concept of witness because God does not depend on angels for what he does (pp. 485, 493f.). It is understandable, then, that in Barth the cosmic functions of angels are in the background and receive only incidental mention (pp. 462f., 497).

In the biblical writings, however, what is said about the actions of angels is basic even to their ministry of witness, and their actions in salvation history seem to rest again on their cosmic functions. Nor is it true that scripture tells us nothing at all about their nature. The NT expressly calls them spirits (pneumata) in Heb. 1:14; 12:9; Rev. 1:4, etc. Barth himself had to recognize that the phrase "ministering spirits" in Heb. 1:14 (leitourgika pneumata) "is virtually a definition of the nature of angels" (p. 452). We have to agree with Barth that the emphasis is on service. Yet we should not on that account overlook or suppress the fact that they are defined as spirits. If we could not define their nature at all, then all that is said about their existence and functions would be indeterminate. It is perhaps for this reason that Barth's intensive preoccupation with the theme has not produced any renewal of the concept of angels in theology.

---

264. For example cf. K. E. Grözinger, in TRE, IX (1982), p. 588. On the cosmological functions of angels cf. p. 587.

265. O. Böcher calls them "personified forces of nature" (TRE, IX [1982], p. 597).

The description of angels as spirits raises the question of their relation to the absolute Spirit, the Spirit of God.[266] This question then merges into the wider one of the relation of angels to God's working in general. Insofar as they are distinct from God, angels are creatures. This is self-evident in Jewish thinking, and it is everywhere presupposed in the NT. The NT alludes to it at least once in Col. 1:16, and it is stated more clearly in the postapostolic period, e.g., in 1 Clem. 59:3 (cf. Heb. 12:9). Their status as creatures, however, is a unique one in the biblical statements, since God himself is directly present in them as his instruments and messengers, so that in some cases it is not clear whether God himself is acting or one who is different from him (Gen. 18:2ff.; 21:17ff.; 31:11ff.; Exod. 3:2ff.; Judg. 13:21f.).[267]

On this basis Barth advanced his thesis that angels, unlike earthly creatures, have no independent being (*CD*, III/3, 480): "They do not exist and act independently or autonomously." But if not, how can they be creatures, as Barth himself calls them (pp. 420, 513)? In spite of denying their independence so sharply, Barth perceived here something that was hardly grasped in the older doctrine, or at least in the *Celestial Hierarchy* of Pseudo-Dionysius the Areopagite, a work for which Barth had more sympathy, notwithstanding his opposition to the idea of any angelic hierarchy (pp. 385ff.), than he found in Aquinas. Barth viewed the angels as "distinct creatures," yet not so clearly separate from one another as earthly individuals (pp. 450ff.). They form the host of heaven (pp. 448ff.). "Individual figures . . . exist only as they are specifically summoned and separated from the rest with a specific commission and in a specific relationship to the earthly history of salvation, disappearing again into the general body as soon as their work is accomplished" (p. 455). This is how Barth takes the famous view of Dionysius that the world of angel is a "dynamically motivated system" (p. 387) and translates it into the language of salvation history (pp. 448ff.). Instead of the angelic hierarchy, in which the light that emanates from God is passed down from above to below, Barth has the kingdom of heaven (pp. 418ff.), which as "a movement which has its origin in God and its target and goal in the creature" (p. 429) forms a multiple unity (p. 447).

Individual angels, then, seem to be more or less ephemeral manifestations of this unitary movement. Materially, then, is not the kingdom of heaven in its

---

266. Barth found hints of an answer especially in Revelation (*CD*, III/3, 465, cf. 502). But there also indications that the development of the Holy Spirit as *the* Pneuma helped to crowd out the idea of angels in primitive Christianity (Böcher, *TRE*, IX [1982], 598).

267. Cf. the discussion in Barth, *CD*, III/3, 488ff.

coming a dynamic field that finds specific manifestation in the angels? No matter how special centers may form within the unity of the field as parts of the whole, we would in this case be viewing each manifestation of God's lordship over the cosmos and history in the form of an angel. But with the emergence of specific gravitational fields within the total field of the divine lordship, there would need to be linked some creaturely independence, without which we could hardly distinguish the angels as creatures. What this independence is, we shall have to work out in what follows.

If we understand the description of angels as spirits in analogy to what we have said about the Spirit as field, what is meant is not in the first instance a personal figure but a force. Thus the NT relates angels to such terms as "principalities" and "powers" (1 Pet. 3:22; cf. 1 Cor. 15:24; Eph. 1:21; also Rom. 8:28). All these powers are set under the dominion of the exalted Christ. This does not seem to be self-evident. The forces that are in the service of God's lordship over creation may obviously become autonomous centers of power whose attraction believers may well find to be threatening (Rom. 8:38f.).[268]

To the astonishment of many observers, such experiences have produced in 20th-century theology a revival of the doctrine of angels and demons. Paul Tillich linked them to the archetypes of depth psychology and to a new awareness of the suprahuman power of the demonic in literature.[269] Gerhard Ebeling related them to the experience that forces are at work in our relation to God and the world that are hidden from us but nonetheless active.[270] Paul Althaus said that the reality

---

268. Barth does not take into account the ambivalence of principalities and powers for the concept of angels, in spite of the obvious biblical evidence not merely directly in 1 Pet. 3:22 but also indirectly in the reference to the disobedience of angels in Gen. 6:1-4, which led to the idea of a fall of angels in Jewish apocalyptic, echoed also perhaps in 1 Pet. 3:19 (cf. L. Goppelt, *Der Erste Petrusbrief* [1978], pp. 247ff., with examples, though Goppelt himself refers the passage to souls of the dead [p. 250]). The disobedience of angels is also presupposed in NT allusions to their fall (cf. Böcher, *TRE,* IX [1982], 596; on the underlying Jewish views cf. Grözinger and Böcher in *TRE,* VIII [1981], pp. 279-86, esp. 279ff.). Barth may well be right when he says that "a true and orderly angel does not do this" (*CD,* III/3, 481, cf. 530). According to the biblical witness, however, which Barth was trying to follow more strictly than the classical doctrine of angels in the theological tradition, not all angels seem to have been "orderly," though not on that account at once forfeiting all reality. The Jewish and Christian doctrine of the disobedience of some angels was a way of avoiding dualism in explaining the presence of the demonic in the world — a dualism that seems to be lurking again in Barth's teaching on nothingness and demons. Even demonic powers are God's creatures, in this case creatures that have proved to be disobedient.

269. *Systematic Theology,* I (New York, 1967).

270. *Dogmatik des christlichen Glaubens,* p. 333.

of angels was a matter not merely of faith but also of experience.[271] Hans-Georg
Fritzsche used the term "field of force" in this connection, though without clari-
fying the link to scientific usage. We stand, he said, in a field of force that embraces
the ego, which is where angels and demons belong.[272]

The greatest difficulty besetting the traditional doctrine of angels
lies in the idea that angels are personal spirits or subjects that serve God
or, in the case of demons, that have turned against him. Nevertheless, if
we remember that the use of personal predicates originates in the experience of being under the influence of not-wholly-explicable forces — an
influence that works in a certain direction and thus shows itself to involve
will[273] — then the idea should not present us with insoluble problems. It
is at any rate secondary to the experience.

D. F. Strauss argued that the activity of angels in the world is in
contradiction with modern science. Science does not view natural phenomena like thunder and lightning, earthquakes, pestilence, etc. as special
acts of God but traces them to natural causes.[274] This objection, however,
is against the special activity of God in natural events no less than that of
angels. It presupposes that the nexus of nature is a closed system, as in a
mechanistic view of the universe. It assumes that theological statements
about the activity of God or angels in cosmic events, or at least in specific
events in nature, are simply explanations of natural processes that compete
with scientific descriptions and the factors that these assert.

If we allow, however, that scientific descriptions are not an exhaus-
tive explanation of events and that the causal relation of events does not
rule out but presupposes the contingency of individual events, and if we
view the nexus of nature itself as a system that is open to contingency and
not closed, then there need be no rivalry between scientific and theological
statements. Both may well relate to the same events. Fundamentally the
angels of the biblical traditions are natural forces that from another angle
might be the object of scientific descriptions. If we define forces like wind
or fire or stars as angels of God, then we are relating them to God their
Creator and to the human experience of being affected by them as servants
of God or as demonic powers that oppose his will. Why should not natural

271. *Christliche Wahrheit*, p. 317.
272. *Lehrbuch der Dogmatik*, II (1967; 2nd ed., Göttingen, 1982), § 12.9 (p. 352).
273. Cf. vol. I, 381f.
274. Cf. *Die christliche Glaubenslehre in ihrer geschichtlichen Entwicklung und im
Kampfe mit der modernen Wissenschaft dargestellt*, I (1840), p. 671.

forces in the forms in which we now know them be viewed as God's servants and messengers, i.e., as angels?

The biblical testimonies relate angels to the heaven in which God dwells and from which he is present and at work in his earthly creation (vol. I, 410ff.). Angels form the divinely created host of heaven (Ps. 33:6; cf. Gen. 2:1; Isa. 45:12; Jer. 33:22; Neh. 9:6, etc.). But heaven is the sphere of creation that is not under human control. Unlike earth, "it exists as invisible creaturely reality. It is invisible and therefore incomprehensible and inaccessible, outside the limits of human capacity."[275] But is not the world of natural forces accessible to modern science? The cosmic forces that science investigates, however, are not simply those of earth. Perhaps the biblical statements themselves do not view heaven as wholly incomprehensible. God's ways and thoughts are higher than ours (Isa. 55:8f.), but they are still manifest to us. It is precisely in view of revelation (Rom. 11:25ff.) that Paul extols the unsearchability of God's ways (v. 35). The order of times that may be read off from the course of the stars (Gen. 1:14) may be known by us, even though it is an order of heaven. All the same, though this order is accessible to human knowledge, it is of a height and depth surpassing this knowledge. The best scientists of our own time admit this regarding the relation of science to nature. Nature constantly presents us with new riddles and mysteries as our knowledge of it increases.

J. Moltmann has related specifically to the future of the world the fundamental indeterminacy of creation on this side.[276] This is in keeping with Jesus' distinctive message of the kingdom of heaven as an imminent future reality that still has an impact on the present. The relation of earth to heaven is the side of creation that is open to God, and heaven is the sphere of God's creative possibilities. Along these lines Moltmann takes up the view of the universe advanced in discussions of the thermodynamic structure of natural occurrence, i.e., as a system open to the future.[277] His

275. Barth, CD, III/3, 424, like the Nicene Creed, following Col. 1:16, which sees the difference between heaven and earth as that between the invisible and the visible. Cf. also M. Welker, *Universalität Gottes und Relativität der Welt* (Neukirchen-Vluyn, 1981), pp. 203ff.

276. *God in Creation*, p. 159.

277. Ibid., p. 163. Cf. the reference to the two volumes *Offene Systeme*, ed. E. von Weizsäcker (1974-81), on pp. 63f. On the thermodynamic concept of open as opposed to closed systems cf. the contribution of H. Wehrt in these volumes ("Über Irreversibilität, Naturprozesse und Zeitstruktur," pp. 135ff.). We find different terms in American discussions; cf. J. F. Wicken, *Evolution, Thermodynamics, and Information: Extending the Darwinian Program* (New York, 1987). Wicken sees three instead of two forms of systems, namely, isolated,

basis is a theological interpretation of the open future of thermodynamics, namely, as the sphere of the creative powers and possibilities of God, which Moltmann regards as an understanding of heaven that is in keeping with present-day knowledge.[278]

This interpretation assumes that the field forces and their activities that direct the course of nature have a temporal structure that is oriented to the future. On the level of microevents this may well be so if what we have said above is correct (see pp. 98ff.). But on this level there may be a reversal of the direction of time as present events restrict the field of possibility. This partial determination of the future by the past and the present, which in classical mechanics and electromagnetics is close to complete determinism, need not be judged negatively from a theological standpoint, even as a temporal inversion of the structure of events vis-à-vis its basis in micro-occurrence. For it is a condition of the continuity of natural events and is thus an expression of the faithfulness of the Creator in his will to bring forth independent creaturely forms. This inversion of the temporal structure and the mode of working of natural forces may thus be regarded as a sign of their creaturely independence in relation to the creative dynamic of the divine Spirit from which they have emerged.

The temporal inversion in the structure of natural forces and their operation causes them to become ungodly and demonic forces only when they close themselves against the future of God, the kingdom of his possibilities, and thus become closed systems. It could well be that world occurrence is at least partially under the influence of such power centers. According to the NT witness the world as a whole has come indeed under the tyranny of an ungodly force, the prince of this world (John 12:31; 14:30; 16:11; cf. Eph. 2:2). The connection between sin and death, which has subjected the whole world to corruption (Rom. 8:20, 22), gives us cause to reckon with the dominion of a destructive power of this nature. If the principle of the increase of entropy in the cosmic process gives

---

open, and closed (p. 34). The isolated are Wehrt's closed, and the closed are those that exchange energy but not matter with their environment. In cosmology we find yet another distinction between open and closed systems, namely, in regard to the question whether the expansion of the universe is infinite, so that either matter loses itself in space or goes on its way without restriction in a "flat" universe, or whether the expansion of the universe will be reversed and end in a Big Crash corresponding to the initial Big Bang because weight will finally overcome the forces of expansion. The latter model is called a closed system, even though time is still irreversible; cf. Tipler, "Omega Point as *Eschaton*," pp. 217-53.

278. Moltmann, *God in Creation*, p. 182.

evidence of this power or its operation (see n. 253), we also see that even this destructive force is still to be understood as a servant of God (Job 1:6) and his will as Creator, though it encounters us as the adversary of God. At any rate, no destructive power is the only determinative ground of the creaturely reality in which it holds sway. Through all other powers and fields of force may be seen also the working of the divine Spirit as the origin of life in the creatures.

In the working of the Spirit, as in that of the divine Logos, the future of the consummation in the kingdom of God predominates. Theological talk about the dynamic of the Spirit of God in creation differs in this regard from the field theories of physics that work in terms of natural laws. The resultant problem arises also, however, in discussions of scientific theory. Here it takes the form of the question how a field theory relates to the evolution of life and whether it calls for a fresh formulation of physical cosmology. We find approaches to such issues in attempts to arrive at a thermodynamic description of conditions for the rise and evolution of life.

e. Cooperation of Son and Spirit in the Work of Creation

At the beginning of this section we spoke of the mediation of the Son in creation. We ascribed to his working the distinctiveness of each creaturely form as opposed to others and to God the Creator. As the quintessence of such distinctions and relations, the Son is the Logos of creation, the origin and epitome of its order. The concrete order of the cosmic process is thus seen to be related to the incarnation of the Logos, which has its goal in the independence of the creature as the place of its distinction from God and from fellow creatures. We then discussed the function of the Spirit in the work of creation, showing that his field operations are temporally structured, so that each new event proceeds from the future of God, from which all creaturely forms take their origin and seek their fulfillment. As Irenaeus said, the Son and Spirit are the two hands of God by which he created all things.[279] Our only remaining question is how the two cooperate in the work of creation.

For this question we have hardly any direct biblical references,

---

279. *Adv. haer.* 4.20.1. As regards the Spirit, Irenaeus was thinking of wisdom, which he did not then relate to the Logos (cf. 4.20.3, also vol. I, 270f., and n. 40 for other references to the Son and Spirit as God's hands).

though Ps. 33:6 describes both Word and Spirit as organs of God's creative activity. Gen. 1:2f. is our most important passage, for here God's creative speaking is in the power of his Spirit or by his powerful breath (see above, pp. 77ff.). In agreement is the fact that elsewhere the Son is the recipient and bearer of the Spirit (vol. I, 315ff.). Gen. 1:2f. justifies the assumption that the same applies in the work of creation. The Son's mediatorial role in creation takes place in such a way that it is in the power of the Spirit that he is the origin of the different creatures in their specific distinctiveness. Do we find in the philosophy of nature any plausibility for this thought when we view the creative working of the Spirit as the field of force of the divine future from which events proceed contingently?

As a field of force, the creative working of the Spirit of God is linked to time and space in its sphere of operations. Discussion of time and space should give us some idea of the interrelation of divine and creaturely reality, as creaturely existence proceeds from God's creative futurity with its own duration, which like all else subsists in the relations of space. In this regard, however, the idea of a vital creative dynamic is not sufficient to make intelligible to us the uniqueness of creaturely existence (proceeding, as it does, from divinity) in its distinction from all else and its relation to it. For this we need a principle of distinction such as we find in the self-distinction of the Son from the Father, i.e., of the divine Logos. Whereas the creative dynamic in the events of creation relates to the Spirit, the Logos is the origin of the distinguishing form of the creature in the totality of its existence and in the ensemble of distinctions and relations of creatures in the order of nature.

But we cannot separate the creative dynamic and the specific form of its expression. The two go together in the act of creation. In the first creation story this fact comes to expression in the idea of the creative speaking of God by which the dynamic of his Spirit becomes the origin of the specific creaturely reality. In the field concepts of science the same fact finds expression in the working of the field dynamic by natural laws. In this respect the general rules in scientific description can be only approximations to an explanation of the concrete event in its uniqueness. The creative dynamic of the Spirit also has an element of indeterminacy. In it the distinctive form that comes forth from it is concealed before it takes concrete shape in the creature. Nevertheless, it is from the Spirit's dynamic, according to the relations of the Logos, that the distinct, independent, and self-centered form of creaturely operation arises. The event of information constitutes the transition.

The concept of information goes back to the rhetoric of antiquity[280] on the one side and to the Christian Aristotelianism of Scholasticism on the other. Here are the roots of its ontological and scientific use.[281] In Christian Aristotelianism the concept denotes the formation of existing matter, and Aquinas sharply distinguishes this from the act of creation, in which the Creator brought forth the whole substance of a thing, matter as well as form.[282]

In modern use of the term there has been a change from Aristotelian usage because the modern concept of energy goes along with the term, differing profoundly from Aristotle's *energeia*. Energy is no longer the intrinsically self-resting fulfillment of being (Aristotle *Met.* 1048a.31). It is a dynamic that generates change. Increasingly it has thus become the counterpart of matter. When Hermann von Helmholtz in 1847 defined energy as a measure of the ability to do work by overcoming resistance,[283] a dualism of energy and matter was presupposed. It needed Einstein's relativity theory to overcome this dualism, by viewing mass (matter) as a manifestation of energy.[284]

C. F. von Weizsäcker related this concept of energy to information. Information now came to denote the unusual or improbable nature of an event that is being caused, or has been caused, by energy.[285] The amount of energy has to be greater, the higher the information content of the event, i.e., its singularity or, in temporal terms, its novelty. The concept of probability links that of energy to

280. Cf. H. Schnelle, "Information," *HWP*, IV (1976), 356f. For early examples cf. Cicero *De orat.* 2.358 etc. and 1 Tim. 1:16 Vulgate, where the term simply has the sense of verbal communication and instruction.

281. A complex prehistory goes back to Neoplatonism (esp. Proclos). In his commentary on metaphysics Albertus Magnus differentiated the transcendental identity of *ens* and *unum* from the idea of one distinct being over against others. In the case of the latter the defining of its unity is an *informatio* that leads to the concept of being (Opera omnia XVI/2 [1964], 397, pp. 1f.). For the differentiation he referred to the *Liber de Causis* (cf. § 17 in the Bardenhewer ed., 180.5). On the underlying idea of *formatio*, which we also find in the Christian fathers, cf. Beierwaltes, *Denken des Einen*, p. 359, n. 65, and on Plotinus, pp. 52ff.

282. *ST* 1.45.2c and ad 2.

283. *Über die Erhaltung der Kraft* (1847; Leipzig, 1889). On this point see M. Jammer, "Energie," *HWP*, II (1972), 496f.

284. On this development cf. M. Jammer, *Der Begriff der Masse in der Physik* (1961, 1964), pp. 185-205, esp. 190f., 202ff., cf. also 240f.

285. C. F. von Weizsäcker, "Materie, Energie, Information," in *Die Einheit der Natur*, pp. 342-66, esp. 347f. This discussion is especially notable because it links the philosophical background of the concept of form to the modern scientific theory of information. Wicken, *Evolution, Thermodynamics, and Information*, convincingly defends the presupposed distinction (or antithesis) between information and entropy against the fusion of the two by C. E. Shannon (cf. 26ff.). We must regard as exaggerated C. F. von Weizsäcker's correction of his earlier statements in the later "Evolution und Entropiewachstum," in *Offene Systeme*, 2 vols., ed. E. von Weizsäcker (1974-81), I, 200-221, esp. 203ff. Weizsäcker's definition corresponds to the functional definition of information by Wicken (*Evolution, Thermodynamics, and Information*, pp. 40ff., 48).

contingency problems in thermodynamics and quantum theory, but also to openness to the future. The related concept of information fits into our presentation of the field operations of the divine Spirit as the origin of events that derive contingently from the future of God.[286] Aquinas and Albertus Magnus distinguished between creation and information because information presupposed matter, but this reason no longer holds good, since matter itself is a way in which energy manifests itself.

The defining of information in terms of probability theory enables modern theology to view information as a measure of the creaturely new that through the Spirit proceeds with each new event from the creative power of God. As a measure of the creative workings of the divine Spirit, the concept of information is subject to the Logos. The differing information content of events constitutes their uniqueness by which they are an expression of the creative activity of the Logos.

From the standpoint of creatures the continued event of creation proceeding from the power of the future of God suffers a temporal inversion whereby it seems to be a process moving from the past to the future. From this angle it is marked by tension between increasing entropy on the one side and ever higher structuring on the other. In its independence all creaturely reality is subject to the fate of destructuring, of dissolution according to the law of entropy. Because of the openness of process structures to future events,[287] however, new structures are constantly formed, since processes take place in open rather than closed systems.[288]

Although the beginnings of this building of structure may be rare and small, they can decisively determine the further course of natural events. As an example we might cite the 1:1,000,000,000 preponderance in the production of electrons,

---

286. At the end of his "Materie, Energie, Information," C. F. von Weizsäcker calls God the nonobjectifiable basis of form (p. 366) but not the quintessence of forms. From the standpoint of patristic Logos theology, this distinction would seem to be problematic, for God is not without the Logos, and the Logos is the quintessence as well as the basis of creaturely *logoi* (see above, pp. 25f.). We have here an application of the unity of transcendence and immanence in the infinity of the divine essence.

287. Wehrt, "Über Irreversibilität, Naturprozesse und Zeitstruktur," p. 174.

288. Ibid., p. 140. Cf. also E. Lüscher, in *Die Zeit,* ed. A. Preisl and A. Mohler (1983), p. 367. In self-organization as a struggle to use the thermodynamic flow of energy, Wicken finds a "response" to the situation and a means to reduce the turnover of energy (*Evolution, Thermodynamics, and Information,* p. 68). According to Wicken, "Whereas the universe is steadily running downhill in the sense of reducing thermodynamic potential, it is also running uphill in the sense of building structure. The two are coupled through the Second Law" (p. 72).

protons, and neutrons over their antibodies in the early days of the universe, when, in the extreme heat, collisions of photons constantly broke them up into parts and antiparts that destroyed each other and gave rise to new photons. The slight preponderance of electrons, protons, and neutrons led with increasing cooling to the formation of matter uniting atoms and molecules.[289]

Similarly in the history of the earth the development of organized life and the continued higher structuring of its forms may be seen as a chain of events that were at first exceptions but that gradually changed the face of the earth. Vegetation covered it with green, molluscs and crustaceans abounded over it, reptiles became dominant, mammals followed, and then humans. Theologians find in this story of the continued higher structuring of forms an analogy to God's history of election. In both cases the improbable exception becomes the intimation of a new norm, a new creation: "God chose what is weak in the world to shame the strong" (1 Cor. 1:27). Is not this true in the history of creation and not just in human salvation history?

The chain of higher structuring in the process of building forms, from atoms and stars to humans, and especially in the development of life, has often given the impression from the very early days of modern thermodynamics that we have here a kind of countertrend to the increase of entropy in natural processes. Whereas the movement is downward in the destructuring and dissolution of forms through increasing entropy, the evolution of life seems to represent an upward movement toward increasingly higher and more complex forms of organization.[290] Nevertheless, we do not have here something to which the principle of increasing entropy does not apply. An increase of entropy in the total structure balances the rise of new partial structures.[291] Hence we are to see the process of higher structuring itself within the general increase of entropy. Higher structuring in the sense of increasing complexity is an open possibility within this framework.[292] That it should actually

289. S. Weinberg, *The First Three Minutes* (New York, 1977), pp. 89ff., cf. 97f.

290. Cf. H. Bergson, *L'évolution créatrice* (1907; Paris, 1948), pp. 243ff., esp. 246f.; cf. 368f. We find the same thought in Teilhard de Chardin. Although he noted that structuring is at the cost of increased entropy in nature as a whole (*The Phenomenon of Man* [New York, 1959]), he found in the upward development of life "escape from entropy by turning back to Omega" (p. 272).

291. Wehrt, "Über Irreversibilität, Naturprozesse und Zeitstruktur," pp. 158ff. Cf. also A. Peacocke, *God and the New Biology* (San Francisco, 1986), p. 140, and the quotation from Wicken in n. 288.

292. In addition to Wicken, *Evolution, Thermodynamics, and Information,* cf. esp. C. F. von Weizsäcker, "Evolution und Entropiewachstum," pp. 203ff. For a more precise description see the works of I. Prigogine on thermodynamics, which were epoch making with their suggestion that conditions of more complex local order arose out of oscillations in equal systems that can lead by way of bifurcation to new dissipative structures of higher stability; cf. *From Being to Becoming: Time and Complexity in the Physical Sciences* (San Francisco, 1980), esp. pp. 77-154.

take place, however, was by no means certain, for thermodynamics has to do only with possibilities and probabilities.[293] The history of the universe within its laws is always, then, a system of indeterminacy in which chance rules.[294] Nevertheless, we find in it an interplay of chance and regularity that lends to the rise and development of life on earth an ineluctability[295] in which Christians recognize the work of the divine Logos.[296]

Theologically one may see in the rise of each particular form a direct expression in creaturely reality of the working of the Logos, of the divine Word of Creation. This development finds its completed form only in the self-distinction by which the individual creature affirms its uniqueness vis-à-vis all others. Only thus can it also affirm God to be the origin of everything finite in his distinction from all that is creaturely, thus paying him the honor of his deity. For this reason the Logos does not find full manifestation in the isolated uniqueness of an individual phenomenon but in its relations to everything else, i.e., in the total order, which as such extols its Creator.

Through the Logos, then, everything acquires its appropriate form and place in the order of creation. In this regard the Spirit mediates the working of the Logos in creation as also in the incarnation. The incarnation is simply the theologically highest instance of creation, the perfect realization of the Logos in the singularity of an individual creaturely form that is not just factually different from all others but that gives validity to all others alongside itself, yet that especially validates itself before God and all creation, assuming the limiting of its own finitude by other creatures. The fact that God is thus honored in his creation as a whole is indissolubly linked to the incarnation of the Logos in a specific creature. In this light we can also understand why it is only in the event of the incarnation that the working of the Logos throughout creation comes to fulfillment.

The working of the Logos in creation has, then, a temporal structure in the sense of an increasing inwardness of the Logos in creation. The history of creation might be described as the way in which the relation to

---

293. Peacocke, *God and the New Biology,* pp. 158f.

294. Cf. W. Stegmüller in the chapter "Die Evolution des Kosmos" in his *Hauptströmungen,* pp. 495-617, esp. 583ff.

295. Ibid., p. 694. Cf. Peacocke, *Creation and the World of Science,* pp. 103f., also 69ff.

296. Peacocke, *Creation and the World of Science,* pp. 105, cf. 205ff.

God the Father, which is proper to the creature as a representation of the Logos, comes to fulfillment. In their own uniqueness not all creatures achieve the full structure of the relation of the Son to the Father. This is the special destiny of humans in creation, and this destiny found fulfillment in the one man Jesus of Nazareth. Others can share in this fulfillment only by fellowship with Jesus. But because the destiny of creation for fellowship with God takes definitive shape in humans, the order of creation in time might be seen as a form of the way to make humanity possible.

This is the element of truth in the assertion of an "anthropic principle" in the history of the universe (see nn. 177ff.). The thesis cannot claim much value as a physical explanation, but it shows very impressively that de facto the universe is so oriented as to provide conditions for the emergence of intelligent beings. Theological interpretation may go further and say that we see here the economy of the divine work of creation relative to the incarnation of the divine Logos in a man.

The way of creation to humans, seen from the creaturely angle as a temporal inversion of the divine act of creation, takes the concrete shape of a succession of forms. Each of these is called into existence as an independent creature. None is simply a means to human existence. Not every line in the sequence leads to humanity, but as a whole they all form a basis for its emergence. The multiplicity of forms expresses the inexhaustible wealth of God's creative power. As a representation of this wealth, the world of creation lauds the Creator by its mere existence. If they do not join in creation's praise of God, humans fail to be what they ought to be according to their destiny, namely, settings and mediators for creation's fellowship with God.

§ 3. Sequence of Forms

Creatures are related to one another inasmuch as they are referred to one another. On the one hand each individual creature has others before it and with it; on the other hand it has the justification of its own existence in service to the others that live before it. From the outset, of course, the coexistence of natural events and forms in the history of the universe has

involved conflict, and their succession has meant destruction and reconstruction. Basic to the formation of all more organized forms, however,
is the repetition of elementary forms and their entry into lasting combi-
nations. Only on the basis of the duration of elementary forms and the
incalculable number of their products is it possible to move above vacil-
lations in fixed states, by way of stabilization on a new level, to a sequence
of forms of which the more complex (or higher) rise above the more
simple (or lower). Through all this, in spite of conflicts, creatures are still
referred, and thus related, to one another. Humans themselves are to live
not only *off* lower creatures but also *for* them as the basis of their own
superior life. They are to carry out God's creative will in the world that
he has made. Thus the second creation story puts Adam in the garden "to
till it and keep it" (Gen. 2:15). Humans have never done full justice to this
task. According to the NT only the Spirit of Christ can enable them to
fulfill this destiny of theirs.

The first creation story depicts the creation of the world already
as a sequence of forms. As the days of creation follow one another, we
first have light and darkness, then water and the firmament, then the earth,
vegetation, and stars, then fishes and birds, finally land animals, and last
of all humans. Modern science might change the order to some extent.[297]
It is astonishing, however, how much agreement there is as to the fact of
a sequence. The story carries the features of a view of nature that was
widespread in the Near East in the first millennium B.C., and one might
have thought that the presuppositions would be much further apart from
modern science than is actually the case.

A particularly striking example of a time-bound insight that we
have now abandoned may be found in the idea of a separation of the
waters of the primal flood by a firmament (Gen. 1:6f.).[298] This firmament
explains mechanically why the waters beneath it, which cover the earth,
retreat and gather together and thus let dry ground emerge, for no masses
of water can now pour down upon them through the heavenly "bell" or
vault (1:6, 9f.). The story of the flood tells us what happens when leaks
in the vault occur and are not stopped (7:11).

The cosmology that finds expression in the idea of the firmament
bears impressive testimony to the science of antiquity, which rationally
relates the order of the universe to human engineering. For this reason it

297. For a short survey cf. I. Asimov, *In the Beginning.*
298. Von Rad, *Genesis*, p. 53.

is a misunderstanding to try to base theology on the literal sense. A theological doctrine of creation should follow where the biblical witness leads by claiming current knowledge of the world for a description of the divine work of creation, using the resources that are actually at hand. Theology will not do justice to the authority of the biblical witness if it tries to preserve the time-bound ideas with which the biblical account of creation works instead of repeating in its own day the act of theologically appropriating contemporary knowledge.[299]

Putting the creation of the stars on the fourth day is another example of a time-bound statement (Gen. 1:14ff.). Here it is not so much a matter of outdated cosmology as it is one of outdated controversy. In opposition to the Babylonian creation epic, which relates the creation of the stars to the formation of the firmament, the creation story puts first the dividing of land and sea (1:10) and the creation of plants (1:11ff.). One might see here a result of the exactitude with which the mechanical function of the firmament is described. The erection of the vault of heaven means that the waters under it gather, and therefore in other places dry land appears (1:9)[300] and vegetation can sprout upon it (1:11f.).[301] The surprising later placing of the stars[302] is meant to depreciate them in comparison with the divine rank that the stars had in the religious world around Israel, especially Babylon. In the Bible the stars simply have the lower function of lamps or signs for the seasons.[303] The controversy here as to the divinity or creatureliness of the stars is no longer relevant in modern thought. But the interest of the story in an inner nexus in the sequence of the individual acts of creation finds natural expression in a

299. Cf. Schlink, *Ökumenische Dogmatik*, pp. 75f.

300. Apart from the ref. in Gen. 1:1, we read only of a separation of water and land rather than a creation of the earth, the two preceding acts being related to this separation; cf. Schmidt, *Schöpfungsgeschichte*, pp. 25f., also Westermann, *Genesis 1–11*, pp. 166, 168, and on creation as separation (pp. 46ff.). Westermann (p. 166) argues that the separations of the first three days form time (light from darkness) and space (above from below, and here from there).

301. Schmidt, *Schöpfungsgeschichte*, p. 108, n. 4. The material reason for the placing of plants before the stars in Gen. 1 is that they belong closely to the earth. See the similar sequence in Ps. 104, which Schmidt cites as an example of the traditional background of Gen. 1 (p. 44).

302. H. Gunkel, *Genesis* (3rd ed.; Göttingen, 1910), p. 127, notes that the stars are created much earlier in the Babylonian story than in the Hebrew (cf. pp. 108f.).

303. Ibid., p. 109. G. von Rad especially stresses the polemical point of Gen. 1:14-19 (*Genesis*, p. 558). Cf. also Schmidt, *Schöpfungsgeschichte*, pp. 119f. Westermann has rightly noted that calling the stars "lamps" does not actually degrade them, but he still thinks that the reduction in function expresses their creatureliness (*Genesis 1–11*, pp. 131f.).

modern depiction of the world of creation. This time, however, the formation of the earth comes after that of the stars and galaxies, and within the galaxies the solar system.

More surprising than the difference in order at this point between science and the early Genesis story is the measure of material agreement, e.g., light at the beginning, humans at the end, light prior to the stars, plants springing forth from the earth, the function of vegetation as a presupposition of animal life,[304] and the close relation between humans and land animals on the sixth day,[305] as distinct from fishes and birds on the fifth. Even more astonishing than these detailed agreements is agreement in the basic idea of a sequence in the development of creaturely forms. The sequence may be different at some points from that of modern science, but science today has also arrived at its own idea of a sequence in its understanding of the world.

According to E. Schlink the chief difference between the sequence in the modern view and that in the Genesis story is that according to the biblical understanding the individual working of the creatures is according to concrete orders that are already set, whereas modern research has increasingly come to think that the orders proceed from the working.[306] The creation story itself is already acquainted with the idea of creaturely agencies' sharing in the work of creation. Thus the earth brings forth both vegetation (Gen. 1:11f.) and land animals (1:24).[307] In this account, however, the thought of an ongoing development in the course of which different forms of creaturely reality arise out of those that precede is a totally alien one. This is not because God's creative activity rules out any creaturely participation. The fact that the earth brings forth plants and animals proves the contrary.

The reason for the remoteness of the text from the idea of an evolution of the forms of creaturely reality is that in the Genesis account the initial creation established an order for all time so that each of the works of

304. The OT, however, does not specifically list plants with animals as living things; cf. Schmidt, *Schöpfungsgeschichte*, pp. 150ff. on Gen. 1:29.

305. In Gen. 1:24f., however, no distinction is made between mammals and other land animals, the distinction being between wild and domestic animals, and between these and all the rest (cf. ibid., pp. 124ff.).

306. Schlink, *Ökumenische Dogmatik*, p. 93.

307. For the tension between command and execution in Gen. 1:24f., cf. Schmidt, *Schöpfungsgeschichte*, p. 126, who points out that the command is given to the earth but that the execution is God's own creative act. Cf. also Steck, *Schöpfungsbericht*, pp. 118ff.

creation would have lasting duration.[308] Connected specifically with this concern is the fact that the different creaturely forms and the species of living creatures received at the outset the lasting forms of their existence. In this regard the first story has a different emphasis from that of other biblical accounts, which do not limit God's creative activity to the beginning but see it as an ongoing activity that finds expression especially in his present acts in history (see above, pp. 40ff.). If it is to do justice to the full biblical witness, then, the doctrine of creation has the task of uniting the interest of this account in the constancy of the order that God has established once and for all with the concept of ongoing creative activity. In the context of modern science the idea of a fixed and constant order no longer need imply an immutability of the divinely created forms in their different genres and species. Though the story does not mention these, the idea of unbreakable natural laws does sufficient justice to that concern.[309] The theory of evolution has given theology an opportunity to see God's ongoing creative activity not merely in the preservation of a fixed order but in the constant bringing forth of things that are new.

In the 19th and early 20th centuries Christian churches and theologians were painfully slow to recognize this opportunity that evolution had given theology relative to natural science. The fight against Darwinism was a momentous mistake in the relations between science and theology.[310] German Protestant theology in

308. Steck lays special emphasis on this motif (*Schöpfungsbericht,* pp. 68ff., cf. also 94, 110, 121f., 126f.). This is why in the creation of living creatures we find a second act of blessing with reference to their continued multiplication (1:22, cf. 1:28). Their duration depends on this (pp. 82f.).

309. At the end of the flood story Gen. 9:11 confirms the idea that relative to living creatures, the will of the Creator is that the creation should endure. Cf. also the thought of a natural order in the rhythms of seedtime and harvest, summer and winter, frost and heat, day and night (8:22). These rhythms are perhaps based on the ruling of day and night by the sun and moon (1:16) and the way in which the sun and moon give us knowledge of the seasons (1:14). This may be why they are not mentioned again in 9:11. In this regard 8:22 is closer to the idea of a regularity of nature that it is the function of the heavenly bodies to indicate.

310. We may say this in spite of the hypothetical character of the theory of evolution. For the difficulties that still beset the attempt to prove evolution empirically, cf. A. Hayward, *Creation and Evolution: The Facts and the Fallacies* (1985), pp. 21ff. Cf. also Peacocke, *God and the New Biology,* pp. 44ff., the reference in Wicken, *Evolution, Thermodynamics, and Information,* p. 209, to E. Mayr, *Principles of Systematic Zoology* (New York, 1969), also *The Growth of Biological Thought* (Cambridge, MA, 1982). The reasons why theologians rejected the theory, however, had little to do with the problems of empirical demonstration.

particular must share some blame for this, although we can understand its resistance to some degree as a reaction to the one-sided interpretation of the theory
by leading biologists. As G. Altner has shown, both sides should have seen in
Darwin's theory the breakthrough to a new, historical view of nature in contrast
to that of classical physics. Instead, biologists found in it the victory for the
mechanistic explanation of classical physics, and theologians reacted to Darwin
with polemics and rejection because they were trapped in the philosophical premises of constancy (immutable species from the beginning of the world) and
blinded by an idealistic overestimation of humanity.[311]

In particular, theology was alarmed by the threat that Darwin's theory of
descent posed to the special position of humans. It found the core of the antithesis
in the replacement of a teleological view of nature (in the light of God's purposeful
positing) by an emphasis on the contingency of many events in the interplay of
inheritance and selection. In this latter respect it was right. With his insights into
the mechanism of selection, Darwin himself had moved away from the teleological
view of nature that in the *Natural Theology* (1802) of William Paley, a book that
Darwin had studied and admired, had been the basis of a proof of God in the
form of the argument from design.[312] The combination of inheritance and selection explained the element of purpose in organic life, which the teleological proof
regarded as explicable only in terms of rational planning. To friends and foes alike,
then, the selection theory seemed to contradict the theistic concept of God. To
both sides it seemed as if the theory of selection in evolution offered in principle
a purely mechanistic explanation of the development of the species. As Altner
points out, they overlooked the fact that the new evolutionary worldview was
giving them the possibility of thinking of the dynamic process of creation as a
process that is open in time.

This is especially true of German theologians, with a few exceptions such
as Karl Beth in Erlangen.[313] In English theology, however, there were early efforts
to link Christian teaching to the new perspective of evolutionary theory. Salvation

---

311. G. Altner, "Wer ist's, der dies alles zusammenhält?," in *Die Welt als offenes
System*, ed. Altner (1986), pp. 161-71, esp. 164f. The developments I cite in what follows
are based on Altner's succinct account of the problem. Cf. also his *Schöpfungsglaube und
Entwicklungsglaube in der protestantischen Theologie zwischen Ernst Haeckel und Teilhard de
Chardin* (1965).

312. R. H. Overman, *Evolution and the Christian Doctrine of Creation: A White-
headian Interpretation* (Philadelphia, 1967), pp. 57ff., on Paley (p. 58), with a survey of the
debate between theology and the theory of evolution subsequent to the work of Darwin
(pp. 69-116). Cf. also J. Dillenberger, *Protestant Thought and Natural Science* (Garden City,
NY, 1960), pp. 217-53; Barbour, *Issues in Science and Religion*, pp. 80-114; E. Benz, *Schöpfungsglaube und Endzeiterwartung. Antwort auf Teilhard de Chardins Theologie der Evolution*
(1965), pp. 157-83; J. Hübner, *Theologie und biologische Entwicklungslehre* (1966). For additional bibliography cf. S. M. Daecke, "Entwicklung," *TRE*, IX (1982), pp. 705-16, esp. 714f.

313. K. Beth, *Der Entwicklungsgedanke und das Christentum* (1909).

history was seen as a continuation of evolution, which reached its culmination in Jesus Christ as the new man. This approach related the theistic concept of God and his rational plans and purposes to the total process rather than to individual constructs with their own ends.

A pioneering work in this regard was *Lux Mundi* (New York, 1889), edited by Charles Gore. This work hailed the theory of evolution as liberation from a mechanistic view of nature that presented God deistically as the initial author of the natural order but not as one who continues to work creatively in the process of natural events.[314] In the 20th century the English tradition of a theology of evolution along the lines of *Lux Mundi* found its most important champions in William Temple and Charles Raven, and more recently in Arthur R. Peacocke.[315]

In England and North America, creationists have offered resistance, rejecting the theory of evolution as incompatible with a literal biblical belief. From the time of Henry M. Morris and John C. Whitcomb (*The Genesis Flood* [1961]), they have tried to explain geological and paleological findings with the help of the biblical flood story (Gen. 6:13–8:22). Creation science has thus come into competition with the geological and biological theory of evolution.[316] The controversy rests primarily on a fundamentalist view of the authority and texts of the Bible. Belief in God's saving action in history, however, involves recognition of the historical nature of the biblical writings and the relation of the concepts we find in them to those dominant at the time.

Comparable in many ways to what we find in Britain and North America is the work of Teilhard de Chardin.[317] Teilhard linked God as the omega of evolution to the future of the world, toward which the dynamic of evolution thrusts (with its radial energy), and the working of which we see in the increasing complexity and inwardness of the forms of life, and also at the human stage in their increasingly social structure.

Although the Roman Catholic Church initially rejected the theory of evolution and its theology,[318] discussion of the thoughts of Teilhard, though at first prohibited and difficult, has now brought a change. In 1959 Hermann Volk

---

314. Cf. Overman, *Evolution and the Christian Doctrine of Creation*, pp. 78f.

315. W. Temple, *Nature, Man, and God;* C. E. Raven, *Natural Religion and Christian Theology*, I (Cambridge, 1953); Peacocke, *Science and the Christian Experiment;* idem, *Creation and the World of Science.*

316. In criticism cf. Hayward, *Creation and Evolution*, pp. 69-157, and R. L. Numbers, "The Creationists," *Zygon* 22 (1987) 133-64, esp. 153ff.

317. We may refer esp. to his main work, *Der Mensch im Kosmos.* Cf. S. M. Daecke, *Teilhard de Chardin und die evangelische Theologie* (1967); also A. Gosztonyi, *Der Mensch und die Evolution. Teilhard de Chardins philosophische Anthropologie* (1968).

318. Cf. the 1950 encyclical *Humani Generis*, DS, 3875ff. = ND, 144-48, 238f., 419f., 858f., 1571, 1998 (pp. 54-57, 82f., 120f., 238f., 409, 544). See also Z. Alszeghy, "Development in the Doctrinal Formulation of the Church Concerning the Theory of Evolution," in *The Evolving World and Theology*, ed. J. B. Metz (Concilium 26; New York, 1967).

could say of the relation between creation and evolution that the former has to do with beginning and not becoming, whereas evolution presupposes beginning.[319] Ten years later Joseph Ratzinger could write that seen from the standpoint of our understanding of the world, creation is not a remote beginning or a beginning divided up into several stages. It has to do with being as both temporal and becoming. Temporal being as a whole is embraced by the one creative act of God, which gives it unity in its division and in which it has its meaning.[320] This view of things has now found wide acceptance in Roman Catholic theology.[321] In it emphasis falls on the rise of what is truly and formally new in evolution[322] by application and extension of the older concept of continuous creation, though Leo Scheffczyk, unlike British theologians, relates this only to the preservation of what has been created in distinction from the original act of creation.[323]

In applying the idea of evolution to creation, we might appeal to statements in the OT, especially in Deutero-Isaiah, about the creative nature of God's acts in history, presupposing that in the process of evolution new things emerge step by step that we cannot reduce to already-existent things. This presupposition comes to expression in the description

319. H. Volk, "Entwicklung," *LThK*, III, 907.

320. J. Ratzinger, "Schöpfungsglaube und Evolutionstheorie," in *Wer ist das eigentlich — Gott?*, ed. H. J. Schultz (1969), p. 242. According to Ratzinger different views of the course of creation show that in the Bible itself faith and worldview are not identical (p. 239). He allows that since Darwin the idea of fixed species is no longer tenable (p. 233, cf. 235).

321. K. Rahner took the lead. Cf. his article "Evolution/Evolutionismus (2)," *Sacramentum Mundi* 1 (1969) 1251-62, preceded by many contributions to thinking on the significance of the theory of evolution for individual themes in dogmatics, esp. *Theological Investigations*, V, pp. 157ff. Cf. also Scheffczyk, *Einführung in die Schöpfungslehre*, pp. 59ff.; S. N. Bosshard, "Evolution und Schöpfung," *Christlicher Glaube in moderner Gesellschaft* 3 (1981) 87-127; idem, *Erschafft die Welt sich selbst?* (Freiburg, 1985); cf. too A. Ganoczy, *Schöpfungslehre* (1983), pp. 143ff., esp. 150f., cf. the 2nd ed. (1987), pp. 196ff.

322. Scheffczyk, *Einführung in die Schöpfungslehre*, pp. 6f.; cf. Ganoczy, *Schöpfungslehre* (1983), pp. 154f. (1987), pp. 213f.

323. Scheffczyk, *Einführung in die Schöpfungslehre*, p. 61, rightly emphasizes that this evolutionary interpretation of the concept of continuous creation is a theological novelty insofar as it enriches the concept dynamically. The British and American theology of evolution went much further by treating continuous creation as an alternative to creation out of nothing (cf. Barbour, *Issues in Science and Religion*, p. 384, and cf. above, pp. 13f. and 38ff.). If we argue that continuous creation presupposes creation out of nothing, we do not have to restrict it to preservation as opposed to initial creation. Along the lines of Ratzinger ("Schöpfungsglaube und Evolutionstheorie"), we might relate creation out of nothing to the whole span of creaturely time and view continuous creation as a more precise definition of creation out of nothing. In this sense we might agree with Barbour (*Issues in Science and Religion*, pp. 365ff., esp. 383ff., 414f., also 456ff.) and bring the whole history of the universe under the rubric of evolution and creation.

of evolution as emergent evolution.[324] Its point is rejection of a reductionist understanding of evolution. The element of chance that Jacques Monod stressed so strongly in antithesis to theological understandings of evolution[325] is important for a theological interpretation of the steps of evolution as an expression of the ongoing creative action of God. The thorough regularity of evolutionary processes and the proceeding of each new form out of those that precede it in the evolutionary chain are no obstacles. The first Genesis story shows familiarity already with the idea that God does his creative work through creaturely agencies. The epigenetic character of evolution, i.e., the arrival of something totally new at each stage, is decisive for the possibility of a theological interpretation of evolutionary processes along the lines of God's creative work in history.

The main difference between the modern view of natural events and the creation story is that modern science traces back all forms in the world of nature to elementary processes and constituents. This approach has its roots in the atom theory of Democritus, which regarded all natural constructs as made up of very small parts, their differences being due to differences in combination. This idea that all complex constructs are made up of elemental parts has decisively influenced the outlook of modern science. Without it we could no longer conceive of a step-by-step sequence in the development of creaturely forms.

The sequence begins with the elementary and least complex phenomena, on which all the others rest. But neither the chemical elements nor the underlying atoms — in which for many years science sought the original, indivisible elementary parts — offer any conclusive answer as to the final building blocks. What were thought to be atoms are themselves made up of many smaller parts, and these again may be divided into "quarks" or "strings" that are qualitatively different, so that they too fail to meet the demand of the atomic theory of Democritus for equal building blocks of matter, to the combination of which all differences may be traced.

---

324. C. L. Morgan, *Emergent Evolution* (New York, 1923). Cf. on this E. C. Rust, *Evolutionary Philosophies and Contemporary Theology* (Philadelphia, 1969), pp. 77ff. In view of the contingent nature of the steps in evolution, T. Dobzhansky, *The Biology of Ultimate Concern* (New York, 1967, 2nd ed. 1969), p. 33, could call evolution "a source of novelty." M. Eigen, "Evolution und Zeitlichkeit," in *Die Zeit*, ed. A. Preisl and A. Mohler (1983), pp. 35-57, esp. 52, agrees in his "game" theory.

325. Monod, *Chance and Necessity*. Cf. on this Peacocke, *Creation and the World of Science*, pp. 95ff., with references to W. G. Pollard as well as Bosshard, "Evolution und Schöpfung," pp. 94ff.

Can we think of the ultimate elementary factor as enduring spatial form, as the smallest body or corpuscle? Or is it something momentary that we cannot plainly localize? There is much in favor of the view that all corpuscular matter comes from elementary events, which for their part are manifestations of fields.

It was the merit of A. N. Whitehead to draw from the revolution in quantum physics the philosophical conclusion that momentary events and sequences of events precede the formation of all lasting bodies in space.[326] Only the incessant repetition of events of a certain kind can form lasting bodies. Whereas H. Bergson regarded continuous duration as the basic phenomenon of all living reality and criticized its breaking up into a sequence, which like a film would create an illusion of constancy, on the ground that divisive reason is here treating time as space, and that on these conditions we cannot reconstruct real movement as in Zeno's famous paradox of Achilles and tortoise,[327] Whitehead seems not to view the cinematographic parallel as erroneous but as a very apt illustration of the coming into being of continuous phenomena, and especially the continuity of the body.[328]

With his thesis of the priority of fleeting events and sequences of events over the emergence of spatial forms that endure in time, Whitehead has gained many adherents. The problem is that this approach tends to become a dogmatic atomism of events that regards momentary and discrete events as ultimately all that may be called real.[329] The extensive continuum of space-time rests on the emergence of events,[330] but we should also regard it as the condition of their emergence. Whitehead did not regard the field of possibility out of which events proceed as their creative origin. Instead, he viewed events as self-creative. Whitehead's cosmology finds no place for the ontological primacy of the field over the event or the infinite over the finite, nor for the nonderivability of the whole from the parts in the emergence of enduring forms.[331]

326. Cf. *Science and the Modern World* (New York, 1925); also *Process and Reality* (Cambridge, 1929). On these works cf. Welker, *Universalität Gottes*, esp. pp. 35-137; also R. Wiehl's Introduction to the 1971 German ed. of Whitehead's *Adventures of Ideas* (New York, 1933).

327. *L'évolution créatrice*, pp. 304ff., 308ff.

328. *Process and Reality: An Essay in Cosmology* (New York, 1929, repr. 1960), p. 53.

329. Ibid., p. 27, also 53 and 95: "Continuity concerns what is potential, whereas actuality is incurably atomic."

330. Ibid., p. 103: The extensive continuum is "real" only as it is derived from the "actual world" of elementary events. Cf. also pp. 123f. on the field concept as a particular form of the extensive continuum.

331. Cf. my "Atom, Duration, Form: Difficulties with Process Philosophy," *Process Studies* 14 (1984) 21-30.

Although all natural constructs are made up of much smaller parts, these parts always belong to a larger context out of which larger and more complex forms emerge that as totalities cannot simply be reduced to their parts. Theologically one might put this fact in terms of the bringing forth of creaturely forms by God's creative action, which does not compete with the scientific explanation of the conditions of their emergence or postulate that there are gaps in principle in the scientific account. The statements of theology about creaturely reality in its individual forms do not just refer externally, however, to the things described by science. They are also oriented to the structural links that tie creaturely forms to the totality of creation. Not least of all, then, theology can help to keep us aware of the need for further advances in the scientific explanation of the reality of nature.

Although all material constructs are made up of atoms and their constituent parts and processes, today we can no longer simply say that the parts that in certain circumstances pass (or decay) into one another are in every respect clearly and continuously distinct building blocks of matter of which more complex structures are formed.[332] Instead, we have to ascribe to subatomic processes and conditions a holistic character.[333] This undefined totality expresses itself in individual phenomena but is not made up of these. We can localize neither it nor its expressions.[334] Naturally, then, we may view the parts as local manifestations of a field that fills all space.[335]

As a result we see links between microphysics and physical cosmology. The early universe, crowded into a small space, must have been so extremely hot that lasting and complex forms could not develop out of the elementary processes.[336] This universe forms the natural total context of such a state. Only with its expansion and the associated cooling could atoms and molecules arise and then combine into galaxies and constellations by way of gravity.[337] Again the total state of the universe must be seen as the total condition for the emergence of such forms.

332. Stegmüller, "Evolution des Kosmos," pp. 599ff.

333. Russell, "Quantum Physics," pp. 350ff.; cf. Barbour, *Issues in Science and Religion*, pp. 295ff.

334. Russell, "Quantum Physics," pp. 351f., referring to J. S. Bell et al.

335. Stegmüller, "Evolution des Kosmos," p. 603; cf. Russell, "Quantum Physics," pp. 356f.

336. Weinberg, *First Three Minutes*, pp. 14ff.

337. Hawking, *Brief History of Time*, pp. 117ff. The formation of the first cores of deuterium and helium would occur not more than two minutes after the Big Bang, but millions of years would be needed for electrons and cores to combine. On the formation of the galaxies and constellations cf. Stegmüller, "Evolution des Kosmos," pp. 526-74.

The same applies to the peripheral conditions that made possible the emergence of a biosphere on earth: the protection of the earth's surface from cosmic radiation by the solar wind, whose effects are reduced again by the earth's magnetic sphere under the influence of the moon;[338] the formation of large molecules under the impact of ultraviolet rays and their filtering by means of the enrichment of the earth's atmosphere with oxygen through the photodissociation of water;[339] and finally the increase of the oxygen in the atmosphere by means of the photosynthesis of plants, a condition of all higher animal life.[340]

Under these special conditions living phenomena came into being by using the decline in thermodynamic energy that was taking place with the expansion of the universe and that had made possible the development of the galaxies and constellations.[341] Above all other constructs, living creatures are marked by the fact that they emerge as the products of active self-formation by self-organization.[342] Preforms might be found in fluctuations that occur and achieve self-movement for a time in dynamic processes. Thus flames have rightly been seen as a parallel. In flames we find an interchange of energy and matter that increases as the flammable material is consumed and that may at times produce itself.[343] Thus a candle flame is a picture of life as a dissipative structure that is made possible and that stabilizes itself by the consumption of energy, or more exactly by the catalytic mediation of the changing of potential energy into heat.[344] Organisms, of course, are much more complex and produce their forms and states by using information as well as accumulated energy (see above, n. 342).

The fact that the emergence of living forms, including humans, depends on the total situation of the universe and its expansion has been pointedly brought to light by the anthropic principle (see above, pp. 74ff.). Even though this does not imply a causal explanation of the agreement of basic constants in nature with conditions for the rise of life and intelligence, at least it expresses the fact that the universe is a totality and is thus the comprehensive condition for all the forms and phenomena that occur in it. This does not mean that in virtue of its dynamic order the universe compels us to accept an intelligent author along the lines of the cosmoteleological proof. But the agreement does seem to tell us that we must view the universe as an "end" in Kant's sense, the parts and the totality condition-

---

338. Stegmüller, *Hauptströmungen*, pp. 693ff., esp. 700.

339. Ibid., pp. 606f.

340. Ibid., p. 715.

341. Wicken, *Evolution, Thermodynamics, and Information*, p. 72.

342. Ibid., pp. 31f.

343. Süssmann, "Geist und Materie," p. 23; also Wicken, *Evolution, Thermodynamics, and Information*, pp. 115f.

344. Wicken, *Evolution, Thermodynamics, and Information*, p. 116: "The stability of a kinetic (dissipative) structure is a function of its ability to concentrate and dissipate thermodynamic potential." On dissipative structures cf. Prigogine, *From Being to Becoming*, pp. 90ff.

ing one another,[345] so that the emergence of life and humans cannot be adjudged to be a matter of chance that might well not have happened.

No matter what may be the final reason for the existence of the universe, we have to think of it as the basis of the cosmic process both as a whole and in all its parts. In this regard organisms have central importance inasmuch as they are themselves ends in a special sense.[346] There is thus a core of truth in the old idea that life, and in particular human life, is a microcosm,[347] though less in the sense of sharing in all the layers of creaturely reality and more in respect of the structure of humans as living beings, and that simply as a development of the structure expressed in the concept of a natural end, since life means self-organization that cannot be ascribed in the same way to the universe as a whole.

Theologically we may view the expansion of the universe as the Creator's means to the bringing forth of independent forms of creaturely reality. This applies not merely in the sense that cosmic expansion offers space to an increasing number of creatures. The emergence of the actual forms is conditional upon the cooling associated with expansion. As distinct from the transitory existence of elementary parts, duration is the basic form of independent existence, whether in the form of integrated systems, as in the case of atoms and molecules, or in the form of mere aggregates, as in that of stars, mountains, and oceans, which are lessened when parts are taken away, but not destroyed. A higher stage of independence of creaturely existence is reached, however, only with organisms whose life takes the form of the self-organization of catalytic processes, i.e., of autocatalysis.

345. Cf. Kant's *Critique of Judgment* (Oxford, 1952) § 64. Kant defines a thing as an end when of itself (although in an ambivalent sense) it is both cause and effect (extended in the 2nd and 3rd editions of 1793 and 1799). But he expands the definition in the next paragraphs, saying that the parts (in their existence and form) are possible only by their relation to the whole. With his mechanistic view of events Kant could extend his idea of end to nature as a whole only as a matter for reflective judgment (§ 75). Here statements extending the findings discussed under the formula of an anthropic principle perhaps have constitutive significance for natural occurrence itself.

346. Wicken, *Evolution, Thermodynamics, and Information,* p. 31, said of Kant's view of the living creature as natural end that as modern research now stands, it is "an extremely useful definition." He advanced as his own more precise definition the idea that the living creature is "an informed autocatalytic system" that forms and maintains itself by "participation in the dissipative flow of nature," but he saw in this a more concrete development of Kant's formal definition.

347. Cf. the article "Makrokosmos/Mikrokosmos," by M. Gatzemeier and H. Holtzhey, in *HWP,* V (1980), 640-49.

We have already stressed the kinship of organic life to dynamic constructs. Organisms are catalyzers. They release dynamic processes that themselves presuppose dynamic cosmic transfers of energy for their formation. They are autocatalytic systems because they produce and reproduce themselves.[348] They do this by information-directed structure building and activity.[349] According to Wicken the genetic information of the DNA double helix must be developed in connection with its use in catalytic processes.[350] We cannot understand living processes, then, only in terms of the replication of the bearers of genetic information. Already in the origin of life there is needed the relation to a totality that links the different functions of RNA and proteins in their development.[351] At all stages in the development of life, then, the parts depend on the whole to which they are functionally related.[352]

Obviously related to the spontaneity of vital processes as the building of forms by self-organization is the multiplicity of living creatures that emerge in such abundance and compete with one another for use of the energy in their environment. The mechanism of selection sets in here,[353] which in Darwin's theory of evolution produced the development of the

348. M. Eigen, "Self-Organization of Matter and the Evolution of Biological Macromolecules," *Die Naturwissenschaften* 58, no. 10 (1971) 465-523.

349. Ibid., pp. 502ff. Wicken, *Evolution, Thermodynamics, and Information*, p. 41, can thus define organization as "informed constraint for functional activity."

350. Wicken, *Evolution, Thermodynamics, and Information*, p. 104: "Information evolves only within a context of utilization," cf. pp. 105f. Wicken thus opposes the hypercycle theory of Eigen, who relates his reconstruction of the formation of autocatalytic systems too one-sidedly to the transfer of information from DNA to RNA to proteins (pp. 98ff.). This model fits only parasitic processes in which RNA phases use alien proteins to reproduce themselves (pp. 102f.). We see this in virus infections, whose study has seen the starting point for modern genetics; cf. Stegmüller, *Hauptströmungen*, pp. 620ff. But Wicken does not think that we have yet explained the extension of the information programs of DNA and RNA to the many protein functions of an organism, nor then the link between RNA and proteins in the organization of a living creature (p. 104). He conjectures that we should look first at proteins (pp. 110ff.).

351. Wicken, *Evolution, Thermodynamics, and Information*, p. 106, refers to "catalytic microspheres" that in the emergence of life are finally distinguished from the formation of cells delimited by a membrane from their environment (p. 125). For a similar picture cf. H. Kuhn, "Entstehung des Lebens Bildung von Molekülgesellschaften," *Forschung* 74 (1973) 78-104.

352. "Organismic wholes cannot be built piecemeal from molecular parts. The whole provides rules and contexts in which parts emerge and acquire functional significance" (Wicken, *Evolution, Thermodynamics, and Information*, p. 130, cf. 136, 166ff., 207). On the relation between the concept of integrated totality and that of system, cf. Bosshard, *Erschafft die Welt sich selbst?*, pp. 110ff., 117ff., in opposition to the "finalistic" tendency in the use of the concept of totality in vitalism. Cf. the antithesis of holistic and reductionist tendencies in biology, according to Peacocke, *God and the New Biology*, pp. 32ff., 57ff.

353. Wicken, *Evolution, Thermodynamics, and Information*, p. 109, sees it as functioning before the development of the ability to replicate.

forms of life through competition for natural resources and opportunities for multiplication. The source of variety, however, is spontaneous productivity. We cannot say that the superabundant wealth of forms is simply characterized by a thrust toward adjustment to the environment.[354] In connection with the drive of living creatures toward increasing complexity it is marked by the fact that living forms have the dignity of fairly easily coming into existence for their own sakes, as ends in themselves. This is an important aspect of their distinctive beauty. The wealth of forms cannot be reduced to the function of adaptation to the environment, significant though this function may be for the process of selection. Indeed, the reverse is true, namely, that the wealth of new forms contains as a byproduct new possibilities of utilizing the conditions of life.

In the biblical belief in creation the richness of life in the variety of its forms plays an important role. Thus Ps. 104 expressly finds in the multiplicity of the animal world an occasion to praise the Creator (vv. 11ff.). In the speech of God that forces complaining Job to recognize and praise the fact that God is above all the detailed claims that individual creatures might bring,[355] the list of the wonders of creation reaches a climax with variety in the animal kingdom (38:29–39:30), and especially with the astonishing size of the hippopotamus and crocodile (40:10–41:25). In the message of Jesus, too, the goodness of the Creator and the paternal care of God, which are so manifest in plants and animals, are an answer to the human tendency to be anxious (Luke 12:24-28; Matt. 6:26-30).

Since biblical piety finds the variety and grandeur of the forms of life so fascinating, it is not surprising that the first creation story mentions expressly the creation of the different kinds of plants and animals. Though the story says that animals alone have the breath of life (Gen. 1:30), plants and animals alike are created after their kind. In this way the variety of creaturely forms in this sphere of creation comes to expression. The classifying angle from which this is done shows interest in the point that this variety as a whole is God's creation.[356] It is not, as in the view of

354. Ibid., p. 179: "The drive toward complexity is constrained by fitness, but not moving on its behalf. . . . The important point is that experiments in organizational complexity provide access to new adaptive zones."

355. R. Rendtorff thinks that this is the point of the speech: "Where were you when I laid the foundation of the earth?" ("Schöpfung und Heilsgeschichte," in *Frieden in der Schöpfung. Das Naturverständnis protestantischer Theologie*, ed. G. Rau et al. [1987], pp. 35-57, esp. 49ff.).

356. Westermann, *Genesis 1–11*, pp. 123ff., 134ff., 141ff., finds in this approach to systematic classifying a step on the way to scientific explanation of the development of

modern science, a product of the self-organization and evolution of life but was there from the very beginning.

Certainly the account does not think that plants and animals simply maintain the same form for all time. By way of seed (Gen. 1:12) or, in the case of animals, the blessing of fruitfulness (1:22), they propagate themselves and increase. But this procedure links the experience of the ongoing renewal and new formation of life to the initial establishment of life.[357] It also restricts it to the circle of species created at the start. We have noted already that this feature of the story expresses time-bound dependence on a mythical approach that traces back all that now exists to a basic primal period (see above, pp. 118f.). In view of the tension with the thought of God's continued creativity in other biblical statements, we cannot regard this as the core of the biblical belief in creation.

More important is the interest in the variety of the forms of life and the concern to grasp them in their totality from the standpoint of the power of life to renew and expand by way of propagation. The modern view brings all these points together under the rubric of the self-organization of living things in their evolution. In this regard it touches on the thought in the story that the blessing of God gave to living things (at least to animals) the power of fruitfulness.[358] The only point is that now the idea of the creative working of God through a vital creative force granted to living creatures themselves is so generalized that it embraces the actual bringing forth of living forms in all their variety.

In this production of life in varied new forms the modern view attaches special importance to the development of the sexual form of propagation and increase. By linking the inheritance of two individuals and by meiosis, greater variety is possible, allowing the inheritance of the individual to be combined with what is common to the species.[359] By the selectivity of the sexual unions of individuals within a species, the prop-

---

plants (p. 123) and animals (p. 141). The commentaries usually pay no particular attention to the interest in the multiplicity of creatures as such.

357. Steck, Schöpfungsbericht, pp. 65ff., 94f., 121ff.

358. Westermann, Genesis 1–11, pp. 139ff. According to Steck, Schöpfungsbericht, pp. 121f. and 126ff., instead of the blessing, we have the command to the earth (Gen. 1:24) to put forth the decisive power of propagation so that land animals may continue in existence (p. 121); only after the flood is the blessing extended to animals (Gen. 8:17).

359. Cf. M. Ghiselin, The Economy of Nature and the Evolution of Sex (Berkeley, CA, 1974), p. 57, followed by Wicken, Evolution, Thermodynamics, and Information, p. 218, who sees in sexuality "a means of mobilizing genetic variability" that "makes evolutionary novelties public property" (p. 213).

agation of life acquires a historical dimension and creatively opens up space within which life can expand.[360] This goes far beyond the function that the first creation story assigns to the blessing of fruitfulness. The main point there was the continued existence of the life that God created at the first after its kinds. Life is in a special way the work of God's creative power. The story brings this out by its readoption of the term *bara'* (Gen. 1:21). For the continuation of life, too, a special divine blessing is required because creatures share in God's creative and sustaining work.[361] Modern evolutionary theory would add that sharing in God's creative work includes the bringing forth of new variants and forms of life that were not there at the first. This extension does justice to the Christian interest in the uniqueness of each individual that passes on life — more so than a restriction of creaturely cooperation in God's creative activity to the mere reproduction of existing forms.

This sharing in the creative force that comes from God does not rule out, of course, the possibility of a bad use of the gift, even to the point of demonic perversion. Creative participation in God's creative working does not of itself mean fellowship with God and his will. It is no surprise, then, that the blessing of fruitfulness that is given to humans as well, and that is even made a matter of their own responsibility (Gen. 1:28), is carefully distinguished from the human destiny of divine likeness, and subordinated to it.[362] Only with the closeness to God that is given with divine likeness do we have a basis for the special position of humanity in God's creation as its conclusion and crown, and also for the relation of humanity to other creatures that comes with the charge to have dominion over the realm of living creatures (1:26) and even over the earth itself (1:28). We cannot detach this charge from the link to God's creative will.

We shall deal expressly with the divine likeness in the next chapter. In our present discussion the related charge to have dominion arises only in respect of the manifested independence of humans as creatures in comparison with the rest of creation. We must emphasize here, however, that in the story the charge does not

---

360. Wicken, *Evolution, Thermodynamics, and Information*, pp. 218f.

361. Von Rad, *Genesis*, p. 60. In the case of land animals Gen. 1:24 says that the earth mediates participation in the vital force that comes from God (cf. Steck, *Schöpfungsbericht*, pp. 126ff.). Westermann, *Genesis 1–11*, pp. 139ff. and 221f., resists the idea of a restriction of the blessing to the mere preservation of what has already been created.

362. Von Rad, *Genesis*, p. 60, on Gen. 1:27f. This is true even if we agree with Steck, *Schöpfungsbericht*, pp. 142f., that the blessing given to humans carries with it an authorization beyond that of 1:22.

mean that humans may do as they like with other creatures or with the earth itself. The fact that Gen. 1:29 gives humans plants alone as food and not animals rules out this conclusion. Only after the flood is the eating of flesh permitted (Gen. 9:3). The original commission does not have in view a dominion of force but a relation such as we find with domestic animals or flocks, and which includes caring for the continued existence of animals as in the case of Noah when he is told to build the ark (6:19f.).[363]

The primary reference in the case of dominion over the earth is to agriculture.[364] It also includes mining. The charge basically embraces a technical handling of earth's treasures. All such phenomena of human cultural activity bear witness to the fact of human dominion over the earth and the animal kingdom. Only the emancipation of the modern West from commitment to the God of the Bible has replaced the thought that we are God's stewards in our rule over his creation by the idea that we have a right to unrestricted exploitation of nature. It is illegitimate, then, to make the biblical picture of humanity responsible for the unrestricted exploitation of the earth by humanity today.[365] Called to have dominion over the earth and all living things, humans are also members of God's creation and in the exercise of dominion are responsible for the preservation of its order.[366] Unlike the Genesis story we may relate this responsibility less to the order established at the beginning and see it more as responsibility for the destiny of creation in its creative development. But in this form it is truly linked to the will of the Creator and its orientation to the reconciliation and redemption of his creation.

Humans are the most highly developed of living creatures. This is true biologically when we compare them with animals.[367] It does not necessarily follow from this that they are the goal of the evolution of life, let alone of the whole universe. It is not impossible that evolution might lead

363. Steck, *Schöpfungsbericht,* p. 145 n. 584; cf. 143f. n. 579; also 151ff.

364. Ibid., p. 156.

365. As we see in Lynn White, "The Historical Roots of our Ecological Crisis," in *The Environmental Handbook,* ed. G. DeBell (New York, 1970), also C. Amery, *Das Ende der Vorsehung. Die gnadenlosen Folgen des Christentums* (Hamburg, 1972). In criticism cf. G. Altner, *Schöpfung am Abgrund* (1974), pp. 58ff., 81f.

366. On the anthropological basis of this statement cf. my *Anthropology,* pp. 43ff., esp. 77ff.

367. Peacocke, *Creation and the World of Science,* p. 157. The evolutionary scientist G. G. Simpson (*The Meaning of Evolution* [New Haven, 1971], p. 236), to whom Peacocke makes special reference, judges indeed that the sum of "basic diagnostic features" that separate us from other species not only involves a sharp distinction but results in "an absolute difference in kind and not only a relative difference in degree." Cf. also Peacocke's *God and the New Biology,* pp. 51f.

beyond humanity to other forms of intelligent life. Yet there are no empirical grounds on which to support this. It is just that theoretically we cannot simply reject such a possibility in view of biological evolution. The thesis that normative constants in nature are so constituted that their values make possible the rise of life and intelligence by no means forces us, in spite of the implied anthropic principle of physical cosmology, to the conclusion that the world was created for our sake or in orientation to us. It simply tells us that in our universe the development of organic life and its human form has become possible and has given an essential feature to the world. The development of life and its human form is not a matter of mere chance in nature, as people used to think in virtue of the vastness of the universe. That this development is a special feature of the world as a whole is something that demands explanation: Why is this so?

We can make such a statement only if we know the origin of the universe as a whole and can define the relation of the development of life and humanity to it. These both are premises of the biblical story of creation, and in the light of the Christian belief in the deity of Jesus Christ and his mediation in creation, the Jewish tradition takes on special and even sharper contours as regards the theme of our position in creation as a whole. Christian theology can thus take the step of maintaining that the rise and development of life and the appearance of humanity bring fully to light for the first time the meaning of all creaturely reality.

If we orient ourselves to the statements of the first creation story regarding humans in relation to creation as a whole, it is natural that we should seek the meaning of creaturely existence in the agreement of the creature with the will of God as Creator. For this is the standard for the dominion over creation that is entrusted to us. But what is the will of God as Creator? In the multiplicity of individual concrete cases it is beyond the grasp of our human understanding to answer this question. Nevertheless, it is plain at least that the will of the Creator is that the creature should be. In other words, the Creator's will is oriented to the independent existence of the creature. Only to this extent do creatures have their own reality in distinction from that of the Creator and other creatures.

At this point we may say that the development of living creatures and especially animals, notwithstanding the frailty and vulnerability of their existence, carries with it a higher degree of independence than we find in atoms, molecules, stars, rivers, seas, or mountains. We do not refer to greater duration, in terms of which other forms of creation are far superior to living creatures. Nevertheless, independent existence reaches a higher stage with living creatures, i.e., independence as self-organization of the forms of existence. With living creatures we have for the first time self-directed activity that is not merely an effect of external causes. This type of activity is aimed at something outside, at the environment in and by which these creatures live.[368] In plants independent activity is limited by the fact that they are spatially fixed. Animals, in contrast, can move about freely. In relating to their environment, therefore, animals also relate to themselves, to the future of their own lives, as we see very clearly in their search for food. The reality around them, and with it the conditions of their own survival, is no longer simply external to them. Nevertheless, an express self-relation is still lacking prior to the stage of the human form of life, except perhaps in the case of chimpanzees.[369] There is not yet any consistent distinguishing of other things in objective reality as really other. Correspondingly there is no distinguishing of the future as future from the immediate present.

Related again is the fact that only humans learned to see divine reality in its distinction from everything finite. Only humans, it seems, have religion. Nevertheless, the vital movement of animals is already oriented to God. Young lions seek their meat from God when they roar after their prey (Ps. 104:21). As the relation to the environment and the future of personal life becomes more inward, so too does that to the Creator and his life-giving Spirit. Animals already have the breath of life in them so long as they breathe (Gen. 1:30).

The stage of the independence of creaturely existence that is reached with living creatures presupposes the elementary forms of enduring existence, i.e., atoms and molecules. Moreover, the spontaneity of the self-organization of living creatures rests on the ongoing working of the forces and laws that govern nonorganic events. It is not by direct divine creation, but by the detour of the expansion and cooling of the universe, the formation of atoms, molecules, and stars, and the development of planet earth with its atmospheric conditions that the independence of

---

368. Wicken, *Evolution, Thermodynamics, and Information*, p. 129: "With the emergence of autocatalytic organization, 'function' became a part of nature. The emergence of AOs [autocatalytic organizations] was accompanied by a gradual shift from the deterministic responses to impressed energy gradients that dominated the prebiotic phase of evolution to the exploitative transformations of environments that characterized its biotic phase."

369. Cf. D. R. Griffin, *The Question of Animal Awareness* (New York, 1976), pp. 30-33; also J. C. Eccles, "Animal Consciousness and Human Self-Consciousness," *Experientia* 38 (1982) 1384-91, esp. 1386ff.

creaturely existence became possible that took shape in plant and animal and finally human life.

If the act of creation aimed at the independence of creaturely existence, then in a certain sense we may justifiably say that we are to see the vastness of the expanding universe and its wealth of forms as a means to the development of organic life. This is not to say that the constructs of inorganic nature do not have their own beauty and meaning. By their very existence they praise God as their Creator. What we are saying is that full creaturely independence comes only with living creatures, and among them in a special sense with humans.

Of us, too, it must be said that our origin in the evolution of life is a condition of the independence of our existence as creatures. This being so, it is hard to see the point of the struggle against the evolutionary theory. Our evolutionary derivation does not rule out the immediacy of our relation to God. If animals already are related in their life's course to God and his Spirit, this is especially true of us. In us, however, there is the further fact that our relation to God is an express theme as a condition of our own creaturely life and our survival. We humans deal thematically with something that is a fact for all creaturely existence. All creatures owe their existence to the creative activity of God. Like us, they are referred to their relation to God and the working of his Spirit. Not just our human existence but the existence of all creatures before God is a theme as we realize and accept the fact that we stand before God as creatures. This is true as we set ourselves alongside all other creatures and speak on behalf of all of them by recognizing that we are creatures of God. For this reason, too, we are called to represent God in his rule over all his creation.

Creaturely independence[370] cannot exist without God or against him. It does not have to be won from God, for it is the goal of his creative work.[371] Apart from God the creature inevitably falls victim to its own corruptibility. To survive, it needs fellowship with the eternal God. This theme arises, of course, only when the creature can distinguish itself and

---

370. With it the creature attains individuality in the sense of D. Henrich, "Ding an sich," in *Vernunft des Glaubens. Wissenschaftliche Theologie und kirchliche Lehre*, ed. J. Rohls and G. Wenz (1988), pp. 42-92, esp. 55ff., 83ff.

371. There is a difference here from the Mesopotamian creation epic, in which humans are created to be slaves of the gods, doing their field work for them (Tablet VI, ll. 6-10 and 35f., in *ANET*, p. 68). Cf. the observations of T. Jacobsen in *Frühlich des Geistes*, ed. H. Frankfort, J. A. Wilson, and T. Jacobsen (1946; Stuttgart, 1954) on the relations between humans and gods in Mesopotamian religion.

all creaturely things in their finitude from the God who is eternal. This takes place at the human stage. When we distinguish ourselves and all creaturely things from God and thus subject ourselves with all creatures to God as Creator, thereby paying God the honor of his deity, the self-distinction of the eternal Son from the Father finds expression. Hence our determination as creatures aims at the incarnation of the Son and therefore at participation in the eternal fellowship of the Son with the Father. Involved, too, is the destiny of all creation, for all creatures are taken up with us into our self-distinction as creatures from God, so that with us they might be differentiated from God but also at the same time related to him as Creator.

Only in the light of the incarnation of the Son in our relation to God may it be said theologically that creation comes to fulfillment in us and that the whole universe was created with a view to us. For reasons that have yet to be discussed, this goal has not yet been fully attained. It has thus become the theme of a history with humanity and, in relation to humanity as a whole, the object of eschatological hope. The present reality of human life does not yet accord with it.

With these statements we are already moving by way of anthropology to christology and eschatology. But before we deal with anthropology as the next step on the way to explication of the revelation of God in Jesus Christ, we must again discuss creation from the standpoint of the whole process of its history, i.e., the creaturely world in the sequence of its forms. We shall need to take a final look at the constitution of the world as a whole in the light of its Creator.

III. CREATION AND ESCHATOLOGY

§ 1. Unity and Distinction of the Act of Creation and the Eschaton

The goal of all creation, not just humanity, is to share in the life of God. Why else should it sigh under the burden of corruptibility (Rom. 8:21f.)? As in the case of our own fall (8:26), we may view this sighing as an expression of the presence of the life-giving Spirit of God in creatures. The creative divine Spirit is vitally at work throughout creation, but also suffers with his creatures on account of their corruptibility prior to taking creative shape in humanity, in one man. Only thus, according to Paul, can the rest of creation participate in the liberty of the children of God (8:19, 21), i.e., in the eschatological future of the resurrection of the dead, which has already come in Jesus Christ but toward which Christians, like all others, are still moving.[372]

According to Paul, faith knows that God himself is present in his creation as its Creator and that the creation thus groans and feels pain because of the contradiction between its state and the goal that he set for it. Yet faith also has expectation and even hope that in due time God will set aside this contradiction.[373] Oriented to the eschatological consummation, this creative presence of God in the immanence of the creaturely world and its forms has given us occasion today to speak of a "sacramental" view of nature in Christianity.[374] Like the matter of the sacraments, the material universe is not just an outwardly visible sign of an invisible grace (God's presence) but a means to communicate it.[375] The related protest against a purely instrumental view of nature that abstracts away from God's creative working in nature and its constructs[376] is undoubtedly justified. It corresponds to the opposition of the Christian belief in creation to the secularist misinterpretation of the divine command to have dominion (Gen. 1:28), as though this handed over nature to us to exploit it as we wish (see above, pp. 131f.).

Nevertheless, in view of the related tendency to slip back into veneration of nature,[377] the term "sacramental" is not a happy one to express this truth. What is denoted by a sacrament is not the fact that the visibly material is a general sign of the invisibly spiritual, or that the former effectively mediates the latter. The term has a specific content, as we see plainly from the need that a sacramental sign be instituted. There is nothing of this kind relative to a sacramental universe. Institution singles out certain material elements and actions from the rest of

372. Cf. Wilckens, *Römer,* II, 152ff.
373. Ibid., p. 156; see also K. Koch, "The OT View of Nature," in *Anticipation* 25 (Geneva, 1979).
374. Cf. W. Temple, *Nature, Man, and God,* pp. 482ff.; Peacocke, *Science and the Christian Experiment,* pp. 178-88; and S. M. Daecke, "Profane and Sacramental Views of Nature," in *The Sciences and Theology in the Twentieth Century,* ed. A. R. Peacocke (Notre Dame, IN, 1981), pp. 127-40, esp. 134ff.
375. Temple, *Nature, Man, and God,* pp. 482ff. Cf. Peacocke, *Creation and the World of Science,* p. 290: "The world of matter, in its relation to God, has both the symbolic function of expressing his mind and the instrumental function of being the means whereby he effects his purpose."
376. Daecke, "Profane and Sacramental Views of Nature," p. 131, in connection with the ecumenical consultation on humanity, nature, and God held at Zurich in 1977. Cf. also Daecke's "Anthrozentrik oder Eigenwert der Natur?," in *Ökologische Theologie. Perspektiven zur Orientierung,* ed. G. Altner (1989), pp. 277-99.
377. Paul Verghese comes close to this in his *The Human Presence: An Orthodox View of Nature* (Geneva, 1978).

material reality and gives them a special function, i.e., that of being signs of God's saving decree on the world's behalf as we see it in Jesus Christ, and of being means of incorporation into his divine purpose.

General references to the sacramental nature of the universe generally omit the eschatological reference that is decisive for the understanding of nature in Rom. 8:19ff. But even a stress on this aspect does not justify the use of the word "sacramental." As creatures of God, constructs in the world of nature are both less than this and more — less because they do not have the specific orientation to the presence of future eschatological salvation in Jesus Christ that is bound up with the institution of a sacrament, more because natural forms themselves are the object of the divine will in creation and do not have their meaning in orientation to something else. We must thus reject any talk of the sacramental reality of creaturely things as too general and imprecise. Nevertheless, we may take a positive view of the thought that Teilhard de Chardin emphasizes, namely, that in the sacraments of the new covenant, and above all in the eucharistic bread and wine, all creation is taken up into the sacramental action of thanksgiving to God.

Creation's destiny of being in fellowship with God, in the sense of sharing in the fellowship of the eternal Son with the Father through the Spirit, has not yet found direct fulfillment in the existence of each individual creature. It could not do so because only at the human stage in the sequence of creaturely forms did express distinction come to be seen between God and all creaturely reality. Without this distinction there can be no creaturely participation in the self-distinction of the Son from the Father. Hence in Romans (8:21f.) all creation is waiting for the manifestation of sonship (8:15) in us, by which the creatures themselves will also be "sons" (8:19; cf. Gal. 4:5f.). Nevertheless, even with the rise of humanity in the sequence of creatures, participation in the Son's fellowship with the Father has not yet been attained. Not the first Adam, but only the last eschatological man who appeared in the person of Jesus Christ will be taken up by the Spirit into the fellowship of the Son with the Father (cf. 1 Cor. 15:45f.).

The tension between the emergence of humanity as the last link in the chain of creaturely forms and the fulfillment of humanity's destiny is connected with the fact that humans as creatures are meant to be independent beings. This is generally true of all creatures. But in this regard humans are the climax of the creaturely sequence. In order to enter into the relation of the Son to the Father as something other than God, the creature needed a prehistory of growing independence in a sequence of creaturely forms. Humans came into existence at the end of this sequence. But then their own independence had to be developed if the relation of the Son to the Father was to find manifestation in it. Certainly Jesus told us that if we do not receive the kingdom of God as little children, we cannot enter it (Mark 10:15). But he addressed this saying to the disciples, i.e., to adults. It is as creatures that have ripened to independence that we are to relate to God as children who expect and receive all things from the Father. Presupposed at least here is that we have learned to differentiate God from all else, from the whole sphere of creaturely reality. Presupposed, too, is the development of a general faculty of discernment, the ability to distinguish the otherness of things in their relations to each other and to the self. Included is the differentiation of everything finite, including the self, from the eternal God.

Creation and eschatology belong together because it is only in the eschatological consummation that the destiny of the creature, especially the human creature, will come to fulfillment. Yet creation and eschatology are not directly identical, at least from the creature's standpoint. For the creature, its origin is the past, in which it has the roots of its existence. It is thus inclined to orient itself to the past. This is true of humans in the early stages of the history of their self-awareness, as we see from its mythical form. For the creature, the future is open and uncertain. Nevertheless, creatures that are awakened to independence (i.e., living creatures) open themselves to the future as the dimension from which alone their existence can achieve content and fulfillment. In the creature's experience, however, the origin and the consummation do not coincide. They form a unity only from the standpoint of the divine act of creation. Even in this regard the structure of their unity demands more precise explanation.

We already touched on this theme in discussing creation as the act of God (see above, pp. 34 and 38ff.). The creation, preservation, and rule of the world are related aspects of the one divine act by which the three persons of the Trinity together bring forth the reality of the creaturely world that is distinct from God. In this regard we saw that the concept of creation relates to the overarching unity of the divine act, that the concept of preservation relates the existence of creatures to their beginning, and that the divine rule aims at the future consummation (see above, pp. 57f.). As regards the divine rule, we saw that creation ends only with the eschatological consummation. But what does that mean for the structure of the divine act of creation itself and for the resultant emergence of the creaturely world?

We can clarify this issue only now that we have discussed the world of creatures in terms of its general structure and the sequence of its forms. For in God's preserving and ruling the world, we have seen already ways in which God enters into the forms of the creatures' existence. Only in the light of our examination of creaturely reality, then, can we define more accurately the relation between creation and eschatology as it is grounded in the unity of the act of creation and as it develops in the history of the created world.

The unity of the divine act of creation precedes time and therefore also the distinction of beginning and end in the sense of logical precedence. For this reason God is said to the First and the Last (Isa. 44:6; 48:12; Rev. 1:8; cf. 21:6; 22:13). He is not restricted to being the First, nor is he only the Last (i.e., as a result of the cosmic process). He stands above the alternative of beginning and end and is Lord of both. But how are we to understand the relation of beginning and end in God's action and in regard to the cosmic process? How does the eternal God embrace the beginning and end of the creaturely world by not only bringing forth time as the form of existence for creation but by himself entering it in his preserving and ruling?

Insofar as the theological tradition has formulated such questions at all, it has either answered that the future of creation is grounded in its beginning or it has adduced the doctrine of divine foreknowledge. We find both answers together in Augustine. The difference is that the first response puts the reference to the future in created reality itself, whereas the second simply refers to the understanding of divine knowledge as foreknowledge.

The reference of the statement about creation to the world as a whole, and therefore to its ongoing in time and not just its beginning, repeatedly occupied Augustine in his exposition of Genesis. Manichean criticism of the first creation story, namely, that a beginning of the world seems to be the result of a capricious divine act and negates the eternity of God, evoked the reply of Augustine that time itself was created with the creatures (De Gen. contra Manich. 1.2.3 [PL, 34, 174f.; cf. also 53f.]). In this regard Augustine was following Ambrose's exposition of the creation of the world in six days (Hex. 1.6.20 [PL, 14, 132]), cf. also Basil (Hex. 1.5 [PG, 29, 13]). He pointed out that whereas the first account has six days, the second has only one (Gen. 2:4 Vulgate [PL, 34, 197f.]).

If he there related this statement specifically to the creation of time, in his final commentary on Genesis, like Ambrose and Basil before him, Augustine linked it to the unity of the act of creation in God's eternity, appealing to Sir. 18:1:

"Qui vivit in aeternum creavit omnia simul" (*De Gen. ad litt.* 4.33-35 [PL, 34, 317-20]; cf. 5.3 [PL, 34, 222f.]). He thus equated the sequence of creaturely times with the one day of God's creation (*De Gen. ad litt.* 4.35 [PL, 34, 320]; cf. above, n. 89). This statement, however, refers only to the sixth day of the first story relative to the one day of Gen. 2:4 (Sir. 18:1). As regards the ongoing cosmic process, Augustine thought he was tied to the biblical statement that creation ended on the sixth day (Gen. 2:1f.). He explained that no species have emerged since, though God continually produces new individuals as examples of the species (*De Gen. ad litt.* 5.20 [PL, 34, 325f., cf. 337f.]). Everything that follows the sixth day in time is grounded on the one hand in God's providence (5.18, 21ff. [PL, 34, 334, 336ff.]) and set on the other hand in the seeds and causes of the future, which belong to all things with their creation (6.8, 10f. [PL, 34, 344, 346]).[378]

The two ideas link (1) the thought that creation, as an eternal act, is simultaneous with the process of time and (2) the view of the first creation story that creation ended on the sixth day as world history commenced. This would subject all following events to an ineluctable necessity either of natural causes or of divine foreknowledge.[379] If all creaturely conduct is fixed by the past, there can be no true contingency or creaturely freedom in the course of events. This does not have to be so if divine knowledge, as in Augustine, is thought to be eternally simultaneous with all times. It is unavoidable, however, if this knowledge, as an ordaining foreknowledge, is linked to the idea of a creation that was completed at the beginning of time.[380] For then it is settled at the very beginning what must take place in the future.

The theology of the Latin Middle Ages constantly tackled this problem with great perspicacity, asking whether that which is contingently future in relation to preceding creaturely causes is robbed of its contingency by the divine prescience and thus takes place of necessity.[381] To avoid this conclusion it is not enough to point out that God foreknows

---

378. On Augustine's doctrine of *rationes seminales* (cf. *De Gen. ad litt.* 9.17.32 [PL, 34, 406]), cf. E. Gilson, *Introduction à l'étude de S. Augustin* (Paris, 1929), pp. 261ff., and esp. the antithesis to the modern theory of an evolution of species (p. 263). Augustine could not arrive at such a theory because of his conviction that creation ended on the sixth day. Cf. also A. Mitterer, *Der Entwicklungslehre Augustins* (1956).

379. Augustine *De Gen. ad litt.* 6.17.28 (PL, 34, 350).

380. This might be the reason for the fact, noted by L. Scheffczyk, that Augustine gives little prominence to the divine economy of salvation in his doctrine of creation; cf. "Schöpfung und Vorsehung," *HDG,* II/2a (1963), pp. 64f.

381. Cf. my dissertation *Die Prädestinationslehre des Duns Scotus* (1954), esp. pp. 17f., 90ff., 116ff.; also Bannach, *Lehre,* pp. 182ff., 249-75.

what is contingent *as* contingent, nor to argue that his eternity is simultaneous with everything creaturely, so that linking divine foreknowledge with the completion of the work of creation on the sixth day does not have to have deterministic implications. If, however, the immediacy of the divine action in creation to every creaturely present is emphasized by abolishing the distinction between creation and preservation and by rejecting any linkage of the divine action to a closed and actualized cosmic order,[382] the question of the unity of the divine action arises if the individual acts are not to seem to be completely arbitrary.

The question of the unity of the world on the basis of the act of creation, and also of the resultant structure, does not find an answer in the idea of an original creation supplemented by continuous creation. This is true even if, in distinction from the first creation story, we view the beginning of the world simply as the commencement of a continued act of creation. It was the function of the story to offer a basis for the unity of the creaturely world by depiction of the original creation. An established order formed this basis. From the outset, however, this idea stood in tension with other aspects of the divine action to which Israel's traditions bore witness. Taken alone, however, these themselves did not offer any self-enclosed understanding of the unity of cosmic reality.

The starting point of another view of God's creative work lay in Israel's traditions of God's saving acts in its history and in the prophetic idea of God's continued historical action. The history of God's acts of salvation and guidance, which was basic to the life of the people, was certainly thought to be a unity along with the promises to the fathers and the nationhood in Palestine that was fully achieved in the reign of David. But during the ensuing period of the monarchy this concept was replaced by the concept of judgment, which developed out of the message of the classical prophets. The disastrous end of the monarchy, which seemed to be out of tune with the basic promises, could thus be viewed as the result of a chain of constant transgressions of divine law. Furthermore, knowledge of an earlier history arising out of the election of Abraham could not be embodied without further development into a historical unity grounded in the correspondence of promise and fulfillment. Only the apocalyptic doctrine of the sequence of world empires (Dan. 2:36-45)

382. See Bannach, *Lehre*, on William of Occam (pp. 255ff., also 221ff.). As regards the divine act as such, Occam contested the difference between creation and preservation (pp. 213f.).

made possible a concept of the unity of universal history at all comparable with the universality of the first creation story.

This story for its part, however, was related in its total conception to the associated history of Israel. It carried with it a view of this history that saw a climax in the cultic laws of Sinai and especially in the sabbath command that was given there (Exod. 31:15-17).[383]

In a similar way, though with a different structure, Karl Barth related completed creation to the concept of the covenant (the epitome of God's saving will respecting creation). Barth did not view the covenant as a copy of the order of creation or of its completion in God's rest on the seventh day. He saw it instead as the goal of creation. In so doing he depicted the relation between creation and covenant as complementary, the covenant being the internal basis of creation, creation the external basis of the covenant.[384] As the determinative goal of creation, the covenant is its internal basis. In the divine counsel God's decree of election, and with it the covenant, precedes the creation of the world. In the execution of this decree the creation of the world makes possible the actualizing of the covenant. Barth thus extends the relation between creation and covenant to the covenant history of Israel and on to the new covenant set up by Jesus Christ. The creation of the world and humanity took place for the sake of the human fellowship with God that was achieved in Jesus Christ. Conversely, creation formed the starting point of the divine covenant history that aimed at Jesus Christ.

Though closely related, creation and the covenant were distinct for Barth because creation was limited to the world's beginning and could thus be no more than an external basis for the covenant history that followed. As in Augustine, the completion of creation at the beginning of the world meant that God's relation to the world was seen from the standpoint of the beginning, or rather of the divine foreknowledge that lies behind the beginning. Foreknowledge and foreordination thus take on the literal sense that from a standpoint prior to the beginning of the world, God foresees its course. Though the use of such terms may well express the origin of salvation in the eternity of God prior to all the chances of history (Matt. 25:34; Eph. 1:4; 1 Pet. 1:20), their literal application to the concept of God leads to an unfittingly anthropomorphic view of God, as though from some standpoint before the world's beginning God were looking ahead to a different future. Such a thought is hardly compatible with God's eternity and infinity.

383. Steck, *Schöpfungsbericht*, p. 253. The thought of a divine original for the sabbath (Exod. 31:17) finds a parallel in the idea of a heavenly sanctuary as a model for the earthly (25:9).

384. *CD*, III/1, 94ff., 228ff., cf. earlier on pp. 72f. We need not go into Barth's exegesis in linking the first story to creation as the external basis of the covenant and the second story to the covenant as the internal basis of creation.

No less problematical is that in his distinction between creation and covenant, Barth seemed to view only the latter and not the former directly as an expression of the love of God (*CD*, III/1, 97f.). If, according to Jesus' message, God's work as the Creator and Sustainer who causes his sun to shine on the good and the bad is a model and basis for the commandment of love (Matt. 5:44ff.), then we must see the creation of the world as already an expression of the love of God. The love with which God loved the world in sending his Son (John 3:16) does not differ in kind from the fatherly love of the Creator for his creatures. The sending of the Son proclaims the radical resoluteness of God's love as Creator for his creatures. Instead of separating God's covenant history from creation, the sending of the Son, from the incarnation to the resurrection, ascension, and glorious return, is to be seen as the fulfillment of God's creative work. But this, of course, demands a view of creation that does not limit it to the world's beginning.

An extension of the concept of creation to the whole history of the world was pioneered already in Jewish exposition of the seven days of the first creation story. In the ten-week apocalypse of 1 Enoch 91:11-17 and 93:1-10, the seven-day week of creation provided a key to the chronology of universal history and its division into ten weeks of years.[385] On the one hand the seven-day schema of the creation story was seen as a model of universal history. On the other hand the whole cosmic time of ʿolam (or ʿalam) was seen as the divinely appointed unity of space and time within which human life is lived.[386] Here the principle of presentation seems to be the division of time according to the sabbath command. Its role in creation constitutes only a special instance.

Some forms of apocalyptic expectation linked the eschatological consummation of the world to the idea of an eighth day of creation, which as the first day of a new week corresponds to the first day of creation in its function as a new beginning (4 Esdr. 7:31).[387] Others set the final consummation under the sign of the seventh day of God's sabbath rest. In this regard we may think of Hebrews and its description of the consummation of salvation for which Christians hope as an entry into the

---

385. K. Koch, "Sabbatstruktur der Geschichte: Die sogenannte Zehn-Wochen-Apokalypse (1. Hen. 93:1-10; 91:11-17) und das Ringen um die alttestamentlichen Chronologień im späten Israelitentum," *ZAW* 95 (1983) 404-30. Cf. Dan. 9:24-27.

386. Ibid., p. 427.

387. Cf. E. Lohse in *TDNT*, VII, 19ff. Such ideas may lie behind Rev. 20:2f., 7 and the idea of the millennial reign of Christ followed by the new creation in 21:1ff. Cf. E. Lohse, *Die Offenbarung Johannes*, NTD 11 (1960), p. 96.

rest of God (4:3-10).[388] A saying in 1 Enoch goes even further. It not only relates the completion of the world on the seventh day to the eschatological consummation of the world but sees the latter as the source of peace, i.e., as the origin of all consummation from the beginning. From the creation of the world peace issues forth from the coming aeon (71:15).

Clement of Alexandria reached a similar conclusion when he saw a correspondence between the first day of creation, the day of the creation of light, and the eighth day, the day of the new creation, which he equated with the day of the rest of God (*Strom.* 6.16.138f. [PG, 9, 346f.]). Clement called this the primal beginning of all that comes into being, the day that is also in truth the day of the creation of the light by which all is seen and all things are attained as an inheritance (138.1). We have here something like an attempt to think of the eschaton as the creative beginning of the cosmic process.

Such an attempt would correspond to the proclamation of God by Jesus to the effect that the eschatological coming of God is the starting point of a fresh assessment of everything past and present. Eschatology in the proclamation of Jesus is no longer an extrapolation of a tradition grounded in past salvation history and presupposing its authority. Its core content — the coming rule of God and our human relation to its future — is the criterion of a critical sifting and reinterpreting of everything that has been handed down. In Jesus, creation itself is set in the light of the eschatological future and becomes a parable of the divine rule.[389] To be sure, Jesus does not directly call creation the work of the coming God, but this view rests on the sense that typifies his message and that runs from the future of God to the world's past and present.

The universe and its history are thus set in a different light from that of the first creation story. The issue there, too, was the totality of world occurrence and not just the beginning. But the totality was seen to be grounded in the beginning. Such a view is characteristic of mythical conceptions, which trace back a normative order of the world to a basic

---

388. Cf. K.-H. Schwarte on Christian exposition of the seven weeks of Dan. 9:24-27 in Irenaeus and Hippolytus (*TRE*, III [1978], pp. 269f.); also his *Die Vorgeschichte der augustinischen Weltalterlehre* (Bonn, 1966). On the Middle Ages cf. J. Ratzinger, *Die Geschichtstheologie des Heiligen Bonaventura* (1959), pp. 16ff.

389. Cf. the observation of U. Wilckens in his "Understanding of Revelation within the History of Primitive Christianity," in *Revelation as History*, ed. W. Pannenberg (New York, 1968), p. 117 n. 35, on the inner connection in Jesus between the motifs of creation, providence, and the everyday on the one side, and the imminence of the rule of God on the other.

primal time that is both the beginning and the model of all that follows.[390]
Certainly the biblical creation stories are not myths in a technical sense,
but in their view of time we see parallels to the mythical understanding.
With their concept of a completion of the primal history they stand in
some tension with Israel's sense of election, which looks back from God's
deeds in the history of Israel to the beginning of the world as his first
historical act. For prophecy and apocalyptic, the divine action that decides
the meaning of history is oriented to the future of a definitive revelation
of God and his righteousness, not merely for the people of God but for
the world.

If the eschatological future of God in the coming of his kingdom
is the standpoint from which to understand the world as a whole, the view
of its beginning cannot be unaffected. This beginning loses its function
as an unalterably valid basis of unity in the whole process. It is now merely
the beginning of that which will achieve its full form and true individuality
only at the end. Only in the light of the eschatological consummation can
we of the world understand the meaning of its beginning. As R. Prenter
has rightly stressed, this comes to expression in the primitive Christian
proclamation that we must believe in Jesus Christ as the mediator of
creation as well as the eschatological bringer of salvation.[391] From the
standpoint of Christian typology all that preceded the earthly appearance
of Jesus is thus a shadowy prefiguration of the truth that came to light in
him. But can we reconcile this view of the relation between eschatology
and creation with the scientific description of the universe?

§ 2. Beginning and End of the Universe

Theological statements about the relation between creation and eschatology presuppose that it is meaningful to speak in some sense about the
beginning and end of the universe. But this presupposition is by no means
self-evident. Already in the patristic era Christian theology ran up against
views that held that the universe had no beginning and that it will be of
unlimited duration.

---

390. On this point cf. my "Christentum und Mythos," pp. 29f., 31ff.
391. R. Prenter, *Schöpfung und Erlösung. Dogmatik 1: Prolegomena. Die Lehre von
der Schöpfung* (1958), pp. 184ff.

Arguments for such ideas were found in both the view of the world and the concept of God. Aristotle found reasons in his *Physics* (8.1) for the view that time and movement have no beginning and will not end. He was aware that in this regard he agreed with most of his predecessors[392] but not at all with Plato, who alone had taught that time itself had a beginning (*Phys.* 251b.17f.; cf. *Tim.* 37d). Decisive for Aristotle was the argument that each Now in the time sequence is related to a Before and After (*Phys.* 251b.20ff.). Since time counts movement, the eternity of time means the eternity of movement as well (251b.13, cf. 27f.).

On Platonic presuppositions discussions of the immutability and eternity of God produced the same result. Thus Origen in Christian theology regarded the fact that the world had no beginning as a condition of calling God omnipotent, in no way restricted to a time that begins with the world's beginning (*De princ.* 1.2.10, cf. 1.4.5). Plotinus taught the eternity of the world as an implication of the fact that the origin of time from eternity must itself be thought of as timeless (*Enn.* 3.7.6), whereas everything temporal has to have something before it in time. In this view, which Proclus also adopted,[393] Neoplatonic and Aristotelian lines of argument converged.

Patristic theology argued against Origen's view that to make God dependent on the world as regards his attributes is to destroy the very concept of God.[394] In other respects, patristics, with its thesis that God created time in a timeless act,[395] could certainly meet the Aristotelian criticism of Plato's statement that time is creaturely, but it could not prove a beginning of time (and creation)[396]

392. Cf. W. Wieland, "Die Ewigkeit der Welt," in *Die Gegenwart der Griechen im neueren Denken. Festschrift H.-G. Gadamer* (Tübingen, 1960), pp. 297f.

393. See Beierwaltes, *Denken des Einen*, p. 169. Plotinus, he says, argued that if the world came into being with time and if the beginning of time is seen as a timeless event, then the world can have no beginning in time. Cf. also his *Plotin über Ewigkeit und Zeit (Enneade III, 7)* (1967), pp. 213f.

394. Methodios of Olympos, *Liber de creatis,* fragment II (PG, 18, 336B; cf. also fragment V [340B]). John Philoponos in his work *De aeternitate mundi contra Proclum* (529) was the first to offer a cogent argument against the thesis that there is contradiction between the immutability of God and a temporal beginning of creation, his point being that there is no link between an essential attribute and its exercise in an act (cf. E. Behler, *Die Ewigkeit der Welt. Problemgeschichtliche Untersuchungen zu den Kontroversen um Weltanfang und Weltunendlichkeit in der arabischen und jüdischen Philosophie des Mittelalters* [1965], pp. 134f.).

395. Cf. already Clement of Alexandria *Strom.* 6.16.142.2, 4 (PG, 9, 369C, 372 A), following Philo in *Leg. all.* 1.2.

396. Against the argument that the circular form of celestial movements shows that they have neither beginning nor end, Basil pointed out that the circles that we draw in fact have a beginning (*Hex.* 1.3 [PG, 9A-C]; cf. Ambrose *Hex.* 1.3.10 [PL, 14, 127B-C]). But this could no more rank as a rational refutation of philosophical arguments for a nonbeginning of time than the thesis that since the parts of the world are corruptible, so is the whole (Ambrose *Hex.* 1.3.11 [PL, 14, 127]; cf. Basil *Hex.* [PG, 11A]).

such as the biblical creation story seemed to imply. The Neoplatonists had inferred a nonbeginning of time from the timelessness of its origin. Against this one might advance the biblical statement that "in the beginning" God created heaven and earth (Gen. 1:1). One might also point christologically to Christ as the beginning of creation (John 1:1). The difficulty might thus be avoided.[397]

In his Genesis commentary Augustine actually related the beginning of time (in the narrow sense) to the fourth day of creation, the creation of the stars,[398] whereas Basil and Ambrose linked it to the creation of heaven and earth (Gen. 1:1).[399] In a broader sense of time that is not linked to the heavenly bodies, Augustine took the same view, having regard to the creation of angels, who were created before heaven and earth, for among spiritual beings, too, there is change and movement, though not corporeal.[400] In *The City of God* Augustine allows that angels always were. Yet they are not eternal like the Creator, because the mutability of time is not the same as immutable eternity.[401] Everything else, for Augustine, has a beginning in time. Time itself is not without a beginning (though not in the temporal sense), because it is a creature.[402]

The Middle Ages hotly debated the question whether the world has no beginning, as we see already in the Arab and Jewish philosophy and theology of the 11th and 12th centuries.[403] Christian Scholasticism had to wrestle more intensively with the Aristotelian and Neoplatonic arguments against a temporal beginning of the world. Most theologians accepted the doctrine, made obligatory at the Fourth Lateran Council in 1215, that the world had a temporal beginning. They thought that they could demonstrate this rationally.[404] Aquinas, however, did not regard the stated arguments as adequate. He thought it enough to maintain the

---

397. *De Gen. ad litt.* 1.2.6, 4.9, and 9.15ff.

398. Ibid., 2.14.28f.

399. Ambrose *Hex.* 1.6.20 (PL, 14, 132A). Cf. Basil *Hex.* 1.5 [PG, 29, 13C]). Augustine shared this view in his commentary on Genesis against the Manichees (1.2.3 [PL, 34, 174f.]).

400. *De Gen. ad litt.* 3.8 (PL, 34, 222f.).

401. *Civ. Dei* 12.16 (CChrSL, 48, 372). Cf. 11.6 (CChrSL, 48, 326).

402. *De Gen. ad litt.* 3.8 (PL, 34, 323).

403. High points in the discussion were Al-Gazali's indication of contradictions in the Aristotelian arguments, the defense of Aristotle against this criticism by Averroes, and the thesis of Moses Maimonides that there are limits to the teaching of Aristotle and that the doctrine of creation that views the whole world as a contingent result of the divine will has greater explanatory force. Cf. Behler, *Die Ewigkeit der Welt*, pp. 149ff., 212ff., 262ff.

404. DS § 800 = ND § 19: "the creator . . . who by His almighty power from the beginning of time made at once out of nothing both orders of creatures, the spiritual and the corporeal, that is, the angelic and the earthly. . . ." Cf. DS § 3002 = ND § 412.

possibility of a beginning of the world in time after refuting arguments to the contrary.[405]

A beginning of the world does not follow necessarily from the eternity and immutability of its divine origin if this is an act of will whose content and result are contingent.[406] On the same basis God, if he had so willed, might have created a world with no beginning in time. We can prove that the world is creaturely and dependent on God as the first cause, but not that it had a beginning in time.[407] We can treat this only as an empirical fact or, since no one was there at the beginning, as a matter of faith.

Thus far the view of Aquinas prevailed in the age that followed.[408] It helped considerably to sharpen the sense of the dependence of the existing order on God's creative will and thus prepared the way for the late medieval voluntarism that the younger Franciscan school, especially Scotus and Occam, carried much further than Aquinas did initially.[409] Yet Aquinas did not weaken the empirical-phenomenological arguments of Aristotelian physics against a beginning of movement and time with the same force as he did the arguments based on the concept of God. This is especially true relative to the argument from the nature of time (*Phys.* 251b.20ff.). Against the argument that the continuity of movement rules out any beginning (251b.28-252a.5) Aquinas objected that the creative will of God can create a movement that no other movement precedes.[410] But the argument from the nature of time is to the effect that no time is conceivable in which a Now does not follow something else. Christian

---

405. *SCG* 2.31-38, cf. 2.1.1.5. In *De pot. Dei* 3.17 Aquinas appeals directly to Maimonides.

406. *ST* 1.46.1.

407. Ibid. 1.46.2. Cf. *Quodl.* 12.6.1, and esp. 12.2.2 with the thesis that God might very well create something that in some sense (but not every sense) is infinite. Cf. *De pot. Dei* 3.14c.

408. Most instructive in this regard is the treatment of Aquinas in Duns Scotus *Ord.* 2 d 1, q. 3 (Vatican ed. [1973], VII, 50-91), esp. the answering of the objection that the idea of a reality that is different from God but unlimited in time implies a contradiction (pp. 77f., nn. 154f.).

409. For this reason there is no force to the objections of Friedrich Schlegel, A. Günther, and J. Frohschammer against Aquinas that by not giving a rational proof for the beginning of the world in time, he undercut the metaphysical basis of the Christian faith both as regards the intention of its teaching and the function of this teaching in the history of theology. Cf. Behler, *Die Ewigkeit der Welt*, pp. 22ff.

410. *SCG* 2.34; cf. *ST* 1.46.1 ad 5.

Scholasticism viewed this merely as an auxiliary argument to that from motion, the Before and After of time being dependent on motion.[411] In the Physics of Aristotle, however, the argument from motion rested on the argument from time. The question arose, then, whether the idea of the creation of a first movement does not contain a contradiction, since the idea of a first in time seems to be against the nature of time, in which there must be a Before and After for every Now.

The Aristotelian argument from time also formed the starting point for opposing a beginning of the world in the antithesis of the first cosmological antinomy of Kant.[412] The argument could also be used against the resultant notion of an empty time before the beginning of the world. For Kant, too, such a time was purely imaginary, for there was nothing in it to make the beginning possible.[413] What is before in time is obviously not detachable from regress in the sequence of causes.[414] This relation is presupposed in Kant's later note regarding the unsatisfactory nature of a view of the world that includes its beginning in time. As Kant saw it, such a view is not big enough for our concept of understanding in the necessary empirical regress. For the beginning always presupposes a preceding time, hence it is not unconditioned, and the law of the empirical use of the understanding demands that we ask concerning some higher condition in time (*Critique of Pure Reason,* B 514f.).

Kant's argument, of course, could not rule out the possibility of this law being a matter of subjectivity, or at least of subjectivity as Kantian philosophy describes it. If, with Hegel, limit (beginning and end) and its crossing are of the nature of the finite (see n. 414), and if that which exists

411. *ST* 1.46.1 ad 7, cf. Scotus *Ord.* 2 d 1, q. 3 ad 2 (Vatican ed. [1973], VII, 88, n. 174). In itself, the Before in time is merely imaginary.

412. *Critique of Pure Reason,* pp. 266f. Since the beginning is something preceded by a time in which there is nothing, there must have been a preceding time in which the world did not exist, i.e., an empty time.

413. Ibid. In empty time nothing can come into being, since no part of such a time has, in contrast to any other part, any distinct condition of existence rather than nonexistence.

414. This fact caused Hegel to comment that the argument of the antithesis in Kant's first antinomy rests on the presupposition that there is no unconditioned existence, no absolute limit, but the existence of the world always demands a preceding cause (*Science of Logic* [London, 1969], pp. 254ff.). The thesis and antithesis together tell us that there is a limit and that this limit is crossed only to the extent that it has something beyond it with which it nevertheless is in relation (ibid.). For Hegel this contradiction was of the very nature of finitude (*Encyclopädie,* PhB, 33 [1959], pp. 209f., *Encyclopedia* § 258). He criticized Kant for laying the burden of this contradiction on reason only in order to free nature from it (*Science of Logic,* pp. 237f.).

finitely is temporal and corruptible to the degree that its transcending remains outside it,[415] then the question unavoidably arises afresh whether a beginning in time is not in any case of the very nature of the finite. Whether this applies to the world as a whole then depends on whether the world as a whole is finite or infinite. This is the real issue behind the debates about the beginning or nonbeginning of the world, whether in the older controversies or in the alternative models of modern physical cosmology.

Modern belief in the infinity of the world is a result of the link between the Copernican revolution in our view of the world and the geometric conception of space in modern science.[416] When Giordano Bruno came to view unlimited Euclidian space as natural space filled with an incalculable number of solar systems, the idea arose of the infinity of the spatial universe. Carrying over the idea to time was secondary, and it took place only hesitantly.[417] The precritical Kant still accepted a beginning (though not an end) of the world[418] but thought of the planetary system as the result of mechanical processes and not as the direct work of an intelligent Author, as Newton did.

415. For Hegel the finite is corruptible and temporal because, unlike the concept, it is not in itself total negativity but has it in itself as its general nature, yet not one-sidedly, relating to it as its *power* (*Encyclopedia* § 258).

416. For the history of this process see A. Koryé, *From the Closed World to the Infinite Universe* (New York, 1958). In contrast to the view commonly expressed after Descartes that Nicholas of Cusa had argued earlier for an infinite world (cf. C. F. von Weizsäcker, *World View of Physics*, pp. 136ff., 149f.), Koyré shows that Nicholas deliberately avoided such a thesis, saying only that the world is unlimited (*interminatum*) (*Newtonian Studies*, pp. 48f.). The step to an infinite world was taken only under the influence of Copernican cosmology (in opposition, however, to Kepler [pp. 55ff.]), specifically by Thomas Digges in 1576, even before Bruno (pp. 35ff.), who was nevertheless the first to think of geometric space as the space of the universe (pp. 46f.). The 14th-century infinitists had contended only for the possibility of an infinite world as an expression of the infinite power of God as Creator (A. Maier, *Die Vorläufer Galileis im 14. Jahrhundert* [1949], pp. 155-215). Bruno argued that there is a necessary correspondence between God's actual work as Creator and the scope of his power (Koyré, *Closed World*, pp. 42f.).

417. We do not find it in Bruno, at any rate not in the quotation adduced by Blumenberg, *Legitimität der Neuzeit*, pp. 551f., from Bruno's *De la causa, principio e uno*, III (*Dialoghi italiani*, ed. G. Gentile [3rd ed. 1958], pp. 280f.), which simply refers to the correspondence between the world and God in the schema of explication and complication, cf. pp. 281f.

418. *Allgemeine Naturgeschichte und Theorie des Himmels* (1755), p. 114 (ET *Universal Natural History and Theory of the Heavens* [Ann Arbor, MI, 1969]), where Kant argues that creation is never complete. It began at one point but will never end. The restriction is the more remarkable in view of Kant's statement that the revelation of the divine qualities is as infinite as they themselves are (p. 106).

The victorious march of the idea of an infinity of the world was first arrested by the traditional distinction between unlimited series of spatial and temporal conditions on the one hand and the intensive, perfect, simple, and indivisible infinity of God on the other. Bruno and Descartes still clung to this Augustinian distinction.[419] The distinction faded only when Henry More equated infinite geometric space with the incommensurability and omnipresence of God and when Isaac Newton made the absoluteness of space and time the basis of his physics. More, and even Spinoza, indeed still distinguished between the spiritual extension of God and bodily space,[420] but when 18th-century physics, departing from Newton's spiritual interpretation of force, and especially gravity,[421] detached the idea of absolute space and time from the concept of God, there resulted the concept of a universe that may be thought of as unlimited in time and space. Kant's doctrine of the antinomies again related the idea of the infinity of the world to that of unlimited space and time[422] and in so doing distinguished it from the perfection of God. No answer was hereby given to More's question to Descartes whether an unlimited continuation of determinations in space and time does not presuppose that in the universe there is neither a beginning nor a limit to cosmic space.[423] This is the case only if, unlike Kant, we think of the world as a whole.[424]

A final chapter in the story of the development of belief in the infinity of the world deals with the mathematical theory attributable to Bernhard Bolzano. Although this theory does not relate directly to cosmology, it formed the climax and conclusion of the transfer of the idea of infinity from God to the world because it seemed to permit a mathematical definition of the actual infinite and therefore its physical application. Bolzano viewed the

419. Cf. Koyré, *Closed World*, pp. 56f., on Bruno's *De immenso et innumerabilibus* (Opera lat. I/1, 286f., 291), also pp. 101ff. on Descartes's *Principia philosophiae*, II, § 22, cf. I, § 26; see also pp. 111ff. On Augustine cf. nn. 400f. above.

420. Koyré, *Closed World*, pp. 143f.

421. See above, pp. 79f.; also N. J. Buckley, "The Newtonian Settlement and the Origin of Atheism," in *Physics, Philosophy, and Theology,* ed. R. J. Russell et al. (Notre Dame, IN, 1988), pp. 81-99.

422. *Critique of Pure Reason*, pp. 268f. A. Antweiler, *Die Anfangslosigkeit der Welt nach Thomas von Aquin und Kant* (1961), p. 113, rightly points out that Kant is here implicitly adopting a concept of infinity along the lines of Anselm's "than which no greater can be thought."

423. For More's letter to Descartes see Descartes's *Oeuvres,* ed. Adam-Tannery, V, 235ff. Cf. Koyré, *Closed World*, pp. 109, 242.

424. Kant, *Critique of Pure Reason,* § B 550f.; cf. § B 532f.: "The world, then, is not an unconditioned totality, nor does it exist as such, whether with infinite or finite size."

actual infinite as the epitome or aggregate of a plurality made up of infinitely many parts.[425] For the first time, then, it seemed possible, contrary to the tradition deriving from Aristotle, to regard the universe as not merely potentially but actually infinite.[426] On this theory, again, the universe is not the only infinite mass. Hence the idea of the infinity of the world lost its conceptually extraordinary character.

An objection to this idea of an infinite mass or aggregate is that underlying it is the concept of the finite parts of which it is composed. The ostensibly actual infinity of the aggregate thus depends on the potential infinity of the synthesis of finite parts or their infinite divisibility. This is the basis of intuitionist criticism of the theory. In addition to showing contradictions and paradoxes in the idea of infinite aggregates,[427] intuitionist mathematics also argued that there can be no actually infinite totalities, since such cannot be constructed out of elements. Certainly we can always construct more than we have already constructed, which always remains only finitely many.[428] In fact, then, the concept of an infinite

425. R. Bolzano, *Paradoxien des Unendlichen* (1851, 1964), 15f. (§ 14). Unlike Descartes (*Med.* III, 28), Bolzano thought the concept of the infinite derived from that of the finite and denoted an aggregate or multiplicity of finite units (§ 2, cf. §§ 10f.). He did not consider the philosophical concept of the infinite as the condition for conceiving of anything finite.

426. Thus Bolzano spoke of the infinite also in the sphere of reality itself (*Paradoxien des Unendlichen,* p. 36, § 25), primarily with reference to God, but also to creatures, in view of the infinity of God's will and power. For the aggregate of these creatures has to be infinite, as also that of the conditions that they individually experience over no matter how short a time (p. 36). On space and time cf. pp. 38, 77f. (§§ 27, 39). Kant could still say that an infinite and unlimited world is too large for any empirical concept (*Critique of Pure Reason,* § B 515).

Georg Cantor, however, who developed Bolzano's theory mathematically, in opposition to Kant's doctrine of antinomies argued for using the concept of infinity without distinction as regards the actual infinite (letter to G. Eneström, 4 November 1885, in G. Cantor, *Zur Lehre vom Transfiniten. Gesammelte Abhandlungen aus der Zeitschrift für Philosophie und philosophische Kritik 1* (Halle, 1890), quoted in H. Meschkowski, *Das Problem des Unendlichen. Mathematische und philosophische Texte von Bolzano, Gutberlet, Cantor, Dedekind* (1974), p. 122. Cantor distinguished between the potential and the actual infinite, defining the former as a mutable, finite quantity that moves out beyond all finite limits, the latter as a fixed and constant quantum that lies beyond all finite limits (p. 121). Cantor liked to speak of the transfinite rather than the actual infinite but expressly equated the two (pp. 118ff.). Only the absolute cannot be increased by the addition of any other elements, not the actual infinite in its distinction from the potential (pp. 121f.).

427. Cf. H. G. Steiner, "Mengenlehre," *HWP,* V (1980), 1053f.

428. This is how C. F. von Weizsäcker (*World View of Physics,* pp. 172f.) summarizes the intuitionist argument. Cf. M. Dummett, *Elements of Intuitionism* (Oxford, 1977), pp. 55-65. We find no claim to actual infinity in the type theory of A. N. Whitehead and

aggregate amounts to no more than potential infinity as an unlimited continuation of finite steps.

The insight into the paradoxes of the aggregate theory might be taken today as an illustration of the way in which physical cosmology has abandoned the idea of an infinite universe. The change came with the theory of relativity, which taught us to see space and time as dependent on the mass and velocity of bodies and thus permitted us to think of the world as spatially unlimited yet finite.[429] Then came E. Hubble's discovery of the expansion of the universe and with it the conclusion that the movement had a beginning when all cosmic matter must have been compressed into the smallest possible space. From the middle of the 20th century the Big Bang as the beginning of expansion — first five billion, then fifteen billion years ago — has become the standard model for physical cosmology.[430]

For the first time cosmology could now make the whole universe in both its spatial and its temporal extension a subject of empirical research.[431] A new situation thus arose for the philosophical question as to the world in its totality. Kant rejected an idea of this kind as empirically meaningless, and this was the basis of his discussion of the cosmological antinomies (see n. 424). For him the unity of the world was no more than a way of linking experiences. Against this it could, of course, be argued that rational thought requires more definite ideas of the world as a whole. But only modern physics has actually demonstrated that such an idea does not in any way go beyond the limits of empirical knowledge or lead to an untenable illusion, but that it is empirically indispensable as well as possible.

Does the now-standard model of an expanding universe mean that the world had a temporal beginning? At first glance, the answer seems

---

B. Russell, *Principia Mathematica* (Cambridge, 1913, repr. 1961), pp. 37ff. Cf. also D. Hilbert, "Über das Unendliche" (1925), in *Hilbertiana. Fünf Aufsätze* (Darmstadt, 1964), pp. 79-108, esp. 82f., 108.

429. On the cosmological application of Riemann's views of space that made this possible, cf. Stegmüller, "Evolution des Kosmos," pp. 501f.; also the succinct remarks of B. Kanitscheider, *Kosmologie. Geschichte und Systematik in philosophischer Perspektive* (1984), p. 156.

430. For a history of the model from its inception with A. Friedmann (1922) and for the most important variants, cf. Hawking, *Brief History of Time*, pp. 40ff. Cf. also J. S. Trefil, *Im Augenblick der Schöpfung*, and esp. Weinberg's classic *First Three Minutes*.

431. Stegmüller, "Evolution des Kosmos," p. 505, and Kanitscheider, *Kosmologie*, p. 148, quoting D. W. Sciama's judgment; cf. also Sciama's *Modern Cosmology* (1971; New York, 1975).

unquestionably to be yes. The world is said to be some fifteen billion years old. In a statement that attracted much attention Pius XII on 22 November 1951 claimed that the new physics confirms the Christian belief in creation with its theory of a beginning of the world in finite time, and that we thus have the basis of a new proof of the existence of God.[432] This statement ran into much criticism.[433] In fact the assumption of a temporal beginning is less clear and not so inescapable as might appear at first glance. And even if the universe did have a temporal beginning, we cannot immediately see here the basis of a proof of God's existence. Different interpretations are possible.

The difficulties in the question of a temporal beginning rest on the fact that the flux of time does not depend on material processes. As temporal measures are relative according to relativity theory,[434] the time of the early universe with its elementary processes raises special problems for the understanding of the flux of time. It is true that in the standard model of an expanding universe the curve of the expansion, if we follow it backward in time, leads to a point where mass is infinitely dense and space infinitely compressed. But reconstructions of this history lead only to proximity to this point, not to $t = 0$, since we cannot determine any physical state for the actual starting point.[435] It is possible that close to the beginning, subjective time is extended according to the degree of closeness, as in the proximity of the event-horizon

432. *Acta Apostolicae Sedis* 44 (1952) 31ff. Cf. esp. the section (C) on the universe and its development and the conclusions, i.e., creation in time, a Creator, and therefore God — the message that the papacy demanded of science, though not expressly, and that most people expected. See, however, the more cautious utterance of John Paul II in his message on 1 July 1988 to the director of the Vatican Observatory, Rev. Georg V. Coyng, on the three hundredth anniversary of the publication of Newton's *Principia;* cf. R. J. Russell et al., eds., *Physics, Philosophy, and Theology,* pp. 11f. John Paul II pointed out that the dialogue of theologians with scientists "would prevent them from making uncritical and overhasty use for apologetic purposes of such recent theories as that of the 'Big Bang' in cosmology."

433. Cf. the examples in Hawking, *Brief History of Time,* pp. 54ff. Many suggest that scientists were feverishly looking for alternatives, since they did not think the findings of science could be in harmony with church teaching. On such reactions cf. S. L. Jaki, *Science and Creation: From Eternal Cycles to an Oscillating Universe* (New York, 1974), pp. 346ff.

434. Hawking, *Brief History of Time,* p. 33, says rather inexactly that the theory of relativity did away with the idea of absolute time. As we have shown, it is only the measure or duration of time that is relative as a result of its dependence on the velocity of light. The temporal sequence of events is not affected.

435. Kanitscheider, *Kosmologie,* p. 309; cf. Weinberg, *First Three Minutes,* pp. 133, 148f.

of black holes.[436] Thus the question of an absolutely first event may not be nonsensical, but it is also not answerable.

Nevertheless, every finite process in time has a beginning. Insofar as we think of the universe in toto as a finite process, to that extent we must assume that as such it had a temporal beginning, notwithstanding the relativity of temporal processes and measures. Modern ideas of a universe that is unlimited in space and time (not just in one direction but in every direction) see the parts of the world as finite but do not see the world in toto as a finite process. In contrast, physical cosmology with its standard model of an expanding universe suggests finitude at least as regards the beginning. There is no empirical reason to view the expanding universe as part of a total pulsating movement in which phases of expansion and contraction succeed one another, so that fresh expansion comes after contraction. The cyclical model certainly cannot be applied to the course of time in the sense that the processes in time will be the same in each cycle. In view of the irreversibility of the course of time, the finitude of the cosmic process carries with it a distinction of the beginning from the end.

Physics perhaps cannot determine the beginning. For this reason we cannot base the thesis that there was a beginning in time directly on the findings or implications of physics. Nor can we infer it conceptually from the nature of the finite, for it depends on whether we can transfer such a concept from finitude to the world as a whole. Nor can we justify the theory as a truth of revelation outside the natural events that we can

436. On the problem of time close to black holes cf. Hawking, *Brief History of Time*, pp. 87ff. For quantum processes Hawking proposes what he calls imaginary time. A reconstruction of cosmology on this basis might depict the universe as a space-time of finite size but with no limit or margin (pp. 134ff.) and also with no beginning or end. For the relevance of this in physics and theology cf. the discussion in C. I. Isham, "Creation of the Universe as a Quantum Process," in *Physics, Philosophy, and Theology*, ed. R. J. Russell et al. (Notre Dame, IN, 1988), pp. 374-408, esp. 397ff. On problems in postulating a first event cf. R. Torretti, "Kosmologie als ein Zweig der Physik," in *Moderne Naturphilosophie*, ed. B. Kanitscheider (1984), pp. 183-200, esp. 197. On similar problems as regards the end in the model of a closed universe, cf. Tipler, "Omega Point as *Eschaton*," p. 227: "Closed universes end in a finite singularity of infinite density, and the temperature diverges to infinity as this final singularity is approached. This means that an ever increasing amount of energy is required per bit near the final singularity." With approach to the singularity, as much free energy is available as suffices "for an infinite amount of information processing between now and the end of time in a closed universe. Thus although a closed universe exists for only a finite proper time, it nevertheless could exist for an infinite subjective time, which is the measure of time that is significant for human beings."

observe and reconstruct. It needs an empirical basis. In fact modern cosmology has given it such a basis. If, in spite of Kant, it is meaningful and necessary to think of the whole process of the universe as a totality, and if this total process is finite in space and time, then it has to have a temporal beginning. We should not say a beginning "in" time as though an empty time preceded it, but a beginning of time itself, yet a beginning that for its part is already temporally defined as the beginning of a sequence of moments in time. The theory suggests itself that in such a beginning phase time itself takes shape as a sequence of events and a measurable flow. Subjective or imaginary time may thus extend itself to infinity close to the beginning. But objectively, i.e., relative to the total process of the universe, the beginning fixes a boundary separating it not from some preceding time but from eternity.[437]

Similar problems arise with the idea of an end of the world. At the latest with the rise of apocalyptic, the biblical tradition is acquainted with the concept of an end of the world, which it linked to hope of the future of the kingdom of God. For Christian theology the expectation that is determined by such ideas and that has been fused with the belief in Christ's return has retained its fundamental significance, notwithstanding great differences in views regarding the span of time still remaining until the end. More precise discussion of this theme must wait until we reach our chapter on eschatology. We mention it here only from a special standpoint, namely, in relation to the fact that the finitude of the world, insofar as its has a temporal structure, includes its end.

For modern thinking this idea has seemed to be much more alien than that of a beginning of the world. The reason probably lies in the relatively lesser prominence that 17th-century science gave to final explanations of the world, and especially in its understanding of the world of nature in general. Thus Descartes conceived of the world as originally created by God. In view of God's immutability, however, Descartes thought that he should trace back all further changes to created things themselves and their

437. Kanitscheider, *Kosmologie,* p. 440, criticizes Kant's argument in the antithesis of the first antinomy on the ground that with the statement that an empty time has to precede a beginning of the world, Kant overlooked the Augustinian alternative that space-time itself came into being with the first event. He refers in support to G. J. Whitrow, "The Age of the Universe," *British Journal for the Philosophy of Science* 5, no. 19 (1954) 215-25, and to B. Ellis, "Has the Universe a Beginning in Time?," *Australian Journal of Philosophy* 33 (1955) 32-37. Cf. Weinberg, *First Three Minutes,* p. 149: "It is at least logically possible that there was a beginning and that time itself has no meaning before that moment."

interactions.[438] The idea of unchanging laws of nature also followed from the divine immutability.[439] Kant, too, in his *Allgemeine Naturgeschichte* of 1755 spoke quite naturally of a beginning of creation but added at once that it would never end (see n. 418). Only with the second law of thermodynamics has physics come to take into account again an end to the world, though primarily only in the sense of a state of thermodynamic equilibrium, the so-called death of heat.[440] The cosmological model of an expanding universe in one of its variants then led to an essentially more radical idea of a world's end, at least in some still far distant future.

The question arose whether the movement of expansion, though prolonged, would continue forever, or whether through the effect of gravity it would be braked to a standstill and then enter a phase of contraction that would finally bring it to a singularity similar to the beginning, a point of unlimited density and compression. Since the discovery and investigation of so-called black holes, examples have been found of processes that might result in this kind of future for the universe.[441] Along with the possibility of continued cosmic expansion throughout space-time and the opposing possibility of a reversal to contraction until the collapse of matter brings the history of the universe to an end, there is also the possibility of a flattening of the curve of expansion and an indefinite stable phase when the forces of expansion come into balance with gravitation.[442] Choosing between these models depends on the as yet unclarified question of the total mass or density of matter in the universe. Although physical cosmology has thus far inclined to opt for a flat universe, newer findings suggest a greater mass than hitherto suspected, with the implication that the operation of gravity might lead to a reversal from expansion to contraction.

Do such considerations have any relevance for the theological

438. Descartes, *Principia philosophiae*, II, §§ 36f.

439. Ibid., § 37.

440. C. F. von Weizsäcker, *Geschichte der Natur*, pp. 37f. Cf. also K. Heim, *Weltschöpfung und Weltende* (1952, 2nd ed. 1958), pp. 114ff., 121ff., who, in the words of Dubois-Reymond, found in the thermodynamic process of the world's end a "scientific eschatology."

441. S. W. Hawking and R. Penrose, "The Singularities of Gravitational Collapse and Cosmology," *Proceedings of the Royal Society of London* (A) 314 (1969/70) 529-48. Cf. Hawking, *Brief History of Time*, pp. 81ff.

442. On the three options of an open, closed, or flat curve of cosmic expansion, cf. Hawking, *Brief History of Time*, pp. 42ff. Hawking himself favored an open or flat curve because, on the basis of the information available at the time of writing, the mass of matter did not seem to be enough to cause a reversal to contraction.

question of the end of the world? Already in discussions of the heat death of the universe it has rightly been pointed out that such an event would be well beyond our human future, since the conditions of organic life would come to an end much sooner. In biblical expectation, however, the end of the world stands closely related to that of human history, and it is an object of more or less imminent expectation. If our world is to correspond to the model of a closed universe that after a phase of contraction collapses into a final singularity analogous to the beginning, this end would be billions of years after the point has been reached when organic life, and with it human life, would no longer be possible.

In connection with discussion of the anthropic principle of Barrow and Tipler, the thought has been advanced that the emergence of intelligent life cannot be a transitory phenomenon. If the whole universe is oriented to such life, it will continue until intellectual dominion is attained over the whole universe, even though the basis of organic life is lost.[443] But would this be a human form of existence? In a more developed version of the anthropic model Tipler has related the end point of full intellectual dominion over the universe to the concept of God rather than to a higher development of human intelligence.[444] Nevertheless, an important point that lends cogency to his argument is his relating of the intelligence that has emerged in the universe with humanity to possible participation in the reality of God that comes to fulfillment in the omega of the universe. This participation would not be possible without assuming that intelligent life continues to the end of the universe, since the divine reality, according to Tipler, does not come into being only at the omega but is to be thought of as free from all the restrictions of time at the omega. Therefore, in terms of the eschatological future, this divine reality is present at each phase of the cosmic process, and hence as already the creative origin of the universe at the beginning of its course.

The presupposition of a continuation of human life is necessary from another standpoint as well, namely, from that of the postulate (accepted by Barrow and Tipler) that the emergence of human or intelligent life in the process of the evolution of the universe must have constitutive and not just ephemeral significance for the process as a whole. Human

---

443. Barrow and Tipler, *Anthropic Cosmological Principle*, pp. 266ff.

444. Tipler, "Omega Point as *Eschaton*," pp. 229f. For an intermediate phase in this development cf. his essay "The Omega Point Theory: A Model of an Evolving God," in *Physics, Philosophy, and Theology*, ed. R. J. Russell et al. (Notre Dame, IN, 1988), pp. 313-31.

life, then, has to be in a position to grasp and determine the total process. On Christian soil the resurrection and exaltation of Jesus Christ as the new man met this condition.[445] Hence we no longer need to assume that there will have to be future forms of development of the intelligence that emerged in the cosmic process with us, this time on a different basis from that of organic life as we know it.

The related detailed discussion must wait until we come to eschatology. It must be clear already, however, that a temporal end of the universe parallel to its temporal beginning is conceivable in physics, so that we can conceive of the universe as finite in its whole process. Moreover, it is clear that the future of the universe rather than its beginning is the place where the whole process from the very beginning has its basis. The anthropic approach, which regards the emergence of intelligent life as essential to the total character of the universe, leads to a view of its basic structure that ascribes to eschatology a constitutive function for the whole universe, for only in the omega of the cosmic process can we conceive of the complete form of the intellectual dominion over the universe that first took shape in us but that, if our emergence was really significant for the universe as a whole, will have to be achieved in some other form that is determinative for the universe in its total range. Only in the omega of the cosmic process is an intellectual dominion over the whole process conceivable that is also the basis of its beginning because it is no longer under the limitations of time.

It might be objected that we can link directly to the beginning the idea of a God who has given the universe its laws and existence. In fact Tipler's theory of the omega point leads ultimately to such an idea. But it has the advantage of leading to this idea by way of the guiding thread of the anthropic principle. Without this path by way of eschatology, it would have to be by leaps of thought and anthropomorphic analogies such as we find in the teleological proof, in which we move from the order of the universe to the postulate of an intelligent author. Over against the traditional line of thinking we have to concede to Tipler's argument that it does not depend on analogies and does not result in an anthropomorphic idea of God. For the rest, we have here only a possible theoretical nexus that is an alternative to other cosmological models, not a proof of God's existence in the traditional sense.

445. On this cf. my "Theological Appropriation of Scientific Understandings: Response to Hefner, Wicken, Eaves, and Tipler," *Zygon* 24 (1989) 255-71, esp. 267f.

For theology there can be no question of adopting such a model. The argument moves on a different plane from that of theology. Nevertheless, it is undeniable that the basic thoughts sustaining it converge with the theological arguments that we have developed here. Hence theology can use the possibility of cosmological deliberations of this kind to elucidate its thesis concerning the future of God as the creative origin of the universe, and to show how relevant this is. In Tipler's model, of course, the way in which God, in terms of the eschaton of the universe, is creatively present to his creatures in the cosmic process still needs much fuller elucidation. No proposals in this regard are as yet present. We are perhaps to look in the direction of the field concept that we have described here from the standpoint of the creative activity of the divine Spirit (see above, pp. 79ff.).[446]

§ 3. Belief in Creation and Theodicy

With good reason we can argue and claim that the world as it offers itself to human experience and knowledge is the creation of the God of the Bible. To show this is the task of the doctrine of creation as it presents the world as God's handiwork. In the process it makes a contribution that we should not

---

446. A reinterpretation of the cosmic field (Tipler, "Omega Point as *Eschaton*," p. 229) along the lines of the constitutive relevance of omega for its structure might offer a solution to the problem of contingency in quantum physics that would make superfluous Tipler's recourse (pp. 235f.) to the "Many Worlds Interpretation" of Hugh Everett (1957) and give more weight than Tipler has thus far done (p. 236) to the temporal contingency of individual events (not in relation to the universal wave function, but to its processes). In criticism of Everett's hypothesis cf. Mary B. Hesse, "Physics, Philosophy, and Myth," in *Physics, Philosophy, and Theology,* ed. Russell et al. (Notre Dame, IN, 1988), pp. 185-202, esp. 192ff. We might perhaps find hints in the right direction in J. A. Wheeler's discussion of the retroactive decision of quantum events if we link this decision with omega and if it is only secondarily that humans share in it in their relation to the world of nature, as in the biblical idea of the divine likeness and the associated dominion in nature. Cf. J. A. Wheeler, "Die Experimente der verzögerten Entscheidung und der Dialog zwischen Bohr und Einstein," in *Moderne Naturphilosophie,* ed. B. Kanitscheider (1984), pp. 203-22, esp. 214ff.; also idem, "World as System Self-Synthesized by Quantum-Networking," *IBM Journal of Research and Development* 32 (1988) 4-15, where Wheeler opposes the idea of a continuous space-time (pp. 13f.) but continues to speak of events (p. 13) that are not conceivable without time, so that his criticism of the concept of time might be viewed rather as a demand for its revision in the sense of a discrete sequence of moments of time, thus allowing us to take contingency into account in our views of time.

underestimate to keeping open the possibility of speaking about God in a way that is intellectually responsible. When theology fails to take up this task the danger threatens that the word "God" will lose any credible meaning.

Even if it is successful, however, the theological doctrine of creation cannot show that the praise of God in nature (Ps. 19) is evident in the sense that we can read it off plainly from our knowledge of nature as it now stands. Though Paul says that we may all see God's eternal power and deity in the works of nature (Rom. 1:20), the express claim that the reality of nature (and human history) is the work of God is in fact debatable. There are many reasons for this. According to Paul, ingratitude and unrighteousness prevent us from paying the Creator of the world the honor of his deity (1:18, 21). Before making such final judgments we might say that different understandings of the world are partly conditioned by the different approaches of the interpreters. Reasons grounded in the very nature of the matter also lie in the way of our recognizing the Creator in the works of creation. Some of these have to do with the independence of creaturely forms and processes, which leave the impression that they need no divine Creator to explain them.

Again, there is the apparently senseless suffering of creatures and the entrance and at least temporary success of evil in creation. This fact makes difficult the postulate of a Creator who is both omnipotent and good. A belief in creation has to assume that the work of creation is good according to the creative will of God. But suffering and evil cast doubt on this conviction. As we shall see, this second problem stands related to the first. But we can explain the relation only by first defining more precisely the challenge that is put to the belief in creation by doubt as to the goodness of the work of creation.

After each individual act of creation the first Genesis story says that its execution is in accord with the divine purpose, and it describes with approval the resultant work as "good."[447] At the end of the story, with the creation of humans, a general approval replaces the specific approval: All creation is said to be "very good" (Gen. 1:31). Humans are naturally included, and emphasis is given in this way to the special importance of their creation as the conclusion of the whole work of creation (2:2).[448] The goodness of all creation obviously depends on that of humans and their being in accord with the divine purpose in creation.

---

447. Gen. 1:4, 10, 12, 18, 25, 31. Cf. Schmidt, *Schöpfungsgeschichte*, pp. 59ff.
448. Steck, *Schöpfungsbericht*, p. 183, cf. 131, n. 521.

According to the Genesis record, the historical form and experience of humanity do not show unambiguously the goodness that the Creator ascribes to it. At the beginning of the flood story we read, "And God saw the earth, and behold it was corrupt, for all flesh had corrupted their way upon the earth" (Gen. 6:12). The reference seems to be not merely to humans but to all living things.[449] All living things are entangled in the guilt that brings down the judgment of the flood. God made the world good, but creatures — and especially humans, in whom the goodness of creation reached its climax — have corrupted it.

Since an original perfection is ascribed to creation, the evil that is present in the world had to come later. The opposite of this corruption would be keeping God's law, especially the sabbath (Exod. 20:11), for this is to uphold the original order of creation. The Christian view goes beyond this by viewing the coming of the eschatological new man in Jesus Christ (1 Cor. 15:46f.) as the completion of creation that overcomes all the corruption that has come into it. On this ground a Christian theology of creation does not have to insist on a perfect state at the first. But the authoritative statements of the biblical creation story concerning the goodness of creation force it in this direction, even though tension might arise with what Paul says in 1 Cor. 15:45ff.

The faith of Israel and primitive Christianity never entertained the thought of accusing the Creator himself of the evil that had come into his creation. It is worth noting that this was not just because the creature, especially the human creature, was seen to be responsible. It was also because the creature has no right to make itself the judge of God's creative action: "Woe to him who strives with his Maker, an earthen vessel with the potter: Does the clay say to him who fashions it, 'What are you making'? or 'Your work has no handles'" (Isa. 45:9; cf. Jer. 18:6; Rom. 9:20). "Behold, he snatches away; who can hinder him? Who will say to him, 'What doest thou'?" (Job 9:12).

On the soil of belief in God the Creator a problem of theodicy — a demand for God's justification of the world he has created — cannot seriously arise.[450] Yet this fact does not prevent the question from forcing itself even upon believers as an assault upon their faith, just as the fact

449. Schmidt, *Schöpfungsgeschichte*, p. 63, n. 1, quoting Gen. 6:17. Schmidt sees here a point of difference from 6:5.
450. Hence Barth reversed the theme, justifying the existence of creatures by the very fact of their creation (*CD*, III/1, § 42.3). God the Creator needs no justification even vis-à-vis the apostasy of his creature from him (p. 266).

(and possibility) of unbelief accompanies belief like a shadow. For clearly there is an open denial of belief in God the Creator, and not without reason this unbelief appeals to the fact of evil in the world, recalling the innocent and disproportionate suffering especially of creatures whose lives could not develop at all. The pitiful suffering and death of children is the most cogent argument against belief in a Creator of the world who is both wise and good.[451]

The objection that uses such arguments and interpretations is by no means theoretical. The meaningless suffering of so many creatures forms a very real obstacle to faith in an almighty, wise, and good Creator. If the objection is to be met, then it will be met only by a real overcoming of evil and suffering such as Christian eschatology hopes for in faith in the resurrection of the dead. A purely theoretical theodicy is exposed to the criticism that Barth brings against Leibniz and his 18th-century followers, namely, that they reinterpret reality by trivializing its shadow side.[452] Suffering, guilt, and tears cry out for a real overcoming of evil. Hence it is only the union of creation and redemption against the background of eschatology that makes possible a tenable answer to the question of theodicy, the question of the righteousness of God in his works.[453] More accurately, it is only God himself who can give a truly satisfying answer to this question, and he gives it through the history of his acts in the world, and especially through their consummation with the establishment of his kingdom in creation.

So long as the world looks only at its uncompleted and unredeemed present on the one hand, and from the standpoint of its original emergence from the hands of the Creator on the other, the fact of wickedness and evil in the world remains an insoluble riddle and offense. The most serious defect of the traditional treatment of the problem of theodicy, precisely in the classical form that Leibniz gave it, is that it has thought it could give a proof of the righteousness of God in his works

451. For a classic formulation of this objection cf. Ivan Karamazov's conversation with his brother in F. M. Dostoyevsky's *Brothers Karamazov,* bk. 5, ch. 4. In Albert Camus's *The Plague* (New York, 1948), pp. 198ff., we find only an echo of this revolt (4.3, 4), since the physician Rieux has already abandoned faith in order to devote himself to helping sufferers (2.6). In Ivan Karamazov, too, the human god that replaces God and seeks human happiness is a correlate of rejection of faith, as we see from the legend of the Grand Inquisitor that immediately follows. Cf. W. Rehm, *Jean Paul, Dostojewski. Eine Studie zur dichterischen Gestaltung des Unglaubens* (Göttingen, 1962), pp. 62ff.

452. *CD,* III/1, 388ff.

453. W. Trillhaas, *Dogmatik,* 3rd ed. (1972), pp. 172ff.

exclusively from the standpoint of the origin of the world and its order in God's creative work,[454] instead of taking into consideration the history of God's saving action and the eschatological fulfillment that has dawned already in Jesus Christ.[455]

Even from the standpoint of reconciliation and eschatological consummation, of course, it is an open question why the Creator did not create a world in which there could be no pain or guilt. From this angle the problem of theodicy is still related to the world's origin. It is thus understandable that Christian theology should first tackle it from this standpoint.

Clement of Alexandria was already asking why wickedness and evil could gain an entry into the world that God created good (*Strom.* 1.17.82ff.). He gave an answer that others would often repeat, namely, that evil and suffering are the result of sin. Responsibility for the coming of wickedness and evil among creatures does not fall on the Creator but on those who do wicked things, since souls are free in their decisions (83.5).

Both parts of this answer are inadequate. Pain and suffering are widespread among other living things in the prehuman world and cannot, then, be the result of human sin.[456] We must resort to a fall of angels and their dominion

---

454. We do not object to the attempt to trace the righteousness of God in his works. Creatures do not transgress their limits in so doing. Indeed, creatures — especially human creatures — are summoned to bear witness to the wisdom, goodness, and righteousness of God in his works. Hence inquiring into these things cannot be blameworthy. The objection is to the one-sidedness of the procedure in traditional discussions of theodicy. This gives the impression we rationally can excuse God for defects in his works instead of letting reason take the same path as God himself takes in justification of his deity.

455. This seems to be Barth's final objection to the Christian optimism in 18th-century literature, in spite of his remarkably positive evaluation of it; cf. *CD*, III/1, 406.

456. In his important book *Evil and the God of Love* (New York, 1966), John Hick tried to defend the early Christian position against the cogent criticism of David Hume in *Dialogues concerning Natural Religion* (1779; ed. H. D. Aiken, London, 1948 and 1977), pt. 11, pp. 73ff. Hick distinguished between the *pain* that living creatures feel (at least vertebrates) and *suffering* (pp. 328ff., 354ff.), the latter being specifically human (p. 355) and the result of sin, in contrast to the momentary pain that is environmentally unavoidable. But this argument is not wholly convincing. It may be doubted whether we can make such a sharp distinction as Hick attempted. There are no theological reasons for so doing. Paul referred to the suffering of nonhuman creatures in Rom. 8:22, and to their sharing in our human redemption. Nor is all human suffering an expression of sinful egocentricity that will not accept its own finitude. In his later *Death and Eternal Life* (New York, 1976) Hick laid stress on compensation for what we miss in the present life as a basic motif of eschatological expectation (pp. 152ff., cf. 390f.). This is in keeping with a fundamental thought in the message of Jesus (Matt. 5:3ff.). It leaves room for a suffering that is not the result of sin, i.e., suffering from the inauthenticity and deficient

over the present world (or over the aeon of fallen creation) if we are to view evil as the result of a free decision of creatures to turn aside from the Creator.[457] But even then limiting responsibility for an evil deed to the doer is not convincing if another might have prevented the doer from doing it. This is especially true in the case of the Creator, who does not stand apart from his creatures but brought them into being. If an act is the result of a free decision on the part of the doer, the freedom is itself a work of the creator, and we cannot think of its exercise apart from his cooperation. Why did not God so order the world that his creatures are protected against sin and evil?

To point out that evil has its origin in the freedom of creatures to decide and act is not to absolve the Creator of responsibility for this creation of his. Although creatures may be free, even in their freedom they are still God's creatures. Concern to absolve the Creator has been a mistake in Christian theodicy. The attempt cannot succeed, nor does it accord with the NT testimony, for in and with the crucifixion of his Son God accepted and bore responsibility for the world that he had created.

From another angle, however, there is an important element of truth in the reference to the freedom of creatures. We need to make a sharp distinction here from the erroneous concern to absolve the Creator. Only then can we see the real significance of the reference. For if the Creator wanted free and independent creatures that can spontaneously acknowledge him in his deity, and thus correspond for their part to the fellowship of the Son with the Father that is realized in Jesus, the decision to create carried with it the risk of a misuse of this creaturely freedom.[458] This argument implies a way of looking at things that leads us into the

---

integrity of the present life. G. Süssmann in "Materie und Vergänglichkeit. Über das Böse als kosmisch-geistige Realität," in *Das Böse in der Evolution und die Güte Gottes*, ed. W. Böhme (1983), pp. 26-43, has rightly pointed out that Jesus' handling of the events recorded in Luke 13:1-5, and his rejection of sin as a reason for blindness in John 9:1ff., do not allow us to attribute human suffering directly or in every case to sin (p. 43, n. 15).

457. Unlike C. S. Lewis, L. Hodgson, E. L. Mascall et al., Hick rejects this idea in his *Evil and the God of Love* (367ff.), and it is in fact unnecessary if we accept his distinction between pain and suffering.

458. For discussion of this problem in British philosophy of religion during the 1950s and 1960s, cf. J. L. Mackie, A. Flew, N. Smart, et al., esp. Mackie, "Evil and Omnipotence," in *The Philosophy of Religion*, ed. B. Mitchell (New York, 1971), pp. 92-104, 106ff.; A. Plantinga, "The Free Will Defense," in ibid., pp. 105-20; and Hick, *Evil and the God of Love*, pp. 308ff. Cf. also Plantinga's *God, Freedom, and Evil* (New York, 1975), pp. 29ff., also 27f., where he distinguishes between the limited goal of the free-will defense and the broader goal of theodicy.

sphere of the doctrine of providence, namely, that the Creator accepts the risk of sin and evil as a condition of realizing the goal of a free fellowship of the creature with himself. God did not will wickedness and evil as such. He could not take pleasure in them. They are not an object of his will. Nevertheless, they are in fact accompanying phenomena. As such they are conditions[459] of the realizing of his purpose for the creature, and they come under his world government, which can bring good out of evil, being oriented to the reconciliation and redemption of the world through Jesus Christ.

Origen was the first to introduce the thought of the divine world government into discussion of the problem of theodicy. In some sense the Stoic doctrine of providence had preceded him.[460] But only on the soil of the Christian belief in creation did the problem become especially acute. Appealing to Job 1:13, Origen declared that God did not merely not prevent the operations of evil and hostile forces ("malignas et contrarias virtutes") in his creation, but actually permitted them ("non solum non prohibet deus, sed et permittit facere haec" [*De princ.* 3.2.7]). This was part of our testing by the providence of God (2.3), and God's patience with sinners can lead them to see their own weakness and thus confer on them the blessing of healing (1.12). Origen did not relate this concept of permission to the origin of evil.

Gregory of Nyssa so related these ideas, however, extending the thought of a permission of evil by divine providence to the creation of human beings, in spite of a foreseeing of the fall (*Or. cat. magna* 8.3 [PG, 45, 37B-C]). He did this in order to meet Manichean objections to the creation of human beings by the good God (7.1 [PG, 45, 29f.]). Augustine then referred expressly to a permission of the fall by the providence of God (*Civ. Dei* 14.27). In so doing, he did not use the idea of permission as a means of absolving God from the emergence of evil in creation.[461] Instead he related the concept of permission to the goal of divine providence, i.e., to the foreseen victory over the devil that would be won by

459. For emphasis on the function of a condition in the permission of evil by God, cf. esp. the *Theodicy* (1710) of Leibniz. Leibniz argued that the evil permitted by God was an object of his will neither as end nor as means, but solely as condition (n. 336; cf. pp. 119, 209; also *Causa Dei*, p. 36).

460. Cf. the comments of R. Schottlaender on Chrysippus (specifically on the fragment in H. von Arnim, *Stoicorum Veterum Fragmenta* [1903-], II, 1177), in his article "Malum," *HWP*, V (1980), 664.

461. This was the interpretation of Blumenberg, *Legitimität der Neuzeit*, pp. 85f., who argued that Augustine was excusing God at our expense. The passages he quoted from *De lib. arb.* and *Conf.* do indeed speak of our responsibility for that which we voluntarily will. But this does not have to go hand in hand with absolving God from responsibility for his creation. We see this plainly in the passages in *Civ. Dei* to which we refer in n. 462.

Christ.[462] Unfortunately we cannot deny that in other places Augustine justified that which seems to be evil to us as part of the multiple perfection of the universe (*Civ. Dei* 12.4), and he could find a place aesthetically even for sin and evil, which are like the dark spots that bring out the colors of a picture all the more brilliantly (11.23.1). These statements belong to a wholly different line of argument from that which appeals to the aims of divine providence and the risk that these might entail creaturely evil.

Considerations aiming at vindication of the goodness of creation, however, should not be isolated or detached from the permission of evil for the purpose of salvation, and in this isolation depicted as characteristic of Augustine's doctrine of providence.[463] It is worth noting that Augustine did not go so far as to say that sin and the existence of the reprobate were necessary to the perfection of the universe.[464] It was left for medieval Augustinianism to take this last step, which threatens to obscure the thought of the love of God as Creator.[465] Nevertheless, even in Augustine's case we may rightly object against the independent treatment of the order and aesthetic harmony of the universe and the rendering of wickedness and evil innocuous by their integration into this order. Augustine thought that the statements about the goodness of creation in the first creation story forced him into considerations of this kind (*Civ. Dei* 9.23). Christian theology, however, may see in this judgment of God on his work an anticipation of its eschatological consummation after it is reconciled and redeemed by the Son. Only then will this judgment have plausibility, notwithstanding the present state of creation.

The theological tradition has described evil as ontologically null and void because it is not work of the divine will or an object of the divine

---

462. *Civ. Dei* 14.27, cf. 22.1.

463. Hick, *Evil and the God of Love,* pp. 88-95, does not avoid this danger because he takes too little notice of the link with the salvation-oriented doctrine of providence, reducing this to the special theme of predestination (pp. 70-75), instead of letting it function as a theme related to every approach. Neglect of the structure of Augustine's doctrine of providence in terms of salvation history makes it easier for Hick to see contrast and opposition between an Augustinian and an Irenean type of theodicy (pp. 217ff.). Hick has to confess, however, that one cannot speak of any express or developed theodicy in Irenaeus (pp. 211, 216). As noted above, we find the first steps in this direction in Clement of Alexandria. The thesis of an Irenean type of theodicy is a construction of Hick himself, inspired more by Schleiermacher than Irenaeus (pp. 225-41). We may agree with Hick that the Irenean idea of imperfect human beginnings is preferable to the Augustinian view of our first estate, but in this regard Irenaeus was not making any contribution to theodicy.

464. Stressed by Hick, *Evil and the God of Love,* p. 94.

465. Cf. as one example among many Aquinas *ST* 1.23.5 ad 3, and cf. Hick's statements (*Evil and the God of Love,* pp. 101-4) on the role of the aesthetic motif in the integrating of evil into the perfection of the universe.

good pleasure. Wickedness and evil have no doubt entered creation with God's knowledge and permission, but they are not objects of his will in the sense of reflecting his creative pleasure. The fact that theology in the West after Augustine, and earlier in the East,[466] used the means of Neoplatonic ontology to describe this situation is no good reason to reject the thesis of ontological nullity. This is true at least so long as we do not link it with an attempt to absolve God from responsibility for the coming of evil into his creation nor to argue that wickedness and evil are not a dangerous reality for creatures.[467]

Responsibility for the coming of evil into creation unavoidably falls on the God who foresees and permits it, even though creaturely action is the immediate cause. God did not shirk the responsibility but shouldered it by sending and giving up his Son to the cross. In this way, as Creator, he stands by his responsibility for the work that he has made. Evil is thus real and costly enough for God himself as well as for creatures. The crucifixion of his Son makes this plain. Evil may be null and void for his creative will, but this nullity is sealed only by his victory over it in the event of reconciliation and in the eschatological consummation of creation.

To say all this, however, is not to answer the question why God permits wickedness and evil. What we have seen is that the two cannot be positive objects of his creative will and that by foreseeing and allowing them, he bears coresponsibility for their coming and stands by this through the death of his Son. But why did he permit them in the first place?

To answer this question the theological tradition has pointed to the ontological constitution of created reality. In comparison with the Creator, the creature is mutable.[468] Measured by God's eternal selfhood, the creature's mutability is an expression of its ontological weakness, of a lack of ontic power. This is particularly true of the human will. By nature[469] it strives after the good that is the true object of its willing, but it

466. Cf. Gregory of Nyssa *Or. cat. magna* 6.2, cf. 7.2.

467. Gregory of Nyssa does not avoid the first danger. To avoid the second, Barth in *CD*, III/3, § 50, views nothingness as a power that is real, even though negated by God. In criticism cf. Hick, *Evil and the God of Love*, pp. 132ff., esp. 141ff.

468. Cf. esp. Augustine *Civ. Dei* 14.13, and on this theme Hick, *Evil and the God of Love*, pp. 44ff., esp. 52ff.

469. On sin and the will, and the rooting of sin in the natural conditions of human existence, cf. my *Anthropology*, pp. 104ff.

has the possibility of actually turning to the worse. This points to its ontological deficiency. That which can turn from the good will at some time really do so.[470]

Leibniz gave this thought a different and more general form. The deeper reason for the possibility of sin, and therefore for the coming of evil into creation with all its consequences, is that there is an original imperfection in the creature because the creature is ontically limited, cannot know all things, may be mistaken about many things, and can thus be guilty of other failings. Leibniz saw here metaphysical as distinct from physical and moral evil.[471] Limitation is a necessary part of creaturehood insofar as every creature is different from God and his perfection. God could not give the creature all things without making it itself a god.[472] Leibniz derived from this fact the limitation of creaturely being in general and also the distinction and variety of creaturely forms as an expression of various forms of limitation. In so doing, he distanced himself from the Neoplatonic explanation of creaturely imperfection as a consequence of the making of creatures out of nothing. The finitude of the creaturely form of existence rather than the weakness of nullity carried with it the possibility of the bad and evil, even if this is not at all the same as sin and evil.

John Hick has brought against Leibniz the objection that to trace back metaphysical evil to the limits of all creaturely being that are inescapably grounded in what the divine understanding knew to be possible is to deny in fact the infinite power of God.[473] This objection fails to do justice to Leibniz, who says expressly that God's omnipotence extends to anything that does not involve a contradiction (*Theodicy*, § 227). For Leibniz, tying the power of God to his understanding of what is possible, and therefore to what is possible in creaturely being without contradiction, is simply an expression of the fact that God does nothing that is self-contradictory. Hick himself recognizes this (*Evil and the God of Love*, pp. 301f.). His criticism of Leibniz thus fails.

One might argue against Leibniz when he says that ideas are not brought forth by an act of the divine will, since understanding precedes will (*Theodicy*,

---

470. Aquinas *ST* 1.48.2c.
471. Leibniz, *Theodicy*, §§ 20f., cf. §§ 156 and 288.
472. Ibid., p. 31, also *Causa Dei*, p. 69.
473. Hick, *Evil and the God of Love*, pp. 176f. In reply see the arguments of Plantinga, *God, Freedom, and Evil*, pp. 34ff., which are not unlike those of Leibniz. Oddly, Plantinga ascribes to Leibniz the view that in his omnipotence God might have created any possible world (p. 33).

§ 335). This statement misses the point that understanding and will are not ontically distinct in God. Even if we are content, however, with the more modest objection that understanding and will are in agreement in God, as their real identity with the divine essence demands, it is nevertheless true enough that God does nothing contradictory, and it would involve contradiction to demand that God should have created creatures without creaturely limits.

Hick otherwise makes the excellent point that we are hardly right to call the argument of Leibniz optimistic (*Evil and the God of Love*, p. 172). Only a superficial view of the thesis that this is the best of all possible worlds can result in this misunderstanding. The true point of the thesis of Leibniz is that under the limiting conditions of creaturely imperfection, this is relatively the best world. It would be foolish to ask for a better. Such a view is hardly optimistic. Instead, we should regard it as the expression of a Christian realism. Face to face with the infinite possibilities open to the divine wisdom, one may doubt whether any of the possible worlds can rank definitely as the best. The objection of Leibniz that then God could not have created any universe at all, since he could want only the best (*Theodicy* § 196), is no real answer.

At this point, instead, theological voluntarism comes into its own. On this view the divine will, as the origin of the contingency of everything outside God, is itself the rule of the good for creaturely reality. Face to face with the infinity of the possible, the creative will of God is itself the basis of the goodness of the existence of creatures. In spite of its shadows, the world is good because God willed and affirmed it, a truth that Barth rightly stressed. The only limit attaching to this principle is that we may not ascribe to the divine will any abstract freedom to act against what is known to be better, or to do anything contradictory. This is the element of truth in Leibniz's criticism of nominalistic voluntarism.

There is some truth in the tracing back of evil, including the moral evil of sin, to the conditions of existence bound up with creatureliness. Nevertheless, it is not enough simply to advance the limitation of creatures as a reason for the possibility of evil. As Leibniz himself knew well, the limit of finitude is not yet itself evil, and if evil came from it, then we must define evil as error and not as a fall from God. At this point Leibniz, too, was caught in the Neoplatonic understanding of evil as defect.

We are to seek the root of evil, rather, in revolt against the limit of finitude, in the refusal to accept one's own finitude, and in the related illusion of being like God (Gen. 3:5). We thus need to reconstruct the thought that would see the possibility of evil in the very nature of creaturehood. Not limitation but the independence for which creatures were made forms the basis of the possibility of evil. This fact sets the relation between creaturehood and evil in an even sharper light than in Leibniz. The independence of creatures expresses their perfection as such as this is basically determined by their possession of existence. But connected with it is also the risk of their apostasy from the Creator. It thus carries with it the temptation to regard themselves as absolute in asserting their own existence.

The source of suffering and evil lies in the transition from God-given independence to self-independence. Here also is the source of the further sufferings that creatures bring on themselves beyond the measure of their finitude.

As regards so-called physical evil and suffering from it, we have already noted the relation between entropy and evil (see above, pp. 96ff.). We may now say that by making themselves independent, creatures fall victim to entropy. Those that cannot take on new energy and thus transcend themselves come under the neutralizing sway of entropy. Even in the case of living creatures that specialize in using the gradient of energy in natural processes and nourish their lives thereby, the related self-assertion is accompanied by a self-independence that finally results in the ossifying of vital systems by aging and death. The more continued existence is internalized in the series of creaturely norms, the more painful corruptibility and the experience of perishing becomes, not merely in the sense of a feeling of momentary pain, but as something that colors our feeling for life as a whole.[474]

The fact that the interdependence of creatures is part of the finitude of existence makes this situation even more acute. Creatures live off and for one another. They build on the existence of others, and others build on them. In the realm of organisms there is also strife for access to the sources of life, competition for nourishment and pleasure in which each maintains itself at the expense of others, even to the point of killing and eating them. The suffering of corruptibility that affects all living things, and that forms the background even to joy in life, culminates in the suffering that others add to it.

Like pain and suffering, evil is possible because of the finitude of existence, and especially of living creatures that seek to maintain themselves autonomously and thus incline to aim at a radical independence. Here is the origin of both suffering and evil.

---

474. Here lies an objection to Hick's restriction of pain to a momentary feeling (see n. 456 above). We must either concede to pain an element of continuity in connection with its effect on our feeling for life or relate the concept of suffering to this instead of limiting it to the reflective self-awareness that we ascribe to humans alone. Cf. the debate with C. S. Lewis in P. Gesch, *Providence and Evil* (1977), pp. 67ff.

Asserting themselves against one another, creatures do so also against the Creator. We see this on the ascending line of forms of life, and it comes to a climax in human sin, for among us the relation to God has become thematic. For the autonomous creature self-independence conceals dependence on God, just as for the scientific observer the autonomy of natural processes hides their origin in God. At the same time, the results of creaturely autonomy in the form of suffering and iniquity seem to refute belief in a good Creator of this world. We have here two aspects of one and the same fact.

If the Creator willed a world of finite creatures and their independence, then he had to accept their corruptibility and suffering, and the possibility of evil as a result of their striving for autonomy. He also had to accept the concealment of his own deity in his creation, its covering over and questioning by the independence of his creatures.

On the stage of human existence the human ability to distinguish others from the self and the self from others, and thus to be aware of human finitude in distinction from the infinite God, opens up the possibility of an acceptance of finitude, corruptibility, and suffering in humility before the eternal God. But praising God for making this world presupposes dissatisfaction with the present state. W. Trillhaas rightly says that there is no theodicy without eschatology.[475] A belief in creation that does not go hand in hand with hope of eschatological victory over the reality of evil and sin, which are related to finitude, can give no answer to the question of theodicy. An answer is possible only when we see that creation is linked to the divine work of the reconciling and redeeming of the world. If creation comes to completion only with the world's reconciliation and redemption, then the Creator is allied to us in the battle to overcome evil and to reduce and heal suffering in the world. Only the eschatological consummation of the world can definitively demonstrate the righteousness of God, and therefore his deity, in the work of creation.

Creation praise of God to which the Psalms refer is always in anticipation of the eschatological consummation. In the light of this, creation already praises God by its continuation as a finite reality, for in this way creatures are as God willed them to be. They also praise God in their perishing, because this is part of their finitude. As creatures accept the finite existence God has given them, they live it out as an existence that is not grounded in itself but owed to another. As they thank God for

475. *Dogmatik*, p. 166.

their existence even in their perishing, in transcendence of their finitude they are in relation to the eternal will of God as Creator, and herein they participate in God's imperishable glory.

CHAPTER 8

The Dignity and Misery of Humanity

The productivity of life, which continually expresses itself in the emergence of new forms, pushes evolution forward. This fact does not of itself mean that in the sequence of forms one of them will be the climax beyond which there can be no further advance. Humans are certainly the most developed form. By intelligent adaptation to different conditions of existence, they have steadily extended their dominion over nature and thus represent the culmination of the evolution of organic life on this earth. Unless a disaster exterminates all humanity without also destroying all organic life, it is hard to imagine in principle any evolutionary advance beyond them. Only from the standpoint of the religiously and biblically grounded awareness of their destiny of fellowship with God, the author of the universe, can we say assuredly, however, that all creation culminates in humanity. To say this, we must (1) be able to look at the world as a whole, notwithstanding the openness of nature; (2) show that humans stand in a unique relation to the origin of the universe; and (3) assume that in them the purpose of finite life is both comprehended and fulfilled.

Knowledge of God as the Creator of the world fulfills the first of these conditions. The second and third are closely related, for the uniqueness of humans among other creatures has its basis in the third condition, i.e., in the definitive actualizing of the relation to the Creator, which is meant for all creatures as such, in the human relation to God.

Only in the light of the incarnation of the eternal Son as a man, however, can we say that the relation of creatures to the Creator finds its supreme and final realization in humanity. The relation of the Son to the

175

Father cannot be transcended by any other form of relation to God. As the eternal God took form in a man, and through him made acceptance as children of God accessible to all other men and women, the relation of the creature to the Creator has found in principle the highest fulfillment that we can possibly imagine.

From the standpoint of our human nature we can claim this distinction only because we are the same species as the one man in whom the eternal Son took shape. This event is not external, however, to our being as humans. In it we see our destiny as individuals and as a species. The human destiny for fellowship with God, which finds definitive realization in the incarnation of the Son, means that humanity as such, and each individual within it, is lifted above the natural world and even also above the social relations in which we exist. The destiny of fellowship with God confers inviolability on human life in the person of each individual.[1] It is the basis of the inalienable dignity of each human person.

The idea of a dignity not merely of individuals by their office and authority but of human beings in general as rational creatures is of pre-Christian origin. Cicero in *De off.* 1.30.106 based it on the gift of rationality, which pledges us to a life directed by reason. Yet Cicero did not link this dignity, as modern usage does, to the idea of the inviolability of human life in each individual. This thought arose only with the idea that we are under a supreme authority that releases us from obligation to other powers, and especially from being controlled by other people or by society. Rightly, then, the Christian tradition sought the basis of personal dignity in our creation in the image of God.[2] Our destiny of fellowship with God forms the indispensable premise of the function of human dignity as the content of a supreme legal principle and a basis for individual

1. Gen. 9:6 relates the prohibition of murder to our being created in the divine likeness. Such a basis is more general than one rooted in christology. Yet according to 2 Cor. 4:4 the likeness of God in human form found manifestation only in Jesus Christ. In him alone do we see that our destiny of fellowship with God is the point of the divine likeness, which Gen. 9:6 adduces as a basis for the inviolability of the human person and therefore for human dignity.
2. Cf. Theophilus of Antioch *Ad Autol.* 2.18, then Gregory of Nyssa in his work on the creation of humanity (PG, 44, 123-256) and Ambrose in his little book *De dignitate conditionis humanae* (PL, 17, 1105-8). For the dignity of human nature on the basis of divine likeness, cf. also Leo the Great (*Sermons* 24.2 [PL, 54, 205A]; cf. 27.6 [PL, 54, 220B]) and Gregory the Great (*Mor.* 9.49 [PL, 75, 900]). Among Scholastics, Bonaventura especially stressed this point (*Sent.* 1.25.2.1 opp. 2, Opera ed. Quaracchi, I, 442]). Aquinas links human dignity to the goal of knowledge and love of God (*SCG* 3.1.11). It is also a sign of the person in virtue of our intellectual nature (*De pot. Dei* 8.4 and 9.3 etc.), but it plays no other role in the doctrine of the divine likeness.

human rights, e.g., in modern declarations of such rights.[3] Modern constitutions (e.g., the West German Constitution of 1949) avoid express references of this kind.

It may well be pointed out that the concept of human dignity has other than Christian roots. Thus S. Pufendorf and I. Kant, basing ethics on the autonomy of reason, adopted and developed the thought of Cicero that human reason gives us a dignity that lays obligations upon us in our conduct.[4] Yet Kant's demand that we treat all individuals as ends in themselves and not means can hardly be inferred simply from their rational nature.[5] This demand is in fact a legacy of the Christian spirit, for which Kant (with dubious success) tried to find a rational basis. The same applies to the modern view that human dignity is the supreme standard of law. We cannot detach the link between this thought and the idea of individual inviolability from its basis in the Bible without depriving it of any solid basis at all. The idea goes far beyond the concept of natural law that we are all equal as rational beings or that we should do to others as we would have them do to us (the Golden Rule). It gives to human dignity an absolute constitutive authority. Reason can claim no such absoluteness. Kant might try to base the idea of the inviolable dignity of each individual on the self-legislation of reason, but such self-legislation soon became the self-determination of individual caprice, with pluralism as the final result. Nevertheless, in the respect that modern constitutional states show to the personal rights of individuals we still see something of the religious basis of these rights to freedom.

A feature of the dignity that accrues to us by virtue of our being destined for fellowship with God is that no actual humiliation that might befall us can extinguish it. In a special way, because they have nothing else that commands respect, the faces of the suffering and humbled and deprived are ennobled by the reflection of this dignity that none of us has by merit, that none of us can receive from others, and that no one can take from us.

3. The United Nations Charter of 26 June 1945 expressly relates belief in "the dignity and worth of the human person" to belief in fundamental human rights (F. Hartung, *Die Entwicklung der Menschen- und Bürgerrechte von 1776 bis zur Gegenwart* [4th ed. 1972], p. 130). In the preamble to the Declaration of Human Rights on 10 December 1948, recognition of the "inherent dignity" of each individual underlies one's equal and inalienable rights (ibid., p. 144; for later references, cf. pp. 265 and 283). The German Constitution of 1949 maintains the inviolability of human dignity in Art. 1.1 and finds here a starting point for the obligatory nature of human rights in Art. 1.2.

4. On Pufendorf's basing of human rights on human dignity, cf. H. Welzel, "John Wise und Samuel Pufendorf," in *Rechtsprobleme in Staat und Kirche* (1952), pp. 392f. On Kant, cf. his *Fundamental Principle of Metaphysics* (New York, 1949), pp. 45f.

5. Kant, *Fundamental Principle of Metaphysics*, p. 251.

The situation is different where no regard is paid to the dignity of our divine destiny and people act without dignity. In this case human life is more marred than it is by oppression, mistreatment, or miserable outward conditions. Such conditions may indeed be unworthy, unjust, and humiliating for us. Although misery of this kind runs contrary to our divine destiny, it does not of itself alienate us from this destiny. That alienation takes place only when we live our lives in antithesis to our destiny. Even then, of course, we cannot simply throw off our dignity. But the dignity of our destiny then becomes a judgment on our unworthy conduct. Only then do we reach the deepest plight of our human situation. It is neither want and oppression, nor the frailty and corruptibility of life, but human conduct that contradicts our human destiny that causes the apostle Paul to cry out: "Wretched man that I am: Who will deliver me from this body of death?" (Rom. 7:24). Mortality characterizes the misery to which all human life is subject, no matter how different human situations may be. The root of this misery lies in death's opposition to our human destiny of fellowship with God.[6]

According to Augustine, misery means being deprived of what we desire and love (*Enn. in Ps.* 26.2.7: *miser quisque dicitur quando illi subtrahitur quod amat* [CChrSL, 38, 157]). But many people also experience the misery of striving after that which in truth is not worth loving. When they have achieved the goods they seek, they are still more unhappy and more miserable than others, for they are so lacking in the true good that they are not even aware of the lack (ibid. and *Civ. Dei* 12.8: *qui perverse amat cuiuslibet naturae bonum, etiamsi adipiscatur, ipse fit in bono malus, et miser meliore privatus*). We can thus see why Augustine thinks that misery is our inevitable lot as long as death threatens life (*Civ. Dei* 11.15.1), for whether we know it or not, we all want a life that death does not end. The reason for this misery, however, is the sin of turning from God (22.24.3), for those who do not serve God are miserable because they are robbed of fellowship with God by their conduct (10.3.2: *Si ergo non colit Deum, misera est, quia Deo privatur*).

Misery, then, is the lot of those who are deprived of the fellowship with God that is the destiny of human life. Alienation from this destiny does not abolish it. Its continued presence is the basis of our misery, for

---

6. Cf. 2 Clem. 11:1. Along with the distress experienced by those who do not serve God, this letter also acknowledges misery in the more general sense, to which the godly and the godless are equally subject (9:4).

in alienation from God we are robbed of our true identity. According to Augustine's acute analysis, we are thus most miserable when we are not aware of our plight — i.e., not in misfortune, sickness, or closeness to death, but when the goods of this world cause us to forget God; we are miserable in the midst of prosperity and affluence because we find life empty and meaningless.

To speak of human misery is better than using the classical theological doctrine of sin to describe our situation of lostness when we are far from God. The term "misery" sums up our detachment from God, our autonomy, and all the resultant consequences. It brings out more clearly than the term "sin" itself the relation between sin and its ramifications. The term "alienation" has a similar breadth.[7] It has two sides, both an action we can take and a situation we can find ourselves in. We can alienate ourselves from someone, and we can also be in a state of alienation. In German the equivalent *Entfremdung* is etymologically close to *die Fremde* (the foreign country), with the implied thought of being away from one's own country (cf. the English "alien"). Alienated from God, we live in the misery of separation from God, far away from the home of our own identity.

In the NT, alienation describes the state of the Gentiles, who "are alienated from the life of God *[apēllontriōmenoi tēs zōēs tou theou]* because of the ignorance that is in them, due to their hardness of heart" (Eph. 4:18; cf. 2:12 and Col. 1:21). In the fathers, too, the concept of alienation is linked to the relationship with God.

P. Tillich, then, ought not to have seen Hegel as the originator of the term when he used it to elucidate the doctrine of sin.[8] Hegel (and later Marx) indeed emphasized the relation to the self, which has been implied in the term from the days of medieval mysticism.[9] In so doing, Hegel, and Marx after him, depicted self-alienation as the human activity that is the origin of the state of alienation. But the implied analogy to the theological doctrine of sin is limited here by the linking of self-alienation to alienation in the sense of alienation of property. This alienation presupposes prior possession. Hegel and Marx thus presuppose an original self-identity that we lose by alienation and self-alienation. Perhaps the Christian idea of an original state and a fall has had some influence here. In a Christian view, however, we never possess our own identity directly. We participate in it only by relation to God as to him who is other than ourselves and all finite things.

7. Cf. my *Anthropology in Theological Perspective* (Philadelphia, 1985), pp. 265ff.
8. P. Tillich, *Systematic Theology*, 3 vols. (repr. Chicago, 1961), II, 45.
9. For examples, see my *Anthropology*, p. 268.

We moderns are well aware of the experiences of misery and self-alienation in our human situation. Especially in literature and art the nature of existence that finds expression in such experiences has been impressively depicted. In its doctrine of sin, theology deals with the origin of this situation in our relation to God. In so doing it always presupposes our destiny of fellowship with God, which Christian teaching has developed on the basis of what the Bible says about our creation in the divine image (Gen. 1:26f.).

Together the two basic anthropological statements in Christian theology — the statements about our creation in the divine image and about our sin — are the presupposition of God's redeeming work for us through Jesus Christ. We need redemption because of sin, which is the root of our alienation from God and the self. But we can speak of redemption only in relation to an event that creates freedom for the redeemed. The fellowship with God mediated through Jesus Christ can mean redemption only on the condition that we thereby become free. This is so when fellowship with God helps us to self-identity, and this in turn presupposes that we are destined by nature for fellowship with God.

This destiny is the subject of the doctrine of our creation in the image of God. But presentation of this doctrine needs a more general anthropological basis that will ensure the connection between theological anthropology and the doctrine of creation on the one side, and christology on the other. In the theological tradition from patristic times the doctrine of our human nature as spiritual and not just psychosomatic has performed this function, forming the framework for an interpretation of the biblical statements about our divine likeness. Our presentation will thus begin at this point. The concrete relation of human life to the life-giving Spirit of God will then be dealt with at the end of the chapter and will form a transition to christology.

This chapter in Christian doctrine does not have the task of developing a complete anthropology. That would require more than a description of our destiny and the situation of alienation from it. A full theological anthropology would have to include as well the actualizing of this destiny, which is the theme of God's redeeming work, its appropriation to and by us, and its goal in the eschatological consummation.[10]

10. Rightly, then, O. H. Pesch put the themes of sin and grace at the center of his depiction of a theological anthropology, *Frei sein aus Gnade. Theologische Anthropologie* (1983). Christology and eschatology then of course must be brought into anthropology, the former as a basis for being in grace, the latter as its consummation. Nor must ecclesiology be left out, for it describes the community life within which our being in grace is actually lived.

A full anthropology would also include not only the biological foundations of the human form of life, its nature, and its position in the world but also the social relations in which human life is lived and which help to condition individual identity in the process of socialization.[11] We will constantly touch on this aspect in the systematic presentation that we are now offering. It will be a specific theme in connection with the concept of the church.[12] Nevertheless, our social nature will not be an independent theme in the discussion. Similarly, the themes of our historicity and our relations to the history of humanity as a means of the concrete actualizing of human life will run through all the remaining chapters of our presentation of Christian doctrine, but they will not be independent themes.

§ 1. Personal Unity of Body and Soul

Any interpretation of human reality must take into account the fact that we live and lead our lives consciously. One may try, as in radical behaviorism,[13] to reduce all conscious experience to outwardly observable conduct and try to explain it as an epiphenomenon of brain functions. One may also view it as the expression of a soul that is different in principle from the body.[14] At all events the fact of consciousness is a basic one in human life for which any anthropology must find a suitable interpretation. At the same time no one can deny that we know conscious and self-conscious life only as bodily life. Modern science also argues that bodily functions condition all psychological

---

11. Cf. part III of my *Anthropology*, pp. 315ff., esp. chs. 7 and 8 on the foundations of culture and the institutional order of life in society.

12. This theme does not belong under a doctrine of creation and preservation. Like the church, the social and political order of our common life must be discussed theologically under the criterion of the kingdom of God and in association with it. Similarly the theological place of sex relations is in the doctrine of marriage. As something given at creation, however, sexuality itself belongs among the prehuman principles of the productivity of life (see ch. 7 above, pp. 130f.).

13. Philosophically G. Ryle advocated radical behaviorism on the basis of linguistic analysis; see his *Concept of Mind* (New York, 1949). He specifically took issue with the Cartesian dualism that sees us as minds in machines. On psychological behaviorism from J. B. Watson to B. F. Skinner and for criticism of the basic assumptions, cf. my *Anthropology*, pp. 28ff.

14. Cf. J. Seifert, *Das Leib-Seele-Problem in der gegenwärtigen philosophischen Diskussion. Eine kritische Analyse* (1979), pp. 79ff.

experience. This is true even of self-consciousness. Yet this fact has not always been evident to us. Many earlier cultures gave the self-conscious human soul a greater measure of independence vis-à-vis the body than our modern knowledge of the close mutual interrelations of physical and psychological occurrence will permit.

In the history of modern thought, advances in nuanced knowledge of these interrelations have robbed of their credibility the traditional ideas of the soul as a substance that is distinct from the body and that is detached from it in death.[15] When the life of the soul is conditioned in every detail by bodily organs and processes, how can it be detached from the body and survive without it? Prevailing trends in modern anthropology see the soul and body as constitutive elements of the unity of human life that belong together and cannot be reduced to one another. The soul and consciousness are deeply rooted in our corporeality. Conversely, the body is not a corpse. It is an ensouled body in all its expressions in life.[16]

We may view this modern understanding as in line with the intentions of the earliest Christian anthropology. Over against Platonism, which was becoming the dominant philosophy of late antiquity by the middle of the 2nd century, the early fathers defended our psychosomatic unity as a basic principle of Christian anthropology. They did, of course, accept the view of the soul as an independent entity, which they corrected only to the extent of regarding both soul and body as partial principles of human reality, so that only the two together constitute the one human person. In spite of this emphasis on psychosomatic unity, however, the dualism of soul and body invaded Christian anthropology. This process illustrates the acceptance by early Christian thinking of ideas that the Hellenistic culture of the age took for granted; it is not an interpretation that has any essential place in Christian anthropology.

15. In favor of the idea that body and soul are two different substances, Seifert cites not only Plato, Plotinus, and Descartes but also Augustine and even Aquinas, in spite of the latter's view that the soul is an essential form of the body (ibid., pp. 126f.).

16. A pioneer of this approach was H. Bergson, *Matière et Mémoire. Essai sur la relation du corps à l'espirit* (1896). Close in many respects is the psychology of W. James, with its thesis that the body is the nucleus of the self of which we are conscious (*The Principles of Psychology* [1890; Cambridge, MA, 1981], pp. 400ff., cf. 341). On the relation between James and Bergson, cf. H. Ey, *La conscience* (Paris, 1963). Ey himself follows up Bergson's lead. In a different way the same is true of M. Merlau-Ponty and, in Germany, of the Scheler school of philosophical anthropology; cf. M. Scheler's works *Wesen und Formen der Sympathie* (1913) and *Die Stellung des Menschen im Kosmos* (1928).

Tertullian already was referring to body and soul as two separate if related substances (*De an.* 27.1f. [CChrSL, 2, 1954, 822f.]). Like Tatian before him,[17] he understood their relation along Stoic lines. The soul is the breath of the body, which manifests itself in the body (cf. Gen. 2:7). Like Irenaeus (*Adv. haer.* 2.34), Tertullian also regarded the soul as immortal (*De an.* 22.2 [CChrSL, 2, 814]) in contrast to Tatian's acceptance of its mortality (*Ad Graec.* 13.1). In support of this view Irenaeus appealed to the parable of Dives and Lazarus (Luke 16:19-31), whose fates after death presuppose their souls' immortality.

In early Christian theologians the interrelation of body and soul in the unity of the person received emphasis especially in apologetic arguments for the Christian hope of resurrection. Athenagoras claimed that the Creator purposed eternal life for the whole person. Hence a resurrection of the body is necessary, for the soul alone is not the whole person (*De res.* 15).

With its doctrine of psychosomatic unity Christian theology at many points had to oppose Platonism, which had a very similar doctrine of God.[18] First, except in Gnostic trends, it could not follow the Orphic teaching that Plato adopted, which viewed the body as the prison or grave of the soul (*Gorg.* 493a; *Crat.* 400b-c) and death as the liberation of the soul (*Phaed.* 64e; *Gorg.* 524b). In opposition Christian doctrine argued that the body as well as the soul is God's good creation and that the union of the two expresses his creative will.

Second, the soul is not divine, as in Plato (*Rep.* 611e). Rather, it is part of our created human nature. Already in Justin's *Dialogue with Trypho* the old man on the shore at Ephesus was stressing that the soul is created and therefore that it is corruptible like everything except God (*Dial.* 5). Although it is the vital principle of the body, it neither lives nor moves of itself (*Dial.* 6), as against Plato's view (*Phaed.* 245e). Later Christian theology certainly took over the doctrine of the soul's immortality but made it dependent on the will of the Creator and thus rejected its supposed inherent divinity. For the soul to attain to divine likeness, and therewith to participate in the immortal life of God, it needed gracious illuminating and elevating by the divine Spirit.[19]

A third difference between Christian and Platonic anthropology was closely related to the first two. Christians rejected the preexistence of souls and the connected Platonic doctrine of their transmigration and reincorporation (cf. *Phaed.* 76e-77d, also 80c ff.). Irenaeus expressly opposed Plato on this issue, contesting both memory of life before birth and the related preexistence of the soul (*Adv. haer.* 2.33.2 and 5). Origen, however, took over the idea of preexistence; along the lines of Plato (*Phaed.* 248c-d) he understood the linking of souls to

17. On Tatian's anthropology, cf. M. Elze, *Tatian und seine Theologie* (Göttingen, 1960), pp. 88ff.

18. Cf. my "Christentum und Platonismus," *ZKG* 96 (1985) 147ff., esp. 150ff.

19. Ibid., pp. 151f.

bodies as a consequence of earlier defects (*De princ.* 2.9.6f.; 1.7.4f.).[20] But Origen soon ran into opposition, and in the 6th century the church condemned him for this view.[21] In contrast, the church's own teaching maintained that the soul is created with the body. Two variations of this position are Tertullian's traducianism, which teaches that the individual soul is created with the body through conception, and creationism, which argues that each soul is directly created by God. Clement of Alexandria paved the way for the latter view, and Lactantius upheld it more decisively,[22] while to the very end Augustine remained undecided on the question.[23]

Though correcting Hellenistic and especially Platonic views, patristic anthropology did not attain fully to the biblical idea of psychosomatic unity, for it was limited by its model of a linking of two substances. Of all the philosophical positions held in antiquity, only the Aristotelian approach could lead to the right conclusion. This took place with the Christian Aristotelianism of High Scholasticism, when Aquinas advanced the thesis that the soul is the essential form of the body,[24] a position that the Council of Vienna (1312) affirmed to be the church's teaching (DS § 902 = ND § 405). On this view the soul is not just a partial principle but that which makes us human in our bodily reality. Conversely, the body is the concrete form in which our humanity, the soul, finds appropriate expression.[25]

For all the closeness to the biblical view of our bodily reality, there is still a shift of accent in Aquinas. It is not so much that he interprets the

20. In interpretation, cf. P. Kübel, *Schuld und Schicksal bei Origenes, Gnostikern, und Platonikern* (1973), pp. 88ff., 95f.

21. At Constantinople in 543 (DS §§ 403, 410 = ND § 401/1, 8). Cf. F. P. Fiorenza and J. B. Metz, "Der Mensch als Einheit von Leib und Seele," in *Mysterium Salutis*, II (1967), p. 615.

22. H. Karpp, *Probleme altchristlicher Anthropologie. Biblische Anthropologie und philosophische Psychologie bei den Kirchenvätern des dritten Jahrhunderts* (1950), pp. 92ff., esp. on Clement (pp. 96f.), Lactantius (pp. 135f., 143ff.), and Tertullian (49ff., 59f.).

23. Ibid., pp. 243f. The real reason why, even in 418, in his letter to Optatus (*Ep.* 190), Augustine would not commit himself to creationism is to be sought in his doctrine of original sin (p. 246). Following Augustine, and for the same reason, Luther inclined to traducianism (cf. G. Ebeling, *Lutherstudien*, 3 vols. [Tübingen, 1971-89], II/2, 46-59).

24. In *ST* 1.76.1 the *anima intellectiva* is the essential form of the human body (*humani corporis forma*). Art. 4 of the same question claims that it is the only essential form. Cf. Fiorenza and Metz in *Mysterium Salutis*, II, 610ff.; also K. Rahner, *Geist in Welt. Zur Metaphysik der endlichen Erkenntnis bei Thomas von Aquin* (2nd ed. 1957), pp. 325ff., esp. 329.

25. Cf. K. Rahner, *Theological Investigations*, 23 vols. (London, 1961-92), IV, 245f.

totality of this reality in terms of the soul.[26] The second creation story could use "living soul" *(nephesh ḥayya)* for this reality (Gen. 2:7). The real difference lies in the understanding of the soul, and especially its spiritual or intellectual character *(anima intellectiva)*. The biblical account certainly relates the soul to spirit, but in a very different sense.

In Gen. 2:7 the soul is not merely the vital principle of the body but the ensouled body itself, the living being as a whole. Hence it does not have the autonomy expressed by the Aristotelian-Thomistic concept of substance. The description of Adam as *nephesh ḥayya* represents him as needy and therefore desirous; his life has the form of need and desire. The basic meaning of *nephesh* as throat, gullet, or larynx has in view the dry throat or hungry gullet. "Like cold water to a thirsty *nephesh*, so is good news from a far country" (Prov. 25:25). "A sated *nephesh* loathes honey, but to one who is hungry, everything bitter is sweet" (27:7). A human being as *nephesh* is a being of desires oriented to things that might meet the desires, and one that is searching for them. Hence an ensouled body does not live of itself but by the Spirit of God who breathes life into it.

In many ways the description of life as need and desire corresponds to the teleological description of living creatures in Aristotelian philosophy. Yet we must not link it to the idea of an organic development of living things in the sense of the Aristotelian concept of entelechy. A point of contact with the Christian Aristotelianism of Aquinas is that God alone can satisfy the desire for life that constitutes the life of the soul (Ps. 107:9; cf. 42:1f.). From the biblical standpoint to desire God is of the very nature of creaturely life as such, transcendent and unattainable though the divine reality may be to living creatures unless it addresses them itself with creative power.

In the biblical sense "spirit" does not mean intellect but vital creative force. Its nature is that of the wind.[27] This is the obvious point of Gen. 2:7. God blows into Adam the breath of life, and this gives life to what he has formed (Job 33:4). "Only the Creator's breathing makes him . . . a living being, a living person, a living individual."[28] The wind of the Spirit or the breath of God is something that the creature always needs. It does not control the blowing of this wind. If the wind stops, death

---

26. Cf. Fiorenza and Metz in *Mysterium Salutis,* II, 613.
27. See vol. I, 373f.
28. H. W. Wolff, *Anthropology of the OT* (Philadelphia, 1974), p. 22.

follows. If God "should take back his spirit to himself, and gather to himself his breath, all flesh would perish together, and man would return to dust" (Job 34:14f.). This does in fact happen when we die. "The dust returns to the earth as it was, and the spirit *[ruah]* returns to God who gave it" (Eccl. 12:7).

The texts just quoted show that the breath of life *(nishmat hayyim)* to which Gen. 2:7 refers cannot be separated from the Spirit *(ruah)*. The two terms describe the same reality (cf. Gen. 6:17). The mortality of human life results from the fact that the Spirit of God is not always at work in it (Gen. 6:3). As "flesh," we are perishable like all other living creatures. Conversely, as long as human life lasts, it is due to the continued activity of the breath of life that comes from the Spirit of God.

The working of the Spirit in living creatures does not mean that he is a constituent part of the creature. Rather, it means that creaturely life has an eccentric character, that it is referred to the divine power of the Spirit that works upon it. Living creatures have the breath of life in them, but it is not at their disposal. God is always the Lord of creaturely life.

The Spanish church of late antiquity rejected the view ascribed to Priscillian that the human soul is a part of God or a divine substance (*Dei portionem vel Dei esse substantiam,* DS § 201; cf. §§ 190 and 455 = ND § 402/5). This was in keeping with the opposition at the very beginnings of Christian theology to the Platonic teaching of the soul's divinity, which seemed to be incompatible with an assertion of its creatureliness. What was not rejected, however, was the idea of a vital operation of the divine Spirit in creaturely life as a principle transcending humanity. On this view the Spirit is not to be understood as a power of the soul but as the power of God that generates and sustains the life of both soul and body and is thus at work in it.

There is, of course, a group of OT sayings that depicts the special measure of the divine Spirit in some people as a charisma conferred upon them and as having some degree of independence vis-à-vis the transcendence of the Spirit of God.[29] This independence is particularly noticeable in the case of what we might call a negative charisma, e.g., the evil *ruah* sent by God to King Saul (1 Sam. 16:14; cf. 1 Kgs. 22:20ff.; Isa. 19:14). In a broader generalization the Spirit that works for a limited time in us might also be called "our" spirit.[30] But nowhere does the OT make any

29. Ibid., p. 36.
30. Ibid., pp. 36ff.

basic distinction between the divine *ruaḥ* and the independent creaturely *ruaḥ* as an essential constituent of living things. It was Hellenism that first brought into Jewish thinking the idea of vital processes as functions of essential constituents of human beings and their souls. The pneuma that works in us could then be regarded either as an essential creaturely element or as an essential divine part of the creaturely soul.

We find the first of these views in rabbinic writings[31] as well as in the apostle Paul. Paul could describe human beings comprehensively as spirit, soul, and body (1 Thess. 5:23) and contrast the divine Spirit with the human spirit (Rom. 8:16ff.), even setting the two in opposition (1 Cor. 2:10f.).[32] Did he see in the latter a divinely given pneuma that is finally alien to us?[33] Did he make his statements on the self-evident but unexpressed presupposition that the pneuma at work in creatures derives totally from the Creator Spirit of God? If so, we would expect this presupposition to be stated at least in connection with the appeal to Gen. 2:7 in 1 Cor. 15:45. But that is not the case. Paul did not say that the living soul was breathed into the first Adam by the Spirit of God. He mentioned the life-giving Spirit *(pneuma zōopoioun),* not at the creation of the first man, but as a distinctive feature of the eschatological man. But how is it that the natural man, who is after the manner of the first Adam, can be or have pneuma (1 Cor. 2:11) if he was created only as a living soul without the Spirit, the Spirit being reserved for the eschatological man? At this point we obviously need an interpretation that goes beyond the express statements of the apostle. Only thus can we reconstruct their material unity.

We can hardly seek this material unity in Paul's use of the term "spirit" along the lines of the second interpretation above, namely, the idea that the spirit is an essential part of human beings or human souls. This was the understanding of Gen. 2:7 that Hellenistic Judaism developed, seeing in the inbreathing of the breath of life into Adam an imparting of the divine Spirit.[34] Typical of this line of interpretation is the linking of the imparting of the Spirit to the knowledge of God. We find

---

31. Cf. E. Sjöberg in *TDNT,* VI, 377, 379, on the related idea of preexisting spirit-souls created directly by God.

32. For further examples, cf. R. Bultmann, *Theology of the NT* (New York, 1951), pp. 205ff.

33. E. Schweizer takes this view in *TDNT,* VI, 435, contra Bultmann.

34. On what follows, esp. Philo, cf. W.-D. Hauschild, *Gottes Geist und der Mensch. Studien zur frühchristlichen Pneumatologie* (1972), pp. 256ff.

this in the Qumran texts.[35] Behind it lies the understanding of wisdom as a charisma that the Spirit of God imparts to us. The number of years does not impart wisdom. "The Spirit enlightens men, the breath of the Almighty makes them understand" (Job 32:8; cf. Deut. 34:9). The Wisdom of Solomon even equates wisdom with the Pneuma.[36] Hence humans, having received the breath of life, ought to know God instead of worshiping idols (Wis. 15:11). Linking Spirit and wisdom according to a Hellenizing interpretation suggests that reason should be viewed as the divine Pneuma that is breathed into us at creation. Philo either made or came close to this momentous linking.[37]

The interpreting of Gen. 2:7 as an imparting of reason by the Creator was the basis of equating the human spirit and reason, which led Christian theology to see in the spirit-soul a higher part of our human constitution. But this theology rejected the idea that the spirit-soul is divine. Christian Gnosticism might have played an important role in this regard.

For Gnostics the spirit imparted at creation (Gen. 2:7) could not be the true divine Pneuma because they ascribed creation to the demiurge and not to the Redeemer God. Only unnoticed by the demiurge could a true divine Spirit have also slipped in.[38] Clement of Alexandria then distinguished between the breath of life in Gen. 2:7 and the imparting of the divine Spirit, viewing the former, like Philo, as an inbreathing of *nous* and reserving the latter for redemption.[39] Similarly Tertullian in his work on the soul stressed against Hermogenes the origin of the soul in the breath of God (Gen. 2:7)[40] but distinguishes between Spirit *(spiritus)* and breath *(flatus)* as between cause and effect, equating breath with the soul.[41] Augustine

35. 1QH frag. 3, 14; cf. J. Maier, *Die Texte vom Toten Meer,* I (1960), p. 120; also Hauschild, *Gottes Geist,* p. 257.

36. For examples, cf. W. Bieder in *TDNT,* VI, 371. Cf. also Sir. 24:3, which describes wisdom as the breath that proceeds from the mouth of God.

37. Hauschild, *Gottes Geist,* pp. 258ff. Bieder in *TDNT,* VI, 373, understands *Op. mundi* 35 rather differently. In another place (*Her.* 55) Philo, according to Bieder (p. 374), even equates *nous* in its guiding function as *hegemonikon* with the divine Pneuma.

38. Hauschild, *Gottes Geist,* pp. 263ff.

39. Ibid., pp. 18ff. and 268f.; cf. Clement of Alexandria *Strom* 5.94.3 etc. See also pp. 28ff. on the role of the Spirit in redemption.

40. Tertullian *De an.* 1.1 (CChrSL, 2, 781).

41. Ibid. 11.3 (CChrSL, 2, 797). Cf. also 4.1 (786), where Tertullian stressed against Plato the creatureliness of the soul. In speaking of the *hegemonikon* of the soul (15.1ff. [801]), Tertullian referred to the biblical view of the heart as the seat of thoughts and aspirations. On Tertullian's dependence on Stoic psychology, cf. H. Karpp, *Probleme alt-christlicher Anthropologie,* pp. 71ff.

took much the same view (*Civ. Dei* 13.24.2ff.). In Origen, however, Gen. 2:7 was no longer normative for anthropology because Origen taught the preexistence of souls.[42] He thus based our spiritual nature on our creation in the divine rational image according to Gen. 1:26. Later theology followed the same line of argument (e.g., Gregory of Nyssa), although rejecting preexistence.[43]

Under the influence of Augustine, Latin Scholasticism rejected the understanding of Gen. 2:7 along the lines of an imparting of the divine Spirit (Aquinas *ST* 1.91.4 ad 3) on the ground that the apostle differentiated the result of this inbreathing by the Creator (a living soul) from the life of the new Adam that is permeated by the Spirit (1 Cor. 15:45; cf. Augustine *Civ. Dei* 13.24.4 n. 6). It needed a return to the Hebrew wording and the uninhibited exegesis of Luther to find the Spirit of God again in the breathing in of the breath of life in Gen. 2:7, though still, of course, with a distinction between this work in creation and the eschatological work in the new Adam. Even Luther failed to see, however, that the life-giving work of the divine Spirit in creation extends to all living things.[44]

The profound difference between the patristic idea of a human spirit-soul and the biblical view of the relation between soul and spirit may be seen in the fact that neither the description of Adam as a living soul in Gen. 2:7 nor the view that life is a work of the divine breath of life gives humans any uniqueness as compared with other living creatures.[45] Animals, too, rank as *nephesh ḥayya* (Gen. 2:19) and have the spirit of life in them (1:20; cf. 6:17; 7:22). In this regard humans simply share in what distinguishes all living things from the rest of creation. According to the first creation story, it is the divine likeness and the associated dominion over all other earthly creatures that distinguishes humans from animals. We find a similar view in Ps. 8:6ff. Similarly, in the second story the man has the privilege of being allowed to name the animals (Gen. 2:19).[46] In view here is the distinctive faculty of speech and the related knowledge. Elsewhere, too, the OT finds a place for the significance of

42. Hauschild, *Gottes Geist*, p. 269, cf. 86ff., esp. 91ff.
43. For Origen only the spiritual part of the soul was created in the divine image (*De princ.* 2.10.7; cf. 3.1.13). Gregory of Nyssa regarded our rational nature as a copy of the divine Nous and Logos (*De hom. op.* 5 [PG, 44, 137B-C). On his rejection of preexistence, cf. 28 (PG, 44, 229ff.).
44. On Luther's exposition of Gen. 2:7 in the 1535/45 Genesis Lectures (esp. WA, 42, 63ff., LW 1 on 2:7), cf. G. Ebeling, *Lutherstudien*, II/2, 34-46.
45. Wolff, *Anthropology*, p. 22. J. Moltmann stresses this point that all living things share in the breath of life (*God in Creation* [San Francisco, 1985], p. 187).
46. G. von Rad, *Genesis: A Commentary* (Philadelphia, 1961), p. 83.

knowing and planning reason in human life, even though it is located in the heart and not the head.[47]

But when it is a matter of the advantage of humans over all other creatures, the emphasis is not on intellectual ability but on the destiny of fellowship with God and the position of rule associated with closeness to God. Materially, of course, the latter is connected, as we see it, to the work of reason. But there can be no question of an autonomy of reason. Like all other expressions of human life, the work of reason is referred to the life-giving working of the divine Spirit. Even the Wisdom literature, which regards understanding as a particularly valuable gift of the Spirit (cf. Job 32:8; 33:4; Prov. 2:6; also the Wisdom of Solomon), does not equate this with our intellectual capacity but sees in it a gift that is not native to us.

The biblical data thus differentiate between spirit and reason. But they give us little help in working out the distinction. Though what they say about the human heart gives evidence of its ability to know and judge, clarification of these points was to a much higher degree a concern of Greek thinking. Rightly, then, patristic theology gave a bigger place in their anthropology to Greek ideas of *nous* and its relevance. In so doing they linked the faculty of knowledge to the concept of the specifically human soul. They found a basis for this in the use of the term "reason" in Paul (Rom. 7:23; cf. 1:20; 12:2, etc.).

The Johannine doctrine of the Logos also suggested that along the lines of Greek ideas of the relation between *logos* and *nous,* they might view human reason as a sharing in the *logos* that comes to fulfillment in one man with the incarnation of the Logos. In this light it seemed to be plausible to see in the divine likeness an expression of the sharing of the *nous* in the Logos. What they had to avoid, however, was identifying reason and spirit. The life-giving working of the divine Spirit in us is not the same as our reason. Like all other living functions, our reason, too, needs to be actualized by the Creator Spirit of God.[48] This fact does not rule out, however, a natural disposition of reason for such actualization nor a leading role for it, as the dominant function of the human soul, in the relation of the whole person to the Spirit.

---

47. Wolff, *Anthropology,* pp. 40-58, esp. 46ff.
48. Rightly K. Barth stressed an equation of the Spirit with God and the difference of the Spirit from creaturely reality. He thus opposed trichotomism on the ground that it forces us to see in the Spirit a part of ourselves (along with the soul and body) or of our souls (*CD,* III/2, 355ff.).

Materially, though with no link to Gen. 2:7 or distinction between spirit and reason, we find the first of these two thoughts expressed in Augustine's doctrine that reason has an aptitude for enlightenment by the divine light of truth.[49] On the basis of Plato's view of enlightenment Augustine developed here a conception analogous in many respects to what we find in the Bible (cf. John 1:9). As a theological interpretation of human reason, it was much superior to the view of knowledge in Christian Aristotelianism worked out by Latin High Scholasticism. On that view reason is an independent entity, though secondarily referred to God as its supernatural goal. Albert the Great and Aquinas, however, viewed the active intellect, which alone is immortal according to Aristotle,[50] as part of the human soul and not as a superhuman power working on the soul from without. They thus laid the foundation for an understanding along Christian lines of our subjective freedom in acts of knowing,[51] in contrast to the views of knowledge in antiquity, which regarded it as in some way the reception of a given truth of things.[52]

Later, in Nicholas of Cusa, even sharper emphasis fell on the activity of reason in thinking knowledge as spontaneous productivity reflecting the creative freedom of the divine Spirit.[53] Cusa's developed conception of a freedom of rational knowledge that approximates to the thoughts of the Creator with its conjectures on the reality of created things[54] offered the model of an understanding that merely applied given, a priori forms of thought to the material of the senses. The argument has in its favor that it better took into account the freedom and historicity of rational activity. In the process the imagination became the true creative principle in intellectual activity. The understanding simply provided it with logical rules. But the activity of the imagination rested on a higher form of receptivity,[55] not just on receptivity to sense impressions, nor on their reproduction by the memory in a free recombining of their contents, but on an openness that relates the infinite ground of subjectivity to finite data of the

---

49. For the parallels between Augustine's doctrine of knowledge and his doctrine of grace, cf. R. Lorenz, "Gnade und Erkenntnis bei Augustin," *ZKG* 75 (1964) 21ff.

50. Aristotle *De an.* 430a.23.

51. Albertus Magnus *Meta.* 11.1.9, Opera omnia 16/2 (1964, ed. B. Geyer), 472, pp. 69f.; Aquinas *SCG* 2.76 and 78, and *ST* 1.79.4. Especially in Albert, decision on this matter is closely linked to the theme of individual immortality, the active intellect alone being immortal in Aristotle.

52. Cf. my essay "Rezeptive Vernunft. Die antike Deutung der Erkenntnis als Hinnahme vorgegebener Wahrheit," in *Überlieferung und Aufgabe. Festschrift für E. Heintel zum 70. Geburtstag,* ed. H. Nagl-Docekal (1982), I, 265-301.

53. Nicholas of Cusa, *De Beryllo* 6; cf. *Idiota de mente* 7.

54. Cf. on this M. de Gandillac, *Nikolaus von Kues. Studien zu seiner Philosophie und philosophischen Weltanschauung* (1953), pp. 153ff., 164; also Cusa's *De coniec.*

55. H. Kunz, *Die anthropologische Bedeutung der Phantasie,* I (Basel, 1946), and on this my *Anthropology,* pp. 377ff.

consciousness.[56] This line of thinking could see itself as true to the theological intentions of Augustine's doctrine of enlightenment.

The crucial role of the life of the imagination, which unites receptivity and freedom, in the activity of reason and understanding, helps to elucidate the dependence of reason on the working of the Spirit as the basis of our subjective freedom. For a more precise understanding, however, it is necessary to attain some clarity on the relation of the Spirit to the general functions of the consciousness.

The basic relation of the consciousness to the infinite basis of life may well lie in the sense of life that in adult experience grasps the distinction between the self and the world, while in the symbiotic sphere of early childhood no clear distinction is yet made between the objective and the subjective aspects of the relation to the world.[57] Feelings of pleasure and pain very early provide a self-reference, of course, which serves as a starting point for the later development of a sense of the self as distinct from an awareness of the world.[58] This self-acquaintance, which is implicitly given

56. In the first version of his *Wissenschaftslehre* (ET *Science of Knowledge* [New York, 1970]), J. G. Fichte described imagination as a faculty that hovers between definition and nondefinition, between the finite and the infinite (*Werke*, I [ed. I. H. Fichte, 1845-46], p. 216, ET 193f.). He ascribed it to the activity of the I reaching out into the infinite, though the element of receptivity in its phenomenology would suggest that as Fichte conceives of it, it is to be related to feeling (pp. 289ff.; cf. 314ff., ET 254, 275). Fichte himself paid no regard to the receptive element in the life of the imagination. It is instructive in this respect to adduce what Fichte said later about feeling (*Wissenschaftslehre*, 1797-98, ed. P. Baumann [PhB, 239, 70f.]; also the 1801-2 version, ed. R. Lauth [PhB, 302, 75ff., 179f.]). Materially cf. the discussion in my *Anthropology*, pp. 244ff. (on feeling) and 377ff. (on imagination).

57. On the transcending of the subject-object distinction that characterizes the phenomenon of feeling, cf. my *Anthropology*, pp. 250f., and on the underlying symbiotic link to the environment, pp. 226ff., 261f.

58. In his *Christian Faith*, § 54, Schleiermacher thought the distinction between pleasure and its opposite depended on the relation of sensory self-awareness to feeling. In § 3, however, he defined feeling as direct self-consciousness. In the light of modern descriptions of feeling, we must take a critical view of both positions. Feeling is not just self-awareness as distinct from awareness of the world. In feeling, the self and the world are not separate. The relation to the self becomes explicit only in self-awareness, but insofar as it is defined by the qualities of pleasure and the opposite that are already there, it exists as a predisposition in feeling (cf. my *Anthropology*, pp. 247ff.). In *Christian Faith*, § 5.1, Schleiermacher shows interest in the fact that in feeling we do not stand opposed to others, but he relates this only to the element of dependence, which in his view is contained already in the immediate self-consciousness (§ 4), whereas in fact, as his own argument shows in § 4.2 (interaction with others), the distinction of the self and the object is presupposed already in sensory awareness. More radically than Schleiermacher, we must root the priority of the distinction of I and subject in the concept of feeling itself, which we cannot characterize as self-awareness but

in feeling,[59] is something that we share with animal life and perhaps with all living things, for all living things, as autocatalysts, are processes of self-organization that are characterized as such by a relation to the totality of their own existence.[60] To form an explicit self-consciousness, however, a link seems to be needed to a nonimpulsive objectivity of object-consciousness that is typical of humans and may be seen in children at play.[61] Being with others as others makes possible the distinction and relation of different objects and also their distinction from one's own body as signified by the proper name and the use of "I,"[62] along with the placing of this body in the world of objects.

The being with others as others mediated by perception awareness[63] thus seems to include, along with the distinction of objects from one another and from the I of one's own body, a field of consciousness in which the basic relation of I and world takes on its contours. The feeling for life as an expression of the presence of spirit with that of the indefinite totality of life that precedes and overarches the subject-object distinction underlies, then, the formation of the field of consciousness within which a survey of different contents is possible.[64] In the experience of encounter with others, this world of consciousness is ascribed to one's own ego and is thus relativized as the world of this ego as distinct from others. The I-relativity of the world of consciousness and its difference from the real world are not constitutive of the consciousness of objects as such but become thematic only in the light of the different worldviews bound up with intersubjectivity. The presence of the infinite ground of being, the

---

merely as a basis for this by means of the qualities of pleasure and its opposite. Cf. my *Anthropology*, pp. 250f. The awareness of dependence, which for Schleiermacher provided the key in his description of religious awareness, is not an original element in feeling but presupposes already the differentiation of I and object.

59. The Stoic doctrine of *oikeiōsis* depicted this as at work already in animals in the form of the striving for self-preservation. Cf. M. Pohlenz, *Die Stoa* (Göttingen, 1959), pp. 57f. W. James built on this in his *Principles of Psychology*, pp. 316f.

60. See above, pp. 126ff.

61. Cf. my *Anthropology*, pp. 62ff., 323ff., 358f.

62. Ibid., pp. 220ff.

63. Ibid., p. 62. Barth describes the human ability to grasp the other as such as our rational nature, which is presupposed in the event of our encounter with God (*CD*, III/2, 402). Conversely, the final cause of our presupposed rationality is that we are destined to perceive God. In distinction from the view above, Barth regarded self-awareness as the basis of the act of perception, which he described as taking up another into one's own self-awareness (p. 399). In contrast, I argue that awareness of the object precedes awareness of the self.

64. Cf. T. Nagel, *The View from Nowhere* (New York, 1986), esp. pp. 13-27.

Spirit, which declares itself in the feeling for life, transcends, however, the difference of subjects; nor is this true only of one's own I, since awareness of this I is itself a product of the differentiating of the unity of the feeling for life in the process of experience.[65]

Only in the field of intersubjectivity and in consequence of the awareness of the I-relativity of one's own self-consciousness can a distinction be made between body and soul. Over against the soul as the inner world of the consciousness stands the body, which, like the things of the world and in distinction from the inner world of my consciousness, is there for others as well as myself. It is tempting to regard the inner world of the consciousness as the true I in distinction from the body. But this is unduly to restrict the concept of the soul as well as that of the ego. In pointing to the speaker, the word "I" always indicates the physical individuality of the speaker.[66] If we are to view the living body as ensouled inasmuch as it is living, then the term "soul" must cover more than the inner world of the consciousness. It must include also the unconscious, which is related to one's own corporeality and its history. It is possible here to relate the idea of the soul that is oriented to experience of an inner world of consciousness with the concept of the soul as the vital principle of the body. Yet the impression that the soul confronts the body as something independent might well derive from treating the inner world of consciousness as independently related to the I.

The inner world of consciousness is ascribed to the I as its own. In the tradition of Kantian transcendental philosophy the I (as in "I think") even rates as the basis of its unity, the unity of experience. But is this really true? Does not the world of the consciousness in some sense have its unity in itself, in its contents and its basic thoughts? Is not the consciousness of the I that thinks the thoughts actually the ground of the conscious experience of these contents and thus responsible for the way in which their apprehension deviates from their objective truth? In fact differentiation always implies a unity of that which is differentiated. This is not the external addition of the consciousness in its synthetic function. Naturally we do not self-evidently become aware of this unity. As the young Hegel would put it, we need perception, or specific per-

---

65. Cf. my "Bewusstsein und Geist," *ZTK* 80 (1983) 332-51, on K. R. Popper's argument in discussion with J. C. Eccles, *The Self and Its Brain: An Argument for Interaction* (New York, 1977).

66. James, *Principles of Psychology,* p. 323, also 378.

ceptions.[67] From the infinity of feeling these come through the imagination, which according to Fichte hovers between that infinity and the
finite data that the consciousness distinguishes. But in the process, as
Hegel emphasized, the perceptions generated by the imagination need
disciplining by the differentiating work of reflection. Only thus do they
take on content as a grasping of the unity of what is differentiated.

Since the exact determining of what is distinct itself depends on
an awareness of the unity, the perceptions of the imagination must relate
both to the different members in their particularity and to the unity that
binds them together for all their distinctiveness. The unity is thus something other than the distinction. Grasping the unity in distinction is a
function of the ability to keep one's distance in an awareness of otherness.
The unity of what is distinct is thus a different thing from the consciousness. It is not owed to the unity of the ego. This unity, as the basis of all
experience that underlies the unity of its contents subjectively and gives
them unity in the course of life, is correlative to the objective unity of the
"concept" that comprehends in its unity what is objectively distinct. There
is thus formed an awareness of the unity of all that which is specific and
distinct, of the "world" as the epitome of everything finite and limited, in
contrast to which we can think of the infinite as something distinct from
it. A further step in reflection then leads us to the insight that we can
distinguish the infinite from the finite (and thus from every "something"
as opposed to something else) only on the condition that it is not just
something other than the finite, in which case it would itself be finite, but
that it also comprehends everything finite. This thought of the infinite
One gives expression to that which is always present to the consciousness
as the indefinite Infinite. It thus forms the mental space in which there
can be distance from the other and definition of its otherness and relationship, of the space that is opened thereby for the consciousness.

We can hardly regard the authority of the ego as a precondition of
every form of objective awareness. It is developed in the process of objective experience and by distinction from everything else. In individual
experience the social nexus precedes the use of the term "I," though an
implicit self-reference such as we have in the feeling for life is a condition
of learning to use this word. With the use of the word the self-reference
becomes an explicit theme for the individual, and secondarily the I be-

67. G. W. F. Hegel, *The Difference between Fichte's and Schelling's System of Philosophy* (1801), PhB, 62a, 31ff. (Albany, NY, 1977), pp. 110ff.

comes the soil of all the contents of the consciousness. But first the multiplicity of the world and the living reality of the individual in distinction therefrom are opened up to the consciousness by the infinity of the feeling for life that underlies the difference of subject and object in the consciousness and thus transcends them in every situation in life. In this respect we should perhaps redefine the relation between spirit and consciousness if the feeling for life expresses the living presence of the Creator Spirit in living creatures. Not the I but the divine Spirit is the ultimate basis for the interrelatedness of that which is distinct in the consciousness, of the interrelatedness also of the I and the things of the world, especially similar living creatures.

Awareness of the infinite as such in its distinction from the finite rests on the fact that we are always "ecstatic" in relation to the other — always apart from the other. We can know the other as such, not merely as our own correlate. We thus learn to distinguish each from the other in its own particularity. Finally, relative to the whole sphere of the finite that is defined and limited by this difference from the other, we form the thought of the infinite. In grasping the finite there is always a nonthematic sense of the infinite as that which is other than the finite. We are aware of the infinite in the religious awareness of a divine power at work in every finite phenomenon. In all knowledge of the world we always see God's eternal power and deity in his works (Rom. 1:20), which is true even though we do not glorify God as God or give him thanks but become foolish and irrational in our religious ideas (v. 21). When this happens we do not distinguish the infinite reality of God (or do so only inadequately) from the medium of creaturely things in whose finitude it may be seen, nor are we aware of our own finitude as beings that, along with the whole world of finite phenomena, owe their existence totally to the one infinite God.

Nevertheless, in a rational distinction of each finite thing from every other, and of all finite things, including ourselves, from the infinite, the divine Logos is at work, who creates and rules all creaturely existence in its individuality. In spite of all the perversion due to sin, of which we must speak later, human intelligence in its perception of the otherness of the other participates in the self-distinction of the eternal Son from the Father by which he is not merely united to the Father but is also the principle of all creaturely existence in its individuality. Human reason, of course, can generate only thoughts and not directly the reality of finite things. But these thoughts do not simply represent finite objects in their distinction from one another. They can also form a basis for the constructs of human technology.

As the Son, in his self-distinction from the Father, is united with him by the Spirit in the unity of the divine life, and as, in his creative activity, he unites what is distinct by the power of the Spirit, so the differentiating activity of human reason needs the Spirit who enables it, by mediating the imagination, to name each thing in its particularity, and in all the distinction to be aware of the unity that holds together what is different. In the process human reason is not of itself filled with the Spirit. In its creatureliness it needs, like every other vital function, to be quickened by the living power of the Spirit if it is to be active, and it also needs the inspiration that lifts it above its own finitude and that in all its limitation makes it aware of the presence of truth and totality in the individual.

The biblical view of the Spirit of God as the creative principle of everything living insofar as it has soul and has life in itself may also be explained in terms of the varied nature of the consciousness and the activity of reason, i.e., those dimensions of the soul that attracted the special attention of Greek philosophy and still form a central sphere of the life of the soul according to our modern understanding. In this respect the view of the soul as the vital principle of the body forces us to inquire into the function of the consciousness for life in general. We best approach this question by recalling the relation of all the phenomena of life to their environment. Environmental reality becomes a theme for living creatures in their perceptive consciousness. By the perception that internalizes what is around us, life also becomes "ecstatic" — that which stands outside of us. The more the life of the consciousness develops, the more we move outward in our consciousness, and the more the world around us moves inward and becomes present in us. The same applies to social relations, for our knowing the human self-consciousness forms the highest stage of the relation of outwardness and inwardness. The objectivity of our relation to objects is the condition on which, in terms of the world, we can become objective to ourselves as members of it.

The "ecstasy" of consciousness — that it "stands outside" — means enhanced and more inward life and therefore more intense participation in the Spirit, the creative origin of all life. This participation does not have to involve being snatched out of the world, as in the extreme case of a sense of the antithesis of the infinite to everything finite. Instead, it expands the soul by experience of the world, which the Spirit creatively permeates, and especially by the experience of human fellowship in face of the infinite ground of the world. Only in others do we meet a life that in its feeling for life is permeated in some way by the infinite ground of the world and the associated promise of the totality of life that is common to each and to all. The presence of this dimension characterizes all encounter with others, even though it is in the negative mode of a cramping or corrupting of their spiritual potential. It runs through all social relations, beginning with those of the family. Not least of all it gives personal depth to the encounter of the sexes.

Without the works of the divine Spirit in us there could be no personality in the deeper sense of the term. For personality has to do with the manifestation of the truth and totality of individual life in the moment of its existence. We are not persons simply because we have self-consciousness and can distinguish and maintain our own ego apart from others.[68] We do not cease to be persons where we no longer have this identity in the self-consciousness, nor are we without personality where it is not present.[69] Personality is grounded in the destiny that transcends our empirical reality. It is primarily experienced in the other, the Thou, as the secret of an inwardness that goes beyond all that we perceive outwardly of the other, so that this other meets us as a being that is active not merely of itself but in terms of a ground of existence that we cannot finally see externally.[70]

Although psychological knowledge explains much in the conduct of the other, psychology cannot lay hold of a final origin of its freedom. That which meets me in this way touches me as personal reality.[71] Part of this is that a totality of existence that I cannot control meets me through that which is externally present to the senses, and does so in such a way that I am also claimed with my own life. We can understand this only on

68. Contra Kant, *Anthropology from a Pragmatic Point of View* (1798), § 1.

69. See my "Der Mensch als Person," in *Das Verhältnis der Psychiatrie zu ihren Nachbardisziplinen,* ed. H. Heimann and H. J. Gaertner (1986), pp. 4f., and my essay "Die Theologie und die neue Frage nach der Subjectivität," *Stimmen der Zeit* 202 (1984) 805ff., esp. 515f.

70. On this cf. D. Henrich, "Ding an sich. Ein Prolegomenon zur Metaphysik des Endlichen," in *Vernunft des Glaubens,* ed. J. Rohls and G. Wenz (1988), pp. 42-92, esp. 69ff., 89ff.

71. Cf. my article "Person," *RGG,* V (3rd ed. 1961), pp. 230ff., for emphasis on this point as regards experience of the personality of God. On the anthropological application, cf. my *Anthropology,* p. 235, and also J. Zizioulas, "Human Capacity and Incapacity: A Theological Exploration of Personhood," *SJT* 28 (1975) 401-47.

the premise that the ground of my own existence meets me in the person of the other.[72] Encounter with the other can thus stimulate inner awareness of my own personality, and it can also be an occasion for critical independence vis-à-vis all intersubjective dependencies.[73]

Although all human life is personal in its individual concretions, it took a long time before the concept of person became a theme of basic anthropological reflection. In the history of Western culture this fact was perhaps related to the further fact that only under the impact of biblical faith was the individual as such — each individual — viewed as a target of the divine address. Materially this was a consequence of the divine likeness. In expression of it the faith of Israel, in virtue of the divine likeness, declared individual life to be sacrosanct (Gen. 9:6). Yet this did not yet imply that each individual human life in its uniqueness has infinite worth for God. The decisive breakthrough to this insight came with the message of Jesus that God reaches out to each of his creatures with eternal love, which we see pointedly in his love for those who have gone astray and are lost.[74] Only in Christian thinking does this characterization of human life then come into relation to the concept of person. The historical starting point for this is christology, with its insistence on the personal unity of Jesus with the divine Logos.[75]

Investigation of the pre-Christian use of *prosōpon* in Greek and *persona* in Latin has shown that the concept of personality was linked to the role that the individual embodied on the stage or in social life. As a generalized term for the individual in the rhetorical and legal language of late antiquity, the word had no real content, since no regard was had to the decisive content supplied by social roles.[76] The same applies to the famous definition of Boethius that the person is a rational individual.[77] This simply added to the general definition of a human being as a

---

72. In 1929 F. Gogarten developed the thesis that in the claim of the other, the Thou encounters God ("Das Problem einer theologischen Anthropologie," *Zwischen den Zeiten* 7 [1929] 493-511). See also E. Lévinas, *Ethics and Infinity* (Pittsburgh, 1985), pp. 95ff.; *Totality and Infinity* (Pittsburgh, 1969).

73. *Anthropology*, p. 241.

74. Cf. my book *Die Bestimmung des Menschen* (1978), pp. 7ff.

75. On the discussion initiated by Chalcedon (451), cf. S. Otto, *Person und Subsistenz. Die philosophische Anthropologie des Leontios von Byzanz* (1968).

76. Cf. M. Fuhrmann, "Persona, ein römischer Rollenbegriff," in *Identität,* Poetik und Hermeneutik 8, ed. O. Marquard and K. Stierle (Munich, 1979), pp. 83ff., on the vocabulary of rhetoric and law.

77. Boethius, *De persona et duabus naturis,* 3: "Persona est naturae rationalis individua substantia" (PL, 64, 1343C).

rational animal, or even more generally as a rational nature, an abstract definition of individuality according to which the concept of person is a matter of indifference compared to all other differences.

The christological use, however, found in "person" a term for the relation to God that was constitutive for the human existence of Jesus. In more general anthropological application this meant that each individual is a person in virtue of the special relation to God, either (like Jesus) in openness to fellowship with him, or in being closed to this destiny.[78] Trinitarian discussion of the term also had an anthropological impact as "person" came to denote what was specific to Father, Son, and Spirit in their mutual relations.[79] If the personhood of Jesus is that of the eternal Son in relation to the Father, all individuals are persons in virtue of the relation to God, which is the basis of their whole existence, or in emancipation from this relation, for even in turning from God they are held to their destiny of fellowship with God, though now in the mode of alienation, of a life that misses its destiny.

We are all persons in our psychosomatic totality as this finds manifestation at each moment of our existence. Totality and personhood are linked, for as we understand it today, "person" means not an exchangeable role but the human self. Selfhood, however, means identity in all individual life. This is true even over a stretch of time, hence selfhood never achieves definitive manifestation in life. It does not yet appear who we truly are, but we exist now as persons.[80] This is possible only in anticipation of the truth of our existence, which is mediated to us now through the Spirit by means of our feeling for life.

We can attain to the totality of our own lives, notwithstanding its fragmentary form at each moment, only in the relation to our Creator. But we achieve our particularity in our encounter with others. Both types of relation are in their own ways constitutive for our individual personhood. We are all persons in our necessary particularity as husbands and wives; fathers, mothers, and children; friends and foes; teachers and students; commanding and obeying; in work, renunciation, and pleasure. Yet personhood transcends all the singularities and changes of circumstances because it finally draws upon the relation to God as the source of its integrity. Thus in every detailed concretion it can coincide with being

78. H. Mühlen, *Sein und Person nach Johannes Duns Scotus. Beitrag zur Grundlegung einer Metaphysik der Person* (1954), pp. 106ff.

79. Cf. Richard of St. Victor *De trin.* 4.12ff. (PL, 196, 937f.). See also vol. I, 278 (on Athanasius), and pp. 320ff. (on the issue itself).

80. Cf. my *Anthropology,* pp. 235ff.

human as such, so that encounter with others can be a summons to be a person who accepts the particularity of individual existence. The special circumstances of life and relations to others are no longer, then, external roles that we may exchange at will. In them, however, the definitiveness of the selfhood that is grounded by God takes on its impress in all its individuality.

In the person, then, the integration of the individual moments of life results in an identity of authentic selfhood. In this process the rational consciousness takes the lead, for by recollection and expectation it can hold the moments of life together in the present and reflect on their compatibility. The philosophical and theological tradition discussed the leadership role of the rational consciousness from the standpoint of the governing of the body by the soul.[81] Like all forms of rule, this can take the perverted form of oppression — in this case the oppression of the body and its needs by a tyrannical "I."[82] But this is no argument against the need for this rule as the integration of otherwise opposing elements in life. Without self-rule there can be no unity or integrity of life.[83]

Personal unity of life is not, however, the product of self-discipline. We need the unity of selfhood to constitute the identity of an ongoing

81. The ancient view of the intellect as the *hegemonikon* of the soul (Plato *Phaed.* 246a-b) suggested this to patristic anthropology, as already in Tertullian (*De an.* 15.1 [CChrSL, 2, 801], cf. 12.1 [CChrSL, 2, 797f.]) and Clement of Alexandria (*Strom.* 6.134.2, 135.4, and 136.4). According to Augustine, who cited Cicero in favor of this view, the rule of the soul over the body was an easy one in paradise, but it is now harder as the resistance of the body shames the soul (*Civ. Dei* 14.23.2).

82. On this ground J. Moltmann rejects the rule of the soul over the body (*God in Creation*, pp. 244ff.). He takes issue especially with the view of K. Barth at this point, describing Barth's teaching in *CD*, III/2, § 46 as one of theological sovereignty corresponding to the intratrinitarian order of a ruling Father and obedient Son (p. 254). Rightly he notes that Barth nowhere mentions any right of the misused body to resist, or any right to feeling to have a voice in the decisions of the rational soul, or any desirable agreement of the body with the soul that governs it (p. 254). Nevertheless, Moltmann's own idea of a partnership of mutual influencing (p. 258) entails far too ideal a notion of harmony and agreement without any problems. The aim of all just government is to achieve such an agreement when it is not self-evident at the outset. Furthermore, as regards intratrinitarian relations, we cannot reject out of hand the thought of the Father's rule, to which the Son obediently subjects himself, without also ignoring basic NT statements, and especially the fundamental concept of a kingdom of God. The important point is that the monarchy of the Father is mediated through the free obedience of the Son (see vol. I, 324ff.).

83. We recall here the work on ethics by W. Herrmann, first published in 1901. A leading thought in this work was the demand, developed out of the concept of self-preservation, that humans as rational beings should achieve self-mastery ([5th ed. 1921], § 5, pp. 19ff.).

and constant ego, which for its part can manifest itself as the subject of acts. All action presupposes the identity of those who act, at least to the extent that this identity is needed to bridge the difference in time between the planning and execution of an act.[84] The longer the period of action, the more constant the identity must be if the goal is to be reached. Those who make a promise that they can keep only many years later, or over a whole life, have to retain their identity if they are to meet the promise. Actions owe their unity to the time-bridging identity of their subjects. Hence the identity must be already constituted if the action is to take place. At the same time, the identity of the person is only in the process of coming to be during our whole life-history, which demands that we evaluate soberly the place of the concept of action. For all our inclination to control our own lives and those of others by action, we do not have here a basic anthropological concept.[85] The possibilities of action and achievement are limited in many ways. Biblical wisdom often tells us how much the success of our plans depends upon the overruling of divine providence. The same is still fundamentally true for us today, even though modern science and technology have extended the range of human activity. The unity and integrity of human life are constituted in another sphere that precedes all action.

§ 2. Human Destiny

Basic to the personality of each individual is the destiny of fellowship with God. That this is the destiny of all of us as God's creatures is finally clear only from the NT message of Christ, which links the coming of the Son of God in the flesh to overcome sin and death with the matter of the goal of human life. The OT writings speak more cautiously of the closeness to

---

84. Cf. *Anthropology*, pp. 367ff.

85. In ibid. (pp. 367ff. and many other places) I oppose the dominant trend in the humanities to overvalue the concept of action, e.g., in the classical thesis of A. Gehlen's anthropology that we are acting beings (*Der Mensch. Seine Natur und seine Stellung in der Welt* [1940, 6th ed. 1958], pp. 19f., 33f., 42ff., 65ff., 130, 200f., etc.). It is a mistake to think that I uncritically follow Gehlen here; cf. C. Frey, *Arbeitsbuch Anthropologie. Christliche Lehre vom Menschen und humanwissenschaftliche Forschung* (1979), p. 81. For my emphatic divergence from Gehlen, cf. "The Christological Foundation of Christian Anthropology," in *Humanism and Christianity*, ed. C. Geffré (Concilium; New York, 1973), pp. 86-100 (in comparison with Herder).

God that characterizes us as creatures and underlies our special position among other creatures.

a. The Image of God in Adam and Christ

Ps. 8 says of man: "Thou hast made him little less than God [or than divine beings, angels] and dost crown him with glory and honor. Thou hast given him dominion over the works of thy hands; thou hast put all things under his feet" (vv. 5f.). This ruling position among other creatures expresses our closeness to God. We are called upon to share and exercise God's dominion over his creation. Ps. 8 does not expressly say this, but the first creation story derives our task of rule directly from the fact that we are representatives of God in his own rule over creation. This is the point of the statement that God made us in his own image and likeness and gave us the function of ruling over other earthly creatures (Gen. 1:26f.; cf. Sir. 17:3f.). In this way our human dominion is linked to God's own dominion. As the image of God, we are God's vicars preparing the way for his own dominion in the world.

The specific reference of the term *zelem* (Gen. 1:26f.) is to an idol or statue of God (cf. 2 Kgs. 11:18; Amos 5:26). The related *demut* is an abstract plural and means "likeness." Exegetical research on the relation between the two terms inclines overwhelmingly to the view that there is no discernible difference between them.[86] If there is any distinction, it is simply that *demut* limits to mere likeness the correspondence of the image to the original as it is present in the image.[87]

The function of the image is to depict the original that is represented. Images of kings in the territories they ruled offer a model. But according to W. H. Schmidt, the actual rule of Pharaoh in Egypt, insofar as he was a living image of God on earth, embodied the divine rule of Amun-Re.[88] The use of the term for our position in creation means on this view that what is otherwise ascribed only to the king is here transferred to all of us.[89]

If, however, the function of the divine image is to represent God's rule in

86. Cf. W. H. Schmidt, *Die Schöpfungsgeschichte der Priesterschrift* (1964), pp. 133, 143.

87. Wolff, *Anthropology*, p. 161.

88. Schmidt, *Die Schöpfungsgeschichte*, p. 137; cf. also O. H. Steck, *Der Schöpfungsbericht der Priesterschrift* (Göttingen, 1975), p. 150, contra K. Westermann, *Genesis*, I (1974), pp. 214ff., ET 148ff.; also *Genesis 1–11* (1972), pp. 24ff.

89. Schmidt, *Die Schöpfungsgeschichte*, p. 139.

his creation, we cannot simply equate the image and the function of rule.[90] If the concept of the image is the basis (and limit) of the function, we must define the function as a consequence of the divine likeness.[91] What the latter really consists of, Gen. 1:26f. does not tell us and does not need to tell us, since the point of the statement is to provide a basis for the function. It might be considered, perhaps, whether the addition of "likeness" is not to be explained in terms of the intention. If so, we may understand that our rule over creation is "like" that of the Creator.

In view of these findings the criticism of biblical anthropology that blames the giving of dominion in Gen. 1:28 for the unrestricted exploitation of nature by modern technology and industrial society, and for the resultant ecological crisis,[92] must be rejected as without merit. Modern industrial society has its basis in modern secular culture, which after the religious wars of the 16th and 17th centuries cut itself off from its historical roots in Christianity. Emancipation from religious ties and considerations, and from the conditions of social life that had their basis in them, has been one of the presuppositions of the autonomous development of economic life in the modern age. Contemporary secularism, while boasting of its emancipation from religious ties, at the same time places responsibility for the consequences of its absolutizing of the striving for possessions on the religious origins from which it has broken free. Certainly faith in the one transcendental God of the Bible has in fact dedivinized the world of nature and handed it over to us as a sphere over which to rule.[93] But this world is still

90. In modern exegesis Wolff claims that it is precisely as ruler that Adam is the image of God (*Anthropology,* p. 160). Socinians took a similar view in their exposition (cf. Faustus Socinus, *De statu primi hominis ante lapsum disputatio* [Racoviae, 1610], p. 93). The same view also seems to have played a role in the Reformation period, for Calvin found it necessary to oppose it (*Inst.* 1.15.4) on the ground that the likeness must lie in the self (*penes ipsum, non extra*). In modern theological writing H. Thielicke recognizes that if the divine likeness serves as a basis for the commission to rule, there must be a difference between them (*Theological Ethics* [Philadelphia, 1966-69], I, 155ff.).

91. Schmidt, *Die Schöpfungsgeschichte,* pp. 142f.; Steck, *Der Schöpfungsbericht,* p. 151.

92. For one of the first instances of this criticism, cf. Lynn White, "The Historical Roots of the Ecological Crisis," in *The Environmental Handbook* (New York, 1970). In German cf. esp. Carl Amery, *Das Ende der Vorsehung. Die gnadenlosen Folgen des Christentums* (Hamburg, 1972). For reasoned dialogue with the charge, cf. G. Altner, *Schöpfung am Abgrund* (1974), pp. 58ff., 81f. Cf. also my *Anthropology,* pp. 74ff.

93. This was the central theme of F. Gogarten's *Despair and Hope for Our Time* (Philadelphia, 1970). It is often overlooked that although Gogarten justified our modern understanding of the world under the impact of science and technology as a valid implication of the biblical belief in God, he opposed the movement from secularization to secularism resulting from our modern apostasy from God (cf. esp. pp. 109ff.). Cf. also his

the Creator's, and God's will as Creator is still the standard for the dominion we exercise as God's image.

This dominion, then, excludes arbitrary control or exploitation.[94] It is like the work of a gardener, as in the second creation story (Gen. 2:15). Because the world of nature is still God's, in spite of being handed over to us to rule, our self-glorious misuse of the power we have been given by God rebounds upon ourselves and plunges us into ruin. In this sense we may view the ecological crisis at the end of the modern age of emancipation as a reminder that God is still the Lord of creation and that human arbitrariness in dealing with it is not without limits or consequences.

If the divine likeness is a standard for our ordination to rule over creation and is therefore prior to it, what exactly is this likeness? Understandably theology has not been ready to accept the silence of the creation story on this matter and has sought data by which to answer the question. Thus far, however, none of the attempts has led to a satisfactory result.

The latest attempt has been that of Dietrich Bonhoeffer (*Creation and Fall* [3rd ed. 1955], pp. 39f.) and Karl Barth. Barth linked the plural of the divine saying in Gen. 1:26 ("Let *us* make man . . .") to the following statement about the making of humanity as male and female, deducing that humankind is the image of God in the plurality of co-human encounter in its basic form as the distinction and relation of male and female (*CD*, III/1, 191ff., esp. 205f.; III/2, 323f.). Barth has attracted some followers,[95] but exegetically one can hardly justify his interpretation.[96] The reference to the creation of humankind as male and female is an

---

Der Mensch zwischen Gott und Welt (Stuttgart, 1952), pp. 175ff. For a different view of the roots of secularization and secularism, but one that takes up the same central concern, cf. my *Christianity in a Secularized World* (New York, 1989), pp. 1-21.

94. Cf. also O. H. Steck, *Gott und Umwelt* (1978), pp. 146ff.

95. P. Trible, *God and the Rhetoric of Sexuality* (Philadelphia, 1978), p. 19, followed by Moltmann, *God in Creation*, pp. 222f. But cf. the criticism by P. A. Bird, " 'Male and Female He Created Them': Gen. 1:27b in the Context of the Priestly Account of Creation," *HTR* 74, no. 2 (1981) 129ff., esp. 136ff., 145ff.

96. Schmidt emphasizes that except in 5:1, which repeats 1:27 word for word, there is no further mention of divine likeness and dual sexual nature together (*Die Schöpfungsgeschichte*, p. 146 n. 4). Gen. 1:26 and Sir. 17:3 simply mention the divine likeness alone or, in the case of Sirach, relate it to the command to have dominion. As regards the plural (ibid., pp. 129f.), we may note that it does not occur in 1:27, where creation as male and female follows creation in the divine image. Bird argues that the creation of man as male and female is an addition to the preceding statement about creation in the divine image ("Male and Female," p. 150).

addition to the statement that humankind is made in the image of God.[97] It allows us to conclude that both man and woman are created equally in the divine image but not that the likeness consists of the relation between the sexes. If we want to agree with Barth that the sexual relation corresponds to the trinitarian relation of the Father and the Son, then we must subordinate woman to man as Barth subordinates the Son to the Father. The story, however, implies an equality of man and woman in principle inasmuch as the divine likeness applies to both, irrespective of sexual distinction.

The classical understanding of the divine likeness in Christian theology relates it to the soul. Thus in the Wisdom of Solomon (9:2) the gift of wisdom replaces the divine likeness and is an equivalent of it as endowment for rule over other creatures (cf. also 2:23 with 8:13, 17, where the destiny of immortality is connected with the gift of wisdom). Similarly the twofold view of wisdom as preexistent (9:9) and as a gift to us led Philo to the idea of the preexistent Logos on the one side and the human *nous* as its image on the other.[98] Following him, Christian Alexandrian theology limited the divine image to human reason (Clement *Strom.* 5.94.5; Origen *De princ.* 1.1.7.24). Gregory of Nyssa (*De hom. op.* 5 [PG, 44, 137C]) made this the normative view in the East, as did Augustine in the West.[99] Patristic thinking concerning the likeness to the trinitarian God to be found in differentiation within the human soul[100] gave it a special turn in Western theology under the influence of Augustine. Latin Scholasticism gave particular emphasis to the fact that the likeness lies primarily in the soul,[101] and this came to be presupposed in Reformation and post-Reformation theology.[102] The Reformers' modifications of the traditional view, to which we shall return later, were all within the basic understanding. Yet this understanding does not accord with

97. There is an analogy here to the "according to their kinds" in the case of animals (Gen. 1:21, 24). Cf. Schmidt, *Die Schöpfungsgeschichte*, p. 146; Steck, *Der Schöpfungsbericht*, p. 154; and Bird, "Male and Female." Yet there is not really a material parallel.

98. *Op. mundi* 69. On the conceptual context of this thought in Philo, cf. J. Jervell, "Bild Gottes I," *TRE*, VI (1980), pp. 493f. Cf. also the extended presentation of Philo's views in Jervell's *Imago Dei. Gen. 1:26f. im Spätjudentum, in der Gnosis und in den paulinischen Briefen* (Göttingen, 1960), pp. 52-70.

99. Augustine *Civ. Dei* 13.24.2; cf. 12.24 and *In Joann.* 3.4 (PL, 35, 1398).

100. Ambrose *De dig. hom.* 2 (PL, 17, 1105-8), and Augustine *De trin.* 9.4ff. and 12.6.6, etc. Cf. P. Hadot, "L'image de la Trinité dans l'âme chez Victorinus et chez St. Augustin," *SP* 6 (1962) 409-42.

101. By way of example, cf. Aquinas *ST* 1.93.6, also 1.93.3 ad 2.

102. Against Osiander, Calvin wrote that although God's glory is reflected outwardly in us, there is no doubt that the soul is the proper seat of the image (*Inst.* 1.15.3). Reformation theology certainly found the true nature of the image in the actual relation to God, but even later Lutherans allowed that strictly the rationality of the soul underlies its divine likeness (D. Hollaz, *Examen theologicum acroamaticum* [Stargard, 1707], I, 2.3) or has its seat there (§ 18 q. 13). Cf. also J. F. Buddeus, *Compendium Institutionum theologiae dogmaticae* (Lepizig, 1724), pp. 365f.

what Gen. 1:26f. actually says. The reference of the passage is to the whole person, with no differentiation of body and soul nor localizing of the image in the soul.

The plasticity of the thought has found expression in the proposal that the divine likeness lies in the upright stance, which visibly manifests our destiny of rule.[103] E. Jüngel has given emphasis to this idea, citing patristic references.[104] Even Augustine found in the upright stance a visible expression of the divine likeness that distinguishes the soul (*De Gen. ad litt.* 6.12 [CSEL 28.1.187]), though more in the sense of looking up to heaven than with reference to dominion over earthly creation. In fact the reference is a good and impressive explanation of the biblical statement, though there can be no certainty that this is what the story had in view.

Irenaeus also emphasized the bodily dimension of the divine likeness when trying to hold together the body-soul and pneumatic aspects, which the Valentinians were separating. In the process Irenaeus dealt with the two terms "image" and "likeness" in Gen. 1:26. The Valentinians saw in these terms two different material aspects (*Adv. haer.* 1.5.5). They did so in the Platonic sense that the Greek renderings (*eikōn* and *homoiōsis*) readily suggested, namely, that only ethical striving for *homoiōsis* can overcome the distance from the original contained in the term "image" (*Rep.* 613a, 4ff., *Theaet.* 176a, 5). Like the Valentinians, Irenaeus referred the likeness to the spirit but also argued that the spirit (1 Thess. 5:23) is part of the whole person along with the soul and body. If we lack spirit, we are only psychic and, since we are still fleshly, will be imperfect. We carry the image of God in the body but do not have likeness to God through the spirit (*Adv. haer.* 5.6.1).

This view, later adopted by Clement (*Strom.* 2.131.6) and Origen (*De princ.* 3.6.1), is certainly not in keeping with the statement in Gen. 1:26, whether in its understanding of the likeness as closeness to God or in its tripartite anthropology. Yet it has the systematic merit of linking the OT statements about our creation to NT statements about Jesus Christ as the image of God and about our destiny of being transformed into this image. This theory is the anthropological basis of Irenaeus's theology of salvation history. In the process the postulate of a doctrinal unity of all biblical statements obscured the difference between the views

103. L. Köhler, *OT Theology* (London, 1957), p. 147. H. Gunkel earlier related the concept to our bodily form (*Genesis* [3rd ed. Göttingen, 1910], p. 112).

104. E. Jüngel, "Der Gott entsprechende Mensch," in *Neue Anthropologie* 6, ed. H. G. Gadamer and P. Vogler (1975), pp. 342ff., esp. 354ff. Jüngel quoted the work of Lactantius *On the Wrath of God* 7.4f. (cf. *Sources chrétiennes* 289 [1982] 112). This interpretation found support from the 18th century onward. S. J. Baumgarten referred to our free rational soul and our upright stance (in contrast to animals) as features of the divine likeness that remain after the fall (*Evangelische Glaubenslehre*, ed. J. S. Semler [Halle, 1759; 2nd ed. 1764], II, 442). C. G. Ammon put this feature first in his description of the divine likeness (*Summa theologiae Christianae* [Göttingen, 1803], 109). Nor should we forget J. G. Herder, *Älteste Urkunde des Menschengeschlechts* (1774), *Sämtliche Werke*, ed. B. Suphan (1883), VI, 249, cf. 316.

of the image in the first creation story and in Paul by an unbiblical understanding of the likeness as something more than the image in place of a changing and deepening of the concept of the image itself.

Christian theology must read the OT saying about our divine likeness in the light of the Pauline statements that call Jesus Christ the image of God (2 Cor. 4:4; Col. 1:15; cf. Heb. 1:3) and that speak of the transforming of believers into this image (Rom. 8:29; 1 Cor. 15:49; 2 Cor. 3:18). These statements do not specifically show the relevance of the history of Jesus Christ to our understanding of humanity as such. Participation in the likeness attributed to Jesus Christ is promised only to believers. Nevertheless, as it corresponds to the rooting of the concept of the image in the creation story, it is related to the concept of humanity generally by what is said about the eschatological new man who is manifested in Jesus Christ (1 Cor. 15:45ff.).[105] To that extent, the idea of Jesus Christ as the image of God in which believers have a share through the Spirit (2 Cor. 3:18) has a general anthropological significance that the NT statements develop. When we inquire into this, unavoidably the question arises with which 1 Cor. 15:45f. does not deal, namely, that of the relation of the divine likeness that characterizes Jesus Christ and is mediated through him to that which according to Gen. 1:26f. is a feature of all of us by creation. In the primitive Christian writings recollections of this (1 Cor. 11:7; Jas. 3:9) stand side by side with the christological and soteriological concept of the divine likeness. Christian theology had to work out the connections between them if it was to cling to the interrelation of our creation and redemption.

The theology of Irenaeus took up this task in controversy with Gnosticism and offered the solution, on the one hand, of distinguishing between Christ as original and Adam as copy[106] and, on the other hand, of interpreting likeness as *homoiōsis*, of linking the copy to the original. As Adam the copy was related to the original, the divine likeness acquired the meaning of a destiny, or goal, that would be achieved by way of assimilation to the original in the process of moral striving. Our first parents failed to reach this goal, and it has been attained only by the actual incarnation of the image itself in Jesus Christ.

Jewish exegesis had already pioneered a distinction between image and likeness in Gen. 1:26f. by relating the statement to wisdom as preexistent wisdom

---

105. Cf. U. Wilckens, "Christus, der 'letzte Adam' und der Menschensohn," in *Jesus und der Menschensohn. Für Anton Vogtle*, ed. R. Pesch et al. (1975), pp. 387ff., esp. 402.
106. Irenaeus *Adv. haer.* 5.12.4 on the basis of Col. 3:9f.; also 5.15.4 and esp. 5.16.2.

on the one side (Prov. 8:22ff.) and to wisdom as a gift (or *nous*) that confers human participation on the other (see above). The only specifically Christian feature was the thesis of an incarnation of the preexistent divine image in a man along with the assertion that only thus could we attain to the destiny that differentiates us from all other creatures. Along these lines Irenaeus related the Pauline sayings about Jesus Christ as the image of God to the incarnate Logos rather than primarily to the preexistent Logos (*Adv. haer.* 5.16.2).[107]

Origen, however, and Athanasius after him, referred them to the *logos asarkos,* the eternal Logos as such.[108] In this case the christological statements about Jesus Christ as the image of the eternal God no longer had any relevance to our general divine likeness. At this point, at least, christology and anthropology had to go their separate ways, in spite of their relation at other points (e.g., the concept of the Logos, in which we all participate as logos-beings). If the divine likeness is then referred, not to the Logos, but to the divine essence or to the whole Trinity, as in the later fathers and especially Augustine,[109] and if the understanding of human reason is further detached from the idea of the divine Logos, then our divine likeness can be viewed as a theme essentially different from that of the Logos in relation to the Father.[110] The incarnation of the Logos, of course, would still have an anthropological function, but only that of a means of restoring the condition of grace that Adam lost at the fall and thus perfecting the divine image. The saving work of Christ won back the lost likeness, providing fellowship with God by assimilation to him and the related immortality, as a divine grace, mediating this grace to us by the church's sacraments. By a detour our created destiny, shattered at the fall, was thus fulfilled. The fulfillment, however, did not transcend the original destiny.

This thought of a mere restoration of the original perfection of Adam

---

107. Cf. P. Schwanz, *Imago Dei als christologisch-anthropologisches Problem in der Geschichte der Alten Kirche von Paulus bis Clemens von Alexandrien* (1970), pp. 131f.

108. Origen *De princ.* 1.2.6; Athanasius *De inc.* 13.7. Cf. J. Roldanus, *Le Christ et l'homme dans la théologie d'Athanase d'Alexandrie* (Leiden, 1968), pp. 40ff.

109. Augustine *De Gen. ad litt.* imperf. liber 16 (CSEL, 28/1, 502); cf. 3.19 (85). From the time of *Barn.* 5.5 and 6.12, early Christian theology found in the plural of Gen. 1:26 an address of the Father to the Son (and Spirit); cf. Justin *Dial.* 6.2; Theophilus *Ad Autol.* 2.18; Irenaeus *Adv. haer.* 4 pref. 4 and 4.20.1; 5.1.3. Irenaeus took this to mean that the image was that of the Son (4.15.4. and 16.1f.). Cf. Tertullian *De res. carn.* 6 (PL, 2, 802). On this point cf. A. Struker, *Die Gottebenbildlichkeit des Menschen in der christlichen Literatur der ersten zwei Jahrhunderte* (1913), pp. 81ff. The later fathers preferred to relate the likeness at creation to the divine nature, referring participation in sonship to the order of redemption; cf. W. J. Burghardt, *The Image of God in Man according to Cyril of Alexandria* (1957), pp. 120ff.

110. Cf. the observations of Aquinas in *ST* 1.93.1 ad 2, along with the assigning of the two themes to the doctrine of the Trinity on the one side and anthropology on the other. The older Protestant dogmaticians took a similar course; cf. Hollaz, *Examen* II c 1 q 9 (§§ 11-15), and H. H. Schmid, *Doctrinal Theology of the Evangelical Lutheran Church* (Philadelphia, 1961), p. 222.

even played a part in the theology of Irenaeus, whose starting point was that the first man had *homoiōsis* as well as the *eikōn*.[111] Yet recapitulation, as the bishop of Lyons understood it, meant more than simply restoration. The fulfillment brought with it more than Adam's original state with its childlike weakness.[112] All the same, the idea of a first perfection that was there at the beginning of human history, and then lost, introduced ambiguity into Irenaeus's concept of anthropological development.[113] He himself failed to see this because of his interest in the typological correspondence between redemption and creation. The theology that followed, however, found in him no clear direction. It could see in Irenaeus the thought of redemption as both restoration and the transcending of Adam's first estate. There was no clear resolution of the tension between the OT concept of the likeness and the NT christological concept.

b. The Image of God and Our First Estate

In Paul's sayings about Christ as the image of God into which all others must be transformed, the Christian doctrine of the divine likeness must see an elucidation of our general destiny of divine likeness. But in so doing it may not expunge the differences between the fulfilling of our divine likeness in and by Jesus Christ on the one hand, and the OT statements about Adam's divine likeness on the other. To do this is to miss the point that our destiny as creatures is brought to fulfillment by Jesus Christ.[114]

The Reformation doctrine of the divine likeness did not avoid this danger. It agreed with Irenaeus, over against Latin Scholasticism, in orienting itself to what Paul says about Christ as the image of God.[115] It also rejected the distinction

111. Schwanz, *Imago Dei,* pp. 124f., 133f.; cf. Irenaeus *Adv. haer.* 3.18.1, also 4.10.1.

112. Schwanz, *Imago Dei,* p. 134, with the illuminating observation that in Irenaeus the *homoiōsis* is in the process of becoming and is not yet perfect. This is wholly in line with the Platonic concept. On the idea that growth is necessary for us, cf. the typical remarks in *Adv. haer.* 4.38.1-4.

113. Schwanz, *Imago Dei,* p. 141 sees a rift at this point in Irenaeus's doctrine of the divine likeness.

114. For this reason A. Ritschl rejected the doctrine of an original perfection. A theology, he said, that finds at the outset the moral state that is possible only in Christianity, declaring this to be our natural condition, has the unfortunate implication that the person of Christ must be viewed as an irregular phenomenon in human history. On this basis Christ must be understood merely as the agent of God's reaction to sin. *The Christian Doctrine of Justification and Reconciliation* (ET of *Die christliche Lehre von der Rechtfertigung und Versöhnung* III [1883]; Clifton, NJ, 1966), pp. 324f., cf. 4f.

115. So said Luther in a 1523 sermon (WA, 14, 110f.).

between *imago* and *similitudo* that Scholasticism had taken over from John of Damascus (*Fid. orth.* 2.12) and linked to Augustine's doctrine of an original state of grace. Reformation exegesis saw the two terms of Gen. 1:26 as equivalents. In this respect they followed a patristic tradition that deviated from Irenaeus[116] and achieved greater accuracy according to modern exegetical judgment. Nevertheless, the thesis of an identity of image and likeness led them to equate the statement of the first creation story in Gen. 1:26 with what Colossians says about the renewing of believers in the knowledge of God according to the image of their Creator (3:10) and with what Ephesians says about the new man as God created him in true righteousness and holiness (4:24; cf. 5:9).[117] The result was not merely that the divine likeness of our first parents included the idea of an original righteousness but that we are to see in renewal through Jesus Christ a restoration of this original relationship with God. In contrast, less prominence was given to the line of thinking in Irenaeus that viewed the incarnation as a fulfillment transcending our first weakness. The stronger the emphasis on our original perfection,[118] the deeper was the fall from it through sin as a result of the first sin.[119]

With such ideas post-Reformation theology followed the teaching of Augustine and Latin Scholasticism. But since image and likeness were one and the same, it had to argue that as a result of sin, the image had been lost as well as the gracious divine likeness.[120] No change came therewith to our created nature, for — in spite of Flacius — we are still human, even as sinners.[121] The older dogmaticians thus had to see both the likeness and our sinfulness as *acci-*

116. Clement and Origen adopted the distinction, but not the later Alexandrians or the three Cappadocians; cf. Burghardt, *Image of God,* pp. 2ff.

117. Cf. Melanchthon's Apology to CA 2.18-22, with appeal to Irenaeus and Ambrose; see also Luther WA, 42, 46, and Calvin *Inst.* 1.15.3f. The older Protestant dogmatics also described the divine likeness of Adam in terms of esp. Eph. 4:24 (J. Gerhard, *Loci theologici* [Leipzig, 1885], II, 110 n. 23, 112 n. 30; A. Calov, *Systema locorum theologicorum,* IV [Wittenberg, 1659], pp. 569ff.; Hollaz, *Examen* II, c. 1 q 6 [§ 5]).

118. On the idealizing depictions of the older Protestant dogmatics, cf. K. G. Bretschneider, *Systematische Entwicklung aller in der Dogmatik vorkommenden Begriffe nach den symbolischen Schriften der evangelisch-lutherischen Kirche und den wichtigsten dogmatischen Lehrbüchern ihrer Theologen* (1805, 3rd ed. 1825), pp. 513ff. A typical example may be found in Hollaz, *Examen,* II c. 1 q 15-24 (§§ 19-51); cf. Schmid, *Doctrinal Theology,* pp. 218, 225.

119. As Ritschl observes, the more lofty the predicates, the more extensive the state of sin into which transgression of the prohibition brought our first parents and their descendants (*Christian Doctrine,* pp. 324f.).

120. Formula of Concord SD 1.2f. (BSLK, 848). Cf. occasionally Augustine, since he did not differentiate image from likeness (*De Gen. ad litt.* 6.27 [CSEL, 28/1, 199]). The older Protestant dogmaticians thought the loss of the likeness was presupposed in NT statements about its renewal in Eph. 4:24 and Col. 3:10; cf. Hollaz, *Examen,* q 25 (§ 51).

121. Cf. W. Sparn, "Begründung und Verwirklichung. Zur anthropologischen Thematik der lutherischen Bekenntnisse," in *Bekenntnis und Einheit der Kirche. Studien zum Konkordienbuch,* ed. M. Brecht and R. Schwarz (Stuttgart, 1980), pp. 143f.

dental determinations of human nature.[122] This was hardly reconcilable, however, with either Gen. 1:26f. or the NT statements about our renewal according to the image manifested in Jesus Christ. Both refer to our specific nature and its actualizing. What Luther said on the theme pointed in a totally different direction.[123] In this matter post-Reformation Lutheran dogmatics failed to equal the theological insight that Irenaeus had already reached. It was left to Schleiermacher to recapture this insight in his pertinent formula that we must see in Christ for the first time the completed creation of human nature.[124]

There is no real biblical basis for the emphasis of the older Protestant dogmatics on a paradisaic perfection and integrity of human life before the fall in consequence of Adam's original righteousness.[125] The shortening of human life in consequence of the first transgression (Gen. 3:16-19) indeed presupposed a prior state in which this judgment did not apply,[126] but this did not have to include either perfect knowledge and holiness or immortality before the fall. The fruits of the tree of life (2:9) were not forbidden to Adam and Eve, but they do not seem to have discovered these fruits before they became sinners (3:22).[127] The Wisdom of Solomon might say that God created us for immortality and closely relate this fact to the divine likeness (2:23), but the second creation story does not allow us to conclude that our first parents possessed immortality, only that they were destined to attain it in the future. Even the threat of death as a result of eating the forbidden fruit does not necessarily imply that our first parents would have been immortal if they had not transgressed. The threat is not to the effect that they become mortal but that they die on the day of transgression, i.e., that they are punished with an early death.[128]

122. Calov, *Systema*, p. 56; Hollaz, *Examen*, II c. 1 q 4 (§ 2). Hollaz argues that the likeness was accidental because it could be lost (Rom. 3:23). J. Gerhard devoted a whole chapter to the thesis that the likeness is not part of our human substance (*Loci theologici*, II, 126f.; cf. Schmid, *Doctrinal Theology*, pp. 222f., 229).

123. In his 1523 *Disputatio de Homine*, Luther called humanity in the present life the mere matter out of which God would fashion the glorious form of eschatological humanity (WA, 39/1, 177, 3-12). Cf. G. Ebeling, "Das Leben — Fragment und Vollendung," *ZTK* 72 (1975) 310ff., esp. 316f., 326ff., also *Lutherstudien*, II/3, 98ff. Luther of course spoke about the restoring of the image, adding in the spirit of Irenaeus that it would also be perfected.

124. Schleiermacher, *Christian Faith*, § 89.

125. On this point cf. Ritschl, *Christian Doctrine*, pp. 514-18, and before him J. Müller, *Die christliche Lehre von der Sünde* (1838, 1844; 3rd ed. Breslau, 1849), II, 483-88.

126. O. H. Steck, *Die Paradieserzählung. Eine Auslegung von Genesis 2:4b–3:24* (1970), pp. 59f., 118ff.

127. Ibid., p. 117, where Steck perspicaciously notes that only autonomous and self-determining humans want immortality, so that inaccessibility to the tree of life makes the limitation of life, which is neutrally presupposed throughout the story but expressly stated only in the curse, definitive and inviolable for the sinner. On the tree of life, cf. pp. 47f., 61ff.

128. K. G. Bretschneider, *Handbuch der Dogmatik der evangelisch-lutherischen Kirche* (1814, 1822; 3rd ed. Leipzig, 1828), I, 747. Cf. von Rad, *Genesis*, p. 95, who takes the

Only in Israel's postexilic wisdom and apocalyptic texts do we find the view that Adam possessed immortality before the fall. Thus 1 Enoch 69:11 says that humans were originally created no different from angels and that death would not have touched them had they not sinned. According to Wis. 1:13, God did not create death. The verse already mentioned (2:23), which states that we were created for immortality, carries not only the Hellenistic sense that they were destined for it but also, unlike Gen. 3, the implication that they originally possessed it; it was only through the envy of the devil that death came into the world (2:24). In contrast, it is worth noting that Paul regarded death as a consequence of sin (Rom. 6:23) and that while he could speak freely of Adam's own fate (5:12),[129] he did not refer to Adam's original immortality. Instead Paul said that the first man was of the earth (1 Cor. 15:47; cf. Gen. 2:7). In line with Paul's argument this means corruptibility. Paul ascribes immortality only to the second eschatological man, who has been manifested in the resurrection of Jesus and whose life is permeated by the creative Spirit of life (1 Cor. 15:52ff.). Unfortunately the fathers in general did not follow Paul at this point but preferred rather the idea of an original immortality of Adam even without and before Jesus Christ, at least in the sense that with participation in the Logos, Adam had a disposition for immortality and would have shared in it had he held fast to the knowledge of God.[130]

Again, we cannot find support in scripture for the view of the older Protestant dogmaticians that our first parents possessed perfect knowledge and holiness. As regards capacity for knowledge, biblically based criticism of the doctrine of the first estate has rightly pointed out that the paradise story links knowledge to eating the forbidden fruit (3:5).[131] Nor do we read anything concerning an original righteousness. The story of the first sin traces it to a lack of affective agreement with the will of God. The serpent simply brings to light an inclination to turn aside from this will (3:5f.).[132] The argument that the renewal to which the NT bears witness allows us to infer an original state, so that we may claim

---

view that the threat of Gen. 2:17 was not that the man and woman would die the same day but simply that they would die, the concern of the author being that God does not carry out the dreadful threat but gives way to grace, since they did not die immediately. Cf. Steck, *Die Paradieserzählung*, p. 110.

129. Cf. U. Wilckens, *Der Brief an die Römer*, 3 vols., EKK (Zurich/Neukirchen, 1978-82), I, 316, also the history of the theme, 310ff.

130. Athanasius *De inc.* 3; cf. Tatian *Or.* 13.1 and 7.1 (cf. Elze, *Tatian*, pp. 90f.), Justin *Dial.* 5f., and Irenaeus *Adv. haer.* 3.20.1f., though Irenaeus did not claim that our first parents were immortal (Struker, *Die Gottebenbildlichkeit des Menschen*, p. 121), nor is this implied in 3.23.6. According to *Epid.* 1.15, immortality depended on observing the command. Irenaeus did view the soul as immortal, but only by participation in the life that comes from God (*Adv. haer.* 2.34).

131. Bretschneider, *Handbuch*, I, 747.

132. Schleiermacher made this point impressively in his criticism of the attempt to explain the beginning of sin apart from a prior sinfulness (*Christian Faith*, § 72.2).

statements about the knowledge, righteousness, and holiness of those who are renewed (Col. 3:10; Eph. 4:24) in favor of Adam's former state,[133] is simply assuming without proof that we may see the NT sayings about the image of God as on the same plane as those in the original story. Around 1800 even a conservative theologian like F. V. Reinhard thought this doubtful. As he put it, there is no certainty that these passages have in view our first parents and their perfection.[134] But does not the OT itself, in Eccl. 7:30, say that God created us upright but that we sought out many inventions? Yes, but the reference here is a general one to our human opposition to God's creative activity, not to a state prior to this fatal drift.

Little is left of the traditional dogma of a perfect first estate when we submit it to the test of biblical theology. As soon as Protestant theology called for a biblical theology in the 18th century,[135] the dogma began to disintegrate. It did not simply fall victim to the application of historical criticism to the text of the biblical account. The development of an understanding of the account as a saga or myth from the time of J. G. Eichhorn and J. P. Gabler[136] was no more than an additional factor in the process of disintegration. The same might be said of criticism of the idea of a loss of the divine image through the fall.

We do not find this idea in the biblical writings, or find it clearly if two debated Pauline texts are taken into account. The list of the generations from Adam to Noah in Gen. 5:1ff. repeats 1:26 and thus implies that the image is still true of Adam's descendants. In saying that Adam begot Seth in his own image (5:3), the text does not necessarily refer to the divine likeness. The wording carries no limitations, however, and thus does not rule out the divine likeness. Indeed, the point of the express reference to the likeness at the head of the list would seem to be that it is passed on to posterity.[137] Support for this view is found in the prohibition of murder in 9:6 on the basis of the divine likeness of each individual. In Paul, too, it would seem to be taken for granted that the likeness is a fact for his own generation (1 Cor. 11:7), even though he offends modern sensibilities and departs from Gen. 1:26 by relating the image primarily to the male. The idea that women share in the image only by way of men (11:7b)[138]

133. Calov, *Systema*, p. 598; Hollaz, *Examen*, II c. 1 q 6 (§ 5) and q 7 (§§ 6, 8); cf. Schmid, *Doctrinal Theology*, p. 222.

134. F. V. Reinhard, *Vorlesungen über die Dogmatik* (1801), p. 261. Müller took a similar view some decades later (*Die christliche Lehre*, I, 485ff.), though under no suspicion as a biblical theologian.

135. Cf. my *Theology and the Philosophy of Science* (London, 1976), pp. 355ff.

136. J. P. Gabler, *J. G. Eichhorns Urgeschichte* (1790-93).

137. Von Rad, *Genesis*, p. 70, contra Barth, *CD*, III/1, 193f., 197ff.; cf. also Schmidt, *Die Schöpfungsgeschichte*, pp. 143f. Barth himself, who in *CD*, I/1, 238ff. and I/2, 307f. had espoused the Reformation doctrine of the loss of the divine image, abandoned this view in his doctrine of creation. Cf. A. Peters, "Bild Gottes IV," *TRE*, VI (1980), pp. 512f.

138. Cf. on this Jervell, "Bild Gottes," pp. 497f. 4 Ezra 5:54 and Wis. 10:1 speak only of a creation of Adam in the divine image.

perhaps rests on a combining of Gen. 1:26 with the account of woman's creation out of Adam's rib (cf. 1 Cor. 11:8). Gen. 1:26, of course, links the creation of both male and female directly to the image. Augustine, and after him medieval and the older Protestant theology, stressed that male and female were created equally in the divine image.[139] Even if materially the divine likeness is not achieved in the relation of male and female, it applies irrespective of the difference between them. Though the point of Gen. 1:26 is not clear, Paul in 1 Cor. 11:7 can regard as a self-evident fact the divine likeness grounded in creation. His statements that believers are changed by the Spirit into the likeness of Christ, who is God's image (2 Cor. 4:4; cf. 3:18 etc.), must have in view, not merely restoration of the image, but a closeness to God that goes beyond the divine likeness grounded in creation, a view that 1 Cor. 15:45ff. confirms. Nor do Rom. 1:23 and 3:23 serve as refutation,[140] though the older Protestant dogmatics appealed to them in favor of the thesis of loss of the image.[141] The perverting of the glory of God by human sin, and especially by idolatry, does not alter the fact that ordination to be in the image of God characterizes human beings as creatures.

If we are to take into account the total biblical testimony to our orientation to God as this comes to expression in the thought of the divine likeness, allowing for all its variety, then we must fully relate the ongoing reality of creation in the divine image to our interpretation of the Pauline thesis that not we as such but only Jesus Christ is the image of God, and that all others need to be renewed after this image in their relation to God. But how can we reconcile the two? A possible starting point is the fact that in Gen. 1:26f. (also 5:1 and 9:6) we are said not simply to *be* the image of God but to be *according to* (בְּ) the image of God. Implied here is a distinction between copy and original. We are the copy. The original is

---

139. Augustine *De Gen. ad litt.* 3.22 (CSEL, 28/1, 89) on the premise that in Christ there is neither male nor female (Gal. 3:28). Among older Protestant theologians, cf. Calov, *Systema* 4.2.10, and Gerhard, *Loci theologici* 8.6 (II, 688-91).

140. But cf. Jervell, *Imago Dei*, pp. 320-31; and Wilckens, *Römer*, I, 107f. P. Schwanz points out, however, that in Rom. 1:23 *doxa* refers to God's own glory and not to a glory given to us, as in 3:23 (*Imago Dei*, p. 55). The statement that all of us fall short of (participation in) God's glory because we sin does not speak of a glory that we have lost (p. 57), as Wilckens supposes (*Römer*, I, 188), interpreting Paul in the light of Jewish ideas such as we find in *Apoc. Mos.* 20f. If this were so, there would be a striking contrast to 1 Cor. 15:45ff., which avoids any idea of a preceding likeness lost through sin.

141. Hollaz, *Examen*, II c. 1 q 7 prob. 2 (§ 6) and q 25 (§ 52); cf. Schmid, *Doctrinal Theology*, p. 238. The older Protestant proof for a loss of the image relied primarily on Gen. 5:3 (cf. above, p. 214) and on the reference to our being renewed in the image of God in Col. 3:10 (cf. Eph. 4:24). Augustine had already used this argument in *De Gen. ad litt.* 3.20 (CSEL, 28/1, 87). He had also taught a loss of the divine likeness in 6.27 (28/1, 199).

left vague, for the plural does not tell us plainly whether the Creator is meant or a quality of deity (cf. Ps. 8:5). This imprecision leaves the door open as regards the original. In Jewish wisdom literature (Wis. 7:26) and in Philo and Paul (2 Cor. 4:4), precision is given along different lines — respectively, preexistent wisdom, the preexistent Logos, or the exalted Christ.

But how does the human copy relate to the divine original? In weighing this question, we must consider that the image must represent the original. This can be done only if it is like it. But the likeness may be greater or less. The greater it is, the clearer the image and the more intensive the presence of the original in it.

The theology of Irenaeus rightly relied on the openness of the similarity to different degrees of intensity. It found a certain likeness to God in the first Adam but its fullness only in Jesus Christ, in whom the original manifested itself. The view of Irenaeus raises problems only insofar as it not merely distinguishes between more or less similarity but makes a categorical distinction between image and likeness, so that after transgressing, Adam could lose the likeness but still retain the image. This view is not tenable either exegetically or materially — exegetically because the two terms are parallel in Gen. 1:26f., and materially because an image ceases to be an image if it bears no similarity to what it depicts.[142] There may be poor images that bear little similarity to their original, but a total loss of similarity eliminates the whole idea of an image.[143] Conversely, the image is the sharper, the greater the similarity. The original may then be the more clearly seen, for the image is a better representation of it. It is more of an image; representation is of its very essence.

When the text speaks of humans' representing God, the point is that humans are according to God's image, but not to the same degree. In the early days of humanity the likeness was perhaps still imperfect. Through sin there was then increasing distortion in individuals. Only in Jesus, as Christian anthropology sees it, did the image of God appear with full clarity.

142. In his discussion of this question, Aquinas saw two kinds of similarity — a more general one that does not concern the relation and one that is closer to the thought of an image insofar as the image may be more or less similar to the original (*ST* 1.93.9). But this view misses the point that similarity is in some sense constitutive for the whole concept of an image.

143. Cf. Augustine in *De Gen. ad litt.* imperf. liber 16 (CSEL, 28/1, 497f., also 503).

In the story of the human race, then, the image of God was not achieved fully at the outset. It was still in process. This is true not only of the likeness but of the image itself. But since likeness is essential to an image, our creation in the image of God stands implicitly related to full similarity. This full actualization is our destiny, one that was historically achieved with Jesus Christ and in which others may participate by transformation into the image of Christ.

Materially the interpretation of Irenaeus, and of others who followed him, expresses the unfinished nature of the image. Renaissance thinkers gave special emphasis to this point. Thus Pico della Mirandola said that Adam was created as a being of imprecise form *(indiscretae opus imaginis).*[144] What he had in view was that by nature human beings fix their own destiny according to their own free judgment. According to Pico, however, the only successful form of this self-fulfillment consists of assimilation to God, so that he too found a full achievement of our divine likeness only in Jesus Christ.[145]

In a different way, almost three hundred years later, J. G. Herder took up again the idea that humans are not fixed beings, though he restricted the element of self-determination by a reference to divine providence. As he put it, God gave instinct to animals, but humans he carved as his own image: religion and humanity in the soul. The outline of the statue is obscure, deep in the marble, but it cannot hew itself out or fashion itself. Tradition and teaching, reason and experience must do this, and God does not leave us without the means to this end.[146] Yet Herder did not relate our growth into the image of God to the manifestation of Jesus Christ as the fulfillment of the likeness. Instead of making this reference, he advanced the more general thought of a direction of human history by divine providence, with humanity, and also immortality, as the goal.

144. G. Pico della Mirandola, *De dignitate hominis* (1486).

145. Cf. C. Trinkaus, *In Our Image and Likeness: Humanity and Divinity in Italian Humanist Thought,* 2 vols. (Chicago, 1970), II, 505ff., 734. E. Cassirer traced back this christocentric humanism to the thinking of Cusa (*Individuum und Kosmos in der Philosophie der Renaissance* [Leipzig, 1927; 3rd ed. 1963], pp. 40ff.). In fact Nicholas of Cusa did relate the concept of the firstborn of all creation not merely to the Logos but, like Irenaeus, to the God-man Christ, because in him the destiny of humanity and every creature came to fulfillment (cf. R. Haubst, *Die Christologie des Nikolaus von Kues* [1956], pp. 169f.).

146. J. G. Herder, *Ideen der Geschichte der Menschheit* (1784) 9.5. Already in his *Älteste Urkunde* (1774) Herder argued that God's decree concerning us is that everything in us should not yet be developed. The image of God exists as yet only in a poor figure of clay. Here, too, it is a fact that by the counsel of God it does not yet appear what we shall be one day and eternally (*Sämmtliche Werke,* VI, 253f.). Cf. my "Gottebenbildlichkeit als Bestimmung des Menschen in der neueren Theologiegeschichte," SBAW 1979/8, 3f.

c. Divine Likeness as Human Destiny

The view that the divine likeness in us is still in a historical process of becoming links the whole theme to the thought of human destiny.[147] This is not an obvious link inasmuch as destiny relates to our definitive future, to the goal and end of our creation, whereas the divine likeness has to do with our original endowment as creatures. If we think of the divine likeness as being already achieved in Adam's first estate, we cannot view it as our final destiny in a process of history.

In this regard the handling of the theme in Aquinas is especially instructive precisely because he tried in his own way to connect the divine likeness and human destiny. He regarded the doctrine of the divine likeness as an answer to the question of the aim of our creation.[148] But because he assumed that the likeness related to Adam's first estate, he could think of our destiny only in terms of the first realization of the image being the aim of creation. This is very surprising, for although such a view was theologically a natural one, the whole of part 2 of the *Summa theologiae* deals with our striving after God. In the prologue to part 2 this striving is in fact linked to the divine likeness, but as the starting point and not the goal. In the process Aquinas occasionally interprets the traditional distinction between the different forms of the image along the lines of a sequence in salvation history that ends only with the state of future felicity.[149] But in depicting our divine likeness as creatures, this approach obviously would not work because it tied the idea to the first estate.

147. Herder was relating the divine likeness and destiny already in 1769 (*Sämmtliche Werke*, VI, 28) and 1774 (VI, 2153). Cf. also *Ideen* 11.1.

148. Aquinas *ST* 1.93 (title and introduction).

149. In *ST* 1.93.4, Aquinas called the likeness of glory the supreme stage beyond natural aptitude and the conformity of grace. He followed here the differentiating of the images of creation, re-creation, and likeness in the *Glossa ordinaria* of Anselm of Laon on Ps. 4:7 (PL, 113, 8490). In Anselm, however, there is no sequence of salvation history. In distinction from the image of creation, which consists of reason, that of re-creation is indeed a grace, but the image of likeness is not related to future glory but to the image of the Trinity in the human soul, as in Augustine. Peter Lombard takes a similar view in his *Commentarium in psalmos Davidicos*, where he relates the image of likeness, not to the Father or Son alone, but to the whole Trinity (PL, 191, 88B). The *Summa* of Alexander of Hales (ca. the middle of the 13th century) relates the image of likeness to the eternal Son and only indirectly to us. This image, he says, is wisdom, which is the Son of God, into whose image we are conformed (*Summa theologiae*, IV [1949] n. 632, p. 999). It was by no means self-evident, then, that Scholasticism would see the three forms of the image in terms of a sequence in salvation history.

If the thought of our destiny is linked to our creation in the divine image, this destiny cannot consist only of our rule over the rest of creation; it relates also and above all to our fellowship with God. This is more than is actually stated in Gen. 1:26f. In the related OT stories fellowship with God has its basis in the covenant with Abraham and applies, not to all people, but only to Abraham's posterity (17:7). While the Noachic covenant simply guarantees the continuation of earthly orders (9:8ff.), God says to Abraham and to Abraham's descendants that he will be "their God." He thus establishes a special relation between himself and the recipients of the covenant that enables the psalmist to say later that God is his rock and "portion for ever" (Ps. 73:26).

It was left for Jewish wisdom to extend this special relation to humanity as a whole, and the starting point for this step was our creation in the divine image. In fact the idea of an image necessitated the question, left open by the first creation story, wherein the likeness consists that connects the original and copy. Simply to point to our upright stance did not supply an adequate answer to this question. This stance might signify dominion over creation or a searching beyond earthly reality. But even these things hardly justify the thesis of likeness to the invisible God. Speaking of humans as God's image must have a basis in a likeness to God's eternal being. Only then is it tenable. Along this line Jewish wisdom literature, at least in its later phase in the Wisdom of Solomon, understood the divine likeness as participation in God's glory[150] and incorruptibility (Wis. 2:23). The Wisdom of Solomon related this participation to our endowment with wisdom at creation (9:2).[151] It is said of wisdom: "For your sake I will attain to immortality" (8:13). Also linked to wisdom is righteousness, and this "is immortal" (1:15). Divine likeness thus means sharing in God's wisdom and righteousness, which also means fellowship with his incorruptible being.

In the context of Jewish exposition these statements refer to the glory of Adam before the invasion of the world by sin and death (cf. Wis. 2:24 and 1:13). The Pauline message about Christ, however, relates such statements, along with what they say about the divine likeness, to the manifestation of the image of God in Jesus Christ (2 Cor. 4:4). The Easter message explains this, for new and imperishable life was manifested with

150. On this cf. Jervell, *Imago Dei*, pp. 45ff., also 100ff. on rabbinic interpretation.
151. In Wis. 9:2 wisdom represents and elucidates the divine likeness of Gen. 1:26f., as may be seen from the goal of dominion over the rest of creation in 9:2b.

the resurrection of Jesus. The image of this second Adam that all are meant to bear (1 Cor. 15:49) is that of the Creator in the sense of Gen. 1:26f., after which we are now to be renewed or refashioned (Col. 3:10). As in Wis. 1:15, this includes righteousness (Eph. 4:24), the basis for which now is the manifestation of new and incorruptible life in the resurrection of Jesus. The hope of participation in this life is guaranteed to believers by the fact that even now they put on the new man in the power of the Spirit (cf. 1 Cor. 15:53f.; Gal. 3:27), namely, by righteousness and true holiness, by mercy, kindness, gentleness, and generosity, as Christ has taught and shown them (Col. 3:12f.).

Here an eschatological turn is given to the fellowship with God that Jewish wisdom viewed as the deeper meaning of the divine image and likeness of Adam before the fall. It is reinterpreted as our final destiny, which is manifested already in Jesus Christ and in which believers share already through the power of the Spirit, who is already effecting the eschatological reality of the new man in them.

Here, then, is the context of the NT statements to which the early interpretation of the likeness and the Reformation and post-Reformation understanding of the image were mainly oriented (cf. esp. Col. 3:9ff. and Eph. 4:24). Decisive for this theological interpretation was the basic eschatological reference that the incursion of eternal life in the resurrection of Christ provided for eschatological hope. If we detach the ethical statements of Col. 3 and Eph. 4 from this basic christological and eschatological relation, then, reversing the Pauline intention in what is said about the new man, we can use them only to describe the original divine likeness of Adam. Furthermore, we promote a purely moral understanding of human destiny such as had developed in much of modern Protestant theology (see below).

Patristic theology, however, rightly clung to the relation between the divine likeness and immortality, although unfortunately not in such a way as to see them, even with a reference to creation, as our eschatological destiny that is actualized only in Jesus Christ, and even then only proleptically. Always in the fathers we also find the consideration that Adam in his first estate, without Jesus Christ, or at any rate without the incarnation and resurrection, might have attained to immortality if he had not broken God's command. In spite of speculation regarding the tree of life in the paradise story,[152] this thesis was not easily reconcilable with the christological faith of the church. Over against Platonic ideas of the soul as inherently immortal, it was no doubt an incisive correction to see in immortality a divine grace dependent on human conduct and not something intrinsic to our

152. Cf. Gen. 2:9 and 3:22 and n. 127 above.

created nature.[153] In this way early theologians expressed the truth that immortality and incorruptibility, applying to the whole person and not just the soul, are elements in our destiny of fellowship with the eternal God. But apart from the line of thinking in Irenaeus to which we referred above (see pp. 207f.), they did not relate this destiny to the future manifestation of the Son of God in the flesh. Once again the reason for this is to be sought in the overdrawn depiction of the original glory of Adam.

Because of ideas that the divine likeness was fully realized at the beginning of human history, the destiny of immortality was necessarily detached from the doctrine of our creation in the image of God. This was at least the case when it was thought that the divine likeness, being originally posited by God, continues after the fall, whereas immortality as fellowship with the eternal life of God became an unattainable goal after the fall until Christ made it accessible again. The problems were complicated by the fact that from the 3rd century onward, under the influence of Platonism, the idea of an immortality of the soul by nature gained support in theology and even became normative, as a result especially of the influence of Gregory of Nyssa in the East and Augustine in the West.

This intrinsic immortality of the soul, however, could not guarantee participation in God's eternal life and therefore in salvation.[154] Our destiny of eternal life and blessedness had to be distinguished from the natural immortality of the soul, which is ambivalent as regards eternal bliss.[155] At the same time the destiny of supreme bliss as our goal could also serve as a basis for the immortality of the human soul, since the soul is oriented to this final goal.[156] The older Protestant dogmaticians often deduced this doctrine of Bonaventura as an argument for the

---

153. Cf. the contesting of a natural immortality of the soul in Justin *Dial.* 5, Tatian *Or.* 13.1, and Irenaeus *Adv. haer.* 3.20.1 (immortality is a gift of divine grace, not a natural property, in 3.20.2). Even in Clement of Alexandria the soul can attain to immortality only through knowledge of God (*Strom.* 6.68.3). Tertullian was one of the first to view the soul as immortal by nature (*De an.* 51.5). He regarded death as the separation of soul and body (51.1 and 52.1), though the soul moves on to a lesser state (53.3) that can hardly be called life (43.4f.). Later theologians like Origen and Augustine accepted the Platonic doctrine of the immortality of the soul but saw its life as dependent on God as a result of its creatureliness (*Civ. Dei* 10.31).

154. *Civ. Dei* 13.24.6.

155. At Lateran V in 1513 the medieval church in the West made the immortality of the soul a dogma (DS § 1440 = ND § 410), but modern Roman Catholic theologians do not think that in so doing the church was defining a philosophical doctrine of the soul's immortality by nature but maintaining the relation of human life to the eternal God, which continues even beyond death. Cf. J. Ratzinger, *Eschatologie — Tod und ewiges Leben* (1977), pp. 127ff. Hence Ratzinger speaks only of a "determination" for immortality by creation (129ff.). Cf. also Fiorenza and Metz in *Mysterium Salutis*, II, 615ff.; also H. Mayr in *LThK*, X, 527f.

156. Bonaventura *Sent.* 2.19.1.1 (Opera omnia, II, 457ff., esp. 460). While Bonaventura finds the final basis of the soul's immortality in its destiny of blessedness, the divine likeness is the formal basis. In this way he can relate the likeness and our destiny, even though distinguishing them.

thesis that immortality, like the divine likeness, belongs to our human nature and is not to be regarded as a supernatural addition.[157] Up to the 18th century it was a common conviction that our destiny, the goal of our creation, points beyond earthly life to a future blessedness as participation in the eternal life of God.

If our eschatological destiny of participation in God's eternal life is no longer viewed as constitutive for the divine likeness, this instead being found in the virtues of a righteous life, then the question might be raised whether the divine likeness in this sense does not form a basis for the understanding of our destiny. The question is then precisely whether our destiny relates primarily to a future life or is to be regarded primarily as the destiny for a moral life in the present world. In the 18th century a debate raged over this question,[158] whose history has not yet been written and in the course of which, under the particular influence of Kant and Fichte, the thesis that our moral destiny is primary gained the upper hand.[159] This process is of interest for our theme of the divine likeness because in modern Protestant theology interpretation of the concept in relation to destiny followed in part the thesis of a moral destiny.

In his understanding of the divine likeness as destiny, Herder described it particularly in terms of religion and humanity,[160] though he also had the goal of eternal life in view. Some later theologians spoke of an earthly as opposed to a heavenly destiny. Thus K. G. Bretschneider saw it as our original destiny to develop our given forces and aptitudes of body as well as spirit in accordance with the laws of the true, the good, and the beautiful.[161] We also find the distinction of an ethically understood

---

157. Calov, *Systema* 4.2.10 (p. 444); also Hollaz, *Examen,* II c. 1 q 20. Cf. also the earlier remarks of Hollaz on eternal salvation as the formal end of theology (I c. 7, 664ff.) along the lines of the so-called analytical method of theology (see vol. I, 3f.).

158. Cf. Bretschneider, *Systematische Entwicklung,* pp. 504f. An especially influential work in the transition to a primarily moral destiny was J. J. Spalding's *Die Bestimmung des Menschen* (1748, 1769). Cf. my "Gottebenbildlichkeit als Bestimmung des Menschen," pp. 16f.

159. Kant uses the phrase "moral destiny" fairly often, e.g., in *Critique of Practical Reason* (1788), *Critique of Judgment* (1790), *Religion within the Limits of Reason Alone* (1793), also *Anthropologie in pragmatischer Hinsicht* (1798). Above all, he gave material primacy to our moral destiny as against a destiny of future happiness, even though regarding the latter as a consequence of the former. As regards Fichte, cf. his *Die Bestimmung des Menschen* (1800).

160. Herder, *Ideen* 9.5.

161. Bretschneider, *Handbuch,* I, 752; cf. 748, where he links the earthly to the eternal destiny; cf. also his *Systematische Entwicklung,* p. 504. As in Kant, fulfilling our earthly destiny is the basis of achieving our eternal destiny.

earthly destiny from a heavenly destiny in C. I. Nitzsch.[162] Materially J. T. Beck even viewed our created divine likeness primarily in terms of our earthly destiny. He had in view a relation between our disposition for divine likeness and the original divine likeness of Christ, but he took this to mean that the disposition must develop into a personal quality of virtue by means of our own actions (i.e., ethically).[163] I. A. Dorner, too, saw us as potentially the image of God, i.e., in accordance with our ethical destiny as this comes to expression in ethical action.[164] For Dorner, however, the religious relation was the cardinal point in the image as destiny, since this gives us the power to unite and fulfill the other aspects. Hence Dorner could closely link our destiny as likeness to the destiny of immortality.[165]

The tendency to direct attention solely to our earthly or moral destiny went hand in hand with the viewing of personality as a finished product. Along these lines R. Seeberg equated the divine likeness and personality, so that the relation to God is our goal only inasmuch as our spiritual nature includes a religious and moral disposition.[166] In the 20th century P. Althaus thought he could find the divine image in our personhood. Yet in this he saw the constitution in which we are destined for the fellowship with God that has been achieved in Jesus Christ.[167] This could mean that the personal constitution of human reality is not to be seen as a finished product but is to be related to its future destiny. In Althaus, however, it is the presupposition and basis of this destiny. E. Brunner, too, viewed the image as our being subjects or persons in the finished sense, understanding personal being as responsible being in Kant's sense.[168] He also emphasized that our being in self-knowledge and self-determination is not primary but secondary. It is subordinate to the relation to God, yet not in the sense of being grounded in the relation to the future of our destiny of fellowship with God.[169]

162. C. I. Nitzsch, *System of Christian Doctrine* (1829, 3rd ed. 1837, ET 1899), pp. 203f.

163. J. T. Beck, *Vorlesungen über Christliche Glaubenslehre,* ed. I. Lindenmeyer (1887), II, 328ff.

164. I. A. Dorner, *A System of Christian Doctrine,* 4 vols. (Edinburgh, 1880-82), II, 80. Dorner maintained that our free acts are not productive in relation to God, but also that as "acts of receiving," they may be either done or left undone (pp. 79f.).

165. Ibid., 82ff.

166. R. Seeberg, *Christliche Dogmatik* (1924), I, 483ff. (the quotation is from p. 501). For a similar equation cf. Nitzsch, *System,* p. 201, and J. Müller, *Die christliche Lehre,* II, 188, 489. The Roman Catholic Tübingen school of F. A. Staudenmaier adopted the same view, though, in controversy with F. C. Baur, rejecting the Protestant interpretation of the divine likeness as human destiny; cf. A. Burkhardt *Der Mensch — Gottes Ebenbild und Gleichnis* (1962), pp. 133ff., 155ff.

167. P. Althaus, *Die christliche Wahrheit. Lehrbuch der Dogmatik* (1947, 3rd ed. 1952), pp. 336f.

168. E. Brunner, "Nature and Grace," in *Natural Theology* (London, 1946), pp. 31f.; cf. also *Man in Revolt* (New York, 1959), pp. 97ff., and *Dogmatics* (London, 1952), II, 55ff.

169. *Man in Revolt,* p. 98. Brunner did not interpret the divine image as destiny because he could break free only gradually from the doctrine of the first estate (cf.

If our destiny is set with our creation in the divine image so that descriptions of it must be oriented to the implications of the relation of the image to God, then from the very first as God's creatures we are destined for fellowship with God, for "life with God."[170] The point of likeness to God is fellowship with him. We must understand our present life, and especially our personality, in terms of this future destiny. It is thus that our future destiny now manifests itself. All other aspects are secondary to this one. Relating the thought of the image to immortality rests on the fact that the relatedness to God has its inner *telos* in fellowship with him. Even the obligatory righteousness that might be called our moral destiny has its basis in the fact that it is a condition of remaining in hope of the fellowship with God that God himself grants. This condition concerns not only our relation to God but also our relation to others, since humanity as a whole, and not just this or that individual, is destined for fellowship with God. The destiny is not just an isolated one. Its aim is the incorporation of humanity into the kingdom of God. Thus the common destiny of fellowship with God underlies and governs human relations. Only in the relation to God, and therefore in terms of the eschatological future of our destiny, does our moral self-determination or ethical autonomy find a firm and solid basis.

If the relation is reversed, as happened with momentous consequences in Kant, moral norms cease to have binding force for individuals. In the course of history the moral autonomy of reason was finally replaced by the caprice of individual self-determination.[171] Our destiny of fellowship with God forms an indestructible basis for an understanding of morality that resists such disintegrating trends. The

---

pp. 104f.). He thus developed an unfortunate distinction between the material image that was lost at the fall and a formal image that consists of our personality and that remains intact. The latter doctrine replaces the older Protestant view of a remnant left after the fall (on this cf. his "Nature and Grace," pp. 32f., 35ff.). Brunner clung to his distinction even after abandoning the idea of a first estate (*Dogmatics,* II, 48ff.). The distinction is an unhappy one compared to that between disposition and actualization because the continuity of the form as something that defines the content stands opposed to the Pauline thought of a transformation of the old I into the new (Phil. 3:21; cf. 1 Cor. 15:51ff.; Rom. 8:29). Barth rightly rejected the formal-material distinction relative to the image (*Natural Theology,* pp. 87ff.; cf. *CD,* III/2, 135ff.).

170. Barth, *CD,* III/2, § 45 thesis.

171. We may study this in terms of fluctuations in the concept of autonomy after Kant. They resulted in a philosophically reflected form of existentialism in J.-P. Sartre. Cf. C. Grawe's article on human destiny in *HWP,* I (1971), pp. 856ff.

presupposition is, first, that religion is not dispensable in the search for a proper understanding of human reality, that it is not a relic of a past age, but that it is constitutive of our being as humans.[172] Second, it is presupposed that there are sufficient reasons for regarding the God of the Bible as the definitive revelation of the reality of God that is otherwise hidden in the unsearchable depths of the world and of human life.[173]

If our creation in the divine image implies our destiny of fellowship with the eternal God, then the incarnation of God in Jesus of Nazareth may be seen as a fulfillment of this destiny. The union of God and humanity in the life of a man obviously cannot be surpassed by any other form of fellowship between God and us. Yet obviously we cannot presuppose at this point the church's doctrine of the unity of God and humanity in the person of Jesus Christ. We may say only that if this doctrine is true, then it implies the fulfillment of our human destiny as God's image. We may thus see why Pauline statements could speak about Jesus Christ as the image of God. They did not do it on the premise of the later doctrine of the deity of Jesus but in the context of the gospel of the resurrection of the crucified One, which also formed the starting point for the doctrine of the eternal sonship of Jesus.

If, however, our destiny as we were created in God's image has found its fulfillment — proleptically as regards all other members of the race — in the fellowship of God and man in Jesus Christ, then we must say that our creation in God's image was related from the very outset to this fulfillment that has come, or broken in, in the history of Jesus of Nazareth.[174] But how are we to understand this relation more precisely? Does it simply mean that in the divine purpose our creation was related to God's fellowship with us as it was fulfilled in the incarnation of the

172. Cf. the following volume, which I edited: *Sind wir von Natur aus religiös?* Schriften der Katholischen Akademie in Bayern 120 (1986); also my *Anthropology.* A reference to the constitutive relevance of religion for the various aspects of human reality, whether implicit or explicit, is the central theme of this book.

173. Cf. vol. I, ch. 4 in connection with the preceding discussion of the competing truth claims of the religions, and the explication of the concept of revelation in terms of the doctrine of God in chs. 5 and 6. The credibility of the truth claims of Christian doctrine relative to the deity of the God of the Bible is not adequately confirmed, however, by a mere clarification of the thought of God. More pertinent is the possibility of understanding this God as the Author and Finisher of the human world, which is the theme of the Christian doctrine of God's economy of salvation from creation to eschatology.

174. We shall discuss more precisely in the next chapter that which is only rather vaguely indicated here.

Son? Or does it mean that our creaturely reality was characterized from the very first by a reference to God and the fellowship with him that was actualized in Jesus Christ?

Karl Barth described fellowship with God (which was pioneered by God's covenant with Israel and brought to fulfillment in Jesus Christ) as a purpose for us creatures that is external to our essential nature.[175] He could thus abandon the idea that the divine image was lost at the fall, a position he had earlier shared (*CD*, I/1, 189, 199) with Reformation and post-Reformation teachers. "What man does not possess he can neither bequeath nor forfeit. And on the other hand the divine intention at the creation of man, and the consequent promise and pledge given with it, cannot be lost or subjected to partial or complete destruction" (*CD*, III/1, 200). The view of the divine likeness as the promise and pledge that simply accompanies "the physical sequence of the generations" has its basis in Barth's rejection of the exegetically more obvious view that the reference in Gen. 5:1-3 is to a handing down of the likeness in that sequence (pp. 198f.).

Barth indeed wanted to retain the correspondence of our creaturely nature to our divine destiny (*CD*, III/2, 204). He found this in the fact that humanity comprises beings in encounter with others (p. 243), as may be seen in the inter-relation of male and female (§ 45.3). The understanding of the likeness thus rests on this interrelation, which we have already dismissed as exegetically untenable. Ephesians (5:31f.) does indeed refer the fellowship of husband and wife that is grounded in creation to the relation between Christ and the church (*CD*, III/2, 312ff.), but this is only indirectly connected with the divine likeness and the destiny that rests upon it, namely, to the extent that this basic statement relates to humanity in the plurality of its members (see above, pp. 214f.). We shall discuss this in another context.

Our main concern at this point is that Barth finds in co-humanity a parable of our destiny of fellowship with God but one that is not perceptible in and of itself, "a reality which encloses the declaration of his ordination to be with God, but only encloses it, and therefore conceals no less than discloses it, and discloses it only when it is expressed by the grace and revelation of God, and in the knowledge of faith thereby awakened" (*CD*, III/2, 321). Hence the divine purpose remains external to the creaturely reality of our lives. In the sense of the divine purpose, this reality is not of itself oriented to God and to being with God. According to Barth, the parable of our ordination for fellowship with God as we see it in our creaturely nature does not lie in religion but in the neutral sphere of co-humanity, with its focus in the sexual relation. Co-humanity replaces our religious determination, as it may well do relative to human conduct in a secu-

---

175. Cf. also H. Thielicke's *Theological Ethics*, I, 147ff.

larized culture, though there in a perversion of our ordination for a knowledge of God that means differentiating him from everything creaturely.

As Paul sees it, the failure to differentiate God from the forms of creaturely reality, and to glorify and thank him as God, is a sign and expression of our human sin and folly (Rom. 1:21ff.). This statement presupposes the truth that as creatures of God, we are summoned to honor and thank him as God in distinction from everything creaturely. This is the religious theme of human life that is remarkably and significantly lacking in Barth's theological anthropology. Even in its distortion, which Paul and the prophetic critics of religion before him brought to light, this theme shows itself to be the content of our destiny as creatures.

If our creation in God's image means that we are to seek God, to honor him as God (i.e., as the Creator and Lord of all things), and to thank him as the Author of life and of every good gift, then we may assume that there is a disposition to do so in every human life, no matter how little we see of it in a given case. Our destiny of fellowship with God on the basis of our creation in the divine image cannot remain external to the actual living of our lives. It does not consist of a purpose of the Creator for us that is external to our creaturely nature and that may be seen on the level of human reality only with the coming of Jesus Christ. If that were so, the Creator would obviously not have succeeded in giving form to his purpose in his work, or at least in setting this work in motion toward the appointed goal. The purpose of the Creator cannot be as impotent or external as that in relation to the creature. We must think of the life of the creature as inwardly moved by its divine destiny, even though, for reasons yet to be discussed, the fulfillment of the destiny did not take place at the beginning of human history but will come only as the goal and consummation of this history. At the beginning there must have been at least an inclination toward this goal.

Since it came to interpret the divine likeness as our destiny, modern Protestant theology has also spoken about an inclination of human nature toward this goal. Thus C. I. Nitzsch said that we are to understand the image as inclination as well as destiny.[176] Similarly Dorner regarded the image as an object of destiny but also as an original gift.[177] Althaus spoke of our human constitution, in which we are destined for fellowship with God.[178] The only question is that of the connection

176. Nitzsch, *System*, p. 201.
177. Dorner, *System*, II, 77.
178. Althaus, *Die christliche Wahrheit*, p. 337. Cf. also Schlink's remarks concerning the image as origin and destiny in *Ökumenische Dogmatik* (Göttingen, 1983), pp. 117f.

between the inclination and its development and fulfillment. Not a few theologians have sought the link in our own activation of the inclination we have been given. The destiny is achieved not merely by development of the inclination but by its free activation.[179] Or, as Dorner put it, there is a mediation by which the ethically necessary — that which belongs to our nature — is to become a reality in our will.[180] M. Kähler, too, spoke of the image as a disposition that includes the task of realizing it. As persons, we have the ability to enter into fellowship with God.[181] Naturally these theologians presupposed dependence on our Creator. Yet not unjustly H. L. Martensen claimed that such views of the fulfillment of the image by our own human activity derived from "Pelagian dogmatics." He himself preferred to speak, not of an inclination or disposition, but of a vital beginning of the true relation to God in our origins.[182]

No matter what terms we choose to use, however, the final insight must always be that actualizing the disposition for divine likeness is not merely a task that we are to perform on our own, even though our participation — our active participation in the process of our own history — is not to be excluded. Only God can cause the image of himself to shine in us. A warning that theology must take to heart is Herder's observation that we cannot on our own hew out or fashion the image of God that has been set in us (see above n. 146) but are referred to the working of divine providence through tradition and teaching, reason and experience. The moment we take our destiny of fellowship with God into our own hands, we are already sinners and have missed the mark.

Our disposition for the destiny of fellowship with God is not left to us to develop on our own. On the way to our destiny and in relation to it, we are not just subjects. We are the theme of a history in which we become what we already are.[183] At present the goal is indistinct. It is not even present to us as a goal but only in an indefinite trust that opens up the horizon of world experience and intersubjectivity,[184] and also in a restless thrust toward overcoming the finite. This unrest and the related feeling of dissatisfaction can certainly be the expression of a human weak-

179. Cf. T. Haering, *The Christian Faith* (1906, ET London, 1913), I, 392.

180. Dorner, *System*, II, 77.

181. M. Kähler, *Die Wissenschaft der christlichen Lehre* (1883, 2nd ed. 1893), §§ 300f. (p. 262).

182. H. L. Martensen, *Christian Dogmatics* (Edinburgh, 1898), p. 152.

183. Nitzsch, *System*, p. 203 put this very acutely when he insisted that we must think of our divine likeness or personality as also disposition and destiny, stating that "the human and therefore the spiritual soul is also to become what it is." But the decisive point is that this becoming of our own identity is not a producing of the self but a history of its formation. Cf. my *Anthropology*, pp. 502ff.

184. Cf. my *Anthropology*, pp. 226f.

ness, namely, of an inability to accept the finitude of life's possibilities and therefore the danger of missing them.[185] Nevertheless, it also gives evidence of a knowledge that the final horizon in which we see the true meaning of the data of life transcends the whole compass of the finite.

It is of the nature of our human form of life to be "eccentric" relative to other things and beings,[186] in awareness of a horizon that transcends their finitude, and hence to be able to move on constantly to new experiences. An expression for this is "openness to the world."[187] More precisely we should speak of an openness beyond everything finite that itself also transcends the horizon of the world because only in awareness of the infinite can we think the thought of the world as the epitome of everything finite. The reference to a finite being or object is already mediated by an unthematic awareness of a field that greatly transcends each such object, and it comes back to the object in the light of the infinite.[188] Only thus, with an enhanced awareness of this movement, can we also perceive the beauty of finite things and beings.

In our own lives we are subject to many limitations and can fall victim to one or another form of limitation that hardens into complete closure, which is no objection to the constitutional openness of our conscious life to the infinity of the Spirit and his work. The phenomenon of human limitation can be understood only against the background of our constitutional openness. This applies also to the innate and implicit openness to God,[189] which we discussed earlier as *notitia Dei insita*.[190] It is not present to the consciousness from the very outset as a reference to God. Only in retrospect, in the light of historically concrete experience of God, can we identify it. In this regard it underlies the different forms of explicit religion. It is also a condition of the possibility of unbelief and of existential closure against God.

185. I am correcting here a certain one-sidedness in what I said in *What Is Man?* (Philadelphia, 1970), pp. 8ff. concerning "openness to the world" as a transcending of the finite.

186. *Anthropology*, pp. 61ff.

187. Ibid., pp. 33ff. and 60ff. on H. Plessner's criticism of an undifferentiated use of the term "world openness" to characterize human conduct.

188. Cf. K. Rahner's discussion of the *excessus* of knowledge of sensory objects as a condition of grasping them (*Geist in Welt*, pp. 153-72). Cf. also his *Foundations of Christian Faith* (New York, 1978), pp. 32ff., on the fact that we are beings with an infinite horizon. Yet to speak of an anticipatory grasping of this horizon is misleading inasmuch as this seems to be presupposed. Rahner himself views the movement of the infinite horizon of being from out of itself as constituting human subjectivity (p. 34).

189. Cf. my *Anthropology*, pp. 69f.

190. Vol. I, 107ff.

Religious characterization of the focus of this constitutional openness of ours is ambivalent, as is every other aspect of human life.[191] It is undoubtedly grounded in a self-declaration of divine reality, yet something about it means that we take our destiny of fellowship with God into our own hands with a view to sharing in the divine life. Being with God is indeed our destiny, yet for this very reason it is a temptation for us (Gen. 3:5). When we snatch it to us as our prey (Phil. 2:6), whether by way of the religious cultus or by emancipation from all religious ties, we miss it. For this reason, we cannot achieve it directly by human action. It can be achieved only when we know that we are distinct from God and, in our finitude over against him, accept ourselves as his creatures. By thus distinguishing God from everything finite, we pay him the honor of his deity.

This sounds simple. But it is not readily compatible with the self-assertion of a finite being, even though acceptance of difference from God presupposes the independence of the creature, even its active independence in awareness of its own finitude. With our ability to transcend ourselves, to mount above all finite things, we humans are summoned to conduct ourselves according to our own choices. But in so doing we may cross every boundary in asserting ourselves. We can thus distinguish ourselves from God only where we are already lifted above ourselves by the Spirit of God and are thus enabled to accept our own finitude.

Only by distinguishing itself from God by accepting its own finitude can the creature be in accord with the will of God the Creator, which willed the creature's distinctiveness and finitude. Only thus does the creature give God the glory that is his due as Creator and at the same time thank him for all that the creature is and has. Only by accepting our finitude as God-given do we attain to the fellowship with God that is implied in our destiny of divine likeness. In other words, we must be fashioned into the image of the Son, of his self-distinction from the Father. We participate thus in the fellowship of the Son with the Father.

In the Son the image is achieved in the sense of full likeness, not because God made himself the same or similar, but because the Son distinguished himself from the Father and the Father from himself in order to reveal the Father as the one God. In this way the Son is so in accord with the being of God as Father that only in relation to him is the Father eternally Father and God. Only to the degree that the self-distinction of the Son from the Father takes human form in the human

191. Vol. I, 172ff.

distinction from God do we find a person who corresponds to God,[192] who as the image of God is destined for fellowship with him.

Our destiny of fellowship with God thus means that we are ordered by the fact that the Son assumes human form in his life, as took place definitively in the incarnation. The incarnation of the Son is not a supernatural event in the sense that it has nothing whatever to do with the nature of the creature, and especially of the human creature, or that it concerns this only externally. In the incarnation of the Son creaturely existence in its distinction from God, but also in its destiny of fellowship with him, comes to fulfillment — to an anticipatory fulfillment, as we have yet to show.

Thus the charge that we are to have dominion over other creatures takes a new turn. We can rightly take up this charge as God's vice-gerents in his rule over creation only by accepting our own finitude, thus attaining the fellowship with the eternal God by which all the creatures that suffer the pain of their corruptibility will be reconciled to their Creator (Rom. 8:19ff.). Acceptance of our own finitude must also mean giving to all other creatures the respect that is their due within the limits of their finitude. In view here is the multiplicity of creatures as an order in which each has its own place. Only thus can we include all creation in praise of its Creator. In thanking the Creator for our own existence, we offer him thanks at the same time for all his creatures.

§ 3. Sin and Original Sin

a. The Difficulty of the Topic

No other theme in Christian anthropology has been so obscured for us today than that of sin and our approach to it. This is not just because of

192. Cf. E. Jüngel's "Bemerkungen zur Gottebenbildlichkeit des Menschen als Grundfigur theologischer Anthropologie," in *Neue Anthropologie* 6, ed. H. G. Gadamer and P. Vogler (1975), pp. 342ff. Jüngel says that by the incarnation of God we are defined as beings that are open to God (p. 349). The truth here is that we are to see the incarnation as the realization of our destiny and that only thus can we see unambivalently the point of this destiny. Nevertheless, we are human from creation, even in the sense of being destined for fellowship with God. Hence for Jüngel, too, openness to God includes openness to the world. In his statement that God's identification with the man Jesus brings sharply to light for the first time our distinction from God (p. 350), we catch the motif that we are stressing here, i.e., self-distinction as a condition of unity, though not expressly with reference to our human self-distinction from God (though cf. p. 351).

the problems that beset the doctrine of original sin and led to the dissolution of the doctrine in 18th-century Protestant theology and also, with
a shift of emphasis, in 20th-century Roman Catholic theology.[193] With
the decline of this doctrine the weight that Reformation theology and
Protestant piety attached to recognition of sin as a condition of assurance
of salvation became truly problematic for the first time. Certain emphases
arose, especially in the piety of the awakening, that sought to renew the
focus on sin as a condition of faith in redemption under the new conditions of modern development, i.e., on the basis of individual experience.[194] For innumerable people this type of piety seems to have led to a
story of suffering under spiritual oppression. In some, a spiritual potential
for emancipation from such pressures was established. But in many instances the emancipation led not merely to the rejection of revivalist piety
as a source of inauthentic guilt feelings but to a turning aside from
Christianity altogether. As a broadly influential example we may cite the
pastor's son Friedrich Nietzsche.[195] The Protestant churches themselves
understood the profound significance of this warning signal only very
late, if at all, so that in them the problems related to revivalist piety caused
many to leave the church and made the rest uncertain. Furthermore, the
problems have been only alleviated, never fully resolved. We must keep
this in mind if we wish to understand why an emotional taboo surrounds
the theme of sin in the public consciousness of the secular societies issuing
from cultures that have been under Christian influence.

The dissolution of the traditional doctrine of sin, especially the
idea of original sin, preceded the development of the piety of the awakening in Protestantism and is one of its preconditions. Already in the 16th
century some groups, particularly the Socinians, described the doctrine
of original sin as unbiblical and rejected it as offensive to human sensibilities.[196] They found it morally objectionable that God should impute
the sin of Adam to his descendants even before they had committed any

---

193. On Roman Catholic developments, cf. H. M. Köster, *Urstand, Fall, und Erbsünde in der katholischen Theologie unseres Jahrhunderts* (Regensburg, 1983).

194. Cf. my "Protestantische Bussfrömmigkeit," in *Christliche Spiritualität. Theologische Aspekte* (1986), pp. 5-25; cf. also J. Werbick, *Schulderfahrung und Busssakrament*
(Mainz, 1985), pp. 7ff.

195. On the significance of ethical criticism for the atheism of Nietzsche, cf.
B. Lauret, *Schulderfahrung und Gottesfrage bei Nietzsche und Freud* (1977), esp. pp. 129-90.

196. Cf. Faustus Socinus, *Praelectiones theologicae* (Racov, 1609), ch. 4, pp. 10ff.,
esp. 13f. Socinus claimed that we must interpret Ps. 51:5 figuratively (p. 12) and take the
eph hō of Rom. 5:12 in the sense of *eo quod* or *quatenus* (p. 14).

evil act themselves. Such an idea seemed to violate the principle that people can be responsible only for acts done by themselves or with their consent, not for the acts of others, especially ancestors, upon whose conduct they could have no possible influence. That God should act against this principle by imputing Adam's sin to his descendants seemed to be incompatible with the belief in his justice and his pardoning love.

In the 18th century, Protestant theology, both Lutheran and Reformed, could no longer escape the force of this argument. This was connected to the fact that the biblical basis of the idea, especially the exegesis of Rom. 5:12,[197] now seemed to be doubtful. In principle Protestant theology was ready to criticize official Protestant as well as Roman Catholic teaching according to the witness of scripture and to investigate the meaning of texts of scripture without preconceptions. The less scripture provided an adequate basis for original sin, the more seriously it fell victim to material criticism.[198] All that remained was the finding of a preponderance of sensual strivings over against reason, as this might be seen in Rom. 7:7ff., 14ff. and as experience confirmed it.[199] Even the practical philosophy of Kant seemed to leave room for an inheriting of this imbalance.[200] The only question was whether this inheritance could be counted as sin if part of the concept of sin as guilt is that it can be imputed to the doer of the act only on the basis of a free decision of the will.[201]

197. J. G. Töllner developed an incisive and significant study of this verse (*Theologische Untersuchungen* [1773], I/2, 56ff. [on Rom. 5:12-19]). His exegesis, like that of many modern scholars, is that death came upon all because all sinned (p. 62).

198. Töllner's "Die Erbsünde" (ibid., pp. 105-59) was a pioneering work in this regard. Materially J. F. W. Jerusalem had anticipated Töllner at important points in his *Betrachtungen über die vornehmsten Wahrheit en der Religion* (Brunswick, 1779), 2.1.4, pp. 465ff., esp. 513ff., 531ff.

199. Töllner, "Die Erbsünde," pp. 116, 122ff.

200. Reinhard regarded the disproportion as a moral sickness handed down to us by our first parents (*Vorlesungen,* p. 196, cf. 301ff.) and caused by eating the poisoned fruit of the tree in paradise (pp. 287f., cf. 276). But he strongly opposed an imputing of the guilt of Adam's sin to his descendants (pp. 288f., § 81), appealing in pp. 384ff. to J. D. Michaelis, *Gedanken über die Lehre der Heiligen Schrift von Sünde und Genugthuung als eine der Vernunft gemässe Lehre* (2nd ed. 1799), §§ 40-43. Töllner had already expressed himself sharply on this issue ("Die Erbsünde," p. 154).

201. Töllner preferred to relate the idea of inheritance to an inherited evil or weakness or sinfulness ("Die Erbsünde," p. 125). Others, like Reinhard, thought Paul's use of "sin" in Rom. 7 for the sensuality that we call original sin (*Vorlesungen,* p. 303) compelled him to cling to the word "sin." For a survey of opinions, cf. Bretschneider, *Systematische Entwicklung,* pp. 544f.

This question agitated 19th-century theology for a long time. K. G. Bretschneider answered in the negative,[202] as did R. Rothe.[203] W. M. L. de Wette, however, thought that our own conscience imputes our innate weakness to us as our own choice and guilt.[204] J. Müller insisted that guilt presupposes an origin of evil in the free choice of the one that commits it. On this ground he also criticized Schleiermacher's talk of a common guilt of the race, which found an echo in Kierkegaard's concept of dread. He postulated instead a preexistence of souls with primal individual decisions for evil. This enabled him to view the evil tendency within us as guilty and therefore to call it sin.[205]

We see impressively here the inclination of the whole century to reduce original sin to individual sin. A. Ritschl then adopted this approach without the premise of preexistence, which most theologians rejected as fantastic and unnecessary. Ritschl accepted the existence of an inclination to selfishness in individuals but also stressed the propagation of sin by the social interaction resulting from acts of sin.[206] Because of this interaction, Ritschl thought, individuals can feel guilty for the acts of others. In a large measure, he believed, Christianity was ready for this.[207] But because he linked sin to personal acts he did not think it necessary to extend the sense of guilt in this way, so that his presentation leaves the impression of exaggerated guilt feelings in Christian piety.

The decay of the doctrine of original sin led to the anchoring of the concept of sin in acts of sin, and finally the concept was reduced to the individual act. We see this plainly in the failure of theological attempts to retain the dimension of universal sin on the basis of a concept of individual responsibility limited to individual conduct. These attempts could result only in generating a false sense of a vaguely universal guilt linked to moralism. The moralism that resulted from anchoring the concept of sin in sinful acts fell victim to criticism of a Christian "Pharisaism"

202. Bretschneider, *Handbuch*, II, 87f. We are not to regard this as an imputation or punishment but simply as an evil (subjective for us).

203. R. Rothe, *Theologische Ethik* (2nd ed. Wittenberg, 1867-70), III, 44, also 158ff.

204. De Wette, *Christliche Sittenlehre* (1819), I, 104ff., 119ff.

205. Müller, *Die christliche Lehre*, II, 485ff., cf. 553ff.; also on Schleiermacher, pp. 432ff. Cf. Schleiermacher's *Christian Faith*, § 71; also S. Kierkegaard, *The Concept of Anxiety* (Princeton, 1980), p. 28, where we read that individuals are both themselves and the whole race (pp. 96ff.). In criticism of Müller, cf. G. Wenz, "Vom Unwesen der Sünde," *KuD* 30 (1984) 298-329, esp. 305 n. 13 with a reference to Rothe's reaction.

206. Ritschl, *Christian Doctrine*, pp. 342f.

207. Ibid., pp. 349, 344. The basis is still the individual act of sin. In this light we can understand Ritschl's criticism of the doctrine of original sin, i.e., that it knows only an impersonal obligation to be punished (cf. his *Die christliche Lehre von Rechtfertigung und Versöhnung* [1883], I, 407, cf. 436f., as well as the criticism of Schleiermacher on 502ff.).

that judged the moral failures of others without any psychological or social understanding of the causes. It was also robbed of its basis by increasing doubts about the premise that moral norms were based on anything more than convention. Christian moralism could thus seem to be a life-denying rigidity, and extended guilt feelings seemed to be simply neurotic. Especially influential in this regard were Nietzsche and Freud with their different but converging lines of argument in moral criticism. The dissolution of an awareness of moral norms applied especially to traditional norms in sexual conduct. To many people the unmasking of the neurotic character of the Christian sense of guilt demonstrated the oppressive nature of the entire Christian belief in God.[208]

We must take into account this history of the decay of the Christian sense of sin if we are to understand what the marginalizing of the term "sin" in current speech implies and why the term has for the most part only a formal sense except in church usage, or can even be used lightly to describe the attractive defying of ill-grounded prohibitions. The formal use is the result of the moralizing of the concept along with the reduction of moral norms to the status of social conventions. The lighthearted use is an expression of liberation from the prohibition of pleasures associated with traditional morality.

Christian theology should not take this decline in usage too lightly, e.g., as though it were merely a confirmation that Christian truth is not accessible to the world. To take this line is to overlook the fact that the linguistic decay is the result of an erosion of the credibility of traditional Christian talk about sin.[209] For this reason an esoteric withdrawal of theology into itself is not an appropriate reaction. Again, it is certainly not enough merely to complain about the linguistic decay and loss of meaning. Theology must instead draw from this process self-critical inferences that relate not merely to traditional teaching and the reformula-

---

208. In addition to Nietzsche, and after him, cf. T. Moser, *Gottesvergiftung* (Frankfurt am Main, 1976).

209. It might be claimed that we are shown here that talk about sin is not necessary from a secular standpoint. This is the view of G. Schneider-Flume, *Die Identität des Sünders. Eine Auseinandersetzung theologischer Anthropologie mit dem Konzept der psychosozialen Identität Erik H. Ericksons* (Göttingen, 1985), p. 13. The writer sees not only in dominant talk about self-development (pp. 16ff.) but also in the mistaken theological development of a moralistic and legalistic understanding of sin (pp. 18ff.) an obstacle to appropriate theological discussion of sin, and on both counts we must agree. But no account is taken of the dissolution of the doctrine of original sin in the modern era, though this underlies the moralistic and legalistic tendencies in handling the theme of sin.

tion of its essential content but also to the premises of those forms of penitential piety and their expression in liturgy that stand in need of criticism.

To win new credibility for the core content of traditional Christian terms in this field might be more difficult than many theological utterances on the matter suggest. Those who declare that the fact of sin is simply a matter of the knowledge of faith that does not need support in the human reality that is accessible to universal experience[210] fail to see that Christian faith does not create the fact of sin but presupposes it,[211] even though awareness of its depth comes only in the light of the knowledge of God mediated through Jesus Christ. Hence those who have not yet attained to faith in Jesus Christ are not thereby freed from the tie to the corruption in the structure of their conduct to which the word "sin" refers. If this matter were not independent of the knowledge of faith (even if its nature as unbelief and disregard for God comes to light only in that knowledge), then what Christians say about sin would in fact fall victim to the complaint of Nietzsche and his followers that we have here a calumniating of life. What Christians say about human beings as sinners is true to life only if it relates to something that characterizes the whole phenomenon of human life and that may be known even without the premise of God's revelation, even if this revelation is necessary to bring its true significance to light.

It has been rightly stressed that the loss of meaning that the term "sin" has suffered in the modern consciousness does not mean at all that people today are no longer aware of the reality of evil.[212] On the contrary, evil, though often perceived only diffusely and partially, is one of our main problems today. More precisely, the problem is that of our inability to master the fact of evil that manifests itself in its destructive effects. The turning away from God has made the problem all the more severe, for it

210. Ibid., pp. 27ff.; cf. also nn. 258f. below.
211. A theology that thinks it can evade this issue in virtue of the christocentricity of the understanding of revelation is betrayed into exegetical distortion as well. Thus G. Freund infers from Rom. 5:12ff. that through Christ's death we can regard the reality of sin as passing, and for this reason guilt can first come with Adam and be inherited (*Sünde im Erbe* [Stuttgart, 1979], p. 187). It is true enough that through Christ's death, or rather through the resurrection of the crucified and dead Christ (Rom. 5:10: "through his life"), sin has been overcome by God and is destined to perish. But it is not a Pauline thought that only thus is a link forged with Adam. What Paul says is that sin was in the world before the law came (Rom. 4:13). Cf. Wilckens, *Römer*, I, 319f.
212. C. Gestrich, *Die Wiederkehr des Glanzes in der Welt* (Tübingen, 1989), pp. 40f.

means that we alone and not the Creator are now responsible for evil in the world, or for the victory over it that we have not yet achieved.[213]

As much as the reality of evil strikes us, however, the blame is typically put on others — on more or less specific others, or preferably on anonymous structures and pressures in the social system. We can understand the placing of blame on structures to some extent because the system of modern secular societies claims individuals in many respects but no longer links the claim to any giving of meaning to individual life or grounds and justifies it, e.g., by the recourse to some authority that can give meaning. Individuals, then, may well feel that the demands of society are cold and alien or that they even repress self-development. As a result the social system and its representatives can very well appear to be evil and can be regarded as responsible for all the individual failures in life. This kind of mentality that localizes evil in others or in groups easily leads to violent upheavals. A point that differentiates this deep-seated inclination to seek evil in others, and to exculpate oneself or one's group, from the biblical and especially the Christian treatment of evil as sin, is that the latter finds the root of evil in the human individual, and indeed in each individual as such, not in someone else.

Naturally evil does not always manifest itself with all its destructive force.[214] This fact can easily give rise to the misunderstanding that evil as a whole is only a marginal phenomenon in the human world. If this were so, evil could be eliminated by singling out and isolating or destroying the perpetrators. The more radically this is done, however, the more easily evil manifests itself even in what is supposed to be good, and especially in the apparatus that is set up to repress it. It is realistic, then, to reckon with a much wider compass of latent evil. The term embraces much more than the forms of its manifestation. Superficially it may even seem to be something good. It may seem to have a place in the free development of the human personality, or it may at least seem to be value neutral. This impression fades, however, when we take into account the innate consequences as they gradually take their effect.

The classical prophets of Israel initiated a view of the universal dissemination of sin among us that some trends in pre-Christian Judaism developed and to which Paul gave a final form. On this view it is, of course,

213. Ibid., p. 41.
214. Ibid., p. 190. Gestrich defines absolute evil as the destroying and profaning of human life, including the soul, for no obvious reason (p. 186).

surprising that evil so seldom manifests itself to the full extent of its destructive nature. The biblical explanation for this is that God constantly protects his creatures, in spite of their sin, against the extreme consequences of what they do. Thus in the paradise story death is the penalty for eating the forbidden fruit, but the entry of death is delayed, so that what we now have is a limited life span. Similarly Cain, after murdering his brother, is protected, though his life is forfeited (Gen. 4:15). The biblical history offers a series of examples of God's limiting the destructive results of the sins of his people. In view of the universality of sin, the rareness of manifest outbreaks of evil is by no means self-evident. It is the consequence of God's gracious sparing and protecting, and human ingratitude for this in the form of taking for granted the good things that happen is yet another expression of sin.

The universality of sin forbids the moralism that will not accept solidarity with those who become the instruments of the destructive power of evil. Sin's universality shows such a moralistic attitude to be hypocrisy. The Christian doctrine of the universality of sin has the specific function, for all the need to check manifest evil and its consequences, of helping to preserve solidarity with evildoers, in whose conduct the sin that is latently at work in all of us finds expression. This antimoralistic function of the doctrine has often been underrated. In the modern world it has fallen victim to the dissolution of the doctrine of original sin when a different doctrine of sin's universality has not replaced it. If such views for their part are based on the idea of actual sin, moralism can be advocated only in part and at the cost of enhanced guilt feelings. Weakening of the conviction that a universality of sin precedes all individual acts has opened the door to the moralism that either seeks evil in others or by inward aggression produces self-destructive guilt feelings.

But what is the sin that is more universal than manifest evil but that also contains its root?

b. Forms of Sin and the Question of Their Root

Whereas Greek translations of the OT and also the NT writings bring all our different failings under the one word "sin" *(hamartia)*, Hebrew offers many different words for the many different forms of sin.[215] The closest

---

215. For instructive survey, cf. Köhler, *OT Theology,* pp. 166ff., and G. von Rad, *OT Theology,* 2 vols. (New York, 1962-65), I, 247f.

to *hamartia* as missing the mark is *ḥaṭṭaʾt*, which in contrast to *ʿawon* suggests carelessness. The term *ʿawon* itself means willful and therefore culpable failure to hit the mark. Common to both words, however, is their reference to individual acts. This also defines the distinction. At the same time the thought of guilt behind the individual act points to a common root in the motivation of the doer. The gravity of the act differs accordingly. Unintentional transgression can be expiated by sacrifice, but the guilt of those who act intentionally remains.[216] This applies even more sharply when the act has the character of revolt against the norm itself, i.e., against the underlying authority. In this case the Hebrew term is *peshaʿ* (apostasy). In Isa. 1:2 all of God's people are in a state of apostasy and revolt against their God (cf. Jer. 2:29 and Hos. 8:1; Amos 4:4).

All these different concepts relate to transgression of norms of conduct. One may thus say that when the OT talks about sin, transgression is always in view.[217] This is true even in statements that depict a universal evil disposition as coming to expression in the transgression (Gen. 6:5; 8:21). The thought of the wickedness of the heart undoubtedly points behind and beyond the individual act, as do the ideas of guilt and revolt. Thus the psalmist prays for a clean heart (51:10), and Jeremiah (32:39) and Ezekiel (11:19; 36:26) hope that in the coming age of salvation God will give us a new and different heart that will not contend against his commands. Jews repent not merely of their deeds but of the root of their deeds.[218] Nevertheless, the idea of the heart that is intent upon evil and that of the new heart that is in harmony with God's command refer always to our relation to the command of God, whether in the form of breaking it or keeping it.

Only in Paul does sin come to be seen as something that precedes commands and that is manifested and discovered by means of the law (Rom. 7:7-11). The OT view of the corruption of the heart as the root of transgressions prepared the ground for this teaching, yet in principle that detaching of the concept of sin from that of the law was a step toward a new idea of sin as an anthropological condition. Only through the law, of course, did the character of this condition come to light. The summing

216. Cf. R. Rendtorff, *Studien zur Geschichte des Opfers im Alten Israel* (Neukirchen-Vluyn, 1967), pp. 20ff.

217. Cf. G. Quell in *TDNT*, I, 278. Sin is "what is contrary to the norm." Köhler explained the infrequent use of *peshaʿ* as due to the orientation to individual sins, but behind these he saw the revolt of the human will against God's will (*OT Theology*, pp. 166f.).

218. P. Ricoeur, *The Symbolism of Evil* (New York, 1967), pp. 240f.

up of all the law's commandments in the one commandment "Thou shalt
not covet" (Rom. 7:7) shows us the perverted nature of sin, i.e., evil desire.
More precisely, sin expresses itself in desires that are against the commands
of God and therefore against the God who issues them.[219] Sin, stirred up
by the law, stimulates desires in me (7:8). Thus latent sin becomes blatant
sin in the desires that are contrary to God's commands. One cannot, of
course, conclude that these desires as such are not sin. On the contrary,
they are the manifest form of sin.

   This Pauline understanding gave orientation to the Christian doctrine of sin. Most of the fathers, at any rate, saw in desire (*epithymia* or
cupiditas, concupiscentia) the consequence of Adam's transgression and
therefore a punishment, the fall of Adam having damaged or destroyed
the dominion over the affections that we enjoyed under the direction of
divine grace.[220] Yet this is not what Paul himself said. In Rom. 7:7 the
condition as such is already an expression of sin.

In the 16th century this theme became the subject of mutual condemnation on
the part of the Reformers and the Roman Catholics. The Reformation view,
oriented to Augustine, was that selfish concupiscence is already sin as such. This
meant that original sin remains even in those who are baptized, though it is no
longer imputed.[221] On this ground the bull of 1520 condemned the relevant
statements in Luther (DS § 1452f. = ND § 1923/2f.). The Council of Trent dealt
with the relation between concupiscence and sin from the standpoint of the
efficacy of baptismal grace and thus arrived at the conclusion that, notwithstanding Paul's description of concupiscence as sin, it is not sin in the strict sense but
the "tinder" (*fomes*) of sin, deriving from sin and inclining to it (DS § 1515 = ND
§ 512). The Lutheran Reformers, however, insisted on the Augustinian and Pauline

219. On Rom. 7:7 and the Pauline view of desire, cf. Wilckens, *Römer*, II, 81f. Cf.
also Rom. 7:17, 20, where the sin that dwells in me is undoubtedly the same as that which
7:7 describes.
   220. Cf. J. Gross, *Entstehungsgeschichte des Erbsündendogmas von der Bibel bis
Augustinus*, Geschichte des Erbsündendogmas 1 (1960), pp. 110f. (on Methodius of Olympus), 137 (Didymus the Blind), 142f. (Basil), and 145 (Gregory of Nazianzus). Athanasius,
however, viewed desire as sin only in an improper sense, since no guilt attaches to it (pp.
132f.). On Methodius cf. also L. Scheffczyk, "Urstand, Fall, und Erbsünde," *HDG*, II/3a
(1981), pt. 1, pp. 85f. Later fathers like Nemesius of Emesa, whose statements John of
Damascus adopted in his account of the orthodox faith (*Fid. orth.* 2.13), distinguished
between natural and unnatural or good and evil desires.
   221. Cf. Melanchthon, Apology to CA 2.35f. (BSLK, 154), appealing to Augustine's
De nupt. et concup. 1.25 (PL, 44, 430). On Luther, cf. G. Ebeling, *Lutherstudien*, II/3, 287f.;
also P. Althaus, *The Theology of Martin Luther* (Philadelphia, 1966), 153-55. On the imputation of sin in Augustine, cf. Gross, *Entstehungsgeschichte des Erbsündendogmas*, pp. 330f.

usage, to which the apology of the Confession of Augsburg had appealed (2.40 [BSLK, 155, 11ff.]). The Formula of Concord thus condemned the opposing doctrine that evil desires are not sin (Epitome 1.11f. [Schaff, *Creeds,* III, 104f.]).

Modern discussion should note that the Roman Catholic interest is in the efficacy of the grace of baptism, which Protestants do not dispute or negate, but simply want to describe differently.[222] As regards the relation between concupiscence and sin, Protestants can concede that the concept of concupiscence does not of itself adequately describe the nature of sin.

According to the Augsburg Confession, we must define sin in relation to God as a lack of "fear of God" and "trust in him" (Schaff, *Creeds,* III, 8). Only then do we read of a "fleshly appetite" *(concupiscentia).* Alone, then, concupiscence does not fully define sin. Yet it is already sin, i.e., a form of its manifestation, even though the core of the nature or perversion of sin may be still hidden. Calling concupiscence a manifestation of sin fits the facts better than the High Scholastic distinction between material and formal aspects of sin, in which concupiscence is the material side, and lack of the righteousness that we owe to God is the formal side.[223] This distinction had the unfortunate implication that concupiscence itself is not sin, in spite of Paul's statements, especially in Rom. 7, for it is only the form that makes a thing what it is. As a manifestation of sin, concupiscence is in fact sin, though the core and root of its perverted nature may still be hidden.

The classical significance of Augustine for the Christian doctrine of sin consists in the fact that he viewed and analyzed the Pauline link between sin and desire more deeply than Christian theology had hitherto managed to do. The many aspects of his teaching that call for criticism should not blind us to this extraordinary achievement. We certainly cannot accept unquestioningly his idea of an inheriting of Adam's sin by succeeding generations, his resultant tendency to see the sinfulness of desire exclusively in sexual terms, and his much too undifferentiated interpretation of the responsibility for decisions of the will (which is necessary to any concept of sin), an interpretation that sometimes prevented him, at the cost of linguistic consistency, from describing desire itself as sin rather than the acts to which it gives rise. Rightly have these

---

222. Cf. G. Wenz, "Damnamus? Die Verwerfungssätze in den Bekenntnisschriften der evangelisch-lutherischen Kirche als Problem des ökumenischen Dialogs zwischen der evangelisch-lutherischen und der römisch-katholischen Kirche," in *Lehrverurteilungen — kirchentrennend?* II, ed. K. Lehmann (1989), pp. 68ff., esp. 88ff.

223. We find the distinction in many 13th-century theologians, e.g., Aquinas *ST* 2.1.82.3. The argument of Aquinas that we are to define sin in terms of its cause — the breach in the relation to God, with concupiscence being a result of this breach — corresponds in fact to the Lutheran statement in CA 2.

aspects of his teaching come under attack. Nevertheless, theology must grasp the important basic thought that lies behind them and assert it apart from the dubious aspects.[224] No discussion of the Christian doctrine of sin can fail to attempt this. Many modern treatments have been unsuccessful because they have overhastily dismissed Augustine's teaching.

From the time of his baptism in 387 and his ensuing work on free will, Augustine viewed immoderate (!) desire, which he often simply called desire (*libido* or *cupiditas*), as the basic form of human sin.[225] His relevant statements, in which immoderate desire is either sin or simply the cause or result of sin, are not wholly consistent[226] because he linked the guilt of sin to acts flowing from the free decision of the will, so that it is hard to find sin proper in desire in infants, which precedes any responsible decision of the will. All the same, the general tendency of Augustine is to equate concupiscence and sin.[227] At the same time concupiscence should not simply be equated with sexuality, as has often happened.[228] Though Augustine liked to take sexual desire as an example that shows the perverted nature of concupiscence, some of his less frequent statements about concupiscence as a structural deformation of the will must be regarded as more basic to his systematic thinking.[229]

224. I tried to do this in my *Anthropology*, pp. 87ff. In what follows I work out more clearly the reasons for my interpretation and its particular character. Cf. also H. Häring, *Die Macht des Bösen. Das Erbe Augustins* (1979), pp. 153-61.

225. *De lib. arb.* 1.3f., 3.17-19. Augustine emphasizes expressly that those who desire what is good, e.g., a life without fear, are not blameworthy (1.4). He then calls immoderate cupidity the expression of a corrupt will (3.17). For a general survey and evaluation, cf. Gross, *Entstehungsgeschichte des Erbsündendogmas*, pp. 322ff. Scheffczyk says that Augustine exaggerates the evil in concupiscence ("Urstand, Fall, und Erbsünde," pp. 218ff.), but he relates Augustine's view too closely to earlier patristic theories and does not adequately account for the inner relation to the sin of pride.

226. Cf. Gross, *Entstehungsgeschichte des Erbsündendogmas*, pp. 325ff.

227. This applies even to the passage in the later work against Julian in which he defined original sin as concupiscence that incurs guilt *(reatus)* (*C. Julian op. imperf.* 1.71 [CSEL, 8/4, 1974, 84]), which in Neo-Scholastic Roman dogmatics is taken to mean that only *reatus*, which in Christians is removed by baptism, makes desire sin (F. Diekamp, *Katholische Dogmatik nach den Grundsätzen des heiligen Thomas,* II [1930], p. 156). Aquinas himself used against this idea (*ST* 2.1.82.3) a similar formulation from Augustine's retractions 1.15 in favor of the idea that concupiscence is original sin. Here, as in the work against Julian, the state of guilt is not just outwardly linked to desire but has its inner basis in it. Gross, *Entstehungsgeschichte des Erbsündendogmas*, p. 330, failed to see this, though we may refer to his discussion of the imputation of sin.

228. Cf. Gross, *Entstehungsgeschichte des Erbsündendogmas*, pp. 324ff. In opposition, cf. the very general sense of libido in *Civ. Dei* 14.15.2.

229. Cf. my *Anthropology*, pp. 87ff. Gross, *Entstehungsgeschichte des Erbsündendogmas,* p. 324, refers to some of these statements, but since they are rare, he reaches the mistaken conclusion that they have little relevance to Augustine's understanding of sin.

According to Augustine, the perversion of sinful desire rests on a perversion of the will. In assessing priorities, the will sets lesser (worldly) good above the supreme good (God)[230] and even uses the latter as a means to attain the former. This is where we see the immoderate nature of the sinful will,[231] for the result is a corruption of the order of nature, which Augustine viewed as a hierarchy of values in which the lesser serves the greater. Since we no longer accept this hierarchical view of the cosmos in a Platonic sense, it might seem that Augustine's thesis that sinful desire has perverted the order is now obsolete. Yet Augustine's analysis culminated in a thought that was independent of the Platonic hierarchy and that would outlast its rejection. In the nonobservance of the orders of nature Augustine found an autonomy of the will that puts the self in the center and uses everything else as a means to the self as an end. This is pride, which makes the self the principle of all things and thus sets itself in the place of God.[232]

For Augustine, pride is the core of perverted desire.[233] Those who desire seek everything that they desire on their own behalf, and this functions implicitly as the final goal of desiring. The self-relation in the structure of desire that comes to expression in the term "concupiscence," even though formally the reference might seem to be to something else (i.e., God as the supreme good), is usually implied rather than stated in Augustine's use of the term. Because the excessive self-affirmation of pride is for the most part only implicitly present and active in desire, the sinful will that is active in the desire for external things does not initially or universally attain to the deepest depth and consistency of a sinful will, namely, hatred of God as a result of the pride that sets itself in the place of God and that will inevitably fail in the attempt. In this regard Augustine thought that the situation of human sinners differs from that of fallen angels, who, as purely spiritual beings, do not sin by way of concupiscence

---

230. Augustine *De div. quaest.* 35.1 (PL, 40, 23); cf. also *Civ. Dei* 12.8.
231. *Conf.* 2.5.
232. *Civ. Dei* 14.13.
233. *De trin.* 12.9.14. V. S. Goldstein, "The Human Situation: A Feminine View," *Journal of Religion* 40 (1960) 100-112, and S. N. Dunfee, "The Sin of Hiding: A Feminist Critique of Reinhold Niebuhr's Account of the Sin of Pride," *Soundings* 65 (1982) 321ff., have argued that the sin of pride is a particularly masculine one and that women are tempted to underdevelop or reject the self. This view fails to see that in Augustine *superbia* is not just one form of sin among others but a general structure that underlies all sins, even the sin mentioned by the two writers. In Kierkegaardian terms, it might be regarded as a despairing not wanting to be oneself (see below, pp. 248ff.).

but directly through pride.[234] In the last resort, however, sin drives even us humans to hatred of God. In the kingdom of the world, then, love of self finally means hatred of God, while in the kingdom of God love of God puts the self in its proper place.[235]

The structural principle of perverted desire — which forms the climax of Augustine's analysis of the Pauline concept of sin as desire — is the idea that wanting to be as God, which in its end result is love of self, implies hatred of God. Unfortunately attention was not always paid to the relation between love of self (or pride) on the one side and concupiscence on the other in Augustine's understanding of human sin.[236] Only the structural unity of the concept that manifests itself in this relation makes it possible, however, to evaluate properly Augustine's achievement in his interpretation of the Pauline definition of sin as desire. The Augustinian understanding of desire differs at an important point from that of the apostle, yet precisely in so doing it brings out the deeper meaning of the Pauline concept, and it does so with greater universality and psychological validity.

Paul equates desire and sin by referring to the law of God — more accurately, to the striving against this law. Augustine's statements about

234. *De Gen. ad litt.* 11.14 and 16 (CSEL, 28/1, 346 and 348f.).

235. *Civ. Dei* 14.28: *amor sui* leads to *contemptum Dei*, and *amor Dei* to *contemptum sui*. R. Holte, *Béatitude et sagesse. Augustin et le problème de la fin de l'homme dans la philosophie ancienne* (1962), has pointed to the Stoic background of the Augustinian concept of love of self. Originally it simply involved self-preservation (p. 239, cf. 33f.); with the perversion of the will, however, it became *superbia* (pp. 248ff.)

236. In the Latin Middle Ages, discussion of original sin found Augustine's position mainly in the definition in terms of concupiscence (cf. Peter Lombard *Sent.* 2.30.8 [PL, 192, 722]). On this trend, cf. H. Köster, "Urstand, Fall, und Erbünde. In der Scholastik," *HDG*, II/3b (1979), pp. 125ff. Aquinas, too, dealt with concupiscence in relation to original sin, though only as its material (*ST* 2.1.82.3). He did not mention an excessive love of self (pride) that implies hatred of God. If, like Augustine, we view pride as the core of concupiscence, the latter cannot be merely the material of sin. It must be itself sin. In a different context (i.e., the discussion of sin as such), Aquinas did refer to inordinate love of self as the true principle of sin and also of concupiscence, inasmuch as excessive striving for temporal goods results from excessive love of self (*ST* 2.1.77.4c and ad 2). The link between concupiscence and self-love is thoroughly Augustinian here, but in the handling of original sin concupiscence is understood more along the line of the pre-Augustinian fathers as a disorder of the powers of the soul.

Modern theology shows a defective understanding of the inner relation of concupiscence to self-love. We see this in the debate between J. Müller and R. Rothe as to the nature of sin. The former saw in self-seeking the principle of sin (*Die christliche Lehre*, I, 177ff.); the latter traced back all sin to sensual sin (*Theologische Ethik*, III, 2ff.). The two parts of the Augustinian concept thus broke apart and came into opposition. Cf. my *Anthropology*, pp. 88ff.

concupiscence relate to desire more generally as an anthropological phenomenon. Certainly in Rom. 7:7ff. Paul was dealing with the human
situation as such. His description takes a narrative form with reminiscences of early biblical history and the revelation of the law. In contrast,
Augustine's statements about the connection between concupiscence and
immoderate self-love (amor sui, superbia) have the form of a philosophical
analysis of the structure of a phenomenon. In the process Augustine was
able to bring to light the opposition to God in the general structure of
desire rather than the opposition of desire to the law as in Paul.

    Augustine thus arrived at the thought of a corruption of the order
of things in their subjection to God as the supreme good. As the root of
this corruption, he pointed to the overevaluation of the self that wills. The
pride that is implicitly at work in perverted concupiscence could even be
claimed directly as a usurping of God's position without taking the detour
by way of the hierarchy of things. Opposition to the commands of a
positive divine law became rejection of the position that belongs to God
by right in relation to his creatures, including his human creatures. In this
way Augustine translated the core of Paul's statements from the narrative
form of Rom. 7:7ff. into a more general conceptual form, a structural
statement regarding universal conduct relative to the reality of God. The
universal extent of sin that Paul could maintain in view of the universality
of death as its effect (Rom. 5:12) became for Augustine a conclusion that
he drew from his anthropological analysis of sin itself.

    The scope of this thought was obscured in the history of Christian
theology by the related concept of an inheriting of sin and by the struggle
to overcome the implied problems. The universality of human sin was
thought to be dependent on its transmission from generation to generation. It was overlooked, however, that the Augustinian discovery of the
link between love of self and concupiscence itself implies a structure of
human conduct that is common to all individuals. Materially, then, no
theory of inheritance was needed. It is self-evident that the universal
structure of human conduct is of the very nature of the humanity that
passes down to individuals from generation to generation. The doctrine
of inherited sin has a tendency to derive the general propagation of sin
from the common origin of the race in Adam. This tendency, however,
obscured the significance of the actual universality of sin as an expression
of the universally applicable structure of conduct. Only when Enlightenment criticism had discredited the doctrine of inherited sin could the
structural universality of sin become a theme in its own right apart from

the idea of inheritance. Kant's doctrine of radical evil played a normative role in this regard.

Kant defined the radical evil according to which we are bad by nature as a perversion in the ranking of the impulses of action, i.e., the subordinating of the moral law, which ought to be supreme, to agreement with self-love, i.e., with the impulses of sensuality that demand happiness.[237] This description is structurally analogous to the Augustinian concept of evil. For Kant, too, evil consists of a perversion in the ranking of goods by the evil will. As in the case of concupiscence in Augustine, sensual aspirations that are rooted in self-love are dominant. The difference from Augustine is that according to Kant's description, the perversion takes place only in our human subjectivity. It is not a perversion of the order of the universe that is manifested in the hierarchy of goods, as in Augustine. We see here that the Platonic cosmos of ontic steps was not an option for Kant's cosmology. More basically, we also note the focus of modern thought on the subjectivity with which we humans encounter the world in freedom. Theology should not conclude too hastily that this development and the related anchoring of the question of God in anthropology were mistaken.[238] It ought to recognize in principle here an extension of biblical motifs in fixing our relation to the world.

As regards the structural description of sin, we may also see progress in the subjective treatment of sin as a failure of the self. Kant prepared the ground for this approach with his thesis of radical evil. A serious weakness as compared to the Augustinian description, however, is that in Kant the perversion of a proper human relation to God was no longer constitutive for sin as it is for Augustine with his phenomenon of concupiscence. For the relation to God Kant substituted the relation to the voice of the moral law that speaks to us. The switch in the ranking of religion and morality, of God and the moral law — although Kant seriously tried to base religion on morality — is something that Christian theology cannot accept.[239] But this defect should not prevent theology from recognizing the service that Kant has rendered. After the collapse of the doctrine of inherited sin, he reopened the question of a general struc-

---

237. I. Kant, *Religion within the Limits of Reason Alone* (1793), pp. 31ff.

238. I take issue at this point with Gestrich's observations in *Die Wiederkehr des Glanzes*, pp. 136f.

239. I agree here with Gestrich, *Die Wiederkehr des Glanzes*. In my *Anthropology* I did not deal with this defect in Kant because I was not there offering a theological evaluation but was dealing with the structural parallels in philosophy and the humanities.

ture of human conduct (over and above individual failings) as one of an intrinsic corruption of subjectivity.

Hegel took up the subjective approach in describing evil and developed and extended the theme by reflecting both on the universal nature of the self-consciousness and on the relation of the finite self-consciousness to the Absolute.[240] We can no longer bring against Hegel, as we can against Kant and his conception of radical evil, the charge that he defined evil or sin without regard to the relation to God. Hegel, too, started with human subjectivity, though not just the moral consciousness, but the individual as a being that is conscious of itself. For Hegel the self-consciousness was the basis of the unity of all the contents of the consciousness of objects. It is thus above each specific content. The same applies to its practical realization in the form of desire.[241] Desire characterizes our natural human will. In this respect we are not what we ought to be. We ought to lift ourselves above our own and every other specificity to the thought of the intrinsically universal, the true Infinite, as opposed to all the finite contents of the consciousness, including the self. The self, however, also has the ability to handle the Absolute as a special content of the consciousness among others, and to take the infinite unity of the I-consciousness, which transcends all its specific contents, as the true Infinite, thus actually making a principle of its own specificity over and above the universal and putting it into practice in its acts. In other words, it has the ability to be evil.[242]

Hegel's concept of desire brings further differentiation into Augustine's doctrine by ascribing to human desire, as an expression of the self-consciousness, a thrust toward the Infinite, which helps us to see why the I can put itself in the place of the true Infinite and Absolute. Desire is not bad in itself. What is bad is the will that identifies itself with it instead of raising itself above mere self-seeking. It ought to be motivated in this direction by the thought of the Absolute that the theoretical con-

240. Cf. esp. Hegel's *Philosophy of Right*, § 139; his *Lectures on the Philosophy of Religion*, III (London, 1896), p. 53; and the fine presentation of his thought in J. Ringleben, *Hegels Theorie der Sünde* (1977), esp. pp. 65ff., and also pp. 116ff. on the relation between sin and the concept of God.
241. Cf. Hegel's *Encyclopedia*, §§ 426ff.; *Phenomenology of Spirit* (Oxford, 1977), pp. 132f.; and, on desire as the natural will that we have to overcome, his *Lecture on the Philosophy of Religion*, 53ff.
242. Cf. Hegel's *Philosophy of Right*, § 139; also the stress on the guilt of the evil will that grasps this final possibility in the *Lectures on the Philosophy of Religion*.

sciousness develops. But is not elevation to the concept of the Absolute always riveted to finite subjectivity as its basis?

It was here that Kierkegaard developed and deepened Hegel's description of sin.[243] The opening sentences of his work *Sickness unto Death* (1849) describe human subjectivity as a relation that relates itself to itself. As a human being, I am a relation of the finitude of my I to the Infinite and Eternal. And I have a relation to this relation that I am by having a consciousness of the self. On my own, then, I cannot attain to harmony and rest because I cannot base the unity of myself on my self-consciousness, for my human existence is posited by the Eternal as a relation to the Eternal. If I try to achieve the unity of the self on my own, it is always on the basis of my own finitude.

In this way Kierkegaard, like Hegel before him, adopts the Augustinian concept of sin as a perversion of the structure of our nature as creatures. But now the form is new. Self-fulfillment on the basis of our finitude is a perversion of the basic relation that the Infinite and Eternal has posited and that makes our existence a relation to the Infinite and Eternal. The result is the desperate character of all our strivings for self-fulfillment on the basis of our finite existence. All such efforts take place in opposition to the constitution of our existence, which comes from the Eternal and his infinity. In our efforts at self-fulfillment we fail desperately for one of two reasons. First, it may be because we are contradicting the grounding of our existence in the Eternal and trying to be our own selves, based on our own finitude. Second, we may perhaps grasp at eternity as our destiny in place of our own finitude and try not to be ourselves, since we can be so only as finite beings, unable really to break free from our own finitude or to attain to eternity.

Kierkegaard did, of course, see a way out of this situation, i.e., the clear grounding of the self in God.[244] But can the self achieve this possibility of faith on its own as a self-grounding on the basis of its own finitude? Has not Kierkegaard shown that the subjectivity that seeks its own self-actualization cannot escape the tie to its finitude?

Kierkegaard has described the desperate situation of the human attempt to actualize identity in view of the divine constitution of the self.

243. On the close link to Hegel in the *Sickness unto Death* (1849; Princeton, 1980), notwithstanding the criticism, cf. Ringleben, *Hegels Theorie der Sünde*, pp. 248f. and 112ff. On what follows, cf. the discussion in my *Anthropology*, pp. 97ff.
244. *Sickness unto Death*, pp. 38ff.

On the soil of subjectivity theory this description has renewed Luther's thesis regarding the bondage of the human will.[245] Though we have a formal ability to choose, on the basis of our finite subjectivity and by our own action we cannot be righteous before God. As Kierkegaard puts it, on our own we cannot achieve our own identity.

Kierkegaard's uncovering of despair in the various forms of human attempts at selfhood contains a radical criticism of all faith in the power of selfhood long before the rise of modern identity psychology, with its descriptions and therapeutic evaluations of the processes of developing identity. At any rate, neither descriptions of the processes nor the therapeutic aids based upon them must be taken to mean that the developing of our own identity is to be viewed as a personal achievement.[246] Excessive focusing on our own identity must be regarded as a deformation of the theme of human life, since the goods and tasks to which life should be devoted ought to come first, not identity. It is from these, and ultimately from God, that personal life can gain an identity that is unattainable to those who are simply concerned about their own identity. We note here the old theme that striving for the idea of the good takes priority over the search for happiness or pleasure.[247] The pursuit of happiness for its own sake is egocentric and leads astray. Only those who seek the good for its own sake will thereby find happiness and identity.[248] "For what will it profit a man if he gains the whole world and forfeits his life? Or what shall a man give in return for his life?" (Matt. 16:26).

Reversing the order of seeking the good and of concern for identity and happiness is at the bottom of the phenomenon of anxiety that Kierkegaard tried to describe as a psychological state midway between innocence and sin.[249] The sin that goes with finitude does not derive from anxiety, as Kierkegaard thought, but constitutes the essence of anxiety, which is concerned about one's own ability. Anxiety fixes on the self and leads to the concern that Jesus criticizes in Matt. 6:25-27 and Luke 12:22-26. Jesus op-

245. Luther, *De servo arbitrio* (1525).
246. Schneider-Flume, *Die Identität des Sünders*, takes issue with the identity psychology of Erikson but unfortunately does not try to integrate his descriptions into a theological anthropology. This is because finding identity is assumed to be an achievement (pp. 73f., 79f., 110ff.), and theological rejection automatically follows.
247. Cf. the dialogue between Socrates and Callicles in Plato's *Gorgias* 491b ff., esp. 506c.7ff. and 470e.9f.: The upright and good are happy.
248. As Gestrich says, true faith is first interested in God himself, not in the believer's maturity, freedom, happiness, or identity (*Die Wiederkehr des Glanzes*, p. 78).
249. *Concept of Anxiety* (1844). Cf. my *Anthropology*, pp. 101ff.

poses this concern with his summons: "Seek first God's kingdom and righteousness, and all these things will be yours as well" (Matt. 6:33; Luke 12:31).

For a subjectivist description of the structural perversion that marks the essence of sin, anxiety has the same basic significance as concupiscence does in Augustine's presentation. As the latter is the root of such concrete sins as greed, envy, and hatred, so anxiety is the source of despair and care, but also aggression.[250] Since subjectivist analyses may be read as a deepening of the Augustinian psychology of sin, anxiety, an expression of excessive self-love, is probably to be seen as the reason for the emergence of concupiscence. We humans are naturally characterized by need and desire. But the step to excessive desire that sin takes may well be based on an anxiety about our own ability that leads to attempts to ensure the self by possession of what we desire.

Anxiety and the related fixation on the self also lie behind the search for confirmation by others, which rightly is stressed today as an important manifestation of sin.[251] Because of the openness of identity in the process of a history that is not yet over, we want recognition by others. When this is sincerely given and expresses loving acceptance, there is nothing bad about it.[252] But when we seek it at any price to secure our own identity, the search springs from an anxiety about the self that, linked to concern for the securing of the self, expresses a self-fixation along the lines of Augustine's love of self.

Striving to safeguard the ego by recognition on the part of others must be distinguished from the related theme of the striving for self-righteousness.[253] It is more basic than the latter, for we need righteousness only before a court that accuses and possibly condemns us. At root, however, the striving for recognition has as its goal the love of the other, though often it must be content with an outward sign of well-wishing. The thirst for confirmation of one's own goodness by those around us is not the root from which all evil grows,[254] although in fact destructive

250. *Anthropology,* pp. 142ff.
251. Gestrich, *Die Wiederkehr des Glanzes,* pp. 199-203.
252. Ibid., p. 201.
253. Gestrich is mistaken on this point (ibid., pp. 202ff.).
254. In this regard Gestrich's statement are off the mark (ibid., p. 203). If he wanted to say that the search for recognition is the basic manifestation of sin, he needed a better argument against the competing traditional claims of concupiscence, self-seeking, and anxiety. The fact that self-seeking and anxiety play a part in the search for recognition shows that they are in fact basic to the structure of sin, whereas the search for recognition is simply one form of manifestation among others.

wickedness may derive in many cases from a disappointed search for recognition, just as it may derive from other forms of sin's manifestation. The search for recognition is one of these forms of manifestation, and perhaps even a special form of concupiscence, related to the theme of our identity as self-conscious beings. At any rate, anxiety about our own ability is already presupposed here as an expression and aspect of exaggerated self-love.

Fixation on the self cannot be derived from anxiety, since it is already contained in it.[255] But in the situation of temporality anxiety constantly reproduces the fixation. The uncertainty of the future and the incomplete nature of our identity feed the anxiety. By anxiety, then, we are caught fast in the self.[256] The alternative is confidence in the future and a present life based on such confidence. But if this were not constantly given to us, we would not be capable of it. We also continually close off ourselves against it in anxiety about ourselves.

Thus far Reformation theology was right to call unbelief the root of sin.[257] In anxiety about themselves we either refuse, or are unable, to accept our own lives as a gift, to be thankful, and to move on confidently to the future. Trust in this sense, of course, is not yet faith in the sense of turning to the God of the Bible. Faith in this express sense is possible only on the basis of the historical revelation of God. If unbelief as a general fact of anthropology is to have a place in the theological description of sin as something common to all humanity, then we must accept a primary imprecision of the object and basis of confidence on the one side and of our inability to trust on the other. The God of the Bible is not yet as a concrete Other. Nevertheless, the biblical belief in creation demands that

255. Along with anxiety, the fixation on the self also takes the form of self-glorying, which is the *hybris* or *superbia* of antiquity.

256. In his three-volume *Strukturen des Bösen* (Munich, 1977-78), E. Drewermann has shown how great are the effects of this over the broad spectrum of neurotic behavior. He rightly emphasizes that for a radical solution to the problem we need a conversion to God. Acknowledging this, however, does not mean that we should follow him in his anti-rationalist campaign or his mixture of biblical and mythical materials on the basis of Jung's psychology. Augustine had already seen the basic significance of anxiety as a root form of sin, though he did not distinguish between fear *(timor)* and anxiety.

257. Luther found in unbelief a sin against the first commandment, as faith is its observance. For references, cf. Althaus, *Theology of Martin Luther*, pp. 144-46; and esp. G. Ebeling, *Lutherstudien*, II/3, 114ff., and *Der Mensch als Sünder*, in *Lutherstudien*, III, 74-107. Calvin took a similar view (*Inst.* 2.1.3). Along the same lines Barth interpreted sin as pride in terms of unbelief (*CD*, IV/1, § 60.2). For sin as unbelief cf. also Pesch, *Frei sein aus Gnade*, pp. 16ff.

we reckon with a reference of all creatures to the biblical God as their Creator, even though they cannot know that he is the one from whom their life derives and to whom it returns. In a correspondingly indefinite way creatures can thus have faith or not, whether in thankful acceptance of life and confident openness on the one side, or in anxiety about their own ability on the other.

In the situation of the universal failure to achieve our human destiny that theology calls sin, unbelief is not always, then, the theme as the final basis. It is this only in encounter with the God of historical revelation.[258] Again, the concrete starting point of sinning does not lie in the naked hubris of our human wanting to be as God. At many points this hubris is at work only implicitly in desire and in anxiety about our own lives. When it comes out into the open, it can have destructive and even murderous effects. But in the everyday manifestations of sin its true nature and the depths of its wickedness are for the most part concealed.[259] How else could it seduce us? We indeed suffer the consequence of a life in anxiety, unbridled desire, and aggressiveness, but only in encounter with the God of historical revelation may we say that this unnatural manner of life is sin against God and in so doing identify unbelief as its root.

c. The Universality of Sin and the Problem of Guilt

Demonstrating the structural universality of sin by means of the link between desire and self-seeking intensifies the problem of responsibility for sin that has always occupied Christian teaching on the matter right up to our modern discussion of the theme. To speak about sin seems to make sense only if conduct is at issue to which guilt may be ascribed. Otherwise it

258. *Anthropology*, pp. 91ff., 135ff. Cf. also Ringleben, *Hegels Theorie der Sünde*, pp. 252ff. on the relation between Kierkegaard and Hegel at this point. For Kierkegaard, cf. esp. *Sickness unto Death*, pp. 99f. Barth charged the theology of the Reformation and post-Reformation, and especially modern Protestant theology (apart from Kähler), with failing to base the knowledge of sin decidedly and exclusively on Christ (*CD*, IV/1, § 60.1). In his own christological grounding of the knowledge of sin (p. 389 thesis), however, he did not see that uncovering sin in the light of the revelation in Christ relates to something that is more universal by nature and that precedes the revelation. Failure to see this means making the fact of sin a mere postulate of the Christian faith. Cf. also Gestrich, *Die Wiederkehr des Glanzes*, pp. 85f.

259. According to Luther, these manifestations of sin may be generally perceived, though blinded reason easily misses them (WA 29/1, 85). Cf. Ebeling, *Lutherstudien*, III, 275f. and 296-300.

would be better to talk about sickness or a sorry situation. But according to Augustine's first work on the free will, there is responsibility only where we do things voluntarily. Sin can be justly imputed only to the sinner, or, more accurately, to the sinning will. For how do we sin if we cannot avoid doing something?[260] Augustine's Pelagian opponents could later quote his statements to this effect. In view of such basic principles, how can there be guilt for a situation in which we find ourselves through nothing we have done and even from birth? In reply Augustine referred to scripture, which says that even careless offenses are worthy of punishment, and, indeed, those that we would have liked to avoid but could not (Rom. 7:15).[261]

This is no answer, of course, to the material argument that links responsibility and guilt to the will of the doer. The only way out that offered itself was to reflect on the freedom of Adam to decide before the fall along with the supposedly Pauline idea that all Adam's descendants were present in him and therefore participated in his free decision to sin, i.e., sinned "in him" (5:12 Vulgate).[262] The question of responsibility for the present dominion of sin has thus become the strongest reason for recourse to Adam and to the participation of his descendants in his sin.

All the same, Augustine did not first develop the doctrine of original sin in order to solve the problem of individual responsibility for our present state. From the time of his work on the free will he shared the idea of the origin of death in Adam's fall, which was very common in patristic theology, and also the idea of the inheriting of a nature corrupted by sin, which Tertullian had linked to traducianism (the origin of the soul by transmission from one generation to another).[263] In the Pelagian controversy Augustine contended with increasing

260. Augustine, *De lib. arb.* 3.18. On the relation between free decision and responsibility in the early Augustine, cf. Häring, *Die Macht des Bösen*, pp. 139ff., 150ff.

261. Augustine, *Retr.* 1.9. On the development of Augustine's later position on guilt and responsibility, cf. Häring, *Die Macht des Bösen*, pp. 189-218.

262. *Civ. Dei* 13.14. For further examples, cf. Gross, *Entstehungsgeschichte des Erbsündendogmas*, pp. 319ff. Gross rightly distinguishes this view from the further line of thought that sees in original sin simply an inheriting of the greedy desire of Adam (p. 322), but he regards the two views as contradictory (pp. 327f.) instead of complementary because he takes too little into account the element of pride in concupiscence. The sin of Adam was already a sin of pride, with which all sin begins (Sir 10:13; *Civ. Dei* 14.13.1). Pride, however, is a corrupt appetite that wants more for the self than is its due, thus forming the core of concupiscence.

263. *De lib. arb.* 3.20; cf. Gross, *Entstehungsgeschichte des Erbsündendogmas*, pp. 266ff., and Tertullian *De an.* 40.1 (CChrSL, 2, 843). In Tertullian we find the Pauline idea of the flesh lusting against the Spirit (38.2f. [841]), whereas *libido* is the main term in Augustine (3.18), or the difficulty of obeying God's will, associated with ignorance.

sharpness for a direct connection between the inheriting of concupiscence and participation in Adam's sin.[264] To that extent the doctrine of original sin came to full development under the pressure of the question of guilt. Only at this point is the thought of inheritance important in Augustine's doctrinal system. He did not need it to explain the universal spread of the corruption of the will involved in concupiscence. The universality of sin remained even without appeal to Adam.

Medieval discussion of the concept of original sin showed, however, that a reference to Adam's freedom of decision before the fall did not by any means solve the problem of responsibility for sin. The idea of a presence of all descendants in Adam in the sense of free participation in his fateful act posed strictly the demand for a preexistence of souls. Augustine's idea of a seminal presence of descendants in Adam could claim some measure of plausibility only on the premise of the traducian view that souls are transmitted from generation to generation, though even then it was in some sense bizarre to think of seminal souls taking part in Adam's decision. On a creationist view a wholly new theory had to be advanced to explain why each soul, created afresh by God for each individual, still bore guilt for Adam's sin. Anselm thought he could give an explanation along Augustinian lines with the thesis that each newly created soul owes to God the original righteousness that had been given to humanity as a species and that had been lost through Adam's fall.[265]

Theologians in the age that followed increasingly adopted this thesis, tying the lack of the righteousness that each descendant owed to God more or less closely to the concupiscence that was passed down from one generation to another.[266] The older Protestant theology, too, followed the same line, though with a special emphasis on the complementary nature of the two aspects of sin.[267] Yet the thought of an inherited culpability for the lack of part of our original endowment could not really solve the problem of individual responsibility of sin. The arguments that have

264. Cf. Gross, *Entstehungsgeschichte des Erbsündendogmas,* pp. 268f., 273, 301ff., esp. 305ff. on the importance of the Augustinian exegesis of Rom. 5:12 for this theme.

265. Cf. Anselm's *De conceptu virginali et de originali peccato* 2-6.

266. On this, cf. H. Köster, "Urstand, Fall, und Erbsünde. In der Scholastik," pp. 129ff.

267. Cf. J. A. Quenstedt, *Theologia didactico-polemica sive systema theologicum,* I (1685, repr. Leipzig, 1715), p. 918, th. 34. In the explanation, concupiscence is part of the corruption that is mentioned here (cf. also th. 35). Quenstedt devoted a whole *quaestio* (11.1029ff.) to the issue of whether original sin consists solely of the lack of original righteousness or has something positive about it; cf. Schmid, *Doctrinal Theology,* p. 244.

been urged against the doctrine of original sin from the time of Socinian criticism, which have brought about its decay, make this plain. Nevertheless, the struggle to reconcile individual responsibility and the universality of sin did not end. The problem of individual responsibility arose with every fresh attempt to give credibility to a universal sinfulness that precedes individual acts, once the traditional ideas of original sin and guilt had disintegrated.

Here lies the deeper reason why the history of the doctrine of sin in modern theology has finally reached the point where sin is reduced to the act of sin (see above, p. 234). Already in the Augustinian presentation original sin had ultimately been traced back to one act of sin, namely, that of Adam. Dropping the idea of inheritance, modern theology has applied the concept of acts of sin to individuals. Sin is the act of each individual that also shapes all individual life, or the "life-act."[268] But is life as a whole an act? Is it not rather a history that is characterized by experiences and happenings and encounters as well as acts?[269] The solution suggested by J. Müller, then, is still instructive. Müller thought that the only way in which he could cling to both the universality and totality of sin on the one hand and responsibility for it on the other was by postulating a prebirth decision of the individual as the origin of sinfulness in life as a whole (see n. 205 above).

The most influential substitutes today for a doctrine of original sin rest on a combination of the supraindividual aspects of sin and the individual setting in the social context. In place of the natural transmission of sin from generation to generation we have the concept of its mediation through social relations between individuals. The social nexus can then be viewed as deformed. We can hardly deny this.[270] As there can be no separating individual and social life, the former being always co-constituted by social relations, so sin also works itself out in the social forms of life. The only question is whether we have here the expression of something that has

268. Cf. Barth, *CD*, IV/1, 500ff. and 403ff. The concept of the life-act replaces that of inherited sin, which Barth too saw to be an "extremely unfortunate and mistaken one" (p. 500).

269. Cf. *Anthropology*, pp. 502ff.

270. Gestrich, *Die Wiederkehr des Glanzes*, pp. 88f., rightly stresses this with reference to interpretations of sin in liberation theology. Cf. M. Sievernich, *Schuld und Sünde in der Theologie der Gegenwart* (Frankfurt am Main, 1982), pp. 249ff., 256ff., and in criticism, 265ff. As an example of a political understanding of original sin on the basis of a view of our situation in the social nexus (cf. below, nn. 279ff.), cf. W. Eichinger, *Erbsündentheologie. Rekonstruktion neuer Modelle und eine politisch orientierte Skizze* (1980), pp. 187-228.

its roots in the life of each individual or whether society itself is the real seat of evil. At this point the question of individual responsibility unavoidably arises as the criterion of the applicability of the concept of sin. Only with the consent of the individual will does the evil influence of society become the sin of the individual. If the individual can basically escape this influence, then there is no difference from the Pelagian view, which recognized the mediation of sin in the social nexus by the infection of bad examples and set this in opposition to the Augustinian doctrine of original sin.[271]

Yet even if the individual cannot escape the influence of society, it may still be regarded as an alien power from which to hold aloof. In this case the individual will not regard the self as intrinsically evil. Evil will seem to be a structural sin apart from the individual. It needs no detailed proof to show that this does not accord with what the Bible says about sin. The biblical statements may vary at specific points, but in no case can we separate ourselves from sin. We have to recognize that the evil of sin is our own evil, whether as our own act or as the power that dwells within us (Rom. 7:17). Sin has its origin in the individual "heart." To explain the universality of sin in terms of the social nexus fails to make this point, even though we still find a place for an inclination to sin in each individual.

We see this in Kant, who, with his idea of a social actualizing of the evil principle in a kingdom of evil,[272] was the most important forerunner of theological constructs along these lines. Kant sought the reason for the development and spread of this kingdom — which we must overcome by founding an ethical kingdom of God, a common life according to the laws of virtue — in the inclination of individuals to pervert the order of impulses.[273] Similarly, Schleiermacher thought that obstruction of the God-consciousness by the individual sensual self-consciousness was a correlate of the communal nature of sin, which results from the interaction of individuals and presents itself as a common life of sinfulness[274] from which individuals can be freed only by integration into another common life that derives from the Redeemer.

Unlike Kant, Schleiermacher places the main accent on the communal aspect. For him the sinfulness that is present in individuals prior to sinful acts,

---

271. On this, cf. G. Greshake, *Gnade als konkrete Freiheit. Eine Untersuchung zur Gnadenlehre des Pelagius* (1972), pp. 81ff.

272. Kant, *Religion within the Limits of Reason Alone*, pp. 73ff.

273. Ibid., pp. 54ff. and on the concept of the ethical kingdom of God.

274. Schleiermacher, *Christian Faith*, § 71.1f., cf. § 69.3. On the idea of common life, cf. § 82.3.

and that has its basis outside their own existence (§ 70), is the common act and guilt of the human race (§ 71). Yet this sinfulness is also present in individuals.[275] A. Ritschl related the thought of Schleiermacher much more decidedly to social interaction inasmuch as the self-seeking action of individuals is what brings them into incalculable interaction with all others and leads them into relations with others in communal evil.[276] The resultant entanglement Ritschl called a kingdom of sin.[277] The distance here from the doctrine of original sin is clearer than that from the Pelagian view of the spread of sin by example and imitation.[278]

In the 19th century only Protestant theology adopted the Kantian interpretation of the supraindividual aspects of the doctrine of sin by way of the social involvement of individuals. Nevertheless, there was a counterpart in Roman Catholic theology, especially in the highly regarded thesis of Piet Schoonenberg that there is a "sin of the world" in which we are all entangled by being situated in the social nexus.[279] In a striking way Schoonenberg's deliberations are very close to the ideas of Ritschl, the only difference being that Ritschl advanced his view as an alternative to original sin, not as an interpretation of it. Even if we think with K. Rahner that the dogmatically binding content of the definition of original sin at Trent (DS § 1513 = ND § 510) is limited to a rejection of the transmission of sin by mere imitation,[280] it is still doubtful whether an understanding of sin as social situation really rules out the view that is rejected. Rejection of a spread of sin by mere imitation ought to safeguard the point that sin is thought of as intrinsically our own sin.[281]

Precisely here lies the problem with interpretations of sin as situation. Although Schoonenberg sought to understand the situation as an inner determination,[282] it is doubtful whether this is conceptually demonstrable unless there is actualization in individual life, and within this an individual inclination corresponding to the situation. We can uphold the element of truth in the Augustinian position as opposed to the Pelagian only if we recognize in sin a basic state of the natural constitution of the perverted life in the individual. Only thus do individuals have to identify themselves with sin as part of themselves, since their own existence in the body is the basic form of the self that identifies them as individuals,

275. Schleiermacher did not think he could call individual participation in the sin of the race guilty (ibid., § 71.2). Only insofar as it continues with our will or arises through us can it properly be called our own guilt (§ 71.1).

276. Ritschl, *Christian Doctrine*, 328f.

277. Ibid.

278. Ritschl's concern to delimit himself on this side (ibid., p. 305) results at best in a further development of the aspect of social interaction.

279. P. Schoonenberg, "Der Mensch in der Sünde," in *Mysterium Salutis*, II, 845-941, esp. 886ff., 890f., 928f. Cf. also K.-H. Weger, *Theologie der Erbsünde* (1970).

280. K. Rahner, in *Theological Investigations*, I, 229ff., 246, 270f.

281. For the description of original sin at Trent cf. DS § 1513 = ND § 510 (p. 130).

282. Schoonenberg, "Der Mensch in der Sünde," p. 924, cf. 891.

the basic form on which all the other aspects of selfhood build.[283] But still this does not give any answer to the question how individual responsibility is possible for the way we are, though it does offer the indispensable premise for a meaningful putting of the question.

New efforts must obviously be devoted to the question in what sense we are to regard the thing we understand as sin as leading to guilt. This question leads on to the further question in what sense guilt and responsibility depend on the freedom of action or are grounded in it. Only in the course of discussing such questions can we judge whether we may speak of guilt and responsibility with reference to anything but acts.

J. Müller thought that for the responsibility and guilt of action we need the premise of "formal" freedom facing alternatives between which we must choose, so that of itself it has the power to produce evil as well as good.[284] For this it is not necessary that those who choose be indifferent as regards the possibilities of choice before actually choosing. The only requirement is that they may choose differently as regards either possibility[285] and that this means the possibility of choosing evil vis-à-vis the norm of the good.[286]

Müller did not make it clear that a will that can choose differently when face to face with the norm of the good cannot be in fact a good will. It is more than weak because it is not firmly set upon the good.[287] To the extent that it can choose differently face to face with the given norm of the good, it is already sinful because it is emancipated from commitment to the good.[288] We may thus understand sin as our human weakness relative to our destiny.[289] Naturally this is not to equate sin with naked wickedness. But we cannot say that this weakness of the will relative to the good is neutral as concerns that antithesis of good and evil.[290] The

283. *Anthropology,* pp. 205ff.

284. Müller, *Die christliche Lehre,* II, 15; cf. 17f.

285. Ibid., pp. 32ff.; cf. 41.

286. Ibid., p. 35.

287. This widespread patristic idea may be found, e.g., in Athanasius *De inc.* 3f. and Augustine *Ench.* 28 (105) (CChrSL, 46, 106). For Augustine the will that cannot sin at all is more free than the will that can either sin or not sin.

288. Cf. the critical conclusion of G. Wenz regarding J. Müller's idea of formal freedom in "Vom Unwesen der Sünde," p. 307.

289. So Irenaeus *Adv. haer.* 4.38.1f. and 4.

290. Barth, *CD,* III/2, 234f., where Barth argues that freedom is never the freedom to sin (p. 235). It is confusing, however, that Barth cannot quite shake off this model of choice as the origin of sin, even though he describes it as the choice between the one and

will that can choose other than the good is already entangled in evil. Hence it will not suffice to appeal to an act of free choice in explanation of the origin of evil and responsibility for it.[291] If we do this, responsibility for a disposition that comes to expression in acts is confused with responsibility for an individual act. This applies no less to Adam than to us today. The insight has a long reach. It affects not only Müller or Kierkegaard but also Augustine and the arguments of the anti-Gnostic fathers. It rules out derivation of responsibility for sin from a decision of the will.

Not contested herewith is the ability of the will to choose between alternatives. This ability and the use of it are in fact typical features of human behavior. They are rooted in our ability to distance ourselves from objects of perception, from conceived objects, and from our behavior relative to them. The possibility of choice, however, is tied to things being present to the consciousness. Only then can we relate in some way to them.[292] But we cannot bring everything before our consciousness in such a way as to make it an object of choice. This fact applies to things both done and not done. We do or do not do many things, without there being any choice in the true sense of deciding after weighing possibilities. In many such cases deliberation and choice are fundamentally possible. They do not take place because we focus the energies demanded on truly important matters. Other things by their very nature evade full perception and therefore choice. This applies especially to our own states as those who choose. We can choose between acts and their objects but not so easily between the moods and feelings to which we are subject. Nor can we readily or directly influence our attitudes to the world by decisions. The same goes for our situation in the world. We can choose how to relate to it, but we cannot alter it in detail, or only to a more or less limited extent.

Primarily, too, our relation to God as the origin of the world and of our own lives is not determined by any choice of ours. As the divine

---

only possibility and our own impossibility (ibid.). Unfortunately W. Krötke in his *Sünde und Nichtiges bei Karl Barth* (1970, 2nd ed. Neukirchen-Vluyn, 1983), pp. 66ff. did not go into the problem of Barth's view of freedom in this regard.

291. In distinction from the line of argument here, Barth criticized J. Müller for attempting any answer at all to the question of the possibility of sin (*Protestant Theology in the Nineteenth Century: Its Background and History* [London, 1972], pp. 594f.). But Christian theology can hardly avoid tackling this question. In the controversy with Gnosticism it long ago attempted such an answer. The only question is how tenable the answer provided is on the ground on which Müller still stands.

292. Cf. James, *The Principles of Psychology* (1983 impression), p. 277; also my "Sünde, Freiheit, Identität. Eine Antwort an Thomas Pröpper," *TQ* 170 (1990) 289ff., esp. 294f.

mystery that encircles and supports our lives on all sides, God is not an object of our consciousness, or is so only diffusely. Hence he is not an object of an attitude that we select. Only insofar as we grasp the divine reality in a specific form of the religious consciousness can it be the object of an attitude that we choose. It is part of the religious consciousness, however, that the divine reality transcends all conceptions of it. The possibility of an attitude toward it is thus limited, for beyond all attitudes of ours the divine reality incomprehensibly encircles and permeates our lives. We may turn aside from the revelation of deity, from the declaration of the divine will. We have already done so when we do not weigh the possibility of it. But we cannot turn aside so directly from the divine mystery that is most inwardly present to our lives. Nevertheless, there is that turning away from God that we call sin. It takes place indirectly, however, as an implication of our human willing of the self when we put the self in the place that is properly God's.

Even our self-willing is not a matter of choice in the sense that we may refrain from it. Self-loathing is itself a form of selfhood, though after the manner of despair. Suicide cannot avoid qualifying the existence of the self by act. All that we can choose is the way in which we will be ourselves, at least within limits, and mostly indirectly by way of the objects and activities to which we devote ourselves, and always in admixture with illusions because we never have ourselves before us as objects, except partially. Always we are like those who look in a mirror.

Is this kind of human self-willing always sin? Is it not rather an expression of the self-centeredness of life that reaches ever higher stages, especially in animals, and finally in humans in the form of self-awareness, which includes identification and is thus a self-willing, relating all else to the I as the center? In this self-centeredness of life, have we not been created by God as beings that to a particularly high degree are capable of independence and dominion over our environment? This is undoubtedly true, and for that reason we may not say that the self-centeredness of life is itself sinful.[293] Nor does it stand in simple opposition to our distinct destiny of elevation above everything finite, including our own finitude, for this movement of life is constitutive for the I itself.[294]

293. So rightly Dorner, *System,* II, 379. In my own first work on anthropology, *What Is Man,* I tied the self-reference of human conduct to the theme of sin (pp. 54ff.) but did not identify the self-reference as such as sin (p. 56), only the self-reference that is enclosed in itself and its secular possessions (146). Cf. also my *Anthropology,* pp. 105ff.
294. *Anthropology,* pp. 105f., 240ff.

Nevertheless, the perversion of the relation of the finitude of the self to the Infinite and Absolute is so close that except in the case of express distinction of the self in its finitude from God, the self does in fact become the infinite basis and reference point for all objects, thus usurping the place of God.[295] Usually this does not take place in the form of revolt against the God of religion but in that of the anxiety of the self about itself, in that of the excessive nature of its desires. At work here is the implicit form of the absolute self-willing that alienates us from God by putting the self in the place that is God's alone, even though the relation to God is not an object of decision.

Wherever the willing of self takes place without existential self-distinction from God, it does in fact take the form of an unrestricted self-affirmation, even though this expresses itself only as unlimited anxiety and care relative to one's own life. To that extent sin is bound up with the natural conditions of human existence.[296] But how, then, can there be human responsibility for sin?

When we talk about responsibility and guilt,[297] we refer primarily to things done or not done insofar as they involve choice and decision. Such things do at least allow of a possibility of choice. In the judicial process, for example, the consideration of possible alternatives of action also plays a role. From the link between talk about responsibility and guilt on the one side and actions on the other, it follows that a direct application to the theme of sin is possible only to the extent that the concept of sin relates to things done or not done, to transgressions of a norm. OT usage meets this requirement to a large extent,[298] as in the paradise story. Incompatible, however, is the state of the wicked heart or of rebellion against God as the background of individual actions, or the Pauline concept of sin as a power that rules and indwells us.

Behind responsibility for our own actions lie certain conditions, without which the mere doing of actions does not imply guilt. Reflection

295. See above, pp. 247f.
296. *Anthropology,* pp. 107ff.; also Gestrich, *Die Wiederkehr des Glanzes,* pp. 75ff.
297. On what follows cf. the section on guilt and the sense of guilt in my *Anthropology,* pp. 285ff., esp. 288ff.
298. I am ignoring here the fact that the OT texts are strongly influenced by the sense that we are tied to the consequences of what we do, irrespective of our ability to avoid doing it. A principle of guilt based on that ability and thus offering a more just judgment of acts was later detached from the thought of consequences. Cf. *Anthropology,* pp. 288ff., with the story of Achan in Josh. 7:16ff. as an example. Basic in this regard is P. Fauconnet's *La responsabilité. Étude de sociologie* (Paris, 1920).

on the historical, psychological, and social circumstances in which acts are performed always makes it seem that the acts are the result of the combination of these factors, so that those who do them are absolved. Responsibility and guilt arise only when there is a valid norm that we should follow or should have followed. The penal system argues in the name of society that we can and should act in accordance with the norm. Objective guilt is thus imputed. If we accept the norm inwardly in the moral consciousness or conscience, then we impute guilt to ourselves. Only then can there be a subjective acceptance of guilt. Thus the sense of guilt, the conscience, and responsibility in some sense concern the linking of awareness of our own identity as an obligation to certain norms and to the demands that they make on our conduct.[299]

In this way what is described as sin comes into relation to the whole sphere of responsibility and guilt. The knowledge of God and of our destiny of fellowship with him shows that the state of opposition to God in sin and separation from him is one that ought not to be and that must be overcome.[300] Guilt may first be ascribed, then, in the form of an outward condemnation of conduct, as with Paul in Rom. 1:18-32. There can be description of the basic situation, however, only from the standpoint of subjective acceptance of the divine requirement. Hence there follows the presentation of our inner division (Rom. 7:15ff.) as we consent mentally to the divine norm but in our conduct take the way of sin.

According to Rom. 7:7ff., sin does not consist merely of individual offenses. Nor can we trace it back to these. It precedes all human acts as a power that dwells in us, that possesses us like our own subjectivity as it overpowers us. It is a state of alienation from God. Yet this alienation does not come about without our own cooperation and therefore our own — even if divided — consent. Paul does not spend time wondering if we might have done differently. All that is important to him is that though we consent to the law of God, we still follow the path of sin. Why do we

---

299. *Anthropology,* pp. 112f., and on conscience, 293ff. Cf. also G. Condrau and F. Böckle, "Schuld und Sünde," *Christlicher Glaube in moderner Gesellschaft* 12 (1981) 91ff., esp. 127-30.

300. Gestrich, *Die Wiederkehr des Glanzes,* pp. 162f., has rightly drawn attention to the danger that modern theology might moralize evil by no longer seeing it as a falling from a good first estate but as a falling behind our spiritual calling and social goals. To avoid this danger we must think of our destiny as not primarily ethical but eschatological, so that it will be achieved in salvation history. This does not have to mean, of course, that there are no ethical ramifications.

do that? Because it promises us life. But in so doing it deceives us (7:11). In truth it brings death.[301]

We engage in sin because of the deception. Our voluntary committing of it is enough to make us guilty. There does not have to be a primal and once-for-all event of a fall for which Adam was guilty quite apart from all entanglement in sin. Paul certainly follows the paradise story when he says that "one man's trespass led to condemnation for all men" (Rom. 5:18). But this was because "all men sinned" as Adam did (5:12). Adam was simply the first sinner. In him began the temptation by the power of sin that still seduces us all today. All of us sin because we think we can attain a full and true life thereby. In this sense the story of Adam is the story of the whole race. It is repeated in each individual. The point is not Adam's first state of innocence in contrast to that of all his descendants. The analogy of the story of all of us to that of Adam stands in the way of such a reading in Rom. 7:7ff. As the first sinner, Adam is the original of all of us in our sinning.

This seems to be the real point of the Genesis story, too. If we take it etiologically, it is an explanation not of the origin of sin but of the origin of death and of the difficulty involved in work and reproduction. Sin explains these things. It is not itself being explained, though the explanation depicts in an illustrative way how it constantly arises in all of us. On this ground doubts have been raised as to whether we really have in this story the account of a once-for-all event of a fall.[302] Dogmatics should also consider that according to the story, sin does not attain by one event its dominion over the human race. It does so in a sequence that reaches a first climax with Cain's murdering of his own brother Abel (4:7ff.) and the final climax in the event of the flood. We are not to look at Gen. 3 in isolation and derive from it the idea of a single fall. We are to look at the whole process whereby sin increases in the race and God takes countermeasures against its aggression to preserve the race from the ruinous consequences of its own acts. This approach is more in keeping with the biblical text in these stories of the early days of human history.

In the history of Christian theology the idea of the origin of sin in the freedom of the creaturely will, and especially in its misuse by Adam,

301. Cf. pp. 292f. in my essay cited above in n. 292.
302. Cf. Köhler, *OT Theology*, pp. 115ff.; C. Westermann, *Genesis* (2nd ed. 1976), p. 376, ET 235; also his *Elements of OT Theology* (Atlanta, 1982), pp. 95f. Cf. also H. Haag, *Schöpfungslehre und kirchliche Erbsündenlehre* (1966), pp. 44ff., 55ff., and the remarks of Häring, *Die Macht des Bösen*, p. 221 on discussion of the theme in OT exegesis.

has served another purpose, namely, that of absolving the Creator from responsibility for evil and its consequences in his good creation.[303] But the references to Adam's freedom of choice can hardly meet this goal, since God's omniscience must have foreseen the fall prior to creation. Augustine had the courage not to resort to evasions at this point but even to emphasize the responsibility of the Creator for the development of things in his creation, though adding that God in his omniscience must have foreseen not only the fall of Adam but beyond it the further course of history until at last a descendant of Adam, with the help of God's grace, would overcome the devil.[304] Along these lines Augustine met doubts as to the Creator's goodness and wisdom on account of the coming of sin in a far more convincing way than did Clement of Alexandria. He also did so in harmony with Paul's theology of the divine mystery of salvation, of the divine plan for history that came to fulfillment in Jesus Christ, in which God "has consigned all men to disobedience, that he may have mercy on all" (Rom. 11:32). In the process Augustine emphasized that God did not force us to sin. Had he done so, it would not be our own sin, and the very concept of sin would be shattered. What Augustine plainly had in view was that in creation God took our foreseen sin into account but was looking ahead to his own future redemption and consummation. Schleiermacher ventured to think along similar lines in the 19th century.[305]

If we ignore here the danger of a deterministic misunderstanding and the absurdities to which it leads,[306] we can see in such thoughts a worthier expression of faith in an omnipotent Creator God than in the approach that views the entry of sin and evil into creation as an event that takes the Creator by surprise, that is inexplicable in terms of faith in God, that cannot be regarded as divinely possible, but that in its supposed isolation seems to be a real counterforce to the Creator in the experience of his creatures. Instead of cherishing this kind of dualism, Christian theology ought to find in the permission of sin the cost of the creaturely independence at which God's creative action aims.[307] As creatures that have attained to full independence, we humans must develop and become what we are and ought to be. In the process we can all too easily give our

---

303. Cf. Clement of Alexandria *Strom.* 1.82-84 (see above, p. 165).

304. *Civ. Dei* 14.27, cf. 14.11.1.

305. Schleiermacher, *Christian Faith,* §§ 79ff.

306. The danger arises with an anthropomorphic idea of a plan that fixes the whole future course from the very beginning; cf. vol. I, 387ff.

307. See above, pp. 166ff.

independence the form of an autonomy in which we put ourselves in the place of God and his dominion over creation. But without creaturely independence the relation of the Son to the Father cannot manifest itself in the medium of creaturely existence.

§ 4. Sin, Death, and Life

The power of sin over us humans rests on the fact that it promises us life, a fuller and richer life. As we have said, this is its deception (Rom. 7:11).[308] Only thus can we explain Paul's statement that sin can use the law as a "pretext" in overpowering us. The command of God was given to us with a view to life. Keeping it should help us to safeguard the life that we have received from God (Deut. 32:47; Lev. 18:5). But the desire that is oriented to what is forbidden thinks it has a better knowledge of what will promote life. It forces us to think that the command has a tendency that is inimical to life, as though observing it would involve renouncing that which is part of life's riches (cf. Gen. 3:4ff.). According to Paul, then, the law becomes a means whereby sin achieves dominion, setting life before our eyes and giving desire an occasion to orient itself to it, but in such a way as to set the law aside — the law of reason as well as the traditional moral order (cf. 4 Ezra 7:62-72). Under the pressure of a keen desire for life, we thus come into collision not merely with a law that seems to hamper our development but with our own reason, which, as Paul says, agrees with the law of God (Rom. 7:22) and yet is hopelessly subject to the blind drive for self-fulfillment.

Even after two thousand years this description is still so true to life that commentary is hardly needed. The different forms of frenzied conduct offer impressive examples of the way in which the drive for self-fulfillment leads to a frenzy that will finally spoil life, narrow the actual field of freedom of decision, and not infrequently end in death. In spite of some obvious differences whose significance we shall have to discuss later, all of us according to Paul have ultimately fallen victim in some way

308. See G. Bornkamm's study of sin, law, and death *Das Ende des Gesetzes,* Paulusstudien I (Munich, 1952), 51ff., esp. 54ff.; also Wilckens's *Römer,* II, 81ff. Wilckens thinks the paradise story lies behind Paul's statements, as also behind similar NT references to the deceitfulness of sin (Eph. 4:22; 2 Thess. 2:10; Heb. 3:13).

to a greediness for life that in all cases ends in death. "The wages of sin is death" (Rom. 6:23; cf. 7:11).

The inner logic of the link between sin and death as Paul stated it arises on the presupposition that all life comes from God.[309] Since sin is turning from God, sinners separate themselves not only from the commanding will of God but also from the source of their own lives. Death, then, is not just a penalty that an external authority imposes on them but lies in the nature of sin as its consequence.[310] Paul was undoubtedly thinking of physical death. Certainly the death that comes as a result of sin is not just a natural process. Its severity lies in separation from God. This is in line with the OT view that death separates from God (Ps. 88:5; cf. 6:5; 115:17; also Isa. 38:18). The explanation that it results from sin simply offers the reason for this separation. It does not mean that natural mortality has nothing at all to do with death in this sense.[311] In separation from God in death, we see the deeper nature of physical death, which is posited already in the nature of sin as separation from God.[312] Only on this premise could Paul in Rom. 5:12 adduce the universality of the fate of death in proof of the universal propagation of sin in the human race.

Later theology, however, distinguished between physical and spiritual death on the one side and temporal and eternal death (or damnation at the last judgment) on the other.[313] The latter distinction appears in Revelation. The idea of the "second death" (2:11; cf. 20:14, 21:8) presupposes a general resurrection to judgment followed by the second death for the damned, with no ensuing resurrection. The former distinction, however, developed in patristic theology as a result of the concept of the immortality of the soul. We find the idea of physical death as the separation of the soul from the body (Plato *Gorg.* 524b.3f.; *Phaed.* 67d.3f., 88b.1f.)

309. Cf. Jewish wisdom (Wis. 2:24; cf. Sir. 25:24) and apocalyptic (4 Ezra 3:7; 7:118ff.; 11ff., also Syr. Bar. 23:4), as well as Baruch (54:15; 56:6), though more in the sense of premature death, as in Gen. 2:17; 3:3f. On this, cf. E. Brandenburger, *Adam und Christus, Exegetisch-religionsgeschichtliche Untersuchung zu Röm 5.12-21 (1. Kor 15)* (1962), pp. 49ff., also 58ff. on rabbinical writings.

310. Cf. my "Tod und Auferstehung in der Sicht christlicher Dogmatik," in *Grundfragen systematischer Theologie,* 2 vols. (Göttingen, 1967-80), II, 146ff.; also *Anthropology,* pp. 140f.

311. Bultmann makes this distinction in his article *thanatos* in *TDNT,* III, 15, though he admits that Paul "does not say this expressly."

312. In a transferred sense we may thus say that the sinner is already dead (1 Tim. 5:6; cf. 1 John 3:14; also Luke 9:60/Matt. 8:22).

313. So also the older Protestant theologians, e.g., Hollaz, *Examen,* III, sect. 2 c. 9 q 2 (§ 373); cf. Schmid, *Doctrinal Theology,* pp. 237f.

already in Tertullian (*De an.* 51.1, cf. 52.1) and Clement of Alexandria (*Strom.* 7.71.3). Unlike Tertullian, however, Clement called physical death natural (4.12.5, cf. 3.64.2) and contrasted it with the death of the soul, which consists of sin (3.64.1) and ignorance of the Father (5.63.8) and separates the soul from wisdom (2.34.2). Origen held similar views.[314]

A middle position that became normative later may be found in Athanasius (*De inc.* 4). On this view mortality is natural to us but not the actual entry of death. Because of our participation in the Logos, even our body would have had immortality had not Adam fallen into sin. Though human nature is mortal, then, the fact of physical death is the consequence of sin. Gregory of Nyssa adopted this view in his *Great Catechism* (8.1f.).

Augustine pointed the way in the West. In the main he took a view similar to that of Athanasius and Gregory of Nyssa. Like the two Greek fathers, he distinguished between a death of the soul resulting from sin, and physical death. The latter rests on the separation of the soul from the body, the former on the separation of God from the soul.[315] Yet the death of the body is not just natural. It, too, results from sin (*Civ. Dei* 13.6). The death of the soul through sin as a present state is not to be confused with the second death, which will separate the damned eternally from God after the judgment (13.2; cf. 20.9.4 and 14.1). Already in Augustine, then, we find the three forms of death of later doctrine.

Up to the threshold of the modern era the church clung to the view that physical death is the result of sin.[316] From the 18th century onward, however, the opinion gained ground in Protestant theology that for us, as for other forms of life, death is part of the finitude of our nature. Only for sinners does natural death become an expression of God's judgment on sin. Not the objective fact of death but our subjective experience of it is understood as the consequence of sin.

C. M. Pfaff in 1722 and J. E. Schubert in 1743 had no trouble in combining the idea that death is natural with the thesis that it originates in consequence of Adam's sin.[317] Half a century later, however, the church theologian K. G. Bretschneider

---

314. Cf. his commentary on John, also *De princ.* 1.2.4, and on this Karpp, *Probleme altchristlicher Anthropologie,* pp. 198f.

315. *Civ. Dei* 13.2. Cf. the Council of Orange (529), canon 2 (DS § 372 = ND § 505).

316. Cf. Trent (DS §§ 1511f. = ND §§ 508f.) and Melanchthon's Apology to CA 2.46f.

317. C. M. Pfaff, *Schediasma orthodoxum . . . de morte naturali* (Tübingen, 1722), pp. 36ff.; J. E. Schubert, *Vernünftige und schriftmässige Gedanken vom Tod* (Jena, 1743), pp. 32ff., 36ff.

adopted the view that previously had been held mainly by Socinians and Arminians, namely, that in Paul as well as the OT and the Gospels, physical death is something natural, since in 1 Cor. 15:35-38 the earthly body must die in order that we may attain to the resurrection. Hence we are not to relate what the apostle says about death as the consequence of sin to the death of the body.[318]

In his *Christian Faith* Schleiermacher asserted that objectively natural evils do not derive from sin, because we find death and pain even where there is no sin.[319] Only on account of sin and its dominion over the life of the senses do we experience the unavoidable imperfection that obstructs this life as an evil, so that subjectively it is for us a punishment for sin.[320] A. Ritschl stressed even more strongly the fact that the concepts of sin and evil do not go together.[321] For the rest he followed Schleiermacher. He gave more precision to Schleiermacher's thesis, however, by arguing that the sense of guilt for sin is what explains our regarding of evils as divine punishments.[322]

The cost of this psychologizing of the traditional view of natural evil, and especially death, was the loss of the sense that our relation to God is a life-and-death matter. The relation came to be focused on the moral life.[323] The understanding of natural evils, and especially death, as consequences of sin seemed to theologians to be at least psychologically justified. But it might appear to be more accurate to set this view aside, along with the accompanying sense of guilt, as simply neurotic. If a real, nonpsychological connection between sin and death is questioned, then it is natural to dismiss this whole complex of thought as the product of more or less sick imaginings. The psychological criticism could also extend to the validity of moral norms themselves, as we see in Nietzsche's description in his *Genealogy of Morals*.

A different way of severing the traditional link between death and sin may be seen in the distinction between natural death and the death of judgment in many 20th-century Protestant theologians. In P. Althaus, E. Brunner, K. Barth, and E. Jüngel the idea of death as a divine judgment on sinners is not just a result of

---

318. Bretschneider, *Handbuch*, I, 551; cf. 747 (on Gen. 3:19).

319. *Christian Faith*, § 76.2.

320. Ibid., § 75.3.

321. Ritschl, *Christian Doctrine*, pp. 347f.

322. Ibid., pp. 354-58.

323. This is true despite the insistence on the originality of the Schleiermacher theme in view of the presentation of Christianity as an ethical system oriented to the teleological thrust of piety (*Christian Faith*, § 11), with an ethical understanding of the kingdom of God as the basis.

the human sense of guilt but an expression of the wrath of God.[324] Only believers, however, are aware of the wrathful God. Only to the consciousness of faith, which includes a sense of sin, is death seen to be God's judgment on sin. This is not so far from the positions of Schleiermacher and Ritschl as might appear at a first glance. For these and others, death is part of our human finitude.[325] Only for sinners, which we know ourselves to be only in faith, and therefore only for the consciousness of faith does death become an expression of divine judgment.

To prove the biblical legitimacy of the idea of a psychological link between sin and death as its consequence, reference has been made to other evaluations of death in scripture. Appeal might be made to the fact that in the OT the patriarchs are said to have died full of years (Gen. 25:8; 35:29; cf. 46:30). Then in the NT Paul took a positive view of death, namely, as liberation from this mortal life, which is distant from the risen Lord.[326] Thus in Phil. 1:21 the apostle says that to die is gain, since it is to be with Christ. In Rom. 14:8, too, the antithesis of earthly life and dying is relativized by belonging to Jesus Christ. According to Ritschl, then, we may not cling to the objective view of the link between sin and evil as a norm. Indeed, Ritschl added, any person of energy and integrity, and not just the regenerate in the Christian sense, can turn evil into good.[327]

Ritschl completely failed to see, however, that the transforming of death in the sayings of Paul has its basis in the fact — objective for Paul at least — that humanity and creation now have been set in a totally new light, namely, that of the resurrection of Jesus. Thus the requalifying of death for Christians in the light of the Easter faith in no way contradicts the general view of death as the consequence of sin in Rom. 5:12 (cf. 6:23).[328] This evaluation still applies, indeed, to the earthly path of Chris-

---

324. P. Althaus, *Die letzten Dinge* (1922, 4th ed. 1933), pp. 81ff.; Brunner, *Man in Revolt*, p. 474; Barth, *CD*, III/2, 602f., 608, 627; E. Jüngel, *Death* (Philadelphia, 1974), pp. 74ff.

325. P. Althaus, "Tod," *RGG*, VI (3rd ed. 1962), p. 918, also *Die christliche Wahrheit*, pp. 409ff.; Brunner, *Dogmatics*, II, 128ff.; Barth, *CD*, III/2, 587ff., 627ff., esp. 632; Jüngel, *Death*, p. 92. Cf. Tillich, *Systematic Theology*, II, 66. On Tillich, cf. my *Anthroplogy*, pp. 141ff.; on the subject matter, cf. my "Tod und Auferstehung," pp. 146ff.

326. Ritschl, *Christian Doctrine*, pp. 350-52, cf. 43f. See also Barth, *CD*, III/2, 634ff., and Bretschneider, *Handbuch*, I, 751.

327. Ritschl, *Christian Doctrine*, pp. 347f.

328. Ritschl does not think the Pauline derivation of death from Adam's sin is theologically binding (ibid., pp. 353f.). R. Niebuhr, *The Nature and Destiny of Man*, I (1961, 1964), pp. 176f., also took a critical view of the Pauline "idea that physical death is a consequence of sin." Brunner, *Dogmatics*, II, 129, did not think the death that Paul calls the wages of sin (Rom. 6:23) can be physical death.

tians (7:1-6). Only by the resurrection of Jesus, and by the linking of
Christians to the death of him who in dying overcame death (Rom. 6:5ff.),
was the tie between sin and death set in another context and thus given
a new significance inasmuch as death no longer involves the end of the
human person (cf. Rom. 7:6).

More important is the reference to the fact that in 1 Cor. 15:44-49 "it sounds as
though Adamic humanity was created subject to death from the very first."[329] Yet
we must remember that Paul does not refer here to a first estate preceding Adam's
sin. For Paul, Adam was the first to sin and die.

The traditional idea of the consequences of sin[330] has the concept
of punishment in view because this term carries with it the thought of a
sanction imposed on those who commit sin. Yet the thought of punishment does not do justice to the biblical idea of a natural connection
between deeds and their consequences.[331] The link between sin and death
as Paul maintained it is as follows. Sin as separation from God already
implies death as its consequence. Death is the result of the break with
God, who is the source of life. It is to be seen in concert with the other
results of sin. Being in opposition to the Creator, we are also in opposition
to our fellow creatures, to the earth, to animals, and to other people (cf.
Gen. 3:14-19). These are not penalties imposed from without and having
no connection with the nature of sin. The conflict of sinners with creation,
with other people, and even with themselves follows from the nature of
sin as a breaking of the relationship to God. There is an inner logic here.
The law of nature that leads from sin to death takes place without any
special divine intervention. The intimation of death as a consequence in
the paradise story (Gen. 2:17) is to be understood as a warning of what
will happen in case of transgression. In this story the intervention of God

329. R. Bultmann in *TDNT*, III, 15.
330. At root many prominent theologians in the 19th and 20th centuries have
taken this view, e.g., Beck, *Vorlesungen über Christliche Glaubenslehre*, II, 456ff., with profound observations on the changed relation between individual and species in Müller, *Die
christliche Lehre*, II, 388ff., who in many things agrees with and appeals to O. Krabbe, *Die
Lehre von der Sünde und vom Tode* . . . (Hamburg, 1836), esp. 7ff., 68ff., 187-327. See also
Dorner and his justifiable stressing of the wrath of God over against Ritschl, *System*, III,
114ff., 119f.; cf. Kähler, *Die Wissenschaft der christlichen Lehre*, §§ 326f. (pp. 280ff.), who
developed the idea of sin as a lack of relationship, which Jüngel took up (*Death*, pp. 78ff.).
331. On this matter, see K. Koch, "Gibt es ein Vergeltungsdogma im AT?" *ZTK* 52
(1955) 1-42.

has the function of limiting the consequences that sin itself unleashes (cf. Gen. 3:19 with 2:17).

This elucidation of the concept of death as the consequence of sin brings to light, however, the full strength of the objection that can be made against the concept. For death seems to be an ineluctable consequence of our finitude, not our sin. All multiple-cell life must die. It is not just that organisms age and wear out. They also must make way for future generations. Life cannot go on without the death of individuals. This is true in human history as well. Individual death is a condition of the continually self-renewing multiplicity of the phenomena of life.

Barth made the link between finitude and death his decisive argument on behalf of the thesis that we die by nature. "Finitude means mortality" (*CD*, III/2, 625). Barth's christological basis for the view that death is not just God's judgment on us but that finitude is part of our creaturely nature (pp. 628ff.) has not unjustly become the subject of criticism.[332] Yet here as elsewhere Barth's anthropology contains a true and important insight even apart from the christological grounding. Our finitude in time as well is indeed part of our nature as creatures (p. 632).

Against the thesis that death is natural on account of the finitude of human life, there is, however, a weighty theological argument. Christian hope expects a life without death (1 Cor. 15:52ff.). This life in fellowship with God cannot involve a total absorption of creaturely existence in God but expects its renewal and definitive establishment. The finitude that is part of creaturely life will not be set aside by participation in the divine life. It follows, however, that finitude does not always have to include mortality. The eschatological hope of Christians knows a finitude of creaturely existence without death. Hence death cannot be necessarily a part

332. H. Vogel in "Ecce Homo. Die Anthropologie Karl Barths," *VF*, 1949/50, p. 124, was already urging against a derivation of creaturely finitude (as distinct from subjection to judgment for sin) from the vicarious meaning of the crucifixion of Jesus (*CD*, III/2, 627ff.). The point is that the vicariousness consists precisely of God in Jesus Christ taking wholly and unreservedly to himself our situation under his judgment, so that no different finitude can be claimed for his humanity. K. Stock rejected this criticism on somewhat inadequate grounds (*Anthropologie der Verheissung. Karl Barths Lehre vom Menschen als dogmatisches Problem* [Munich, 1980], pp. 228f.) but did not himself think that the derivation of human finitude from christology was successful (p. 233). It might have been more successful if it had advanced the self-distinction of the Logos from the Father as the basis of human (as of all creaturely) finitude instead of arguing from the incarnation as the condition of the vicarious death of Jesus.

of the finitude of creaturely existence.[333] Only of existence in time is it true that the finitude of life and mortality go together. But how are we to understand this?

The existence without death that Christian hope expects is characterized not merely by fellowship with God but also by participation in the wholeness that flows from God's eternity. As the life of creatures in the totality of its temporal span stands open to the eyes of the eternal God, so the redeemed will also themselves stand before God in the totality of their existence and glorify him as the Creator of their lives.

This wholeness of existence is not attainable by creatures who are subject to the process of time. This is true at any rate of us humans because we know that our present, as well as the present state of other creaturely existence, differs from the future and the past. Knowing the future and the past, we rise above the narrowness and transitoriness of the present moment. Yet by this knowledge we are also more deeply than other beings differentiated from what is not yet or no longer. The difference between our present and the future, not only of God, but of our own lives so far as they are still hidden in God's future, prevents us from definitively achieving the totality of our finite existence. We can certainly anticipate this totality. Only thus can we have any duration and identity of existence in the process of time. But even with our anticipations we are tied to the standpoint of the present moment, which in the process of time is succeeded constantly by new moments as we move into an open future.

The temporality of creaturely existence is a condition of the independence that we have yet to achieve (see above, pp. 95f.). Only as a result of becoming in time can finite existence, on the condition of its link to the eternal God, stand independently before God in the totality of its temporal span. In passing through temporality, the creature with the finite future of its life that is yet before it also has an end outside itself. But the end of our existence, as the externally appointed limit of our duration, is death. Death is not itself external to our existence. The end that has yet to come casts a shadow in advance and defines the whole path of life as a being for death in the sense that our end is not integrated into our existence but threatens each moment of our living self-affirmation with nothingness. We thus lead our temporal lives under the shadow of death (Luke 1:79; cf. Matt. 4:16).

333. On this point, cf. my observations in *Grundfragen*, II, 153f.

At the same time in each moment of our present our self-affirmation of life is marked by the antithesis to our end in death. Death is the last enemy of all living things (1 Cor. 15:26). Fear of death pierces deep into life. On the one hand it motivates us to unrestricted self-affirmation, regardless of our own finitude; on the other hand, it robs us of the power to accept life. Either way we see a close link between sin and death. The link is rooted in sin to the extent that only the nonacceptance of our own finitude makes the inescapable end of finite existence a manifestation of the power of death that threatens us with nothingness. The fear of death also pushes us more deeply into sin. The fact that the acceptance of our own finitude is so hard for us who know ourselves to be living beings and affirm ourselves as such is connected with the structure of temporality in which our end, and with it our wholeness, is still ahead of us. That the end and totality of finite existence in time are still ahead of us characterizes the situation in which sin actually arises, that is, the unrestricted self-affirmation that with apostasy from God implies death as the end of our existence.

One of the finest efforts of 20th-century theology to achieve a deeper understanding of the links between creaturely life, sin, and death is Karl Rahner's *Theologie des Todes,* with its relating of the theme of death to the question of the wholeness of human existence. Rahner was spurred on to this study by the analysis of existence in M. Heidegger's *Being and Time,* which based the ability to achieve the totality of our existence on the prior knowledge of our own death.[334] Rahner altered Heidegger's thesis by linking the ability to achieve wholeness to the relation to God either in the mode of being open to him or in that of being closed against him.[335] In the process, however, he adopted Heidegger's premise that death brings existence to completion and viewed death as an act of our own in which we complete life from within.[336]

Both theses stand in need of criticism. First, it is God, not death, who can bring to its totality the existence of the creature that he has posited. Rahner rightly linked the question of the totality of life to the relation to God, for only from God can we receive "salvation" in spite our finitude, and in this way we share in the totality of God. The relation between this theme and the problem of death is that it is a matter of the salvation of finite existence and that, negatively, death breaks off this existence. Achieving salvation means overcoming death. Second, however,

334. *Being and Time* (New York, 1962), pp. 279ff.
335. *Zur Theologie des Todes* (1958), pp. 36ff.
336. Ibid., also pp. 29f., 65, 76f. On what follows, cf. my *Grundfragen,* I, 145f. (ET *Basic Questions in Theology,* 2 vols. [Philadelphia, 1970-71], I, 165f.); also II, 154f.

the totality cannot be our own act, not even as regards death, for death is not our own act. We have to suffer it.[337]

As distinct from the finitude of creaturely existence, death is part of God's creation only in connection with sin. The Wisdom of Solomon says categorically that God did not create death (1:13). Theology, of course, must recognize something analogous to death throughout creation, for all living things stand under the burden of corruptibility (Rom. 8:20ff.). Like human sin, the link between sin and death has a prehuman history. In this history a demonic dynamic seems to have developed that culminates in human sin and the dominion of sin and death over humanity.[338]

The more important point at this juncture is one we touched on above, namely, that death is an essential consequence of sin rather than a punishment that God has arbitrarily set and imposed. A mark of God's intervention in the history of his creatures is that he has constantly limited the results of sin and evil so as to make the life of his creatures possible under the limiting conditions they face.

We see here not only the outworking of God's patience with sinners but his continued creative activity in his government of the world, which again and again brings good out of evil. Traditional Christian dogmatics has paid far too little attention to this truth in its discussion of our fallen plight. Much too often it has given an overly negative portrayal of human life under the conditions of the coming of sin and its consequences. The measures that God the Creator has taken against the powers of sin and evil that have invaded his creation have been largely neglected. Human abilities remaining after the fall, especially the freedom of the will, have naturally come into question. But the primary issue ought not to be that of human abilities but the continued creative activity of the good Creator and his providence.

Important in this regard is the fact that by the continued creative activity of his Spirit, God constantly rescues his creatures from the entanglement in self-centeredness that comes as a result of their anxieties

337. E. Jüngel has rightly called death an ending that comes upon us and therefore something that is "anthropologically passive" ("Der Tod als Geheimnis des Lebens," in *Entsprechungen: Gott — Wahrheit — Mensch. Theologische Erörterungen* [Munich, 1980], p. 344; cf. *Death*, pp. 91f.). Of the actual process of dying this is perhaps true only with reservations, of course. One can always invest one's dying with dignity. Yet only in the case of suicide is dying an act.

338. See ch. 7, pp. 108f., 172ff.

and desires. In spite of sin and its ramifications, then, we may again and again know the original joy in life, joy in the richness, breadth, and beauty of creation and in each new day, joy in the illuminations of the life of the spirit, power for action within the order of community life, and a turning to others and participation in their joys and sorrows. In a way analogous to Luther's doctrine of the two kingdoms we are here given responsibility for the social order and its justice, and even in regard to the rational shaping of individual life we are given a share in the activity of the divine world government that limits sin and its consequences.

In the biblical history the command not to let sin rule over us but to master it was given specifically to Cain (Gen. 4:7), and it thus applies even in the world that is not yet redeemed and not merely among Christians. If Cain did not measure up to the demand, this is an illustration of the constant danger that sin will break out in destructive wickedness. Its effects can accumulate and at times bring whole peoples within its orbit. Yet reason and law can restrain them. In our human story, notwithstanding the covert and open outworkings of sin and the outbreaks of destructive wickedness, we have achieved astonishing things and known periods of high cultural blossoming. This does not alter the fact that even at the best of times dark forces have been at work in life that by means of anxiety and desire have finally brought death and destruction. We cannot achieve liberation from these sinister forces merely by breaking the fetters that oppressors put on us from outside, though doing this might bring temporary alleviation. We achieve liberation from sin and death only where the image of the Son takes shape in human life through the operation of the Spirit of God.

CHAPTER 9

Anthropology and Christology

hristology begins with the primitive Christian interpretation of the person and work of Jesus of Nazareth as God's Messiah.[1] The title "Messiah" implies the thought of divine sonship. On the Christian view it early had the sense that in the man Jesus the preexistent Son of God came to earth. Only God himself could be behind this event, i.e., by sending his Son into the world (Gal. 4:4; Rom. 8:3).[2] Yet we can know that it actually happened only as it took place on the plane of our human, creaturely reality.

This fact poses first the methodological problem of christology. Should we begin with the basis in God and his initiative in sending the Son, or should we move on the plane of human reality, on which we must show that the event took place, if it really took place at all? But second, we have here the question of the special nature of the humanity of the Son of God as distinct from all other human reality, and yet also in relation to it. In this introductory chapter on christology, we deal with the connection between the methodological question and that of the uniqueness of the humanity of the Son of God in relation to our human nature and destiny in general. Chapter 10 then discusses the special humanity of Jesus as the basis of what we are to say about his deity, and chapter 11 looks at his special history from

---

1. Cf. my *Jesus — God and Man* (Philadelphia, 1968), pp. 11ff.; also W. Kasper, *Jesus the Christ,* quoted by I. U. Dalferth in his important essay on recent English criticism of incarnational christology, "Der Mythos vom inkarnierten Gott und das Thema der Christologie," *ZTK* 84 (1987) 329. On the subject, cf. also J. Moltmann, *The Way of Jesus Christ* (New York, 1990), pp. 1ff., 37.

2. On this point, see below, pp. 367ff.

the standpoint of what God did in it to reconcile the world, but still in the general context of anthropology and the doctrine of creation.

§ 1. The Method of Christology

The apostolic proclamation of Jesus of Nazareth as the Son of God began with his earthly coming, his fate at the end of his earthly path, and the divine action in raising him from the dead. The church's christology, however, developed from the 2nd century onward chiefly out of discussions about the relation of the preexistent Son of God to God himself, his proceeding from the Father, his relation to creation, and his incarnation. There was good reason for this. In the Gentile mission the belief in one God, which Christians shared with the Jews, was basic in the debate with popular polytheistic ideas (cf. 1 Thess. 1:9f.). Reconciling this belief with the Christian confession of the divine sonship and deity of Jesus Christ was thus bound to be a central theme and problem in early Christian thought.[3] With the upsurge of Logos christology in the 3rd century,[4] a decision was fully made in favor of interpreting the whole NT witness to Christ from the standpoint of this sending of the preexistent Son into the world, i.e., for the basic type of christological statement that has come to be known as christology "from above." A framework was thus set up within which all the further christological controversies of the early church and the Latin Middle Ages would take place.

Another way of grounding christological statements was needed only with the Reformation, when antitrinitarians and Socinians threw doubt on the trinitarian understanding of the confession of Christ's deity and to a large extent on the whole idea of his preexistence.[5] Since the criticism was made on the basis of a strict scripture principle, debate with

3. Cf. A. Grillmeier, *Christ in Christian Tradition* (London, 1964), pp. 108ff., on the importance of the apologetic Logos doctrine in the development of christology (also on Justin).

4. The price paid was the detaching of the concept of the Son from the historical person of Jesus Christ. Cf. the critical observations of F. Loofs in his article "Christologie, Kirchenlehre," *RE,* IV (3rd ed. 1898), p. 35, on the combining of the concepts of Son and Logos. Loofs, however, underestimated the link between the Logos concept and ideas of the preexistence of the Son that were current already in the primitive church.

5. For a survey and bibliography, cf. G. A. Benrath, "Antitrinitarier," *TRE,* III (1978), pp. 168-74.

it had to be in terms of biblical exposition. Hence the messiahship of Jesus as the core of the NT witness and the basis of dogmatic statements about his person came increasingly to the fore.

Helping to make this possible was the use of the title "Christ" in traditional dogmatics at this point, e.g., *De Christo* or *De persona Christi*. Hollaz was still content merely to give an introductory explanation of the title as part of the name of Jesus Christ.[6] Buddeus put a doctrine of the covenant of grace (not one of predestination) before christology and made Christ as the mediator of this covenant the theme of christology; he stressed the fact that the title "Christ" denotes his office.[7] His emphasis on the concept of Christ as mediator, however, brought him at once into a traditional doctrine of the person of Christ as a union of the divine and human natures.

In 1777, however, Semler replaced the doctrinal section on Christ's person by a chapter on his history that identified his messiahship as the true theme of the doctrine concerning him.[8] Semler discussed the doctrinal statements about Jesus as God and man as an interpretation of this basic theme but with critical insights. Other theologians of the later 18th century such as F. V. Reinhard followed the same procedure, viewing the statements of Christian dogma as a correct interpretation of the messiahship of Jesus.[9] Reinhard's pupil K. G. Bretschneider was more critical and urged a limitation of dogmatic christology to what the Bible actually says about the messiahship of Jesus, though he allowed that this included a confession of his deity and of the incarnation of the preexistent Son.[10] C. I. Nitzsch took essentially the same position in 1829.[11]

We have here a way of grounding christological statements that since the debate about the theology of A. Ritschl has been called christology "from below to above."[12] In such an approach the historical Jesus

6. D. Hollaz, *Examen theologicum acroamaticum* (Stargard, 1707), III, 113f.

7. J. F. Buddeus, *Compendium Institutionum theologiae dogmaticae* (Leipzig, 1724), pp. 521ff.; cf. H. H. Schmid, *Doctrinal Theology of the Evangelical Lutheran Church* (Philadelphia, 1961), p. 293.

8. J. S. Semler, *Versuch einer freiern theologischen Lehrart* (1777), pp. 387ff., cf. 440ff. Semler went much further than his teacher S. J. Baumgarten, whose *Evangelische Glaubenslehre* (Halle, 1759; 2nd ed. 1764), which Semler edited, followed traditional lines except for starting at the incarnation (II, 6-23).

9. F. V. Reinhard, *Vorlesungen über die Dogmatik* (1801), pp. 332ff., 336ff.

10. *Handbuch der Dogmatik der evangelisch-lutherischen Kirche* (1814, 1822, 3rd ed. Leipzig, 1828), II, 163ff., 183f. Bretschneider thought it best not to go into the nature of the union of the two natures (pp. 186f.).

11. *System of Christian Doctrine* (1829, 3rd ed. 1837, ET 1899), pp. 247ff.

12. F. H. R. Frank in his *Zur Theologie A. Ritschl's* (1888, 3rd ed. 1891), p. 27, formulated in this way a basic principle that he accepted along with Ritschl: "Our knowledge

Christ is the starting point and the measure of all christological statements about his person; christological statements themselves are viewed as an interpretation of his historical reality. As Ritschl puts it, we could not know what Christ is eternally, or what he does for us according to his exaltation to God, if these things were not at work in his temporal and historical existence.[13] Theology in the early 19th century thought it could appeal solely to the testimony of the Gospels concerning Jesus, and above all to his sayings about himself, particularly in John. With the advancing development of historico-critical exegesis, it became necessary to go back instead to the total character of the coming of Jesus and his history in order to find a basis for confession of his deity.

In Ritschl this approach became highly polemical in opposition to the speculative christology influenced by Hegel and Schelling[14] and the kenosis doctrine of the Erlangen dogmaticians. In the process Ritschl appealed to the historical person of Jesus as the starting point of all christological statements and argued that knowledge of his deity is possible only by faith in him.[15] For this reason Ritschl could have come very close to Schleiermacher in his way of finding a basis for christology.[16]

The actual parallels were slight, however, apart from the opposition to Logos christology and to the new speculative christology. Schleiermacher had constructed the concept of the Redeemer and his attributes out of the community's sense of redemption as the premise of its existence.[17] Ritschl gave much more emphasis to the uniqueness of Jesus as the origin of the community's faith in him. In so doing he distinguished between the historical work of Jesus in

---

of Christ, as of God, moves from below to above," parallel to Ritschl's liking for the famous saying of Melanchthon that to know Christ is to know his benefits (CR, 21, 85, quoted by Ritschl, *The Christian Doctrine of Justification and Reconciliation*, III [ET of *Die christliche Lehre von der Rechtfertigung und Versöhnung*, III (1883); Clifton, NJ, 1966], pp. 396f.).

13. Ritschl, *Christian Doctrine*, pp. 405f., cf. 430-32.

14. For a discussion of the problem of "from above" and "from below" that is still instructive, cf. O. Weber, *Foundations of Dogmatics*, 2 vols. (Grand Rapids, 1982-83), II, 12-26, esp. 16f.

15. Ritschl, *Christian Doctrine*, pp. 392-94. Cf. E. Günther, *Die Entwicklung der Lehre von der Person Christi im XIX. Jahrhundert* (1911), pp. 296f.

16. Cf. J. Kaftan, *Dogmatik* (1897, 3rd ed. 1901), pp. 411ff.; also *Zur Dogmatik* (1904), pp. 247ff.

17. *The Christian Faith*, §§ 87f. Thus Schleiermacher begins with the Christian consciousness and asks how the Redeemer is posited according to it (§ 91.2). This leads him to the idea of the Redeemer as original in relation to the common life founded by him (§ 93), a status that involves the constant force of his God-consciousness, the true being of God in him (§ 94).

connection with his proclamation of the kingdom of God and the work of the risen Christ as believers experience it. He viewed all statements about the work that we experience today as statements about the continuation of his historical work on earth, which must be mediated to individuals through the church, which traces its origin back to Jesus.[18] This presentation has more in common with those of Reinhard, Bretschneider, and the younger Nitzsch than with that of Schleiermacher.

Unfortunately the history of theology has neglected the christological approaches before and contemporary with Schleiermacher,[19] so that an erroneous picture has resulted that sees in Schleiermacher the one who renewed the linking of faith to Jesus Christ in response to the rationalistic dissolving of the older christology. Part of Schleiermacher's christology is indeed the suppression of a historical grounding in favor of a reconstruction of christology in terms of the faith-consciousness. In this respect W. Herrmann's christology, especially in the later period,[20] is close to Schleiermacher's, but not at root that of Ritschl.

Ignoring the difference between the approach of Ritschl and that of Schleiermacher has made it possible to suspect an anthropocentric projection in the christology from below that developed in Ritschl's school, and to set in antithesis to it the thesis that we can understand the person of Christ only from above, namely, as the person of the divine Logos.[21] This is to leap past the justifiable demand that all christological statements about Jesus Christ must be vindicated in terms of his historical reality and an exposition of it. The demand applies even to the assertion that the person of Jesus is that of the divine Logos. We can know even God himself only in that which took place here below, in the human history of Jesus of Nazareth.[22] Hence P. Althaus among others has stood by the demand that christology must move from below to above. Like NT christology, it must begin with the man Jesus and his story and consider how

18. Ritschl, *Christian Doctrine*, pp. 417f., 414f., 449ff., 463-66, cf. 3f.
19. Thus the influential work of E. Günther (see n. 15) begins with Schleiermacher and does not mention earlier attempts to find an exegetical and historical basis for christology. Typical are the accounts in F. A. B. Nitzsch and H. Stephan, *Lehrbuch der evangelischen Dogmatik* (3rd ed. Tübingen, 1912), pp. 527ff., which present Schleiermacher as the reviver of christology in opposition to rationalism.
20. On Herrmann's christology, cf. W. Greive, *Der Grund des Glaubens. Die Christologie Wilhelm Herrmanns* (Göttingen, 1976).
21. K. Barth, *Theology and Church* (New York, 1962), p. 265, concluded that "no other way whatever exists except the road from above downwards." He clung to this tenet in his *CD*. But Herrmann did not want to begin from above and thus make a fruit of redemption the root (*The Communion of the Christian with God* [Philadelphia, 1971], pp. 81ff.).
22. According to O. Weber, classical christology has paid too little attention to this (*Foundations*, II, 15-16, 23). Fundamentally it does not reach us where we are, namely, without any restriction whatever below. Does Barth really make good this lack, as Weber thinks (ibid., p. 23, n. 78)?

he requires and gains our faith. It cannot take a course of trinitarian deduction and begin with Christ's eternal deity. For us humans, knowledge of preexistence and the Trinity does not come before knowledge of the man Jesus but rests upon it.[23]

This line of argument presupposes that the history of Jesus that took place here below has an upward thrust, i.e., that it is open to the reality of God. The question thus unavoidably arises whether this is true uniquely of the history of Jesus or whether it applies to human history as a whole.[24] If the latter is the case, then the further question arises why the mediation of Jesus is necessary for the relationship of others to God. If the former is the case, we have to ask how we can move from the human reality of Jesus to the presence of God in him. According to Althaus, this takes place through the venture of faith, which is adequately grounded in the self-testimony of Jesus and the message of his resurrection, but without any need of proof thereby.[25] If this is so, however, is not faith itself in the last analysis the starting point of what we say about God in Jesus Christ rather than the actual history of Jesus?

To test and justify christological statements about Jesus, christology must get behind the confessional statements and titles of the primitive Christian tradition, reaching the foundation to which these point, which underlies faith in Jesus. This foundation is the history of Jesus. Christology must ask and show how far this history of Jesus is the basis of faith. It does so by inquiring into the actual inner necessity of christological development in the NT[26] and the continuation of this logic in the christology of the early church. We have here the task of a theory of the christological tradition.[27] Such a theory traces the inner systematic consistency of the development of christology into a confession and clarification of the deity of Jesus Christ; it also can function as a standard by which to judge the aberrations and errors that have arisen in the

---

23. P. Althaus, *Die christliche Wahrheit. Lehrbuch der Dogmatik* (1947, 3rd ed. 1952), p. 424.

24. Weber, *Foundations*, II, 18.

25. Althaus, *Die christliche Wahrheit*, pp. 425ff. Althaus's uncertainty here, as his intention of basing faith on the history of Jesus changes into a dependence of the theological understanding of the history on the act of faith, is finally due to his view that we cannot prove the resurrection historically (p. 426). We find the same uncertainty in his otherwise important work *Das sogennante Kerygma und der historische Jesus* (Gütersloh, 1958). Debating this point is the main aim of my reply to Althaus in "Insight and Faith," in *Basic Questions in Theology*, 2 vols. (Philadelphia, 1970-71), II, 28ff. Cf. also *Jesus — God and Man*, pp. 26ff.

26. Althaus, *Die christliche Wahrheit*, p. 424.

27. *Jesus — God and Man*, pp. 13f.

course of christological development. As a historical presentation, such a theory would also have a systematic character.[28] Depictions of christology from below that simply focus on the systematic core of the basic nexus of christological statements emanating from the history of Jesus, and give a systematic account of this core,[29] do at least presuppose the possibility of a theory of this kind.

We can develop such a theory only if we assume that the christological confessional statements of primitive Christianity may be understood as an explication of the content of meaning implicit in the appearance and history of Jesus.[30] Given its premise of an inner relation between the apostolic message about Jesus and Jesus himself and his proclamation, the theory calls for investigation of the necessary assumption that there is correspondence between the community's confession of Christ and a messianic consciousness that Jesus himself expressly proclaimed. But it is possible to reconstruct the link between the apostolic message about Christ and the proclamation and history of Jesus in terms of an explication of implicit meaning only if we include the primitive Christian witness to the resurrection of Jesus as the raising of Jesus to a form of fellowship with God that legitimates his pre-Easter work.[31] Only by his resurrection from the dead did the Crucified attain to the dignity of the Kyrios (Phil. 2:9-11). Only thus was he appointed the Son of God in power (Rom. 1:4). Only in the light of the resurrection is he the preexistent Son. Only as the risen Lord is he always the living Lord of his community.[32]

28. Thus far we have no presentation of this kind. Grillmeier's fine work *Christ in Christian Tradition* does have a systematic purpose inasmuch as the history of christology before 451 is presented as a prehistory of the Chalcedonian dogma, but the contents of meaning implicit in the history of Jesus do not serve as a standard of doctrinal development and evaluation.

29. *Jesus — God and Man*, pp. 21ff.

30. Cf. Bultmann, *Faith and Understanding*, I (Philadelphia, 1969), p. 206, where he argues that in Jesus' call for decision for the divine rule that he proclaims we have an implied christology. Bultmann, however, was not thinking of the confessional statements of the post-Easter community, which he rightly viewed as an expression of Easter faith.

31. The weakness of the new quest for the historical Jesus, which occupied Bultmann's followers as they studied the relation between the message of Jesus and the Christ-kerygma of his community, was that like Bultmann (in his *Faith and Understanding*), they left out of account the Easter message because of its dubious historicity. Cf. J. M. Robinson, *A New Quest of the Historical Jesus* (Philadelphia, 1983).

32. R. Slenczka has stressed that in the NT witness the personal being of Jesus Christ is not limited to his earthly history (*Geschichtlichkeit und Personsein Jesu Christi* [Göttingen, 1967], pp. 294ff. [on the controversy between Kähler and Herrmann], also 316ff., 333f.). Cf. also Moltmann, *The Way of Jesus Christ*, pp. 40f. Dalferth rightly opposes

It is not self-evident that the resurrection of Jesus is part of the historical basis of a christology from below. There was hot debate on this point in the controversies regarding the christology of Ritschl and his school. Ritschl himself built his christology solely on Jesus' proclaiming and founding (as he thought) of the kingdom of God among us. Without recourse to the resurrection, he inferred the deity of Jesus directly from the involved agreement with the will of God.[33] In reply, Kähler emphasized that in its development and impact, our certainty in confessing Jesus as Lord is linked to the certainty that he is the living Lord, crucified and risen.[34]

In a famous essay on the historical Christ as the basis of our faith, Herrmann defended the view of Ritschl on the ground that he was trying to understand the picture of the inner life of Jesus that the NT gives — i.e., the personal life of Jesus or the historical Christ — as the answer to the question how we today may see in Jesus the basis of the belief that there is a God who will deliver us from all need and sin.[35] Herrmann, then, expressly did not find in the resurrection of Jesus a basis of faith. For him, the resurrection was one of the thoughts of faith that the community of believers in Jesus developed.[36]

Even more strongly and unequivocally Max Reischle argued along the same lines,[37] though H. Cremer objected — with good reason — that the apostles did not preach the inner life of Jesus but the Crucified, who died for our sins according to the scriptures, who on the third day rose again according to the scriptures, and who, exalted to God's right hand, has poured forth that which is

---

the truncating of the basis of christology in the history of Jesus by excluding the Easter event ("Der Mythos vom inkarnierten Gott," pp. 339ff.). English critics of incarnational teaching have so excluded it, especially J. Hick, "Incarnation and Mythology," in *God and the Universe of Faiths* (New York, 1973), pp. 165ff., as well as the contributions to the volume *The Myth of God Incarnate* (Philadelphia, 1977), edited by Hick.

33. Ritschl, *Christian Doctrine*, § 48 (pp. 442-52), esp. pp. 449ff. Ritschl could thus maintain that valuing the ethical calling of Jesus (to preach and found the kingdom) leads to a religious evaluation of his person as the Son of God (cf. § 50).

34. Kähler, *The So-called Historical Jesus and the Historical, Biblical Christ* (Philadelphia, 1964), p. 64. Kähler at once equated the risen Lord with the Christ of apostolic preaching and all the NT, without leaving space for a development of christology in primitive Christianity or for the inner structure of the process. At this point the inquiry of Ritschl and his school is superior.

35. W. Herrmann, "Der geschichtliche Christus der Grund unseres Glaubens," *ZTK* 2 (1892) 256 and 261, cf. 263, 272, and 233.

36. Regarding Kähler's view that the risen and exalted Christ is the final support and basis of our faith, Herrmann commented that this is not correct (ibid., p. 250), for Christ's resurrection and exaltation are the content of faith but not its final basis (p. 251; on the difference, cf. 247f. and 263). By content of faith Herrmann meant a thought of faith (*Communion*, p. 47).

37. M. Reischle, "Der Streit über die Begründung des Glaubens auf den 'geschichtlichen' Jesus Christus," *ZTK* 7 (1897) 171ff., esp. 202f.

now seen and heard. As Cremer put it, he is the risen and living Christ who stands before us in the presence of God and the Holy Spirit, in whom God grasps us.[38] Even within Ritschl's school, objections were now brought against the exclusion of the resurrection as a basis of faith. According to T. Häring, we cannot speak of the revelation of God in Jesus apart from his resurrection, so that this event must be regarded as the basis of faith.[39] Reischle and Häring agreed that the individual elements in the basis of faith form a graduated whole and that we cannot detach from this the proof of the power of Jesus over death.[40]

We cannot separate the question whether the resurrection is part of the basis of faith from that of the facticity or historicity of the event.[41] Understandably, then, the controversy did not lay the latter to rest. If the resurrection was not a historical event but was still the decisive starting point of primitive Christian proclamation, as Bultmann assumed, then we can ascribe no significance at all to historical knowledge as the basis of our confession of Christ. If, however, we must go back to the historical Jesus to protect the kerygma against the suspicion that it is a mere myth,[42] then, assuming that the resurrection is not historical, we must seek agreement between the kerygma and the message of Jesus without including the subject of Easter. In this case, of course, the development of the christological tradition would be unintelligible as a historical process. But if we can establish the facticity of the Easter event (in a way that has yet to be described), then it is possible that the history of the confession of Christ up to the formation of the christological and trinitarian dogma of the church can be viewed as an explication of the meaning that is intrinsic to the history of Jesus in the light of the Easter event.[43]

38. H. Cremer, *Glaube, Schrift, und heilige Geschichte* (1898), pp. 44f.; on this, cf. Reischle, "Der Streit," p. 195. The thesis that the impress of the inner life of Jesus precedes faith Cremer called a hypothesis that stands in need of forceful criticism if it is to become the true picture of Christ, free from misunderstandings or perversions (*Glaube*, p. 89).

39. T. Haering, "Gehört die Auferstehung Jesu zum Glaubensgrund?" *ZTK* 7 (1897) 331ff., esp. 341.

40. T. Haering and M. Reischle, "Glaubensgrund und Auferstehung," *ZTK* 8 (1898) 129ff. On this whole controversy, cf. Greive, *Der Grund des Glaubens*, pp. 106-11.

41. We shall discuss this theme more fully in the next chapter.

42. E. Käsemann, "The Problem of the Historical Jesus," in *Essays on NT Themes* (London, 1965), pp. 33-34.

43. This is a basic thesis of my *Jesus — God and Man*. For a similar thesis, cf. C. F. D. Moule, *The Origin of Christology* (Cambridge, 1977), esp. pp. 135-41. The contributions to *The Myth of the Incarnate God* did not even consider the question whether there might be continuity in the sense of a progressive explication of a content implicit from the very first; rather, they assumed that a series of ideas originating in the culture were attached to the person of Jesus from outside. Moule repeated his thesis in discussion with the author; cf. "Three Points of Conflict in the Christological Debate," in *Incarnation and Myth: The Debate Continued*, ed. M. Goulder (Grand Rapids, 1979), pp. 131ff., esp. 137f. But no answer was reached apart from the concluding observations of the leader of the discussion, Basil Mitchell (p. 236), who recognized that the question is an open one (cf. also Goulder's preface [p. x]).

There are, of course, many forms of a christology from below. Unlike the classical Logos christology, however, they all start with the historical Jesus and seek to find in his proclamation and history the basis of the community's confession of Christ.[44] Many of these christologies focus solely on the proclamation of Jesus and especially on the related claim to authority, ignoring the inner reasons for the offense that so often came as a reaction to Jesus. Others concentrate on Jesus' way to the cross as an expression of the love of God that he proclaimed, though without adequately considering that without the Easter event, this interpretation of his execution is absurd and that in the biblical testimony it was formulated only in the light of that event. Not infrequently the response of faith to the proclamation of Jesus is seen as the origin and basis of the confession of faith in the Easter event, though in fact the biblical testimony presents the Easter event as the basis of the faith of the disciples.

Supplementing everywhere the reference to the historical Jesus by the faith of individuals or the church is the most common form of a christology from below. On this view, it is faith alone that fills out the picture of the human, historical Jesus. Faith sees more than a mere man. This may be regarded as a response to Jesus' claim to authority, but the reference to the productivity of faith hardly serves as an adequate basis of confessional christological statements in a christology from below. In the last analysis this type of argument appeals to a principle of authority and thus despairs of offering any real basis. It also agrees that the call of Jesus for decision goes out not merely to Jewish hearers in his own day but to all people at all times, an extension that can be vindicated and actually carried out only on the basis of the Easter message.

---

44. Cf. R. Slenczka, *Geschichtlichkeit und Personsein Jesu Christi*, pp. 310ff., who rightly points out that the phrase "christology from below" can mean many things (p. 309) but notes the various points in common in the different positions (p. 311). On christology from below in recent Roman Catholic theology, cf. W. Kasper, "Christologie von unten?" in *Grundfragen der Christologie heute*, ed. L. Scheffczyk (1975), pp. 141-70. In fact we might call the basic argument of W. Kasper's *Jesus the Christ* that of a christology from below, in spite of our criticism of Kasper in n. 45. In his presentation Kasper adopts a pneumatologically colored interpretive vocabulary. We see this even more strongly in Moltmann's *Way of Jesus Christ*, esp. pp. 73ff. Yet this presentation too is a christology from below rather than from above, in spite of the criticism of the methodological distinction as superficial and misleading (p. 69). If we could avoid the distinction of theological basis in the facile way in which Moltmann and others do, it is surprising that it has left such deep traces in the history of theology as we have seen above, and as we find in Moltmann's own discussion (pp. 49ff., 55ff.). Starting with the messiahship of Jesus after the manner of Moltmann himself is typical of the switch to a christology from below in the history of modern theology (e.g., in Bretschneider, *Handbuch*).

It is certainly understandable that many modern Christians find it hard to burden their argument for faith in Jesus Christ with something so philosophically debatable as the fact of the resurrection of a dead person. Historically and substantively, however, we cannot understand in any other way the origin of the Christian confession and its christological statements.[45] In the history of the development of Christianity, this is the fundamental character[46] of the christological statements of the Christian confession, which can be reconstructed but not replaced in Christian theology. Individual faith is certainly not tied to this basic argument. We can believe without it. But faith of that kind is not theology. Only arguments count in theology. Theology cannot ignore the question of the foundation of faith in Jesus Christ. It cannot ignore the underlying relation that leads to the rise of faith and the statements of the christological confession. The truth of Christian doctrine is at issue in theology. Of service in this regard is the discovery and reconstruction of the actual nature of the church's christological confession. Theological argument neither here nor elsewhere makes faith or the Holy Spirit superfluous. Nevertheless, it is also true that appeal to faith and the Holy Spirit is not of itself an argument.

In his campaign against the methodological demand for a christology from below, especially with reference to the version advocated by me, but also by Karl Rahner,[47]

---

45. Strangely Kasper (*Jesus the Christ*) says of my *Jesus — God and Man* that for the sake of a traditional conception, I am forced to make the resurrection an event that (on certain hermeneutical premises) I can prove. Forced? Up to the 18th century the whole Christian tradition regarded the resurrection of Jesus as an event that took place (i.e., a historical event) in human history. The modern reconstruction of the rise of Christianity and the confession of Christ cannot ignore this. Furthermore, Kasper did not accurately present my argument. I did not claim that we can prove the resurrection from the ambivalent fact of the empty tomb (the appearances are more persuasive), nor did I ascribe a confirmative function to it as regards Jesus' claim to authority. Kasper expressed himself much more guardedly in *Jesus the Christ*.

46. It belongs to the historicity of faith in Christ that we cannot detach this relation of the statements from its historical origin. In the process that leads from this origin to the confession of Christ's deity, we do not have a different, subjective relation of discovery such as we find in the conversion and development of some theologians. On the theoretical distinction, cf. W. Pannenberg, G. Sauter, S. M. Daecke, and H. N. Janowski, *Grundlagen der Theologie — ein Diskurs* (1974), pp. 86-97.

47. K. Rahner and W. Thüsing, *Christologie — systematisch und exegetische* (1972), p. 47. Rahner here bases his "ascent christology" on the unity of the (historically knowable) claims of Jesus and the experience of his resurrection. It is here, in his later writings, that he comes close to my *Jesus — God and Man*. Even though his basis in transcendental anthropology points in another direction, there is still some correspondence to my own deliberations (as will become clear later).

which links the message and history of Jesus to his resurrection from the dead, Kasper speaks of the danger of undervaluing the abiding presence of Christ in the Spirit.[48] In opposition to a reconstruction of the tradition as regards the underlying relation of christology, he stresses that apostolic proclamation is itself a constitutive element in the Christ event,[49] obviously in the sense of the witness of the Spirit that supplements the history of Jesus Christ. He thus demands a pneumatologically determined christology, thinking that this will erase the distinction between a christology from above and a christology from below.[50]

We must concede that the apostolic gospel is very closely related to the Christ event. We shall deal with this connection in the next chapter. But to maintain that apostolic proclamation has a *constitutive* function for the Christ event is not in keeping with the apostolic witness itself. The Easter message *follows* the Easter event; it does not constitute it. It is itself constituted by the event and by the self-declaration of the risen Lord (Gal. 1:16; cf. Matt. 28:19). John's Gospel says of the witness of the Spirit that he will not speak of himself but will take and proclaim what Jesus is (16:13f.).

The underlying relation of christological argumentation to the historical reconstruction of the material foundations of the statements of the christological confession, and especially the confession of the deity of Jesus, clearly has not yet been fully developed. If christology from below does not manage to develop material alternatives to confession of the deity of Christ but shows that this confession, and consequently the concept of the incarnation, is a relevant expression of the implied significance of the coming and history of Jesus, then this means that the human and historical reality of Jesus of Nazareth can be appropriately understood only in the light of his coming from God.[51] We then must think of his history as the action of God that has its basis in God. Hence we cannot regard a christology from below as ruling out completely the classical christology of the incarnation.[52] It is simply reconstructing the revelatory historical basis

48. Kasper, "Christologie von unten?" p. 151.
49. Ibid., p. 150.
50. Ibid., p. 169; cf. also Moltmann, *The Way of Jesus Christ* (see n. 44 above).
51. Cf. the remarks of G. Sauter, "Fragestellungen der Christologie," *VF* 11 (1966) 61, on my *Grundzüge der Christologie* (ET: *Jesus — God and Man*); cf. also the epilogue to the 5th German edition of *Grundzüge*, pp. 421f.
52. Thus Althaus wrote that when dogmatics has done its work of reflecting on the basis of faith in Jesus Christ, it can and should consider what faith can know of his nature and thus move from above to below as NT christology did in its statements about the incarnation of the preexistent One (*Die christliche Wahrheit*, p. 425). Cf. also K. Rahner, *Foundations of Christian Faith* (New York, 1978), pp. 177, 299f.

that classical christology has always in fact presupposed, though never properly explained. Only methodologically do we give precedence to arguing from below,[53] presupposing, of course, that this procedure leads to the conclusion that the concept of incarnation is not a falsification but a pertinent development of the meaning implicit in the coming and history of Jesus. In truth, material primacy belongs to the eternal Son, who has become man by his incarnation in Jesus of Nazareth.

Rightly understood, then, the two lines of argument from above and from below are complementary. A systematic reconstruction of the history of the christological tradition in terms of its origin, however, at least permits us to differentiate critically between the essential content of christological dogma and secondary features or distortions. In so doing it has furthered development of an interpretation of the dogma in the light of the biblical witness, as classical christology also did.

The task of interpreting the appearance and history of Jesus in relation to God, as the act of God, must be to the fore when we deal with christology within a total presentation of Christian doctrine. Since the overarching context in which we handle christology has a more or less explicitly trinitarian structure according to the church's confessions of faith — in terms of the economy of the divine action in the creation, reconciliation, and consummation of the world — the result for christology is that it depicts the appearance and history of Jesus of Nazareth as the action of the trinitarian God for human salvation. But as in the case of the doctrine of the Trinity, does not this actually presuppose a christology from below? Conversely, in a monographic presentation of christology, in which it is best to give christological statements a grounding from below, is not the thought of God necessarily presupposed?[54] The latter premise is unavoidable because discussion of the themes involved in the doctrine of God goes far beyond the compass of the special task of christology. Nevertheless, a total presentation of Christian doctrine must try to integrate christology from below into the context of its overarching themes, i.e., into the context of the doctrine of God and the economy of his work in and with the world. A total presentation of Christian doctrine of this kind cannot allow the traditional underlying relation of the statements of the Christian confession to retain the status of a presupposition

---

53. Rahner, *Foundations*, p. 177, and the critical remarks about a classical christology of descent (pp. 289f.).

54. Cf. *Jesus — God and Man*, pp. 21ff.

that is external to itself. Summarily at least, it must take up this presupposition into the course of its own presentation by giving it its place in the context of the economy of the divine action.

In the process, theology may not begin with a concept of God that is not shaped for its part by the revelation of God in the human history of Jesus. For Christian faith, only through Jesus is it manifest who or what God is. A temptation of classical christology from above has always been to violate this basic rule precisely in describing the event of the incarnation by laying as a foundation a general, rather than a specifically Christian, concept of God, in terms of which the incarnation is then stated. But the same applies to the concept of humanity as well. Those who speak about God becoming man must have some preconceptions of what is meant by the two terms.

Christology from below faces the same problem. It, too, must have similar preconceptions in describing the message and history of Jesus. In particular, it is exposed to the danger of using a general anthropology that is not conceived in terms of the God of the revelation in Christ as the basis of its interpretation of the coming and the special history of Jesus.[55] To do this is to offend against faith in the God revealed in Jesus as the Creator of all things, ourselves included. The historical reality of Jesus of Nazareth is necessarily distorted on the basis of an anthropology and historiography that ignores the relation to the Creator. "No one knows who the Son is except the Father, or who the Father is except the Son and any one to whom the Son chooses to reveal him" (Luke 10:22).

Is, then, the relation between theology and anthropology a circular one of reciprocal conditioning? In fact, regard for the reciprocal conditioning of concepts of God and concepts of human nature and destiny is a methodological premise if we are to achieve a systematically comprehensive christology. The circle here, if we may call it such, is not the vicious circle of a logically defective argument that assumes what it must prove. Rather, we have here a relation of real mutual conditioning between an idea of God and a human self-understanding.[56] This relation does not arise only in relation to the special problem of christology. Light is shed on it in scripture by our being destined for divine likeness. On the premise of the deity of the biblical God, this means that not Christians alone but all of us, including atheists

---

55. Cf. my "Christologie und Theologie," in *Grundfragen systematischer Theologie,* 2 vols. (Göttingen, 1967-80), II, 131ff., 135ff.

56. *Basic Questions,* I, 8; also *Jesus — God and Man,* pp. 201f.

and agnostics with their views of the world, move always in a world that is the creation of the biblical God and to which we humans also belong. The primary proof of this thesis is that all nonreligious views of humans and their world rest on reductions that suppress constitutive conditions and characteristics of human reality, that show themselves to be reductions, and that are thus vulnerable to argument.[57]

On a secular view of human reality, by gradual removal of the restrictions (but without circular argument) it is thus possible to achieve an awareness of the actual reciprocal relation of theology and anthropology that characterizes human self-understanding.[58] Only on this stage of awareness does the question become urgent as to the true form of divine reality, a question that can be answered only by the illuminating power of this reality's own revelation. But part of the illuminating power of the Christian understanding of God is that the special relation between Jesus of Nazareth and the Father whom he proclaimed embraces all humanity and its world and forms a special theme within the field that is thus opened up. In the course of developing Christian doctrine, the question also arises as to the deity of Jesus. Although this question already formed the starting point for the formulation of the trinitarian God, as a theme of christology it now arises in a different way, namely, in the context of an understanding of the world as God's creation as this results from a trinitarian concept of God.

Among all other creatures, we humans have the distinction of being related in a special way to God. On this fact rests our calling to have dominion over other creatures and our equipment for this task. To be sure, all other creatures are also related to God as their Creator inasmuch as they owe their existence to him and are continually referred to him for its preservation and development. This is why the world of creatures praises the Creator by its very existence. But for us the relation to God is an explicit theme inasmuch as we differentiate God from our existence and from everything finite. For us, then, thanksgiving and praise are a theme in the fulfillment of life. We are religious by nature. The fact that some people live without religion does not refute this fact. Atheists are human too. Yet from the standpoint of Christian faith, we must say that human nature does not come to full development in their lives. Even to us, it is not fully clear what humanity is without religion.

57. Cf. my *Anthropology in Theological Perspective* (Philadelphia, 1985) for analysis and demonstration.
58. Cf. vol. I, 107ff., 136ff.

The constitutive significance of religion for our humanity is closely related to the fact that we are beings endowed with consciousness and self-consciousness. We distinguish things in our world from ourselves and ourselves from the other things and beings to which we know we are related. In making this distinction, we see that things and beings are finite and distinguished from other things. But always related to the thought of finitude is that of the Infinite. Hence our human awareness is essentially a transcendent awareness that rises above the finitude of objects. In grasping finite objects in their distinction, we are also aware of the Infinite as the condition of their knowledge and existence. In our essential constitution as conscious beings, then, we are already destined to be religious.

In this constitution of conscious life, the Logos is present in a special way. As the generative principle of differentiation, he establishes and permeates the distinctive existence of all creatures. To us who are conscious beings in relation to others, the distinction of things and beings from all else is a theme of the consciousness, whereas in the case of all other creaturely existence, it is no more than factually determinative. In our conscious life, then, we are especially within the Logos who permeates all creation.

This is a thesis that we find in the tradition of Greek logos philosophy, developed particularly in the thinking of Heraclitus and Stoicism. But in John 1:4b, 9 also the Logos is "the light of men." We humans, then, participate in a special way in the Logos, to whom all things owe their existence or life (1:3). Athanasius rightly made this sharing in the Logos that was given us at creation the starting point of his doctrine of the incarnation of the Logos.[59] Without this premise the incarnation of the Logos would be alien to our nature. We could not say of him that "he came to his own possession" (1:11). The immediate continuation is that "his own people received him not," but the unheard-of aspect of this fact is that by creation we belong to the Logos and are thus "his own."

Our specifically human participation in the Logos is thus in terms of the human consciousness that differentiates things and that also links what it differentiates. Behind such an understanding is the theological premise of the self-distinction from the Father that constitutes the sonship of Jesus as we developed this thought in our presentation of the doctrine of the Trinity. Already in the doctrine of creation we claimed this self-

59. *De inc.* 3 and 7f.

distinction from the Father as the key to an understanding of the cosmological function of the Logos as the mediator of creation. In christology we shall test, confirm, and develop in different ways the thesis that this self-distinction is of basic significance.

From the standpoint of our relation to the Logos, the appearance of Jesus Christ may be understood as the completion of creation. No one in 20th-century theology has seen or formulated this truth more impressively than Karl Rahner. According to Rahner, we are to understand the incarnation as the free, unmerited, unique, and absolutely supreme fulfillment of what humanity means. Rahner adds that when we see this, we more readily and intelligibly dispel the false appearance of something marvelous and mythological that otherwise attaches much too easily to the concept of the incarnation.[60] This insight is of special relevance vis-à-vis recent English criticism of the concept and the ensuing debate.[61] The concept of the mythical is often very vague and is claimed to be relevant metaphorically, not cognitively.[62] Structurally, however, the concept of incarnation is not metaphor. Yet it has a mythological appearance when it is equated with the notion of the miraculous birth of the Son of God in analogy to similar mythical and poetic notions of Greek and Near Eastern origin, and when it is introduced without careful thought. Rahner meets the demand for thought in part, i.e., in a general form that still needs to be grounded in the uniqueness of the person and history of Jesus, when he says that the incarnation of God is the one supreme case of the fulfillment of human reality.[63] For Rahner, then, anthropology is defective

---

60. Rahner, "Jesus Christus, III B," *LThK*, V, 956.

61. Cf. Hick, *The Myth of God Incarnate,* and A. Goulder, ed., *Incarnation and Myth: The Debate Continued.* For further bibliography on this debate, see Dalferth, "Der Mythos vom inkarnierten Gott," pp. 320f. n. 4.

62. Cf. Hick, "Incarnation and Mythology," pp. 165ff. Related but less precise is the discussion, borrowing from D. F. Strauss, of M. Wiles, "Myth in Theology," in *The Myth of God Incarnate,* pp. pp. 150ff., 163f. Cf. Dalferth, "Der Mythos vom inkarnierten Gott," pp. 336ff. In a different sense, as a sensory portrayal of the nonsensory, Bultmann used the concept of the mythological in his *Gospel of John* (Philadelphia, 1971), pp. 60f. I myself plead for a specific theological use of the term "myth" that will be in keeping with the history and science of religion in my essay "Die weltgründende Function des Mythos und der christliche Offenbarungsglaube," in *Mythos und Rationalität,* ed. H. H. Schmid (1987), pp. 108ff. I base this on my earlier study of Christianity and myth (1971), now published in *Grundfragen,* II, 1980, 13ff., esp. 28ff., and on the relation to the idea of incarnation (pp. 59ff.).

63. *Theological Investigations,* 23 vols. (London, 1961-92), IV, 109. Rahner goes on to say that this supreme case involves being as self-giving, as set forth in christology.

christology[64] insofar as its theme is not our unity with God in distinction from him.

Rahner presented these statements about the relation of anthropology to christology as the expression of a "transcendental" anthropology and christology.[65] But the term "transcendental" is misleading here, since it suggests an a priori positing of forms of experience.[66] Rahner intended by the term the structural relation of anthropology, theology, and christology that transcends detailed historical findings, the basis of which is to be sought in anthropology. In later statements he recognized the historical mediation of this structural factor.[67] But if we take this concession strictly, the term "transcendental" is no longer suitable.

In a different way John Cobb has formulated the unity of anthropology and christology through the Logos concept on the basis of the process philosophy of A. N. Whitehead. Cobb interprets the Logos as the call of God to each creature for a "creative transformation" of its existence in the sense of realizing its divinely given possibilities of self-fulfillment.[68] For Cobb, Jesus is one with the Logos because he is unrestrictedly open to the divinely given possibility of existence;[69] he thus offers an example of human existence in its relation to God. Because Whitehead's view of God is nontrinitarian, in the course of the argument Cobb, unlike Rahner, does not commit himself to the deity of Jesus Christ, in virtue of which Christ can be for us more than just an exemplary person. Hence Cobb does not arrive at a full concept of incarnation.[70]

Logos christology and anthropology are so close that the question naturally arises whether the individual particularity of Jesus of Nazareth

64. Ibid., I, 164 n. 1. But it does not follow, as Moltmann surmises in *The Way of Jesus Christ*, p. 51 n. 23, that human personality, other than in the case of the incarnation, is necessarily characterized by the sin of egocentricity. We are sinners only as in our defectiveness we strive after autonomy and make ourselves absolute.

65. Rahner, *Theological Investigations*, I, 185ff., and *Foundations*, pp. 206ff.

66. On the tension between transcendental structure and contigent historicity, cf. the critical observations of W. Kasper, "Christologie von unten?" pp. 156f.; and on the general problem of Rahner's use of "transcendental," cf. F. Greiner, *Die Menschlichkeit der Offenbarung* (1978) (cf. pp. 250ff. on christology). Yet to find in Rahner (as in Schleiermacher) a kind of anthropological christology (Moltmann, *The Way of Jesus Christ*, pp. 61f.) is doubtful, since Rahner had in view a divinely constituted humanity and could speak not merely of the God-consciousness of Jesus but also in a trinitarian sense of the true deity of the Logos incarnate in Jesus.

67. *Foundations*, pp. 207f.

68. J. Cobb, *Christ in a Pluralistic Age* (Philadelphia, 1975), pp. 62-81.

69. Ibid., pp. 140f.

70. See my essay "A Liberal Logos Christology: The Christology of John Cobb," in *John Cobb's Theology in Process*, ed. D. R. Griffin and T. J. J. Altizer (1977), pp. 141ff.

is not simply that he definitively expresses essential humanity as participation in the Logos. Nevertheless, according to the prologue to John, our human sin, i.e., alienation from the Logos, must be overcome by the incarnation of the Logos. The resistance of darkness even to the incarnate Logos means that he is not received by us (John 1:11) unless we are born anew of the Spirit of God (1:13; cf. 3:5).

The relation of our created destiny to the incarnation of the Logos in Jesus of Nazareth is not, then, a direct one of disposition and actualization. The way from disposition to actualization is broken by sin. Because we are alienated from the Logos, we learn to know the Logos — who is still the origin of our life and the light of our consciousness — only through Jesus. It is not as if, before meeting Jesus, we had no general concepts of our nature and destiny, of God, of the Logos as the epitome of the world's order, or of our relation to God. Only through Jesus, however, do these general concepts acquire their true content. It is herein that the specific person and history of Jesus have universal relevance. This universal relevance is part of the particularity of the historical person of Jesus.

We might express this as follows. In antithesis to the concept of humanity, the particularity of Jesus is the origin of a new human image. We see this in Paul's contrasting of Christ and Adam in 1 Cor. 15:45ff. and Rom. 5:12-19. Here again sin breaks the unity of human reality. On account of it, the Adam of Genesis becomes the first Adam, and opposed to him in Jesus Christ is the second Adam, the definitive form of human reality that has overcome sin and death.

In Romans, Paul emphasized the contrast between Christ and the man of sin so strongly that there was little place for the relation of the person and history of Jesus to God's creative purpose.[71] With his act of obedience the one man Jesus Christ (5:15) is the direct opposite of the first man Adam.[72] No mention is made of a positive relation between them[73] unless we take into account the earlier

71. Things are different in 1 Cor. 15:45-49, where it is necessarily stated that the earthly man must precede the spiritual man (v. 46) as sowing precedes harvest (vv. 42ff.).

72. E. Brandenburger, *Adam und Christus, Exegetisch-religionsgeschichtliche Untersuchung zu Röm 5.12-21 (1. Kor 15)* (1962), pp. 158ff., esp. 219ff., 231.

73. Along these lines Brandenburger (ibid., pp. 267-78) sharply opposes Barth's interpretation in *Christ and Adam* (New York, 1956), esp. Barth's theses relating to Adam as a model and likeness of Christ (pp. 58f.) and the graduated relation of the two (pp. 34f.). Brandenburger thought that in Rom. 5, Paul was interested not in human nature as such (p. 273) but in the contrast between the act of Adam and the obedient act of Christ (p. 271, cf. 269). Barth's discussion is closer to that of Irenaeus (Brandenburger, *Adam und Christus*, p. 272) and 1 Cor. 15:45-49 than to Rom. 5:12ff. (see n. 72).

statements of Paul about the reconciliation to God of those who because of Adam had fallen victim to sin and death (vv. 8-10). But the link here lies not in our created nature and destiny but in the eschatological event of the death of Christ. God's gracious turning to those who were lost under the dominion of sin forges the link. Yet there is at least an implicit connection between Christ's act of obedience (v. 19) and Adam's sin. Adam ought to have proved himself by obedience to God. Instead, he inaugurated the rule of death by his transgression (v. 17). Thus the Son's act of obedience did what Adam ought to have done but failed to do.

But what was the Son's act of obedience? In context it was his taking to himself the death of sinners (Rom. 5:6ff.). The material relation to the disobedient act of Adam is not wholly clear, for Adam's obedience did not consist in the fact that he died. Instead, he was threatened with death if he transgressed the divine command (Gen. 2:17).

In another passage Paul does allude to the relation between Christ's obedience unto death and the sin of Adam, namely, in the hymn to Christ in Phil. 2:6-11. There it says of Christ that he did not lay hold of equality with God as his booty (v. 6) but in obedience to God humbled himself to the death of the cross (v. 8). Undoubtedly we have here an allusion to the temptation of Eve by the serpent, who offered her the hope of being like God (Gen. 3:5), which led to her and Adam's sin. The obedience of Jesus Christ the Son (Phil. 2:8), then, reverses the act of Adam. Unlike the first man, Jesus did not fall into the temptation of wanting to be like God, even though in his preexistence, unlike Adam, he was in the form of God (v. 6). Although his obedience perhaps had a different content from that required of Adam, yet there is an antithetical correspondence between his act and that of Adam inasmuch as the obedience springs from the mind of Christ that does not seek to be like God but accepts distinction from God in subordination to him. We may thus say that in Rom. 5, too, Christ sheds light on the original situation of Adam and therefore on our human nature and destiny in relation to God.

Paul's contrasting of the new man in Jesus Christ with the first Adam served in patristic theology as a frame within which to discuss the uniqueness of Jesus Christ compared to the rest of us. It is important that we should keep before us both the distinctive features of the developed procedure and its limitations. Only thus can we properly evaluate the different course taken by modern christology, which starts with the historical particularity of the public work of Jesus and seeks there his universal significance for the race and a basis for confession of his deity. Both approaches have the same task of pinpointing the uniqueness of the person and history of Jesus Christ in relation to human nature and destiny.

As already in Paul and the Johannine doctrine of the incarnation of the divine Logos, demonstrating this relation serves to show us what is the universally human and even (in John) the cosmic significance of the special history of Jesus and his person.

§ 2. The "New Man" in the Person and History of Jesus Christ

a. The New Man from Above

Paul described Jesus Christ as the eschatological form of humanity that in contrast to the previous Adamic humanity, obeys God and overcomes mortality. Such a description, like John's view of Jesus as the incarnate Logos, expressed the claim of a universal relevance for Jesus' person and history that goes far beyond the sphere of Jewish faith.[74] In Romans especially this is done by way of setting the eschatological man, who has appeared in Jesus Christ, in antithesis to the first Adam as the Genesis story depicts him. In the controversy with dualistic Gnosticism, the church of the 2nd century had to emphasize the relation between the new man from heaven who had come in Jesus Christ (1 Cor. 15:47) and the earthly man of the first creation.

Quite apart from its immediate context, the church in this regard made a decision of fundamental importance for the development of christology in keeping with the total biblical witness to the unity of God and his work. If the God of redemption who is revealed in Jesus Christ is the same as the Creator of the world and the human race, then we must view his saving work as an expression of his faithfulness to his creative work. In that case the sending of the new eschatological man must be seen in relation to the creation of Adam at the first. In harmony with this is the idea of a salvation history that aims at human fulfillment in Jesus Christ — an idea that presented itself to Melito of Sardis and Justin Martyr,[75] and perhaps also to Ignatius of Antioch, when he told the Ephesians that he was declaring to them the divine plan of salvation (oikonomia), which aims at the new man Jesus Christ (Eph. 20:1). We owe the classical development of this concept to Irenaeus.

74. Emphasized by Brandenburger, *Adam und Christus,* pp. 237ff., on Rom. 5:12.
75. On Melito and Justin, cf. Grillmeier, *Christ in Christian Tradition,* pp. 89ff., 94ff.

According to Irenaeus, the incarnation of the Son fulfilled the whole ordinance of salvation *(oikonomia)* regarding human beings (*Adv. haer.* 3.17.4; cf. 16.6) in a salvation history that began with our creation and came to completion with the "recapitulation" of fallen humanity in Jesus Christ.[76] Irenaeus explained that we did not reach completion at the first because, as finite beings, we were unable to receive, or achieve by ourselves, perfect fellowship with God. We were like children (4.18.1f.).[77] We had to wait until we reached maturity (4.83.3f.). It was because of this original weakness, as God foresaw, that sin came, and death as a result (4.83.4). But the Creator could not abandon us to death (3.23.1). He thus sent the Logos, in whose image we were originally created (5.16.2; cf. 12.6 and 15.4). The Logos saved us from the dominion of death and perfected us by uniting us with the image (5.9.3; cf. 36.3). Thus there are stages on our path to perfect fellowship with God (4.9.3). The path leads by way of the carnal to the spiritual (4.14.3). It was under this motto that Irenaeus, following the lead of Paul (2 Cor. 3) and in line with other early Christian theologians, integrated the covenant history of God with Israel into his picture of human history as a whole.

The Platonizing interpretation of the divine likeness, which we have discussed already, formed the leading systematic concept in this account of human development.[78] By differentiating original and copy and subordinating the latter to the former, Irenaeus linked the OT statements about Adam's creation to Paul's statements about Jesus Christ as the last and definitive Adam. He could hardly appeal here to Rom. 5:12ff. but certainly to 1 Cor. 15:45-49 (also v. 22). For Paul's antithesis between the first and second Adam was not so sharp in 1 Corinthians as in Romans. What we have in 1 Corinthians is more of a sequence[79] — first the Adam who is a living soul (Gen. 2:7), then the spiritual man (1 Cor. 15:46).

Irenaeus took up this thought and related it to 15:49, 53. Nature, he said, had to come first, then the mortal and corruptible had to be overcome and swallowed up by the immortal and incorruptible. Humanity had to become according to God's image and likeness, having first attained to the knowledge

---

76. *Adv. haer.* 5.14.2; cf. 3.18.1 on the basis of the event in God himself; also 3.22.3. On the whole concept, cf. J. T. Nielsen, *Adam and Christ in the Theology of Irenaeus of Lyons* (Assen, 1968).

77. Cf. Theophilus of Antioch *Ad Autol.* 2.25 and his stress on the need for the education of Adam by God (2.26). Cf. Nielsen, *Adam and Christ*, pp. 88f.

78. Cf. pp. 208ff. above; cf. also Irenaeus *Adv. haer.* 5.6.1 and 16.1.

79. Most exegetes see in this sequence an antithesis to the reverse sequence found in Philo and some Gnostic texts, and obviously known in a similar form at Corinth, whereby the creation of a heavenly man comes first, along the lines of Gen. 1:26f., followed by the earthly Adam, who falls into sin (Gen. 2:7). On 1 Cor. 15:46, cf. Brandenburger, *Adam und Christus*, pp. 71ff., esp. 74f. on Gnostic parallels, and 117ff. on Philo, though cf. R. Scroggs, *The Last Adam: A Study in Pauline Anthropology* (Philadelphia, 1966), who viewed Paul's thinking as closer to rabbinic interpretation of Gen. 2:7 and tried to explain the antithesis accordingly.

of good and evil (4.38.4; cf. 5.9.3 and 11.2). Along the lines of such a sequence Irenaeus quoted 1 Cor. 15:22. We are all to receive life in the spiritual Adam as we all died in the psychic Adam (5.1.3). But Irenaeus went further than Paul by seeing in the coming of the two Adams stages in the history of the same humanity that Jesus Christ was leading to perfect fellowship with God. Hence in Irenaeus, unlike Paul (Rom. 5:18f.), Adam's sin was an interlude[80] that God foresaw in his plan for human fulfillment, so that it could not alter the course of salvation history.

In this view, made possible by his understanding of the divine likeness, Irenaeus presented human nature materially as a history whose character we know from its outcome, i.e., from Jesus Christ. Or is it the case that in fact the end of the history is determined by the beginning, namely, by our essential relation to the Logos as the divine original? At any rate — and this is the second difference between the account in Irenaeus and the statements of Paul in 1 Cor. 15:45ff. — the perfecting of humanity does not come only with the dawning of eschatological life in the resurrection of Jesus, nor with the Son's act of obedience as in Rom. 5; it has its basis already in the incarnation of the divine Logos (5.15.4). Here Irenaeus combines Pauline and Johannine motifs and relates them to his concept of the image (cf. 5.16.2).

The linking of Adam typology and Logos christology that Irenaeus initiated is found again in the 4th century in Athanasius's work *The Incarnation of the Word*, with an emphasis now on the subtler doctrine of the Logos that Alexandrian theology had meantime developed.[81] The function of this linking was no longer anti-Gnostic but apologetic.[82] The incarnation of God through his Logos was not unworthy of his deity because what was at issue in this event was none other than the restoration and completion of the participation in the Logos that is related to our human nature, that guarantees our immortality, and that had been lost

80. Cf. Nielsen, *Adam and Christ*, pp. 75f. Nielsen rightly emphasized that in Irenaeus the solidarity of the two Adams aims at the integration of the flesh into the saving will of God, contrary to the Gnostics (p. 76). But he was wrong to see here an antithesis to Paul (Rom. 8:10). Irenaeus rightly derived from 1 Cor. 15:49ff. the fact that the corruptible does not share in the salvation of resurrection as such, but only as it is changed.

81. R. A. Norris, *God and World in Early Christian Theology: A Study in Justin Martyr, Irenaeus, Tertullian, and Origen* (New York, 1965), pp. 70ff., underlines Irenaeus's reservations as regards the Logos doctrine in view of his opposition to Gnostic ideas of emanation. On the role of the Logos in the cosmology and anthropology of Athanasius in his double apology *Contra Graecos* and *De incarnatione*, cf. J. Roldanus, *Le Christ et l'homme dans la théologie d'Athanase d'Alexandrie* (Leiden, 1968), pp. 43ff.

82. On the place of the work of Athanasius in apologetics, see ibid., pp. 11ff., esp. 16ff.

through the sin of Adam and its consequences.[83] On the one side here we find an expression of the solidarity of the Logos with humanity (cf. *De inc.* 8). But on the other side we see the difference between Christ and all others. Jesus Christ is the new man from heaven who has overcome death. He is this because in him the Logos has come from heaven in the flesh and could not be mastered by death.[84] What distinguishes him from all others and makes him the one who defeats death is thus his union with the divine Logos.

Like Apollinaris of Laodicea,[85] Cyril of Alexandria worked out the meaning of the uniqueness of Jesus Christ as the new Adam. As he saw it, the uniqueness is that Jesus is not a "mere man" but the Son of God, the Logos. He stressed this first in controversy with Jewish understandings and then soon found occasion to protest, too, against Judaizing trends in the Antioch school of theology, especially Nestorius and his rejection of the title *theotokos,* the God-bearer, for the mother of Jesus.[86] In reality, however, the Antioch theology that Cyril fought in the person of Nestorius was controlled by the same basic thought that the distinction of Jesus from all others rests on his union with the divine Logos. The Antioch position as stated by Theodore of Mopsuestia, however, stressed that this union made it possible for Jesus to be obedient to God in his human life, even to the death of the cross,[87] whereas the Alexandrians regarded the death of Jesus directly as an act of the Logos who had appeared in him.

To all appearances the christology of Antioch did not first develop a purely human uniqueness of Jesus that manifested itself in his suffering

83. *De inc.* 7. Athanasius could speak of the loss of our share in the divine likeness of the Logos because that share is not part of our corruptible and mortal nature but is added to it as a divine gift (*De inc.* 4). Yet the loss did not involve any loss of the rationality in which the participation finds expression. On this complex matter, cf. Roldanus, *Le Christ et l'homme,* pp. 74-98.

84. Athansius *C. Arian.* 1.44. Cf. R. L. Wilken, *Judaism and the Early Christian Mind: A Study of Cyril of Alexandria's Exegesis and Theology* (New Haven, 1971), pp. 103f.

85. Grillmeier, *Christ in Christian Tradition,* pp. 329ff.; also E. Mühlenberg, *Apollinaris von Laodicaea* (1969), pp. 143f., 146f., 208.

86. Wilken, *Judaism and the Early Christian Mind,* pp. 106ff., 119ff.; also 138ff., 160f., 173ff. on the importance of the controversy with Judaism, and 201ff. on the controversy with Nestorius.

87. R. A. Norris, *Manhood and Christ: A Study in the Christology of Theodore of Mopsuestia* (Oxford, 1963), pp. 191ff., 207f., stresses that the root of Theodore's christological "dualism" lies in his interest in the obedient suffering of the human Christ. The context was the doctrine of two ages (corresponding to the Adam-Christ typology) — the present age and the future eschatological age (pp. 160-72). Cf. also G. Koch, *Die Heilsverwirklichung bei Theodor von Mopsuestia* (1965), pp. 75-89.

obedience, or that underlay this, and then make this the basis of statements about his deity, as done in a modern christology from below. It certainly did not do this in the sense of leaving the deity an open question in the history of Jesus, so that it would not be present as his presupposed divine nature in his acts up to his resurrection and ascension. This theology, like that of Alexandria, firmly accepted the deity of Jesus, even before his birth, as a presupposition throughout his human history. There was thus no need to make a special theme of the human uniqueness of Jesus and his history and to treat this as a basis for what was said about his deity. In the 5th century such a view would have been suspected of being close to the christology of Paul of Samosata, though this did not lead to an assertion of the full deity of Jesus Christ. The theology of Antioch, with its relatively modest demands for attention to the historical humanity of Jesus, came under suspicions of this kind.

In the history of early christology the equation of the incarnation of the Logos with the birth of Jesus blocked the way to any evaluating of the human uniqueness of Jesus of Nazareth as a medium of the revelation of the divine Logos as we see this already in the Adam typology of Paul and as it might have been further developed. This equation is not in keeping with the basis of the doctrine of the incarnation in John 1:14.[88] Neither here nor in 1 John 4:2 is there any specific relation to the birth of Jesus. The reference is to the totality of his life and work, which reflects the "grace and truth" of God as Father (John 1:14). Similarly the saying about the sending of the Son into the world (3:16) refers to the passion and death of Jesus (cf. also 1 John 4:9), not to his human birth, of which there is no special account in John's gospel.

The same applies to the pre-Pauline reference to the sending of the preexistent Son of God into the world, a reference that we often find

88. The commentaries on John rarely discuss this issue. We do not find it in L. Morris, *The Gospel according to John* (Grand Rapids, 1971), pp. 102ff., or R. Schnackenburg, *The Gospel according to St. John*, 3 vols. (New York, 1980-82), I, pp. 265-73. This is the more surprising in view of the reference to being born of God in v. 13, though not with reference to Jesus, since the plural relates to those who receive the Logos. Some texts substitute a singular to make this a reference to the birth of Jesus (cf. commentaries by Morris, pp. 100ff., and by Schnackenburg, pp. 264f.). Perhaps this was because copyists missed a reference to the birth of Jesus in 1:14. It is the more remarkable that where one would have expected some mention of the miraculous birth of Jesus, the text puts a plural instead and speaks of the spiritual rather than the earthly birth of believers. Among the few commentaries that go into the question whether 1:14 refers to the birth of Jesus, cf. Bultmann, *Gospel of John*, p. 62 n. 2. Bultmann dismisses as irrelevant all questions as to the how of the *egeneto*. All that we are told is that the Revealer appeared in the sphere of *sarx* (p. 62).

in Paul. Thus we read in Rom. 8:3 of the sending of the Son into the flesh of sin[89] that he might liberate us from sin. Only in Gal. 4:4 do we find an express relating of the sending to the birth of Jesus, and even here the reference is not simply to the beginning of his course. The point is that the Son of God has entered the sphere of earthly existence with its conditions and relations. This applies to all his earthly course, so that in Gal. 4:4 we find mention not merely of his birth but also of the subjection of his earthly course to the Mosaic Torah ("born under the law").[90] In view of these findings, one must speak of a plain shift of accent in the early church interpretation of the incarnational event to the degree that it was now primarily, if not exclusively, associated with the birth of Jesus, and the demonstrations of divine glory and power were found in his earthly works and his resurrection from the dead as consequences of this.

The only NT support for such a view is in the Lucan account of the conception and birth of Jesus, where the angel in his message to Mary bases the divine sonship of Jesus on the act of conception in the power of the divine Spirit (Luke 1:35). Theology must evaluate this tradition in tension with the other NT accounts of the incarnation and sending instead of grounding its understanding of the incarnation solely on the birth story. We must see in the Lucan story testimony to the fact that Jesus was the Son of God from the very first and did not become so later, whether by his baptism or his resurrection.

But this is not to say that we may equate the event of the incarnation with the isolated event of the birth. Instead, the significance of the birth is dependent on the story of his overall earthly course. Only in the light of what followed may we say whose birth this truly was, namely, that of the Son of God. This is not just a matter of the subsequent knowability of something that was true from the very first. No one has full personal identity from the moment of birth. Who we are or were, whose birth will be recalled, is seen and decided only in the course of life and in view of its end. Even though we may say that this man or woman was from the very first this specific person, the truth of the statement is related to later

89. Cf. Wilckens, *Der Brief an die Römer*, 3 vols., EKK (Zurich/Neukirchen, 1978-82), II, 124f., esp. also on the significance of the phrase *homoiōma sarkos hamartias*, not as mere similarity, but as being equally under the conditions of those who live in the sphere of sin's dominion (p. 125).

90. Cf. W. Kramer, *Christ, Lord, Son of God*, SBT, 1/50 (London/Naperville, 1966), pp. 111ff., esp. 112f.

events in that person's life.[91] In the case of Jesus, too, the particular identity of his person is related to the course of his history, and especially to its outcome in the passion and the Easter event. Only in the light of this outcome may we say, then, that the child Jesus who was born of Mary was the Messiah and the Son of God.[92] In other words, the history of his earthly work and his passion, which in the light of the Easter event shows him to be the Son of God, is not something accidental in relation to the identity of his person.

Rightly the christology of the early church found the uniqueness of Jesus in his divine sonship. It did not succeed, however, in fittingly describing the relation of this to the human and historical distinctiveness of his public appearance as we have it in the gospel tradition. From the very first it put the whole earthly path of Jesus under the sign of the incarnation of the Logos in his birth. For this reason even the interpretation of Pauline Adam typology could not do justice to the fact that the appearance of the second eschatological Adam was linked in 1 Cor. 15:45ff. to the new life of the risen Lord, and in Rom. 5:12ff. to the filial obedience of Jesus Christ on his way to the cross, but in neither case to his birth.

The exposition of scripture at Antioch tried best to make room for the historical humanity of Jesus, but even then it did so on the assumption that already at the beginning of his path, in his birth, the incarnation of the Logos had taken place, so that the concern to preserve the features of a historical human life seemed to involve bifurcation, a christology of division, a questioning of the personal unity of the Incarnate. Nor did the christological work of the Middle Ages and the older Protestantism raise freely enough the question as to the human distinctiveness of Jesus in his

91. Cf. *Anthropology,* pp. 508ff.

92. We have here what I called "retroactive force" in *Jesus — God and Man,* pp. 135ff., 141. I perhaps did not make plain enough that the basis of this idea of a retroactive change of significance (and nature) lies in the hermeneutic of historical experience, for many reviewers thought I was advancing a notion that was conceptually unclear. Thus Moltmann in *The Way of Jesus Christ* spoke of a "forced assumption" (p. 77), though he had earlier found it a "helpful thought" (*The Crucified God* [London, 1973], p. 181). I had something in mind along the lines of Dilthey's hermeneutic of historical experience, namely, a descriptively demonstrable fact with ontological implications. The significance of an event as we see it later (in which it is always a matter of its *ti en einai*) is not independent of the events in the light of whose (provisional) conclusion we look back upon it. The thesis of a retroactive force corresponds to the constitutive significance of anticipation (which Moltmann himself assumed). On this and the links to the Aristotelian analysis of movement, cf. my *Metaphysics and the Idea of God* (Grand Rapids, 1988), pp. 71ff.

work and destiny, for this too took for granted the equation of the conception and birth of Jesus Christ with his incarnation. It was the biblically based criticism of this picture by the Socinians, along with new approaches in the christology of the late 18th and 19th centuries, that first made possible an inquiry into the distinctiveness of Jesus untrammeled by that presupposition. Paul's Adam typology could have pointed the church much earlier in this direction.

b. The Author of a New Humanity

Paul's view of Jesus Christ as the new eschatological or last Adam has a social reference oriented to human community. It tells us that "we" all shall "bear" the image of the new and heavenly man (1 Cor. 15:49) and shall be changed into his likeness (2 Cor. 3:18). As the last Adam *(eschatos Adam)*, Jesus Christ is thus the original of a new humanity that is made anew in his image by participation in his obedience, in his death and resurrection. In Paul this thought formed the soteriological motif of his Adam christology, and the motif still had an impact in patristic christology.

Taken alone, the concept of the image or original is ambivalent. Like the idea of a species, it may apply equally and directly to all the individuals involved. Paul, however, stressed mediation from the one to the many. In the case of Adam, each of us sins as Adam did, and death has thus come upon all (Rom. 5:12). The participation of the many in the image of the eschatological man, however, is by being changed into his likeness (2 Cor. 3:18; also Rom. 8:29). This leads us easily to think of the church as the sphere in which, and by the missionary preaching of which to the whole world, the many are changed into the new man by baptism and faith. But Paul did not develop this relation to ecclesiology in connection with Adam typology, though he hinted at it in what he said about the elect being destined to be conformed to the image of the Son (Rom. 8:29).

Irenaeus related participation in the image of the heavenly man to the baptism and moral renewal of individual believers,[93] but not expressly to the church as a fellowship. Methodius of Olympus was the first to take up Irenaeus's extension of the Adam typology to Mary as the new Eve[94]

93. *Adv. haer.* 5.11.2 and 9.3.
94. Ibid. 3.22.4.

and to extend it to the church,[95] depicting the church as the new Eve, the mother of a renewed humanity. Athanasius linked the Adam typology to ecclesiology in a different way with his thought of a new creation of humanity in Christ (2 Cor. 5:17).[96] Nevertheless, he hardly went beyond Irenaeus's reference to baptism, and he certainly did not raise the question of the relation of the distinctive earthly history of Jesus to the rise of the church. This question seems to have been blocked by the idea of the function of Christ, the new Adam, as a prototype.

At one point, however, Paul's line of argument in Romans leads us further. If the sin of the one Adam means judgment on the whole of humanity (the many), and the obedience of Christ means justification for all (Rom. 5:18f.), there is still the difference that the gift of grace presupposes the sin of the many, so taking it to itself that the many achieve justification (5:16).[97] This implies a historical link between the appearance of Jesus Christ and the consequences of Adam's sin. It also implies an orientation of his mission to the saving of the many who live under the yoke of sin and death. Early christology undoubtedly stressed this orientation, but it did so especially in connection with the incarnation of the Logos. Since it equated the incarnation with the birth of Jesus, it did so with reference to the birth. In Paul, however, what is at issue is the obedient suffering of Jesus. The relation of this to the many and their salvation is what the Father had in mind in sending the Son. In Paul it was also the will and work of the Son (Rom. 5:6; cf. Gal. 2:20).

In view of the total NT witness, theology must evaluate the orientation of the obedient suffering of Jesus to the salvation of the many within the context of his earthly message and activity, which led him to the cross. But here again the question arises as to the human distinctiveness of Jesus that corresponds to the statements of faith regarding the manifestation of the divine Logos or Son in him. This cannot be a distinctiveness that characterizes Jesus in isolation but must be one that relates his earthly history to humanity (the many). Again at this point, then, we must diverge from the type of discussion that predominated in early christology.

Although early christology sought the uniqueness of Jesus as a man

95. Cf. Wilken, *Judaism and the Early Christian Mind,* pp. 100f.

96. On Adam typology and 2 Cor. 5:17 in Athanasius, cf. Roldanus, *Le Christ et l'homme,* pp. 138ff., cf. 210. On christology and ecclesiology, see L. Malevez, "L'église dans le Christ. Étude de théologie historique et théorique," *Recherches de science religieuse* 25 (1935) 257-91 and 418-40.

97. Cf. Brandenburger, *Adam und Christus,* p. 226.

from heaven primarily in his deity, it did also know and stress one quality that differentiated the human nature of Jesus from all others, even in its distinction from the Logos, i.e., the sinlessness of Jesus. As we learn from Heb. 4:15, sinlessness differentiates the human nature of Jesus from that of all others. He was tempted as we are, yet without sin. From the days of Irenaeus and Tertullian,[98] attention focused on sinlessness as the distinguishing attribute of Jesus, and Chalcedon (451) emphasized this point in its famous Definition: By his incarnation the Son of God became like us in all things, sin excepted (DS § 301 = ND § 614). But what is the material basis of this statement that Jesus was without sin? Early christology sought it in his moral perfection, in the immutable fellowship of his soul with God.[99] On this view the one quality that distinguishes the humanity of Jesus relates to his individual life, and this thought has influenced modern ideas of the sinless holiness of Jesus.[100] It does not regard the relation to others as constitutive for the uniqueness of the humanity of Jesus, though the goal of the incarnation of the Logos is the lifting of the human race out of the grip of sin and death.

Yet the situation has now changed. Theologians began to relate the person of Jesus as Messiah and Savior from the very first to the covenant of grace that he has set up,[101] and therefore to the covenant people of the Redeemer that has taken historical shape in the community of the church. The tendency here, however, is to view the person of the Redeemer as a human personality, so that his work in inaugurating the kingdom of God among us is seen as an expression of his human particularity.

In Schleiermacher the concept of the Redeemer is governed by his relation to the fellowship of the redeemed that he founded (*Christian Faith*, § 88.4). Incorporation into this community life is essential to the redemption of individuals because individuals alone cannot free themselves from entanglement in the social nexus of sin (§ 87). On account of our social dependence on others, our liberation must

---

98. Irenaeus *Adv. haer.* 5.14.3 and Tertullian *De carne Christi* 16 (PL, 2, 780). Cf. more scripture passages and patristic references in my *Jesus — God and Man*, pp. 354ff.

99. Origen *De princ.* 2.6.4f.

100. Cf. Schleiermacher's *Christian Faith*, § 98. We may also think of the influential work of C. Ullmann, *Die Sündlosigkeit Jesu. Eine apologetische Betrachtung* (1828, 7th ed. 1863), which bases confession of the deity of Jesus as well as his uniqueness on his sinlessness (pp. 178ff.). Cf. my *Jesus — God and Man*, pp. 359f., esp. on W. Herrmann and Ullmann (pp. 360f.).

101. Buddeus, *Compendium*, pp. 513f. (4.1.318). Underlying this view is Reformed federal theology; cf. Calvin *Inst.* 2.9-11.

be grounded in a new fellowship. In the history of this concept, which developed from Rousseau by way of Kant to Marx, Schleiermacher, along with Kant's philosophy of religion and following it, represented a Christian variation. The new fellowship cannot have the form of the state as in Rousseau. As distinct from the external constitutional order of the state, it must be a community with a common mind (Kant) or a community of piety (Schleiermacher). Like Kant before him, Schleiermacher described it as the kingdom of God.[102] In both Schleiermacher and Kant the common life of the church is oriented beyond historical particularity to the idea of humanity as a whole.[103] Thus Schleiermacher could write that the new common life that is founded by the Redeemer and characterized by the dominion of God-consciousness, beyond all relations to terrestrial objects and data, is a new stage in human development (§ 88.4) and may even be regarded as the completed creation of human nature (§ 89 Thesis).

As everything that is posited by Christ in the human sphere is set forth as the new creation, Christ himself is the second Adam, the Initiator and Author of this more complete human life, or the completing of human creation (§ 89.1). In a way that is remarkably similar to that of early Alexandrian theology,[104] Schleiermacher thus related Paul's description of the existence of believers as a "new creation" in Christ (2 Cor. 5:17) to the depiction of Christ as the Author of a new humanity, the second Adam (§ 89.1). Like Athanasius or Cyril, he presented the implied particularity of Jesus Christ primarily as a description of his individual life, thinking of the social function of the Redeemer in founding the fellowship of the redeemed along causal lines as an imparting of the sinless perfection that characterizes him as an individual (§ 88 Thesis).

The idea of redemption as a transferring of the Redeemer's own state to believers was possible, of course, only because Schleiermacher substituted the thesis of a prototypical perfection of God-consciousness for the doctrine of Christ's deity (§ 93.2). Whereas the christology of the early church found the uniqueness of Jesus in his deity, Schleiermacher saw it as a purely human uniqueness, i.e., as the constant power of his God-consciousness, as a true being of God in him (§ 94 Thesis). Schleiermacher's describing of the distinctiveness of Jesus in human terms was at the cost of minimizing the early confession of the deity

---

102. *Christian Faith*, § 87.3; cf. the thesis of § 117. For Kant see *Religion within the Limits of Reason Alone* (1793), pp. 85ff., on the difference from the state. Already in Kant the idea of a moral people of God can be put into practice only in the form of a church. With this distinction between church and state, which Kant based on that between legality and morality, Kant, and Schleiermacher after him (and unlike Rousseau and his successors), follows the tradition of the Lutheran two-kingdoms doctrine.

103. Thus Kant said that the concept of an ethical common life relates always to the ideal of a human totality, and it differs in this respect from that of a political common life (*Religion within the Limits of Reason Alone*, p. 88).

104. On Athansius, cf. Roldanus, *Le Christ et l'homme*, pp. 131ff., esp. 139ff. On Cyril, cf. Wilken, *Judaism and the Early Christian Mind*, pp. 104ff.

of Jesus. Apart from this alteration, his view of the Redeemer bears a striking resemblance to what we find in Alexandrian christology, especially in the linking of the perfect power of his God-consciousness (which replaces the deity) to his sinlessness (§ 98). Among these parallels is also the unimportance of the details of the story of Jesus for the concept of the person of the Redeemer (§ 99). If Schleiermacher had adhered to the early confession of Christ's deity without diminution, his doctrine of the person of the Redeemer would have been monophysite in structure, since he would have seen the uniqueness of the humanity of Jesus directly in his deity. In his case, however, the reference is not to the deity but simply to the being of God in the human God-consciousness of the Redeemer.

In describing the activity of the Redeemer in founding a new human fellowship in God's kingdom that is freed from the dominion of sin, Schleiermacher ignored the features of the proclamation, work, and history of Jesus that characterize his historical reality. Focusing on the marks of perfection (of God-consciousness) and sinlessness that the concept of the Redeemer demands, he neglected the distinction between his earthly work and his impact after his crucifixion and resurrection.

In the theological tradition, on the basis of Phil. 2:6-11, this distinction between the two phases of the history of Jesus has been described in terms of the two states of humiliation and exaltation.[105] The former state covers the earthly proclamation and work of Jesus and his suffering obedience on the way to the cross.[106] Schleiermacher could make nothing of this distinction because he rejected the idea of a preexistence of Christ in relation to which the earthly history of Jesus would necessarily be a humbling.[107] Yet he did take note of the difference between the humility of his path of suffering and the exaltation of his resurrection. He thus found a place for the distinctiveness of his human history as a whole. Within his earthly history his work is that of establishing a new human fellowship in the kingdom of God. A more nuanced definition of this fellowship is needed, however, in view of the situation of the earthly proclamation of Jesus on the one side and the apostolic message of Christ on the other.

105. Cf. esp. the Lutheran doctrine of the two states and the revival of kenosis teaching in the 19th and 20th centuries (*Jesus — God and Man*, pp. 312ff.). Patristic theology had already related the humiliation of the Son of God to the incarnation, though with no implied renunciation of divine attributes.

106. The older Protestant dogmatics linked the distinction of states to the doctrine of the threefold office that Christ exercises in both humiliation and exaltation.

107. *Christian Faith*, § 105 App.

Ritschl objected against Schleiermacher's new version of the doctrine of Christ's person that he did not clearly differentiate and integrate the thought of the redemption brought by Christ and the ethical aim of the kingdom of God.[108] Ritschl himself regarded the redemption of sin by its remission simply as a means to the final purpose of a kingdom of God among us that was the final end of God as well as of Christ's ministry. Schleiermacher could not see it this way because for him redemption consisted not merely of the sense of sin forgiven but positively of the renewed force and dominance of the God-consciousness, i.e., of a being of God in us, as in Jesus, which could not be regarded simply as a means to something else.

Ritschl, however, found in Schleiermacher a real tension between the neutral concept of religion that came to expression in his talk about the power of the God-consciousness and his stress on the fact that Christianity is a moral religion and that as such it is teleologically oriented to the kingdom of God.[109] This latter point, which Ritschl found to be neglected in Schleiermacher's actual presentation, and especially in his christology, came to the fore in Ritschl's own depiction of the work of Jesus and the person that it characterized. According to Ritschl, Jesus proclaimed that the kingdom of God was not only near but that it was already present in his own person and work — to the degree that as the expected Messiah, he founded a community that acknowledges him as the Son of God and the bearer of God's rule, thus actualizing the rule of God within it.[110] For Ritschl, then, the messiahship of Jesus and the establishment of the kingdom of God by the founding of the community belong very closely together.[111] In the community, by the exercising of righteousness, the kingdom of God comes into being in a temporal process like the growth of a plant or the action of leaven on dough.[112]

After Johannes Weiss showed in 1892 that we must view the coming of God's kingdom that Jesus proclaimed as the eschatological future that comes from God alone,[113] not as the result of human action, and therefore not as an ethical goal, it has been easy to criticize Ritschl in terms of NT exegesis. Furthermore, the parables of growth that Jesus told do not have as their point the growth of the circle of disciples until the kingdom is achieved, but the contrast between the unassuming present and the overwhelming greatness of the future of God.[114] Above all, we cannot speak of a founding or establishing of the kingdom of God by Jesus, or at least not in relation to his founding of the Christian community.[115]

---

108. Ritschl, *Christian Doctrine*, pp. 9f.
109. *Christian Faith*, §§ 11, 92.
110. Ritschl, *Christliche Lehre*, II, 31f.
111. Ibid., pp. 39f.
112. Ibid., p. 40.
113. J. Weiss, *Die Predigt Jesu vom Reiche Gottes* (1892, 2nd ed. 1900, newly ed. by F. Hahn, 1964), pp. 74ff., cf. 105f.; ET, Philadelphia, 1971, pp. 67ff., 81ff.
114. Ibid., pp. 82ff.; ET, pp. 72ff.
115. Ibid., p. 105; cf. 1st ed., pp. 24f.; ET, pp. 81ff.

The rise of the church is the result of the appearances of the risen Lord and the imparting of the Spirit, though it had its root, perhaps, in the fellowship of Jesus with his disciples. Ritschl himself, then, made too little distinction between the earthly sending of Jesus and the impact made by his resurrection. By tracing back the founding of the church to Jesus' earthly work and equating it with the kingdom of God that Jesus proclaimed, Ritschl viewed the work of the risen and ascended Lord as flowing too smoothly from the earthly ministry of Jesus between his baptism and his crucifixion.

Nevertheless, Ritschl was right in his criticism of Schleiermacher insofar as he missed in Schleiermacher a due regard for the central theme of the procla-mation and the whole earthly history of Jesus, namely, its relation to the rule of God, which he preached as imminent. Much too hastily Schleiermacher reduced this theme to that of the constant power of Jesus' God-consciousness,[116] and in so doing neglected the difference between the appearance of Jesus and the future of the divine rule. Ritschl was also right in stressing against Schleiermacher the link between the message of Jesus and the OT expectation of the rule of God.[117]

It is in this light that we are to see Ritschl's legitimate stress on the relation of the sending of Jesus to the community. In the OT history of the covenant and the message of the prophets, belonging to God and the hope of his royal dominion are linked to the actualizing of his divine law in the life of the covenant people. Similarly, the eschatological message of Jesus regarding the imminence of the kingdom of God was linked to a new exposition of the law of God in the light of this imminence. In his historical work, however, Jesus did not found the church as a community distinct from Israel. He was conscious instead of being sent to the lost sheep of the house of Israel (Matt. 15:24; cf. 10:6). In contrast to the Jewish movements of his day, Jesus did not gather a remnant of the true righteous. He held himself and his disciples open to the people to whom he directed his message.

Neither Schleiermacher nor Ritschl grasped this properly because both of them let themselves be guided by the idea, as Schleiermacher formulated it, that a relation to the whole human race is essentially posited by faith in Christ[118] and that this relation takes concrete shape in the rise of the Christian community. The only difference was that Ritschl tried to make this relation the theme of the earthly sending of Jesus and in this way to find a basis for confession of the deity.[119] In fact, however, the messianic title, whose link to the person of Jesus we have yet

116. *Christian Faith,* § 94 Thesis.
117. Ritschl, *Christian Doctrine,* pp. 9f. refers to Schleiermacher's undervaluing of the OT; cf. *Christian Faith,* § 132.
118. *Christian Faith,* III, § 94.2.
119. Ritschl called the founding of the kingdom of God by Jesus a moral vocation (*Christian Doctrine,* § 47 [pp. 434-42]) and linked to this definition the thesis that in accordance with this vocation, the ethical evaluation of Jesus becomes religious self-evaluation (pp. 438ff.). Cf. § 45.

to discuss, was an expression of the hope for a restoration of the Jewish people, and the message of the imminence of the kingdom of God grew out of the faith tradition of Israel and was directed to this people, even though it might have broader implications. Bultmann rightly integrated the appearance of Jesus into the nexus of the Jewish religion. Jesus, he said, was "no Christ but a Jew," and his preaching moves within the worldviews and conceptions of Judaism, even where it stands in antithesis to traditional Jewish religion.[120] It was the post-Easter community that took the message of the risen Lord beyond the confines of the Jewish people, and even then not without profound inner conflicts.

With his proclamation of the imminence of the rule of God and its dawning in his own work in Israel, Jesus came to move the covenant people to conversion to its God.[121] For this reason his message and his person carry with them a question to the self-understanding of Jews that still remains an open one. Jesus and his message and the implied challenge are not in the first instance a matter for Christians. They apply primarily to the Jewish people. The question that is posed to its self-understanding by Jesus and his message is this: How radically does the faith of Judaism take the first commandment in relation to all other concerns, even its own religious tradition? How the two differ we cannot go into here. But the message of Jesus puts the question, and it is still an open one, for, apart from a small group of followers, Jesus and his message met with rejection from his people.

The basis of this rejection and its connections with the trial that ended with the crucifixion need careful consideration in view of the controversies regarding the theme. At this point we may simply emphasize that it was only as the mission of Jesus met with rejection by his people,

---

120. R. Bultmann, *Das Urchristentum im Rahmen der antiken Religionen* (Zurich, 1949), p. 78. Bultmann drew from this insight the inference that we must view the proclamation of Jesus as a presupposition of NT theology but not as a part of it (*Theology of the NT* [New York, 1951], p. 3). This verdict justifies the attempt to place Jesus in the tradition of Jewish faith. But this effort can be successful only if it also presents the challenges that the message, conduct, and history of Jesus put to the Jewish people of his day (see below).

121. The prophetic theme of conversion is not prominent in the message of Jesus (as distinct from that of the Baptist, Mark 1:4 par.), though it is to the fore in Mark 1:15 (cf. E. P. Sanders, *Jesus and Judaism* [Philadelphia, 1985], pp. 108ff.). All the same, sayings like the summons to subordinate all concerns to seeking God's kingdom (Matt. 6:33) naturally imply very strongly a conversion to God. If the theme is not an independent one, this is perhaps because conversion is not for Jesus, as for the Baptist, a precondition of participation in the kingdom. At the center of his message is the imminence and even the presence of the rule of God for believers.

and he went to the cross and passion, that he became the Savior of the nations. Only as the crucified and risen Lord is he the new and eschatologically definitive man. Here we have the leading example of the divine overruling that brings good out of evil (Gen. 50:20). Precisely by the event of the passion he became a figure that transcends the national and religious differences between Jews and non-Jews (Eph. 2:14). Because of his rejection by his own people, salvation has come to the Gentiles (Rom. 11:11). Paul saw here a demonstration of the divine plan for history (the *mystērion,* Rom. 11:25), which, in virtue of God's covenant faithfulness to his election, will finally give Israel a part in the salvation of God's kingdom, namely, when it recognizes its promised Messiah in the Crucified.

The messianic title came to be finally linked to Jesus only by his condemnation as a messianic pretender. Previously Jesus had held aloof from expectations that he was the Messiah. But he had to be handed over to the Romans as a messianic pretender. The inscription on the cross especially makes it plain that this was the basis of his condemnation (Mark 15:26 par.). In the light of his resurrection from the dead, he was then believed to be divinely recognized as the coming Messiah and given his dignity as such (Rom. 1:3f.),[122] so that confession of his messiahship soon came to be associated with his name, became a part of this name, and influenced the recounting of his earthly history. In his pre-Easter ministry Jesus himself, as stated, rejected the title and the associated expectations (Mark 8:29-31).[123] The meaning of the title first had to be revised by linking it to the Crucified,[124] so that instead of a political liberator, a messianic king, there would be seen a suffering Messiah adapted to Jesus and forever afterward related to his name.

Following Otto Betz, but in opposition to the dominant view of NT exegetes, Moltmann has recently advocated the thesis that by orchestrating his entry into Jerusalem along the lines of Zech. 9:9 (Mark 11:1-11), and by his symbolic cleansing of the temple (11:15-17), Jesus proclaimed himself to be the Messiah and confessed himself to be so in his trial before Caiaphas (14:61f.) and Pilate

---

122. On Rom. 1:3f., cf. M. Hengel, *The Son of God: The Origin of Christology and the History of Jewish-Hellenistic Religion* (Philadelphia, 1976), pp. 59ff.

123. F. Hahn, *The Titles of Jesus in Christology: Their History in Early Christianity* (London, 1969), pp. 157f., 223-28.

124. Moltmann, *The Way of Jesus Christ,* pp. 138f. We can thus see why Moltmann calls Jesus "a messianic person in process" (pp. 136ff.), though this phrase does not do full justice to the fact that the Gospels retroactively see him as the Messiah from the very first.

(15:2).[125] This is certainly in keeping with what the Evangelists say, but whether it accords with the historical facts may be questioned.[126]

The entry into Jerusalem may be seen as a prophetic sign that presents the coming of the rule of God along the lines of Zech. 9:9, in contrast to a display of political and military power. But if it was meant to proclaim the messiahship of Jesus, it is strange that Jesus was not arrested at once by the Romans as a rebel.[127] The overturning of the money changers' tables in the temple court may also be seen as a prophetic sign, but one symbolizing the predicted destruction of the temple (13:2) rather than its cleansing.[128] No messianic authority was required for this action. It stood in the authentic prophetic tradition (cf. Jer. 7:11ff.).

The answer to the high priest's question in Mark 14:62, and especially in the versions in Matt. 26:64 and Luke 22:67ff., is ambivalent insofar as it replies to the question of messiahship with a statement about the coming of the Son of Man.[129] Even if this is seen as an affirmative answer, it is still difficult to see why Caiaphas should have found it to be blasphemous.[130] Moltmann himself thinks the messianic claim of Jesus seemed to be blasphemous to the high priest only because he regarded it as false and thus construed it as blasphemous presumption.[131] But how did

125. Ibid., pp. 182ff. This thesis does not seem to agree with the statement quoted in n. 124 that only in the light of the cross does the title take on its Christian sense and come to be linked to the name of Jesus. But we do have to consider that Jesus might have revised the title himself and given it a new interpretation before the entry into Jerusalem.

126. See Hahn, Titles, pp. 155ff., and Sanders, Jesus and Judaism, pp. 296-308, esp. 297ff. on the problems raised by the Synoptic accounts of the hearings before Caiaphas.

127. Hahn, Titles, pp. 156f.; Sanders, Jesus and Judaism, p. 306. Sanders agrees that Jesus proclaimed himself a king (on the model of Zech. 9:9) at the entry, but not in a political sense (p. 307). This is doubtful. Jesus' message suggests rather that a sign was being given of the coming of the kingship of God.

128. Sanders, Jesus and Judaism, pp. 61-76. Whether the saying about the temple and the related symbolic action offer a decisive reason for handing over Jesus to the Romans on a charge of revolt (as a messianic pretender), as Sanders suggests, is very doubtful because it does not agree with the emphatic statement of Mark and Matthew that although the saying played a part in the hearing before Caiaphas, it was not the reason for the verdict (Mark 14:55-60). Sanders himself notes this (p. 297). Even if we have doubts about the historical accuracy of the Gospel accounts, we cannot rule out the possibility that the Evangelists were rightly informed about the role of the threat against the temple in accusations against Jesus. Or did they play down or suppress the significance of this point? But what reason would they have to do so, especially after A.D. 70?

129. Sanders, Jesus and Judaism, p. 297, and D. R. Catchpole, "The Answer of Jesus to Caiaphas (Matt. xxvi, 64)," NT Studies 17 (1971) 213-26.

130. Sanders, Jesus and Judaism, pp. 298 and 55.

131. Moltmann, The Way of Jesus Christ, pp. 161f. There is certainly no messianic equation with Almighty God himself (p. 162) because messiahship did not involve this. John 10:33 contains the accusation that Jesus was making himself equal to God, but not in connection with the question of messiahship. There is thus no basis for Moltmann's combining this verse with Mark 14:61f.

Caiaphas arrive at this conclusion?[132] The only sure point is that Jesus was handed over to the Romans for judgment as a messianic pretender and therefore as a rebel. But it is equally clear that this was a pretext behind which there were other matters that made him unacceptable to the Jewish authorities, though the accounts of the proceedings do not make it wholly clear what these were.[133]

The early Christian confession of Jesus as Messiah corresponds to his pre-Easter ministry precisely in the fact that the mission of Jesus was primarily to God's people of the old covenant. We cannot detach his specific mission from the people of Israel, to whom he brought the message of the imminence of the rule and righteousness of God. This mission had a messianic character, of course, only as a renewing and deepening of the relation of Israel to its God, not as a restoration of its political independence, and certainly not as an establishment of its supremacy among the nations. For this reason the handing over of Jesus to the Romans as a messianic pretender rested on a calumny. But because his condemnation as such attached the messianic title to him, and because there was no place left for any other Messiah after God had confirmed his earthly ministry by raising him from the dead, for the disciples the messianic hope of Israel fused with the picture of the suffering and crucified Son of God.[134] This meant that Israel could have no other Messiah beside him. Not under the sign of political power and messianic rule over the nations, but by faith in the Crucified, the nations, wherever the gospel of Jesus Christ is proclaimed and accepted, will come to worship the God of Israel as the one and only God.

When Israel in the course of its history had constantly been forced to play the part of the Suffering Servant of Isa. 53 in order to witness thus to its God among the nations, why could it not recognize itself again in the picture of the crucified Messiah? Perhaps the content of Jewish messianic expectation provides us with an answer to this question. The messianic hope was oriented to an overcoming of the experience of suffering. It came into association with periods of political

132. Moltmann (ibid., p. 162) agrees with Betz that it is hard to answer this question.

133. Earlier Moltmann himself argued along these lines. In *The Crucified God* he thought we should seek the real reason for the attitude of the Jewish authorities in Jesus' criticism of the law and the implied claiming of plenipotentiary authority.

134. Cf. Kramer, *Christ, Lord, Son of God,* pp. 19-64, for a searching inquiry into pre-Pauline and Pauline usage under the impress of the linking of the title "Christ" to Jesus' crucifixion and resurrection.

revival and independence such as the Zealots were seeking in the days of Jesus. At the same time, as Christians have contributed to the long history of Jewish pogroms, they have not made it easy for the Jewish people to see their Messiah in the crucified Jesus whom Christians worship. In both sections of the one people of God, a temptation to triumphalism has thus stood in the way of reconciliation under the sign of the Crucified.

By depicting Jesus as the new eschatological Adam, and therefore as the definitive form of humanity, the apostle Paul has given expression to the universal significance of the person and history of Jesus in the light of the Easter event — a significance that reaches far beyond the people of Israel. He did not use the concept of the Messiah to achieve this end. In terms of the Jewish tradition he probably found this title too closely linked to the special and particularist hopes of the Jewish people, and especially to their political expectations. For this reason it was not adapted to serve as the symbol of a hope that extends to all people and unites all nations — a hope that he saw to be grounded in the cross and resurrection of Jesus. Nevertheless, he retained the link between the name of Jesus and the title "Christ" (Rom. 5:17, cf. v. 15). This link to the crucified and risen Lord changed the meaning of the title itself, and only thus did it acquire the relation to the whole of the human race that Schleiermacher ascribed to it.[135] As the Messiah who does not exercise dominion through political power but through his vicarious suffering for human sins, Jesus not only changed the Jewish hope in the consciousness of his disciples but also opened it up with a view to the reconciliation of the Gentile world with Israel and its God.

c. The Manifestation of the Son and Human Fellowship

Jesus of Nazareth, the crucified and risen Lord, manifested himself to his disciples as the Christ of God who fulfilled Israel's hope of salvation by altering and extending it through what befell him. As the Messiah of Israel, then, he is also the eschatological new man, the definitive form of humanity that corresponds to the will of God, to our divine orientation by creation to relationship with God. According to 1 Cor. 15:22, 45ff. Jesus Christ as he who is risen from the dead is this final man; by the Spirit he

135. *Christian Faith*, § 94.2.

is filled and transfigured by God's incorruptible life. According to Rom. 5:12ff., he is the new man and he who was obedient to God in his suffering and death (5:19). The two aspects go together, and Paul expressed their unity by describing Jesus as the Son. His resurrection from the dead proved Jesus to be the Son and publicly instituted him as such (1:4). But he was the Son already as he was given up to death for our reconciliation with God (5:10; 8:32), i.e., on the path of his earthly obedience to the Father (5:19).

Hebrews puts it even more clearly: "Although he was a Son, he learned obedience through what he suffered, and being made perfect, he became the source of eternal salvation to all who are related to him in obedience" (5:8f.). The first statement should not be seen as contrasting filial closeness to the Father with obedience to him. Rather, it gives expression to the tension between learning obedience in time and pretemporal sonship. At any rate, the status of sonship and obedience to the Father go together. Obedient subordination to the Father characterizes Jesus as the Son. As Paul puts it, he lets himself be guided by the Spirit of God (Rom. 8:14). His obedience, then, is not the alien obedience of the slave. It is an expression of his free agreement with the Father. By this Spirit, he has in himself the eternal life that shows him to be the living and incorruptible Christ in his resurrection from the dead.

We have emphasized above (see pp. 301f.) that what is said about the sending of the Son in both Paul and John relates to the whole history of Jesus and not just to the event of his birth. Precisely because the totality of the history of Jesus is an expression of his sending, his birth can also be included in the statement (Gal. 4:4f.; cf. Rom. 8:3). But how exactly are we to describe the event of the sending of the Son — the event of his incarnation — in this comprehensive sense?

As we shall show more precisely in chapter 10, section 2, the idea of the sending of the Son presupposes his preexistence, his being in the eternity of God in correspondence with the eternity of the Father. This eternal being of the Son, one may say, finds manifestation in the history of Jesus Christ[136] as the eternal relation of the Son to the Father takes human shape in this history. We do not have here one example of this basic relationship among many others. Only here does the basic relationship find actualization in such a way that we then perceive it in other

---

136. On the more exact meaning of this concept, cf. my "Erscheinung als Ankunft des Zukünftigen," in *Theologie und Reich Gottes* (1971), pp. 79ff., esp. 83ff.

human examples, albeit in what is in many ways a broken and distorted form. If this were not so, we could not present the filial relationship of Jesus to the Father as the basic form of our human destiny of fellowship with God. But if this destiny is manifest in the person and history of Jesus, then precisely because he is the Son, we can call Jesus Christ the new eschatological man.

As a prefiguration of the incarnation of the Son of God in Jesus Christ, the basic filial relationship finds intimation in the history of Israel when the Judean king is called God's son in Nathan's promise to David (2 Sam. 7:14; cf. Ps. 89:26f.), in the formula of legitimation and enthronement in Ps. 2:7, and especially in extensions of the designation to the whole of the covenant people as we find it in the concepts of the exodus tradition (Hos. 11:1; Jer. 31:9, 20; cf. 3:19; Exod. 4:22). All members of the people could be called the children of God, his sons or daughters (Deut. 14:1; Isa. 43:6; 45:11), even apostates (Deut. 32:5, 19f.). Paul's use of this term for Christians (Rom. 8:16; Gal. 4:5f.) is not, then, something totally new in relation to the tradition of Israel's faith.[137] The new thing is simply the inclusion of non-Jews in the filial relation and the linking of the relation to the gift of the Spirit (Rom. 8:14) and to fellowship with Jesus Christ, *the* Son, through whom believers receive the Spirit of sonship (Rom. 8:15; Gal. 4:6). Only in Jesus Christ has the basic filial relationship for which we are destined come to full and definitive manifestation. In him the eternal Son of God has become flesh.

According to the biblical testimonies, it was the Spirit who mediated the taking shape of the divine Son in the person of Jesus, and it is by the Spirit or in connection with his imparting (Gal. 4:6) that believers receive a share in the sonship of Jesus Christ. By the Spirit, in his resurrection from the dead, Jesus Christ has been instituted into authority as the Son (Rom. 1:4). With the reception of the Spirit at his baptism by John came also a declaration of his divine sonship (Mark 1:10f. par.). In the power of the Spirit he was the Son of God already from his birth.

This is the special point of the Lucan account of his birth by the Spirit (Luke 1:32, 35f.).[138] It is only for the sake of this christological concern that the narrative has

---

137. On the use in postexilic Judaism, cf. Hengel, *Son of God*, 41ff.

138. To supplement what follows, and especially patristic and modern theological discussion of the virgin birth, cf. *Jesus — God and Man*, pp. 141-50, and Moltmann's excellent contribution "Christ's Birth in the Spirit," in *The Way of Jesus Christ*, pp. 78-87.

so much to say about Mary. Because Jesus Christ is the Son of God in person and therefore from his very birth, Mary is rightly honored as the "mother of God," as the Council of Ephesus (431) correctly decided (cf. DS § 251 = ND § 605). In this one statement about Mary that became ecumenically binding, the focus is not on the person of Mary as such (as in the Marian dogmas of Roman Catholicism in 1854 and 1950) but on confirmation of the belief in the incarnation of the Son of God. The dignity of Mary as *theotokos* remains unaffected by historical investigations of the infancy stories and their findings, and especially by the thesis that the accounts in Luke and Matthew are legendary.[139]

In the older version of the tradition that underlies Luke, we find a basis for the account in the angelic saying to Mary (1:35) that her promised Son, in virtue of his conception in the power of the divine Spirit with no male participation, will be called the Son of God. Here the title and its link to the person of Jesus are presupposed already, and the story of his conception and birth explains why he is called the Son of God. Even though rumors circulated by opponents regarding the strange circumstances of the origin and birth of Jesus might have played a part in the development of the story,[140] the relevant findings do not permit us to insist on the historical facticity of the virginity of Mary after the conception and birth of Jesus, at least in a medical sense. If we try to make this the real theme of the story of the birth of Jesus (cf. Isa. 7:14 LXX), we are false to the purpose of the narrative. Gynecology is not the issue, but Christian pneumatology.[141] If the story as a whole is legendary, we have to interpret the details in terms of the christological aim and not as facts isolated from the context or from the general interpretative frame. The case is different if historical facticity is at issue, as in the case of the statements about the resurrection in 1 Cor. 15:3ff.

The reason for critical evaluations of the historical facticity of the virgin birth of Jesus is not the philosophical difficulty of regarding such as event as possible but the apparently legendary nature of the narrative. In any case, however, the narrative is not meaningless. It must be approached from other angles. In the

---

139. Cf. M. Dibelius, *Jungfrauensohn und Krippenkind* (1932), and R. E. Brown, *The Birth of the Messiah: A Commentary on the Infancy Narratives in Matthew and Luke* (New York, 1977), esp. pp. 298-309 and 517-33. In principle Brown follows the literary interpretation that Dibelius in particular developed (pp. 307-9). He states, however, that "one must explain why the christology of divine sonship, when it was associated with Jesus' birth, found expression in terms of a virginal conception" (p. 308, n. 36). By way of explanation, Brown suggests some general knowledge of a premature birth that led Jewish opponents of the Christian community to argue that Jesus was illegitimate. The Christian narratives, then, were meant to lay to rest such suspicions (pp. 526f.).

140. Brown, *The Birth of the Messiah,* pp. 534-43, cf. 530.

141. Moltmann, *The Way of Jesus Christ,* p. 78. Cf. also H. Stirnimann, *Marjam. Marienrede an einer Wende* (1989), pp. 210-60, esp. 211ff. According to Stirnimann, the story in the Protevangelium of James 18-20 has the function of warding off interest in physical proofs of the virginity of the mother of Jesus (pp. 231ff.).

background is the topological relation to the Greek rendering of Isa. 7:14. This provided the key word "virgin" as distinct from the "young woman" of the original. In the story the virginity of Mary in her meeting with the angel is a poetic means to depict the proper human attitude of humble reception when the reality of God comes into one's life. It is also an expression of the exclusiveness of commitment to the one God. This is how the Mary of the Lucan story has been depicted in innumerable gripping pictures. Along these lines Luther lauded her as a model of faith.[142] She anticipates the obedience of her Son to his heavenly Father, and in this sense it may be said that in her reaction to the angel's message the Son takes human form, i.e., as regards his relation to his heavenly Father. Essentially this spiritual reality is not dependent on whether there was male participation or not in the conception of the boy Jesus. It is enough on its own, however, to induce all Christians to show loving and reverent regard for Mary as the *theotokos*. Christ is to achieve form in the life of every Christian as in that of her Jesus (Gal. 4:19).

The incarnation of the Son in the figure of Jesus means that this man is the Son of God in person and that he was so throughout his life. As in general we cannot separate the person from the history of a person — only in one's history does the personal identity take shape that gives ongoing distinctiveness to the one whose history is then recounted[143] — so it is with the person of Jesus as the Son of God. The Easter event definitively decided the personal identity of Jesus as the Son of God, but in the light of that event he was the Son of God from the very beginning of his earthly course, and even from eternity (see above, pp. 302f.).

From the standpoint of the eternal Son his identification with the person of Jesus has the form of incarnation. We must not see this, however, as an accidental happening that is external to his eternal essence. It is logically related to his trinitarian self-distinction from the Father. As the free self-distinction of the Son from the Father is the basis of the possibility of all the creaturely reality that is distinct from God, it is also the origin of the incarnation of the Son in Jesus of Nazareth. This is the sense in which we are to understand the self-emptying and self-humbling of the eternal Son of God in the event of his incarnation (Phil. 2:7f.). If we see

---

142. WA, 7, 544-604, *Das Magnificat Vorteutschet und ausgelegt* (1521, LW, 21, 297ff.). H. Räisänen, *Die Mutter Jesu im NT* (1969), p. 154, calls Luke's Mary a kind of prototype of the Christian (cf. pp. 93 and 149ff.).

143. The "retroactive" constitution of the earlier in light of what happened later applies especially to the identity of the person. Moltmann missed this point in my discussion of the significance of the Easter event for the identity of Jesus as a person (*The Crucified God*, p. 182).

here a partial or total renunciation of his divine nature, we not only dissolve the eternal self-identity of God but destroy the concept of incarnation, which is to the effect that the eternal God himself has taken the living form of a mortal man.[144] The self-emptying and self-humbling that we find when we compare the eternal deity of the Son to his incarnation must not be seen as a limitation but as an expression of the eternal deity. But this is possible only if we understand it in relation to the eternal self-distinction of the Son as the basis of the possibility and reality of creaturely existence in general. The eternal self-distinction from the Father contains already the element of self-emptying. It is precisely thus that the Son became the origin of the difference of a creaturely existence that is distinct from God.

In the sheer difference of creatures from God, however, the self-distinction of the Son finds expression only in a one-sided form, that of difference, not as a medium of fellowship with God. Only in a creature which like us humans knows that it is related to God in the distinction can the self-emptying that goes with the Son's self-distinction from the Father come fully to expression in the form of creaturely existence. In this sense we must view the emptying and humbling of the eternal Son that go with the incarnation as an element in the free self-fulfillment of the Son in self-distinction from the Father. By this self-fulfillment of filial being the destiny of the creature for true independence in fellowship with God is also realized and we are liberated from the confusion of autonomy over against God and the resultant subjection to the power of corruptibility and death.

In the sending of the Son for incarnation in the one man Jesus, the concern is thus with others too. God sent his Son into the world to save it (John 3:17; cf. 6:38f.). The goal of the sending of the Son, then, is to be found in others. According to John, the goal is reached with the proclamation of Jesus, while according to Paul (Rom. 8:3 and Gal. 4:4f.) there is a special link to the death of Jesus by which believers are liberated

144. Still instructive in this regard is I. A. Dorner's criticism of 19th-century Lutheran kenosis teachings in "Über die richtige Fassung des dogmatischen Begriffs der Unveränderlichkeit Gottes," in *Gesammelte Schriften aus dem Gebiet der systematischen Theologie, Exegese und Geschichte* (1883), pp. 188-377, esp. 208-41. Dorner called the underlying thought in these teachings a doctrine of "depotencing" (p. 213, cf. 233ff.). On the origin of the criticism in his correspondence in 1842-45 with H. L. Martensen on Christ's person, cf. C. Axt-Piscalar, *Der Grund des Glaubens. Eine theologiegeschichtliche Untersuchung zum Verhältnis von Glaube und Trinität in der Theologie Isaak August Dorners* (Tübingen, 1990), p. 224 n. 78 and 225ff.

from the dominion of sin, the law, and death. Thus the sending of the Son aims at the reconciliation to God of the world, i.e., of the human world, and by this of all creation. The claim of Christian proclamation that this took place in the history of Jesus needs fuller exposition and demonstration, however, if it is to hold good. This will be our task in the two chapters that follow. For the moment we may provisionally take note of the connection between the sending of the Son to save us and the function of the Messiah relative to the fellowship and renewal of the people of God. These have their counterpart in the saving work of the obedience of the second Adam on behalf of the many (Rom. 5:12ff.). This connection does not merely point to the identity of Christ as the Son of God and the new Adam. It also shows us how far Jesus Christ has given universal relevance to the story of Israel's election and the tradition of Jewish faith.

It has been said already that in Paul the thought of the divine sonship of Jesus combines the primitive Christian confession of the messiahship of Jesus with statements regarding the eschatological form of humanity that reach out beyond the tradition of Jewish faith and claim universal relevance for the history of Jesus. Decisive in this regard was the revision of Jewish messianic expectation by the linking of the concept of the Messiah to the person of the Crucified. In this way the nationalist and particularist limitation of the Jewish hope to the Messiah as the "son" of God (Ps. 2:7) who would exercise divine dominion of earth was transcended, thus freeing messianic expectation from restriction.

Similarly the universal relevance of the Jewish tradition of divine justice was freed from ties to the historically contingent features of the Mosaic law that apply to the Jewish people as part of its historical identity. For not only Paul but primitive Christianity as a whole — after initial hesitation on the part of the Jerusalem community — understood the cross of Jesus Christ as the end of the Mosaic law, at least as it separated Jews and Gentiles, though not at the expense of abandoning the righteous will of God, to which the law bears witness. This process is closely linked to the liberation of the messianic idea from all restriction. By its very origin this idea goes hand in hand with divine justice and the involved function of the messianic king in the righteous community. In the Isaianic tradition especially the monarchy was seen as having the function of establishing the law of God. In Isa. 11:2ff. the messianic hope was oriented to a future king who would truly do justice to this task, who would establish right and peace, and who would thus make Zion a focal point for the nations along the lines of Isa. 2:2-4 (cf. also Zech. 9:9f.).

In the link between messianic expectation and divine law, the latter was the central theme for the faith of Israel. The messianic hope stood in the service of the actualizing of divine law. But this law and its actualization were very closely connected with the election of Israel. Israel's election was the basis of its commitment to divine justice, as we see clearly in Deut. 4:37-40 (cf. 7:11). In the broad conception of Isa. 42:1f. (cf. 42:6), the aim of the election of Israel was that it should proclaim the righteous will of God to the nations. On this view the election of Israel is not an end in itself. It serves the will of God on behalf of the human race as a whole. One might say that it serves the kingdom of God in the world, for the rule of God for which Israel waits was a rule of right and righteousness. This was what Isaiah and Micah foresaw in their visionary picture of a future pilgrimage of the nations to Zion so that the God of Israel might end their conflicts by telling them what is right (Mic. 4:2f.; Isa. 2:3f.).

It is the more regrettable, then, that the law of God as it was preserved in the legal traditions of Israel and observed in Jewish practice should become a sign of difference and separation between Israel and the Gentiles. How we are to understand this process we shall discuss more fully in a later context. The result, however, was the very opposite of the summons to Israel in Isa. 42:1f. to be a witness to the righteous will of God among the nations. Did not a witness of this kind demand that the content of the righteous will of God should be universally binding and not just involve a Jewish particularity sanctified by the authority of the tradition? In such a case does not the establishment of divine right by the Messiah have to begin with a liberation of its content from nationalistic restrictions and the opening up of its binding core for all people? The next chapter will show that this is precisely what took place in Jesus' exposition of the law.

With his exposition of the traditional law of God, Jesus was not contesting the obligatoriness of this law in the faith of Israel. He expounded the traditional law of God in the light of the future of God, who is the Creator of all of us. In the relation of all of us to the one God, all our legal relations have the basis of their validity. Thus our individual destiny for fellowship with the one God goes hand in hand with the preservation and promotion of fellowship among us as this takes lasting shape in legal relations. We cannot work out our destiny of fellowship with God in the isolation of a purely individual relation to God, nor can we work out our destiny for life in fellowship and peace without God. The attempt is often made, but the result has always been the distortion of fellowship by the rule of some over others. The link between fellowship with God and human fellowship forms the central content of Israel's witness among the nations and the basis of the universal relevance of its faith tradition. This universally valid content of Jewish faith traditions, however, lies hidden under encrustations related to the history of their development and exposition. Jesus' exposition of the law broke them free from these encrustations. This is what constitutes its messianic character, though the appearing of Jesus did not meet the messianic hopes and ideas of the people, especially its political expectations.

Jesus criticized the traditions. He did not prove to be the hoped-for political liberator. He thus met with opposition, which finally led to his arrest and execution, as we shall see in more detail in the next chapter. But the end of his earthly career accomplished the liberation of the messianic hope of Israel, which typifies his ministry in the light of his exposition of the law. In chapter 11 we shall see that this was the content of the reconciliation of the world by his death. Having freed the exposition of the law, and also Jewish messianic hope, by relating the messianic idea to the cross, the risen Lord could show himself to be the Messiah not merely of the Jews but of all people, the Son of God who wills to unite all people to himself, and through himself to God, after the image of the new eschatological man that is manifested in him.

CHAPTER 10

The Deity of Jesus Christ

The issue in the question of the deity of Jesus Christ is the deity of the man Jesus. We are not dealing, then, with the divine nature considered in isolation. We must discover the contours of the divine sonship of Jesus in his human reality, which as eternal sonship precedes his historical existence on earth and must be regarded as the creative basis of his human existence. If the human history of Jesus is the revelation of his eternal sonship, we must be able to perceive the latter in the reality of the human life. The deity is not an addition to this reality. It is the reflection that the human relation of Jesus to God the Father casts on his existence, even as it also illumines the eternal being of God. Conversely, the assuming of human existence by the eternal Son is not to be seen as the adding of a nature that is alien to his deity. It is the self-created medium of his extreme self-actualization in consequence of his free self-distinction from the Father, i.e., a way of fulfilling his eternal sonship. It is this precisely because in it he has left the sphere of deity in order that in the medium of creaturely existence, he might be bound to the Father as the one God in his self-distinction from him, and that he thus might fulfill our human destiny as creatures and deliver us from the confusion of sin.

§ 1. Reasons for Maintaining the Unity of Jesus with God

The question of the deity of Jesus, of the relation of the reality of his earthly life to the eternal God, is falsely put if we view the relation solely or even primarily as the fellowship of his human nature with the eternal Son. For the man Jesus, God was there only in the person of the heavenly Father, to whom he knew he was related in his whole existence and by whose Spirit he let himself be guided. Only by way of the relation of Jesus to the Father can we decide how and in what sense he himself may be understood to partake of deity, namely, as the Son of this Father.

a. The Relationship of Jesus to the Father in His Public Ministry

We first begin to see the uniqueness of Jesus as man in the way in which the human relation to God, or the rule of God in human life, was the dominant theme of his life. This is true first of his public proclamation, which he seems to have undertaken only after the imprisonment of John the Baptist.[1] The central thought of this proclamation was the imminence of the divine rule.

Jesus shared expectation of the rule of God with his people's tradition. From the time of Hellenism the hope of an establishment of the royal rule of God over the nations (Ps. 96:10ff.; cf. Isa. 52:7) had taken on eschatological features (Ps. 97:1ff.).[2] God's own coming to rule the world was predicted in Daniel (2:44ff.) as the putting to an end of the sequence of human empires. The apocalyptic Assumption of Moses associated the royal rule of God with the last judgment of all creation (Ass. Mos. 10:1ff.). In general, however, the idea of the divine rule is comparatively rare in apocalyptic. To the fore are notions of the coming of a new aeon, of world judgment, and of the coming of the Son of Man to judgment. To describe coming eschatological events, however, Jesus preferred the hope of the rule of God as we find it expressed in the Jewish Eighteen Benedictions (11th benediction) and the Qaddish Prayer.[3]

There is a difference here from John the Baptist's message of judgment, with which Jesus started and which he retained in the conviction

1. On Mark 1:14, cf. J. Becker, *Johannes der Täufer und Jesus von Nazareth* (1972), pp. 14f.

2. J. Jeremias, *Das Königtum Gottes in den Psalmen* (Göttingen, 1987), pp. 136ff., cf. 121ff. on Ps. 96. Cf. also H. Merklein, *Jesu Botschaft von der Gottesherrschaft. Eine Skizze* (Stuttgart, 1983), pp. 24f., 39ff.

3. H. Leroy, *Jesus. Überlieferung und Deutung* (1978), p. 71. On the coming of the kingdom of God, as distinct from its establishment, cf. N. Perrin, *Rediscovering the Teaching of Jesus* (New York, 1967), pp. 57ff.

that the future of God did not tally with trust in past ideas of salvation. The work of the Baptist, like that of Jesus, focused wholly on the future of God. The Baptist, however, found the content in the imminence of judgment, whereas for Jesus the content of God's future lay in the coming of his rule.[4] For this reason, in distinction from that of the Baptist and in spite of the break with Israel's past, the message of Jesus was essentially one of salvation. This fact found symbolic expression in his return from the desert of the Lower Jordan, where John had taught, to the fertile settlements of Galilee.

Throughout its history Israel's hope of God's own royal rule was motivated by the expectation that its establishment would free the covenant people from foreign domination and thus bring peace and salvation (Isa. 52:7). But according to the prophetic verdict, proclaimed by the Baptist and the Qumran Teacher as well as Jesus, that the people had come under judgment, it was no longer self-evident that the coming of God's rule would mean salvation for Israel as distinct from the Gentiles.[5] Jesus himself did not preach the coming of God's rule as salvation for the covenant people as a whole (on the basis of its covenant relation to God), but as salvation only for those who set their hope wholly on the imminence of the future of God, whether in response to the appeal of his own message or for some other reason, as in the case of those whom he called blessed. For these people the salvation of God's rule was already present and at work. A closer understanding of this complex matter leads us to the very heart of Jesus' message.

We misunderstand this message if at this point, as often happens, we think it enough to say that the inaugurating of present participation in the future salvation of God's rule by Jesus was an expression of the sense of authority that filled him. We should not contest the fact of this sense of authority, regardless of the associated problems that will give us reason to explore it later. But it is of far-reaching significance for an understanding of Jesus and for christology as a whole that this sense of authority was not the basis of the content of his proclamation. On the contrary, it was its consequence or accompaniment. Why this is so we

---

4. Becker, *Johannes der Täufer und Jesus von Nazareth*, pp. 74f. In Matt. 3:2, however, note that the imminence of God's rule is the basis of the Baptist's summons to repentance. This statement blunts the essential point of difference between Jesus and the Baptist (p. 13). On the break with the past in the Baptist, cf. pp. 16ff., in Jesus, 71f. Cf. also the comparison in J. Jeremias, *Die Verkündigung Jesu, Neutestamentliche Theologie,* I (1971, 2nd ed. 1973), p. 56.

5. Merklein, *Jesu Botschaft,* pp. 43f.

shall explain more fully below. But first we should try to see the promise and the event of present participation in salvation, in its relation to the proclamation and work of Jesus, in terms of the content of his message, i.e., in terms of the meaning of his intimation of the rule of God. Arriving at an understanding of this kind is linked to a solving of the much-debated question as to the relation between the future and the present of the rule of God in the proclamation of Jesus.

Unquestionably Jesus referred to the rule of God as coming or future. We may simply adduce the second petition of the Lord's Prayer (Matt. 6:10) in analogy to the daily prayers of Judaism. The common reference to achieving or entering the kingdom (Matt. 5:20; 7:21; Mark 9:33 par.; 10:23f. par.) also has a future sense, referring to participation in the future fellowship of salvation, as J. Weiss has emphasized.[6] The reference to future table fellowship in the kingdom of God (Matt. 8:11; Luke 13:29f.) at festival meals also played implicitly a determinative role to the degree that the meals represented the (future) fellowship of the kingdom and offered advance assurance of participation in its salvation. In Mark 14:25 there is another plain reference to the future meal in the kingdom of God. In many other places where there are no express references to God's future rule, future sayings belong materially to the same context, e.g., the sayings about the future of the Son of Man, whom Matt. 25:34 can call a king. Thus the judgment of Weiss still stands today that both in number and in substance, the future sayings predominate.[7]

The only question is how the less common sayings that speak of God's rule as present relate to the future sayings. The only express statements that the rule of God is present are in Luke 11:20 par. and Luke 17:20. Materially, of course, Luke 10:23f. is to the same effect as 17:20. We may also refer to Jesus' answer to the question the Baptist put to him from prison (7:22 par.) or to Mark 2:19. All such sayings seem to say, as Bultmann cautiously puts it, that the rule of God may not be present but is dawning.[8]

E. Käsemann went further and claimed that we must infer from Matt. 11:12f. that the change of aeons has already come with John the Baptist, that the rule of God has broken in but still faces opposition.[9] Käsemann's view has commanded much agreement.[10] Yet it would be a mistake to make a single, notoriously

6. J. Weiss, *Die Predigt Jesu vom Reiche Gottes* (1892, 2nd ed. 1900, newly ed. by F. Hahn, 1964), pp. 72f.

7. Ibid., p. 71. Cf. E. P. Sanders, *Jesus and Judaism* (Philadelphia, 1985), p. 132.

8. R. Bultmann, *Theology of the NT* (New York, 1951), p. 7.

9. E. Käsemann, "The Problem of the Historical Jesus," in *Essays on NT Themes* (London, 1965), p. 43.

10. Cf. Perrin, *Rediscovering*, p. 76; cf. also Jeremias, *Verkündigung*, pp. 54f.

obscure, and puzzling saying the basis of a thesis that diminishes the plain statements about the future of the divine rule.[11] One-sided emphasis on the presence of the *basileia,* as though the decisive turn had already come, has thus come under justifiable criticism.[12] We must not see statements about the presence of the kingdom as alternatives to the idea of its future coming. The reference is to the inbreaking of the future of God, but we must understand this future itself as the dynamic basis of its becoming present.[13]

The starting point for understanding the breaking into the present of God's future must be this future itself. Do we have here a basis on which to understand, in the ministry of Jesus, the entry of the future of God into the present of his hearers? Luke 11:20 might seem to indicate that his exorcisms were decisive in this regard. Yet Jesus did not simply work as an exorcist.[14] Furthermore, other relevant sayings such as Luke 17:20 refer to the appearance and work of Jesus more generally. Again, the ministry of Jesus in all its aspects was oriented to the call that we should commit ourselves totally to the rule of God that he declared to be imminent: "Seek first his kingdom and his righteousness, and all these things shall be yours as well" (Matt. 6:33; cf. Luke 12:31). In many sayings Jesus gives the imminent rule of God priority over all other human duties and concerns (cf. Luke 9:62). This is the point of the two short parables of the merchant and the pearl and the treasure in the field (Matt. 13:44-46). What is the basis of this priority?

It would seem to be very closely related to the first commandment

11. Cf. Perrin on the second petition of the Lord's Prayer as a petition for the continuation of something that the disciples have already experienced (*Rediscovering,* pp. 160f.).

12. Sanders, *Jesus and Judaism,* pp. 129-56, esp. 150ff. In discussing Luke 11:20, Sanders thus inclines to make the present aspect too questionable (pp. 133ff.). It is merely possible or even conceivable (p. 140). Weiss had already pointed out how hard it is to distinguish clearly between *ephtasen* and *ēngiken* for the imminent coming of the kingdom (*Die Predigt Jesu,* p. 70), but only to support this thesis that the future coming and the present inbreaking are not contradictory (pp. 69f.). On the present inbreaking of God's rule and similar (if more cultically oriented) ideas at Qumran, cf. H.-W. Kuhn, *Enderwartung und gegenwärtiges Heil. Untersuchungen zu den Gemeindeliedern von Qumran mit einem Anhang über Eschatologie und Gegenwart in der Verkündigung Jesu* (Göttingen, 1966), pp. 189-204.

13. The related inverting of the usual view of the future as an outworking of the present helps us to understand why it is hard to state this matter more precisely, as we see in Merklein, *Jesu Botschaft,* p. 65 (cf. p. 68, etc.). Trying to combine the two German words *Geschehen* and *Ereignis* into *Geschehensereignis* is no help, for the former means no more and no less than the latter, so that combining them adds nothing.

14. So rightly Sanders, *Jesus and Judaism,* p. 135.

(Exod. 20:3) and the uniqueness of Yahweh that this proclaims. Possibly this commandment was the motivating force behind the development of the thought of Yahweh's royal rule in ancient Israel, along with the associated concept of the holy jealousy of the God of Israel.[15,16] This is especially true of the eschatological form of the notion as we find it in Zech. 14:9: "And the Lord will become king over all the earth; on that day the Lord will be one and his name one." The uniqueness of God, however, demands the undivided turning to him that is required in Deut. 6:4f.: "Hear, O Israel: The Lord our God is one Lord, and you shall love the Lord your God with all your heart, and with all your soul, and with all your might."

It is perhaps not without profound significance that in answer to the question of a scribe, Jesus called Deut. 6:4f. the first commandment rather than Exod. 20:3.[17] In it the basis of the demand made upon the people is not the saving act of the exodus but the uniqueness of Yahweh. Linked to this is an express requirement of total commitment to this God. The basic demand of Jesus was the same, namely, that we should seek first the kingdom of God (Matt. 6:33). The direct result is that the uniqueness of the God who comes to rule excludes all competing concerns. It also follows that to those who open themselves to this summons, God already comes with his rule.[18] The particular dynamic of Jesus' message of the *basileia*, then, is that the rule of God is imminent but that it also emerges from its futurity as present. The basis is that the oneness of God is the content of this future, and his rule is the outworking of his claim to the present life of the creature.

We can hardly rate too highly the bearing of this matter on an understanding of the message of Jesus. It shows that the supposed contradictions between what he says about the future of the *basileia* and its presence are groundless. It also tells us that in order to explain the presence

15. On Exod. 20:4; 34:14; Deut. 6:14f., cf. G. von Rad, *OT Theology*, 2 vols. (New York, 1962-65), I, 203ff.

16. Cf. W. H. Schmidt, "Die Frage nach der Einheit des Alten Testaments — im Spannungsfeld von Religionsgeschichte und Theologie," *Jahrbuch für biblische Theologie* 2 (1987) 33-57, esp. 52. Schmidt's translation is followed by a rendering of the verse in Zechariah, to which we refer in the next sentence.

17. Mark 12:29f.; Matt. 22:37f. (in Luke 10:26 the scribe gives the answer). I owe the insight into the difference between appeal to Deut. 6:4f. and Exod. 20:3 to a joint seminar with H.-W. Kuhn in the summer of 1989.

18. Cf. H. Merklein, "Die Einzigkeit Gottes als die sachliche Grundlage der Botschaft Jesu," *Jahrbuch für biblische Theologie* 2 (1987) 13-32, esp. 24. Merklein rightly calls it surprising that hardly ever is the question raised as to the theological possibility of Jesus' statements about the eschatological present. The question is not put because it is taken for granted that we must refer here to Jesus' sense of authority.

of the future of God, we do not have to have recourse to Jesus' supposed sense of intrinsic authority. Transition from the future to the present arises out of the matter itself, out of the content of the proclamation of Jesus, out of the claim of the oneness of God upon the present of the hearers.

From the presence of the rule of God in believers who open themselves to its coming along the lines of Deut. 6:4f. and subject themselves to its claim, it follows that thereby believers also participate already in eschatological salvation. To participate in the rule of God, to enter the kingdom, is the quintessence of eschatological salvation. According to the verdict of John the Baptist, the people of Israel had become an unsaved collective[19] that could no longer be certain of participation in the salvation of God's rule (Matt. 8:11f.) but stood under the threat of judgment. Yet to those who now live in the light of God's rule because they open themselves to its proximity, eschatological salvation is also present with this rule. Because the proximity is mediated by the message of Jesus, the time of his presence with his disciples is a time of eschatological joy (Mark 2:19 par.). By his participation table fellowship becomes an anticipation of the eschatological banquet in the kingdom of God.[20]

Although the whole people stands under threat of divine judgment, the message of the imminence of the rule of God opens up participation in eschatological salvation to individuals. In this fact Jesus himself sees a demonstration of the love of God that seeks the lost, in keeping with the goodness of the Creator, who causes his sun to shine on both the good and the bad (Matt. 5:45). This goodness of the Creator becomes saving love in the sending of Jesus to announce God's imminent rule. We see this in the parable of the shepherd seeking the lost sheep (Luke 15:4-7).[21] The point of this parable, as of the parables of the lost coin (vv. 8f.) and the prodigal son (vv. 11-32), is the joy of God ("in heaven," v. 7) at the saving of the lost.[22] Forgiving love that has reached its goal finds expression in this joy.

According to the introduction in Luke 15:1-3, the parables explain the attitude of Jesus to those who were religious (and social) outcasts, i.e.,

---

19. Merklein, *Jesu Botschaft*, pp. 33f., cf. 30.

20. Cf. the comprehensive discussion in Perrin, *Rediscovering*, pp. 102-8, esp. 107f.

21. On God as Shepherd on the one side, Jesus on the other, cf. H. Weder, *Die Gleichnisse Jesu als Metaphern* (Göttingen, 1978; 3rd ed. 1984), pp. 168ff., esp. 174f. Perrin, *Rediscovering*, pp. 97f., opts more decidedly for Jesus, not God.

22. In application of the parables, salvation means conversion (Luke 15:7, 10). Jesus did not teach participation without conversion. But his message did not begin with a demand for conversion. It began with the nearness of the kingdom, in receiving which the salvation is present that includes conversion.

the tax gatherers and sinners. They explain the inclusion of this group in the table fellowship, which guarantees participation in eschatological salvation (Mark 2:15 par.; cf. Matt. 11:19). By addressing this group, Jesus revealed the nature of the participation in salvation that his message of the nearness of God's rule effected in those who received it. The participation is from God himself, and it means in each case the rescuing of the lost. Those who accept the message are no longer outcasts. They share in the salvation of God's rule. The presence of salvation is also related to the removal of the barrier that separates from God. Forgiveness of sins and salvation are thus promised to the lame man who puts his trust in Jesus (Mark 2:5ff.). Scholars are divided on whether the isolated accounts of Jesus' promise of forgiveness to some individuals (cf. also Luke 7:47) actually belong to the historic ministry.[23] But there can be no doubt whatever that the presence of God's rule and participation in its salvation include remission of sins and overcoming of that which separates us from God.[24] The turning of Jesus to tax gatherers and sinners makes it abundantly clear that sinners are included in the saved community; the mention of table fellowship is the most striking expression of the message of the saving love of God.[25]

The love of God that is shown in the nearness of God's rule as present salvation mediated by the work of Jesus also helps us to understand the way in which Jesus interpreted the traditional law of God, or, more precisely, the way in which he gave it a new basis in his eschatological message. The fundamental thought was that those who open themselves to the summons of God's rule, who accept its imminence and thus receive present salvation, must also let themselves be drawn into the movement of the love of God as it aims beyond individual recipients to the world as a whole. We can have fellowship with God and his dominion only as we share in the movement of his love.

Jesus expressed this relation in a parable, for his parables explain different aspects of his message of the nearness of the divine rule.[26] In

---

23. Cf. H. Leroy in *EDNT*, I (1990), pp. 181-83. R. Bultmann's contesting of the authenticity of Mark 2:5 and Luke 7:48 in his *History of the Synoptic Tradition* (New York, 1972) has found much acceptance; cf. also, for Mark 2:5, P. Fiedler, *Jesus und die Sünder* (Frankfurt am Main, 1976), pp. 110f.

24. So rightly Jeremias, *Verkündigung*, pp. 115ff.

25. Ibid., p. 117.

26. Perrin, *Rediscovering*, pp. 186f., contra E. Jüngel, *Paulus und Jesus* (Tübingen, 1962; 3rd ed. 1967), pp. 135-74, who argues that the parables are the way in which the

this case the parable is that of the wicked servant (Matt. 18:22-35). Forgiveness received is related to the readiness to extend forgiveness to others. The fifth petition of the Lord's Prayer expresses the same thought (Luke 11:4; Matt. 6:14). We find it also more generally in the basing of love of enemies on the fatherly goodness of the Creator (Matt. 5:45f.; cf. Luke 5:35f.). Because fellowship with God along the lines of the love of God commanded in Deut. 6:4f. is possible only in connection with personal participation in the movement of God's love to the world, Jesus could directly link the command to love our neighbor (Lev. 19:18) with the love for God that is the supreme commandment (Mark 12:31 par.).

We find similar summaries of the law of God in rabbinic and other texts from the time of Jesus.[27] Jesus' exposition of the will of God is not materially different. We see this from the short dialogue with the scribe in Mark 12:32ff. The difference lies in the basis, for Jesus grounds the demand for love of neighbor, not in the authority of tradition, but in the goodness of the Creator and in the love of God that is manifest in the coming of the *basileia,* a love in which we can have a part only as we are ready to respond to it and to pass it on. The twofold command of love, then, is not just a summary of the main content of traditional law, a summary that presupposes the authority of tradition both as a whole and in detail. Instead, it stands over against tradition as a critical principle. This is why Jesus could say to the scribe, who in fact simply represented a different stage of the tradition as compared to the sacrificial system (Mark 12:33; cf. the prophetic tradition, 1 Sam. 15:22; Hos. 6:6), that he was not far from the kingdom of God (Mark 12:34). This is why he could also set his own "I say to you" over against the law of Moses (Matt. 5:22, 28, 32, 34, 39, 44). Of less significance is the extent to which the antitheses contradict the law or simply follow a line of exposition. The decisive point

---

coming rule of God breaks into the hearer's present. H. Weder in particular *(Die Gleichnisse Jesu)* has developed Jüngel's view. When Weder says, contra A. Jülicher and J. Jeremias, that the truth stated in parables cannot be put in any other way (p. 64), this is contrary to the fact that Jesus obviously did speak about the coming of the rule of God in other ways, which the parables presuppose. Though not all the parables have their origin in defense of the message of the imminence of the kingdom against critics, they still explain aspects of the message in various ways, e.g., the joy associated with its proximity (Perrin on Matt. 13:44-46), the need for decision (Luke 14:15-24; 16:1-13), trust in God (Luke 11:5ff.; 18:1ff.), patient waiting on God's future (Matt. 13), or the right answer to its summons (Luke 10:30-37; Matt. 18:23ff.; Luke 14:28f., 31f.).

27. For examples, cf. E. Lohmeyer, *Das Evangelium des Markus* (11th ed. 1951), pp. 259ff.

is that the authority of tradition no longer functions as the criterion, since in his eschatological message with its revelation of the love of God in the inbreaking of his rule, Jesus found a new basis for interpreting the law of God.

In so doing Jesus in fact claimed unheard of authority for his own person, even if his attitude, as we are trying to show, can be understood in terms of the content of his eschatological message. As he maintained that in his ministry the coming rule of God was present already to the salvation of those who received his message, he knew that he was not only in agreement with God but that he was also the mediator of the inbreaking of the rule and the forgiving love of God. With this awareness he was not afraid to oppose freely the tradition that was sanctified by God's revelation to Moses, trusting that in the process he was in harmony with the will of God. It is not surprising that in this regard he caused offense to devout Jews and that his person became the subject of violent controversies between adherents and opponents.

b. The Unity of Jesus with the Father as a Point of Contention in His History

If the appearance of Jesus and his intimation of the rule of God do not presuppose any claim to special authority for his person, they undoubtedly imply such a claim on account of the light that the content of his message shed on him personally. Jesus did not need to speak about himself or to relate his person to the concepts of Jewish eschatological expectation — his followers did that. He himself treated any such identifications with caution. There were good reasons for this caution, as we shall see.

Jesus could hardly identify himself as the Messiah, given the related political connotations that would necessarily have meant misunderstanding of his mission and message.[28] Like the Baptist, he seems to have distinguished the Son of Man as the future heavenly Judge from his own present appearing, though Luke 12:8 sees correspondence between future

28. Cf. O. Cullmann, *Christology of the NT* (Philadelphia, 1959), pp. 122f., on Mark 8:27ff. E. Dinkler made the point more sharply in his "Petrusbekenntnis und Satanswort," in *Signum Crucis. Aufsätze zum NT und zur christlichen Archäologie* (1967), pp. 293-312, esp. 286ff. Jeremias, *Verkündigung*, pp. 261f., also stressed the rejection of political messianic expectation by Jesus and even related this to the temptation in the wilderness (pp. 76f.). My own view is close to that of Merklein, *Jesu Botschaft*, pp. 146f.

judgment by the Son of Man and the present attitude taken to his person and message.[29] It also seems doubtful whether Jesus viewed himself as the Servant of the Lord along the lines of Isa. 53.[30] But whether he wanted it or not, his message of the imminence of the rule of God unavoidably brought his person into play. This was due above all to the claim that the eschatological salvation of the divine rule was breaking into the present for those that received his message. With this claim he presented himself as the mediator of that salvation. Inevitably, then, a suspicious half-light fell upon his own figure. Could any mere man make himself out to be the place of the presence of God? Did not this claim lack the humility due the God of Israel? The appearance of Jesus necessarily raised the suspicion that he was arrogating to himself the authority and power that in truth came to him only in reflection of his proclamation of God.

We now see how much depends on beginning with the content of the message rather than a supposed claim to authority if we are to understand the proclamation of Jesus. Those who regard his sense of authority as the root of his message and appearing share at bottom the view that caused his opponents to reject him. In the debate about the figure of Jesus it is of decisive importance that we should not put his person at the center. The center, rather, is God, the nearness of his rule, and his fatherly love. The content of the message of Jesus unavoidably implied that he would emerge as the bringer of salvation and the reason for eschatological decision. But there are indications that he himself was aware of the related ambivalence, as though he were allotting his person a position that Jewish faith could find blasphemous. Jesus seems to have tried to avoid equation with the figures associated with Israel's eschatological hope, especially the Messiah. But he could not avoid the ambivalence without abandoning his message of the nearness of the kingdom, which was already becoming present for those who received him.

This ambivalence that surrounds his coming helps us to understand the rejection he encountered, the offense taken at his person. Ac-

---

29. Cf. *Jesus — God and Man*, pp. 58ff.; also Merklein, *Jesu Botschaft*, pp. 152ff., 158ff. On the relation between John's message of the eschatological Judge (Luke 3:16f.) and the Son of Man, cf. Becker, *Johannes der Täufer und Jesus von Nazareth*, pp. 35ff.

30. Jeremias, *Verkündigung*, pp. 62 and 272ff. Jeremias did not maintain that Jesus equated himself with the Servant as a title. His point was that though Jesus spoke about the Son of Man in the third person (pp. 253ff.), he knew himself to be the future Son of Man because his claim to fulfillment ruled out the possibility of any other (p. 263). Cullmann, *Christology*, pp. 161ff., took a similar view.

cording to Mark, main points of tension were his table fellowship with tax collectors and sinners (Mark 2:16) and his claim that he could forgive sins in expression of the presence of the salvation of divine rule (2:5ff.). In both cases it is implied that with him and by him, the future of God's rule is already present, and it is this implication alone that makes explicable the charge of blasphemy (2:7), i.e., equating himself with God. Because of this ambivalence that accompanied his ministry, Jesus could call blessed those that did not take offense at him (Matt. 11:6; Luke 7:23 Q). It was indeed so easy to take offense. Related, perhaps, is the fact that according to Mark, Jesus tried to stop people from telling about his deeds or magnifying his person (Mark 1:43f.; 3:11f.; 5:43; 7:36; 8:27ff.). Since the days of W. Wrede it has been customary to trace these features to the Evangelists and to find in them the theory of a messianic secret that traces back the community's post-Easter knowledge of the majesty of Jesus to nonmessianic traditions of his earthly appearance.[31] Mark, however, refers to the regard that the work of Jesus evoked and that led to the post-Easter awareness of his divine sonship. Possibly the Gospel accounts contain traces of a traditional realization that Jesus was aware of the ambivalence into which his message thrust him and that he tried to counteract it.

In John especially this theme plays a major role. Jesus constantly must meet the objection that he is making himself God's equal. According to 5:17f., the charge rested on the intimacy with which he spoke of God as his Father. In 8:52f. there is outrage that with his eschatological message he sets himself above the authority of the fathers of Israel. "Who do you claim to be?" (v. 53) was the question hurled at him, and behind it stood the suspicion that he was a deceiver of the people (7:12). As the Evangelist records it, Jesus replied that his teaching was not his own but God's (7:16). This is wholly in keeping with what the Synoptists tell us. The accusation in 8:13 that he was bearing witness to himself and that his witness was not true is also in keeping with the Synoptic situation regarding his proclamation of the imminence of the rule of God, because the combining of its dawning with his own appearing made him the mediator of present salvation. For this reason Jesus could not simply repel the criticism in John. He could only appeal to the fact that he did not stand alone with his witness. Another, the Father, would also witness on his behalf (8:16ff.; cf. 5:32; 8:50; 14:24).

31. W. Wrede, *Das Messiasgeheimnis in den Evangelien* (1901, 3rd ed. 1963), pp. 62ff., 224ff.

The appearance of Jesus, then, involves a claim that needed divine confirmation in view of the controversy that it caused. The basic theme of his message — the imminent inbreaking of divine rule — needed confirmation by the intimated event itself. His message was thus in the same position as all that the prophets said in God's name (Deut. 8:21f.; cf. Jer. 28:9). When he claimed that the future rule of God would break in for those who accepted his message, the need for divine confirmation became the more pressing. We see this in his appeal to the coming judgment of the Son of Man, which would justify those who confess him and thus confirm his message (Luke 12:8f. par.).[32] In Jerusalem he would make a similar appeal before his Jewish judges (Luke 22:69).[33] To the charge that he was arrogantly claiming an authority that is properly God's alone, he could finally appeal only to the coming of the Son of Man or, as in John, to the Father's witness on his behalf. The Easter community then viewed the resurrection of Jesus as divine confirmation of the sending of the Crucified. During his earthly ministry, however, Jesus did not have this confirmation. Only as the eschatological events that he intimated came to pass could it be given. He might refer to the mighty acts accompanying his message (Matt. 11:5f.; Luke 11:20), but these could not offer unequivocal confirmation. This is why he blessed those who took no offense at him (Matt. 11:6).[34] According to the witness of John (also of Mark 2:7), his claim to unity with the Father, and to a present inbreaking of the divine rule for those who receive his message, met with the response of an accusation of blasphemy (John 10:3; cf. 19:7).

32. On the authenticity of third-person sayings about the Son of Man, see *Jesus — God and Man*, pp. 58ff.

33. In Luke Jesus thus evaded the question whether he was the Messiah. Only in Mark is there a direct answer to this question ("I am" in 14:62), and in this gospel the reference to the judgment of the Son of Man that follows is perhaps meant to equate Jesus with the Son of Man. The Lucan version is more along the lines of Luke 12:8f., in which the judgment of the Son of Man will confirm the ministry of Jesus but for that very reason is a different authority. Yet the exegetical literature often makes an immediate equation of Jesus with the Son of Man as regards this judgment, e.g., B. A. Strobel, *Die Stunde der Wahrheit*, though cf. Cullmann, *Christology*, pp. 117ff., and Sanders, *Jesus and Judaism*, p. 297. The reaction of the high priest in Mark 14:63f. might suggest such an understanding. But it might also rest on the fact that Jesus' prophetic threat of heavenly judgment on these earthly judges for their abuse of the Jewish courts took effect along the lines of Deut. 17:12. If the saying is authentic, their reaction does not in any case have to mean that they rightly construed the intention of Jesus.

34. *Jesus — God and Man*, pp. 63ff., and on his opponents' demand for a sign in Mark 8:12 par. 63f. Cf. vol. I, 200f. on rejection of this demand as an evasion of the need for decision.

In 1964 the thesis that the claim to authority implicit in the message of Jesus needed verification ran up against the dominant view that it was self-authenticated. The thesis thus encountered much misunderstanding.[35] Especially grotesque was the suspicion that it depreciated the central significance of the crucifixion of Jesus for the Christian understanding of his person and work in that it saw the resurrection, not the crucifixion, as the divine confirmation of his claim to authority.[36] The resurrection, however, presupposes his death; it is the raising again of the Crucified. Again, and above all, the claim to personal authority that was linked to his message and arose out of its content did not at first lead to the confirmation of Jesus but rather to his rejection as a deceiver and finally to his crucifixion.[37] The open question of verification of the unheard of claim to personal authority that the appearance and work of Jesus imply is an important one for christology because the related ambivalence shows that his rejection and therefore his path of suffering even to the cross are essentially and not just accidentally bound up with his destiny. The theology of the cross is thus linked to the earthly sending of Jesus to proclaim the imminent rule of God.

It was one of the merits of A. Ritschl to have pioneered insight into this matter by seeing in the passion of Jesus an expression of faithfulness to his calling.[38] On this view Jesus accepted his passion for the sake of his sending to announce the kingdom of God. A broader historical-exegetical foundation was thus laid for a theology of the cross as compared with the predominant isolation of the crucifixion under the impact of the theory of satisfaction. Yet Ritschl did not work out the inner connection between the offense taken at the appearance of Jesus and the ambivalence of the claim to personal authority. Only in virtue of this inner connection does the path of suffering lose its appearance of being accidental and come to be seen as an essential part of his divine mission.[39] This is the starting point in the next chapter, where we deal with the question of the saving significance of the death of Jesus.

Jesus declared the present inbreaking of the saving future of God's rule, with an implication of its proclaimed imminence and the need to

---

35. Ibid., pp. 53-66.

36. B. Klappert, *Die Auferweckung des Gekreuzigten* (1971), pp. 54ff., esp. 56f.; also J. Moltmann, *The Crucified God*, p. 173. I dealt with this criticism more fully in the epilogue to the 5th German edition of my *Grundzüge der Christologie* (1976), pp. 419f. (not in the ET *Jesus — God and Man*).

37. *Jesus — God and Man*, pp. 251ff.

38. A. Ritschl, *The Christian Doctrine of Justification and Reconciliation* (Clifton, NJ, 1966), § 48 (pp. 442-52), esp. pp. 448ff. We find the first movement in this direction in Schleiermacher's *Christian Faith*, § 101.4. On Ritschl, cf. G. Wenz, *Geschichte der Versöhnungslehre in der evangelischen Theologie der Neuzeit*, 2 vols. (Munich, 1984-86), II, 101ff.

39. Cf. my "Theology of the Cross," *Word and World: Theology for Christian Ministry* 8 (1988) 162-72.

respond to it in faith. Those who miss this implication and instead look only to the man who makes such a claim can very easily be left with an impression of unheard of presumption. We find here not only the explanation of the rejection of Jesus by some of his hearers but also the background of his arrest by the authorities in Jerusalem and the direct ground of the proceedings against him. As regards the latter, a prophetic threat against the temple (perhaps based on Jer. 7:11-14 and 26:6) and the intimation of its destruction (Mark 13:2; cf. 14:58 and John 2:19), along with the accompanying symbolic action,[40] could very well have been the immediate reason for his arrest by the Jewish authorities.[41]

There is no basic reason to question, or to regard as an unhistorical reconstruction, the gospel accounts that implicate the Jewish courts as well as the Romans in the events leading to the execution of Jesus, even though the reports of the proceedings against Jesus before the Sanhedrin and the preceding hearings are not uniform. In his highly regarded address of 1931, which focused on Mark 14 as the only primary source,[42] Hans Lietzmann threw doubt on Mark's account of a night sitting of the Sanhedrin. His observations led him to the conclusion that the only session was the short one of Mark 15:1 in the early morning after the arrest, that there was no formal trial, and that Jesus was then handed over to the procurator.[43] Lietzmann criticized the account in Mark especially for deviations from Jewish procedure and the unbelievability of a formal condemnation for simply claiming messianic dignity (14:61f.).

Many later inquiries into the trial took a similar line, especially the influential work of Paul Winter, *On the Trial of Jesus* (Berlin, 1961). Winter went even further by suggesting that Jesus was handed over to the Romans, not because of his teaching, but because of the unrest he was stirring up among the people (p. 135, cf. 146), the Jewish leaders fearing reprisals from the occupying power (p. 41; cf. John 11:50). An even bolder conjecture on the basis of John 18:3, 12 is that the Romans rather than the Jews might have taken the initiative in arresting Jesus.[44] The idea that the procurator himself initiated the trial, however, is hardly

40. John 2:13-22 could very well have preserved the original context better than the Synoptists, who separated the so-called cleansing of the temple (Mark 11:15-18 par.) from the prediction of its destruction (Mark 13:2 par.).

41. For details, cf. Sanders, *Jesus and Judaism*, pp. 61-90, 301-5, 334f. Sanders thinks that the overturning of the money changers' tables symbolizes the approaching destruction (esp. pp. 69ff.). Cf. also W. H. Kelber, *The Passion in Mark* (Philadelphia, 1976), pp. 168ff.

42. H. Lietzmann, "Der Prozess Jesu," in *Kleine Schriften, II, Studien zum NT,* ed. K. Aland (1958), pp. 251ff.

43. Ibid., p. 260, cf. 254ff.

44. So, with appeal to H. Conzelmann, P. Lapide, *Wer war schuld an Jesu Tod?* (Gütersloh, 1987), pp. 53f.

reconcilable with the account of the proceedings before Pilate in John.[45] Mention of Roman participation in the arrest has a bearing on our historical evaluation. But if the initiative came from the Romans, the part also played by the Jewish temple police is hard to understand. It is more likely that the temple police used Roman support to minimize possible opposition.

The tradition of Peter's denial, whose credibility can hardly be doubted, supports the account of a night hearing in the high priest's palace.[46] Not so easy to defend is Mark's account of a formal hearing before the Sanhedrin in that palace (Mark 14:55).[47] The situation is different, however, with the trial the following morning, to which Luke 22:66 bears witness as well as Mark 15:1.[48] Whether this resulted in a formal condemnation (Mark 14:64) or whether Jesus was handed over to the Romans without formal condemnation but as sufficiently suspect (Luke 22:71) after threatening his judges with the imminent judgment of the Son of Man (Luke 22:69 par.) and being equated with this Son of Man,[49] we can no longer say.[50] In favor of a breaking off of the trial is the consideration that the messianic self-confessions that could be inferred from the words of Jesus

45. R. E. Brown, *The Gospel according to John*, 2 vols., AB (New York, 1966-70), II, 815f.

46. Cf. Strobel, *Die Stunde der Wahrheit*, pp. 7ff.

47. Though cf. Lietzmann, "Der Prozess Jesu," pp. 54ff.; also Strobel, *Die Stunde der Wahrheit*, pp. 16f. and 12. Cf. also D. Catchpole, *The Trial of Jesus: A Study in the Gospels and Jewish Historiography from 1770 to the Present Day* (Leiden, 1971), pp. 186ff., on Luke 22:66. For a different view, cf. R. Pesch, *Das Markusevangelium*, 2 vols. (1977, 2nd ed. 1980), pp. 416ff.

48. Although John has only the hearing before Annas, found only here (John 18:19ff.), and does not expressly refer to a sitting of the Sanhedrin, he does say that Jesus was taken to Caiaphas (18:24) before being handed over to Pilate (18:28). These accounts do not rule out the morning session of the Sanhedrin, on which the Synoptists are agreed. We can hardly reject it merely because of the silence of John. Lapide, *Wer war schuld an Jesu Tod?* pp. 61f., is also wrong to say that both John and Luke have only preliminary hearings and no Jewish trial. We need only cite Luke 22:66 to the contrary.

49. On Jesus' own intention, cf. pp. 337f. above.

50. Contra Strobel, *Die Stunde der Wahrheit*, pp. 76ff., who defends the historicity of Mark apart from the first night sitting of the Sanhedrin, and who offers arguments against the capital powers of the Sanhedrin (pp. 18ff.) and the irreconcilability of the Markan account with Jewish procedure (pp. 46ff.). We may accept the points made by Strobel, also against the theory of J. Blinzler, *Der Prozess Jesu* (4th ed. 1969) that Sadducean penal and trial procedure underlay the trial of Jesus (pp. 48ff.). According to Strobel, differences for special religious offenses are unimportant, as in the case of a deceiver according to Deut. 13:5f. (pp. 55ff., 61, 81ff.). In view of John 7:12, I think it plausible that Jesus was in fact suspected of being a deceiver who was leading people astray from traditional divine revelation. Yet it is hard to accept a formal sentence by the Sanhedrin (as in Mark; cf. Strobel, *Die Stunde der Wahrheit*, pp. 71ff.) because the account in Luke seems to suggest (22:71) that the trial was broken off with no verdict. Cf. also H.-W. Kuhn, "Kreuz II," *TRE*, XIX (1990), pp. 713ff., esp. 719.

made it possible to hand him over to Pilate on a charge of sedition without a formal Jewish verdict. Yet the threat of judgment by the Son of Man (Luke 22:69), even without identification of Jesus as the Son of Man, would have been enough for a death sentence as an insult to the court (Deut. 17:12),[51] but hardly a capital offense in Roman eyes.

At any rate, the threatened destruction of the temple, which along with the symbolic action in the temple might have been the reason for the arrest, does not seem to have been also the basis of the condemnation (cf. Mark 14:55-61). A prophetic threat was not in the last resort an actual offense against the temple such as Jesus allegedly had in mind according to the "false witnesses" of Mark 14:58 (cf. 15:28). Nor would we have here a reason for condemnation by the Romans. For this a declaration of messianic ambitions was needed, such as was suspected in the threat of approaching judgment by the Son of Man (Mark 14:62 par.). This saying might have been decisive for the outcome of the trial in two ways. For his Jewish judges it expressed an intolerable arrogance on the part of Jesus, who threatened the supreme court of the people with the heavenly judgment of the Son of Man. But it also provided a pretext for handing him over to Pilate for an offense that carried a capital sentence by Roman, though not by Jewish, law.

Theological interest in these matters is not dependent on whether or how far we must charge the then official representatives of the Jewish people with personal guilt for the death of Jesus. There would be personal guilt only if they caused the judicial murder of Jesus through personal dislike. It is quite possible that they acted in good faith in regarding Jesus as a deceiver (John 7:12) who was seducing the people into apostasy from the God of Israel along the lines of Deut. 13:5f.[52] Even less can we speak of a guilt of the Jewish people as a whole for the death of Jesus, notwithstanding Matt. 27:25. Even if in the debates about the release of a condemned person the crowd did utter this terrible curse, is God going to hold the crowd and the whole people to it? It is true that Jesus predicted

51. Cf. Pesch, *Markus*, II, 437f. Strobel (*Die Stunde der Wahrheit*, pp. 92f.) does not distinguish between threatening the court with the judgment of the Son of Man and the identifying of Jesus as the Son of Man. According to J. Bowker, *Jesus and the Pharisees* (Cambridge, 1973), pp. 46ff., Deut. 17:12 was the reason for the condemnation. Blinzler, however, favors the prohibition of blasphemy in Exod. 22:28; cf. in *LThK*, IV, 1118. E. Schillebeeckx, *Jesus: An Experiment in Christology* (New York, 1979), pp. 312ff., follows Bowker but assumes that the trial broke off without a formal condemnation (pp. 315ff.).

52. This is the point of Strobel's arguments, *Die Stunde der Wahrheit*, pp. 81-92. They carry weight even if the charge was no reason for official condemnation by the Sanhedrin. We still find an awareness of this decisive accusation in Justin *Dial.* 69.7 and 108.1.

the destruction of the temple and also, given the authenticity of Luke 19:41-44, the besieging and destruction of Jerusalem as a judgment of God on his people (cf. Luke 13:34f.). Early Christianity saw a fulfillment of this prophecy in the siege and overthrow of the city by Titus in A.D. 70.

The reason for the threat of judgment, however, lay in the refusal of Israel to return to its God in answer to the summons of Jesus, not in the personal death that was ahead of him, closely though this was related to rejection of his message. When John says that the Jews sought to kill him (8:40) because his word found no place in them (8:37), we have here something that applies even more to the Gentile world, and especially to secularized humanity today, including secularized Christianity. Underlying rejection of the message of Jesus regarding God's claim upon us is pride in our natural freedom (John 8:34ff.) which, under the sign of an understanding of freedom according to natural law, has alienated us moderns far more deeply from God than the sense of being the freeborn children of Abraham alienated Jews in the time of Jesus.

When the church saw God's judgment on Jerusalem in A.D. 70, it did not weep over it as Jesus did. It did not bow with the Jewish people under the divine judgment that hung over it also. In false self-righteousness it thought that the Jewish people alone had come under divine condemnation for the death of Jesus. In so doing it forgot that Jesus himself had hoped that beyond the judgment there would be an eschatological restoration of Israel.[53] Paul also had affirmed that the God of Israel stood by the election of his people in spite of its rejection of Jesus (Rom. 11:1, cf. v. 11), in expectation that all Israel would finally come to see the work of God for it in the sending of Jesus (11:26). The resurrection of Jesus by the God of Israel not only cancels the condemnation of Jesus as a deceiver but also expresses God's faithfulness to the election of his people. For Paul, then, the cross of Jesus was certainly the end of the law (Rom. 10:4; cf. Gal. 3:13), but not the end of the election of Israel.[54]

53. Sanders, *Jesus and Judaism*, pp. 61-119, 335ff. relates the saying and symbolic action against the temple to this expectation.

54. This distinction is normative for correction of my own 1964 discussion of Paul's doctrine of Christ as the end of the law and the judgment that for Christians the cross of Jesus means the end of Judaism as a religion (*Jesus — God and Man*, pp. 26f.; cf. the epilogue to the 5th German edition, p. 420, and *Das Glaubensbekenntnis, ausgelegt und verantwortet vor den Fragen der Gegenwart* [1972], p. 92). In 1964 I had far too undifferentiated a view of the Jewish religion as a religion of law, which according to Paul had come to end in the cross of Jesus, instead of seeing the essence of Jewish faith in the same way as the proclamation of Jesus, i.e., in terms of faith in the God of Israel, in antithesis if necessary to the legal tradition.

Christian charges of deicide against the Jewish people on the basis of Matt. 27:28 and as a seal of its definitive rejection by God ought never to have arisen, and the Christian churches have rightly distanced themselves from them,[55] unhappily very late, but at least with an expression of shame at the long and painful history of Christian relations to the Jewish people, as charges of this kind have poisoned them.

Theological interest in the connections between the offense caused to many members of his people by the appearance of Jesus and the events leading to his condemnation and crucifixion is on a very different plane. At issue here is not the fixing of Jewish guilt for the death of Jesus but the action of God in his passion. An essential point in this regard is that offense at the message and conduct of Jesus was not accidental. It arose out of the ambivalence into which the message of Jesus thrust his own person. The relation of his crucifixion to the results of the offense forms the basis of Christian faith-statements about the saving significance of the cross. If the cross were an external event unrelated to his message or his work, it would be theologically meaningless, the result of a tragic misunderstanding on the part of the Romans, who regarded Jesus as a political agitator. But if on the basis of his message there is a link between ambivalence regarding his person and the resultant rejection, arrest, and handing over to Pilate for condemnation as a rebel, then all these consequences flow from the divine sending of Jesus and ultimately from God himself. If the offense and the cross were (provisional) results of the claim that the message of Jesus implied for his person, then the presence of God in him (as a mere man) brought him to the cross and thrust him into the situation of dereliction. This is true also and precisely if Jesus' awareness of the presence of God in his work was not a mere illusion. The related ambivalence was set aside only by the resurrection of the Crucified.

c. The Justification of Jesus by the Father in His Resurrection

The resurrection of Jesus from the dead, which was backed by appearances to his disciples and also to Saul their persecutor, forms the starting point of the apostolic proclamation of Christ and also of the history of

55. We may refer primarily here to *Nostra Aetate* 4 of Vatican II in 1965. Cf. also the collection *Die Kirchen und das Judentum. Dokumente von 1945 bis 1985*, ed. R. Rendtorff and H. Henrix (Munich, 1988). Cf. Rendtorff's *Hat denn Gott sein Volk verstossen? Die evangelische Kirche und das Judentum seit 1945. Ein Kommentar* (Munich, 1989).

the primitive Christian community. Without the resurrection the apostles would have had no missionary message, nor would there have been any christology relating to the person of Jesus. Without this event, as Paul wrote to the Corinthians (1 Cor. 15:17), the faith of Christians is vain. This does not mean that faith simply depends on the report of the resurrection of Jesus. In this event the appearance of a new and eternal life is not the only issue. For Christian faith it is not a matter of indifference who it was that was raised from the dead, namely, the Crucified (Mark 16:6; cf. Acts 2:36; 4:10; 1 Cor. 1:13). Nor was this just any person crucified, but the crucified Jesus of Nazareth. Hence the Easter faith of Christians is linked for all time to the earthly history of Jesus of Nazareth, who proclaimed to his people the nearness of the rule of God, who was rejected by his adversaries as a deceiver and handed over to the Romans for execution, who was raised from the dead by God, and who was thus instituted as Messiah (Acts 2:23f., 36; cf. Rom. 1:4). The resurrection of Jesus is the basis of Christian faith, yet not as an isolated event, but in its reference back to the earthly sending of Jesus and his death on the cross.[56]

This reference is not something that was added to the event of the resurrection of Jesus. It is inseparable from the event as such, since it was the crucified Jesus who was raised. If, on the premise of faith in the God of Israel, we see the event as the work of God, this implies directly a canceling of the rejection of Jesus and his message by the representatives of his people, a refutation of the accusation and suspicions that resulted in his being handed over to the Romans and his crucifixion. We cannot detach the fact of the resurrection from its meaning.[57] The Easter event means directly that God himself justified the condemned and executed Jesus, namely, by the Spirit, by whose power he was raised from the dead (1 Tim. 3:16; cf. Rom. 1:4; 4:25).

---

56. Cf. the epilogue to the 5th edition of my *Grundzüge* (pp. 417f.). In 1964 a proper recognition of the constitutive significance of the resurrection of Jesus for christology was apparently so unusual in dogmatic theology that emphasizing it seemed to many readers to be an alternative to basing faith on the earthly work of Jesus.

57. We have here an instance of the general rule that in the historical nexus of event and experience, event and meaning go together, the latter by no means external to the event or arbitrary. But we also have here a special instance of the rule, for the meaning is not always so closely related to the event. Even in the Christian tradition, e.g., the empty tomb is ambivalent when taken alone (cf. John 20:13ff. and Matt. 28:13). The appearances to the disciples could also be interpreted in different ways (Luke 24:39). Only when the event is identified as the resurrection of Jesus is there no longer any ambiguity.

In this way God confirmed the claim that was implicit in the work of Jesus, and that was also expressly made by him, namely, that the imminent rule of God that Jesus proclaimed was about to break in, and in fact was already doing so for those who trusted his message. This is how the first Christians understood it,[58] and there was no other way of understanding the event in the Jewish context in which the report of it arose. Hence acceptance or rejection of the account of the resurrection of Jesus was originally identical with decision for faith in him or for unbelief.[59]

Confirmation is more than disclosure of a meaning that the person and history of Jesus already had on his way to the cross, so that it was his even without the Easter event, though in hidden form. The Easter event certainly shed a new light on the death of Jesus, on his earthly ministry, and therefore on his person. But that does not mean that even without the event of the resurrection these would have been what they are when seen in its light. We depreciate the Easter event if we construe it only as a disclosure or revelation of the meaning that the crucifixion and the earthly history of Jesus already had in themselves.[60] Only the Easter event determines what the meaning was of the pre-Easter history of Jesus and who he was in his relation to God. To do this the event had to be an event with its own weight and content, namely, the resurrection of Jesus from the dead to a new life with God. This event dispelled and removed the

58. Jeremias, *Verkündigung*, p. 285, states summarily that for the primitive church the resurrection of Jesus was divine confirmation of his having been sent. Cf. U. Wilckens, *Resurrection. Biblical Testimony to the Resurrection: An Historical Examination and Explanation* (Atlanta, 1977), pp 124ff.

59. This is the reason why the event of the resurrection of Jesus was reported only by believers. Faith itself was not a presupposition of encounter with the risen Lord, as the example of Paul adequately testifies. Yet in the context of Jewish experience the meaning of the event was so clear that no one to whom the Lord appeared could acknowledge the event and remain an unbeliever.

60. This is the point of Bultmann's famous statement that the resurrection is an expression of the significance of the cross (*Kerygma and Myth*, ed. H. W. Bartsch [London, 1953], pp. 38ff.). Similarly Barth in the 2nd edition of his *Romans* (London, 1935) wrote that the resurrection was not a historical event like the other events of Jesus' life and death but the nonhistorical relating of his whole historical life to its origin in God (p. 195); cf. my article "Dialektische Theologie," *RGG*, II (1958), pp. 168ff., esp. 170f.). In *CD*, of course, Barth insisted against Bultmann that the resurrection was a second specific event after his crucifixion (III/2, 441ff., esp. 445; cf. IV/1, 304ff.), but even here the content of the event is "the revelation of the mystery of the preceding time of the life and death of the man Jesus" (III/2, 455; cf. IV/2, 118ff., esp. 131ff.). As Barth saw it, "that which took place on the third day . . . lifted up the whole of what took place before in all its particularity . . . into something that took place once and for all" (IV/1, 313).

ambiguity that had earlier clung to the person and history of Jesus and did not simply disclose a meaning that had previously been hidden, but still present, quite apart from the event of the resurrection.

After provisionally describing in this way the basic content of the Christian Easter message, we can turn to the related problems that demand clearer explanation. We need to look first at the terms that are used, then at the concepts they involve. Only thus can we meaningfully tackle the question of the facticity of the event. If the event did not actually take place, of course, then all discussion of its meaning is a waste of time. But we must first know what kind of event it was if we are to throw light on the question of its facticity.[61]

1. *The language of the resurrection of Jesus is that of metaphor.* Thus a word like "raising" suggests a wakening from sleep. When we waken from sleep, we "rise" up. So it is with the dead. Underlying this metaphoric usage is the further metaphor that was common in both Jewish and Greek thinking, namely, the idea of death as a sleep.[62] In the Jewish sphere we find this especially in apocalyptic works (Dan. 12:2; 1 Enoch 49:3; 100:5, etc.; Syr. Bar. 11:4; 21:24, etc.). But there are also isolated instances in Jeremiah (51:39), the Psalms (13:3), and Job (3:13; 14:12). Rising from the sleep of death also occurs (1 Enoch 91:10; 92:3; Syr. Bar. 30:1). Yet in spite of the metaphoric language, a real event was in view, as also in the case of the resurrection of Jesus. It is not, however, an event in everyday experience, and in accordance with common custom it is thus stated metaphorically. The transitive ("to raise") and intransitive ("to rise") forms are not alternatives in this regard; the two go together. The one who is raised rises up. This is true of the resurrection of Jesus. Dead, he does not overcome death in his own power. He must be raised. Awakening by the Father and his Spirit is always presupposed when we read of the "rising" of Jesus (e.g., 1 Thess. 4:14).[63]

61. Notwithstanding the complexity of the theme, I have tried to make the following discussion as succinct as possible. For fuller consideration, cf. *Jesus — God and Man*, pp. 66-114. I will also try, however, to deal with certain misunderstandings of my previous argument.

62. Cf. H. Balz in *TDNT*, VIII, 545ff., esp. 548f., 551; also C. F. Evans, *Resurrection and the NT* (Naperville, IL, 1970), pp. 22ff.

63. Cf. the excellent observations in W. Kasper, *Jesus the Christ* (New York, 1976). Moltmann sees a material difference between raising and rising (*The Crucified God*), following H. Schelkle, "Auferstehung Jesu. Geschichte und Deutung," in *Kirche und Bibel: Festschrift E. Schick* (1979), p. 391. But cf. A. Vögtle in the work he coauthored with R. Pesch, *Wie kam es zum Osterglauben?* (1975), pp. 15ff. Even when the resurrection is depicted as the Son's own act (John 2:19; 10:17f.), it is always done in obedience to the Father and not as an independent act of power (cf. Evans, *Resurrection*, pp. 21f.).

Related to the language is the goal of the process that it describes, namely, a new life, whether in the sense of a return to earthly life (Luke 8:54; Mark 5:41; John 11:11) or in that of a transition to a different life. It is worth noting here that in neither case is the term "life" a metaphor. Only the transition from death to life falls outside the realm of everyday experience and must be stated metaphorically. The new eschatological life (2 Cor. 4:10; 5:4; Rom. 5:10), eternal life (Gal. 6:8; Rom. 2:7; 5:21; 6:22f.), is life in the full sense (cf. John 1:4; 5:26; 14:6, etc. with 3:15, 36; 4:14, etc.; 6:53f.), in comparison with which earthly life can be called life only with reservations. Because the biblical concept of life sees it in terms of the divine Spirit as the origin of all life, life in the full sense is life that is related to its divine origin, permeated by the Spirit, and hence immortal (1 Cor. 15:44: *sōma pneumatikon*), i.e., the new life (Rom. 6:4) of eschatological hope. This new and imperishable life was manifested already with the raising of Jesus to it.

2. *The idea of raising from the dead to a new and eternal life has its roots in Jewish eschatological hope.* Its origins may well be linked to the individualizing of the relation to God in the Babylonian exile. Individuals were now no longer viewed merely as members of the living body of the people within which the merits and offenses of their parents had their impact. The relation between good deed and reward or transgression and judgment took effect in each individual life (Ezek. 18:2ff., 20; cf. Jer. 31:29). But the relation did not work out in human experience. The course of the world showed that the righteous suffer and the ungodly prosper. Israel's faith in the justice of its God had to come to terms with this. It thus arrived at the idea of future reward or punishment for good or bad deeds that do not produce the appropriate fruits in this life. But this thought demanded a resurrection of the dead such as we find expressly in the OT only in Dan. 12:2: "And many of those who sleep in the dust of the earth shall awake, some to everlasting life, and some to shame and everlasting contempt." The Jewish concept of the resurrection arose, then, out of the problems of theodicy, the justice of God, and its demonstration in the lives of individuals.[64]

---

64. Cf. my essay "Tod und Auferstehung in der Sicht christlicher Dogmatik," in *Grundfragen systematischer Theologie*, 2 vols. (Göttingen, 1967-80), II, 147ff. Cf. also Wilckens, *Resurrection*, pp. 85f. J. Moltmann has rightly stressed the relation to the theme of theodicy and the justice of God in his *Way of Jesus Christ* (New York, 1990), p. 225, and also in his essay "Gott und Auferstehung," in *Perspektiven der Theologie, Gesammelte Aufsätze* (Munich, 1968), pp. 36-56.

Nevertheless, Jewish texts present a varied picture regarding the relation between resurrection and eternal life. On the one side, as in Daniel, both the just and the unjust are raised. Resurrection here is simply the presupposition of judgment. On the other side we have the idea of the resurrection of the just (e.g., of martyrs) as a transition to eternal life. We find this first in Isa. 26:19, though perhaps here, as in Ezek. 37:1-14, we may simply have a metaphor for the rebirth of the people and not the concept of individual resurrection.[65] In 1 Enoch 92:3 there is a reference to a raising of the righteous to life,[66] and in 2 Macc. 7:14 to a raising of the martyr to life. Similarly in the dialogue of Jesus with the Sadducees in Mark 12:18-27 the resurrection as such means participation in life, as the example of the patriarchs shows (vv. 26f.). It was in this sense that primitive Christianity spoke of the resurrection of Jesus. According to Paul, believers could expect to be raised in the same way (1 Cor. 15:42ff.).[67] The resurrection of Jesus, then, was not a return to earthly life. It was a transition to the new eschatological life. He is "the first fruits of those that have fallen asleep"(1 Cor. 15:20), "the first-born among many brethren" (Rom. 8:29), "the first-born from the dead" (Col. 1:18; cf. Rev. 1:5), the initiator of a new life (Acts 3:15).

3. *Eschatological expectation of a resurrection from the dead provided linguistic expression and a conceptual framework for the Christian Easter message.*[68] It made it possible for the disciples to identify the appearances

65. Wilckens, *Resurrection,* pp. 86-88, though cf. O. Plöger, *Theokratie und Eschatologie* (1959), p. 85.

66. Wilckens, *Resurrection,* pp. 92f., thinks this is usually the case in references to an end-time resurrection of the dead, e.g., 1 Enoch 51:1 (cf. 46:6), as distinct from 4 Ezra 7:32ff. and Syr. Bar. 50f. Cf. also G. Stemberger, *Der Leib der Auferstehung. Studien zur Anthropologie und Eschatologie des palästinischen Judentums im neutestamentlichen Zeitalter* (1972), and esp. J. Kremer in the book he coauthored with G. Greshake: *Resurrectio Mortuorum. Zum theologischen Verständnis der leiblichen Auferstehung* (1986).

67. That Paul's expectation of a resurrection of Christians in 1 Thess. 4:13ff. arose only out of the Easter message, as P. Hoffmann assumes in *TRE,* IV (1979), pp. 452f., seems hardly credible in view of the fact that expectation of a resurrection of the righteous to life was a presupposition of the Easter message. In 1 Thess. 4:13f. Paul is simply relating this expectation to the situation of Christians. For them the resurrection to life means the continuation and renewal of fellowship with the risen and returning Lord (4:17). His resurrection guarantees them a share in the resurrection to life (4:14). To that extent we have here a very specific modification and concretization of Jewish expectation of the resurrection of the just.

68. Cf. the discussion in *Jesus — God and Man,* p. 77. For a different view, cf. K. Berger, *Die Auferstehung des Propheten und die Erhöhung des Menschensohns* (Göttingen, 1978), pp. 15f., though his arguments against F. Hahn and U. Wilckens (pp. 248ff.) are not convincing. He tries in vain to weaken the connection that is made in 1 Cor. 15:20 between the resurrection of Jesus and the general resurrection (pp. 250f.). If, however, the resurrec-

of the crucified Lord to them. It was not a ghost that appeared (Luke 22:37), nor one who had come back to the reality of this earthly life (John 20:17). It was the Lord who had been raised to the new eschatological life. The nexus of experience that made it possible for the disciples to recognize Jesus when he made himself known in the appearances was ultimately given to them by their sharing in his life and work up to the days of his going to Jerusalem and his arrest.[69] According to the accounts of the Evangelists, the marks of the wounds removed the last doubts as to the identity of Jesus in his appearances to the disciples (Luke 24:40; John 20:20, 25ff.). But without the terminology of the eschatological hope of Israel, the disciples could not have realized that it was in the reality of the life of the resurrection that Jesus made himself known to them.[70]

4. *The relation to the Jewish idea of eschatological resurrection to life, however, was profoundly altered by the linking of this idea to the reality of Jesus encountered in the Easter appearances.*

a. Resurrection to eternal life relative to the crucified Jesus immediately meant the justification and confirmation of his earthly mission and person by God (see above). This confirmation relates especially also to the personal authority implied in his message and work. Suggested already here is the thought of an exaltation[71] to participation in God's

---

tion of Jesus is to be understood as an expression of the eschatological resurrection of the dead, there is no basis for combining it with ideas of the return of prophets such as Elijah or Enoch prior to the coming of the end.

69. Moltmann in *The Way of Jesus Christ* calls this "the immediate personal framework for [the disciples'] interpretation" (p. 221). We cannot easily deny that. The only point that it does not explain is how the disciples could identify the appearances as signs of his *resurrection*. Required for this was eschatological expectation of a resurrection to life. To that extent it is misleading when Moltmann speaks of a "further" background in the "prophetic and apocalyptic tradition" of contemporary Judaism, a framework in which the disciples "also" lived and thought, as though the nature of the reality that they experienced in the appearances could be known by them independently of this framework.

70. Vögtle rightly doubted whether expectation of a general resurrection (of both the good and the bad) would be a sufficient horizon of interpretation for the Easter appearances (*Wie kam es zum Osterglauben?* pp. 107ff., 110). What was needed was expectation of the resurrection of the righteous to life (pp. 112ff.).

71. For a succinct summary of data on the link between resurrection and exaltation statements in primitive Christianity, cf. Kasper, *Jesus the Christ.* We should not see in the idea of exaltation an alternative schema by which to explain the Easter appearances alongside resurrection and rapture (Moltmann, *The Way of Jesus Christ,* pp. 220f.). The only alternatives would be a ghostly apparition or a return to earthly life (see above). Exaltation was certainly an independent concept in Jewish tradition, but in the Easter tradition of Christianity it seems to have been an implication of the resurrection, which it presupposes. The same applies to the idea of rapture, i.e., a snatching up of the Lord to God, from whom he

rule over the world, which primitive Christianity expressed by linking the figure of Jesus to the figures of eschatological expectation. This exaltation was to the dignity of the Messiah (corresponding to the inscription on the cross) and the Son of Man, whose future as Jesus had announced it, along with the manifestation of the Messiah, was now awaited as the return of the risen Jesus. Jewish tradition did, of course, have similar ideas of an exaltation to fellowship with God, e.g., that of Elijah or 1 Enoch, but not in connection with a resurrection from the dead.[72]

b. Jewish expectation of an eschatological resurrection, whether to judgment or to eternal life, did not count on the resurrection of one individual before the end of this aeon. In close connection with the identifying of the appearances of Jesus as eschatological resurrection, primitive Christianity seems to have regarded this event as the beginning of end-time events. Only as the Parousia of Jesus as Messiah and Son of Man, which at first was seen as very imminent, failed to come at once did it accustom itself to the thought of the resurrection of one individual within a history of the world that had not yet reached its end.

c. Nevertheless, belief in the enacted event of the resurrection of Jesus remained linked to expectation of the resurrection of the just (Luke 14:14), or of those who are related to Jesus by faith (1 Thess. 4:14f.; cf. Rom. 6:5, etc.). In the Christian sphere, too, there could be a revival of the more general idea of a resurrection of all the dead as a presupposition of the dispensing of judgment at the return of Christ (Acts 24:15; John 5:29; cf. Rev. 20:12ff.). We shall deal more thoroughly with the detailed aspects of this Christian expectation at a later time in connection with eschatology. The only point of importance here is that we cannot detach the conceptual content of the doctrine of the resurrection of Jesus from the more general expectation of an end-time resurrection of the dead. This is because it is only in this connection that the mode of the reality of life of Jesus that the Easter event proclaims can be upheld in contrast to mere hallucinations or ghostly apparitions.

d. The result is that for its final verification, the Christian message of the resurrection of Jesus needs the event of an eschatological resurrection of

---

will one day return as Messiah (Acts 3:20f.). Moltmann himself does not deny that "raising" and "rising" are the original categories of interpretation for the appearance of Christ (*The Way of Jesus Christ*, p. 221), but his formulations seem to suggest that other ideas could have been chosen instead. In fact, however, they came into consideration only as implications of the message of the resurrection.

72. For details, cf. Wilckens, *Resurrection*, pp. 102ff.

the dead. The enacting of this event is one of the conditions, if not the only condition, on which to maintain the truth of the resurrection of Jesus. Maintaining this truth implies a view of reality that rests on the anticipating of a fulfillment of human life and history that has not yet taken place. Hence the Christian Easter message will be contested as long as the general resurrection of the dead and the coming again of Jesus are still future. At the same time, insight into the proleptic structure of the Easter message strengthens the sense of its appropriateness. It is in keeping with the event of the resurrection of Jesus as an anticipation of eschatological salvation, which for its part stands in significant analogy to anticipation of the coming rule of God in the proclamation of Jesus and his earthly work. The Easter message of Christianity corresponds to the proleptic aspect of the history of Jesus in that as the proclamation of a specific event in the historical past, it always presupposes the universality of a changing and fulfilling of the reality of humanity and the world that is still in the future.[73]

5. *The proclamation of the resurrection of Jesus as the hope of salvation for the human race beyond the confines of the Jewish tradition presupposes the possibility of maintaining with sufficient plausibility the universal validity of Jewish expectation of an eschatological resurrection of the dead, at least in its basic features.* At first glance the early history of Christian mission does not seem to support this thesis. In the first two centuries the message of the resurrection of Jesus was adopted much more readily than the doctrine of an end-time resurrection.[74] Late antiquity gave some plausibility to the message of the resurrection of Jesus with its mythical ideas of deities in the mystery cults dying and rising again. Jewish expectations of a resurrection of the body, especially the flesh, created great difficulties. But there could be no separating the two. Early Christianity could see in the resurrection of Jesus a basis for expecting a future resurrection of the dead (1 Clem. 24:1; Barn. 5:6). In so doing it presupposed the fact of the resurrection of Jesus. Paul had already emphasized that we can reverse the relation between the resurrection of Jesus and the resurrection of the dead: "If there is no resurrection of the dead, then Christ has not been raised" (1 Cor. 15:13). Needed, then, is a more general argument for the plausibility of expecting a future resurrection of the dead.

73. Thus far Moltmann is right to say that for the Easter witnesses Easter was not a fixed and finished event of the past but a future event that in its ambivalent historical form underlay a universal and world-changing hope ("Gott und Auferstehung," p. 44).

74. So R. Staats in "Auferstehung Jesu Christi II.2," *TRE,* IV (1979), pp. 513ff., esp. 523.

Like Paul's controversy with the Corinthians regarding this expectation, the account of the reaction of the philosophers of Athens to Paul's proclamation of the resurrection of Jesus (Acts 17:32) shows how precarious the thesis was in the early days of the Christian mission to the Gentiles. The first letter of Clement, then, tried hard to advance arguments for the Christian expectation of the future and was not at all content merely to say that the beginning of the future resurrection of the dead had come already with Jesus. For Clement, each new day is a kind of resurrection (24:3), as is also the emerging of plants from seeds (24:4f.; cf. 1 Cor. 15:35-38). Even the myth of the phoenix bird bears witness to expectation of resurrection (1 Clem. 25:1ff.). In the second century, defense of the bodily resurrection of Christians against Gnostic spiritualizing became a main theme of Christian theology. A series of works was devoted to it, including especially the tractate of the first head of the Alexandrian catechetical school, Athenagoras, on the resurrection of the dead. Athenagoras saw the need to go beyond an appeal to the omnipotence of God (cf. 2 Clem. 27:5) or a treatment of resurrection as the presupposition of the last judgment.[75] He developed a more broadly based anthropological argument that on the premise of our psychosomatic unity would try to show that our redeeming and fulfilling must include the body as well as the soul, as is possible only by means of a bodily resurrection.[76]

In the modern situation, in which mythical talk of deities who die and rise again has long since lost its credibility, and in which the thesis of the bodily resurrection of Jesus and the future hope of a resurrection of the dead must be maintained in a climate of basic philosophical skepticism, the anthropological argument for a hope after death, and for the appropriateness of including our corporeality in this hope, has gained in importance even for the Easter message.[77] Fuller discussion of this theme belongs to the whole sphere of eschatological problems and hence will have to come later. For the moment we may provisionally presuppose the possibility of this type of argument.[78]

6. *Decisive for confidence in the facticity of the resurrection of Jesus as the Christian message proclaims it are the primitive Christian testimonies*

75. On this see G. Kretschmar, "Auferstehung des Fleisches. Zur Frühgeschichte einer theologischen Lehrformel," in *Leben angesichts des Todes* (1968), pp. 101f.

76. L. W. Barnard, *Athenagoras: A Study in Second Century Christian Apologetic* (Paris, 1972), pp. 122ff., 126ff.; also his article "Apologetik I," *TRE*, III (1978), pp. 371ff., esp. 386-89.

77. Cf. *Jesus — God and Man*, pp. 82ff.; also Kasper, *Jesus the Christ*, for bibliography.

78. Cf. my essay "Constructive and Critical Functions of Christian Eschatology," *HTR* 77 (1984) 119-39.

to the appearances of the risen Lord to his disciples, along with the discovery of the empty tomb of Jesus in Jerusalem. We cannot accept these testimonies blindly on mere authority, of course, but must see whether they hold up to the kind of testing to which we submit, and by which we prove, other reported facts.[79]

The Christian Easter tradition combines very different materials, which seem at first to have been independent and then put together. We have first the resurrection appearances, then the finding of the empty tomb. The accounts of the appearances form the basis of the Easter witness, whereas the mere fact of the empty tomb is subject to different interpretations (John 20:13f.; cf. Matt. 28:13) and takes on significance for the whole subject only in connection with the appearances.[80]

The oldest form of the appearances tradition is Paul's in 1 Cor. 15:3-7. We cannot question the age of the account or the direct derivation of the account from a man who knew personally the witnesses cited,[81] or most of them, being himself the last in the series (1 Cor. 15:8). Paul himself brought them all together on the one list,[82] doing so in order to support his argument in the epistle.

A more difficult question is that of the nature of the appearances, and with it the further question of the relation between the appearance to Paul himself and the appearances recorded in the Gospels, which also differ among themselves.[83] In these accounts we perhaps have a later stage

79. For details, cf. *Jesus — God and Man*, pp. 88-106, and the excellent survey in R. E. Brown, *The Virginal Conception and Bodily Resurrection of Jesus* (Paramus, NJ, 1973), pp. 69-129.

80. I advocated this view already in 1964 in *Jesus — God and Man* (p. 97). I there discussed the historicity of the resurrection on the basis of the appearances (pp. 89ff.) before taking up the question of the empty tomb. I find it hard to see, then, why my book "perhaps gives to the fact of the empty tomb a significance that it is not given in the NT witnesses" (Kasper, *Jesus the Christ*).

81. On understanding *ōphthē* (1 Cor. 15:5ff.; Luke 24:34, etc.) in analogy to OT appearances of God to the patriarchs (Gen. 12:7; 26:24; cf. 17:1; 18:1, etc.) and esp. Moses, cf. Vögtle and Pesch, *Wie kam es zum Osterglauben?* pp. 26-43.

82. For details, cf. Evans, *Resurrection*, pp. 44ff.; Brown, *The Virginal Conception*, pp. 92ff.; and *Jesus — God and Man*, pp. 86f. The analysis of 1 Cor. 15:3ff. that I quote there (pp. 89ff.) is from U. Wilckens in the 3rd edition of his *Die Missionsreden der Apostelgeschichte* (1974), p. 228.

83. The research of J. E. Alsup, *The Post-Resurrection Appearances of the Gospel Tradition* (1975), have caused me to take a more nuanced view of the age and historical value of the individual Gospel accounts than I did in *Jesus — God and Man*, pp. 92ff. I still find it hard to agree with W. L. Craig, "On Doubts about the Resurrection," *Modern Theology* 6 (1989) 53ff., esp. 61ff., that the Gospel accounts of the appearances are as a whole

of the tradition with legendary and in part tendentious features (Luke 24:39ff.). The details have possibly been reshaped, yet a factual core may still underlie the narratives.[84] A common view is that in their form the events in all the stories seem to offer visionary experiences. This is not to deny their reality, however, even though in detail there might be circumstances that are usually associated with hallucinations, whether due to drugs or sickness. The thesis that we must regard all visionary experiences as psychological projections with no basis in reality cannot be regarded in any case an adequately grounded philosophical postulate.

If we start with the biblical material relating to the appearance of the risen Lord to Saul the persecutor, we can arrive at more solid conjectures as to the nature of the Easter appearances. In Acts 9:3 we seem to have a vision of light (along with an audition). The Lord thus appeared from heaven (Gal. 1:16)[85] in distinction from the Gospel appearances, in which Christ came on earth, passing through closed doors. There are two reasons for regarding the reconstructed form of the appearance to Paul as an indication of the original behind the Gospel accounts.[86] First, we have the fact that in the oldest NT witness the resurrection and ascension of Jesus form a single event,[87] as in Phil. 2:9; Acts 2:36; 5:30f.; the self-

---

"fundamentally reliable historically" (p. 61). Craig's decisive argument for his thesis is that there was not enough time between the events and the accounts for legendary development (p. 62). This point, however, rests on an early dating of the Gospels before A.D. 70, for which Craig (p. 74, n. 21) appeals to J. A. T. Robinson, *Redating the NT* (Philadelphia, 1976).

84. Cf. Alsup, *The Post-Resurrection Appearances*, pp. 269f., esp. 272ff., also 211ff.

85. Cf. R. H. Fuller, *The Formation of the Resurrection Narratives* (London, 1971), pp. 47f. We are to see in Gal. 1:16 a reference to the apostle's conversion (cf. H. Schlier, *Der Brief an die Galater* [11th ed.], pp. 26f.; G. Bornkamm, *Paulus* [1969], pp. 40f.). Evans, *Resurrection,* paraphrases: "To reveal his Son through me to the Gentiles" (p. 46), but this is not possible, since v. 16b describes the Gentile mission as the goal and consequence of the imparted revelation, thus distinguishing the two. To call the appearance a light phenomenon on the basis of Acts (esp. 9:3) does not contradict what the apostle says about the corporeality of the risen Lord as *sōma pneumatikon* (1 Cor. 15:44; cf. the shining of the celestial bodies in v. 40). On this see also Evans, *Resurrection,* p. 66. We are perhaps to see a reflection of Paul's experience in 2 Cor. 4:6 (Fuller, *Formation,* p. 47). The closeness of the Acts account to Paul is perhaps greater than Evans allows (pp. 33f., 66; cf. also 182). But in this case Evans is probably right to conclude that Paul understood the other appearances to be like his own. The difference between the author of Acts and Paul is that Luke saw the appearances to the others as more similar to the earthly appearances of Jesus.

86. Cf. E. Schillebeeckx, *Die Auferstehung Jesu als Grund der Erlösung* (1979), p. 90; also my own discussion in *Jesus — God and Man,* p. 92.

87. Evans, *Resurrection,* pp. 136ff. As Evans sees it, the idea of exaltation is earlier, but carries the notion of resurrection with it.

declaration of the risen Lord must thus have been from the concealment of heaven. Second, the Jerusalem disciples seem to have recognized the apostolic commissioning of Paul by the Lord himself in accordance with Paul's own resolute appeal (Gal. 1:1, 12) and on the basis of the appearance of the risen Lord to him (cf. Gal. 2:9). This means that they found sufficient agreement between his experience and the meetings of the original disciples with their Lord.[88] In opposition it might be pointed out that Luke does not seem to have given the same ranking to the appearance of Paul as to the appearances to the other disciples before the ascension. But Luke's sharper distinction between the time *before* and the time *after* the ascension seems perhaps to be a deviation of his own from the original equation of the resurrection and ascension.

Adducing Acts 9, E. Schillebeeckx[89] understands the Easter appearances as conversion visions such as we find elsewhere in Jewish traditions.[90] Yet he does not see them simply as an expression of the conversion experiences of the disciples.[91] In fact the NT presents them, not as an expression, but as the starting point and basis of the conversion of the disciples.[92] Schillebeeckx assumes that the starting point does not lie in the appearances. He argues that after his death, Jesus was identified as the eschatological prophet whose return in the end time was awaited.[93] He finds a Parousia kerygma with this content in Q.[94] The related conviction that Jesus is alive then found secondary expression in the Easter appearances.

Though Schillebeeckx still emphasizes the close connection between the resurrection and the Easter appearances,[95] his reconstruction fails to do justice to the basic significance of the appearances of the risen Lord in both Paul and the gospel accounts. His thesis seems to rest on the source reconstructed from Luke and Matthew and his inferring from the lack of any appearances in this source that the tradition behind it knew of no appearances. But this argument from silence is not a very sure basis for an understanding of the rise of Easter

---

88. Vögtle and Pesch, *Wie kam es zum Osterglauben?* p. 60, emphasizes that this was Paul's claim.

89. Schillebeeckx, *Jesus* (New York, 1979), p. 369; cf. p. 708.

90. Schillebeeckx, *Auferstehung,* pp. 92f.

91. Ibid., pp. 93f.; also *Jesus,* pp. 644ff.

92. As Moltmann puts it, the appearances are not to be explained by the faith of the disciples, but the faith of the disciples by the appearances (*The Way of Jesus Christ,* p. 217; with Schelkle, "Auferstehung Jesu," p. 395).

93. Schillebeeckx, *Auferstehung,* p. 85.

94. Ibid., pp. 50ff.

95. Ibid., pp. 88f.

faith that runs totally counter to the Gospels as well as Paul. We must begin with the fact that the Easter appearances formed the starting point for the kerygma of the resurrection of the Crucified.

Older scholars often viewed the finding of the empty tomb in its earlier form in Mark 16:1-8 as a late Hellenistic legend.[96] But legitimate doubts have arisen regarding this judgment,[97] so that increasingly the story has come to be accepted as old, being regarded as a local Jerusalem tradition and an original part of the passion story.[98] The text of the story does occasion doubt as to whether it may be viewed as simple historical narration.[99] Even so, the present form of the story might well preserve individual recollections that are historically relevant, especially that of the role of the women in finding the empty tomb and that of early appearances in Galilee rather than at the tomb.

R. Pesch is now one of the foremost critics of the historicity of the empty tomb. The skepticism of his judgment as to the age of the tradition merits consideration.[100] According to Pesch, the story of faith in the resurrection of Jesus presupposes his resurrection on the third day, which in turn excludes the idea of finding his body in the tomb.[101] We thus have a reconstructed story providing a scenario for a preexisting truth.[102] Against such interpretations of the tomb

96. Cf. Bultmann, *The History of the Synoptic Tradition*, pp. 287ff.; also H. Grass, *Ostergeschehen und Osterbericht* (1956), pp. 20ff., 173-86.

97. Still a basic work in this regard is H. von Campenhausen's *Der Ablauf der Osterereignisse und das leere Grab* (1952, 2nd ed. 1958). Cf. also Brown, *The Virginal Conception*, pp. 117ff.; and R. H. Fuller, *Formation*, pp. 69f.

98. Cf. Pesch, *Markus*, II, 519f., also 18, 20ff.

99. Cf. the story of the anointing by the women in Mark 16:1, the timing of which Luke explains — not to the satisfaction of all scholars — as due to the preceding sabbath (23:56; cf. Campenhausen, *Der Ablauf der Osterereignisse*, p. 24 n. 84). It seems highly unlikely that only en route would the women have come to realize that they would need help to move the stone (p. 24). Perhaps here and in 16:8b we might have a later addition to bring the story into line with an earlier stage of the tradition (*Jesus — God and Man*, p. 102). Even according to Campenhausen (p. 40), the account as a whole undoubtedly has something of a legendary character. Along with F. Mussner, *Die Auferstehung Jesu* (1969), Schillebeeckx, *Jesus* (on Matt. 28:15), viewed it as the cult legend of an annual celebration at the tomb of Jesus. Cf. also L. Schenke, *Auferstehungsverkündigung und leeres Grab* (1968). In his 1979 *Auferstehung* Schillebeeckx distanced himself from this thesis (pp. 103ff.) and argued more firmly for the historicity of the empty tomb (pp. 104f.).

100. Pesch, *Markus*, II, 522-40; also his "Das 'leere Grab' und der Glaube an Jesu Auferstehung," in *Internationale katholische Zeitschrift Communio* 11 (1982) 6ff., esp. 19.

101. Pesch, "Das 'leere Grab,'" p. 17.

102. Pesch, *Markus*, II, 521.

story the Oxford logician Michael Dummett has protested in a highly regarded article.[103] He attacks the views of Hubert Richards and Fergus Kerr, who argued that the Easter message of the apostles did not contain the report of an empty tomb. In discussions between Christians and Jews there was common recognition that the tomb was empty. The point at issue was not the fact but the explanation. Either Jesus had risen as the apostles maintained, or his body had been stolen to provide the basis of a deception, or so the accusation went.[104] In this matter the drift of the NT texts is sufficiently clear, and it is not convincing to see in them a literary convention, as though they were not really saying what they seem to say.[105]

Historical judgment must take into account not merely an analysis of Mark 16:1-8 but also the situation of the primitive Christian preaching of Easter in Jerusalem, the site of the execution and burial of Jesus. If, according to the contemporary Jewish understanding, the report of the resurrection implied that the tomb was empty,[106] then it is hardly conceivable that the Christian message of the resurrection could have spread abroad in Jerusalem unless the presupposition of the empty tomb were tenable.[107] Confirmation that this fact was generally known and presup-

103. M. Dummett, "Biblische Exegese und Auferstehung," *Internationale katholische Zeitschrift Communio* 13 (1984) 271-83.

104. Ibid., p. 278; cf. *Jesus — God and Man,* pp. 103f.

105. Dummett, "Biblische Exegese und Auferstehung," p. 281. Dummett is here criticizing the abuse of form criticism (cf. p. 271).

106. Cf. Vögtle and Pesch, *Wie kam es zum Osterglauben?* pp. 97, 109, 130. This is also the premise of the theory of Pesch that the story of the empty tomb is a product of belief in the resurrection.

107. Cf. Althaus, *Die Wahrheit des kirchlichen Osterglaubens* (1940), p. 25, quoted in *Jesus — God and Man,* p. 100. Cf. also Moltmann, *The Way of Jesus Christ,* p. 222, who points out that the message of the resurrection that the disciples brought back to Jerusalem could not have survived a single hour if the body could have been shown to be in the tomb. Cf. also Craig, "On Doubts about the Resurrection," pp. 53ff., esp. 59f. Pesch in his commentary dismissed this argument too summarily as an unprovable and refutable postulate (*Markus,* II, 538). He dealt with it more fully in his essay "Zur Entstehung des Glaubens an die Auferstehung Jesu," *TQ* 133 (1973) 206ff. His doubts as to the tomb tradition in this essay do not agree well with the age assigned to it in his commentary, or especially with the role that the tradition ascribes to the women in finding the empty tomb.

Impressive at a first glance is the thesis that the view of Herod expressed in Mark 6:14, 16 — namely, that Jesus was the beheaded Baptist risen again — supports the idea of a resurrection without an empty tomb (p. 208; cf. also K. Berger, *Die Auferstehung des Propheten und die Erhöhung des Menschensohns,* pp. 15ff.). But the reembodiment of a dead person in someone else is very different from an eschatological resurrection of the dead and transformation into a life that is very different from existence on earth. Vögtle thus rejected this thesis (*Wie kam es zum Osterglauben?* pp. 80ff.). Cf. also W. Kasper,

posed by friends and foes alike may be found in references to the debates
between Christians and their Jewish opponents on the theme, e.g., in the
Gospels at Matt. 28:13-15 or John 20:12ff., also v. 2.[108] There is no trace
of any contention against Christians that the body was still in the tomb.
The force of this fact is often underestimated in discussions of the tradition of the finding of the empty tomb, as is also the extent of the link
between the resurrection and corporeality, especially in relation to one
recently deceased, and to the circumstance that the resurrection of Jesus
was believed and proclaimed in Jerusalem.

Those who want to dispute the empty tomb of Jesus must show
that contemporary Jewish witnesses to belief in the resurrection included
some who did not think the resurrection of the dead need have anything
at all to do with the body in the tomb.[109] They must also assume that
such views (not thus far attested) were sufficiently popular in Palestine,
else the first Christians could not have successfully preached the resurrection of Jesus if his body had been intact in the tomb. Even then, an
explanation would still be needed as to why the Gospels present debates

"Der Glaube an die Auferstehung Jesu vor dem Forum historischer Kritik," *TQ* 153 (1973)
229ff., esp. 236: "It is obvious that the NT does not see in the resurrection, after the break
of the crucifixion, a return to the old life but the qualitative irruption of the new life in
the new aeon and a qualitatively new mode of the presence of Jesus in the Spirit. Hence
the resurrection of Jesus was not like a return of Elijah, who according to the OT and
Jewish tradition had not even died, nor was it after the manner of the return of John in
the earthly Jesus, which was a commonly accepted notion."

108. On this cf. Campenhausen, *Der Ablauf der Osterereignisse*, pp. 31ff. The question of Vögtle why in the older tradition prior to Matt. 28:13-15 there is no debate with
Jewish attempts to explain the empty tomb (*Wie kam es zum Osterglauben?* pp. 87ff.) offers
a reason to dispute the assumption of early knowledge of the empty tomb only if Mark and
Luke ought to have mentioned such debates had they occurred. But this is not plausible in
view of the character and the probable recipients of their accounts. Vögtle's further objection
that if the tomb was found open and empty, the disciples ought to have told of an examination and confirmation (pp. 92ff.) is even less plausible, since the predominant view is
that they were in Galilee at the time of the opening and finding according to Mark 16:1-8.
Hence Vögtle's reasons against early knowledge of the empty tomb are unconvincing (cf.
pp. 97f.). His theory that although the Easter proclamation reckoned with the empty tomb,
there was no interest in it in Jerusalem, not even in response to Jewish opponents, is also
intrinsically unconvincing.

109. There might well have been different views to the corporeality; cf. J. Kremer
in G. Greshake and J. Kremer, *Resurrectio Mortuorum*, pp. 68ff. Nor was there perhaps any
great clarity on the antithesis to the Greek idea of the immortality of the soul (pp. 71ff.).
Since expectation of resurrection was linked to the eschatological future, it is not surprising
that the relation to the body in the tomb was not clarified; cf. G. Stemberger, *Der Leib der
Auferstehung*, pp. 115f. Yet the basic concept was that human existence must be corporeal
and can take concrete form only in the same corporeality (p. 116).

between Christians and their opponents regarding what happened to the body. So long as no proofs are offered on these points, we must assume that the tomb of Jesus was in fact empty.

Paul's mention of the burial of Jesus in 1 Cor. 15:4 tells us nothing regarding his knowledge of the finding of the empty tomb. From the fact that he does not expressly mention the empty tomb[110] we cannot infer that he did not know about it, but merely that emphasis on this fact was not theologically important for him as he developed his argument in his epistles. This is not surprising if for Paul the empty tomb was a self-evident implication of what was said about the resurrection of Jesus. Paul found proof of the event in the appearances of the risen Lord, not in the empty tomb. This is understandable in view of the fact that the empty tomb could be explained in different ways. In Jerusalem the empty tomb had to be important as a self-evident fact, but not equally so in Ephesus or Corinth. Furthermore, the fact of the empty tomb has no importance of its own if it is implied already in a raising or rising again or if by itself it cannot sustain the proclaiming of a resurrection.

Though primitive Christian conviction as to the resurrection of Jesus rests not on the finding of his empty tomb but on the appearances, the tomb tradition is significant for the total witness to the Easter event. It creates difficulty for the theory that the appearances of the risen Lord might have been mere hallucinations. It also resists any superficial spiritualizing of the Easter message, though leaving room for the thought of a changing of the earthly corporeality of Jesus into the eschatological reality of a new life. We thus cannot explain the finding of the empty tomb as a product of Easter faith and must recognize that it happened independently of the appearances. Accordingly, even if this tradition developed in the light of Easter faith, we must still assign to the report the function of confirming the identity of the reality of Jesus encountered in the appearances with his resurrection from the dead.

7. *The thesis that Jesus rose again, that the dead Jesus of Nazareth came to a new life, implies already a claim to historicity.* This is true here

---

110. Craig, "On Doubts about the Resurrection," does not think that the stress on the burial as such, but that the sequence "dead, buried, and raised" (1 Cor. 15:3ff.) implies the empty tomb (p. 57). I regard this as an important point. The reference to the burial as well as the death is not just a literary device to stress the reality of the death; it is also a statement of fact (contra J. Broer, *Die Urgemeinde und das Grab Jesu. Eine Analyse der Grablegungsgeschichte im NT* [Munich, 1972], pp. 273ff.).

as it is of all spatiotemporal events insofar as there is confidence that the thesis will stand up to critical testing, that such testing will not negate the alleged facts. If the Christian thesis regarding the resurrection were asserting that something took place that transcends human history in space and time, then the situation would obviously be different. But that is not so. The Easter message certainly states that the resurrection of Jesus was an event of transition from this earthly world to a new and imperishable life with God, yet the event took place in this world, namely, in the tomb of Jesus in Jerusalem before the visit of the women on the Sunday morning after his death.

Paul (1 Cor. 15:4), unlike Mark (8:31; 9:31; 10:34 par.), expressly calls "on the third day" a fulfillment of scripture (cf. also Luke 24:27). Whether he had Hos. 6:2 in mind must remain an open question.[111] The timing in Mark 16:2 ("early in the morning on the first day of the week") can hardly have its origin in that verse, and only with difficulty can it be regarded as the source of the third-day formula, i.e., one reckoning from the death of Jesus.[112]

Any assertion that an event took place in the past implies a historical claim and exposes itself to testing. This necessarily applies, then, to the Christian assertion that Jesus rose again the third day after his death. As regards the proper understanding of this thesis, the following points should be noted.

a. Historicity does not necessarily mean that what is said to have taken place historically must be like other known events.[113] The claim to historicity that is inseparable from the assertion of the facticity of an event

---

111. Cf. G. Delling in *TDNT,* II, 949, and Evans, *Resurrection,* pp. 47ff.; also K. Lehmann, *Auferweckt am dritten Tag nach der Schrift* (1968), pp. 221-30.

112. Cf. E. L. Bode, *The First Easter Morning* (1970), p. 161, to whom Craig, "On Doubts about the Resurrection," p. 54, appeals. Craig refers also to the conjecture of Brown, *John,* II, 980, that the agreed usage of the Gospels regarding the time of finding the empty tomb may be taken as a pointer that "the basic time indication of the finding of the tomb was fixed in Christian memory before the possible symbolism in the three-day reckoning had yet been perceived." This is in opposition to Evans, *Resurrection,* pp. 75f. On the Jewish roots of the idea of the resurrection on the third day, cf. also Lehmann, *Auferweckt am dritten Tag,* pp. 262-90.

113. On this, cf. my rebuttal of E. Troeltsch in *Basic Questions in Theology,* 2 vols. (Philadelphia, 1970-71), I, 53ff., esp. 57f. Cf. also Moltmann, *The Way of Jesus Christ,* pp. 243ff., in spite of his rejection of the historicity of the resurrection (see n. 114). Cf. also D. P. Fuller, "The Resurrection of Jesus and the Historical Method," *Journal of Bible and Religion* 34 (1966) 18-24.

simply involves the fact that it happened at a specific time. The question whether it is like other events may play a role in critical evaluation of the truth of the claim but is not itself a condition of the actual truth claim the assertion makes.

b. Hence a reference to the otherness of the eschatological reality of resurrection life compared to the reality of this passing world does not affect the claim to historicity that is implied in the assertion of the facticity of an event that took place at a specific time.[114] Theological interest in the assertion of the historicity of the resurrection of Jesus, as of his incarnation, depends on the fact that the overcoming of death by the new eschatological life has actually taken place in this world and history of ours.

c. Assertion of the historicity of an event does not mean that its facticity is so sure that there can no longer be any dispute regarding it.[115] Many statements of historical fact are actually debatable. In principle, doubts may exist regarding all such statements. In the case of the resurrection of Jesus, all Christians must realize that the facticity of the event will be contested right up to the eschatological consummation of the world because its uniqueness transcends an understanding of reality that is oriented only to this passing world and because the new reality that has come in the resurrection of Jesus has not yet universally and definitively manifested itself.[116] Nevertheless, Christian faith maintains that the es-

114. Moltmann, *The Way of Jesus Christ*, p. 214, misses this point when he writes that those who call the resurrection of Christ "historical" in the same sense as his death overlook the new creation that begins with it and fail to take into account eschatological hope. The difference from the crucifixion lies in the quality of the event, not in its character as event.

115. This widespread but inappropriate idea is perhaps primarily responsible for skepticism regarding the use of the word "historical" with reference to the Christian affirmation of the resurrection. Thus Kasper wrote that he invited historical research to offer solid proof but insisted that he saw no reason to treat the resurrection of Jesus as a real event if it could not be historically affirmed as such (*Jesus the Christ*). He overlooked the fact that in his excellently stated thesis the main issue is the logical one regarding the facticity of a past event; the degree of decisiveness with which such claims can be made is an entirely separate matter. He thus also thought that I made too great demands on the historical method. But "historically" does not mean "historically provable" (so Moltmann, *The Way of Jesus Christ*, p. 215). It means that an event actually took place. When can we say that something is historically provable, without further doubt? The claim to historicity simply means that an assertion will stand up to historical investigation, even though there may be differences and debates about the judgment.

116. In this sense I can agree with the tenor of Moltmann's description, *The Way of Jesus Christ*, pp. 223 and 240ff. When Moltmann writes of the Christian belief in the resurrection that it remains a hope until verified by the eschatological resurrection of all the dead, so that its language is that of promise and the hope established thereby, not of completed facts

chatological life of the resurrection of the dead has already become an event in the crucified Jesus. As a factual statement about a past event, to say this unavoidably involves therefore a historical claim. It can only cause confusion to deny the claim but hold fast to the statement of facticity.

d. Our judgment regarding the historicity of the resurrection of Jesus depends not only on examining the individual data (and the related reconstruction of the event) but also on our understanding of reality, of what we regard as possible or impossible prior to any evaluation of the details. In this regard Paul is right that if we do not think the dead can rise in any circumstances, then we cannot regard the resurrection of Jesus as a fact (1 Cor. 15:13), no matter how strong the evidence may be that supports it.[117] We must concede, however, that a judgment of this type rests on a prior dogmatic decision and does not deserve to be called critical (in the sense of the evaluating of the transmitted texts).

Certainly historical reconstruction is always oriented to a common-sense view of reality — a view that is in a state of constant flux, that may, e.g., take up new perspectives once they are adopted widely enough.[118] In the Middle Ages the biblical concept of reality was one of the elements in the common understanding. But at the beginning of the Christian tradition, and in the secular culture of our own day, the biblical concept of reality as a field of divine action, including its eschatological consummation, formed and forms a challenge. To respond to this challenge may be difficult for secular historians. But if they are to reach a critical judgment regarding the Easter message, they must distinguish between the degree to which individual findings and the greater coherence of alternative descriptions[119] force them to this judgment, and the degree to which it is the result of a fundamental preconception. Insofar as it is

---

(p. 223), he makes too little of the finished nature of the resurrection of Jesus, which Paul stresses in 1 Cor. 15:12ff. More accurately, we ought to say that the reality that broke in with the resurrection of Jesus is not yet complete, and in this sense the event is thus debatable. Yet we still maintain that it has already happened, and the fact that the new life has come makes Christian hope a well-grounded hope. Moltmann does also say that Jesus was raised before all others (p. 223), thus saying more than his appended elucidation states.

117. For a classic example, cf. ch. 10 ("Of Miracles") of Hume's *Inquiry concerning Human Understanding* (1758).

118. On this, cf. the clear and considered discussion in H. Burhenn's "Pannenberg's Argument for the Historicity of the Resurrection," *Journal of the American Academy of Religion* 40 (1972) 368-79.

119. On the significance of the latter, see A. Dunkel, *Christlicher Glaube und historische Vernunft* (Göttingen, 1989), pp. 288f.

the latter, Christian theology has no reason to shrink from the challenge that its assertion of the historicity of the resurrection of Jesus raises for secular history.

§ 2. The Christological Development of the Unity of Jesus with God

a. The Divine Sonship of Jesus and Its Origin in the Eternity of God

The Easter event became the starting point of apostolic proclamation and the church's christology. Both rest on the distinctive significance of this event in its reference back to the pre-Easter history of Jesus. Specifically, it refers to his work as messenger of the imminent rule of God and to the linking of the messianic title with his person by the accusation that led to his condemnation and execution by the Romans. In content this reference has the character of a divine confirmation and vindication (1 Tim. 3:16) of the pre-Easter person and work of Jesus in view of his rejection and condemnation by the Jews and the Romans. We must now consider in more detail the implications of this event of confirmation and vindication.

If we are to understand the event of the resurrection of Jesus as his divine confirmation and vindication vis-à-vis his condemnation by human judges, then we must first consider it as a repudiation of the accusation that was brought against him. Jesus did not make himself equal to God, not even in the sense of declaring himself to be the Son of God (Mark 14:61). He differentiated himself from God by subordinating himself to the Father so that he might serve the Father's lordship by all that he did. In this way he gave the Father the honor that all creatures owe him as the one God. Only in this self-distinction from the Father by subordination to his royal rule, and in service to it, is he the Son.

Here is the explanation of the ambivalence of the answer of Jesus to the question that in the Synoptic tradition the high priest put to him at the climax of the Jewish hearing: Are you the Messiah, the Son of the Blessed? (Mark 14:61). The ambivalence of the reply finds reflection in the different renderings in the Gospels. The "I am" in Mark 14:62 is clearly positive, but we find reservations, though not rejection, in Luke 22:67f. and Matt. 26:64. The reply in Luke suggests that confession of divine sonship involves the human arrogance of making oneself equal to God. Sonship is not seen in the sense of subordination to the Father as the one

God. The continuation shows this, since the threat of judgment by the Son of Man seems to have been understood as an expression of human arrogance (Matt. 26:65; cf. Luke 22:70f.). Nevertheless, Jesus is the Son of the Father precisely by subjecting himself to the Father's kingly rule and serving it. The divine vindication vis-à-vis the judgment of human judges says first, then, that precisely by not making himself equal to God, he is righteous before God as the "Son" of the Father, as the resurrection discloses. Rom. 1:4 may not expressly say this (though cf. Phil. 2:8f.), but his institution into "sonship" by the resurrection is to be understood as an expression by God himself, confirming directly the divine authorization of Jesus' mission.

The description of Jesus as "the Son" has a basis in the way in which he spoke of God as his Father during his earthly ministry, though the actual use of "the Son" on his own lips (Matt. 11:27; Luke 6:22) may not be historically authentic. The question of the authenticity of this self-description is of secondary importance, since his way of calling the God of his mission "the Father" implied sonship in relation to this Father. In the light of the Easter event, then, it was natural to call the one whom God had justified by raising him from the dead "the Son," especially as the title "Son of God" had played a part in the trial in another connection, namely, in regard to the question of messiahship. The title "Son of God" was a fitting one for the Messiah, for the Davidic king was the "son of God" according to Ps. 2:7 and 2 Sam. 7:14.[120] The title "Son" thus links the messianic title that Jesus did not claim, but that was connected with him as the reason for his condemnation and execution, to the characteristic relation of Jesus to God as his Father.

The divine vindication of the Crucified by his resurrection must also be seen in relation to his condemnation and execution by the Romans as a messianic pretender. Over against the Roman verdict on Jesus, the divine vindication says that he is not the Messiah in the sense of a political ruler and therefore in the sense of the charge of revolt against Roman domination. Nevertheless, the title "Messiah" stuck because of its link to that of "Son." It became, indeed, part of the name of

---

120. In Rom. 1:3f. Davidic sonship is thus a step toward institution to divine sonship, which Ps. 2:7 relates to accession to the throne. On the Davidic descent of Jesus, cf. F. Hahn, *The Titles of Jesus in Christology: Their History in Early Christianity* (London, 1969), pp. 240-78, esp. p. 241; also Cullmann, *Christology*, pp. 127ff., and C. Burger, *Jesus als Davidssohn* (Göttingen, 1970).

Jesus, but reinterpreted in terms of the suffering obedience of the Crucified. Jesus was confirmed as a fully authorized representative of the royal rule of God that he proclaimed. This is the point of his exaltation to messianic dignity by institution into full exercise of divine sonship (Rom. 1:4) in the power of the Spirit, who raised him from the dead. But because the exaltation expresses the vindication of Jesus by his resurrection, being thus related to the charge made against him, which led to his condemnation and crucifixion, we do not have in the messianic rule of the one thus exalted merely a new phase that follows, cancels, and leaves behind that of his passion. At issue here is the messiahship of the Crucified as such, so that in a paradoxical interrelation, John's Gospel can call the crucifixion itself exaltation (3:14; 8:28; 12:32f.). In the sense of John, of course, this is possible only in the light of the resurrection and the return to the Father.

The divine confirmation of Jesus in the Easter event extends also to his earthly ministry and on this basis to his proclamation of the divine rule and of its coming with himself. The implied claim of Jesus for his own person — namely, that the future of God is present in and by him — no longer seems to be human arrogance in the light of the Easter event. The resurrection of Jesus now gives confirmation that already in his earthly ministry he acted on the Father's authority, so that the kingly rule of the Father was indeed present in him. Already in his earthly coming he was the Son of the Father, though first instituted as such with power by his resurrection (Rom. 1:4). Institution into sonship by the resurrection cannot mean that only from that point onward was he the Son of the Father.[121] Such a view fails to see the confirmatory thrust of the resurrection. As an event of confirmation, the Easter event has retroactive force.[122] In the light of the Easter event, then, the divine sonship of Jesus comes into relation to his baptism by John, the starting point of his public work (Mark 1:11 par.).[123] The resurrection of Jesus confirmed not merely his message and work, as though the content of these were detachable from his person, but Jesus himself, the person upon whom his message had cast a half-light. Jesus' filial relation to the Father thus could rightly be dated

---

121. Cf. Paul's interpretation of Rom. 1:3f., U. Wilckens, *Der Brief an die Römer*, 3 vols., EKK (Zurich/Neukirchen, 1978-82), I, 59.

122. See n. 92 in ch. 9 above.

123. For more detail, cf. *Jesus — God and Man*, pp. 137ff. According to Jeremias, *Verkündigung*, pp. 56ff., the baptism was historically the starting point of his sense of divine sonship (pp. 61ff.).

back to the actual beginning of his earthly existence, to his conception and birth (Luke 1:32, 35).[124]

For a proper understanding of this aspect, we must remember that we can validly relate the divine sonship of Jesus to the baptism, or to the origin of his earthly life as the birth of the Son of God, only in the light of the Easter event and as an expression of its confirmatory function. Only when this angle is taken into account do ideas of the basis of the sonship of Jesus in his baptism on the one hand, or his birth on the other, not come into conflict either with one another or with the early statement that he was instituted into the dignity of sonship by his resurrection from the dead. Taken in isolation, the three concepts of the origin of the divine sonship of Jesus come into competition and cancel one another out.[125]

The Easter event also confirms the message of Jesus to the degree that it at least partially fulfills the intimation of the coming divine rule. The end did not actually come before the generation of Jesus passed away (Mark 9:11; 13:30; cf. Matt. 10:23). Nevertheless, for Jesus himself the final salvation of the rule of God became a reality with his resurrection from the dead. For primitive Christianity, then, the delay in the Parousia was not a disappointment that shattered the foundations of its faith, even though the first generation, including Paul (1 Thess. 4:15-17), expected it imminently (cf. 1 Cor. 15:51; Rom. 13:11). Through the risen Lord and his Spirit eschatological salvation had already become a certainty for believers, so that the length of the remaining span of time was a secondary matter. This did not alter the fact, of course, that the future of the final consummation was constitutive for faith in Jesus Christ.

As a consequence of the Easter event and the related reception of the Spirit, the accent in the grounding of participation in salvation came to be focused, not on the eschatological future, but on fellowship with the Lord, who was now present by his Spirit. In Jesus' message the imminence of God's eschatological future had

---

124. The story of the virgin conception in Luke 1:26-38 presupposes the title "Son of God" for the promised child. V. 35b in particular gives us to understand that the story has the character of an etiology of divine sonship. It offers a basis for something already known, namely, that Jesus is the Son of God. On the birth stories, cf. R. E. Brown, *The Birth of the Messiah: A Commentary on the Infancy Narratives in Matthew and Luke* (New York, 1977), pp. 313, 517-31.

125. The idea that the differentiated use of the concept of sonship in the NT gives freedom to dogmatic reflection to go its own way, regardless of the related "contents" (H. Grass, *Christliche Glaubenslehre*, I [1973], pp. 112, 117), expresses a strange notion of the relation of Christian teaching to the biblical witness. The variety shown by the witness does not release us from the obligation but should cause dogmatics to seek the unity behind the variety and the reasons for the development of the varied forms of witness. Insight into this task underlies the procedure in *Jesus — God and Man*, pp. 133-50.

given urgency to the summons to orient oneself to it, but after Easter the message of the reconciliation and redemption enacted in the death and resurrection of Jesus replaced that motif. We must evaluate this development in terms of the anticipatory presence of the future of salvation that is characteristic of the message and work of Jesus. Seen in this way, the development was not a mistaken one. It was a proper building on the foundation that Jesus laid. The Easter event confirmed this feature of the earthly ministry of Jesus both by giving force to the divine authority of Jesus and by repeating the element of anticipation in expecting the irruption of salvation (the new and imperishable life in fellowship with God had indeed come for Jesus, but not yet for all believers). Both motifs come together in the thought of incarnation: the proleptic revelation of salvation amid unfinished world history as an expression of the manifestation of the eternal Son of God in the earthly history of Jesus as this may be seen in the light of the Easter event.

The relation of Jesus to the eternal God as this finds expression in the concept of divine sonship, and as it is the content of the confirmation of his person and mission by the resurrection, may not be limited to the span of his earthly existence. The confirmation of his message by the God who raised him to life says not merely that Jesus acted with divine power but also that God is from all eternity the One whom Jesus proclaimed him to be. The message and history of Jesus contain the eschatologically definitive revelation of the Father and his turning in love to his creation. "No one knows the Father except the Son and anyone to whom the Son chooses to reveal him" (Matt. 11:27 par.). But if the Father is from all eternity the One he is shown historically to be in relation to Jesus his Son, and through him, then we cannot think of the Father apart from the Son. This means on the one hand that the risen Lord is exalted to eternal fellowship with the Father. His relationship to the eternal Father as the Son, however, means on the other hand that the Son was linked to the Father before the beginning of the earthly existence of Jesus. The relation reaches back also to the time before his earthly birth.[126]

126. K.-J. Kuschel, *Geboren vor aller Zeit? Der Streit um Christi Ursprung* (Munich, 1990), agrees with my thesis that we can no longer think of the deity of God apart from Jesus (p. 528, quoting from my *Glaubensbekenntnis,* p. 75). It is an unconditional NT belief that for believers, Jesus is inseparable from the deity of the eternal God. But Kuschel asks whether we are to infer from this that the consubstantiality of Jesus with God means, as I also affirmed, that on the side of his unity with God, Jesus already existed before he became man, before his earthly birth. Does it also mean the participation of this man in the eternity of God, even though he was not eternal as man but, like us, was born in time (p. 528)? We may rightly ask this, but Kuschel advances no argument for evading this conclusion if we take seriously the position that he also accepts, namely, that Jesus as a person is inseparably related to God in his eternity.

If the relation to the historical person of Jesus of Nazareth in eternity characterizes the identity of God as Father, then we must speak of a preexistence of the Son, who was to be historically manifested in Jesus of Nazareth, even before his earthly birth. Then we also must view the earthly existence of Jesus as the event of the incarnation of the preexistent Son. Certainly we may not think of this Son in isolation from the historical filial relation of Jesus to the Father if the affirmation of his preexistence is grounded on this alone. Theologically the eternal relation of the Father to the Son may not be detached from the incarnation of the Son in the historical existence and work of Jesus.[127] Nevertheless, we are to understand this relation as part of the eternal identity of the Father. We can thus speak of a state of preexistence of the Son of God, who was manifested in the history of Jesus, even before his earthly birth, just as for the same reason we may speak of an abiding relation of the Crucified and risen Lord to the Father in consequence of his exaltation to fellowship with the Father and to participation in his lordship.

The question of the religious origin of the idea of preexistence, which we find in Jewish wisdom speculation (Prov. 8:22f.; Sir. 24:3ff.) rather than in non-Jewish Hellenistic concepts,[128] must not crowd out the more basic question of the reasons for linking the idea to the figure of Jesus in the tradition concerning him.[129] Preexistence statements and the confession of the exaltation of Jesus

127. Karl Barth dealt with this link between the thought of preexistence and the historical revelation of God in Jesus Christ in *CD*, I/1, 414ff. He made the connection between the eternal deity of the Son and the historical existence of the man Jesus by means of the doctrine of predestination. The first "object" of predestination is the Son of God as destined to be the Son of Man, the preexistent God-man Jesus Christ, who as such is the eternal basis of the divine election (*CD*, II/2, § 33.1; cf. III/1, 50f.). Along these lines Barth distinctively doubled the concept of preexistence, referring to the deity of Jesus Christ, the eternal Son, in I/1, 414, and to the human reality of Jesus in II/2, 110. But by doing this, and relating the two aspects by means of the concept of election, he did not manage to define conceptually the connection between the preexistence of the eternal Son as such and the historical filial relation of Jesus to the Father. For the act of the election is part and parcel of the freedom of God's relation to the world, so that its content cannot be constitutive for the eternal identity of his divine essence. If it were, the world itself would be the correlate of this essence. Hence we must derive the link to the incarnation from the eternal relation of the Son to the Father and not by the detour of the doctrine of predestination.

128. Cf. G. Schimanowski, *Weisheit und Messias: Die jüdischen Voraussetzungen der urchristlichen Präexistenzchristologie* (Tübingen, 1985), pp. 13-308; also H. v. Lips, *Weisheitliche Traditionen im NT* (Neukirchen-Vluyn, 1990), pp. 150ff.

129. We find the link in Q sayings (Luke 13:34f. par.), but Schimanowski (*Weisheit und Messias*, pp. 313f.) and Lips (*Weisheitliche Traditionen im NT*, pp. 254ff.) regard it as later than Jesus himself.

derive from the confirmation of his divine authority by his resurrection from the dead. For believers, then, exaltation has priority and claims greater interest. Yet preexistence is closely connected with it[130] and, like it, rests directly on the relation of the risen Lord to the eternal God. Here lies the explanation of its early appearance in primitive Christian texts.

In Paul we find the thought not only in Phil. 2:6ff., quoting a pre-Pauline hymn,[131] but also in the statement about Christ's part in creation, "through whom are all things" (1 Cor. 8:6), as well as his activity in Israel's salvation history (1 Cor. 10:4).[132] We may also refer to what is said about the sending of the Son into the world (Gal. 4:4; Rom. 8:3), since these sayings of Paul presuppose preexistence as the starting point of the mission,[133] as is incontestably the case in John (3:17; cf. 1 John 4:10). We certainly do not do justice to the evidence in the primitive Christian tradition if we regard the idea of the preexistence of the Son of God who was manifested in Jesus as a marginal phenomenon that occurs only in the hymns in Col. 1:15-17 and Heb. 1:2 and in John's Gospel.[134] Materially it is in

130. J. Habermann, *Präexistenzaussagen im NT* (1990), pp. 421f., calls the exaltation statements the starting point for preexistence statements.

131. Ibid., pp. 91-157.

132. Ibid., pp. 178ff., 215ff., 221ff.; cf. Schimanowski, *Weisheit und Messias*, pp. 317ff., 320ff.

133. So W. Kramer, *Christ, Lord, Son of God*, SBT, 1/50 (London/Naperville, 1966), pp. 114ff.; also Hahn, *Titles*, pp. 304f. Hahn points out that sending statements as such might be related to prophetic sending (cf. Mark 12:1-9) without presupposing preexistence. But this is not so when, as in Gal. 4:4, the sending is related to the birth, to earthly existence, and to entering into earthly circumstances and relations (Kramer, *Christ, Lord, Son of God*, p. 114; cf. Hahn, *Titles*, loc. cit.). Sending thus presupposes preexistence.

Critics of the linking of Gal. 4:4 and Rom. 8:3 to the presupposition of a preexistent status of the Son have failed to weaken this argument. J. Blank, *Paulus und Jesus* (1968), p. 267, and G. Schneider, "Praexistenz Christi," in *NT und Kirche*, ed. J. Gnilka (1974), p. 408 n. 43, see an analogy to prophetic sending along the lines of Mark 12:4-6 but do not take into account Hahn's arguments against the use of this analogy. J. D. G. Dunn, *Christology in the Making: A NT Inquiry into the Origins of the Doctrine of the Incarnation* (Philadelphia, 1980), pp. 38-46, also appeals to Mark 12:6 as supposedly the closest parallel to Gal. 4:4 (p. 40). He rightly points out that "born of a woman" does not have to refer to the event of the birth as such, but he fails to take up the separate issue that Paul's statement as a whole mentions the conditions of Jesus' earthly existence (as a Jew) as well as his birth of a woman and subjection to the law, thus describing the situation into which the Son was sent. The same applies in a different way to Rom. 8:3.

134. So Kuschel, *Geboren vor aller Zeit?* pp. 526f. Kuschel forgets at this point that he himself finds a Wisdom idea of preexistence in Phil. 2 (p. 329) and that he described a personal preexistence statement as a function of what is said about humiliation and exaltation (p. 326). The fact that this was the central point for Paul does not mean that the preexistence statement was not important for him in this function. Certainly it does not stand alone (p. 335), but this does not imply that Paul rejected the idea. We see in Kuschel a tendency to insist on the main theological point in the context as distinct from preexistence statements, and hence to relativize such statements, to treat them lightly, and finally to

fact very closely related to the apostolic proclamation of the risen and divinely exalted Lord, and this relation finds sufficiently clear expression in the NT texts if we realize that we are not to expect systematic or doctrinal reflection on the theme in these texts. We find no such reflection on other themes either (e.g., that of exaltation).

The idea of a preexistence of the Son of God, who manifested himself historically in Jesus' relation to the Father, is inescapable not only if we assert the fellowship of Jesus with the eternal God but also if we maintain the link between the eternal identity of the Father God whom Jesus proclaimed and the relation to Jesus as his Son. By God's election we too may receive fellowship with the eternal Father, but without preexistence being ascribed to us. But if the relation to a man is constitutive for the eternal identity of God himself, then the correlate in the relation must also be eternal. The result is the preexistence of the son. The idea of preexistence, however, is not required always and everywhere to express this relation to the eternal essence of God. Thus we may speak of an ideal preexistence[135] of divine thoughts of creation prior to their execution in history. Like all creaturely reality, this preexistence in the purposes of God would be on the condition of the divine freedom and would not be constitutive for the identity of the divine essence.[136]

---

eliminate them altogether (cf. 362ff. on 1 Cor. 10:4 and 365ff. on 1 Cor. 8:6, esp. 317ff.). This does not suggest exegetical objectivity.

   Against inquiry into the material connections between the church's later dogmatic statements and the implications of NT texts like those cited, Kuschel raises the charge of misusing in a hermeneutically inconsistent way (p. 528) the history of Jesus as a springboard from which to reach a presupposed metaphysical relation between the Father and the Son (p. 528; cf. 526f.). From such a charge, with its polemical sidetracking, we can deduce only that the author had no sympathy with the inquiry (which itself is by no means intrinsically meaningless) into these relations. Why should one caricature systematic reflection on the implications of NT statements for the message of Christ and Christian teaching? Does not this happen, perhaps, because Kuschel himself wants to purge the picture of Jesus of anything that might lead to the doctrine of the Trinity (cf. pp. 505ff., 666ff.)? Certainly the doctrine of the Trinity does not depend solely upon the occurrence of the idea of preexistence in Paul. The decisive point is that the relation of Jesus to the Father as his Son implies his eternal sonship (see above, n. 126). But if this is so, we may assume that this fact played a part in the history of the tradition, i.e., in the process of developing christological conceptions in primitive Christianity.

   135. For emphasis on the difference between ideal and real preexistence, cf. R. G. Hamerton-Kelly, *Preexistence, Wisdom, and the Son of Man* (Cambridge, 1973).

   136. Cf. n. 127 on Barth's doctrine of Christ's preexistence in the counsel of God (esp. *CD*, III/1, 50f.).

Because the thought of preexistence as such does not express intrinsic relationship to the divine essence, Christian theology, notwithstanding the early appearance of the concept in connection with Jesus Christ, needed a long period of theological discussion before it finally clarified the full deity of the preexistent Son in the 4th century. For many years an obstacle to the attainment of this clarity was the linking of the procession of the Son from the Father to the transition of the eternal God to his action in creation and salvation history. Along these lines the procession of the Son seemed to be the beginning of the work of creation, and consequently it could not stand on the same plane as the eternal deity of the Father. Origen was still trapped at this point, even though he pioneered a way out of the dilemma with his thesis of the eternal generation of the Son by the Father.[137] Only the argument of Athanasius, for which Origen prepared the way, and which was to the effect that the Father cannot be the Father without the Son and hence is never without the Son,[138] made possible a clarification of the Christian confession of the preexistence of the divine Son, who was manifested in Jesus Christ along the lines of his full deity.

The origin of the divine sonship of Jesus can lie, then, only in the eternity of God himself. Though preexistence statements in the NT might be rather vaguely formulated for the most part, this is their true point. Other statements that link the divine sonship to the resurrection, the baptism, or the birth need not be in contradiction if we understand them in relation to their context and their special point, and if we do not read them as definitive answers to the question of the ultimate origin of the divine sonship of Jesus. Only the statement about preexistence led to a definitive answer, and for a long period its content stood in need of clarification. But preexistence statements, along with statements about the divine sonship in connection with the resurrection, baptism, or birth, have one point in common. They all are possible only in the light of the resurrection of Jesus from the dead and the confirmation of his earthly work by this event.

How does it stand, however, with the inner basis of the relationship of Jesus as Son to the eternal essence of the Father? Without this inner basis in the historical relation of Jesus to the Father, even what the apostolic kerygma says in the light of the Easter event concerning the filial

---

137. *De princ.* 1.2.4; cf. vol. I, 275.
138. Athanasius, *C. Arian.* 1.29 etc.; cf. Origen, *De princ.* 1.2.10 and vol. I, 272ff.

dignity of Jesus would be external to his historical reality. No doubt the distinctiveness of the filial relation of Jesus to the Father became an express theme only in the light of his resurrection from the dead. Yet it must still be demonstrable in the relation of the earthly Jesus to the Father if theological statements about the eternal sonship of Jesus are to be truly relevant.

b. The Self-Distinction of Jesus from the Father as the Inner Basis of His Divine Sonship

At the heart of the message of Jesus stood the Father and his coming kingdom, not any dignity that Jesus claimed for his own person that would thus make himself equal to God (John 5:18). Jesus differentiated himself as a mere man from the Father as the one God. He thus subjected himself to the claim of the coming divine rule, just as he required his hearers to do. He could even reject the respectful title "good Master" (Mark 10:18 par.), with a reference to God alone as good. If we still can speak of a sense of sonship in relation to God,[139] this is a reflection of what he says about God as Father. The Son is he who in his relation to the Father corresponds to the latter's fatherly being.

"The Son can do nothing of his own accord, but only what he sees the Father doing" (John 5:19). This Johannine saying excellently charac-terizes the point of the filial relation as we see it also in the Synoptic texts insofar as the special position of Jesus that differentiates him from others is not also intended. Thus Jesus in a Q saying could demand very generally of his hearers that they should show themselves to be the children of their heavenly Father by loving their enemies as God causes his sun to shine on both the good and the bad (Luke 6:35; Matt. 5:45). Again the Q saying in Matt. 11:25 (Luke 10:22) need not originally contain any exclusive claim for the person of Jesus but may be taken as a figurative statement that explains subordination to the Father in terms of a filial relationship as the condition of true knowledge of God. In the present context, of course, it does denote the special dignity of Jesus. In the parable of the wicked husbandmen, too, the son (Mark 12:6 par.) is plainly differentiated from the servants. If the parable really goes back to Jesus, he is perhaps distin-

---

139. Dunn, *Christology in the Making*, pp. 22-33 ("Jesus' Sense of Sonship"), esp. 26ff.

guishing his mission from that of the prophets. In sum, the term "Son" to denote the proper relation to the Father is ambivalent. It may be a general term, or it may denote the special relation of Jesus to the Father. In the trial this ambivalence stands behind the question of divine sonship and the answer of Jesus (Luke 22:70) if the reports in the Gospels rest on historical materials.

In the designation of Jesus as the Son, it was probably the disciples who stressed the uniqueness of his relation to the Father and therefore his difference from all others. From their standpoint, and in the light of the Easter event, this was completely understandable. We easily forget, however, that this uniqueness of Jesus rested on the unconditional subordination of his person to the lordship of God that he proclaimed. If Jesus himself had claimed a distinctive sonship in his relation to God, then there would have been justification for his condemnation (Mark 14:64) for the apparent blasphemy of making himself equal to God.

For Christian faith, then, much depends on whether Jesus avoided making himself equal to God. That is, it depends on whether, as a creature of God, he subordinated himself to the imminent rule of God that he announced with just the same unconditionality as he required of others. Only in this subordination to the rule of the one God is he the Son. As he gave his life in service to the rule of God over his creatures — namely, to prepare the way for its acknowledgment — he is as man the Son of the eternal Father. Rejection of any supracreaturely dignity before God shows itself to be a condition of his sonship. It is mediated by his self-humbling (Phil. 2:8). This constitutes the indirectness of the identity of Jesus with the Son of God.[140]

In the situation of the earthly ministry this matter was not wholly clear because Jesus claimed authority in his proclamation of the imminent rule of God, no less authority than that of God himself. He claimed it, not for his own person, but for the future of God that he proclaimed. This did not alter the fact, however, that he was the one proclaiming the message to

140. For more detail, cf. *Jesus — God and Man*, pp. 226f. In the epilogue to the 5th edition of my *Grundsätze der Christologie*, pp. 423f., I point out that the doctrine of the deity of Jesus Christ is rounded off only with these statements concerning the indirectness of his deity by way of his relation as man to his heavenly Father, and not with the portion of the book devoted to knowledge of his deity. This means that we must view part II ("Jesus the Man before God," pp. 191ff.) as part of the doctrine of his deity precisely because the humanity of Jesus in his difference from the Father, as well as his relation to him, is the revelation of his deity.

which the claim was linked. With the declaration that the divine rule had begun already among believers with his work, the ambivalence of the claim became extreme. Jesus could have avoided the consequences, but not by simply stating that he was not making himself equal to God. Such an assurance would have been credible to his hostile opponents only if he had abandoned his message and ministry. Standing by his mission meant accepting the foreseeable consequences of the ambivalence.

The upshot was that on account of the supposed arrogance of making himself equal to God, he was put to death. Death exposed his finitude as distinct from his alleged equality with God (Matt. 27:40-43 par.). It was a punishment for the sinner and his delusion of being God's equal. It showed his finitude. The light of his resurrection revealed, however, that he had not deserved this sinner's death. This means, then, that in truth he suffered in our place as sinners. In the light of the Easter event the transgressors are those who rejected his message and ministry and contributed to his death. If his judges thought him a blasphemer, they themselves proved to be guilty, not only by blaspheming God himself in his messenger, but by taking his life. Dying a sinner's death, Jesus suffered the fate that he did not deserve but that they deserved, and with them all those who reject the divine claim upon their lives that Jesus proclaimed.[141]

If the death of Jesus was vicarious in this sense, it does not follow at once that we can see it as a saving death for those in whose place he suffered it. In the first instance, it is rather a sign of God's judgment on sin. It is a saving death only for those who are linked to him and his fate through faith in his promise that nothing can separate them from him. Those who by faith in Jesus Christ have fellowship with his death, even in their own, die in the hope of life, of the new life that was manifested already in Jesus with his resurrection from the dead. By his death, and for those who are linked to him by faith, Jesus has conquered the power of death that separates from God and eternal life.[142]

The resurrection effectively reversed the charges against Jesus and confirmed his mission. We thus see that if he had saved his life at the cost of his proclaiming the divine lordship, he would have actually made himself independent of God and put himself in equality with him. "Whoever would save his life will lose it" (Mark 8:35 par.). This was true

141. Ibid., pp. 263ff.
142. Cf. *Grundfragen*, II, 146-59; also ch. 11 below.

of Jesus himself. He could not be the Son of God by an unlimited duration of his finite existence. No finite being can be one with God in infinite reality. Only as he let his earthly existence be consumed in service to his mission could Jesus as a creature be one with God. As he did not cling to his life but chose to accept the ambivalence that his mission meant for his person, with all its consequences, he showed himself, from the standpoint of the Easter event, to be obedient to his mission (Rom. 5:19; Heb. 5:8). This obedience led him into the situation of extreme separation from God and his immortality, into the dereliction of the cross. The remoteness from God on the cross was the climax of his self-distinction from the Father. Rightly, then, we may say that the crucifixion was integral to his earthly existence.[143]

The self-distinction of Jesus from the Father, which was the condition of the manifestation of the eternal Son in Jesus' obedience to the mission he received from the Father to proclaim God's lordship, can be described as his self-emptying and self-humbling along the lines of the early Christian hymn in Phil. 2:6-11. We have here two essential features of Jesus as the new man, the man of obedience to God as distinct from the sin of Adam, who wanted to be like God and who thus forfeited the fellowship with God for which he was destined.

Does the hymn in Phil. 2 sing of the historical path of Jesus Christ or of the path of preexistent being to earthly existence? Or is that a false alternative? How does the statement about the self-humbling of Jesus in the obedience of the passion (v. 8) relate to the preceding statement about self-emptying (v. 7)? These questions arose in post-Reformation controversies, and they are still a matter of exegetical debate in our own time. The self-humbling obviously refers to the earthly path of obedience that led Jesus to the cross, but the self-emptying seems to start with the divine equality of the Son that he renounced so as to take to himself the slave-existence of human conditions of life. Yet the two verses with their two ideas of self-emptying and self-humbling describe one and the same event, namely, the path of Jesus to suffering and crucifixion. We find support for this view in the fact that the self-emptying seems to carry an allusion to Isa. 53:12 and hence to denote the giving up of a life of equality with God to death,[144] so

---

143. Cf. E. Jüngel, "Das Sein Jesu Christi als Ereignis der Versöhnung Gottes mit einer gottlosen Welt. Die Hingabe des Gekreuzigten," in *Entsprechungen: Gott — Wahrheit — Mensch. Theologische Erörterungen* (Munich, 1980), p. 283.

144. Cf. R. P. Martin, *Carmen Christi: Philippians 2:5-11 in Recent Interpretation and in the Setting of Early Christian Worship* (London, 1967), pp. 182-85.

that in part at least it coincides with the result of self-humbling to the obedience of the passion.[145]

Some have even tried to limit the references to the path of earthly obedience and thus have contested any idea of a starting point in preexistence. The main point here is that the statement stands in antithesis to the fall of Adam in Gen. 3.[146] In distinction from the first Adam, Jesus Christ did not have to grasp at the divine likeness as a prey in order to claim equality with God (cf. Gen. 3:5). Instead he humbled himself to the death of the cross in obedience to God (cf. Rom. 5:19; also Heb. 5:8). The basic thought of the hymn thus corresponds to the Pauline contrasting of the second Adam's obedience to God with the disobedience of the first Adam (Rom. 5:12ff.). But does this make the thought of preexistence disruptive or superfluous? Not at all! A broader view is taken of the new man than in Rom. 5 — a view that includes the thought of preexistence (cf. Rom. 8:3). The new man is no mere man, for the eternal Son of God is manifested in his earthly course. The analogy to Gen. 3 is thus transcended. The hymn itself forces us to this conclusion, for the statement in 2:7b that he took human form can refer only to his entry upon a human form of existence (cf. Gal. 4:4).[147]

We thus have to agree with Cullmann that the same thing — the path to the cross — is depicted in two ways in Phil. 2:7f.: as an act of obedience on the part of the man Jesus, and as an act of the Preexistent manifested in him. The text does not further clarify the relation between the two aspects. In narrative form it has them succeed one another, as though the self-humbling to the cross followed the self-emptying. But we may infer their interrelation from the end of the hymn. Because of his obedience the Crucified is exalted by God and receives from him the name of Kyrios (2:9, 11). He is thus shown to be the Preexistent, who is with the Father from all eternity. Otherwise, even in spite of his deity, the Preexistent would be of lesser dignity than the Kyrios, as whom the Crucified is exalted. For such a view the hymn offers no support at all; the state of the Preexistent is depicted as divine with no such restriction. The only remaining option, then, is that the exaltation of the Crucified makes clear that his earthly

---

145. O. Hofius, *Der Christushymnus Phil. 2:6-11* (Tübingen, 1976), p. 63, thinks that in 2:7c-8c we are shown how far the Preexistent, renouncing his riches, was willing to become poor and chose an existence in weakness and dishonor.

146. Cf. Cullmann, *Christology*, pp. 174ff., and Dunn, *Christology in the Making*, pp. 114-21. Unlike Cullmann, Dunn does not think we need find an implication of preexistence in the parallel with Adam (pp. 182f.), since the divine form of life of which Jesus emptied himself corresponds to the divine likeness in which Adam was created (p. 116).

147. So Cullmann, *Christology*, pp. 177ff. When Dunn argues that in the word *genomenos* "a reference to birth is not necessarily implied" (*Christology in the Making*, p. 311 n. 76), this may well be true of the verb as such. It is not true, however, of the specific context in which it is used in Phil. 2:7, for the goal of what is denoted by the verb is entry upon the conditions of earthly life. At this point there is no parallel between the hymn and the story of the fall.

path was already the path of one who was related to God from all eternity and that precisely on this path he was obedient to God. The starting point of the path of Jesus Christ in preexistence has the function of ruling out an adoptionist understanding of the exaltation. Thus the hymn as a whole sings of the earthly path of Jesus as that of the preexistent Son of God.

In his form of life as Jesus, on the path of his obedience to God, the eternal Son appeared as a human being. The relation of the Son to the Father is characterized in eternity by the subordination to the Father, by the self-distinction from the majesty of the Father, which took historical form in the human relation of Jesus to God. This self-distinction of the eternal Son from the Father may be understood as the basis of all creaturely existence in its distinction from God, and therefore as the basis of the human existence of Jesus, which gave adequate embodiment in its course to the self-emptying of the Son in service to the rule of the Father. As the incarnation of the Logos was the result of the self-emptying of the eternal Son in his self-distinction from the Father, so the self-humbling of Jesus in obedience to his sending by the Father is the medium of the manifestation of the Son on the path of his earthly life.

In this regard it is presupposed that the self-emptying of the Preexistent is to be understood as a renunciation not of his divine essence but simply of any equating of himself with the Father. By distinguishing the Father from himself as the one God, the Son certainly moved out of the unity of the deity and became man. But in so doing he actively expressed his divine essence as the Son. The self-emptying of the Preexistent is not a surrender or negation of his deity as the Son. It is its activation.[148] Hence the end of his earthly path in obedience to the Father is the revelation of his deity.

The older Protestant orthodoxy in its Lutheran version understood the self-emptying of the divine Logos at the incarnation as a partial or temporary renouncing of the use or the public manifestation of the attributes of divine majesty that according to the Lutheran view of the incarnate Logos were also attributes of his human nature in virtue of the communication of attributes.[149] The 19th-century kenoticists then regarded the self-limitation of the divine Son at the incarnation as a renouncing even of the possession of the relative attributes of omnipotence, omnipresence, and omniscience that characterize the relation of deity to the world.

148. Cf. Barth, *CD*, IV/1, 129f., 177ff., 179ff.
149. Cf. *Jesus — God and Man*, pp. 308ff. On the theme in the early church, cf. esp. F. Loofs, "Kenosis," *PRE*, X (3rd ed. 1901), pp. 246-63.

Critics of this idea, among them Dorner, rightly saw here a renouncing of deity itself.[150] This would then destroy the whole concept of incarnation. If God is not truly and totally in Christ, what sense does it make to talk of the reconciliation of the world with God in him?[151] Nevertheless, we still find kenotic expressions in modern dogmatic christology, usually in terms of a clear separation from the divine attributes at the incarnation or even from their use.[152] If there is still talk of a *kenōsis* of the Son of God, however, it must be explained how we can think of such self-emptying without renunciation of the possession or use of divine attributes, since what is signified is at any rate a transition from the divine sphere to the limitation of a creaturely form of existence.

This aspect is not clear in Barth's presentation when he describes "The Way of the Son of God into a Far Country" (*CD*, IV/1, § 59.1, pp. 157ff.) from the perspective of the doctrine of election (pp. 170ff.), in virtue of which the Son of God is not only the Elected but also the Rejected (II/2, 161ff.), who took the place of perishing humanity (IV/1, 173). Barth certainly made it clear that it is part of God's deity that in his transcendence and majesty "he can be God and act as God in an exalted and also a lowly way" (p. 187). But being actively present in his creatures, even in their lowliness, is not the same as so accepting the limitations of creaturely existence that they are really limitations of his own being. How can that be, without God ceasing to be God? In spite of Barth's fine discussion of the obedience of the Son (pp. 193ff.) and its rootage in the trinitarian life of God (pp. 202f.), it is no answer to say that in God's eternal decree of election, God resolved upon this, and that the Son then took this path in obedience to the Father.[153] Such an answer is possible only if we understand the obedience of the Son as an expression of his free self-distinction from the Father by which he lets the Father be the one God and by which he became the origin of all that is distinct from God, so that for this reason he himself could be manifested as the Son of the Father in the form of creaturely distinction, in the finite form of creaturely existence as distinct from that of God.[154]

150. *Jesus — God and Man*, pp. 310ff.

151. Cf. Barth, *CD*, IV/1, 183.

152. For examples, cf. *Jesus — God and Man*, pp. 312ff.

153. Nor does Barth offer clarification of this question in his discussion of the event of the incarnation in IV/2, 36ff. Cf. *Jesus — God and Man*, pp. 314f.

154. In *Jesus — God and Man*, pp. 314f., I too did not yet see this possibility of linking the thought of the kenosis to the eternal uniqueness of the Son as such in his relation to the Father, though the starting point for this was present in the discussion in part III about the indirectness of the identity of Jesus with the Son of God (pp. 334-37). For that reason I was then critical of interpretation of the incarnation in terms of the thought of kenosis in Phil. 2:7f., assuming that an ontological understanding of the concept would unavoidably involve restricting the deity of the Logos, or at least of the participation of the assumed man in the deity.

The self-emptying and self-humbling of the Son that found perfect expression in the history of Jesus Christ should not be understood first as an unselfish turning to us, though it is that also. Rather, it is primarily an expression of the self-giving of the Son to the Father in an obedience that desires nothing for self but serves totally the glorifying of God and the coming of his kingdom. Precisely thus the way of the Son is also an expression of the love of God for us. For by the self-distinction of the Son from the Father, God draws near to us. The *kenōsis* of the Son serves the drawing near of the Father. It is thus an expression of the divine love, for we attain to our salvation in the closeness of God to us and in our participation in his life.

c. Two Natures in One Person?

In the light of their divine confirmation and vindication by the resurrection, the implications of the coming and work of Jesus for his own person took on sharper contours and became evident in christological titles, e.g., in confessional statements and hymns. As a result we can reconstruct the development of primitive Christian christology as an unfolding of the significance of the person and history of Jesus as this came to be seen in the light of the Easter event. Research into the tradition, especially as regards the christological titles, has largely brought to light the normative contents of the history of christological development in early Christianity. In accordance with the methodological requirements set out in chapter 9, section 1, the core materials have been worked out in the discussions of the present chapter with a main focus on the divine sonship of Jesus.

It should now be clear that the history of christological development in primitive Christianity does not consist of a disconnected sequence of heterogeneous ideas that were later attached to the person of Jesus and had nothing to do materially with his historical figure, being only the expression of the enthusiastic beliefs of his followers, who, as one might easily assume, were only too ready to give supraterrestrial enhancement to the portrait of their Master. If that were so, the statements of the confession of Christ and christological doctrine would be no more than products of the faith-consciousness of the primitive church. They would then have the truth only of poetic fantasy with no basis in the historical reality of Jesus himself. The church's doctrine of a divine saving event in the person and history of Jesus prior to faith in him, and serving as the basis of that faith, would then be robbed of its substance. But in view of the fact that there is a demonstrable material connection between the implications of the work and history of Jesus on the one side, and on the other the christological titles and statements about his person, as the church formed these in the post-Easter situation, gives us good reason to regard the titles and statements as an explicit naming of the person of Jesus in the eschatological significance that is proper to it in its history.

Can the same be said for the further development of christology in the history of the early church? Do we have there also a process of continued explication and clarification of the unique significance of the historical figure of Jesus in terms of his earthly work, his crucifixion and resurrection?

In this regard we should note first that from the 2nd century onward the development of christological teaching concentrated on the theme of divine sonship in distinction from the many other titles that we encounter in primitive Christianity — e.g., Son of Man, Messiah (Christ), Kyrios, Savior, Servant of the Lord, and Prophet. The variety of these early titles may be explained for the most part[155] as the result of an interpretation in terms of Jewish eschatological expectations based on the OT. Jesus himself did his work on earth in the context of these expectations, the contents of which were related to him after his resurrection from the dead as a fulfillment of OT prophecy as primitive Christianity understood it.[156] On account of the reference to one and the same person, it was natural that the different figures of Jewish expectation should coalesce into one. As a result some descriptions that were originally titular became part of the name of Jesus. This was true primarily of the title "Christ," but also to some extent of "Kyrios," which could become the first part of the name of Jesus, even though the term always denoted the honored position of the risen Jesus as the exalted Lord over all authorities and powers, or at least the Lord of his community ("our Lord"). Other designations were subordinate in one way or another to the divine sonship of Jesus.

A specially instructive example was the reinterpreted title "Son of Man," which already in Ignatius (*Eph.* 20.2) became the correlate of Son of God, being now understood to denote the humanity of the incarnate

---

155. "Savior" (*sōtēr*), with its roots in Hellenistic thinking, is an exception, though cf. in the OT esp. Isa. 45:15, 21 and Zech. 9:9.

156. Involved here, though we cannot show this, were many links between the earthly appearance of Jesus and the various titles of Jewish expectation.

divine Son.[157] Important in the time that followed was the equation, made possible by the concept of preexistence, of the Son of God with the preexistent Logos or the Wisdom of God that had a part in the creation of the world. This equation found open expression in John's Gospel and perhaps underlay Pauline and post-Pauline statements about preexistence. At any rate, the divine sonship of Jesus and discussion of its exact understanding became a central theme of christological doctrinal development from the second century onward.[158] The result of this development was that in the church's baptismal confession the second article increasingly confessed Jesus as the only (or only begotten) Son of God and subordinated "Kyrios"[159] and all other christological designations to this title.

Can we accept this concentration on the divine sonship of Jesus as proper in the light of the NT witnesses? We must answer yes because of the central function of the title "Son of God" from the beginnings of primitive Christian christology (cf. Rom. 1:4) and its connection with Jesus' proclamation of God as Father of his creatures. Even more, in the debate about the person of Jesus, this title gave clearest expression to the subject of Jesus' relationship with God, and therefore also to the subject of his divine justification and confirmation.

If we may regard the preexistence statements of primitive Christianity as a proper development of the relationship that the title "Son of God" denotes, namely, that of Jesus with the Father but also that of the Father, the eternal God, with Jesus as his Son, then we are accepting the need for further clarification of the relation between the divine and the human in the figure of Jesus Christ as the incarnate Son.

For a starting point we might turn to the primitive Christian schema of a twofold evaluation of Jesus "after the flesh" and "after the spirit," which may well lie behind the pre-Pauline formula in Rom. 1:3f.[160]

---

157. Cf. also Justin *Dial.* 100.3f. On Irenaeus, Hippolytus, Tertullian, etc. see A. Grillmeier, *Jesus der Christus im Glauben der Kirche,* I (1979), pp. 49ff.

158. Grillmeier, *Christ in Christian Tradition,* pp. 11f.

159. Cf. DS §§ 3ff. for the texts of early confessions and the table in P. Schaff, *The Creeds of Christendom* (6th ed. New York, 1931), II, 40f. "Kyrios" was often brought in as the first part of the name or added to confession of the divine sonship along with "Savior" (*sōtēr*).

160. Cf. Wilckens, *Römer,* I, 57f. But the formula may also be Pauline in view of the use of *kata sarka* elsewhere in Paul, esp. Gal. 4:21ff. (p. 58). At any rate, R. Schnackenburg, "Christologie des NT," in *Mysterium Salutis,* III/1, 266, has rightly pointed out that the use in Rom. 1:3f., 1 Tim. 3:16, and 1 Pet. 3:18 is complementary, not antithetical as elsewhere in Paul.

and which we also find in 1 Tim. 3:16 and 1 Pet. 3:18.[161] We meet with
the same schema in the apostolic fathers as well, e.g., in the Shepherd of
Hermas,[162] especially in Ignatius (*Eph.* 7.2; cf. 18.2 and 20.2), and also in
2 Clement (9:5). In this light we may well speak of an early Spirit christology that set the divine and the human in Jesus alongside one another
without further differentiation and that might be found in many different
versions.[163]

Later witnesses to this twofold way of looking at Jesus were Melito
of Sardis and Tertullian. Melito was the first to speak of two essences
(ousia) of the one Christ, though he was simply giving expression to the
traditional twofold approach.[164] We find similar expressions in Tertullian,
who described spirit and flesh as the two "substances" that were united
in the person of Jesus.[165] The way was thus prepared for the later two-
natures doctrine of the church's christology, which developed, therefore,
out of the twofold evaluation of Jesus as according to the flesh and according to the spirit.[166] Because of a possible "dynamic" misunderstanding
of the description of the deity that was present in Jesus as "spirit,"[167]
however, the end of the 2nd century saw "Logos" coming into more
common use for the deity of Jesus. It increasingly replaced "spirit" in this
context. In Irenaeus it stands behind the description of the one Christ as
true God and true man, which for the rest follows the schema of twofold
evaluation.[168] Structurally there is agreement here with the statements of

161. F. Loofs, *Leitfaden zum Studium der Dogmengeschichte* (1889; 5th ed. 1950, ed. K. Aland), p. 70, called this twofold evaluation or understanding of the historical Jesus the oldest christological schema that we know, the basic datum of all later christological development. J. N. D. Kelly, *Early Christian Doctrines* (New York, 1958), p. 138, emphatically endorsed this judgment. It is strange that Grillmeier, *Christ in Christian Tradition,* did not deal with this phenomenon, though cf. his "Die theologische und sprachliche Vorbereitung der christologischen Formel von Chalkedon," in *Das Konzil von Chalkedon,* 3 vols., ed. A. Grillmeier and H. Bacht (Würzburg, 1951-54), I, 31.

162. Loofs, *Leitfaden,* pp. 70f.

163. Kelly, *Early Christian Doctrines,* pp. 142ff.; cf. *Jesus — God and Man,* pp. 116-208.

164. Melito Fr. 6 (from a work on the incarnation of Christ). For the text, cf. E. J. Goodspeed, *Die ältesten Apologeter* (1914), p. 310. Loofs, *Leitfaden,* p. 115 n. 7, rightly pointed out, contra Harnack (*History of Dogma* [New York, 1961], II, 190 n. 2), that this formula was only formally new in Melito.

165. Tertullian *Adv. prax.* 27. Interesting here is the christological use of John 3:6. See also *De carne Christi* 18 and on this Kelly, *Early Christian Doctrines,* pp. 150ff.

166. Cf. Kasper, *Jesus the Christ.*

167. Ibid.

168. Irenaeus *Adv. haer.* 4.6.7; cf. 3.16.5, though both texts refer to the Son without any use of the Logos concept.

Melito and Tertullian regarding the union of two substances in the one person.[169] According to Tertullian, a person also consists of two substances, body and soul, so that the union of deity and humanity in the one person does not seem to be completely paradoxical or to raise the problems that would later become unavoidable with Origen's introduction of "two natures."[170]

On the way to the doctrine of the two natures, however, the schema of twofold evaluation "after the flesh" and "after the spirit" underwent profound reinterpretation. Originally it referred to two stages in the history of Jesus — his earthly path to the cross, and then his exaltation by resurrection from the dead.[171] But already in Ignatius succession gave way to simultaneity. The logical presentation now was that of the union in the one person of the Son of God and the man born of Mary. This new version was not simply in opposition to what was found in the NT witnesses. It followed a trend originating in those witnesses inasmuch as the significance of the resurrection as confirmation in primitive Christianity involved a retrospective reference of the divine sonship of Jesus to the whole of his earthly life. In fact, then, the result was that from the very beginning of his earthly history Jesus was not just man but also the Son of God. Still constitutive in this regard was the Easter event and the perspective based upon it.

A fateful change thus took place, or at least a fateful shift of emphasis, when, as in Ignatius *Eph.* 18.2, the birth of Jesus instead of the Easter event became constitutive for the union of deity and humanity in him. Certainly from the standpoint of the Easter event the conception and birth of Jesus had to be seen as the entry of the eternal Son of God into union with this human life (Gal. 4:4). The event did not end, however, with the birth of Jesus. The union of the Logos with this human life continued throughout the whole of the earthly history of Jesus as the eternal Son of God took shape in him through the relation to the Father. We are not to take this to mean that the deity and humanity gradually

---

169. Harnack, who regarded substance and nature as equivalent, was thus speaking loosely when he called Melito the first father to refer to two natures (*History of Dogma;* see the reference in n. 164 above).

170. Origen *In Ioann.* 10.6.24; 32.12.192, and *C. Cels.* 3.28; 2.23; cf. Kelly, *Early Christian Doctrines,* pp. 155f.

171. Schnackenburg, "Christologie des NT," p. 265, rightly points out that in the NT witnesses we have two successive modes of being of Christ, though related to one another, in contrast to the later doctrine of the two natures.

grew together in the course of Jesus' history. But with the development of his human life, a relationship to the Father developed with increasing depth, and with it his divine sonship. We may say the latter because the filial relation of Jesus to the Father came to fulfillment only in the obedience of his life of suffering even to the point of crucifixion.

In the light of Easter, then, it is clear that Jesus was always the Son of the Father, but he was made perfect in sonship only by his suffering (Heb. 5:8-9; cf. 2:10). Only in his life as a whole is he the Son. Hence we must not restrict what we say about the incarnation to his conception and birth at the beginning. If he had followed a different path in his human development, if he had not been baptized by John, if he had not been the herald of the rule of God, if he had not accepted the consequences of his mission by taking the path of suffering, he would not be the Son of God. And he is this only in the light of Easter morning because only in this light is his path defined unequivocally as a path of obedience and not of human arrogance.

If we limit our understanding of the incarnation to the conception and birth of Jesus, then we cannot think of the union of the eternal Son with this human life as mediated by the relation of Jesus to the Father. As in the classical christological controversies on every hand, it will then be presented directly as the assuming of human nature by the Logos. But on this view the dilemma arises that has proved insoluble in the history of christology from the time of the 5th-century christological controversies. At the incarnation the Logos assumed either a complete man or only human nature in general. In the former position, held by the Antiochenes, the full humanity is assumed to be independent. In the latter, held by the Alexandrians, the human nature was fashioned into an individual only at the incarnation, and then Jesus had no specific human individuality, no independence, no creaturely freedom.[172] The dilemma is insuperable as long as we think that the event of the incarnation was complete with the birth of Jesus.[173] The statement about the incarnation of the eternal Son

---

172. *Jesus — God and Man*, pp. 291f.

173. In 1964 I myself related the incarnation exclusively to the beginning of the earthly course of Jesus as the basis of his individual life. I thus concluded that christology should not begin with the concept of the incarnation but should reach its climax there (ibid., p. 291). This was certainly in keeping with the traditional position that the thought of preexistence and incarnation is mediated by the kerygma of the resurrection of the Crucified and grounded in it.

No matter how we reach the concept of the incarnation, however, its own logic demands that we think of the eternal Son as the basis of the earthly existence of Jesus. *Jesus*

in Jesus of Nazareth relates, however, to the whole of his history and not just to its commencement.[174] Can we overcome the dilemma of a christology of union and distinction from this angle?

A presupposition is that we not think of the divine and the human in Jesus Christ as two natures that stand ontologically on the same level and have nothing to do with one another apart from their union in the person of the God-man. This view of the two-natures doctrine came under the very effective criticism of Schleiermacher,[175] and it is likewise opposed by the full weight of the argument discussed in the 4th century and adopted by Apollinaris of Laodicea, namely, that two complete and independently existing essences cannot form a union.[176]

But we cannot think of the relation of human nature to God along such lines when we see it in the light of the biblical belief in creation. As creatures, human beings in their nature are dependent on God as their Creator. This applies no less to the relation to the divine Logos. Hence the eternal Son or Logos is by no means alien to human nature. It is his own possession (John 1:11). Because all creatures owe their independent existence to the creative activity of the Son in virtue of his self-distinction from the Father, because the Logos is the basis of their creaturely independence as the generative principle of otherness, the nature of the Logos can find expression to some extent in all creatures. He can do so in us humans to a higher degree than in other creatures because we are able and destined to distinguish God from ourselves and ourselves from God, so that the self-distinction of the Son from the Father can take shape in us.

Human nature as such is ordained for the incarnation of the

— *God and Man* did not try to do this. Instead it based the identity of Jesus with the eternal Logos on the relationship of obedience with the Father (pp. 334ff.), as in the preceding presentation. Nevertheless, the manifestation of the eternal Son in the history of Jesus must itself be viewed as an expression of the incarnation of the Son if the incarnation is constitutive for the human existence of Jesus. But we cannot do this without prejudice to the creaturely independence of Jesus in his history if this history is predetermined by an event of incarnation at the very outset. Precisely the creaturely independence of the human history of Jesus has to be thought of as the medium of the incarnation, but in such a way that the constitution of the person of Jesus takes place in the whole process of this history. Otherwise Jesus would first be a mere man and would then later become the Son of God by union with his human person.

174. See ch. 9 above, secs. II.1 and II.3.

175. *Christian Faith,* § 96.1. On this see *Jesus — God and Man,* p. 285.

176. Cf. Ps.-Athanasius *C. Apoll.* 1.2 (PG, 26, 1096B), and on this Grillmeier, *Christ in Christian Tradition,* pp. 332ff.

eternal Son in it.[177] Hence the event of the incarnation is no alien thing, although it may seem alien to sinners who are alienated from God, and although it is the infinitely transcendent deity that unites itself to us in this event. Certainly we ourselves cannot fulfill this destiny of ours in our own finite strength. Only the Spirit of God, who lifts a human being above its own finitude, can it accept its finitude, so that the relation of the Son to the Father can take shape in it. If creaturely independence is not thereby harmed or even eliminated, this is because the difference of the creature from God is the product of the eternal Son in his self-distinction from the Father. As the Son is related to the Father only by this self-distinction, so the creature can have fellowship with God only in its distinction from God and in the humble and obedient acceptance of this distinction. But this takes place as the eternal Son takes human form in such acceptance of creatureliness before God. This happened in the history of Jesus, in the whole history of his life from birth to resurrection and ascension.

The special relation of human nature to the Logos as its creative origin is thus the condition of the possibility of the incarnation as the union of the Son with an individual human life, a union that was mediated by our relation to God the Father and that thus had the form of a life history in which this relation unfolded. The process of this history is the concrete form of the human reality of Jesus. Only here does he have identity as a person.[178] In this history he is the Son of the Father, so that of one and the same Jesus Christ we may say that as the one who was crucified, raised, and exalted, he was and is both true man and true God. In this sense, and only in this sense, there is truth in the otherwise misunderstood and misleading doctrine of the two natures of this one person.

The implications of the christological doctrine of the union of two natures in one person were discussed especially in debates regarding the communication of the attributes between the two natures and the person of Christ.[179] On this

---

177. Cf. the formulation by Rahner quoted in n. 63 of ch. 9 above; also Kasper, *Jesus the Christ,* who rightly called it the basic mistake of Apollinaris to understand human nature as a self-enclosed entity.

178. For history as the process of forming identity, cf. my *Anthropology in Theological Perspective* (Philadelphia, 1985), pp. 502ff.; on identity and personality, pp. 224ff.; and for the basis of this understanding, the section on the relation between the I and the self, pp. 200ff.

subject there was already agreement in the 5th century that we must see in the person of Christ the attributes of both natures. Post-Reformation theology called this form of the communication the *genus idiomaticum.* The 5th-century school of Antioch wanted to restrict the exchange to the relation of the two natures as they were united in the one person. Reformed theology took a similar course, including distinctive activities of the natures that must be referred to the person as the acting subject *(genus apotelesmaticum).*[180] Debated, however, was the older Lutheran teaching that rested on Gregory of Nyssa's doctrine of the mutual perichoresis of the two natures in the unity of the person, which would view the human nature as sharing in the majestic attributes of the divine nature such as omnipotence, omnipresence, and omniscience, the *genus maiestaticum.*[181]

Regarding this we may say first that no personal union is conceivable without an indwelling of the Son of God in the human reality of Jesus or the sharing of Jesus as man in the divine attributes of the Son of God. Yet we must also stress here that the mutual perichoresis or indwelling of the natures must be viewed as mediated by the relation of Jesus to the Father and his self-subordination to the Father, which is the condition of the manifestation of the Son in him. It thus follows that only in distinction from the deity of the Father can we speak of a participation in it. It follows further that the mediation of the participation of the humanity of Jesus in the deity of the Logos by Jesus' relation to the Father means that the mutual indwelling of the Son in the human life of Jesus on the one side, and of his humanity and lowliness in the deity of the Son on the other, takes place in the process of his history, so that we cannot think, as the older Lutherans did, that it was achieved already at the very beginning of the way of Jesus, at his birth.

The exalted Lord who sits at the right hand of the Father shares in the kingly rule of God in a different way from the earthly Jesus, who became the locus of this rule as its earthly herald. If identity with the eternal Son, and therefore participation in deity and its attributes, is mediated by the self-distinction of Jesus from the Father in the course of his earthly history, there is no reason to postulate a renunciation of the use of the divine attributes during the period of the earthly

179. For more detail, cf. *Jesus — God and Man,* pp. 296ff. For late patristic discussion, cf. esp. John of Damascus *Fid. orth.* 3.3 and 4 (PG, 94, 993-1000). For an example of the handling of the theme in High Scholasticism, cf. Aquinas *ST* 3.16.1-12. For further development, cf. R. Schwarz, "Gott ist Mensch. Zur Lehre von der Person Christi bei den Ockhamisten und bei Luther," *ZTK* 63 (1966) 289-351.
180. Calvin *Inst.* 2.14.3: "Those things which apply to the office of the Mediator are not spoken simply either of the divine nature or of the human."
181. For a basic statement, cf. the Formula of Concord SD 8.48-96. Cf. also T. Mahlmann, *Das neue Dogma der lutherischen Christologie* (1969). On Luther's own view of the communion of the natures and the unity of the person of Christ, see Schwarz, "Gott ist Mensch."

ministry of Jesus, for postulates of that kind presuppose an unrestricted possession of the attributes at the beginning of the earthly history and find no place for the development of the self-distinction of Jesus from the Father in the process of that history. For the exalted Lord, too, the self-distinction of Jesus from the Father and his deity in the twofold sense of self-distinction as creature and as Son of the Father is still the condition of the divine sonship of Jesus, so that there can be no talk of a mere transfer of the divine attributes to the human nature.[182] We do not need this even for the presence of Christ at the Lord's Supper, as we shall have to show in a later context. At this point Lutheranism, following Melanchthon, spoke of a voluntary presence instead of Luther's ubiquity.[183]

The human nature of Jesus Christ shares, then, in the deity of the Logos, but only through the mediation of self-distinction from God. In the course of the history of Jesus, the eternal Son of God also shares in the creaturely limitations, needs, and sufferings that a human form of existence entails. This is a natural result of the self-distinction of the eternal Son from the Father as the one God, a movement that reached its deepest depths in the incarnation of the Son and the suffering obedience of Jesus. The theological tradition shrank back from the logic of the mutuality of the perichoresis of deity and humanity in the incarnation of the Son.[184] Luther's theology of the cross first faced this logic, and it found a successor in Hegel's thesis of the death of God himself on the cross.[185] Here again, however, we cannot talk of a simple transfer of what we say about one nature to the other (e.g., applying the human predicates of lowliness to the deity of the Son). On the cross the Son of God certainly died and not just the humanity that he assumed. Nevertheless, the Son suffered death in his human reality and not in respect of his deity.[186] In the death of Jesus the deity reached the extreme point

---

182. Cf. the Formula of Concord SD 8.72; cf. also Negativa 2.3, though the formula does not make the necessary deductions regarding the participation of Jesus as man in the divine omnipotence and omniscience (cf. Mark 13:32 par.).

183. On the origin of this thought in Melanchthon, cf. Mahlmann, *Das neue Dogma*, p. 25; on its significance for M. Chemnitz, see pp. 218ff. According to Mahlmann (pp. 222f. n. 71), the term "multivolipresence" for this is of Reformed provenance. Cf. also Formula of Concord SD 8, Negativa 4.

184. This is true of the statement of the Formula of Concord that on account of God's immutability, the incarnation neither adds to him nor takes away from him (SD 8.49).

185. On Luther, cf. Schwarz, "Gott ist Mensch," pp. 305 and 311ff. On Hegel and his relation to Luther, cf. E. Jüngel, *God as the Mystery of the World* (Grand Rapids, 1983), pp. 63ff., 77ff.

186. Cf. the quotation from Luther's 1528 work on the Lord's Supper in Formula of Concord SD 8.41f. to the effect that deity and humanity are one person in Christ and that, in virtue of this personal unity, scripture ascribes to the deity all that happens to the humanity and vice versa. If so, then we must say that the person suffers. But the person is true God; therefore we may rightly say that the Son of God suffers. For although the one part (if we may speak thus) does not suffer as deity, nevertheless the person, who is God,

of the self-distinction from the Father by which the Son is also related to the Father, so that even his humanity could not be held in death.

The person of Jesus Christ is identical with the eternal Son. But this does not mean that the human reality of Jesus lacks personality. Precisely in his human history Jesus has his personal identity solely in being the Son of his heavenly Father. This fact integrates all the features of his earthly existence into a unity. The man Jesus has no other identity than this, though he cannot have been aware of it from the very outset.[187] It is enough that his human life as a whole was lived to and from his heavenly Father. The history of Jesus led him deeper and deeper into this identity of his person as the Son of the Father. Hence his human existence never had its personal identity in itself but always only in the relation to the Father, and therefore in his being the Son of this Father.[188] Herein he was both truly man and true God.

§ 3. The Incarnation of the Son as God's Self-Actualization in the World

The incarnation of the Son is not irrelevant to the deity of the trinitarian God. By it he became manifest to the world. It was also significant for the eternal fellowship of the Father with the Son by the Holy Spirit. It brings creation into the trinitarian fellowship. The creation of the world does not rest on any inner necessity of the divine nature that compelled God to make his creation; rather, the creation is a free act of God on the part of the Son as well as the Father. But the creation of the world carries with it the incarnation of the Son, for it is the means of actualizing the royal

---

suffers in the other part as humanity (WA, 26, 321; LW, 37, 210). Hegel did not observe Luther's rule of the communication of the attributes when he wrote that not the man but the Divine died, becoming man thereby (*Jenaer Realphilosophie* [1805-6], PhB, 67, 268 n. 3; cf. Jüngel, *God as the Mystery of the World*, pp. 102f.). In view of statements of this kind, I spoke in vol. I, 314 of an inverted monophysitism in Hegel.

187. On recent Roman Catholic attempts to describe the human self-consciousness of Jesus in terms of the two-natures doctrine, cf. *Jesus — God and Man*, pp. 328ff.; Kasper, *Jesus the Christ*.

188. In this sense I adopted and modified in *Jesus — God and Man*, pp. 337ff., a concept that goes back to Leontius of Byzantium, that of the *enhypostasis* of the human nature of Jesus in the Logos.

rule of the Father in the world. Without lordship over his creation, God would not be God. The act of creation is certainly a product of the freedom of God, but once the world of creation came into existence, lordship over it became the condition and proof of his deity. If the Creator were only the author of the existence of the world but could not achieve lordship over it, we could not call him truly God or indeed Creator in the full sense of the word.

The monarchy of the Father had been actualized already in the eternal fellowship of the Trinity. It did not need the existence of a world. In all eternity the Son gives the Father the honor of his kingly rule.[189] The rule thus is eternal — not, of course, without the Son and Spirit, but through them. But it now applies to creation as well. The rule of the Father is set up and brought to acknowledgment in creation through the Son and the Spirit.

In its existence and nature, creaturely reality is an expression of the creative act of God and bears witness thereby to his royal lordship. Nevertheless, the independence of creatures both for themselves and for observers of the world of creatures hampers recognition of that lordship. The independence of creatures, though, accords with the will of the Creator. It forms the inner goal of the act of creation. Nevertheless, it can seem that the natural processes of the creaturely world are so automatic that the thought of God is not needed for an understanding of the world of nature.[190] This is particularly true of the human world, which gives supreme embodiment to the independence of creaturely existence. Yet as finite beings and in spite of all our independence, we are inescapably subject to death.

By the incarnation of the Son sinners who are under penalty of death are saved, reconciled, brought into the trinitarian fellowship of God, and thus made participants in eternal life. Our first concern, however, is with the actualizing of the royal rule of God in creation through the event of the incarnation of the Son, or at least with the breaking in of this rule as a present reality in one man. By this one man, in whom the Son took human form, the royal rule of God is present to others and has become a force that determines their lives and fills them with new and eternal content. The actualizing of God's royal rule in the world by the incarnation of the Son and the reconciliation of the world through him are two sides

189. See vol. I, 324ff.
190. Cf. ch. 7 above, sec. I.4b.

of one and the same thing. Without the former there could not be the latter. But the reverse is also true. The kingdom of God is set up in his creation with the reconciliation of the world.

Here we have the task of the Son and the point of his being sent. By him the future of God is already present in the world. He thus opens to us access to our salvation, namely, to participate in the future of God. As the Father has sent the Son, he has entrusted the cause of his royal lordship to him and given him his own plenary power, especially the power of judgment and resurrection (John 5:22, cf. vv. 19ff.). John's Gospel thus gives already to the earthly Jesus the power assigned to the exalted Lord in Matt. 28:18 (but cf. also Matt. 11:27). Because the royal rule of the Father is present in and through Jesus, because the eternal Son has taken human form in him, the power of the Father has also been imparted to him.

With the transferring of his power to the Son who is manifested in Jesus, the Father made his deity dependent on the success of the mission of the Son. Not least of all, then, the Father suffers with the suffering of the Son.[191] The rejection that the Son experiences puts the kingship of the Father in question too. The *basileia* is actualized by the Son as he glorifies the Father (John 17:4), i.e., as he reveals his deity on earth.

As the Father sends the Son, he denotes his own absence, being present in the world through the Son. In some sense we may say the same about the act of creation by which the Creator gives creatures their own being. The love of the Creator is undoubtedly displayed in the existence of creatures, for it is he who gave them their existence. We also see his fatherly care in their preservation. Nevertheless, God, the heavenly Father, is absent for creatures as they grow into independence.

Not at all accidentally, secular culture senses this absence.[192] Creatures that are aware of their independence and rely upon it experience the power of God only as a limit, as their inability to control either their origin or their ultimate future. The absence and hiddenness of God proclaim in truth the judgment to which creatures are inescapably subject when they emancipate themselves from God and trust wholly in their own finite resources. By judgment God remains the Lord of creatures that turn aside from him. But the judgment that sinners cannot escape also expresses the impotence of the Creator. God as Creator does not will the death of sinners

191. I need not repeat here what I said in vol. I, 313f., 329. See there the references to Jüngel and Moltmann.
192. See my *Die Erfahrung der Abwesenheit Gottes in der modernen Kultur* (1984).

(Ezek. 18:23). He wills the existence and life of his creatures. In this sense his deity is tied to the sending of the Son, who with the Spirit is already present to all creatures from creation, but who himself also took creaturely form in order that by his message the future of God might be present to the world, to its salvation and not its judgment. In this way the Son glorifies the Father in the world and completes the work of creation.

The divine absence from the world reached its peak of intensity in the dereliction of the Son on the cross. In that way the Son suffered the fate of sinners. The absence of God as Deliverer means that creatures are delivered up to the consequences of their conduct. Sinners are handed over to death as the fruit of their turning aside from God. On the cross, then, Jesus died the death of sinners as a result of the ambivalence that was part of his historical manifestation. As the Son, he no doubt suffered dereliction much more profoundly than any others. Yet in the light of the Easter event the judgment of God in the crucifixion of Jesus proved to be a sign of the judgment of God on the world that rejected the Father himself in the Son. At the same time, this judgment in the cross of the Son became for the world its access to salvation. All of us can see in the death of Jesus our own death as the price of making our finite lives independent of God. In faith in the promise of Jesus, however, and through fellowship with him in his death, we can also win hope of the new life that was revealed with his resurrection from the dead. Hence the absence of the Father in the dereliction of his Son on the cross — and only here — is itself a factor in his becoming present for the world through the Son. The Father has given up the Son (Rom. 8:32; cf. 4:25) as he gives up sinners to the consequences of their acts and abandons them to the corruption that their conduct entails (Rom. 1:24, 26, 28). Yet in the case of the Son this handing over to death opens up the way of salvation for the world.

As the Father is present to the world for its salvation through the sending and death of the Son, and as his fatherly love is thus revealed, the Son has actualized the deity of God in the world and glorified in it God's name and kingly rule. Certainly this glorifying in the world presupposes constant glorifying in God's eternity. Yet in the world the kingly rule of the Father is first glorified by the Son and Spirit as the incarnate Son, by obedience to his mission, glorifies the name of the Father among us, and as the Spirit teaches us to see herein the mission of the obedient Son. Since we cannot separate the deity of God from his royal lordship, it follows that the irruption of the future of this lordship in the work of the Son has as its content the absolute reality of God in and for the world.

Because, however, the sending of the Son and Spirit is from the Father, in relation to the fulfillment of the mission by the obedience of the Son and the work of the Spirit, we thus may speak of a self-actualization of the trinitarian God in the world.

To speak of a self-actualizing of God in the event of his revelation naturally cannot mean that the trinitarian God had no prior reality in himself. Taken literally, the ambiguous expression says the very opposite, since it names the self as both subject and object of the actualizing. The self thus precedes the fulfillment of its own actualizing. This is the paradox of the idea. The self that is to be actualized, and that thus becomes the result of self-actualizing, must also be thought of as the subject of the action and therefore as already actual at the very beginning.

This paradox is not a familiar one as we normally use the term. By it, however, the term becomes an apt one for theological use, though not for anthropological use. Among us there is no identity of the subject and the result of the action as the expression demands, for we are always in the process of becoming. We are thus on the way to the self and must move forward on this way with our acts. The idea of self-actualization transcends our measure as finite beings. By no means accidentally the origin of the concept is in philosophical theology, in the idea of God as his own cause *(causa sui)*.[193] Even as a term for God, it is not a fitting one relative to God's eternal essence in the unity of his trinitarian life.[194] Nevertheless, the relation of the immanent to the economic Trinity, of God's inner trinitarian life to his acts in salvation history inasmuch as these are not external to his deity but express his presence in the world, may very well be described as self-actualization. For here the subject and result are the same, as the expression demands. The term "self-actualization" is better for what is at issue than Barth's "repetition of God"[195] because it avoids the idea of copying and instead pregnantly expresses the unity of the immanent and economic Trinity. The reality that is achieved in the eternal fellowship of the Trinity and by the economy of its action in the world is one and the same.

A modification of the term is that we do not have a simple subject but the threefold subjectivity of Father, Son, and Spirit as both the origin and the result of the event. The one God acts through the trinitarian persons and precisely thereby creates the paradox. It is certainly true of all the persons specifically that they are there before the process of God's self-actualizing in the world of his creation by historical revelation. It is also true that their deity is the result of this

193. See vol. I, 390f.
194. Ibid., p. 351. I cited there H. Schell's use of the idea of *causa sui* for the inner trinitarian relations; Barth, too, approved of this in *CD*, II/1, 305f.
195. Barth, *CD*, I/1, 299. Cf. E. Jüngel, *The Doctrine of the Trinity: God's Being Is in Becoming* (Grand Rapids, 1976), pp. 27ff., also 103ff.

process. Yet the action of the trinitarian persons is not oriented directly to themselves but to the other persons. In the economy of salvation the same is true of the sending of the Son by the Father, of the Son's obedience to the Father, and of the glorifying of the Father and the Son by the Spirit. Hence the self-actualization of the one God is one of reciprocity in the relations of the persons and the result of their mutual self-giving to one another.

Already in the witness of the Psalms of Israel the kingdom of God is from of old (Ps. 93:2), and yet, as the later royal Psalms increasingly stress, it is being actualized among the nations in the process of history.[196] Israel's election and the giving of the land (Ps. 47:4) could be hailed as the initiation of God's kingly rule over the nations (47:5ff.).[197] The rise of the Persian empire under Cyrus and the return of the exiles saw its renewal.[198] But historical experience repeatedly taught Israel to put its definitive coming to earth in the future, until finally it became the theme of eschatological hope.[199] The message of Jesus expounded this eschatological future of the royal rule of God as a claim upon the conduct of all individuals in present-day life, so that the future came already for those who committed themselves to it in faith. It is constantly present for the community in the obedience of the Son that Jesus demonstrated on his way to his death on the cross. The lordship of God in creation did not come by his chosen one setting up political rule over the nations, beginning with the political liberation of his own people. This lordship relativizes the antitheses between political power and the aspirations of those who are oppressed by it instead of making the aspirations the starting point for fresh rule and oppression. The sending of the Son into the world and the fulfillment of his mission by his death is God's way of actualizing his rule in the world without oppression and with respect for the independence of creatures, even on the part of God himself.

To extend God's rule among us the Son needs the Spirit, who glorifies him (John 16:14). The Spirit of truth who proceeds from the Father bears witness to Jesus (15:26). He teaches the disciples all things

---

196. Jeremias, *Königtum*, pp. 20ff.
197. Ibid., pp. 50ff., where Jeremias states that the kingdom is (1) eternal and universal, (2) actualized in history, and (3) experienced afresh as a reality in the present cultus.
198. Ibid., pp. 121-26, on Isa. 52:7 and Pss. 96 and 98.
199. Zech. 9:9. On Ps. 97:6, cf. ibid., pp. 136ff., esp. 141.

and reminds them of all that Jesus said (14:26). He leads them into all truth (16:13), namely, the truth of God that is manifest in the Son.[200] He thus glorifies the Son in Jesus as the Son has glorified the Father on earth (17:4). When the Johannine Christ prays that the Father will glorify him, the Son (17:1, 5), he means the glorifying by the Spirit referred to in 16:4. For the Spirit proceeds from the Father (15:26). When it is said that the Spirit will take what is the Son's and proclaim it, the reference is not just to the history and words of Jesus. All creation is to be summoned to glorify the Son, for all that the Father has is his (16:15). Hence in the last analysis the glorifying of the Son by the Spirit serves the glory of the Father. The Father will be glorified in the Son. With the prayer for glorifying by the Father who sends the Spirit, the Johannine Christ acts to complete his own sending — "that the Son may glorify thee" (17:1). Everything in the conduct of the Son and the work of the Spirit ultimately serves to glorify the Father and enhance the irruption of his kingdom into the world.

Basic for the glorifying of the Son by the Spirit is the Easter event. For the Spirit does not merely give knowledge that Jesus is the Messiah of Israel and the Son of the eternal Father. The knowledge thus imparted rests on the fact that he creates life. We find this in John (6:63) no less than Paul (Rom. 8:2). The life-giving work of the Spirit relates primarily in this context to Jesus himself, for by the Spirit he was raised from the dead (Rom. 8:11; cf. 1:4 and 1 Pet. 3:18). The same Spirit, then, can guarantee the hope of new life to believers (Rom. 8:11). As the Creator of new life from the resurrection, the Spirit leads to knowledge of the sonship of Jesus in the light of the confirmation and vindication of his pre-Easter work (1 Tim. 3:16). In Johannine terms, we have here the divine glorifying of Jesus in believers.

The glorifying of Jesus by the Spirit is mediated by the apostolic message, which in virtue of its content goes out in the power of the Spirit (1 Thess. 1:5; cf. 1 Pet. 1:12), and by which those who believe in it receive the gift of the Spirit (Gal. 3:2) that establishes in them hope in death-defeating new life in fellowship with the Crucified, whom God raised again. Hence the Spirit gives believers not merely knowledge of the divine dignity of the Son but also, with this knowledge, the beginning of a new filial life in the Spirit, in a fellowship that has a part in the filial relation of Jesus Christ to the Father. The glorifying of the Father and the Son in

200. 1 Cor. 2:10: The *pneuma* searches everything, even the depths of God.

believers that is the work of the Spirit aims, then, at the reconciliation of the world with God. It is linked to the overcoming of mortality and consummation by participation in the eternal life that by the Spirit unites the Son to the Father and that has already come as the future of creation in his resurrection from the dead.

CHAPTER 11

The Reconciliation of the World

§ 1. Salvation and Reconciliation

The Son's sending by the Father and his incarnation had as their goal the salvation of the world (John 3:17). In keeping with this goal was the human distinctiveness of Jesus in his work and his history. For as he made place for God's lordship among us, his work also sought a renewal of human society. Its messianic character as this found expression in his crucifixion and resurrection also meant an expansion of Israel's messianic hope to the whole of the human race. Paul and John represented this expansion by their use of the title "Son." The Son of the heavenly Father, who is the Creator and Father of us all, came to save the world in the person of Jesus. Paul emphasized the universality of this event by calling Jesus the absolute eschatological man, a second Adam.

We cannot separate the question of the particularity of Jesus from the soteriological function of his work and his history and therefore his person. This is true already of his earthly proclamation and impact, and it became plain in the saving activity of Jesus that the Gospels record. The same combination of messianic dignity and soteriological function characterizes the apostolic message concerning Christ. The fact that its soteriological function is already part of the uniqueness of the figure of Jesus does not justify us, of course, in simply projecting on his person various human interests or hopes for salvation, so that Jesus seems to be no more than an exponent and bearer of these expectations. It is certainly true that if Jesus as the Son of God fulfills the universal hope of salvation, he attracts to himself all the different forms of this hope. As we see from Jewish messianic expectation, however, these hopes must be reshaped and newly qualified if they are to be linked to the person of Jesus as the one who fulfills our human hope of salvation. Only in the work and history of Jesus do we see clearly what will really serve our salvation and in what sense he is the universal bringer of salvation, our Redeemer. It is thus and not otherwise that soteriology is to be treated as a function of christology, i.e., independently of existing and historically shifting hopes of salvation.[1]

Along the lines of the message of Jesus, the salvation that he mediates consists of fellowship with God and the related life, which also embraces a renewal of fellowship with others. To have a part in the rule of God (Matt. 5:3 par., 10; 19:14; Luke 6:20), to find access to it (Mark 9:47; 10:14f., 23ff.; cf. Matt. 25:10; John 3:3), is of the very essence of salvation. The understanding of salvation in the apostolic message is similar. In it fellowship with Jesus Christ becomes central, and already in connection with the historical coming of Jesus this fellowship guaranteed participation in the coming rule of God (Luke 12:8 par.), as we find this expressed especially in common table fellowship with Jesus. According to the apostolic message, fellowship with the Crucified is the basis for the hope of participation in the new life that was manifested in his resurrection. For Jesus, too, the resurrection of the dead was already a constituent part of the salvation of God's coming rule (Mark 12:27).

After Easter the overcoming of death by the new life of resurrection became the essence of the future of salvation, as participation in the divine lordship had been in the message of Jesus. Materially there is no difference here, for the new life by resurrection from the dead is life in fellowship with God by his Spirit. In particular, the character of the eschatological future is the same in both definitions of salvation — a future, however, that is already present in the case of believers. This eschatological reference

---

1. See "Christology and Soteriology," in *Jesus — God and Man*, pp. 38ff. When K.-H. Ohlig says in opposition that christology is "a function of soteriology" (*Fundamentalchristologie* [Munich, 1986], p. 27), he does not seem to realize that this thesis can make the contents of christology a projection of various changeable expectations of salvation. In fact Ohlig allows for the critical function of the historical person of Jesus for an understanding of human salvation. Thus salvation is seen to be mediated by history, and salvation is viewed christologically as mediated by a Messiah, specifically by Jesus as the Christ (pp. 28f.). Hence Jesus Christ is the criterion in defining our understanding of salvation precisely in the sense of the subordinating of soteriology to christology that Ohlig criticizes (p. 28 n. 6). As regards the present christology, this means that the filial relation of Jesus to the Father is not a projection upon him of differently based human hopes of salvation. It is grounded in the claim of the first commandment. On this rests also the universal soteriological relevance of the sonship of Jesus.

characterizes the NT term for salvation *(sōtēria)* and underlies the other soteriological concepts of the NT, e.g., what Paul says about our justification, redemption, reconciliation, and liberation by Christ, in which believers now share.

In German the word "Heil" carries the sense of the wholeness or integrity of life, even in the sense of achieving wholeness in the course of our history. Similarly *sōtēria* has the wholeness and integrity of life in view (cf. simply Mark 8:35 par.). It refers not merely to the process of saving but also to the result, to the saved and newly regained life. In the latter respect it is close to the comprehensive sense that the word for peace *(shalom)* bears in the OT.[2] The wholeness of life that a word like "Heil" denotes cannot be achieved, however, in the process of time. It may even be felt to be absent, or at least to be threatened, in the march of history, with no final security. Hence the salvation of human life depends on the future.

Jesus' eschatological message of salvation makes this fact the theme of our human relation to God. The relation to the future of God and his lordship decides the final salvation (or not) of human life. Paradoxically it is thus said that those who try to secure their life in this world without regard to the future of God will lose it, while those who hazard their lives for the future of God's rule and lose it for the sake of this rule on earth will finally gain it (Mark 8:35 par.). The focusing of salvation on the eschatological future of God stands in critical opposition to all achievement of human life in this world alone,[3] for in striving for self-fulfillment in this world, we close ourselves off to God and his future. This is the

---

2. Following W. Caspari, *Vorstellung und Wort "Friede" im AT* (1910), and J. Pedersen, *Israel: Its Life and Culture,* II (1926), pp. 311ff., G. von Rad defined *shalom* as the wholeness of life in fellowship (*OT Theology,* 2 vols. [New York, 1962-65], I, 130). In his contribution to the article in *TDNT,* II, 402ff., he rightly translated *shalom* as "salvation" (cf. esp. p. 403 on Ps. 85). L. Rost took a similar course in the Festschrift for A. Jepsen (1971), pp. 41ff. In the article, von Rad pointed out that the reference may be also to individual well-being and is not limited to social relations. That he did not expressly stress the meaning "salvation" in his OT Theology is surprising, since salvation plays a central role in this work. Cf. also J. I. Durham, "Šalôm and the Presence of God," in *Proclamation and Presence: Festschrift for G. H. Davies* (Richmond, 1970), pp. 272ff.

3. This is the reason for the tension between *sōtēria* and *salus,* which C. Andresen especially dealt with in his article "Erlösung," *RAC,* VI (1966), pp. 54ff., esp. 163ff. Cf. also N. Brox, "Σωτηρία und salus. Heilsvorstellungen in der Alten Kirche," *EvT* 33 (1973) 273ff. On the relevance of the eschatologically oriented concept of salvation as opposed to immanent expectations, cf. G. Ebeling, "Das Verständnis von Heil in säkularisierter Zeit," in *Wort und Glaube,* III (1975), pp. 349ff., and B. Welte, *Heilsverständnis. Philosophische Untersuchungen einiger Voraussetzungen zum Verständnis des Christentums* (Freiburg, 1966).

reason why salvation can be ours only as deliverance from the lostness of life under the powers of sin and death.

If salvation is part of our relation to God's future and must be viewed as deliverance from the present state of existence, from the standpoint of Jewish expectations it is naturally understood as deliverance in the approaching world judgment, with which the future of God will put an end to the present age. In fact Paul predominantly sees *sōtēria* as salvation in the future judgment (Rom. 5:9; cf. 1 Thess. 1:10; 5:9f., etc.). Yet future salvation is already assuredly present for believers through Jesus Christ. Along these lines Pauline theology is in keeping with the relation between future and present divine rule in the message of Jesus. In and by Jesus future salvation is opened up for believers and can be attained now.[4]

Paul, of course, does not understand the presence of salvation as the work of the future of God. In and for itself this future does not seem to be our salvation. Salvation is linked to pardon at the future judgment. It is mediated by the past event of the saving death and resurrection of Jesus Christ. In general its presence is not described as salvation but as the state of justification (Rom. 5:9; cf. 8:3f. etc.) or as peace with God. For Paul the glory of the new life that is the content of *sōtēria* is still a matter of hope. This hope rests on the fact that pardon in the coming judgment is pronounced already for those who believe in the crucified and risen Christ. The state of peace with God that justifies hope for deliverance at the coming judgment rests for its part on the event of reconciliation with God through the death of his Son (Rom. 5:10, cf. v. 18). For the apostle, then, reconciliation, justification, and deliverance in the coming judgment form an indissoluble whole.[5] The differences between them are fluid. Righteousness is not just a result of the obedience of Christ (Rom. 5:18); it also is an object of hope in the sense of the pardon hoped for at the judgment (Gal. 5:5). Again, believers can be said to be saved already (Rom. 8:24), even if also in hope. This is through the power of the gospel (1 Cor. 15:2; cf. 2 Cor. 6:2), which can also be called the word of reconciliation (2 Cor. 5:19).

4. In the thought of the presence of eschatological salvation, E. Jüngel has rightly seen the positive element that Paul's doctrine of justification has, despite all the differences, in common with what Jesus proclaimed (*Paulus und Jesus* [Tübingen, 1962; 3rd ed. 1967], pp. 266f.).

5. On this see W. G. Kümmel, *Die Theologie des NTs nach seinen Hauptzeugen,* NTD supp. 3 (1969), pp. 165-83; and C. Breytenbach, *Versöhnung. Eine Studie zur paulinischen Soteriologie* (Neukirchen-Vluyn, 1989), pp. 170ff., on Rom. 5:9f.

We should not conceal the profound differences between the apostle and Jesus in their descriptions of the way in which salvation is present for believers. But we may view the differences as caused by the fact that the events of the crucifixion and resurrection of Jesus separated the public ministry of the apostle from the earthly manifestation of Jesus, whose message made the salvation of the rule of God present already for believers. These events were before Paul's eyes as the accomplishing of reconciliation, on which the Christian hope of pardon and deliverance at the coming judgment rests.

Theology can connect the Pauline view to the inbreaking of the salvation of God's rule in the message and work of Jesus only if it does not understand the concept of salvation exclusively in terms of the future, which Pauline usage tends to do by relating it to the expectation of approaching judgment. Above all, however, the relating of the Pauline understanding of salvation on the basis of the death of Jesus to the message of Jesus himself has as its premise the fact that there is a connection here. This is so inasmuch as the death of Jesus was a consequence of his message and his earthly work. As we have seen, the inbreaking of the rule of God in the event of the proclamation and work of Jesus involved the ambivalence of his appearance that resulted in his death. Above, we have deliberated concerning the transforming and expanding of the messianic concept by relating it to the Crucified (pp. 312ff., 322), and also concerning the obedient suffering of Jesus as the consequence of the sonship manifested in his self-distinction from the Father (pp. 374f.). Such deliberations might serve as starting points for reconstructing a basic relation to the Pauline interpretation of the crucifixion of Jesus as an expression of the love of God (Rom. 5:8; cf. 8:32). This view of the crucifixion would be based on the revelation of the love of the Father as it was present already in the pre-Easter ministry of Jesus, when the future of his kingdom became present salvation for those who accepted the message of Jesus. We shall have to see how far we can find arguments to support a link of this kind.

In spite of tying *sōtēria* to the event of deliverance at the approaching judgment, Paul himself could sometimes say that this salvation has been imparted to believers already through the gospel (see above). This emphasis is stronger in Ephesians (2:5, 8); Titus 3:4f. can even speak of the deliverance of believers through baptism. Linguistically we see here a shift to the present in the idea of participation in eschatological salvation, though still with a reference to future consummation. This shift makes good sense theologically, since it is closer than Pauline usage to the stand-

point of Jesus' own message, which announced that the saving eschatological future of the rule of God is present already. Since future salvation
is mediated in the present by Jesus, we may extend the term *sōtēria* to his
work, as in John 3:17 and 4:22,[6] and especially in the statement in Heb.
2:3 that *sōtēria* originated in the proclamation of Jesus himself. This
statement is surprisingly close to modern exegetical insights on the theme
of the proleptic presence of the salvation of the divine rule in the message
and work of Jesus. We may even understand the description of Jesus as
the "pioneer" of salvation along these lines (2:10).

Reference to a future consummation of salvation indeed persists.
Yet placing the accent on the origin of salvation in the history of Jesus
and its imparting by the gospel and baptism brought a change in the
content of its understanding (at least as regards *sōtēria*) in comparison
with Paul. The primary reference now is not to the deliverance of believers
at the coming judgment but on the historical event of rescue from the life
of sin for a new life by the Spirit (Titus 3:4ff.). Paul had associated with
deliverance at the coming judgment a definition of *sōtēria*[7] in terms of
participation in the glory of the new life manifested already in Christ (Phil.
3:20f.; cf. Rom. 5:10; 8:30), but the latter concept was now no longer tied
to the time of the future judgment. As a result the Pauline vocabulary of
justification was less prominent in post-Pauline statements regarding the
present participation of believers in salvation. Sharing the new life in
Christ was no longer determined primarily by deliverance at the last
judgment. Hence present salvation was no longer characterized primarily
by anticipation of pardon at the future judgment as distinct from the life
then to be attained. It was now the initial reality of the new life itself which
had come into this world through Jesus Christ.

It may be seen, then, that the sharp Pauline distinctions between
reconciliation, justification, and future salvation in the judgment are not
representative of the NT witness as a whole, nor indeed are they always clear
in Paul himself. Nevertheless, a theological evaluation must keep two points
in view. First, salvation is linked to the future of God, which is already
present in this world in Jesus Christ, though its consummation is still ahead.
Second, participation in salvation is mediated through the history of Jesus

---

6. According to R. Bultmann, *Gospel of John* (Philadelphia, 1971), p. 189 n. 6, the
statement that salvation is of the Jews is an editorial gloss; see, however, R. E. Brown, *The
Gospel according to John*, 2 vols., AB (New York, 1966-70), I, 172, and R. Schnackenburg,
The Gospel according to St. John, 3 vols. (New York, 1980-82), I, 435f.
7. Cf. W. Foerster in *TDNT*, VII, 980-1012, esp. 983.

and especially his crucifixion. Paul in particular tied the latter aspect — the significance of the death of Jesus Christ for assurance of present salvation — to the concept of reconciliation. Reconciliation with God through Christ's death on the cross is the basis of the present form of Christian participation in salvation, which Paul described as justification and as peace with God.[8] To express this basic association the term "reconciliation" and its relation to the death of Jesus have rightly played a normative role in the history of Christian doctrine. In the process, however, the meaning of reconciliation has undergone a shift. Its range has become narrower, and its relation to the death of Jesus has taken on a different sense. Precisely in its original Pauline thrust and breadth, however, it has the potential to serve as the key to an appropriate systematic interpretation of the significance of Jesus and of the whole process of imparting salvation.

§ 2. The Concept and Doctrine of Reconciliation

The Pauline linking of the slogan "reconciliation" to the death of Christ (Rom. 5:10) shows us why Christian theology has understood the death of Jesus in terms of reconciliation, but it also has seen reconciliation in the light of various interpretations of the death of Jesus Christ. In the process, in contrast to Paul, for whom God was the subject of the event of reconciliation (2 Cor. 5:19), the idea could arise that God, having been offended by the sin of Adam, had to be reconciled to humanity by the obedience of the Son, or by the sacrificing of his life on the cross.

The origins of this understanding seem to lie in Irenaeus's theory of "recapitulation." Irenaeus saw a recapitulation of Adam by Christ, i.e., a repetitive restoration and rescuing of what was originally lost in Adam (*Adv. haer.* 5.14.1). Irenaeus could also describe this as a reconciliation of those who were alienated from God. This reconciliation was through Jesus Christ, or through his body given up to death (cf. Col. 1:21f.; *Adv. haer.* 5.14.2f.). The disobedience of the first man at the

---

8. Although in Paul the sayings regarding reconciliation, like the thought of justification, are oriented to the present state of life in faith, the state of peace with God (Rom. 5:1), their relation to the death of Jesus gives them a basic function for justification (2 Cor. 5:21). Only thus can we understand something that Breytenbach stresses (*Versöhnung*, p. 223), namely, that reconciliation as an expression of the love of God precedes faith, whereas justification always stands related to it.

wood of the forbidden tree of paradise was healed by the obedience of the second Adam on the wood of the cross. Thus we were reconciled by the second Adam with the God whom we had offended in the first Adam (5.16.3). For us he reconciled the Father, against whom we had sinned, and made good our disobedience by his obedience (5.17.1). Irenaeus is close here to the thought of Rom. 5:19 that reconciliation takes place through the obedience of Christ.

Rom. 5:19, however, does not speak of any softening of an angry Father by the sacrificial death of Christ. In Irenaeus the only deviation from Paul is that the Father seems to be the object of Christ's reconciling obedience and not the subject of the work of reconciliation as in 2 Cor. 5:19. As Irenaeus sees it, the obedience of the second Adam reconciles the God offended by the sin of Adam. Paul does not say this. The basis of a tendency toward this interpretation of reconciliation in Irenaeus is the development of Paul's antithetical parallel between the second Adam and the first, with a stress in both cases on the relation to God. The limits of the parallel in the difficult passage Rom. 5:12-21 are thus ignored.[9] The obvious trend in Irenaeus was soon strengthened by the interpretation of the death of Jesus as an expiation made to the Father for the sin of humanity.[10] In the Latin church the idea became especially important after Cyprian.[11] Thus Augustine could write that we are under the Father's wrath because of original sin and furthermore that we need a Mediator and Reconciler who can appease this wrath by offering a unique sacrifice.[12] In this way Augustine expressed the basic thought that Anselm, at the beginning of the Scholastic period, presented in different terms in his satisfaction theory.[13]

9. See G. Bornkamm, "Paulinische Anakoluthe im Römerbrief," in *Das Ende des Gesetzes*, Paulusstudien I (Munich, 1952), pp. 80ff., 88ff.

10. Pioneered by Tertullian. Cf. H. Kessler, *Die theologische Bedeutung des Todes Jesu* (1970), pp. 72ff. We find the thought expressly in Origen (ibid., pp. 77ff.) along with that of the death of Christ as a ransom to deliver us from the power of the devil; cf. A. Harnack, *History of Dogma* (New York, 1961).

11. Harnack, *History of Dogma*.

12. Augustine *Ench.* 10.33 (CChrSL, 46, 68). In support Augustine adduced Rom. 5:10, though this mentions neither Mediator nor sacrifice. In view of this statement of Augustine, the claim of O. Scheel is surprising that there is no reconciling of God in Augustine, that he knows nothing of the wrath of God (*Die Anschauung Augustins über Christi Person und Werk* [1901], p. 332).

13. On Anselm's *Cur Deus Homo*, cf. Kessler, *Die theologische Bedeutung des Todes Jesu*, pp. 83-165. Scheel's view that Anselm's line of thinking was remote from Augustine (*Die Anschauung Augustins*, p. 336) and that there is in him no substitutionary theory as in Augustine (p. 337) overstates the differences; the agreement between the two lies especially in the focus on the mediatorial office of the human nature of Christ, as will be shown below. Here we undoubtedly find a form of representation. In view of the systematic implications of this view of Christ's mediatorship, we certainly have here more than an Augustinian "sprinkling," even though one might say that Anselm did not attain to the whole dynamic or depth of Augustinian theology (Kessler, *Die theologische Bedeutung des Todes Jesu*, p. 128).

The linking of the thought of reconciliation with Christ's function as Mediator contributed to the systematic consolidation of the interpretation of the Pauline idea of reconciliation as a softening of God's wrath at Adam's sin by the offering made to him in the death of Jesus. In the concept of Christ as Mediator, Western christology stressed the role of his human nature, by which he represented us before God in his suffering obedience. This view had its basis in Augustine and became normative for Latin Scholasticism.[14]

Linking reconciliation of the Father offended by Adam's sin to the mediatorial office of Christ may be found already in Irenaeus, who, appealing to 1 Tim. 2:5, found the work of the Mediator in the reconciling of the Father (*Adv. haer.* 5.17.1). Augustine early adopted the same thought and the same text (PL, 34, 1070 and 35, 2122; cf. 34, 1245). He expounded the thought in more detail in his *Confessions*, where he argued that Christ, being equal to the Father as Logos, cannot be the Mediator according to his deity but only according to his humanity (10.68). He stated the same thought again in the *City of God* (9.15.2).[15] The idea profoundly influenced Latin Scholasticism. It is presupposed materially in Anselm's satisfaction theory, even though Anselm did not use the Mediator concept.[16]

The issue was discussed and controverted expressly in the 12th century. Note was then taken of Paul's statement that God was in Christ and reconciled the world to himself (2 Cor. 5:19). Hence Peter Lombard argued that the Father or the whole Trinity was the subject in reconciliation.[17] Nevertheless, the idea of appeasing the divine wrath, along with the concept of the Mediator,[18] which Lombard, under Augustine's influence, related to the human nature of Christ, resulted in the statement that in regard to power it is the whole Trinity that is involved in reconciliation but that the Son alone is Mediator according to his human nature through his obedience.[19] The equation of reconciling with Christ's mediatorship also caused the leading 13th-century theologians to relate both

14. On the discussion of this question in early Scholasticism, cf. A. M. Landgraf, *Dogmengeschichte der Frühscholastik*, II/2 (1954), pp. 288ff. ("Die Mittlerschaft Christi").

15. See further examples in Scheel, *Die Anschauung Augustins*, pp. 319f., 124f. Scheel rightly points out that Augustine regarded the divine humanity as constitutive for the idea of a Mediator between God and humanity (pp. 325f.). Yet there is no contradiction, for on the basis of the divine humanity the human nature is decisive for the work of mediating. Scheel recognized that this approach was the main one in Augustine's discussion of the theme (p. 327).

16. *Cur Deus Homo* 2.18 (PL, 158, 762ff.)

17. *Sent.* 2.3 and 4 (Rome, 1981), p. 123 (3.19.6). On the vacillation in Lombard, cf. Landgraf, *Dogmengeschichte*, pp. 300ff.

18. *Sent.* loc. cit.

19. *Sent.* 3.19.7. Lombard adduced Gal. 3:20 and Augustine in support. For the statement in 3.19.6, he appealed to 2 Cor. 5:19.

concepts to his human nature. Bonaventura took this view,[20] and so did Aquinas, who stated that as the one and only Mediator, Christ reconciles us to God by his sacrifice, doing so according to his human nature.[21]

Reformation theology did not follow this relating of the mediatorial office only to Christ's human nature, since it regarded the divine-human person as a whole as the bearer of the office.[22] Nevertheless, the Reformers adopted a view of Christ's reconciling death related to the Scholastic understanding of Christ's mediatorial office, seeing it as an expiation that reconciles God's wrath toward sinners. In Luther we find a revision in terms of the vicarious penal suffering of Christ.[23] Along the lines of Anselm's satisfaction theory, however, Melanchthon could describe the crucifixion of Christ as an offering made to God to appease his anger at sinners.[24] Calvin argued similarly, though he also emphasized the divine initiative in reconciliation, thus coming close to the idea of the death of Christ as a vicarious bearing of our punishment on the Father's commission.[25] The older Protestant dogmatics gave stronger emphasis to the basic structure of Anselm's satisfaction theory by putting the Father at the center as the recipient of Christ's offering of satisfaction. In so doing it contributed not least of all to Socinian criticism of the traditional view of the need of satisfaction for the sin of Adam and his progeny and criticism also of the idea of imputing the merits of Christ to others.[26]

20. Bonaventura *Sent.* 3.19.2.3 (Opera Omnia, III [1887], p. 410).

21. *ST* 3.26.2, cf. 3.49.4.

22. Formula of Concord SD 8.46f. On this topic cf. Melanchthon's Apology to CA 21 ("Mediator" or "Reconciler" in the German text, *propitiator* in the Latin), but with no use of the two-natures doctrine. Calvin is especially clear in *Inst.* 2.14.3. The person of Christ is the bearer of the office, not either the divine or the human nature. On the polemical importance of the question, cf. J. Baur, "Lutherische Christologie im Streit um die neue Bestimmung von Gott und Mensch," *EvT* 41 (1981) 433ff. Yet this relating to the divine-human person is not an innovation, since we often find it in early Scholasticism, and cf. Robert of Melun (Landgraf, *Dogmengeschichte,* pp. 296f.).

23. On Luther and Christ's penal death, cf. O. Tiililä, *Das Strafleiden Christi* (1941), and more briefly *Jesus — God and Man,* pp. 278ff. Luther, however, did not set this view in antithesis to the idea of satisfaction but related the two theories. Cf. P. Althaus, *The Theology of Martin Luther* (Philadelphia, 1966), pp. 202ff.

24. *Loci* (1559; CR, 21, 871f.). Cf. CA 3: He died "that he might reconcile the Father unto us, and might be a sacrifice . . . for all . . . sins."

25. *Inst.* 2.16.6. On the Father's love that aims at reconciliation, cf. esp. 2.16.3. The accent thus shifts from satisfaction to vicarious penal suffering (2.16.2).

26. G. Wenz, *Geschichte der Versöhnungslehre in der evangelischen Theologie der Neuzeit,* 2 vols. (Munich, 1984-86), I, 75f., 79f. On Socinian criticism of the satisfaction theory, cf. pp. 119-27; on the revival of a penal view in Grotius, pp. 128-36.

Only after the destruction of the satisfaction theory by the rational criticism of the Socinians and the adoption of this criticism by the Protestant theology of the Enlightenment[27] did attention begin to focus more widely on the difference between the thought of reconciliation in the NT (including Paul) and later theological usage. *God* did not have to be reconciled; the *world* is reconciled by God in Christ (2 Cor. 5:19). It must be regarded as a merit of modern Protestant theology that after critical destruction of the satisfaction theory it reinstated the Pauline orientation of reconciliation statements to the world, to us who are to be reconciled. It now came to view the reconciliation of the world by Christ as an outworking of the love of God in the face of the opposition of humans who are hostile to God, a love of God that we see operative through Jesus Christ. Even so, however, insufficient account was taken of the fundamental significance of the death of Christ for the Pauline thought of the reconciling of the world by God (Rom. 5:10; 2 Cor. 5:21f., cf. 5:14).

In 1729 J. C. Dippel pointed out that in the NT God was not reconciled to the world by Christ but the world to God.[28] This insight, however, did not fit in with the current linking of reconciliation to Christ's sacrifice, so it was lost again until J. C. Döderlein and G. Menken revived it at the turn of the 19th century.[29] In dogmatics the Heidelberg supernaturalist H. Schwarz[30] and above all Schleiermacher independently attempted to detach the traditional dogmatic concept of reconciliation from the doctrine of satisfaction and to develop it from a new systematic angle.

In *The Christian Faith* Schleiermacher treated reconciliation and redemp-

27. Ibid., pp. 170-216, esp. the discussion of J. G. Töllner (pp. 179ff.). M. Kähler rightly said of this development that in spite of a futile struggle from J. Gerhard (cf. H. H. Schmid, *Doctrinal Theology of the Evangelical Lutheran Church* [Philadelphia, 1961], pp. 356ff.), to Grotius, Socinian teaching became the acknowledged opinion of Lutheran theologians ("Das Wort 'Versöhnung' im Sprachgebrauch der kirchlichen Lehre," in *Zur Lehre von der Versöhnung* [1898, 2nd ed. 1937], pp. 1ff., 24).

28. J. C. Dippel, *Vera Demonstratio Evangelica*, II (1729), p. 676, quoted in Wenz, *Geschichte*, I, 168.

29. G. Menken, *Versuch einer Anleitung zu eignem Unterricht in den Wahrheiten der heiligen Schrift* (1805), quoted in Kähler, "Das Wort 'Versöhnung,'" p. 25. Kähler called Menken the first to work out the antithesis between church usage and the Pauline use of the term "reconciliation." Cf. J. C. Döderlein, *Institutio theologi christiani* (1780, 2nd. ed. 1783), II, 331f. (§ 262).

30. Cf. F. H. C. Schwarz, *Grundriss der Kirchlichen protestantischen Dogmatik* (1816). Kähler ("Das Wort 'Versöhnung,'" p. 25) saw here the first dogmatic attempt to redefine church usage in line with Paul's statements about the reconciliation of the world by God in Christ, but with no express criticism of the traditional understanding.

tion as parallel; the two together constituted Christ's work.[31] Hence the point of reconciliation was not to work on God to appease his wrath but, as in the case of redemption, to communicate the God-consciousness of Christ to us. Interest focused here not merely on the effects in the recipients but on the actions of the Redeemer himself. The Redeemer's work is thus at the forefront of the presentation. It consists of his taking us up into the dynamic of his God-consciousness. The reconciling activity is no different. It is simply a special element in the general work of redemption (§ 101.2), namely, the vanishing of the old man (and his sense of guilt) that accompanies adoption into living fellowship with Christ. The reconciling work of Christ thus confers a sense of the forgiveness of sins.

Schleiermacher thus offered an understanding of the reconciliation effected by Christ that broke with what he called the "magical" satisfaction theory and also with the idea of penal suffering that God imputed to us (§ 101.3). It also was closer to the Pauline idea of an act of reconciliation that originates in God and that through Christ has the world as its target. Schleiermacher's view is thus related to the concepts that Abelard developed in the 12th century in opposition to Anselm.[32] But just as Abelard's critic Bernard of Clairvaux missed in Abelard's teaching any appreciation of the expiatory function of Christ's death,[33] so Schleiermacher's presentation carries no reference to the fundamental significance of the death of Christ, by which we are reconciled to God according to Paul (Rom. 5:10).

Schleiermacher himself did try to meet in advance the objection that there was no reference to Christ's suffering in his understanding of Christ's reconciling work (§ 101.4). His concept of reconciliation does in fact contain an interpretation of the suffering, namely, with reference to the resistance of sin that the work of the Redeemer encounters, and especially with reference to the fact that Christ's work, oriented to the kingdom of God among us, gave ground to no opposition, not even to that which resulted in the destruction of the person. Here, then, the

---

31. *Christian Faith*, §§ 100f. The quotations that follow in the text are from this work. On individual aspects, cf. Wenz, *Geschichte*, I, 366-82.

32. In his *Commentary on Romans*, Abelard took *per fidem* in 3:25 to mean that Jesus is *reconciliator* only for believers (Opera Omnia, ed. E. M. Buytaert, I [1969], pp. 112, 91f.). God's demonstration of his justice by ordaining his son to be the Reconciler by his blood was something Abelard referred to the justifying love of God (pp. 112, 92f.). He thus rejected the ransom theory and avoided any idea of redemption from God's wrath by Christ's death. For Abelard, it is the life of the risen Lord that saves us from wrath (on Rom. 5:10). Cf. J. Turmel, *Histoire des Dogmas*, I (1931), pp. 427-33.

33. In his letter to Pope Innocent, in which he attacked Abelard's doctrine of the Trinity, Bernard also referred to his rejection of the ransom theory (*Ep.* 190.11ff.; cf. *S. Bernardi Opera*, VIII, ed. J. Leclercq and H. Rochais [Rome, 1977], pp. 26ff.). He found in Abelard's polemic against this a rejection of redemption as such (*Ep.* 190.21f.; VIII, 35ff.). Bernard's own view finds expression in his sermons on the Song of Songs (20.3 and 116.10f.). Christ appeased the Father by his patience in suffering (116.13f.).

linking of reconciliation to the obedience of the Son in Paul (Rom. 5:19) finds a place in the form of Christ's faithfulness to his vocational duty as the Redeemer (§ 104.4), but nothing corresponds to Paul's statement that we are reconciled to God by the death of his Son (Rom. 5:10). Schleiermacher himself admitted that the suffering of Christ was not a "primitive element" in his view of reconciliation (§ 101.4). Only very secondarily does Schleiermacher's presentation link the Redeemer's reconciling work to his death and passion.

Among theologians close to Schleiermacher, C. I. Nitzsch thought it necessary to fill out Schleiermacher's concept of reconciliation with the thought of an expiation made by Christ's death, and in this way to do justice to the witness of scripture. Yet in Nitzsch, too, we find any essential connection between expiation and reconciliation limited to the thought of vocational suffering.[34] J. C. K. von Hofmann, too, remained astonishingly close to Schleiermacher, notwithstanding the trinitarian starting point of his own doctrine of reconciliation. Jesus Christ, Hofmann said, was faithful to his divine calling against all resistance, even unto death.[35] Hofmann thought he could introduce the expiatory character of the death of Jesus in this way, though not in a substitutionary sense.[36]

Though some critics accused him of subjectivism, Hofmann clung to the objective character of reconciliation in the sense of Christ's reconciling action. A. Ritschl, however, made the thought of reconciliation totally subjective. He construed reconciliation with God as the effecting of a sense of reconciliation in believers and equated the former with the latter.[37] He still believed that the concept has a broader range to the degree that it expresses the real effect that is the aim of justification and pardon, namely, that those who are pardoned enter into the relationship that is thus established.[38] For him, then, reconciliation with God is not tied to the event of the death of Jesus as the true meaning of this event, or as its effect. It is also no longer thought of as the reconciling work of the Redeemer in the sense of Schleiermacher. It takes place exclusively in the consciousness of believers or the believing community.

34. C. I. Nitzsch, *System of Christian Doctrine* (1829, 3rd ed. 1837, ET 1899), p. 262, §§ 133-35.

35. J. C. K. von Hofmann, *Der Schriftbeweis* (1852, 2nd ed. 1857), I, 46; cf. II, 193ff. Cf. Wenz, *Geschichte*, II, 55.

36. G. Thomasius pointed this out in his evaluation of Hofmann. Cf. Wenz, *Geschichte*, II, 55.

37. A. Ritschl, *The Christian Doctrine of Justification and Reconciliation* (ET of *Die christliche von der Rechtfertigung und Versöhnung*, III [1883]; Clifton, NJ, 1966), § 15 (pp. 72-79). Kähler, "Das Wort 'Versöhnung,' " p. 13, rightly criticized Ritschl's appeal to Melanchthon (pp. 72-74) in support of this equation; cf. also Wenz, *Geschichte*, II, 63-131.

38. Ritschl, *Christian Doctrine*, pp. 76f. At the end of Ritschl's § 16 (p. 85), we read: "In so far as justification is viewed as effective, it must be conceived as reconciliation, of such a nature that . . . the place of mistrust towards God is taken by the positive assent of the will to God and His saving purpose."

410   *11. The Reconciliation of the World*

Ritschl thought that his exegesis of Paul justified this radical break with the theological tradition. Because 2 Cor. 5:19 links the reconciliation saying to God's not imputing transgressions, Ritschl concluded that the reconciliation is not directly related to the sacrificial value of Christ's death but is linked only by means of the sacrificial effect that Paul favored, namely, the forgiveness of sins.[39] For Ritschl the sacrificial value of the death of Christ has its basis in the willingness of Jesus to suffer his fate at the hands of opponents as something that God ordained and that gave supreme proof of fidelity to his calling.[40] In Ritschl, too, this fidelity in service to the kingdom of God was decisive for an understanding of his death. In fact we do have here a very significant thought, for it brings to light the connection between the earthly mission of Jesus and his death. No more than Schleiermacher or Hofmann, however, did Ritschl discuss the ambivalence that the mission of Jesus meant for his person. Hence he could make nothing of the vicarious thinking of 2 Cor. 5:21 or its relation to the thought of reconciliation two verses earlier.[41] The idea of an expression of vocational faithfulness in the death of Jesus does not explain, as Kähler put it, how a new situation is set up in the relation between God and us by the crucifixion. But this is implied when Paul says that though we were the enemies of God, we were reconciled to God by the death of his Son (Rom. 5:10).

Kähler agreed with Ritschl that in Paul reconciliation embraces the restoration of our fellowship with God, but he insisted that for Paul this event rests on a process of the past,[42] namely, the death of Christ. With Paul we must see this historical fact as an action on God's part, so that the whole event of reconciliation is mediated in a divine act in history.[43] Rightly, and especially against Ritschl, Kähler said that the real question is whether Christ rectifies erroneous views concerning an unchangeable fact, namely, the love of God (which, according to Ritschl, sinners cannot believe in because of their sense of guilt), or whether Christ is the author of a changed situation.[44] If the latter is true, then the death of Christ must be seen as a real overcoming of the misery that consists of our having fallen into sin and death and the related estrangement from God. Only

39. Ritschl, *Christliche Lehre*, II, 230ff.
40. Ritschl, *Christian Doctrine*, pp. 469f.
41. Ritschl simply says of 2 Cor. 5:21 that Jesus had the form of sin in his violent death in order that we might attain to the righteousness of God (*Christliche Lehre*, II, 173f.). He avoided linking the passage to Gal. 3:13.
42. Kähler, *Zur Lehre von der Versöhnung* (1898, 2nd ed. 1937), p. 268.
43. Kähler, *Die Wissenschaft der christlichen Lehre* (1883, 2nd ed. 1893), §§ 353, 360; cf. also the statements referred to in the preceding note.
44. Kähler, *Zur Lehre von der Versöhnung*, p. 337.

thus can we see in Christ's death as a historical event the reconciliation of the world to God.

This is the point when we speak of that death as expiation for human sins.[45] Expiation removes the offense, the guilt, and the consequences. In this sense Paul could call Christ's death an expiation (Rom. 3:25).[46]

Like the ancient concept of punishment, the thought of expiation ties in with the idea of a natural link between acts and their consequences.[47] In punishment the acts rebound upon those who do them, so that no harm results for the whole social unit to which the doers belong. In expiation the doers are released from the damaging consequences of their acts. This is what happens in the case of expiatory offerings in the OT (Lev. 4–5). The guilt is transferred to the animal sacrifice, and with the offering it is set aside.[48] The process is especially clear in the ritual of the great Day of Atonement in Lev. 16:21f. The damaging effects of misdeeds are chased out of the world by expiation, punishment, or penitence.[49] But expiation is possible only in certain cases. It presupposes divine permission

45. Kähler, *Wissenschaft,* §§ 411, 428-31, and 436.

46. More exactly, God publicly instituted Jesus Christ as a *hilastērion* in his blood. Paul added "by faith" because only by faith can we share in the expiatory effect of this event. Cf. U. Wilckens, *Der Brief an die Römer,* 3 vols., EKK (Zurich/Neukirchen, 1978-82), I, 190ff. Wilckens saw in *hilastērion* the cover over the ark (Exod. 25:17-22), which is the place of the divine presence that guarantees expiation (p. 192). In his *Versöhnung,* p. 167, Breytenbach (among others) agrees with the rendering "place of expiation," though he does not accept the view of Christ's atoning death as a cultic expiation, a sin offering (pp. 160ff.), because it is an alternative to the temple cultus and brings this to an end (p. 168, cf. 170).

47. For a basic account of the idea of a sphere of fateful actions in view of the link between act and result in OT thinking, cf. K. Koch, "Gibt es ein Vergeltungsdogma im AT?" *ZTK* 52 (1955) 1-42. On sin and expiation, cf. also von Rad's *OT Theology,* I, 262ff.; on consequences and punishment, see pp. 264f.

48. Cf. R. Rendtorff, *Studien zur Geschichte des Opfers im Alten Israel* (Neukirchen-Vluyn, 1967), pp. 199ff. H. Gese, "Die Sühne," in *Zur biblischen Theologie* (1977), pp. 85ff., posited a distinction between personal and material atonement for a fault, but it is open to question whether this thesis is in accord with OT ideas of expiation.

49. On the distinction between punishment and expiation, cf. C. H. Ratschow, "Vom Sinn der Strafe," in *Die weltliche Strafe in der evangelischen Theologie,* ed. H. Dombois (1959), pp. 98-116, esp. 108ff. Because of the common basis, however, punishment may count as expiation in the Jewish tradition, and may be accepted by the offender as such, face to face with the eschatological future of divine judgment. Cf. the references in J. Gnilka, "Wie urteilte Jesus über seinen Tod?" in *Der Tod Jesu. Deutungen im NT,* ed. K. Kertelge (Freiburg, 1976), pp. 13-50, esp. 41f. In modern legal thinking, if an offender accepts and affirms punishment, it can have the function of expiation as reconciliation with society even without reference to judgment after death (cf. the references in H. Hübner, "Sühne und Versöhnung. Anmerkung zu einem umstrittenen Kapitel Biblischer Theologie," *KuD* 29 [1983] 284ff.).

with a view to the gracious sparing of the offenders. When the thought of expiation is applied to the death of Christ, the idea of an inner connection between sin and death is basic (Rom. 6:7, 23). The understanding of Christ's death as expiation for human sins presupposes that as God set up expiatory offerings to make possible the transfer of sins and their consequences to animal sacrifices, so he transferred human sins to Christ in his crucifixion. Yet the thought of an actual offering is not essential here. The death of Jesus can also (though cf. n. 46) be understood as an expiation (or possibility of expiation) that God set up by his action in and by Jesus in competition with the cultic offerings and as their abrogation.

God is the acting subject in this expiatory action, for as we shall show more precisely in the next section, the crucifixion of Jesus has atoning force only in the light of his resurrection by God. In this way God showed himself to be the Victor over sin and death in reconciliation of the world.[50] The premise on which we can talk about reconciliation as the act of God is the relation to the historically unique event of the death of Jesus, for this distinguishes the event of reconciliation as an act of God from a process of reconciling with God that takes place only in the subjectivity of believers. For a long enough time in the history of theology, the death of Christ could also be seen as an expiatory achievement of the man Jesus, who appeased the wrath of God at human sin. To view it instead as the act of God to reconcile the world is to give the event of reconciliation a new orientation. Either way, however, the death of Jesus is significant.

As God's act for the reconciliation of the world, this event is oriented to our entering into the reconciliation that is thus opened up for us. The apostle thus pleads that we be reconciled to God (2 Cor. 5:20). He makes this plea in Christ's stead, for the plea aims at the actualizing of the distinctive meaning of the crucifixion of Christ, its inner *telos* in the world's reconciliation. Only in the form of anticipation can we say

---

50. In his *Christus Victor* (1931), Gustaf Aulén has contributed to the debate between Ritschl and Kähler regarding the term "reconciliation." Aulén there advanced the idea of a divine victory over sin, death, and the devil as a third type of teaching about reconciliation that the Greek fathers favored, an alternative both to the Anselmic satisfaction theory and to the Abelardian subjective doctrine that many moderns adopted. In intention, the thesis of Aulén still stands, in spite of corrections of the depiction of Luther by O. Tiililä, *Das Strafleiden Christi*. In Luther's penal understanding it is God who acts in Christ's death to reconcile the world. Cf. also Aulén's "Die drei Haupttypen des christlichen Versöhnungsgedankens," *ZST* 8 (1930) 501ff.; and K. Heim, "Die Haupttypen des Versöhnungslehre," *ZTK* 19 (1938) 304ff.

that the reconciliation of the world has already taken place in the cross of Jesus. The issue in the history of proclaiming this event is the movement from anticipation to actualization. To this extent the apostolic ministry of reconciliation is itself reconciliation, though it is the reconciliation once and for all effected by Jesus on the cross that is at work through the ministry of the apostles and the proclamation of the church. By the apostolic ministry, then, the event of reconciliation that has its origin and center in the death of Jesus Christ still goes forward. For this reason Paul can say that according to the counsel of God the (temporary) rejection of the Jewish people of God has become the means to the reconciling of the cosmos (Rom. 11:15). For in consequence of it the missionary proclamation of the apostles came to be addressed to the Gentiles. The event of reconciliation thus includes the whole process of the renewing of our fellowship with God that sin had broken — the process that begins at the cross of Christ and continues by means of the ministry of the apostles.[51]

No modern theologian has emphasized more vigorously than Karl Barth that reconciliation is the act of God alone and that as such it took place in the crucifixion of Jesus Christ.[52] For him, however, the event was "self-contained." It was not an ongoing process toward some distant goal (*CD*, IV/1, 76). Hence Barth sharply distinguished the apostolic ministry of reconciliation to which Paul refers in 2 Cor. 5:18ff. from reconciliation itself. The apostolic ministry of reconciliation is not "of itself self-contained, but it begins only with this self-contained and completed event." It is not an "extension" of reconciliation, which was a unique event, and yet "because God in Christ was its subject — it is present in all its fulness in every age" and "is also the immediate future in every age . . . the future which brings every age to an end" (ibid.).

In this connection, at any rate, Barth was not referring like Paul to an eschatological consummation that transcends reconciliation.[53] He could mention Rom. 11:15 in passing (p. 74) but did not go into the fact that here at least the reconciling action of God does not have to do with the event of Christ's crucifix-

---

51. Only the consummation phase of the process transcends reconciliation. As we are reconciled by the death of Christ, we shall receive salvation by his life (Rom. 5:10). Eschatological salvation is more than reconciliation. It is participation in God's own life, which has been manifested already in Jesus Christ by his resurrection from the dead. We find a similar differentiation in Rom. 11:15. If the temporary rejection of Israel has brought the reconciliation of the world, its reacceptance by God will bring more, namely, life from death.

52. Cf. *CD*, IV/1, 76 and elsewhere. Reconciliation is an "act of sovereignty" on God's part (p. 80).

53. Cf. the remarks of Wilckens, *Römer*, II, 245, on Rom. 11:15.

ion. Barth's restriction of reconciliation to this event also comes into contradiction with his main exegetical authority, F. Büchsel.[54] Because the apostolic ministry of reconciliation is not yet complete, Büchsel said of 2 Cor. 5:19f. that "reconciliation must not be thought of as concluded." It is certainly concluded for believers (Rom. 5:9ff.), but not for the world. For the world it is "as little finished as the *apobolē* of the Jews. Both have been begun in the cross of Christ, and both are in course of fulfillment."[55]

Unlike Barth, Kähler tried to link the once-for-allness of the reconciling act of God in the death of Christ[56] with the process of "appropriating" reconciliation[57] in the course of the history that is directed by the kingly rule of the exalted Christ. If on the one side reconciliation is an act of God in the form of a historical fact, on the other side it requires historical continuation and appropriation to humanity in and through its individual members.[58] Kähler could thus view the reconciliation set up in Christ as the "center of God's ways" with us (§ 393). As distinct from Barth, he did not think of God's reconciling act in Christ as directly present and contemporaneous in every ensuing age because it runs through time and history. He saw it as mediated in its effects through the course of history. In this way he wanted to do better justice to the Pauline statements and also to the distinction between reconciliation and consummation.

Kähler's presentation is also more in keeping than Barth's on the human historicity of the death of Christ, an inseparable part of this being that the individual event is related to the process of history before and after it. Theologically basic in Kähler to the link between the reconciling act of God in Christ's death and the historical process of its effective appropriation[59] by human recipients is his interpretation of the vicarious nature of Christ's expiatory death. He understood the vicarious penal suffering of Christ (§ 425) as a "sponsoring representation" oriented to future reception, so that the dedication of our own

54. Barth (*CD*, IV/1, 73) refers directly to Büchsel in *TDNT*, I, 254ff.

55. *TDNT*, I, 257. O. Hofius, "Erwägungen zur Gestalt und Herkunft des paulinischen Versöhnungsgedankens," *ZTK* 77 (1989) 186ff., distinguished (as Barth did) between God's act of reconciliation and the apostles' word of reconciliation. But we properly express the unity of the event as it is oriented to those who are to be reconciled only if we regard the divine act in the death of Christ as open to the word and its acceptance in faith. On Rom. 11:15, cf. also Breytenbach, *Versöhnung*, pp. 176f. Breytenbach calls the death of the Son the basis of the possibility of a new relation to God, which the term "reconciliation" denotes (p. 159; cf. 181f.).

56. Kähler, *Wissenschaft*, §§ 353 and 360.

57. Ibid., § 432, cf. § 441.

58. Ibid., § 360, cf. § 439f.

59. The term "appropriation" does not seem to be quite right inasmuch as through the process of appropriation, reconciliation is first accepted by the human recipients and in this way actualized for them. Elsewhere Kähler speaks of an "offer" (ibid., § 440a, cf. § 432), which again seems to be too weak if God actually set up reconciliation in Christ's death (§ 393).

wills to obedience to God is not superfluous but is for the first time made possible (§ 428). This means that it spans our relation to God for all time (§ 429). This sponsorship on behalf of others is set up by the royal rule of the exalted Christ (§ 439), and consummation of the reconciliation grounded in Christ comes through the work of the Spirit in believers (§ 442). Here, then, the divine action that reconciles humanity forms a trinitarian nexus of events in salvation history.

The more decidedly we think of the reconciliation of the world as an act of God himself, the more urgently the question arises as to the role of the human recipients. Reconciliation cannot take place unless it applies to them. Do we not have to regard not merely God's reconciling act but also its human acceptance as constitutive for the event? Barth put this question as well as Kähler; like Kähler, he sought an answer in the concept of representation. We as recipients of God's reconciling act have a part in it by being represented.[60] We are represented, however, by the Son of God, who himself became man.

But can we be represented by the Son of God as recipients of the act, as sinners and enemies of God, so that he accepts the offer of reconciliation on our behalf? Neither in Barth nor in Kähler do we find a satisfactory answer to this question,[61] i.e., an answer that does justice to the situation of the recipients as human beings, as sinners in need of reconciliation. Connected herewith is the further question whether the thought of representation leaves room for the human creaturely independence of those who are represented, so that they for their part can no longer see God and his claim on their lives as hostile but can reconcile themselves to this claim. If God does not have to be reconciled to us but we to God, then the reason for our hostility to God must be removed if there is to be reconciliation with him.

---

60. *CD*, IV/1, 75. God accomplished the "complete conversion of the world" to himself (p. 74). He did it in the form of an exchange, a substitution, which God "has proposed between the world and Himself present and active in the person of Jesus Christ" (p. 75). Barth found the thought of representation in the basic meaning of the term *katallassein* (p. 74). This means that it is present in the very thought of reconciliation. Jesus Christ "took the place of sinners" (p. 235). He thus "stands under the wrath and judgment of God. He is broken and destroyed on God" (p. 175). He is still the Son of God who fulfilled the righteous judgment on us "by Himself taking our place as man and in our place undergoing the judgment under which we had passed" (p. 222). Wenz rightly stressed that Barth never says that the deity and sinlessness of Jesus Christ were first fully communicated by the self-sacrifice manifest in his suffering obedience (*Geschichte*, II, 245).

61. In his incisive presentation Wenz concludes that we see a "one-sided dominance of the deity of Christ" (*Geschichte*, II, 155) in the interpretation of the crucifixion in both Barth (pp. 242ff.) and Kähler (pp. 154ff.).

Can the concept of representation meet this demand? To answer this question we shall have to clarify the term, its many variants, and its implications for our understanding of ourselves in our relation to God.

§ 3. Representation as the Form of the Salvation Event

a. First Christian Interpretations of the Death of Jesus and the Fact of Representation

Not all strata of the primitive Christian tradition view the death of Jesus as a salvation event. The message of the resurrection of the Crucified could apparently be proclaimed without being linked to a theological understanding of his death.[62] Q seems to have viewed the death as a prophetic destiny known in advance from the OT (Luke 13:34 par.; cf. 11:49ff.).[63] The early tradition behind the passion story seems simply to have recognized the divine necessity of the innocent suffering and death of Jesus in fulfillment of the prophetic testimonies of scripture.[64] We find a similar view in Luke 24:25f. and Mark 8:31 par. Nevertheless, among the many theological interpretations of the death of Jesus that primitive Christianity developed,[65] special significance clearly attaches to the view that the death of Jesus was expiatory, though not primarily as an expiatory sacrifice.[66]

Whether the interpretation goes back to Jesus himself is contested.

62. Cf. G. Friedrich, *Die Verkündigung des Todes Jesu im NT* (Neukirchen-Vluyn, 1982), pp. 14-21.
63. Cf. O. H. Steck, *Israel und das gewaltsame Geschick der Propheten. Untersuchungen zur Überlieferung des deuteronomistischen Geschichtsbildes im AT, Spätjudentum, und Urchristentum* (Neukirchen-Vluyn, 1967). On Luke 13:34f., see pp. 53-58 and 222-39. There were perhaps christological reasons for the inclusion of what might have been a Jewish saying in Q; see Friedrich, *Verkündigung*, pp. 14f.
64. Cf. Kessler, *Die theologische Bedeutung des Todes Jesu*, pp. 243f.
65. In *Jesus — God and Man*, p. 246, I stress the variety as compared with the more uniform message of the resurrection. Cf. also K. Lehmann, "'Er wurde für uns gekreuzigt.' Eine Skizze zur Neubesinnung in der Soteriologie," *TQ* 162 (1982) 300ff. For an excellent survey, cf. Friedrich, *Verkündigung*.
66. Kessler, *Die theologische Bedeutung des Todes Jesu*, pp. 265-96. Kessler does not dispute the dominance of the thought of expiation but criticizes the idea that we must see it as an expiatory offering (pp. 68-71). Cf. esp. Friedrich, *Verkündigung*, on Rom. 3:23-26 (pp. 57-67). With many other exegetes Friedrich found in the tradition regarding the Lord's Supper the starting point for the primitive Christian understanding of the death of Jesus as expiation (p. 35).

He might very well have reckoned with the possibility of an approaching violent death.[67] But it is another matter to have proclaimed his death as a ransom for many (Mark 10:45)[68] or as an expiatory death. Debate has arisen as to the authenticity of the statements that the Gospels attribute to Jesus that ascribe an expiatory function to his death. Certainly we cannot rule out in principle the possibility that he himself saw his death in this way. But the assumption that he actually did so in Mark 10:45 or at the institution of the Lord's Supper (see below) faces considerable difficulties. If he actually spoke in this way, we would have expected that the question of the meaning of his death would have been decided authoritatively and unequivocally in advance for primitive Christianity. Thus it would be hard to see why, according to Luke, the disciples came to see only from the prophetic scriptures why the Messiah had to suffer all these things (Luke 24:26). It might be better for dogmatics, then, to go into the question of the meaning of the death of Jesus, and the reasons for primitive Christian statements regarding its expiatory function, without presupposing that Jesus himself explained his death along these lines. Even if he did not, the widespread expiatory statements in primitive Christianity will prove to be a relevant exposition of the true meaning of the event.

We cannot at once regard all statements that speak of Jesus Christ dying "for us"[69] as the expression of an expiatory function of his death. In the account of the institution of the Lord's Supper in Mark, the "for many" in the cup saying is linked more to the idea of a covenant sacrifice than to that of an expiatory offering.[70] Even if a covenant sacrifice might also have an expiatory function, the main accent falls elsewhere. We must be cautious, then, if we are inclined to find the thought of expiation self-evident when we run across the words "for us" with no further elucidation. The expression

67. Friedrich, *Verkündigung*, pp. 25f.; Kessler, *Die theologische Bedeutung des Todes Jesu*, pp. 232ff. Kessler rightly adds that this does not mean that he directly willed or provoked this violent death (p. 233).

68. On this verse, cf. Friedrich, *Verkündigung*, pp. 11f., who lists commentators who support and those who reject the authenticity of this saying. On problems facing acceptance of its authenticity, see also Gnilka, "Wie urteilte Jesus über seinen Tod?" pp. 41ff.

69. Cf. Friedrich, *Verkündigung*, pp. 72-76; and H. Riesenfeld in *TDNT*, VIII, 510-18.

70. On Mark 14:24, cf. F. Hahn, "Zum Stand der Erforschung des urchristlichen Herrenmahls," *EvT* 35 (1975) 553ff., and F. Lang, "Abendmahl und Bundesgedanke im NT," ibid., pp. 524ff. Lang thinks the covenant idea was a very early part of the tradition (p. 528) but may also have been linked to the motif of purging sin (p. 535). Hahn lays more stress on the difference between covenant and expiation but thinks there might be a linkage in Mark 14:24 because of the added "shed for you" (as distinct from 1 Cor. 11:25).

might well signify no more than "in our favor" or "on our behalf."[71] Thus the bread saying in the Pauline version (1 Cor. 11:24) simply means that Jesus is "for" the recipients and present to them. To seek the origin of the idea of an expiatory meaning for the death of Jesus in the eucharistic tradition and celebration, as many do,[72] is thus a dubious procedure.[73]

Nevertheless, "for us" could easily come to be linked with the motif of expiation and related to the explanatory words at the Supper insofar as signs of the death of Jesus and the shedding of his blood were seen in the breaking of the bread and the pouring of the wine. The motif is plainly present when "for us" is brought into connection with "our sins." If Christ died for our sins, as in the traditional formula in Paul (1 Cor. 15:3), then that undoubtedly means that he made expiation for our sins. The developed formula of Rom. 4:25 says this, as does the way in which 1 Pet. 2:24 understands the "suffered for you" of v. 21. The same thought comes to expression in another form in sayings regarding the giving up of the Son to death (Rom. 8:22; cf. 4:25) or his self-offering on our behalf (Gal. 2:20), though here "our sins" does not seem to be an express part of the formula but may be understood only from the context (cf. also Eph. 5:25). Related materially is the image of the ransom (1 Tim. 2:6; Titus 2:14) that Jesus Christ paid by his death for us (cf. Mark 10:45 par.).

Paul also says in some passages that in his death Christ took the place of sinners. For us, God "made him to be sin who knew no sin" (2 Cor. 5:21). The idea of a change of places is expressly stated here. He took the place of us sinners. This is saying much more than that he gave his life for us (Rom. 5:6f., etc.). That he gave his life for us does not have to mean that he suffered in our place the death that ought to have been ours. Yet "for us, on our behalf" can very easily merge into "in our place," especially in the context of the idea of expiation, i.e., when the expiation that a person makes for others is the

71. It is widely assumed that this is the basic sense; cf. Riesenfeld in *TDNT,* VIII, 511ff., and K. Kertelge, "Das Verständnis des Todes Jesu bei Paulus," in *Der Tod Jesu,* ed. Kertelge (1976), pp. 116ff. Even in Paul's case we can hardly say that the thought of expiation was always present; see Friedrich, *Verkündigung,* p. 73. Without good reason we certainly cannot import it into simple "for us" sayings or 1 Cor. 11:24, though cf. G. Bornkamm, "Herrenmahl und Kirche bei Paulus," in *Studien zur Antike und Urchristentum* (1959), p. 162.

72. Cf. Riesenfeld in *TDNT,* VIII, 513; also Gnilka, "Wie urteilte Jesus über seinen Tod?" pp. 31ff., 50.

73. Especially as regards the parts of the eucharistic tradition that are thought to derive from Jesus himself. Cf. Hahn, "Zum Stand der Erforschung," pp. 558ff.; also his "Das Verständnis des Opfers im NT," in *Das Opfer Jesu Christi und seine Gegenwart in der Kirche,* Dialog der Kirchen, 3, ed. K. Lehmann and H. Schlink (1983), pp. 51ff., 68f.

expiation that they themselves ought to have made. Even so, this does not have to imply that the person who does something for others will in the process, and to that end, enter into the existential conditions of those others on behalf of whom it is done. But that is precisely what Paul was wanting to say in 2 Cor. 5:21. In Romans he could declare that representation in this sense was the very purpose of the sending of the Son. God sent "his own Son in the likeness of sinful flesh and for sin [its expiation]," and God "condemned sin in the [his] flesh" (Rom. 8:3).[74] This statement is very close to the saying in Gal. 3:13 that the Crucified bore the curse of the law "for us" and in that way redeemed us from that curse and from the law in general.[75] In Rom. 8:3 the condemnation of sin in the flesh is the condemnation that came upon the Crucified, the sentence of death that sin merits (cf. also 2 Cor. 5:21).

We clearly must reckon with different stages in the thought of representation. To do something for others that they ought to do is to do it on their behalf, "for them." But it does not have to mean entering into the conditions of their lives. Usually it is possible to do it only because of not being under the limitations that put needy people in a position in which they can no longer help themselves.

What we have here is a co-human solidarity in which some represent others. We find this kind of representation in a broader sense in any social group in which individual members have special functions that both single them out and enable them to contribute to the unit as a whole and to the other members (cf. 1 Cor. 12:12ff.). In a working society the different members do particular jobs for others, and all the members are thus reciprocally related to one another. They are "for" one another and must act in solidarity in this sense, for "if one member suffers, all suffer together" (1 Cor. 12:26). The benefits that the acts of some confer and the harm that the failings of others cause all affect the society as a whole.[76]

---

74. Cf. Wilckens, *Römer*, II, 124ff.; on *peri hamartias*, pp. 126f. Cf. also Friedrich, *Verkündigung*, pp. 68ff., though he is skeptical regarding a technical cultic understanding of the phrase.

75. On Gal. 3:13, cf. Kertelge, "Das Verständnis des Todes Jesu," pp. 128ff.; also H.-W. Kuhn, "Jesus als Gekreuzigter in den frühchristlichen Verkündigung bis zur Mitte des 2. Jahrhunderts," *ZTK* 72 (1975) 1ff., esp. 35.

76. Cf. Friedrich, *Verkündigung*, pp. 41f., and *Jesus — God and Man*, pp. 264ff. ("The Universal Horizon of the Concept of Substitution"), where, like W. Kasper in *Jesus the Christ* (New York, 1976), I stress that the solidarity in good and evil that is basic to us as social beings has recently become a comparatively alien thought with increasing individualism. After Socinian criticism of the church's doctrine of redemption, the idea of representation or substitution thus became an alien one in modern Protestantism.

Giving one's life to save others or society represents a special case. We do not have here a vicarious service on the premise of different social positions. To sacrifice one's life is to offer up one's whole existence, as others would lose theirs without the sacrifice. To do so does not necessarily involve an expiatory function. As a rule, life is sacrificed to save the life of others. Is this true of the death of Jesus "for us" or "for our sins"? No, for those for whom Jesus died also must die themselves. To speak of the death of Jesus "for us" is thus more complex than might appear at a first glance.

The understanding of this death as an expiatory death "for our sins" seems to offer a way out of the difficulty. This expiatory death indeed does not preserve from death the earthly life of those on whose behalf he died, but it does preserve them for eternal life in the judgment of God. This does not mean that because of the death of Christ the death of others ceases to be the judicial consequence of sin. According to Paul, all believers are freed from sin only because and insofar as their own future death is anticipated and linked to the death of Jesus by baptism (Rom. 7:1-4; cf. 6:3f.). At this point the exclusive sense of dying in place of another passes over into the thought of an inclusion. By baptism the (future) death of the baptized is linked to the death of Jesus. Only thus do Christians receive the hope of participation in the life that was already manifested in Jesus in his resurrection (Rom. 6:5).

In 2 Cor. 5:14 Paul expresses as follows this distinctively complex and inclusive meaning of the death of Jesus "for us": "One has died for all, therefore all have died." The structure of this formulation reminds us of the sayings in Rom. 5:17ff. concerning Jesus Christ as the new Adam who by his obedience represents "many." Not merely does he represent them, but by the "abundance of grace" he gives them a share in his righteousness (v. 17). The participation in the obedient suffering and death of Christ that is mediated by baptism and faith is then in 2 Cor. 5:17 the means whereby believers have reconciliation to God through Christ (v. 18). This train of thought helps us to understand the concluding statement that God "for our sake made him to be sin who knew no sin, so that in him we might become the righteousness of God" (v. 21). Taken alone, this verse suggests a simple exchange of places. In the context of the preceding argument, however, the thought is integrated into that of the inclusive significance and effect of the death of Jesus Christ.

We find another nuance of the thought of representation in Rom. 8:3. If in 2 Cor. 5:21 God put the sinless Christ in the place of sinners, so that he had to bear the judgment of sin instead of them (cf. Gal. 3:13), Rom. 8:3

says of the preexistent Son of God that he was sent in the form of human sinfulness in order that judgment upon sin might be executed on the form of this earthly existence of his. Here the vicarious expiatory death of Jesus Christ is the purpose of his whole sending by God. Also, at least implicitly, the entering of the preexistent Son into the conditions of earthly existence that are governed by sin acquires the meaning that he took the place of sinners in order that he might suffer their fate. The incarnation thus becomes an act of representation. Not in his counsel alone does God let the innocent Jesus suffer death in the place of sinners, i.e., the judgment upon sin. Instead we read that (in his Son) God himself took the place of sinners and took to himself the judgment on their sin.

b. Expiation as Vicarious Penal Suffering

The variety of interpretations of the death of Jesus in primitive Christianity might give the impression that the differences have more to do with differing human presuppositions than with the special nature of the event itself. One might then conclude that these presuppositions have changed profoundly over two thousand years and no longer include cultic ideas of sacrifice, expiation, and substitution. It would then seem that today we must speak of the death of Jesus in very different terms.[77] Among the NT interpretations we might still retain, for example, the idea of Jesus Christ as the author and initiator of salvation (Heb. 2:10) or as the prince of life (Acts 3:15), since such thoughts are still intelligible to us today.[78]

This approach, however, assumes that we may adopt any understanding of the death of Jesus that we fancy. Does the distinctiveness of the event that we must interpret offer no starting points or criteria, then, by which to interpret it?[79] If the choice of forms of interpretation is limited

77. Friedrich, *Verkündigung,* pp. 143ff., esp. 145f.
78. Ibid., pp. 156ff., 176.
79. Friedrich did not totally deny this. He simply regarded the various interpretations as unable to comprehend the reality (ibid., p. 144). He rightly referred to the limitations of the ransom image and to the uniqueness of the death of Jesus in distinction from the ideas of mystery religions. He thus concluded that we must reconstruct ideas taken from the world of that day (pp. 144f.). He did not consider whether perhaps some of the interpretations, when adapted, might not bring out the meaning of the event better than others. The dominant role of ideas of expiation and representation in primitive Christian statements regarding the death of Jesus might be in fact the result of the uniqueness of the event serving as a selective principle in the history of its interpretation.

by the nature of the event itself, and their content is shaped by it, then we may not at will replace the results of the process of interpretation by other interpretations. We may replace them only to the extent that we adopt into a new interpretive model the elements of understanding that are expressed in the traditional terms, along with aspects of the event that have not thus far been considered.

As regards the elements of understanding that came to the fore in the ideas of expiation and representation (or substitution), it is hardly likely that they can be fully covered by others that we can supposedly understand more easily today, so that they will no longer be needed in such presentations. But if this is so, then at best new interpretive models can have only a supplementary function. This applies already to the biblical depiction of Jesus Christ as the author or initiator of (the new) life and eternal salvation. The fact that a later age may find it hard to understand traditional ideas is not a sufficient reason for replacing them. It simply shows how necessary it is to open up these ideas to later generations by interpretation and thus to keep their meaning alive. The problems that people have with ideas like expiation and representation (or substitution) in our secularized age rest less on any lack of forcefulness in the traditional terms than on the fact that those who are competent to interpret them do not explain their content with sufficient forcefulness or clarity.

We have pointed out already (see n. 76) that the thought of representation is not so alien to our modern social world as is maintained.[80] The same applies to the idea of vicarious expiation, as may be seen from the works of René Girard on the importance of the scapegoat motif in the history of human culture.[81] As Girard sees it, the significance of the motif changes with the passion of Jesus because Jesus, by suffering vicariously himself, overcame the power that is directed against others and is focused on the scapegoat. This is to interpret the passion in predominantly ethical terms.[82] But notwithstanding the necessary criticism, the works of Girard and the attention they have claimed show that the thought of vicarious expiation is still relevant.

80. Friedrich, *Verkündigung*, pp. 150f.

81. R. Girard, *Violence and the Sacred* (Baltimore, 1977); cf. also "Generative Scapegoating," in *Violent Origins: Ritual Killing and Cultural Formation*, ed. R. G. Hamerton-Kelly (Stanford, CA, 1987), pp. 43-145.

82. In criticism of Girard, cf. M. Herzog, "Religionstheorie und Theologie René Girards," *KuD* 38 (1992) 105-37. Cf. also Girard's *Des choses cachées depuis la fondation du monde* (Paris, 1978), pp. 165ff.

The above remarks imply that in interpreting the death of Jesus, we must make the nature of the event normative for the evaluation, selection, and use of the interpretive models available. This happened already in the process of building the tradition. The variety of NT interpretations of the death of Jesus simply indicates the peculiar difficulties of understanding that the theme posed from the very first. In this case, however, the force of the different interpretations must derive from the event that they were interpreting and must be measured by it. Only thus can we arrive at a well-founded assessment of the essential justifiability of this or that interpretation. The fact that they found a place in primitive Christianity does not guarantee their truth. Nor does their antiquity. The oldest interpretation (possibly that Jesus suffered the fate of a prophet) may not be the most profound or the most true to the facts.

Even the OT derivation of certain ideas (cf. 1 Cor. 15:3) does not guarantee the validity of applying them to the death of Jesus Christ. An OT idea or saying must "fit" this event if it is to bring out its divine significance along the lines of the primitive Christian proof from scripture. No doubt Isa. 53:4f. had a great influence on primitive Christian ideas of the vicarious expiatory meaning of the death of Jesus "for many," but in each case we still must seek the material basis for this kind of understanding in the distinctive constellation of the event itself. Showing a material correspondence does not on its own answer the question whether sayings regarding the expiatory and vicarious significance of the death of Jesus are true. In particular we can expound and support the thesis that the death of Jesus has expiatory significance for all humanity only if we take into account the basic anthropological situation of humanity in relation to sin and death.

Primitive Christian statements regarding the expiatory function of Christ's death presuppose first that we cannot see in the crucifixion of Jesus a punishment for his own faults. This presupposition was fully possible only in the light of the resurrection (see above, pp. 343ff., 363ff.). By raising Jesus from the dead, God himself vindicated Jesus from the charges that led to his execution. He was not a political agitator, nor had he arrogated divine authority to himself as a human being. He did not die, then, for his own sin. By the Easter event — but only in the light of it — he was proved to be sinless.[83] Why, then, did God deliver him up to

---

83. On the sinlessness of Jesus, cf. *Jesus — God and Man*, pp. 354ff. Cf. also the observation of M. Hengel, *The Atonement: A Study of the Origins of the Doctrine in the NT* (London, 1981), pp. 65f.

death? Why indeed — in the light of prophetic indications that primitive Christianity took from the OT — did a divine "must" lie over his path to death? If he did not die for his own sins, Jesus can only have died for others. In the first instance that is perhaps the only alternative open if we are to understand the death of a man whose fate must be seen, not as accidental, but as divinely ordained in the light of the divine confirmation of his sending by his resurrection from the dead. On Jewish presuppositions at any rate, the thought of an expiatory death had to be a relatively natural one.[84] As an expression of the mercy and saving love of God, an expiatory death was also in keeping with the message of Jesus concerning the love of God that his own coming proclaimed (see above, pp. 331f.).

This parallelism does not justify us in viewing the death of Jesus "for us" as simply a special instance of the solidarity with others that characterizes his earthly coming as a whole.[85] To say this is to level down the specific significance of his death "for us." Only from the standpoint of the special meaning could the whole life of Jesus be seen as a way to this death (Phil. 2:6-8; cf. 2 Cor. 8:9). We give an incomplete and even misleading picture of the conduct of Jesus in his pre-Easter ministry if we simply call him "the man for others" or the epitome of co-humanity.[86] In his whole appearance Jesus was first and foremost the man for God; he was the man for others only insofar as he was sent to attest God's coming rule to them and to demonstrate with the dawning of this rule in his own work the love of God for his creatures, even for the creature that was lost. Since his obedience to his divine mission, even to the death on the cross, meant the giving of his life for the world, the whole of his earthly course could later be construed in this sense. This was possible, however, only by interpreting his death as an expiation for the sins of the world.

Even if Jesus did not die for any fault of his own, it is not self-evident that the expiatory function of his death should embrace all humanity. Jewish ideas of the suffering and death of the righteous, and especially of martyrs for the faith, suggest instead that we should think in terms of the

---

84. E. Lohse, *Märtyrer und Gottesknecht. Untersuchungen zur urchristlichen Verkündigung vom Sühnetod Jesu Christi* (Göttingen, 1955; 2nd ed. 1963), esp. pp. 29ff., 66f., 78ff.

85. Cf. Kasper, *Jesus the Christ.* Cf. the critical remarks of Lehmann, "Er wurde für uns gekreuzigt," pp. 306ff.

86. Kasper, *Jesus the Christ,* with an appeal to D. Bonhoeffer, *Letters and Papers from Prison* (third ed.; New York, 1967), pp. 209f. The misleading element in such terms is that they easily merge into a secularized humanism that has little in common with the work of Jesus in either motivation or structure.

suffering and death of Jesus being an expiation for the Jewish people.[87] We actually find traces of such a view in John's Gospel (11:50f.). In the primitive Christian tradition as a whole, however, it is far less prominent than a universal understanding of the phrase "for many" as it is used especially in the tradition concerning the Last Supper (Mark 14:24 par.; cf. also 10:45). The term is in any case an inclusive one, though it is still ambivalent, for, as in Isa. 53:12, it may indicate that the expiatory efficacy is either for all the Jewish people or for all humanity. The latter is undoubtedly the case in 2 Cor. 5:14f. (cf. Rom. 5:14). Almost certainly we must regard the universal scope of the efficacy of the death of Jesus as an expansion of a primary relation to the Jewish people, and not vice versa.

Nor can we immediately find in the thought of expiation for the Jewish people a parallel to Jewish ideas of the expiatory function of the sufferings of the righteous and the Maccabean martyrs. For Jesus died as one who was rejected by his people. In the Jewish tradition support could be found for the understanding of his death as expiation for his people only in Isa. 53:3ff.[88] The circumstances of the death of Jesus provided a reason to go back to this prophetic passage inasmuch as Jesus was in fact despised and rejected by his people (Isa. 53:3) but justified by God with his resurrection. If the Jewish authorities had found in his supposed arrogant claim to equality with God a pretext for handing him over to the Romans for execution, his resurrection showed that with his condemnation and execution his judges had laid violent hands on him who was sent by God and therefore on God himself. They stood under the threat of the imminent judgment of the Son of Man that Jesus himself had invoked against them (Luke 22:69 par.). They themselves had wrongly arrogated to themselves divine authority against God in the person of him whom he had sent. Thus the sentence of death that they had passed on Jesus ought in truth to have been passed on them. The Easter reversal of the significance of the events that had led to the crucifixion of Jesus shows that Jesus literally died in the place of those who condemned him.[89]

If his death was then understood as expiation, this interpretation could easily tie in with the actual substitution of the death of Jesus in the place of his judges and the whole people that they represented. Here might well have been the background of the statements of Paul in Gal.

---

87. Cf. Lohse, *Märtyrer und Gottesknecht,* pp. 94ff., esp. 101.
88. Ibid., p. 114, on 1 Cor. 15:3.
89. See above, p. 374, and *Jesus — God and Man,* pp. 259ff.

3:13; 2 Cor. 5:21; Rom. 8:3. For these statements make little sense apart from a reference to the situation of the condemnation and execution of Jesus, in which he was made the sinner and actually came under the curse of the law. As Paul saw it, God himself by means of the human judges not only made Jesus to be sin but also had him bear in our place (and not merely in that of his Jewish judges or the whole Jewish people) the penalty that is the proper penalty of sin because it follows from its inner nature, i.e., the penalty of death as the consequence of separation from God.

It is in keeping with the eschatological proclamation of Jesus, and not least of all with his reference to the coming judgment of the Son of Man (Luke 22:69 par.), that the expiatory efficacy ascribed to his death relates to that coming judgment of God or the Son of Man. According to Jewish belief, the expiatory death of the righteous could work in favor of the future life of the people and the continuation of the covenant, and in special cases in favor of the participation of individuals in the future life of the resurrection.[90] Yet the fact of the death of Jesus relates so closely to the eschatological message of Jesus, and strife concerning it, that even the sin-canceling power that is ascribed to his death in the light of the Easter event[91] can relate only to the eschatological judgment of God on the living and the dead. For the same reason we must see that the expiatory efficacy of his death is linked to the (at least subsequent) conversion of the people to the God of his eschatological message, and therefore to confession of Jesus himself along the lines of Luke 12:8 par. Expiation for the people of God in the death of Jesus means, then, that in spite of participation in the crucifixion and other sins, access to eschatological salvation is still open on the condition of acceptance of the eschatological message of Jesus and confession of Jesus.

Roman participation in the events leading to the execution of Jesus perhaps was the occasion for extending the understanding of the death of Jesus as expiation to the Gentile world represented by Rome.[92] The one who was handed over as a blasphemer and executed as an agitator suffered death in the place of, and on behalf of, all those who as sinners live in arrogated equality with God and actual rebellion against him and who

---

90. Lohse, *Märtyrer und Gottesknecht*, p. 107, cf. 89f.
91. Ibid., p. 119, with stress on the fact that 1 Cor. 15:17 relates the sin-canceling force of the death of Jesus to his resurrection.
92. *Jesus — God and Man*, pp. 267f.

thus bring death upon themselves.[93] As the Son of God suffered vicariously in his flesh the condemnation of sinners (Rom. 8:3), he did it for all (2 Cor. 5:14) and triumphed for all. In the condemnation and execution of Jesus, God "made him to be sin [for us] who knew no sin, so that in him we might become the righteousness of God" (2 Cor. 5:21). In this situation of condemnation and execution, Jesus (whom, through the resurrection, God showed to be innocent) bore death as the consequence of our sin, thereby effecting representation in the concrete form of a change of place between the innocent and the guilty. The innocent suffered the penalty of death, which, as the harmful result of sin, is the fate of those in whose place he died. This vicarious penal suffering, which is rightly described as the vicarious suffering of the wrath of God at sin, rests on the fellowship that Jesus Christ accepted with all of us as sinners and with our fate as such. This link is the basis on which the death of Jesus can count as expiation for us.[94]

Representation and expiation do not mean that those who are represented do not have to die themselves. It means, rather, that those whom Jesus represents have the possibility in their death, by reason of its linking to the death of Jesus, of attaining to the hope of participating in the new resurrection life that has already become manifest in Jesus (Rom. 6:5). At issue, then, are representation and expiation before the eschatological judgment of God. Recipients of the expiatory working of the death of Jesus may have confidence that their own death will not mean definitive exclusion from God and his life. This confidence expresses itself already in this life in works of righteousness (Rom. 6:13). With the hope of the new resurrection life, the covenant righteousness of God takes effect in sinners (2 Cor. 5:21), for God wills the life of his creatures.

To this extent there is thus in fact an exchange of places between the innocent Jesus, who was executed as a sinner, and the manifestation

93. Lehmann, "Er wurde für uns gekreuzigt," pp. 313f., has rightly pointed out that the modern misunderstanding of the thought of expiation is due to a dwindling sense of its presupposition in the ruining of one's life by guilt (p. 313). On this theme, see pp. 265-75 above on the link between sin and death.

94. It makes no sense that Lehmann upholds the expiatory nature of the death of Jesus ("Er wurde für uns gekreuzigt," pp. 311ff.) and stresses the indispensability of a change of place and destinies (p. 314) but mentions only incidentally the interpretation of the death of Jesus as vicarious penal suffering, finding in it a narrowing down of the complex biblical data (p. 299). Without this vicarious penal suffering, the expiatory function of the death of Jesus is unintelligible, unless we try to understand his death as an equivalent offered to God along the lines of Anselm's satisfaction theory, which has no basis in the biblical data.

of the righteousness of God in those whom he represents before him. This exchange takes place only if, for their part, the sinners for whom Jesus died let their lives, which have fallen victim to death, be linked to the death of Jesus (Phil. 3:10f.). This takes place in baptism (Rom. 6:3f.; Col. 2:12). Only then does the expiation that the death of Jesus makes possible actually come into force for individuals. Paul pregnantly expressed this in Rom. 3:25 by using the term *hilastērion,* even if the word also describes the death of Christ as the place of expiation that God had prepared. The death of Jesus has expiatory efficacy for individual sinners as they for their part link their own deaths to the death of Christ, which became the transition to the new life of the resurrection of the dead.

But here again the question arises as to the relation between vicarious expiation and reconciliation. Note has rightly been taken of the difference between the two concepts. The respective linguistic backgrounds and implications are very different. The idea of reconciliation has no cultic reference but is related to diplomatic processes in concluding peace between enemies.[95] Thus Paul in 2 Cor. 5:20 has the role of an envoy commissioned by God to make peace. Reconciliation is thus effected, but the other side has to agree. There is a remarkable parallel here to the specific problems of the expiatory effect of the death of Jesus, which we have just discussed.

The starting point of the apostle's message of reconciliation lies in the atoning death of Christ.[96] The judgment on sin in the death of the Son is the basis of the possibility of reconciliation.[97] We have seen, however, that the expiatory effect of Christ's death is not just an objectively closed event. It becomes fruitful for individuals only as their own deaths are linked to that of Christ. There is a clear parallel here to the reciprocity in the event of reconciliation. We may thus maintain that the thought of reconciliation explains and clarifies the need for receiving and appropriating the expiation grounded in the death of Jesus. As the offer of reconciliation made by the one side must be accepted by the other if there is to be reconciliation, so the expiation grounded in Christ's vicarious death needs appropriation by confession, baptism, and faith on the part of each individual. Otherwise, neither vicarious expiation nor reconciliation can

95. Cf. the examples in Breytenbach, *Versöhnung,* pp. 45-83.
96. Ibid., pp. 154ff.
97. Ibid., pp. 165, 215; cf. 220ff. Breytenbach emphasizes that we should not relate the idea of the expiatory offering to this (cf. also pp. 204ff.).

be depicted as an event that was concluded in the death of Christ (Rom. 5:10). In both cases we must see an inclusive statement. But the inclusive sense of representation has an anticipatory function. There must be repetition in the process of propagating the gospel by apostolic proclamation and appropriation through faith, confession, and baptism.

c. Representation and Liberation

If we do something that others ought to have done, or suffer something that they ought to have suffered, we have an exclusive sense of representation or substitution. We alone do what must be done, and those whom we represent or replace no longer need to do it. Anselm applied this thought to his interpretation of the reconciling death of Christ. Human beings owe satisfaction to God but cannot pay it because they owe all they have to God. Satisfaction is paid to God, however, by the voluntary death of the God-man.[98] Socinian criticism of this theory argued that no one can represent others as moral subjects. A debt can be repaid either by the debtor or by someone making payment on the debtor's behalf, but there is no restitution for a moral fault unless the one who committed the offense makes it.[99]

Exclusive representation of that type does not correspond to the NT witness. The reconciling death of Christ is not a payment that Christ made to God in place of others. It does not mean that others need not die. Christ's death represents before God the death of all. "One has died for all; therefore all have died" (2 Cor. 5:14). P. K. Marheineke made this thought the basis of his new understanding of the concept of representation. As he saw it, Christ is not the representative of humanity insofar as he is outside it but insofar as he *is* it, representing in himself what is the same in all individuals.[100] The thought here of inclusive representation

98. *Cur Deus Homo* 2.6; cf. 1.24f.
99. This is how D. F. Strauss states the central argument of F. Socinus in Strauss's *Die christliche Glaubenslehre in ihrer geschichtlichen Entwicklung und im Kampfe mit der modernen Wissenschaft*, II (1841), p. 294.
100. P. K. Marheineke, *Die Grundlehren der christlichen Dogmatik als Wissenschaft* (1827), p. 398; cf. Wenz, *Geschichte*, I, 317f. The basic thought of inclusive representation may be found already in Hegel, when he said that an alien sacrifice is not brought and another punished in order that there may be punishment, life negated, otherness removed. Each dies for himself and must be and do what is demanded out of individual subjectivity and guilt. Each grasps the merits of Christ. Doing this, converting, abandoning natural will

makes Jesus the representative of all humanity. This is in keeping with Paul's description of Christ as the second Adam. There takes place in him paradigmatically that which is to be repeated in all the members of the humanity that he represents. At any rate, in Paul Christ's death includes ours in such a way as to change its character. By the linking of our death to Christ's in the act of baptism, our death takes on a new sense that it does not have of itself. It becomes death in hope. We do not see in Jesus only what may be said at once of all of us. What was done in his death does not apply automatically to all others. It needs an express establishing of fellowship with him. To this extent the death of Jesus, to which the change in the meaning of our death may be traced, still has an exclusive aspect that is true of it alone. The death of him whom God raised and justified is the reconciliation of the world.

As distinct from the exclusive representation of vicarious satisfaction, the thought of inclusive representation is not limited to any one interpretation of the death of Jesus. It can cover the whole course of Christ's life in the same way as does Paul's concept of Christ as the second Adam, whose image we all bear. As the image of God and the Son of God — by whom, Paul says, we are to receive sonship (Gal. 4:5; Rom. 8:15; cf. Eph. 1:5) — Jesus Christ is the paradigm of all humanity in its relation to God.[101] Yet as in the case of the new Adam, he is our representative, not as we now are, but as we are to be. In contrast the incarnation of the Son relates to the conditions of our existence as descendants of Adam (Rom. 8:3). It aims at the overcoming of sin in the flesh of him who bore the judgment on sin in our place. This statement, too, has an inclusive sense if we read it in the light of 2 Cor. 5:14, though it again has also an exclusive sense. The old Adam dies in the death of Christ in order, through that death, to be changed into the new Adam (1 Cor. 15:49, cf. vv. 42ff.).

---

and interests, being in infinite love is a matter for the individual (*Lectures on the Philosophy of Religion*, III [London, 1896], p. 95). We may then trace back the thought to G. F. Seiler, *Über den Versöhnungstod Jesu Christi*, 2 vols. (1778-79), who seems to have introduced the German term *Stellvertretung*; cf. K.-H. Menke, *Stellvertretung. Schlüsselbegriff christlichen Lebens und theologische Grundkategorie* (Freiburg, 1992), p. 88. Ritschl, *Christian Doctrine*, pp. 546f. hit on the distinction between inclusive representation and the exclusive representation of the satisfaction theory.

101. Here again we of course must note that in Jesus Christ the preexistent Son of God became flesh, whereas it is only through him that believers receive adoption as children of the Father.

This thought of an inclusive representation relating to the incarnation of the Son in Jesus Christ has shaped the whole history of Christian soteriology. It found classical expression in the early church interpretation of Christ as the new man from heaven (see above, pp. 304ff.). It was also the presupposition of Anselm's satisfaction theory, for only the incarnation of the Son establishes the relation to humanity that is the premise of the transferring of his merits to others (cf. *Cur Deus Homo* 2.19). In Anselm, however, this basic aspect plays only a subordinate part because he sought the basis of redemption in an achievement of the God-man for the Father. In Paul, however, Christ was linked to others precisely by the vicarious suffering of death as the punishment for sin.

The thought of inclusive representation might also lead, however, to a violating of the independence as persons of those that are represented. The exclusive theory of satisfaction teaching did this by assuming that we may be replaced as moral persons. Inclusive representation can similarly result in the notion that Jesus Christ alone is man before God, that he has so taken our place and acted and suffered in our favor that we can add to what he has done nothing of our own. This means the replacement and suppression of those in whose place the Son of God came.

The problems of this tendency in the thought of inclusive representation do not seem to have troubled Karl Barth. How else could he have written that in Jesus Christ, God removed not merely sins but "their very root, the man who commits them" (*CD*, IV/1, 77)? Can Christian theology really say that in the event of his death Jesus Christ "in his own person" "has made an end of us as sinners and therefore of sin itself" (p. 253)? Paul certainly says that sin dies only with the death of the sinners and that this has happened already for believers because of the linking of their death to the fate of Christ (Rom. 7:4). But by ascribing to the event of Christ's death what Paul describes as the work of baptism, Barth has raised the question whether the final result is not the total disappearance of our independent humanity.[102] Barth's concentration of the concept of reconciliation on the death of Jesus Christ as a closed event of the past (see n. 52) has fateful consequences. Because he does not think of the event as open to a process of

102. Wenz, *Geschichte*, II, 247. The core of this criticism of Barth's doctrine of reconciliation was first formulated in 1965 by D. Sölle; see the ET *Christ the Representative: An Essay in Theology after the "Death of God"* (Philadelphia, 1967), pp. 88ff. Sölle called Barth's view "objectivist." She criticized the definitiveness of Jesus Christ as "inevitably totalitarian" (p. 109), demonstrated in the history of Christian anti-Semitism. Along similar lines G. Wagner described Barth's christology as "theological liquidation" ("Theologische Gleichschaltung. Zur Christologie bei Karl Barth," in *Die Realisierung der Freiheit*, ed. T. Rendtorff [1975], pp. 10-43).

reception, the result is that he can view the judgment on sin in the death of Christ as comprehensive and definitive only if in this event God "has delivered up us sinners and sin itself to destruction . . . removed us sinners and sin, negated us, canceled us out" (p. 253).

Against a totalitarian understanding of representation as the replacement of those who are represented, it has been validly argued that a true representative only temporarily takes the place of others and thus leaves open the place that is only representatively occupied.[103] With permanent occupation the representative becomes a replacement.[104] But this argument moves on the level of exclusive representation. It hardly touches the concrete content of the primitive Christian thought of representation, i.e., the expiatory function of the death of Jesus. The idea of temporary representation presupposes the ongoing existence of those who are represented. According to Paul's understanding of the atoning power of the death of Jesus, however, those who are represented can share in its atoning efficacy only through their own death. Above all, there must be a link with the death of Jesus by confession and baptism.[105] To the extent that this reception is already anticipated in intention in the saving event of the death of Jesus, this death has the character of inclusive representation. At the same time, however, it exceeds the limit of purely temporary representation.

The limitation of the idea of temporary representation may be seen in Sölle, especially in its application to the relationship of Jesus with God. On her view, Jesus did not merely take *our* place in his passion or his incarnation. He also represented the absent *God* to us with his message and in his work.[106] But the testimony of the

103. Sölle, *Christ the Representative,* pp. 48ff. A good example of representation is the pedagogical relation between teacher and student. "The teacher is responsible for those who are still immature or incapable. He safeguards the opportunities and interests of those he represents" (p. 116). When students mature, however, teachers become redundant.

104. Ibid., pp. 48f. That Christ becomes a replacement in Barth, leaving us no existence of our own, is shown, according to Sölle, by the fact that our representation by Christ leaves us nothing to do with or after him (pp. 89f.). She touches here on the most critical point in Barth's doctrine of reconciliation.

105. This is what we have to do with and after Christ — the things that Sölle misses in Barth.

106. Sölle, *Christ the Representative,* p. 146. This aspect of her thinking explains the subtitle. The element of modern secularism called the death of God is viewed, of course, as purely temporary, according to Sölle's concept of representation, as it proved to be in the United States in the case of T. Altizer.

Gospels does not depict Jesus as the representative of God. In his message and work the coming kingdom of the Father is already present, a power that determines the present. Jesus is not the representative of the Father but the mediator of his presence. Decisive in this regard is his self-distinction from the Father, by which he shows himself to be the Son — even on his way to death.

As the Son of the heavenly Father, Jesus is also the original of the sonship that all should receive through him in order that they might have no less immediate access to God as the Father (Rom. 8:15). Precisely as the Son, then, Jesus is also the new Adam, in whom our destiny of divine likeness is achieved. Yet as the new Adam, by whose filial obedience God is manifested as the Father, Jesus did not represent others only temporarily. According to the claim of the Christian message, he is the definitive actualizing of our destiny as the incarnation of the Son. His definitiveness leaves room, however, for the individuality of others. They are not suppressed or eliminated. This is because the claim to definitiveness is not directly linked to the individuality of Jesus. That would be so if he had arrogated divine dignity and authority to himself.

We showed above (pp. 334ff.) that this was the great misunder-standing of his appearance and person on the part of his adversaries, the reason why they rejected him as a blasphemer and deceiver. In his appear-ance the claim that God's rule had dawned with his own work made it seem that he was making himself equal to God, in spite of his self-distinction from the Father. The result of this ambivalence was the rejec-tion, condemnation, and execution of Jesus, which set before him and forced upon him his own finitude, which his opponents thought he was trying to escape. (Death is the seal of finitude.) But as Jesus accepted his death as the bitter consequence of his mission, his death became the seal of his self-distinction and therefore also the proof of his unity with God as the Son of the heavenly Father.

Only in the transition through the death of his individual existence as man is Jesus the Son. His human individuality has definitiveness, not as its particularity endures, but only as he offers it up for the sake of God and in the service of the coming of the kingdom. This is why Paul could write to the Corinthians that he no longer knew or judged any one, not even Jesus, according to the flesh, i.e., according to what he was and is for himself (2 Cor. 5:16). By accepting the death of his particular existence, Jesus made room for that of others. At the same time, however, we see by his conduct that others in their individual particularity can share in the filial relation to God and the inheritance of his kingdom only through the death of Jesus and through acceptance of their own death for the sake of God and his kingdom.

In this way, then, we can perhaps understand why we are reconciled to God precisely through the death of the Son, namely, through the death of the man who in his suffering obedience showed himself definitively to be the Son of God. Our enmity against God that was overcome thereby (cf. Rom. 5:10) grew out of the fact that as sinners, as those who wanted to be like God, we find no room alongside God but have fallen victim to death. Through the death of the Son, however, God gives us room alongside himself even after death. Because the Son dies in the particularity of his human existence, all others in their otherness are not crowded out by him as though his human particularity were the measure of all things and excluded all others.

This is how the adversaries of Jesus saw it when they accused him of the presumption of making himself equal to God. No one can tolerate this in others. We all want to be as God, and so sensing it in others, we condemn one another and involve one another in the consequences, for death is the consequence of sin. But as Jesus accepted the death that others inflicted on him as the consequence of his sending to bear witness to the rule of God, he thus sealed the self-distinction from God that he proclaimed. He did not die for his own sin but as an expiation for the sins of others, an expiation that is effective because the separation between God and his life is overcome once others let their own death be linked with his death, in this way gaining assurance of participation in the life of God after death. The death of Jesus, then, means that others no longer have to see themselves as excluded from fellowship with God and therefore as enemies of God. He opens up access for them so that in accepting their own finitude like him, and in fellowship with him, they come to share in life from God and can already live this earthly life assured of the eternal fellowship with God that overcomes the limitation of death.

Hegel's speculative doctrine of reconciliation also viewed the transcending of natural finitude, of direct existence, as the core of the event.[107] By the surrender of finitude the antithesis to the absolute is overcome (see n. 100). But for Hegel, Christ's death was also the death of God himself (PhB, 63, 157f.). He said that we

---

107. Hegel, *Lectures on the Philosophy of Religion*, pp. 93f. On the systematic context, cf. Wenz, *Geschichte*, I, 310ff.

must understand the idea of sacrificial death in the sense of the mutual surrender of God and ourselves, of the absolute and the particular. Only thus can we see in Christ's death that which reconciles — absolute love.[108] But this thought of God's death in that of Christ is alien to the NT, though Paul repeatedly spoke of the death of God's Son (Rom. 5:10, cf. 8:32). Church teaching has rightly referred sayings of this kind to Christ's human nature. The Son of God died on the cross after his human nature.[109] This death was the death of Jesus, who in the light of his resurrection by God is the Son of the eternal Father.

Hegel neglected the careful distinctions of orthodox christology between the divine and human natures in the unity of Christ's person when, without such differentiation, he spoke of Christ's death as that of God himself. At the same time the one event was for him, as a transcending of the self-alienation of God in the incarnation, the return of the divine Idea to itself, the reconciliation of Spirit with itself.[110] Hegel expressly did not want to have Christ's death regarded as the penal suffering of the innocent on behalf of sinners.[111] He thus dogmatically asserted an inclusive view of the event based on the thought of the incarnation and ignored the exclusive element contained in the thought of representative expiation. For this reason he does full justice in his interpretation neither to the historical particularity of the death of Jesus nor to the liberating effect of his death for others as individuals.[112]

In the expiatory character of the death of Jesus the exclusive element of his vicarious death, the death of one who is innocent for sinners, comes to expression. But obedience to God, for the sake of which Jesus accepted death, is paradigmatic for all of us. In it Jesus is the Son, the new Adam, after whose image we are to be renewed. Part of this is the acceptance of our finitude before God, which is actualized in baptism by the

108. Wenz, *Geschichte*, I, 315.

109. This is true for the Lutheran churches; cf. the Formula of Concord (1580), SD 8.20: "Wherefore the Son of God has truly suffered for us, but according to the attribute of human nature" (Schaff, *The Creeds of Christendom* [6th ed. New York, 1931], III, 151).

110. Hegel, *Lectures on the Philosophy of Religion*, p. 159; also *Sämtliche Werke*, ed. H. Glockner, 16:304, and *Encyclopädie*, ed. J. Hoffmeister (PhB, 33), § 566. According to Hegel, the possibility of reconciliation rests on the intrinsic unity of the divine and human natures that achieves awareness in the thought of reconciliation (*Lectures on the Philosophy of Religion*, pp. 93f.). See also the *Lectures on the Philosophy of World History*.

111. *Lectures on the Philosophy of Religion*, p. 95. For Hegel, Christ's death makes satisfaction for us inasmuch as it represents the absolute history of the divine Idea, what has taken place in itself and takes place eternally.

112. In his *Lectures on the Philosophy of World History*, p. 306, Hegel certainly refers to the liberation of the individual as the result of the union of God with us in an individual. But the individual here is simply a general form that is realized in all, not the particularity that distinguishes each person from others.

linking of our own future death to the death of Jesus. Nevertheless, the inclusive vicarious element in the obedience of Jesus as the Son, which led him to the cross, does not mean that the particularity of the individual existence of others alongside Jesus, the normative man, is of no significance or is suppressed. For Jesus is the Son only through the death of his particularity. Hence the independent significance of other individual lives alongside his life is not set aside by the fact that he took the place of all others. Indeed, it is by the exclusive sense of his vicarious death that the independence of others alongside him is made possible. Now, linked to the death of Jesus, we may all live our own lives and follow our own vocations in the certainty of sharing in the life that has overcome death in the resurrection of Jesus.

The independence that the vicarious death of Jesus assures for those who are linked to him is characterized by Christian freedom from the tyranny that sin and death exercise over human life. Believers are free from this dominion in hope of the new life from God that was manifested in the resurrection of Jesus. They are also free from the dominion of the law that holds sin and death in check, for sin will reach its end with death, and it has already done so proleptically for believers, whose future death is linked to the death of Christ.[113] Fellowship with God and his eternal life gives individuals independence of the world and its powers in all the relation of dependence in which they live their finite lives.[114]

It also sets them at a distance from themselves, which enables them to fulfill their individual callings in service to God and to the world, to which his love is addressed. This is the freedom of a new immediacy to God that believers have as his children (Gal. 4:4-6). It is mediated by the sending of the Son and his vicarious death. It is actualized, however, by the Spirit of sonship in believers themselves. The Spirit thus brings the

113. The Christian thought of reconciliation and redemption is thus closely connected to the theme of liberation. This is not primarily liberation in the political sense but, much more radically, liberation from the servitude to sin and death in which all of us live. This liberation, however, is not simply a private, individual matter but has implications also for political government (see n. 114). On this topic, cf. H. Kessler, *Erlösung als Befreiung* (1972), also T. Pröpper, *Erlösungsglaube und Freiheitsgeschichte. Eine Skizze zur Soteriologie* (2nd ed. 1988), pp. 38ff., also M. Seckler, "Theosoterik und Autosoterik," *TQ* 162 (1982) 289-98.

114. Cf. the remark in Hegel's *Lectures in the Philosophy of World History* (p. 308) regarding the infinite inner freedom with which the church of the martyrs confronted the Roman state. This is in keeping with the discussion of the revolutionary political relevance of the cross of Christ in the *Lectures on the Philosophy of Religion*.

mission of the Son to completion. We thus read in John that there is true freedom only through the Son (8:36) but that it is good for Christ's own that he should go away and that the Spirit should come (16:7f.). For the Spirit will lead them into the truth (16:13), which makes them free (8:32). In this regard John agrees with Paul when the latter says that "where the Spirit of the Lord is, there is freedom" (2 Cor. 3:17). Where there is this freedom of the Spirit, our reconciliation to God has reached its goal.

§ 4. The Triune God as Reconciler of the World

In the first section of this chapter I tried to clarify the systematic function of the Pauline concept of reconciliation. We saw that what is at issue is the way to the salvation of the world through overcoming the opposition to God into which sin and death have plunged us. My aim in the second section was then to show that the world must be reconciled to God, not God to the world, and that God's act in reconciling the world certainly took place in Christ's passion. The concept covers not merely the past history of Jesus, however, but also the present apostolic ministry of reconciliation. In the third section I then reached a similar conclusion, namely, that we cannot restrict the significance of the death of Christ as vicarious expiation to the crucifixion of Jesus as a past event but that there is also a dimension of implicit representation that is actualized only with the bringing in of those "for whom" Christ died. Since we have here processes of interpreting, receiving, and understanding the death of Christ on the part of those who are drawn into the event as the recipients of reconciliation with God, the question arises how this history of reception relates to God's own reconciling action in the death of Christ. Is the divine action in Christ's death no more than the object of human interpretation and reception? Or is God himself at work in the proclaiming of Christ's death as the reconciliation of the world to him? If he is, is there still room for the free entry into his reconciliation of those who are to be reconciled?

A trinitarian description of the divine action in the event of reconciliation might be the answer to this whole question. To be sure, 2 Cor. 5:18 causes us in the first instance to think specifically of an action of the Father in the death of Christ. But it may quickly be seen that the Son and Spirit also participated. Can a description of the event in these terms help us to understand our human participation in the making of reconciliation, and also to clarify further the relation between exclusive and inclusive representation in Christ's reconciling death?

a. The Action of the Father and the Son in the Event of Reconciliation

We are to understand from both 2 Cor. 5:18f. and the more passive formulation in Rom. 5:10 that in the death of Jesus, God the Father acted to reconcile the world. In the crucifixion of Jesus the law of action did not rest finally with the human executioners. Through all the baseness, cowardice, and brutality, God the Father was at work in this event according to his providential directing of the course of history. He "gave up" his Son (Rom. 8:32; cf. 4:25).[115] In material agreement is the saying in Rom. 8:3 that he sent the Son in our sinful form of existence[116] in order that he might condemn sin in the Son's flesh. The point here is that the whole earthly path of the Son was from the outset a path to the crucifixion of Jesus according to the providence of God. John 3:16 is to the same effect, though it simply says that God "gave" his only Son out of love for the world so that those who believe in him should have eternal life.[117]

The whole sending of the Son by the Father aims, then, at the vicarious expiatory death on the cross. We may say this on the basis of modern historical and exegetical research into the tradition relating to Jesus insofar as the death of Jesus follows from his proclamation of the imminence of the rule of God and its dawning in his own work. Greater difficulties arise, however, when we speak of the Son instead of the Father as the subject of this loving giving up to death (Gal. 2:20). Ephesians enlarges this thesis into one of self-sacrifice. "Christ loved us and gave himself up for us, a fragrant offering and sacrifice to God" (5:2, cf. v. 25). These statements correspond to the Gospel accounts of the passion as foreknown to Jesus (cf. the predictions in Mark 8:31; 9:31; 10:33 par.) and even planned by him. Yet they are in tension with the historical judgment

---

115. Cf. W. Kramer, *Christ, Lord, Son of God,* SBT, 1/50 (London/Naperville, 1966), pp. 115-19 ("The 'Giving Up' of the Son").

116. Cf. the rendering of *sarx hamartias* in U. Wilckens, *Das NT übersetzt und kommentiert* (1970), p. 525, "In unser von der Sünde bestimmtes Dasein."

117. Bultmann, *Gospel of John,* p. 153 n. 3, has emphasized that *edoken* carries the suggestion of "gave up to death" here, but we can take it more broadly as a reference to the sending of the Son to the cosmos (cf. Kramer, *Christ, Lord, Son of God,* pp. 30, 116f.), as in 1 John 4:9 and Gal. 4:4, though with the special nuance that he "gifted" his Son to the world.

that although Jesus certainly reckoned with the possibility of a violent death and ultimately faced its inevitability, he can hardly have sought it as the goal of his message and ministry (see above, pp. 416f.).

The question also arises, however, as to the relation between the self-giving of the Son to death and the giving up by the Father. Who is the subject of the giving up? If we are not to see any contradiction between the two types of statement, we must suppose that they are saying the same thing in different ways. But this is possible only if the action of the Father in giving up the Son does not make the Son a mere object but implies his active cooperation, and again if the action of the Son does not rule out the fact that the initiative in the event lies with the Father. Paul was already expressly maintaining this cooperation of the Son with the Father on the way to the cross when he described the conduct of Jesus Christ in his relation to the Father in terms of obedience (Rom. 5:19). The obedience of the Son corresponds to the giving up by the Father.[118] Whereas Heb. 5:8 says that the Son learned obedience in the school of suffering, which reminds us of the Gospel accounts of the prayer of Jesus in Gethsemane (Mark 14:32ff.), Paul stresses the existing unity of the will of the Son with that of the Father on the way to the cross.[119] The more pressing, then, is the question of the relation of this view to the human historicity of the person of Jesus.

Even if we assume that Jesus increasingly reckoned with the probability of a violent death, and that his last meal with the disciples stood under the sign of this expectation, it is a big leap from this idea to that of a self-offering that the Son had prepared and planned for a long period beforehand. To understand the relevant NT statements we do well to remember how it came about that the title "Son of God" came to be linked to the person of Jesus. This happened in the context of proclamation of his resurrection from the dead, which was viewed as institution to divine

---

118. In Rom. 5:19, as in Phil. 2:8 and Heb. 5:8f., the Son's obedience relates to the crucifixion. Cf. Wilckens, *Römer,* I, 326f. Nevertheless, it characterizes the whole path of the second Adam, and we therefore should not follow the theological tradition in construing it only as passive obedience and not also as an active doing of the will of God.

119. Unlike the hymnal tradition represented by Phil. 2:8 and Heb. 5:8f., Paul sees the cross totally as the action of God in Christ (2 Cor. 5:19; cf. Rom. 3:25), so that Christ and God are one at the cross. We see there the love of God (Rom. 5:8) and at the same time the love of Christ (Gal. 2:20; 2 Cor. 5:14). God gives him up (Rom. 4:25; 8:32), and Christ gives himself up (Gal. 2:20; cf. 1:4). Yet we have here one and the same event, in which God and Christ cooperate so fully that the work can be called both that of God and that of Christ (Wilckens, *Römer,* I, 326f.).

sonship (Rom. 1:3f.).[120] As a result the pre-Easter history of Jesus was now seen in a new light. For those who looked back from the resurrection of Jesus to his earthly proclamation and ministry, this whole history had to present itself as the earthly path of him who in hidden fashion was already the eternal Son of God.

The Gospel tradition shows how features and traces of his deity came to be detected in his history through the human coming, speaking, and acting. The events of this history were now regarded from the standpoint of the sending of the Preexistent into the world, and from this angle the divine ineluctability of his way to the cross could also seem to be an action of the preexistent Son of God as primitive Christianity found in the prophetic writings of the OT. The Son surely knew of this ineluctability and himself affirmed it. As, then, Jesus accepted his approaching death as a fate imposed not merely by his enemies but by God himself, in a deeper sense the Son of God present but concealed in him was at work, making himself an offering in obedience to the Father and for the salvation of the world (Eph. 5:2).

Let us recall again that this way of looking at the history of Jesus rests on knowledge of his resurrection and exaltation. He who was exalted as Son of God came to be seen as the true subject of the history that led him to the cross. He was detected in the course of events. Exalted, Jesus is also the subject of the history of proclamation in which his death is explained and proclaimed as the reconciliation of the world. Paul rejoices in fellowship with God "through our Lord Jesus Christ, through whom we have now received our reconciliation" (Rom. 5:11). The "now" is the now of apostolic proclamation in the sense of 2 Cor. 5:20 and its acceptance in faith. It is Jesus Christ himself, the exalted Kyrios, who "now" gives us reconciliation through the ministry of the apostles and the preaching of the church — the reconciliation proleptically accomplished once and for all in his death. Hence the apostle says in 2 Cor. 5:20: "We beseech you on behalf of Christ, be reconciled to God." The apostle pleads on Christ's behalf, yet not as though representing an absent Christ, but in such a way that the exalted Lord himself is "now" effecting through him the reconciliation of believers (1 Cor. 1:10; 2 Cor. 10:1).

The past history of Jesus thus becomes also present event in the work of the exalted Christ through apostolic proclamation. We find, then,

120. See above, pp. 363ff.

three levels in the event. We must distinguish these levels and clarify the basis and structure of the way in which they are seen together. This is especially important for an understanding of the gospel tradition as an interpretation of the history of Jesus. We have first the human historical level of the work and fate of Jesus. Then we have the same history as the medium of the eternal Son of God, who is at work in it as he became man in the person of Jesus. Finally we have the same history again as the medium of the active presence of the exalted Lord through the apostolic proclamation that explains to the world at large the saving significance of this history. The interrelation of the three levels is basic for a proper understanding and evaluation of the church's doctrine of Christ's reconciling office. This doctrine views the history on the solid basis of the reality of the eternal Son of God present in Jesus. It also presents the history as the medium of the present work of the exalted Lord for the reconciliation of the world.

b. *The Reconciling Office of Christ*

The question of the divine subject of the event of reconciliation in the crucifixion of Christ leads us back once again to the connection between christology and soteriology (see above, pp. 397ff.). Clearly the Father does not act alone in the offering up of Jesus to death. Jesus himself is not simply passive in this action, for the Son is also acting subject in the event. As such, he is the Savior of the world (1 John 4:14).

Paul describes Jesus as *sōtēr* only in Phil. 3:20. He does this in expectation of the return of Christ to change our mortal life into the new life that is already a reality in him. This is in keeping with Paul's use of *sōtēria* in the future tense (see above, pp. 400ff.). We find the same future reference in the idea of the exalting of the Crucified to be the (future) *sōtēr* (Acts 5:31) of the people of God (cf. Luke 2:11). Nevertheless, in Paul future salvation is linked to the reconciliation that we already experience. It is based on this, and therefore on the death of Jesus Christ (Rom. 5:10). Then in accordance with the increasing tendency to see the present situation of Christians as participation in salvation, Eph. 5:23f. can call Christ the Savior of his body, since he gave up his life for the church. Ignatius, too, related the title to the expiatory death of Christ (*Smyrn.* 7.1). 1 John also calls Jesus *sōtēr* in this sense (4:14; cf. John 3:16f.). But the Johannine sayings see the Son as Savior not merely of the people of God but of the cosmos (John 4:42). His saving work was the purpose of his being sent into the world.

Statements about the action of the Son in the history of Jesus, and especially in his death for the world's salvation, obviously transcend an immediate human interpretation of the coming, work, and destiny of Jesus. In principle, however, this is done already by the christological titles that are ascribed to the Crucified in the light of his resurrection by God. The title "Messiah" already has a soteriological function that, on account of the linking of this title to the crucifixion, is explained specifically by the interpretation of his death as an atoning death. The only new thing in statements about the self-offering of the Son in this event is that "Christ" and "Son of God" not merely function as titles but name the preexistent Son of God who was sent into the world as the acting subject of the history of Jesus, a subject not simply identical with the human reality of Jesus as it may be brought to light by historical research into the Jesus tradition, but still the true subject at work in his human history.

Christology may not simply adduce such assertions as statements of faith that cannot be demonstrated. It must ask whether and how far we can understand and justify them as an expression of the historical uniqueness of Jesus in connection with his work and destiny. But then if the assertion of the divine sonship can be accepted as a proper description of the relation of Jesus to the Father, as it seems to be in the light of his resurrection from the dead, and if in consequence the earthly existence of Jesus must be regarded as the existence of the eternal Son of God, who was sent into the world, then we may rightly speak of the action of the Son of God in his historical existence. From this angle we may also find the action of the Son of God in those aspects of the history that from the standpoint of the human reality of Jesus do not seem to be actively done by him but passively suffered. Nothing unforeseen or unplanned can happen to the Son of God. Only on the side of his human nature may we distinguish between his active coming and work on the one side and the fate that he suffers on the other. Whereas we cannot identify the salvation of the world as an aim that Jesus set himself in the historical humanity of his work, we may well describe the atoning function of his death with a view to the world's salvation as the object and goal of the Son of God, who was at work in the history of Jesus.

Statements of this kind have a prophetic structure. The relevance for all humanity that they ascribe to the special person and history of Jesus anticipates the outcome of human history. In other words, the truth of the content of such statements depends on the work of the Spirit, who will glorify Jesus in human hearts as the Son of God. The christological statements themselves arose in this way as an expression of the initial work of the Spirit in the believing community of primitive Christianity. This is true already of titles such as "Messiah," "Kyrios," or "Son of God." Each of these titles relates the specific figure of Jesus to all humanity, and above all to its future. Each is implicitly soteriological. This is in keeping with the claim, characteristic of the human ministry of Jesus, that the definitive future of God is already breaking in with him for the world's salvation. The primitive Christian kerygma of the resurrection is along the same lines. It tells us that the definitive saving future of the new life from God has come already in him. Hence sayings about the work of the eternal Son of God in the history of Jesus are not isolated in this regard. In them, however, the soteriological relevance of the person and history of Jesus is in a very special way the express theme.

Statements regarding Jesus as the Reconciler who brings salvation to humanity would not be true without their correlate — saved and reconciled humanity. Only in this relation is Jesus in fact the universal Reconciler and Savior. But is humanity really reconciled to God and saved from sin and death? Appearances and the lessons of world history do not seem to support this thesis today. Do they, then, refute the statements that are implied in the christological titles and expressly formulated in what is said about the saving significance of the death and resurrection? There is as yet no definitive proof of the truth of the statements. They anticipate something that is still open to question in the course of history. The reconciliation of the world through Jesus has undoubtedly made itself known to believers, but we cannot as yet advance it as the conclusive result of world history.

Statements regarding Christ's saving work that have the reconciliation of the world as their content find their proper place between the anticipatory soteriological titles of christology ("Son," "second Adam," "image of God," etc.) and the as yet incomplete process of the reconciling of humanity. Specifically at issue is the saving significance of the death of Jesus, not merely in the sense that *God* acted in Christ's death for the reconciliation of the world (2 Cor. 5:18) but also in the sense that the *Son* offered himself up in this event (Gal. 2:20). We have here a saving work of Christ only to the extent that — in the words of Hebrews — Christ "offered up himself" as the high priest who makes atonement for the people's sins (Heb. 7:27; cf. 9:26ff.).

Hebrews gives us plainly to understand that such statements anticipate the actual process of the setting aside of humanity's sins. "Christ, having been offered once to bear the sins of many, will appear a second time, when sin is set aside,[121] to those who are eagerly waiting for him" (9:28). Hebrews, then, stresses not merely the once-for-allness and definitiveness of the sacrificial death of Jesus (9:26) but also the ongoing intercession of the risen Lord before God (v. 24). It thus gives us occasion to develop a view of his saving work or reconciling office that extends beyond the once-for-all event of the crucifixion. Along the same lines we might refer again to the sending sayings already mentioned. Thus sayings like John 3:16f. relate the whole history of Jesus, in the light of the incarnation of the Son of God, to the purpose of saving the world.

The theology of the Latin Middle Ages first differentiated a special doctrine of Christ's work as Mediator from the doctrine of his person.[122] The separate treatment of the theme, which in Reformation theology took the form of a doctrine of Christ's office as Mediator[123] distinct from the doctrine of his divine-human person, has run into vigorous criticism in modern theology because the person and work of the Savior belong indissolubly together.[124] As regards their soteriological implications, the titles "Christ," "Kyrios," and "Son of Man" confirm this, not to speak of the understanding of Jesus Christ as the new Adam who definitively fulfills our destiny of divine likeness.

Nevertheless, there are significant differences between statements about the person of Christ and statements about the saving work that he accomplished, or his reconciling office, not least in their relation to the historical figure and history of Jesus. Christological statements about the

121. The rendering of *chōris hamartias* by Wilckens, *Das NT übersetzt und kommentiert*, p. 795. The meaning cannot be that Jesus himself will be without sin but that in contrast to his first coming, he will no longer have to deal with sin.

122. This took place in the chapter devoted to the theme in Peter Lombard *Sent.* 3.16.6f. (see above, nn. 17ff.). Cf. the interpretation of the union of the two natures in the one person in Leo I (DS § 293).

123. For a systematic handling of the theme in Reformation theology, the account of Christ's office as Mediator in Calvin became normative (*Inst.* 2.12ff.). Like Augustine and Latin Scholasticism, Calvin began with the use of the term "Mediator" in 1 Tim. 2:5 (see above, nn. 15ff.) but in the process emphasized that the divine-human person is the bearer of the office (see above, n. 22). The older Protestant theology widely accepted the concept of a mediatorial office, though *munus* was used at times instead of *officium*. The fathers had sometimes used *munus* for the kingly and priestly offices of Christ (e.g., Augustine, who related both offices to Christ because anointing was required in both [*Enn. in Ps.* 26.2.2]).

124. Cf. Schleiermacher's *Christian Faith*, § 92.2. The thesis of the unity of the person and work then came to be generally recognized; cf. *Jesus — God and Man*, pp. 208ff.

person of Jesus Christ might be reconstructed as an exposition of his historical figure in the light of its history, and especially of the crucifixion of Jesus and his resurrection from the dead. But when we turn to statements about the saving work or reconciling office of the incarnate Son of God, there is the additional problem that behind the human history of Jesus another history comes into view. According to this other history, what seems in the one case to happen to Jesus is now an action of the Son of God that aims no longer, like the earthly sending of Jesus, at the people of God of the old covenant but at the salvation of humanity, and that then finds continuation in the activity of the risen Lord.

If we measure the statements of the theological tradition regarding the saving work or mediatorial office of the incarnate Son of God directly by the measure of the history of Jesus, we reach the overwhelmingly negative result that in all probability the earthly Jesus suffered crucifixion as his fate without himself bringing it about as an act of self-offering. In his earthly existence he was not a priest, nor was he a king. To call him a prophet does justice best to his earthly ministry, but even that levels down what is specific in his coming and message, aware though he was of being in the prophetic tradition. The concern of Jesus was not to announce this or that event in the historical future. His sole concern was with God and God's future. He made this his concern with a transcendent claim. This is why he did not list himself among the prophets (cf. Luke 16:16 par.). The historical Jesus, then, was neither priest nor king nor, in the strict sense, prophet.

In 1964, in light of these findings, I raised a fundamental criticism against the Reformation doctrine of the threefold office of Christ as Priest, King, and Prophet.[125] This criticism was directed not merely against the associating of the three functions, which dated from the time of A. Osiander (1530), which had achieved acceptance especially under the influence of Calvin, and which relied on the requirement of anointing both for these offices and for the Christ. The criticism was directed also against the view expressed here that the divine-human person of Christ is the acting subject of the history of Jesus.[126] The traditional concept of the office of Christ was consequently reduced to the sending of the historical Jesus as it was exercised in his message and public ministry as distinct from his

125. *Jesus — God and Man,* pp. 208ff.
126. Ibid., p. 223. In connection with the kingship of the risen Lord, I of course did allow that one might speak of Jesus as the subject of the effects of his earthly coming (p. 210; cf. 378ff.).

fate.[127] The relation between this concept of sending, analogous to that of the prophets, and what the NT says about the sending of the preexistent Son into the world was left an open one.

A. Ritschl had already tried to link the traditional doctrine of the office of Christ more closely to the historical reality of Jesus and had made a plea in this connection for replacement of the term "office," with its legal and institutional connotations, by the "calling" of Jesus to set up the moral community of the kingdom of God among us.[128] Like Schleiermacher, Ritschl discussed the concept of office or calling from the standpoint that in relation to the existing community of believers, which Jesus aimed to establish by his words and works and suffering, the ongoing basis of its existence lies in its nature.[129] In 1964, however, I myself emphasized the break that came in the relation to the pre-Easter work of Jesus with the events of the crucifixion and resurrection,[130] and I thus limited the term "calling" to the pre-Easter work, though naturally its abiding significance extends to all creation precisely on account of the resurrection of the Crucified.

Deliberations on the fact that looking back from Easter we see that the thought of divine sonship means not only incarnation but also an activity of the Son in the history of Jesus have now forced me to correct the position that I took up in 1964. The only point remaining is that between the human action of Jesus in the context of his earthly history and the action of the Son of God in that history a distinction must be made, and that the relation between the two stands in need of clarification. Naturally the Son of God incarnate in Jesus acts through his human activity, but his action embraces the distinction between the human activity and the fate of Jesus. The earthly activities thus have contexts other than those that appear on a purely historical approach.

Even though we have to speak of an action of the incarnate Son of God in the history of Jesus, and especially in his expiatory death "for us," this does not of itself justify the idea of a threefold office of Christ as King, Priest, and Prophet. Primarily this idea has typological significance. It expresses the fulfillment and consummation of the old covenant in the history of Jesus by uniting the three most important offices of God's people in the one person. The idea thus has more poetic than dogmatic value, since we can hardly show it to be a necessary expression of the content of the history of Jesus. Its grounding in the requirement of anoint-

127. Ibid., pp. 219ff. The office of Jesus covers only "the commission under which the historical Jesus knew himself to stand" (p. 211).
128. Ritschl, Christian Doctrine, pp. 433f. These remarks come at the end of a discussion of the problems involved in the doctrine of the threefold office.
129. Ibid., pp. 430f.
130. Jesus — God and Man, p. 223, cf. 210.

ing both as Christ[131] and for the three offices, which is historically doubtful in the case of the office of prophet,[132] can hardly serve as an argument
for their union in the history of Jesus.

The long history of discussion of the doctrine of the threefold office in modern
theology is a clear indication of the difficulties involved. In 1773 J. A. Ernesti was
already making a plea that we should focus the concept of the mediatorial office
of Christ on his vicarious sacrifice.[133] Materially this meant returning to the
medieval type of teaching on Christ's saving work, though using the term "office"
instead of "work." But even if we see some gain in including other functions in
our understanding of Christ's office as Mediator,[134] the schema of a personal
union of the offices is still off the mark. F. H. R. von Frank formulated incisive
criticism of it. In his view the effecting of saving expiation was materially basic
to the mediatorial office of Christ. This was the basis of his position and power
as King, which he essentially exercises by his Word.[135] When we associate the
three offices, the thought gives the wrong impression that they are three equal
parts of a whole that in fact includes them all, the *officium Christi.*[136]

The Reformation doctrine of Christ's mediatorial office in reconciling the world is superior to the medieval form of the doctrine of the saving

131. As regards king and priest, cf. Augustine (see above, n. 123).

132. On this, and especially Calvin's appeal to Isa. 61:1, cf. *Jesus — God and Man*,
p. 213. The anointing of the prophet can only be a figurative one, referring to the imparting
of the Spirit.

133. J. A. Ernesti, "De officio Christi triplici," in *Opuscula theologica* (1773, 1792),
pp. 413-38. Ritschl, *Christliche Lehre*, I, 522ff., argued against Schleiermacher (*Christian
Faith*, §§ 102ff.) that he had not done justice to the exegetically well-founded criticism of
Ernesti.

134. This is the most important point made by theologians who clung to the
schema, e.g., Schleiermacher (*Christian Faith*, § 102.3) or I. A. Dorner (*A System of Christian
Doctrine*, 4 vols. [Edinburgh, 1880-82], III, 388ff.). But Ritschl rightly observed that linear
listing has the value only of making fully sure that we include everything when pointing
out the significance of Christ as the Mediator of salvation (*Christian Doctrine*, p. 428).

135. F. H. R. von Frank, *System der christlichen Wahrheit*, II (1880), § 35. In contrast
to Ritschl's approach, which highlights the kingly work of Christ in founding and upholding
his religious community (*Christian Doctrine*, p. 405), this way of looking at the matter is to be
preferred, for Ritschl misses the point that though the linking of the title "Messiah" to Jesus
was occasioned by the accusation of the Romans, it rested on his exaltation, also that historically the development of the doctrine of the mediatorial office was by no means accidentally
related to the interpretation of the atoning death of Jesus. It is precisely here that the NT
witnesses speak most plainly of an action of the Son of God in the history of Jesus.

136. Frank, *System*, p. 194. Frank found in the threefold schema a logically divisive
and in truth illogical association of organically interrelated elements. He called this a major
fault of the older dogmatics.

work of the Mediator inasmuch as the concept of office takes up the thought of the sending of the Son by the Father. Fulfilling his mission to reconcile and redeem the world, the Son simply does what the Father sent him to do. The concept of office expresses this much better than the thought of making satisfaction to God for human faults. The one who does the work of reconciliation is the Son of God, who in the human reality of Jesus makes reconciliation by his death on the cross.[137] A further advantage of the doctrine of Christ's threefold office lies in the thought that the old covenant comes to fulfillment in the work of the Reconciler. Finally, there is the third advantage that the reconciling work of the Savior covers not only his sacrificial death but also the earthly course of his witness to the imminence of the divine rule and the work of the exalted Christ, especially his intercession for believers with his sacrificial death on the cross (Heb. 7:25).

The activity of the exalted Christ as Priest, King, and Prophet could not, of course, be seen as coincident with the content of the earthly history of Jesus as it is presented in the witness of the Spirit; it was simply described from the standpoint of a phase of Christ's mediatorial office that objectively follows his earthly history, the reason being that the older Protestant doctrine did not think through the mutual relation between the work of the ascended Christ and that of the Spirit. We see here the one-sidedly christological objectivism of the older doctrine of Christ's office as Reconciler, which prevented it from doing justice to the interrelation of three different levels of meaning in the statements of primitive Christianity regarding Christ's saving work, which we stressed earlier.

If the human and historical level of the history of Jesus is transparent to the presence of the incarnate Son of God concealed in it, as became clear in the light of the exaltation of the Crucified, then not only is the messianic dignity of Jesus Christ in virtue of his kingly office perceived to be present in hidden form in his earthly appearance, but the fate of execution that overtakes Jesus is also seen to be an act of self-offering on the part of the incarnate Son of God, who is at work in this history. This is the content of the activity of the exalted Lord, who rules the world by the word of the gospel and the power of the Spirit, creating faith in the gospel, putting all opposition to it to shame, assembling believers, and in this way preparing the way for the kingdom of the Father in the world, as he had already in his earthly work made the coming rule of God present to believers.

---

137. This is the element of truth in views that relate the work of the Mediator to his human nature.

One might describe the anticipation of the future of God in the work of the earthly and the exalted Christ[138] as the "prophecy" of Jesus Christ,[139] so long as we take into account the distinctiveness of the eschatological proclamation of Jesus as compared with all preceding prophecy. The sole content of this prophecy is the imminence of God. The fulfillment is thus already there in him who grants faith in the intimation. In this sense, Jesus Christ is also present and at work in the proclamation of his gospel as he in whom God is present. Understood thus, the church's proclamation may be regarded as a work of the exalted Christ himself, its word of proclamation as his Word, or rather God's Word (cf. 1 Thess. 2:13).[140] The criterion, of course, is still the history of Jesus in and by which God and his rule are present among us. Where this takes place, however, it does so, not in virtue of the authority and proclamation of the church, but in the power of the Spirit, who bears witness in human hearts to the truth of God in his gospel, and who thus bears witness also to the glory and lordship of the exalted Christ.

c. The Completion of Reconciliation in the Spirit

In the history of the reconciliation of the world to God we have the restoration of the sin-broken fellowship of humanity with its Creator, the source of its life. In the process the creaturely independence of humans

138. To express what we here call anticipation of the future of God, M. Kähler used the thought of the exalted Christ as the new Adam "guaranteeing" the total renewal of the life of humanity (*Wissenschaft*, § 439). Cf. above, pp. 414f. He was following D. Schenkel here in opposition to the Hegelian term *Aufhebung* (cf. Schenkel's *Die christliche Dogmatik vom Standpunkte des Gewissens aus dargestellt*, II/3 [1859], p. 857, and on this Menke, *Stellvertretung*, pp. 148f.). Schenkel expressly emphasized the anticipatory element in Christ's reconciling death (pp. 861f., quoted by Menke, p. 149). Kähler focused one-sidedly, however, on the person of Christ as distinct from the Spirit. As he saw it, the pledging representation of humanity by the second Adam, who embraces humanity, makes humanity itself fit for God's indwelling by the Spirit, and the God-man in his consummated divine spirituality, through God, brings the Spirit into the personal life of humanity (§ 443). My own interpretation of reconciliation, which is close to Kähler's at many points, diverges from it significantly here. By using the term "anticipation," I leave room for a referring of the Son to the independent work of the Spirit.

139. On this theme, cf. Barth *CD*, IV/3, 48ff. Kähler also spoke of the "prophecy" of Christ's reconciling work (*Wissenschaft*, § 440; cf. § 435).

140. At this point my presentation in *Jesus — God and Man*, p. 219, stands in need of correction. We certainly should not treat the church's proclamation of the gospel as "a part of the prophetic office" of Christ in the sense that its work may be "identified with his without distinction." Yet it does serve the lordship of the exalted Christ, who, insofar as the proclamation corresponds to the gospel, is himself at work in and by it.

had to be, not set aside, but renewed. It had been eliminated by the bondage of sin and by death, though sin had deceived us by picturing an autonomy in full possession of life that it would make it possible for us to attain. If, however, our reconciliation to God is to renew us in independent existence, to free us for the first time for true independence, this cannot come solely from the Father, nor can it be achieved solely by the sending of the Son into the world. It must happen on our side as well.

In exemplary fashion this took place in Jesus of Nazareth. As he is united to the Father as the Son precisely in his self-distinction from him, he vicariously reconciles in his own person the independence of humans and all creatures to God. He is thus the Mediator between God and us (1 Tim. 2:5). He is so by his death, for the acceptance of death was the extreme consequence of the self-distinction of the Son from the Father, and by it he made room not only for the glory of God but also for the existence of others alongside Jesus.

But how can others share in the reconciliation that was achieved in exemplary fashion by the incarnation and death of the Son in Jesus Christ? They can do so only as they are taken up into fellowship with the Father of the Son who became man in Jesus Christ (cf. Gal. 3:26f.; 4:5; Rom. 8:14f.). This taking up is not merely in the sense of something that happens to them from outside but as a liberation to their own identity, though not in their own power. This takes place through the Spirit. Through the Spirit reconciliation with God no longer comes upon us solely from outside. We ourselves enter into it.

As the self-offering of the Son for the reconciliation of the world and his being offered up by the Father are one and the same event and form a single process, so we are to see the work of the exalted Christ and that of the Spirit in us as different aspects of one and same divine action for the reconciliation of the world.

We see this first exegetically. In Paul, and also in John's Gospel, the work of the Spirit and that of the exalted Kyrios are to a large extent parallel; in fact they seem to be interchangeable in content.[141] Paul could thus summon us to walk in the

---

141. See I. Hermann, *Kyrios und Pneuma* (Munich, 1961); also E. Schweizer in *TDNT,* VI, 396ff. Schweizer there says of John (pp. 442f.): "As it was said of Jesus (14:20), so it is said of Him [the Spirit] that He is in the disciples, 14:17. These, but not the *kosmos,* know both Him (14:17) and Jesus (16:3). Both He and Jesus are sent by the Father (14:24, 26). Both go forth from the Father (16:27; 15:26), teach (7:14; 14:26), witness (8:14; 15:26), convince the *kosmos* of sin (3:18-20; 16:8-11), yet do not speak of themselves (14:10; 16:13)."

Spirit or to put on Christ, and materially these two things are one and the same. The dwelling of the Spirit in believers (Rom. 8:9) is having the Spirit of Christ, and directly afterward we read of Christ in us (v. 10). The equation of Christ and Spirit finds direct expression in 2 Cor. 3:17: "The Lord is the Spirit," and this statement comes at the end of a section on the difference of the ministry of apostolic proclamation as a ministry of the Spirit from the OT ministry of the letter (cf. 3:8).

Paul could thus view his whole proclamation as a work of the Spirit, which is tantamount to saying that Christ himself is speaking through the apostles (2 Cor. 5:20; cf. 2:17 and 12:19; 13:3). The Spirit effects righteousness in us by creating faith in the message of Christ. In 1 Cor. 6:11 we are righteous through the name of our Lord Jesus Christ and the Spirit of our God. The righteousness of Christ is thus attributed to the Spirit but elsewhere also to the blood of Christ (Rom. 5:9). That is no surprise if through the Spirit Christ himself is present to us, and with the exalted Lord is present also his earthly fate. Paul can thus call the eucharistic cup a drink of the Spirit (1 Cor. 12:13: All have drunk of one Spirit). By the Spirit, God's reconciling that took place in the crucifixion of Jesus Christ is actualized in recipients, in those who had to be reconciled. Hence Paul could write that through our Lord Jesus Christ we have "now" received the reconciliation (Rom. 5:11) that God made in the death of his Son. At issue is not just a later appropriating of the *fruit* of the once-for-all event in the death of Jesus. By baptism believers are inserted into the death of Jesus (Rom. 6:3).[142] This takes place through the Spirit, for by one and the same Spirit we are all baptized into one body (1 Cor. 12:13), and directly after we read that we have all drunk of the one Spirit. By the power of the Spirit, then, Christians are incorporated into the body of Christ (1 Cor. 6:17), which itself by the resurrection is a pneumatic reality (1 Cor. 15:4f.). They are thus recipients of the reconciliation that was made in his death.

The Spirit lifts us above our own finitude, so that in faith we share in him who is outside us, Jesus Christ, and in the event of reconciliation that God accomplished in his death. Believers are "ecstatic," i.e., outside themselves, as they are in Christ (Rom. 6:6, 11). Thus — and only thus — Christ is also in them (8:10).[143] There is nothing unnatural about this "ecstasy," for our spiritual life may well be inherently "ecstatic" and may thus actualize in a special way the distinctiveness of living things (see

142. For Paul, then, reconciliation and justification are closely related. On Rom. 5:9f., cf. pp. 400f. above and Breytenbach, *Versöhnung;* also Kümmel, *Theologie,* pp. 181ff.
143. A more detailed description of this structure of faith and its significance for the doctrine of justification follows in vol. III, ch. 13.

above, pp. 196ff.). Human consciousness in its ability to be itself among others has a thoroughly "ecstatic" structure, and precisely in this way it is given life by the Spirit. As self-consciousness, it knows its own being among others, and by nature it is thus itself when among others, for being with others determines its nature. Not all being outside the self, of course, enables us in a higher sense to come to ourselves by lifting us above our particularity. In this way we may also be estranged from ourselves, not only in extreme states of self-forgetfulness or when fury and frenzy take us outside ourselves, but also in phenomena of bondage and addiction that lead structurally to the basic form of concupiscence as Augustine described it. At the same time self-forgetfulness may also be the supreme form of self-fulfillment when those that forget themselves are wholly dedicated to that which is their destiny as human beings and persons. This is how it is with faith in Jesus Christ.

In "ecstatic" being with Christ, believers are not in bondage to another, for Jesus as the Son of the Father is for his part fully God and therefore the man who gives himself up for others. As believers through the Spirit are with Jesus, they participate in the filial relation of Jesus to the Father, in his acceptance of the world in virtue of the goodness of God as Creator, in his love for the world. Those who believe in Jesus are thus not estranged from themselves, for with Jesus they are with God, who is the origin of the finite existence of all creatures and their specific destiny. For this reason being outside the self through the Spirit and in faith in Jesus Christ means liberation, not merely in the sense of elevation above our own finitude, but also in the sense of attaining afresh by this elevation to our own existence as the Creator has affirmed it and reconciled it to himself. It means liberation from the bondage of the world, sin, and the devil for a life in the world in the power of the Spirit.

If believers are thus "ecstatically" lifted above themselves by the Spirit so as to be in Christ through faith, this does not mean that along the lines of mystical union, they merge into Christ or through him into God, that they are no longer even aware of their own distinction from Christ and from God. Instead, believers know very well that their own existence is different from Jesus Christ in whom they believe, even though they are united to him by faith. An irrevocable part of their union with Christ in faith is awareness of the difference between their own existence and him their Head, just as believers who in Christ share in the filial relation of Jesus to the Father differentiate themselves therein from the

Father as Jesus did. As we showed in chapter 10,[144] this self-distinction from God is the condition of the fellowship of Jesus himself with the Father and the basis of his own divine sonship. Herein is the difference between Jesus and the first Adam, who wanted to be as God and who thus lost both the God who is infinitely above all creatures and also his own creaturely life. Believers share in the filial relation of Jesus to the Father and therefore in his self-distinction from this Father, which found definitive actualization in the incarnation of the Son.

Another part of this sharing in the sonship of Jesus is the realization by believers that they differ from Jesus not only as he is another man but as he is also the one who alone in person is the Son of the Father. Precisely in the awareness of this distinction, and through acceptance of their own creatureliness, believers in Christ share in his sonship in relation to the Father. In other words, participation in the filial relation of Jesus to the Father frees believers for immediacy in relation to God as their Father. This immediacy to God is to be lived out in the particularity of their own life-fulfillment.

By the Spirit, believers are capable of this self-distinction from Jesus, who is in person the eternal Son of the Father, for the Spirit himself differentiates himself from the Son by not openly glorifying himself but glorifying Jesus as the Son of the Father and the Father in the Son.[145] The Spirit, who is himself God, brings with him fellowship with God, but only as he distinguishes himself from the Father and the Son, and with himself all those whose hearts he fills and lifts up to God. Even the "ecstatic" working of the Spirit does not mean that self-distinction from God is no longer a condition of fellowship with him. It makes it possible for us to rejoice in this distinction in peace with God.

The distinction and self-distinction of the Spirit from the Son are first clearly presented in John's Gospel, though Christ and the Spirit are not absolutely identical in Paul.[146] In John, Jesus announces the coming of the Spirit as the *paraklētos* (14:26). He will come only when Jesus has parted from his own (7:39; 16:4). Whereas Jesus was with them only for a short time and will come again only at the consummation (13:33; 16:4; 17:24), the Spirit will stay with them always

---

144. See above, pp. 371ff.
145. See vol. I, 314f.
146. Schweizer does not see full personal identity, even in 2 Cor. 3:17 (*TDNT*, VI, 419), but the way in which the *kyrios* is present to the community (p. 434) or his mode of existence (p. 419).

(14:16). A main point of distinction is that the Spirit will show the disciples the true significance of Jesus (14:26; 16:13) by reminding them of what he said (14:26) and glorifying him (16:14).[147]

Although Jesus himself was filled with the Spirit of God, it was only after he left the disciples that they received the Spirit as an abiding gift. His absence put them in a position in which they could independently recognize the glory of Jesus in his humility and lowliness and thus be reconciled to God in their own lives by accepting his life as paradigmatic for them. Hence the Johannine Christ could say that it was good for them that he should leave them (John 16:7), for they could then attain to the independence of their own relation to the Father by perceiving the glory of the Son in his death and passion. The pain of finitude could then no longer separate them from God, who let his own Son die on the cross to make expiation for the sin of the world, but who also acknowledged his Son even in his death. Hence the Spirit completes our reconciliation with God by enabling us through faith in Jesus Christ to accept our own finite existence before God.

§ 5. The Gospel

Not in himself, but in the other, the Spirit is with himself.[148] Awareness of being reconciled to God is something that Christians do not find on their own but through faith in Jesus Christ. They achieve it as the Spirit teaches them to know the heavenly Father in Jesus the Son. To participate in sonship is the destiny of believers and the source of their freedom. This knowledge is not an explanatory addition from without to the subjectivity of those who believe in the historical reality of Jesus. It simply unfolds the significance that the history of Jesus itself has. The reconciliation of the world has taken place in the death of Christ (2 Cor. 5:19), even though it is completed only by the Spirit in believers. It is anticipated in the significance of the history of Jesus insofar as this has relevance to all humanity. But this significance needs to be unfolded and in fact brought

---

147. Cf. Kümmel, *Theologie,* pp. 278ff.
148. This saying echoes Hegel, and would have been inconceivable without him, but it does not have the same sense as in Hegel. Cf. my chapter "Der Geist und sein Anderes," in *Hegels Logik der Philosophie. Religion und Philosophie in der Theorie des absoluten Geistes,* ed. D. Henrich and R.-P. Horstmann (1984), pp. 151-59.

home to all people. This takes place through the missionary message of the apostles and the church. In the process the apostle does not simply proclaim the reconciliation that has taken place already in the death of Christ. The proclamation is itself part of the making of reconciliation, for in Christ's stead the apostle beseeches his audience to be reconciled to God (2 Cor. 5:20).

The apostolic ministry of reconciliation (2 Cor. 5:18) consists of the proclamation of the gospel, or the message of Christ in which Jesus Christ himself speaks (2 Cor. 2:12; 9:13; 10:14). Because God acted in Christ, Paul can also speak of the "gospel of God" (1 Thess. 2:2, 8; 2 Cor. 11:7; Rom. 1:1, etc.). The content of this good news is the word of reconciliation (2 Cor. 5:19).[149] In the programmatic statement in Rom. 1:15-17 the gospel is the power of God to salvation to those who believe, making manifest the righteousness of God. We find a corresponding statement in 2 Cor. 5:20f., in which the righteousness of God comes to fulfillment as we let ourselves be reconciled to God through the atoning death of Jesus Christ.

If in Paul, then, the gospel is the apostolic missionary message about Jesus Christ, the crucified and risen Lord, in whose death God has reconciled the world to himself, we also find another and at a first glance a very different use of the term "gospel" in the NT. Thus in Mark the gospel of God denotes the message of Jesus himself (1:14). Perhaps for this reason the term "gospel" came to be used for comprehensive presentations of the Jesus tradition.[150]

It was once conjectured that Paul introduced the term "gospel" to primitive Christianity and that it was then transferred from Pauline usage to the message of Jesus and after that to his history (Mark 14:9).[151] But

149. Paul never expressly speaks of the gospel of reconciliation as he does of the gospel of Christ, but the "word of reconciliation" in 2 Cor. 5:19 is unquestionably the same as the gospel, with whose proclamation he is entrusted in Rom. 1:1, and with the "word of the cross" in 1 Cor. 1:18. The statements about the apostolic ministry of reconciliation in 2 Cor. 5:18-21 are the climax of the discussion of the apostolic ministry of proclamation that begins in 2:14 (the *diakonia tou pneumatos,* 3:8) and that comes under the head of the *euangelion tou Christou.*

150. Mark opens, "The beginning of the gospel of Jesus Christ" (1:1). One might also translate "about Jesus Christ," and in this sense we have the starting point of a literary genre — the gospel. But the genitive might also refer to the gospel that Jesus himself proclaimed (cf. J. Schniewind, *Das Evangelium nach Markus* [1933, 6th ed. 1952], p. 43); cf. 1:14. In this case 1:1 is to the effect that the proclamation of Jesus began with the work of the Baptist recorded immediately afterward in 1:4ff.

151. So E. Lohmeyer, *Das Evangelium des Markus* (11th ed. 1951), p. 29 n. 4; but cf. T. Zahn, *Einleitung in das NT,* II (1900, 3rd ed. 1924), pp. 169f.

the origin of the term probably lies in OT prophecy, i.e., in the figure of the messenger of eschatological peace: "Behold on the mountains the feet of him who brings good tidings, who proclaims peace" (Nah. 1:15 [2:1 in Heb.]); "How beautiful upon the mountains are the feet of him who brings good tidings, who publishes peace, who brings good tidings of good, who says to Zion, 'Your God reigns'" (Isa. 52:7).[152] In the latter passage the central content of the message of peace is the dawning of God's kingly reign, indeed in the sense that God has already entered upon it. The similarity to the central theme of Jesus, which Mark 1:15 calls the content of the message that he proclaimed, is striking, although in relation to its future Jesus saw the divine reign as still in the process of dawning.

In Isa. 61:1f. we note that the breaking in of the lordship of God means salvation, and in Luke 4:18f. this saying is the basis of the sermon of Jesus at Nazareth at the beginning of his public preaching: "The Spirit of the Lord God is upon me, because the Lord has anointed me to preach good news to the poor. He has sent me to proclaim release to the captives and recovering of sight to the blind, to set at liberty those who are oppressed, to proclaim the acceptable year of the Lord" (cf. also Matt. 11:5). Since the figure of the messenger of eschatological peace still had a role in Jewish life in the days of Jesus,[153] we certainly cannot rule out the possibility that Jesus understood his own message in these terms.[154] He too proclaimed the kingdom of God to be imminent, breaking in already in his own work and with acceptance of his message, and accompanied by the deeds of salvation to which Isa. 61:1f. referred.

In this case Paul's concept of the gospel is the result of a development that derives from Jesus himself and then from the immediately ensuing usage of primitive Christianity. For the post-Easter community Jesus himself became the content of the gospel because in him the reign of God was already present and salvation was available through him. The gospel of Jesus Christ thus became the gospel concerning Jesus Christ. But Paul, possibly like Jesus himself, could also speak of the gospel of God. At

152. See P. Stuhlmacher, *Das paulinische Evangelium*, I: *Vorgeschichte* (Göttingen, 1968), pp. 116ff.

153. Ibid., pp. 142ff., with a reference to Qumran (Isa. 61:1 and the Teacher of Righteousness of 1QH 18.14).

154. Ibid., p. 243, though Stuhlmacher cautiously does not think it is historically proved that Jesus himself used expressions of this kind. Wilckens thinks we certainly must reckon with the possibility that Jesus saw himself as the messenger of peace of Isa. 61:1f. (*Römer*, I, 75, excursus "Evangelium").

any rate the inbreaking of the rule of God was the original content of the gospel, the reason for the joy that made the news *good* news. Jesus himself, the crucified and risen Lord, became the content of this news because the salvation of the kingdom of God is present already in him.

In Rom. 1:16 Paul said that this message is "the power of God for salvation to every one who has faith" because "in it the righteousness of God is revealed." As the covenant righteousness of the Creator this righteousness of God is the dawning of his new creation, even though for Paul the eschatological manifestation (epiphany) to all the world is still to come.[155] In substance, then, what the apostle says about the righteousness of God and its being revealed through the gospel is close to what Jesus said about the breaking in of the reign of God and its salvation. According to 2 Cor. 5:21, however, the righteousness of God is revealed to us believers because we are reconciled to God through the reconciling death of Jesus Christ, who proclaimed the gospel. It is thus to believers who attain to reconciliation that there is revealed the covenant righteousness of God, the fatherly goodness of the Creator, who does not abandon his creatures to corruption. In this sense the Pauline concept of the gospel — the saving message of the reconciliation of the world through the death of Jesus Christ — is a relevant interpretation of the original meaning of the term, the saving presence of the eschatological rule of God linked to the person and history of Jesus.

In modern dogmatic work G. Ebeling in particular has studied the relation between the term "gospel" and the Isaianic messenger of joy (esp. Isa. 52:7) and has stressed the similarity of the message of Jesus concerning the coming rule of God and its dawning in his own work.[156] Barth earlier drew special attention to the link between the first sermon of Jesus at Nazareth (Luke 4:17f.) and Isa. 61:1f. (*CD*, IV/2, 197f.), although more in the sense of the fulfilling of the salvation there proclaimed in the person of Jesus.[157] Ebeling rightly emphasized that the

155. P. Stuhlmacher, *Gerechtigkeit Gottes bei Paulus* (Göttingen, 1965), pp. 74ff., esp. 75, 81.

156. G. Ebeling, *Dogmatik des christlichen Glaubens* (Tübingen, 1979), II, 93f. The shift from the future sense to the perfect as regards the eschatological event (p. 95) is pertinent only to Pauline usage, not to the message of Jesus himself, in which the future of the rule of God forms the starting point, so that there is no more of a perfect here than in Isa. 52:7.

157. It was not important to Barth that in both the Isaianic messenger of peace and in Jesus there is a distinction between the inbreaking of the rule of God and the person of the messenger (he does not refer to Isa. 52:7). Barth could even state expressly that there

term "gospel" expresses the relation between the apostolic message about Christ and the message of Jesus himself.

He ignored, however, the different definitions of the content of the good news in Jesus and Paul and simply found the constant factor in the fact that it is good news relating to the person of Jesus.[158] But we can hardly say that this is true in the same sense for Jesus and for Paul. In Jesus the saving presence of the rule of God in his ministry was mediated through concentration on the future of God, to which he appealed. In Paul, however, the saving significance of the gospel message concerning Christ rested on the reconciliation of the world to God that had been accomplished in the death of Jesus. If we ignore these differences, we are left with the abstract idea of a "word event" that was inaugurated by Jesus and related to him. Nevertheless, Ebeling rightly stressed the character of the gospel as event.

Similarly E. Schlink, following Paul, underlined the truth that a life-giving work goes hand in hand with the promise of the gospel.[159] In fact Paul called the gospel the power of God for salvation to believers (Rom. 1:16), and already in 1 Thess. 1:5 he said that the gospel had come to them "not only in word but also in power and in the Holy Spirit and with full conviction." Schlink rightly concluded, then, that the gospel is not just a making known of the once-for-all act of salvation in Jesus Christ but that the act of proclamation is itself an act of salvation on God's part. He thus rejected both the reduction of the concept to an act of salvation that follows in the event of proclamation and the opposite tendency to replace an active by a noetic understanding of the gospel that he thought he detected in the later Barth.[160]

One may ask, however, what the basis is of the relation between the active and noetic aspects of the gospel. The only possible basis is the content, which in Paul is the distinctive event of reconciliation that on the one hand is already an event in the death of Christ but that on the other hand is to reach its goal through the apostolic ministry of reconciliation and in its recipients.

The dynamic that characterizes the gospel and is based on its content is a feature already of the message of Jesus concerning the

---

is no distinction between God's lordship and the person of Jesus (*CD*, IV/2, 198). In a certain sense, this may be true christologically (i.e., as regards the relation of the eternal Son to the Father), but it hardly applies to the preaching of Jesus. Barth ignored the self-distinction of Jesus from the Father that is the inalienable condition of his deity and his identity with the kingdom of his Father.

158. Ebeling, *Dogmatik*, II, 93; cf. also III, 290.

159. E. Schlink, *Ökumenische Dogmatik. Grundzüge* (Göttingen, 1983), pp. 421ff., esp. 424f.

160. Ibid., pp. 426f.

coming rule of God because by this word of proclamation the rule itself is present already for those who put their trust in it. The apostolic gospel differs inasmuch as it speaks of an event that has taken place already. Not the future of the rule of God, as in Jesus, but the past event of the history of Jesus, and especially of his death, is now at work through the apostolic gospel. This is possible only because this past event contains within itself the eschatological future inbreaking of the rule of God. Hence the message of the resurrection of the Crucified is itself full of the spiritual reality of the risen Lord. In the case of Paul's gospel, then, its proclamation involves life-giving power emanating from it. The ultimate reason for this is that the eschatological future of God lays hold of the hearers by means of the content of the message. In the history of the crucified and risen Jesus, and by its proclamation, the saving future is now active even after the death of Jesus through the power of the Spirit, who raised him from the dead and who now glorifies him through the gospel message (cf. 2 Cor. 3:7ff.; 4:4-6). It is in this sense that Jesus Christ himself, the Kyrios, speaks and acts through the word of the gospel.[161]

The power that fills the gospel is thus connected with the presence of the future of God in the coming of Jesus, and also with the imparting of this presence of eschatological salvation by the Spirit, who through the gospel leads to knowledge of the Son in the human history of Jesus. Accordingly, we cannot trace back this power to a general concept of the Word of God that is oriented to an OT understanding of the Word.[162] Precisely with respect to the power of the Spirit, which fills the gospel as the eschatological message of the saving future of God that has dawned in Jesus Christ and which radiates from its content according to 2 Cor. 4:4, Paul in 2 Cor. 3:6ff. distinguishes it from the OT ministry of the law. In this regard the gospel is also not the correlate of the law, as though we could speak of it only in relation to the law.[163] The antithesis between gospel and law as Paul made it in Galatians is historically conditioned

161. Cf. Wilckens, *Römer*, II, 229, on Rom. 10:17. "The gospel is the Word of the exalted Christ who speaks to all nations from heaven. His human messengers simply repeat, as it were, his eschatological reality" (p. 230).

162. So Ebeling, *Dogmatik*, III, 254f. The word of the law, which Ebeling in an incisive discussion relates to the word of the gospel, is structurally different even in OT thinking from the concept of the word of active power (Ps. 33:9; cf. Isa. 55:11; Jer. 23:29), as in the view of the prophets. On different biblical ideas of the Word of God, cf. vol. I, 241ff., 251ff.

163. Ebeling, *Dogmatik*, III, 290.

inasmuch as the time of the law ended with the coming of the message of eschatological salvation (Gal. 3:23-25; cf. Rom. 10:4).[164]

The gospel could not have initiated a new epoch in salvation history if in content it had not been independent of the validity of the law. This does not mean that the will of God to which the law bears witness does not remain in force, or that the law of the old covenant does not have a function in the new epoch of the gospel, though naturally a much altered function.[165] But the relation to law is not constitutive for the concept of the gospel as the message of the inbreaking of the reign of God or, in a Pauline sense, as the essence of the missionary message of the apostles concerning Jesus Christ. If we miss this point, we fail to see the distinctiveness of the NT gospel as the message of the saving presence of the divine rule, and we easily come to restrict its content, whether along the lines of a parallel to the law (the new law), or by making it correlative to the accusing and slaying function of the law, in which case it becomes no more than the promise of forgiveness of sins.

At this point we urgently need to revise a key Reformation principle. But Protestant theology, though supposedly subjecting all tradition to the authority of scripture, takes up this task only grudgingly, if at all.

In Luther's Galatians lectures in 1516-17 the comment on 1:11 is to the effect that the gospel preaches the forgiveness of sins and the fulfilling of the law that has already been accomplished, namely, by Christ. The law says: Pay what you owe, but the gospel says: Your sins are forgiven you.[166] For this definition of the content of the gospel Luther had appealed a year earlier, in his Romans lectures, to the quoting of Isa. 52:7 by Paul in Rom. 10:15. The message of salvation is lovable and desirable precisely because of the forgiveness of sins to those made anxious by the law.[167]

But neither Paul nor Isa. 52:7 says anything of the sort. In Rom. 10:17 Paul speaks of the need to proclaim the message of salvation in order to make possible faith in the Lord, who is the content of the message. The reason why this

---

164. Ibid., pp. 291f. Ebeling, however, champions an abiding relation of gospel to law because the law for the first time makes us sinners in a specific sense and thus makes us aware of our unworthiness and our need of grace (p. 292). Paul could describe the law's function in salvation history along similar lines but did not give it a lasting function of preparing for the gospel in the epoch of the message of salvation. Ebeling's account along these lines is certainly in keeping with later Reformation statements about the relation between law and gospel but not with the historical sense of what Paul says.

165. I deal with this theme in detail in vol. III, ch. 12.

166. WA, 57, 60.

167. WA, 56, 424, 8ff.; LW, 25, 416f.

message is a message of salvation is not directly stated but is presupposed: Those who call on the name of the Lord will be saved (10:13). The whole complex of Paul's concept of eschatological *sōtēria* is bound up with this thought. But in Isa. 52:7 the reason for joy is the dawning of the reign of God. To relate this message to the promise of the forgiveness of sins is at best a very spiritualized exposition. We have here an orienting of the gospel to the promise of absolution in penance as it was practiced in the Western church in the Middle Ages.

What is forgotten is that the gospel has to do with the dawning of the reign of God that brings salvation. The forgiveness of sins abolishes the separation between us and God. Basic here is the presence of the rule of God in the work of Jesus. Where the salvation of God's lordship is present, all separation from God is overcome. For believers, then, participating in God's reign means the forgiveness of sins and the new commandment of love. But to restrict the salvation of God's kingdom that found expression in common meals with Jesus to the forgiveness of sins is not in keeping with the message of Jesus and makes sense only against the background of the penitential piety of the Middle Ages. Even the event of reconciliation that is the content of the gospel for Paul does not consist only in the promise of forgiveness. It is a matter of life and death.

In his controversy with Lutheran critics of his thesis that the law is a form of the gospel, Karl Barth rightly opposed the restriction of the gospel to the proclamation of the forgiveness of sins (*CD*, IV/3, 370). But Barth's main point here was that the gospel is also God's claim upon us, so that it is also the "law of faith" (pp. 393-97). Barth's view, like that of his Lutheran opponents, thus moves within the framework of the question of the relation between law and gospel, the only difference being that for him the gospel is the origin of the law as well. In this respect Barth ignored the difference in salvation history, namely, that the law belongs to the old covenant, whereas the gospel is the basis of the new covenant, and in such a way that the law comes to an end when the message of eschatological salvation is proclaimed. When we see this, we can hardly call the law a form of the gospel (*CD*, II/2, 509; cf. pp. 511f., § 36). Nevertheless, Barth rightly perceived that the Lutheran restriction of the gospel to the promise of forgiveness is not in keeping with the breadth of the NT concept.

Barth was also right to point out that in Paul the gospel as the message of reconciliation includes our claiming the new reality by the Spirit. But this cannot be called law in the strict sense. The law of the Spirit in Rom. 8:2 is something very different from the Mosaic Torah, which with the coming of the gospel lost its validity in salvation history. At this point Barth failed to see what it was that caused the Lutheran Reformation to restrict the gospel to the promise of forgiveness instead of interpreting it in traditional fashion as the new law. This approach brings out very well the antithesis that Paul set forth. But we must think of the gospel much more comprehensively in its distinction from the law, namely, in terms of the theme of God's kingly rule, and therefore as the apostolic missionary message concerning the resurrection of the Crucified, the content of which is eschatological salvation in and through him. Forgiveness of sins is one essential element of this, but only one. It is grounded in the saving presence of God in Jesus Christ and comprehended by this. Hence Luther's statement in the Small Catechism also applies in reverse: "Where forgiveness of sins is, there is also life and salvation."

As the message of the reconciliation of the world to God that was made in the death of Jesus, whom God raised up, the apostolic gospel includes the missionary activity that aims at the founding of congregations and the rise of the church. Paul could remind his congregations that they were the product of his proclamation of the gospel (1 Cor. 4:15; cf. 1 Thess. 2:2ff.) and that in it they stood fast (1 Cor. 15:1). The inner link between the gospel and the founding of churches is obscured by the reduction of the gospel to the promise of forgiveness of sins.[168] But it may be seen without difficulty if we begin with the fact that the reign of God and its dawning in Jesus Christ form the content of the gospel.

We are also to understand the definition of the gospel as the message of the reconciliation of the world in the death of Jesus Christ. The world is reconciled to God and his lordship through Christ's death inasmuch as by the death of Christ the lordship of God shows itself to be a love that saves. It is in keeping with the universality of the one God and his lordship as the Creator of the world that what was addressed to Zion and the covenant people of the OT in Isa. 52:7 has now become a missionary message to the "world," which was reconciled to God in Christ's death and which is now to have a part in this reconciliation (2 Cor. 5:18ff.). At issue is the kingdom of God among us. Because the kingdom of God has the concrete form of fellowship with God and others, the gospel as the message of reconciliation to God must everywhere lead to the founding of congregations that have among themselves a fellowship that provisionally and symbolically represents the world-embracing fellowship of the kingdom of God that is the goal of reconciliation. The fellowship of the church that the gospel establishes is

168. It was a merit of Kähler to work out the function of the gospel in founding the church (*Wissenschaft*, § 457) as an expression and actualization of the significance of the reconciling event in Jesus Christ for all humanity (cf. § 443), though he clung to his narrow core definition of the gospel (§ 338), even if expanding it by including the message of the resurrection and the context of all historical revelation. This was in keeping with the Lutheran tradition to the degree that in CA 7 the gospel is the criterion by which to know the true church, and hence the condition of its unity. Neither the Lutheran tradition nor Kähler, however, could make sense of the narrow definition of the gospel as the promise of forgiveness in terms of the link between the gospel and the church.

thus a sign and a provisional form of the humanity that is reconciled in the kingdom of God — the humanity that is the goal of the event of reconciliation in the expiatory death of Jesus Christ.

The gospel thus takes precedence over the church. Over against the church it represents the authority of Jesus Christ, the church's Lord and Head. Though the gospel is proclaimed in the church and by its office bearers, it is not a product of the church; rather, the gospel is the source of the church's existence. This is not just because the church is founded on the gospel of the crucifixion and resurrection of Jesus Christ but even more clearly because the apostolic gospel has its origin in the good news of Jesus himself concerning the imminence and dawning of the salvation of God's reign. The proclamation of the gospel, then, is not merely one thing among others in the church's life. It is the basis of the church's life. The church is a creature of the Word.

Here, again, we find the basis of the authority of the Bible in and over the church. Over against the church, scripture represents the church's origin in the gospel and therewith in Jesus Christ himself. Hence the authority of scripture rests on that of the gospel and its content — the saving presence of God in the person and history of Jesus Christ. Only insofar as they bear witness to this content do the words and sayings of scripture have authority in the church. The question of the extent of the canon is thus a subordinate one. The church's decisions relative to it simply show in what writings the church recognizes the original apostolic witness to the gospel. The OT writings share this authority to the degree that they are to be read as preparation and prophecy relative to the revelation of the God of Israel in Jesus Christ, those of the NT to the degree that they bear witness to the event of this revelation and its meaning. How far this is true must be tested for each writing and each saying in each writing. The authority of the Bible in the church does not guarantee, then, the truth of individual statements in the biblical books. The church endorses the Bible only for the sake of the gospel, and the gospel only for the sake of the reconciliation of the world by God in the death of Jesus Christ, whom God, by raising him from the dead, instituted the Lord and Messiah of a renewed humanity.

As regards the function of the gospel in God's act of reconciling the world, and as regards the function of the NT writings as the deposit and document of the apostolic proclamation of the gospel, i.e., the apostolic preaching that founded the churches,[169] we may say of both scripture

169. Ibid., § 452.

and apostolic proclamation that they were inspired by the Spirit of God. But such a statement regarding the inspiration of scripture is again no guarantee of the truth of individual sayings. On the contrary, the statement that scripture is inspired presupposes conviction as to the truth of the revelation of God in the person and history of Jesus, the deity of Jesus, and the action of the triune God in the reconciling event of the death of Jesus Christ, his resurrection from the dead, and the apostolic ministry of reconciliation. This conviction has its basis elsewhere.[170] Hence the thesis of the divine inspiration of holy scripture and its authority in the church comes at the end of the doctrine of reconciliation and not in the prolegomena to dogmatics[171] or in the doctrine of the church.[172]

The relation of the gospel and holy scripture to the church as we have described it is significant for the fulfilling of the reconciliation that is grounded in the atoning death of the risen Messiah and that is served by the proclamation of the gospel. The precedence of the gospel and scripture over the church promotes the freedom of faith and its immediacy to God relative to all human authority, including the church and its officers. Important though the communication of the gospel by the ministry of the church and its institutions may be, the truth and authority of the gospel do not rest on the authority of the church. This authority derives from that of the gospel, which is linked directly to the tradition and history of Jesus Christ. We must always measure the form of its proclamation by this content. We can do this even though access to this content is made possible only by the proclamation of the gospel and the written record of its basic apostolic form. The same applies to the witness of scripture. We must measure scriptural statements by the content of the gospel to which they bear witness. The gospel is accessible through these statements but differs from them. Hence what we say about the authority of scripture over the church in no way restricts the freedom of individual judgment regarding the content and truth of the scriptural witness. On the contrary, it leaves room for this. For only in the free recognition and acknowledgment of the truth of God in the history of Jesus can the reconciliation of God to the world that is grounded therein reach its goal.

170. I am adopting here a statement of Schleiermacher to the effect that regard for holy scripture cannot be the basis of faith in Christ; rather, faith in Christ must be presupposed to allow for special regard for holy scripture (*Christian Faith*, § 128 Thesis).

171. See vol. I, 28ff., esp. pp. 31ff.

172. As in Schleiermacher, who put the doctrine of holy scripture at the beginning of his treatment of the essential and unalterable features of the church (*Christian Faith*, § 128ff.).

INDEX OF SUBJECTS

465

and reconciliation, 407-8

Reformation, 60, 204, 206, 210-11, 214, 240, 251, 252, 278, 406, 447, 460

Reformed theology, 47, 53, 73, 233, 387

Relativity, 81, 88, 89, 91, 93, 111, 154-55

Religion, 225, 226-27, 229, 291-92, 309
  and morality, 246

Renaissance, 85, 89, 217

Representation, 415-16, 417-21, 425, 427, 429, 430-31, 432
  exclusive, 430-32, 438
  implicit, 437
  inclusive, 429-31, 432, 435, 438
  temporary, 432-33

Reprobate, 168

Reproduction, 263

Responsibility, 259, 261-62

Restoration, 209, 215, 311

Resurrection, 164, 183, 266, 268, 269-70, 283-85, 288, 310, 312, 316, 338, 344-45
  and apostolic message, 343-46
  and ascension, 354-55
  as confirmation, 338, 349-50, 363, 365-66, 374, 383
  and corporeality, 358
  of the dead, 137, 351-52, 398
  end-time, 351
  and eternal life, 347-48
  facticity, 346, 352, 360-62
  historicity, 285, 287, 359-63
  and judgment, 348, 350
  as metaphor, 346, 348
  and Sonship, 363-67, 371

Revelation, 225

Revivalism, 232

Righteousness, 211, 214, 219-20, 254, 400

Roman Catholic theology, 221, 232, 233, 240-41

Sabbath, 143, 144-45, 163

Sacraments, 137-38

Sacrifice, 239, 420, 421-22

See also Expiation

Salvation, 327-28, 331-32, 366-67, 391, 392, 397, 456, 458
  future aspect, 398-402
  history, 36, 68-69, 103, 104, 218, 262, 371, 393, 414-15, 460, 461
  plan, 7
  present aspect, 400-403
  and evolution, 120-21
  See also Soteriology

Satan, 16

Satisfaction, 448

Satisfaction theory, 404-8, 412, 431, 448

Scapegoat motif, 422

Scholasticism, 26, 36, 47, 56, 58, 111, 148, 149-50, 176, 184, 189, 191, 206, 210-11, 218, 241, 405, 444
  See also Aristotelianism

Science:
  and creation story, 116-19, 123
  modern, 44, 74, 99, 106, 151
  See also Physics, Quantum theory

Secular culture, 204, 226-27, 232, 342, 362-63

Selection, 128-29

Self, 200-201
  actualization, 393-94
  affection, 94
  alienation, 179-80, 435
  awareness, 51-52, 139, 192-93, 260
  centeredness, 260, 274
  consciousness, 28, 94, 181-82, 192, 197, 198, 247, 256, 292, 452
  determination, 217, 223, 224
  differentiation, 139
  distinction, 29-31, 139, 452-53
  formation, 126
  fulfillment, 248, 265, 294, 320, 399, 452
  grounding, 248
  identity, 179, 180
  knowledge, 223
  loathing, 260
  love, 244-46, 250-51
  mastery, 201
  movement, 80, 82

Son of Man, 313, 334-35, 337, 340-41, 364, 380, 426, 444
Sōtēr, 441
Sōtēria, 399-402, 441, 461
Soteriology, and christology, 398, 441-43
Soul, 18, 79, 96, 197, 217
   and body, 182-86, 194, 200, 207, 267
   divinity, 186
   as image of God, 206-7
   immortality, 183, 220-21, 266, 358
   origin of time, 93
   preexistence, 183, 189, 254
   and spirit, 185
Space, 84-90, 96, 110, 154
   absolute, 86, 87-88, 89
   compressed, 155
   differentiated from Time, 90-91
   geometric, 85-86, 88-89, 90, 151
   infinite, 85-86
   plurality, 87
   relational, 87-88
   unity, 88
Speech, 189
"spirit," 185-86, 187, 381, 383
   angels, 103-5
   as image of God, 207
   and reason, 190-91
Spirit of God, 104, 275, 366, 386, 392-93
   breath of life, 186
   in creation, 32, 33-34, 61, 77-78, 81-84, 98, 109, 197
   creative principle of movement, 79
   distinction from Son, 83-84
   as field, 105, 110
   freedom, 30
   and future, 101-2
   glorifies Son, 394-96
   and human spirit, 187
   inspiration of Scripture, 464
   and Jesus Christ, 450-51
   life-giving, 76-77, 136, 187, 190
   and Logos in creation, 109-14
   paraklētos, 453
   power, 459
   procession, 2
   in reconciliation, 437, 450-54

   relation to Son, 32
   and resurrection, 98
   and space and time, 88
Spontaneous productivity, 129
Stars, 106, 117-18, 126, 148
State, The, 307
Stewardship, 132
Stoicism, 18, 81, 86, 93, 167, 183, 244, 292
Subject, absolute, 28, 31
Subject-object distinction, 192-93, 196
Subjectivity, 246-47, 248-50
Subordination, 372-73
Substance, 111, 185, 382-83
Substitution, 419, 421-22, 425, 429
Succession, 95
Suffering, 17, 54, 73, 162, 164-66, 172-73, 424
   of Messiah, 312, 314-15, 321
Superbia, 243, 244, 245
Supernatural addition, 222
Synoptics, 313, 336, 340, 363, 372

Technology, 197, 204
Teleology, 57, 160, 309, 412
Theodicy, 56, 163-67, 168, 347
   and eschatology, 173
   See also Suffering
Theology, 287, 289-90
   post-Reformation, 206, 220, 252, 387
   18th Century, 304
   19th Century, 304
   modern, 27, 47, 69, 112, 220, 222, 227, 252, 255, 268, 407, 444
   and anthropology, 290-91
   and law, 44
   and science, 50, 59-60, 69-71, 82-84, 106
Theology of the Cross, 338, 388
Theotokos, 300, 318, 319
Therapy, 249
Thermodynamics, 70-72, 97, 100, 107-8, 109, 112, 126, 158
Time, 57-58, 84-85, 87, 90, 92, 94-95, 102, 108, 110, 140-41, 146, 272

INDEX OF NAMES

INDEX OF SCRIPTURE REFERENCES

1. OLD TESTAMENT

2. INTERTESTAMENTAL WRITINGS

3. QUMRAN

4. NEW TESTAMENT

16:8b	356	14:14	350	1:10b	25
		14:15-24	333	1:11	25, 292, 295, 385
Luke		14:28ff	xvi	1:13	295, 301
1:26-38	366	14:28f	333	1:14	301
1:32	317, 366	14:31f	333	2:13-22	339
1:35	302, 318, 366	15:1-3	331	2:19	339, 346
1:35f	317	15:4-7	331	3:3	398
1:79	272	15:7	331	3:5	295
2:11	441	15:8f	331	3:6	382
3:16f	335	15:10	331	3:14	365
4:17f	457	15:11-32	331	3:15	347
4:18f	456	16:1-13	333	3:16	144, 301, 438
5:35f	333	16:16 (par)	445	3:16f	441, 444
6:20	398	16:19-31	183	3:17	320, 369, 397,
6:22	364	17:18	55		402
6:35	372	17:20	328, 329	3:18-20	450
7:22 (par)	328	18:1ff	333	3:36	347
7:23	336	19:41-44	342	4:14	347
7:47	332	22:37	349	4:22	402
7:48	332	22:66	340	4:42	441
8:54	347	22:67f	363	5:17	36, 41
9:60	266	22:67ff	313	5:17f	336
9:62	329	22:69	337, 341	5:18	372
10:22	290, 372	22:69 (par)	340, 425,	5:19	372
10:23f	328		426	5:19ff	391
10:26	330	22:70	373	5:22	391
10:30-37	333	22:70f	364	5:26	347
11:4	333	22:71	340	5:29	350
11:5ff	333	23:56	356	5:32	336
11:20	329, 337	24:25f	416	6:38f	320
11:20 (par)	328	24:26	417	6:53f	347
11:49ff	416	24:27	360	6:63	395
12:6	35	24:34	353	7:12	336, 340, 341
12:8	334	24:39	344	7:14	450
12:8 (par)	398, 426	24:39ff	354	7:16	336
12:8f	337	24:40	349	7:39	453
12:22-26	249			8:13	336
12:24-28	129	**John**		8:14	450
12:24ff	35	1:1	28, 148	8:16ff	336
12:31	250, 329	1:1ff	24	8:28	363
13:1-5	166	1:2	26	8:32	437
13:29f	328	1:3	22, 292	8:34ff	342
13:34f (par)	368	1:4	347	8:36	437
13:34f	342	1:4b	292	8:37	342
13:34 (par)	416	1:9	292	8:40	342

4:10	347
5:4	347
5:5	98
5:14	407, 420, 427,
	429, 430, 439
5:14f	425
5:16	433
5:17	305, 307, 420
5:18	420, 437, 443, 455
5:18f	438
5:18-21	455
5:18ff	413, 462
5:19	400, 403, 404,
	405, 407, 410,
	439, 454, 455
5:19f	414
5:20	412, 428, 440,
	451, 455
5:21	403, 410, 418, 419,
	420, 426, 427, 457
5:21f	407
6:2	400
8:9	424
9:13	455
10:1	440
10:14	455
11:7	455
12:19	451
13:3	450

Galatians

1:1	355
1:11	460
1:12	355
1:16	288, 354
1:24	439
2:9	355
2:20	305, 418, 438,
	439, 443
3:2	395
3:13	342, 419,
	420, 426
3:20	405
3:23-25	460
3:26f	450

3:27	220
3:28	215
4:4	277, 302, 316,
	369, 376, 383, 438
4:4f	320
4:4-6	436
4:5	430, 450
4:5f	138, 317
4:6	317
4:19	319
5:5	400
6:8	347

Ephesians

1:4	143
1:5	430
1:10	25, 32, 58, 63, 73
1:13f	98
1:21	105
2:2	108
2:5	401
2:8	401
2:9ff	7
2:12	179
2:14	312
4	220
4:18	179
4:22	265
4:24	211, 214, 215, 220
5:2	438, 440
5:9	211
5:23f	441
5:25	418, 438
5:31f	226

Philippians

1:21	269
2:6	230
2:6-8	424
2:6-11	296, 308, 375
2:6ff	369
2:7f	319, 376, 378
2:8	296, 373, 439
2:8f	364
2:9	354, 376

2:9-11	283
2:11	376
3:10f	428
3:20	441
3:20f	402
3:21	224

Colossians

1:15	208
1:15-17	369
1:15-20	24
1:16	25, 104, 107
1:17	35
1:18	348
1:20	25, 73
1:21	179
1:21f	403
2:12	428
3	220
3:9f	208
3:9ff	220
3:10	211, 214, 215, 220
3:12f	220

1 Thessalonians

1:5	395, 458
1:9f	278
1:10	400
2:2	455
2:2ff	462
2:8	455
2:13	449
4:13ff	348
4:14	346
4:14f	350
4:15-17	366
4:17	348
5:9f	400
5:23	187, 207

2 Thessalonians

| 2:10 | 265 |

1 Timothy

| 1:16 [Vulgate] | 111 |

5. APOCRYPHA

6. EARLY CHRISTIAN LITERATURE